PHILOSOPHY LOOKS
TO THE FUTURE

Second Edition

PHILOSOPHY LOOKS TO THE FUTURE

Confrontation, Commitment, and Utopia

Peyton E. Richter
Boston University

Walter L. Fogg
Northeastern University

WAVELAND
PRESS, INC.
Prospect Heights, Illinois

ST. PHILIP'S COLLEGE LIBRARY

For information about this book, write or call:

Waveland Press, Inc.
P.O. Box 400
Prospect Heights, Illinois 60070
(847) 634-0081

Copyright © 1978 by Allyn and Bacon, Inc. Reprinted by arrangement
with Allyn and Bacon, Inc.
1985 reissued by Waveland Press, Inc.

ISBN 0-88133-185-6

*All rights reserved. No part of this book may be reproduced, stored in a retrieval
system, or transmitted in any form or by any means without permission in
writing from the publisher.*

Printed in the United States of America

11

TO THE YOUNG WHO SHALL INHERIT, WE HOPE, A
HABITABLE AND HUMANE WORLD OF THE FUTURE

Stephen, Michelle, Carla, Neal,
Malcolm, Kate, Jennifer, Mary Louise,
Doug, Daphne, Deidre, Dirk,
Todd, Jason, Jimmy, Bettina, Verena,
Carolee, Wendy, Kristin, Kent, Greg, Eric,
Manuel, Midore, Farida, Gopal, Hillary,
Jody, Stephanie, Cindy, Justin, Annie,
Tara, Roas, Amy, Bruce

CONTENTS

PREFACE

Although the reading selections in this expanded second edition of *Philosophy Looks to the Future* are for the most part different from those in the first edition, the purpose of the book remains the same: to introduce beginning students of philosophy to a number of problems which, we believe, are appropriate subjects for reflection. These problems relate to the human condition, human nature, the definition of the good life, authority and freedom, the religious quest, and the future.

We might have selected problems at a lower level of generality and have included readings on specific problems such as the new morality, the population explosion, and the ecological crisis. Instead we have chosen problems of greater generality which are not only relevant to the immediate interests of college students and their teachers but at the same time are of perennial and ultimate concern to all reflective men and women.

We believe that the beginning student's first contact with philosophical writing should not be the razor-sharp arguments of professional specialists. These should come later when the student sees the need for them. Rather, the central purpose of an introductory text should be to show philosophy as working toward an enlargement of the understanding in relation to human experience. Generality may be one of philosophy's greatest vices; but it may also be one of its greatest virtues.

The theme of confrontation and commitment, around which we have organized our topics and selections, hardly needs any justification either as a pedagogical schema or as an ideational choice. It is basically only another formulation of the central concern of the whole philosophical enterprise: the critical scrutiny of belief and of problematic situations as a basis for responsible decisions and defensible choices. The word "confrontation" has unfortunately recently gained currency in its sense of "meeting with hostility" rather than in the more positive sense in which we are using it here: "to bring face to face with" or "to encounter immediately." It is in this sense that we hope to promote a "confrontation" between students and basic issues. We propose to use "commitment" in the sense of "the binding together of agent and belief as a basis for action." As its dictionary meaning would suggest, a commitment is a pledge, something undertaken, but by no means is it to be construed as something pledged in ignorance or undertaken blindly. To the contrary, a commitment ideally should spring from a conviction, and a conviction, in turn, from reflection on values, not from mere happenstance and ignorance. The commited life is the life pledged to the realization and protection of certain values.

The philosopher raises the question: "Why be commited to one kind of life rather than another?"

In answering this question, philosophy must look to the future. However, modern readers often discern their own assumptions and values only by comparison with the assumptions and world views of the past. The editors have accepted the view of philosophy as a discipline which takes place in historical contexts, contexts which have meaningful continuities with the present. Accordingly, the various readings in the book are for the most part arranged chronologically and contain a good deal of traditional material.

Although most of the reading selections included are taken from the works of philosophers, we have drawn also upon the works of novelists (e.g., Dostoyevsky and Camus) and psychologists (e.g., May and Maslow) whenever their treatment of various problems have the merit of originality, profundity, or unusual interest. This will make the book of use, we hope, in enriching the content of introductory philosophy courses. In addition, it will also make available a philosophically oriented source book for general education courses in the humanities and the social sciences as well as provide an unusual adjunct text for particular courses in literature, religion, and psychology. We would like to hope, too, that this book may be of interest to those readers exploring philosophical questions for the first time on their own.

Finally, we believe that students today have practical and idealistic concerns with the future. They are very personally concerned with defining themselves through their commitments to careers and lifestyles. They also show concern with the lure of alternative social philosophies and communal ideals. At the end of the text we have therefore asked the reader to envisage an ideal society, a utopia, in which he or she confronts the future and tests the consequences of commitments, if only in imagination. Utopias, as working hypotheses, not only provide a survey of future possibilities, they also enable the student to coordinate and illustrate concretely social and philosophical commitments.

We are grateful to the many users of the first edition of this book for their helpful comments and criticisms which have aided us, we believe, in increasing the readability and relevance of this second edition. We are grateful also for various acts of assistance to John DeRemigis, Elydia Siegel, Rebecca Freedman, Irene Arman, Joyce Lunde, Richard Sherlock, Stephen Nathanson, and Charles Farquhar. For having commented upon and typed portions of the manuscript, we wish to thank Jane Fogg.

Peyton E. Richter
Walter L. Fogg

INTRODUCTION:
WHY PHILOSOPHY?

Seek and ye shall find.

Jesus Christ

Que sais-je? ("What do I know?")

Michel de Montaigne

Comfort is no criterion of truth.

Anonymous

Be ye lamps unto yourselves.

Gautama, the Buddha

Philosophy begins in wonder.

Socrates

Philosophy takes nothing for granted.

Anonymous

Questions, questions, questions!

Anonymous

The unexamined life is not worth living.

Socrates

You will not learn philosophy from me but how to philosophize — not thoughts to repeat, but how to think. Think for yourselves, inquire for yourselves, stand on your own feet.

Immanuel Kant

Like archers, we stand a better chance of hitting upon the right if we can see it.

Aristotle

A little philosophy inclines a man's mind to atheism, but depth of philosophy leads back to religion.

Francis Bacon

It is better to be a human being dissatisfied than a pig satisfied; better to be a Socrates dissatisfied than a fool satisfied.

John Stuart Mill

No caterpillar could be a sceptic — and walk.

Anonymous

Myself when young did eagerly frequent Doctor and Saint, and heard great argument about it and about: but everymore came out by the same door wherein I went.

Omar Khayam

Introduction: Why Philosophy?

Many students approach the study of philosophy with the idea that it is a kind of game in which they will be required to take seriously such trivial questions as whether there is any sound when a tree falls in a forest when no person is around. Ambrose Bierce defined philosophy in his *Devil's Dictionary* as "a route of many roads leading from nowhere to nothing." Philosophy is, in fact, interested in puzzles and paradoxes, and in some seemingly trivial ones, when the analysis and resolution of these can aid in the resolution of more significant problems, such as the nature of matter and mind.

The source from which philosophical inquiry springs and to which it must return is the human condition. Each of us is acquainted with doubt, human suffering, the need for action, and the anguish of moral decision. Almost everyone experiences hope and fear, a feeling of what is right and wrong, a sense of beauty, a curiosity about unanswered questions, and a desire to exercise powers and continue to develop them. Each individual responds to the human condition in which these experiences occur and attempts to create a life that has meaning and value. In doing this, he or she reflects and speculates, especially when conflicts requiring resolution arise between beliefs, feelings, and actions.

Philosophy is never very far from ordinary reflection. The philosopher insists, however, on reflecting more thoroughly and with as much precision as possible. Consistency of argument, coherence of belief, and clarity of meaning are the hallmarks of philosophical reflection. "Philosophy," wrote Victor Hugo, "is the microscope of thought."

PHILOSOPHIZING

The term *philosophy* literally means "love of wisdom" (*philein,* "to love"; *sophia,* "wisdom"). Philosophy may indeed love and aspire to wisdom, but it never gives its followers the satisfaction of permanent possession of its

ST. PHILIP'S COLLEGE LIBRARY

goal. The philosopher examines beliefs and concepts the way a biologist does magnified cells, some of which may be harmless or healthy while others are dangerous. With his "microscope of thought" he submits them to his most concentrated scrutiny. He makes them give an account of themselves—of their origin, meaning, and value. Committed himself to the life of critical inquiry, he examines commitments in all areas of the human condition no matter how secular or sacred. If his conclusions leave him unhappy, even enraged, he is determined nevertheless to reach them and to make them his own.

PHILOSOPHY AND DOUBT

Philosophers have sometimes been referred to as "dutiful doubters." The spirit of scepticism has undoubtedly always been closely allied with philosophical reflection. "The first step toward philosophy is incredulity," said Diderot. More recently, Alfred North Whitehead has defined philosophy as "an attitude of mind toward doctrines ignorantly entertained."[1] Both of these statements are in the mainstream of Western philosophy, which goes back to the Greeks and Socrates who stressed the importance not only of knowing oneself but of knowing *for* oneself, of arguing and testing one's convictions, and of following the path of truth wherever it might lead. The person who defined philosophy as "a refined sense of one's own ignorance" was Socratic in his inspiration (see Part One).

Several of the great doubters in the history of philosophy will be presented in this book: René Descartes, who doubted his way to certainty; Leo Tolstoy, whose doubts nearly drove him mad; and William James, who overcame the will to doubt with the will to believe. Different though they were, these thinkers would agree that one must confront one's doubts courageously rather than try to run away from them, and that the unflinching confrontation with doubt can lead to many benefits, focal as well as fringe. For only by testing one's beliefs in an air of philosophical scepticism, can one know if the beliefs are not just accepted but acceptable. "I respect faith," someone has said, "but doubt is what gets you an education."

PHILOSOPHY AND FREEDOM

Beginning students of philosophy often wonder why philosophers get so excited over philosophical theories and why they resist so vehemently any attempt by authorities to interfere with their freedom of inquiry. Isn't philosophy only a matter of ideas, and do ideas really matter? Shouldn't we rely on expert opinion and on reliable authorities who know what they're talking about and can tell us exactly what to believe?

The answers to these questions will be given by various thinkers in Part

Four. Feodor Dostoyevsky suggests in "The Legend of the Grand Inquisitor" that most people really don't want to be free to believe what is true and to do what they please. Among these is certainly not Henry David Thoreau, "the sage of Concord," who will argue for the individual's right and duty to defy all authority and to do his own thinking, insisting that "if I could not doubt, I should not believe." Thoreau's defense of freedom to doubt, to believe, and to act would be strongly supported by John Stuart Mill, who argues in *On Liberty* that freedom of philosophical reflection, among other forms of freedom, is not a luxury but an absolute necessity. Mill, like Clarence Darrow, would consider it a tragedy to teach children not to doubt, since they would in all probability become adults who lack the ability to think critically and to act creatively. They might be "true believers" but they would adhere to false beliefs. They would lack the spontaneity Erich Fromm identified as the pulse of freedom. They would certainly fail to appreciate the importance of thinking for themselves and would not hesitate to impose, by force, if necessary, their own prejudices and beliefs upon those who disagreed with them. Freedom and doubt cannot exist without one another. Neither can tyranny and fraud, for, as Bergen Evans points out:

> In the last analysis all tyranny rests on fraud, on getting someone to accept false assumptions, and any man who for one moment abandons or suspends the questioning spirit has for that moment betrayed humanity.[2]

Philosophers, then, are persons who put a premium on open-mindedness, who entertain interesting ideas as though they were honored guests, and who find the company of provocative questions far more engaging than that of pat answers. Bertrand Russell, himself a great sceptic, saw in this questioning spirit philosophy's chief value and ultimate justification. Philosophy should be studied, Russell believed, not for the sake of its answers, which can never be proved absolutely true, but for the sake of the questions it raises. These questions open and stretch the mind, stimulate the intellectual imagination, and undermine dogmatism and tyranny. Furthermore, Russell concluded, "through the greatness of the universe which philosophy contemplates, the mind also is rendered great, and becomes capable of that union with the universe which constitutes its highest end."[3]

BOUNDARY SITUATIONS

Besides affording countless opportunities to doubt, the human condition has other sources from which philosophy springs. The German pessimist Arthur Schopenhauer held that "undoubtedly it is the knowledge of death, and therewith the consideration of the suffering and misery of life, that give the strongest impulse to philosophical reflection and metaphysical explanations of the world."[4] If our lives were painless and endless, Schopenhauer believed, we would never wonder why the world exists or question the meaning of our existence. We would simply take it all as a matter of course (see Part Two).

Another German philosopher, Karl Jaspers, traced one of the major sources of philosophy to man's sense of "forsakenness," to the anxiety he experiences when he confronts what Jaspers calls "ultimate" or "boundary situations."[5] These are situations that arise from the very nature of the human condition. They are inescapable, insurmountable, and insoluble by ordinary practical or rational means. Struggle, chance, guilt, death—to mention only four of these unique situations—face all of us no matter how hard we may try to avoid them or discount them. Only by confronting them directly and courageously can we become, Jaspers believes, truly human beings. Although these boundary situations can shatter us, causing us to founder, in the process we can commit ourselves to what Paul Tillich calls our "ultimate concern" (see Part Five). Unless we are committed to something, there can no more be meaning to life than there can be intimacy in love without a total personal commitment. As Nietzsche put it, "If one can find a *why* to live for, one can live with almost any *how*." If we can find no meaning to human existence and no end to strive for under the shadow of death, our sufferings would seem horrifying and our predicament absurd. In light of such considerations, Albert Camus argued that the most fundamental philosophical problem is suicide and tried to develop a philosophy of life that would justify creative involvement rather than self-destruction (see Part Four).

PHILOSOPHY FOR ACTION

Other thinkers also have argued that philosophical reflection is developed from the desire to formulate a theoretical basis for action or practice. One of the best examples of this is Karl Marx, who said that whereas previous philosophers had been concerned with understanding the world, he and his fellow communists were concerned with changing it. Confronted with a capitalistic society, Marx and later Edward Bellamy became committed to a revolutionary program that would lead eventually, they were convinced, to a classless society. Following this tradition, the contemporary philosopher Herbert Marcuse has brought Marxism up to date, reinterpreting its implications for American society and presenting a powerfully charged image of a "one-dimensional man" that continues to haunt twentieth-century capitalism.

Like Marx, Bellamy, and Marcuse, the pragmatists William James and John Dewey also stressed the intimate relationships between ideas and consequences and theory and practice. Theory, they held, was valuable only insofar as it clarified and guided practice—and practice, properly observed, should modify and verify theory. Doing and undergoing, observing and reflecting, theorizing and experimenting are continuous not separate activities, and philosophy, therefore, should never be separated from concrete human experience.

Among the other proponents of a philosophy that transforms man and his world, one of the most controversial is the behavioral psychologist B. F. Skinner. Skinner's defense of scientific methods in solving problems, his rejection of the concepts of consciousness, freedom, and human dignity, and his utopian vision of a world ruled by the principles of behavioral engineering are presented far more dispassionately than the doctrines of either the Marxists or the pragmatists. However, his approach is no less radical—and, according to his critics, it is fraught with as many difficulties (see Part Four).

PHILOSOPHY AND LIFE

Despite Marx's strictures against speculative philosophy, philosophers have never really thought merely in order to think. They have always had to think in order to act. Socrates, when he taught that the unexamined life was not worth living, certainly did not mean that one should spend one's life constantly examining one's life without living it. Philosophy's relationship to life is intimate and complex. A philosophy of life inspires action and guides conduct; it also permeates a person's attitude toward himself, toward other people, and ultimately toward the universe. He is not only committed to it, it commits him to a certain stance, a certain perspective, and usually to a certain life style. A person's philosophy of life gives him a base from which to evaluate reflectively past experience, both personal and historical, and a vantage point from which to survey the reality, both physical and mental, in which he lives. It provides him with principles by which he can answer the central moral question, What ought I to do?, thus allowing for resolution of moral conflict and a commitment to acting so as to promote and to attain the good (see Part Three).

CONFRONTATION AND COMMITMENT

After contemplating the human condition, the French mathematician and mystic Blaise Pascal observed:

> When I consider the short duration of my life, swallowed up in the eternity before and after, the little space which I fill, and even can see, engulfed in the infinite immensity of spaces of which I am ignorant, and which know me not, I am frightened, and am astonished at being here rather than there; for there is no reason why here rather than there, why now rather than then. Who has put me here? By whose order and direction have this place and time been allotted to me?[6]

Out of such attempts to fathom and cope with the condition of being human have sprung a wide variety of activities including work and play, education and politics, moral conduct and religious worship, artistic creation and scientific inquiry, and philosophizing. For philosophy, as Socrates once said, begins in wonder. It springs from the same source as science and religion and, like these activities, it attempts to map a previously unexplored territory. As the reflective appraisal of life's meanings and values, philosophy is one of the chief means by which we try to make ourselves feel a little more at home on a tiny planet whirling around a sun in a solar system adrift in a vast and mysterious universe. A philosopher, it has been said, is a person who has waked up to wonder.

There are as many criteria for choosing readings for a philosophy anthology as there are philosophical viewpoints. Viewing philosophy as an instrument of an ideology, Marxist editors would include material on the class struggle, alienation under capitalism, revolution, and the vision of the Marxist reorganization of society. Committed to a conception of philosophy as concerned reflection, existentialists would choose readings that illustrate the ambiguity and anguish of human existence and focus upon the importance and necessity of human choice. Followers of St. Thomas Aquinas would see philosophy as a handmaiden to Christian theology and would include readings on the issues of theology, the relation of reason to faith, the natural to the supernatural world. Logical positivists, viewing philosophy as an adjunct to the sciences, would concentrate on the linguistic and methodological problems that arise from scientific thought. They would perhaps give little attention to religious beliefs except to discuss them within the context of the methods used in the verification of scientific beliefs.

We have chosen "confrontation and commitment" as our underlying theme in order to present philosophy as an activity in which the individual encounters problematic situations that demand resolution. These problems challenge our analytic capabilities and require our total involvement. Philosophy has grown out of man's attempt to understand and to give some meaning to his existence in a mysterious universe. It has thus addressed itself to the human condition and has guided individuals in their search for more reliable beliefs, for a deeper understanding of themselves, for the better life, for freedom, and for something of future worth and ultimate concern. Philosophers have tried to make intelligent, defensible commitments using the approach that John Stuart Mill identified as the spirit of philosophy:

To question all things; never to turn away from any difficulty; to accept no doctrine either from ourselves or from other people without a rigid scrutiny by negative criticism; letting no fallacy, or incoherence, or confusion of thought, step by unperceived; above all, to insist upon having the meaning of a word clearly understood before using it, and the meaning of a proposition before assenting to it. . . .[7]

While confronting human problems, philosophical thinking has attempted to replace obscurity with clarity, fragmentation with coherence, partial understanding with one which is more complete. Although Mill described the critical spirit of philosophy, Alfred North Whitehead gave us a beautiful statement of the wider effects it may have on human life:

> Philosophy begins in wonder. And, at the end, when philosophic thought has done its best, the wonder remains. There have been added, however, some grasp of the immensity of things, some purification of emotion by understanding.[8]

As futurologists often point out, today more than ever before, the present is being invaded by the future. Already the possibilities of genetic and behavioral engineering have become hotly debated political and moral issues. The prospects of indefinite prolongation of human life or of intergalactic communication are no longer considered to be unrealistic or farfetched (see Part Six). More and more studies of the future are being seen as having practical and theoretical value. As Herbert J. Muller has pointed out, there are uses of the future quite as important as uses of the past, and, "man has never had more practical need of visions of ideal possibilities."[9]

"Life must be lived forwards, but can only be understood backwards," wrote the Danish philosopher Sören Kierkegaard. The twentieth century continues to present us with unique social conditions which require new analyses, adjustments, and commitments. Both as an analytical tool and as what Erich Fromm calls "a frame of orientation and devotion," philosophy is indispensable in helping us to meet the demands of our time. Philosophy must look to the past in order to search out and disseminate the insights, knowledge, and methodology that might be useful and relevant in solving the problems of today. Philosophy must also look to the present to bring clarity, coherence, and responsible commitment to contemporary situations and searchers. Philosophy, finally, must look to the future for some tentative advance notion of the tasks it may be asked to perform. Instead of "backing into the future" (which in the past has led us to the predicaments and potential disasters of the present), we can confront the future more constructively by contemplating and choosing from alternative futures.

"The future belongs to him who dares," Alcibiades said proudly.
"The future belongs to him who dares think," Socrates corrected him, smiling ironically.[10]

NOTES

1.   Alfred North Whitehead, *Modes of Thought* (New York: Capricorn Books, Macmillan, 1958), p. 233.

2.   Bergen Evans, *The Natural History of Nonsense* (New York: Vintage Book, Knopf, 1960), p. 262.

3.   Bertrand Russell, *The Problems of Philosophy* (New York: Henry Holt, n.d.), p. 249.

4.   Arthur Schopenhauer, *The World as Will and Representation,* trans. E. F. J. Payne (Indian Hills, Col.: The Falcon's Wing Press, 1958), p. 161.

5.   See Karl Jaspers, *Way to Wisdom* (New Haven, Conn.: Yale University Press, 1954), chap. 2.

6.   Pascal, *Pensées, trans.* W. F. Trotter (New York: Modern Library, Random House, 1941), sec. III, no. 205, pp. 74–75.

7.   Francis W. Garforth, ed., *John Stuart Mill on Education* (New York: Teachers College Press, 1971), p. 177.

8.   Alfred North Whitehead, *Modes of Thought* (New York: Macmillan, 1938), p. 232.

9.   Herbert J. Muller, *The Uses of the Future* (Bloomington, Ind.: University of Indiana Press, 1974), p. 13.

10.   Imaginary Dialogue Between Socrates and Alcibiades, Anonymous.

RELATED READING

Brightman, Edgar S. *An Introduction to Philosophy.* New York: Henry Holt & Co., 1925.

Christian, James L. *Philosophy: An Introduction To the Art of Wondering,* 2d ed. San Francisco, Calif.: Rinehart Press, 1977.

Davidson, Robert F. *Philosophies Men Live By,* 2d ed. New York: Holt, Rinehart, & Winston, 1974.

———. *The Search for the Meaning of Life.* New York: Holt, Rinehart, & Winston, 1962.

Durant, Will. *The Pleasures of Philosophy.* New York: Simon & Schuster, 1953.

———. *The Story of Philosophy.* New York: Pocket Books, 1961.

Edman, Irwin. *Four Ways of Philosophy.* New York: Henry Holt & Co., 1937.

———. *Philosopher's Quest.* New York: Viking Press, 1947.

Edwards, Paul, ed. *Encyclopedia of Philosophy.* New York: Macmillan, 1967.

Ginsberg, Robert. *Welcome to Philosophy: A Handbook for Students.* San Francisco, Calif.: Freeman, Cooper & Co., 1977.

Honer, Stanley M. and Thomas C. Hunt. *Invitation to Philosophy: Issues and Options*, 2d ed. Belmont, Calif.: Wadsworth Publishing Co., 1973.

Jaspers, Karl. *Way to Wisdom*. New Haven, Conn.: Yale University Press, 1954.

Joad, C. E. M. *Guide to Philosophy*. New York: Dover Publications, 1936.

Kaplan, Abraham. *In Pursuit of Wisdom: The Scope of Philosophy*. Beverly Hills, Calif.: Glencoe Press, 1977.

Keen, Sam. *Apology for Wonder*. New York: Harper & Row, 1969.

Koestenbaum, Peter. *Philosophy: A General Introduction*. New York: American Book Company, 1968.

Lawton, Philip and Marie-Louise Bishop. *Living Philosophy*. New York: Canfield Press, 1977.

Maritain, Jacques. *On the Use of Philosophy*. New York: Atheneum Publishers, 1969.

Marti-Ibanez, Felix, ed. *Tales of Philosophy*. New York: Clarkson N. Potter, 1967.

Metha, Ved. *The Fly and the Fly Bottle*. Baltimore: Penguin Books, 1965.

Montague, W. P. *Great Visions of Philosophy*. La Salle, Ill.: Open Court Publishing Co., 1950.

Ortega y Gasset, José. *What is Philosophy?* New York: W. W. Norton & Co., 1960.

Platt, Robert M. *The I-Opener*. Englewood Cliffs, N.J.: Prentice-Hall, 1976.

Rader, Melvin. *The Enduring Questions*, 2d ed. New York: Holt, Rinehart, & Winston, 1969.

Runes, Dagobert, ed. *Dictionary of Philosophy*. Paterson, N.J.: Littlefield, Adams & Co., 1961.

———. *Pictorial History of Philosophy*. Paterson, N.J.: Littlefield, Adams & Co., 1963.

Russell, Bertrand. *A History of Western Philosophy*. New York: Simon & Schuster, 1963.

———. *The Problems of Philosophy*. New York: Oxford Book Co., 1959.

Sparshott, F. E. *Looking for Philosophy*. Montreal: McGill-Queens University Press, 1972

Sprague, Elmer. *What is Philosophy?* New York: Oxford Book Co., 1961.

Titus, Harold H. and M. Smith. *Living Issues in Philosophy*, 6th ed. New York: D. Van Nostrand Company, 1974.

Thomas, Henry. *Biographical Encyclopedia of Philosophy*. Garden City, N.Y.: Doubleday & Co., 1965.

Thomas, Henry and Dana Lee *Living Biographies of Great Philosophers*. Garden City, N.Y.: Halcyon House, 1941.

Urmson, J. O., ed. *A Concise Encyclopedia of Western Philosophy and Philosophers*. New York: Hawthorn Books, 1960.

Voltaire. *Philosophical Dictionary*. Translated by Peter Gay. New York: Basic Books, 1962.

Wheelwright, Philip. *The Way of Philosophy*. New York: Odyssey Press, 1960.

Part 1

CONFRONTATION WITH THE HUMAN CONDITION

Commitment to Philosophical Inquiry

Youth is a blunder, manhood a struggle, old age a regret.

Benjamin Disraeli

To strive, to seek, to find, and not to yield.

Alfred Lloyd Tennyson

We come from a dark abyss, we end in a dark abyss, and we call the luminous interval life.

Nikos Kazantzakis

The only way to escape from the abyss is to look at it, measure it, sound its depths and go down into it.

Caesare Pavese

Try to be one of the people on whom nothing is lost.

Henry James

The first forty years of life gives us the text: the next thirty years supply the commentary.

Arthur Schopenhauer

The isness of things is well worth studying, but it is their whyness that makes life worth living.

William Beebe

Inebriate of air am I,
And debauchee of dew.

Emily Dickinson

Some people have nothing but experience.

Don Herold

Life is the act of drawing sufficient conclusions from insufficient premises.

Samuel Butler

Short is the little that remains of your life. Live as on a mountain.

Marcus Aurelius

The living are the dead on holiday.

Maurice Maeterlinck

Life is easier to take than you'd think; all that's necessary is to accept the impossible, do without the indispensable, and bear the intolerable.

Kathleen Norris

The secret of being miserable is to have leisure to bother about whether you are happy or not.

George Bernard Shaw

Introduction: The Human Condition

One of the best delineations of the human condition today is given by William Snaith in *The Irresponsible Arts*.

> The estrangement of man and art is one facet of the alienated world we live in. The pace of that alienation was increased and its effects intensified in the last half-century. The sense of meaninglessness has grown. . . . Man . . . sees the diminishment of himself on every hand. Once sovereign in his world, he watches a Frankenstein monster, progress, his own invention, rush on inexorably toward some goal of its own, pushing its creator aside. . . . He is being cut off from any meaningful contact with nature. He is leaving the land to be herded into great impersonal cities. He no longer knows the victory of a successful harvest in the face of storm, drought, or flood. He has lost the exultation of the successful hunt for his meat. He has been robbed of his gods and beliefs by his own reasoning and science. He has lost the glory in the strength of his arm, replaced by engine and machine. He turns his back on the problems of his planet—hunger, shelter, pestilence, war—and looks to the planets Venus and Mars for answers. His proud possession, his brain, is being displaced in many daily tasks by the electronic computer. His exotic technology surpasses the physical capacity of his muscles and nervous responses, and he must depend on instruments to make decisions of control. His machines are governed by machines while he idly sits by. His diminishment increases. He has lost his name to a serial number or dog tag, Social Security card and Diners' Club membership. He has lost his oneness in the crowd and cannot see his contribution in a specialist and piece-work system. He feels his sense of outrage blunted and reduced to impotence by the mechanics of his society. He finds his rewards and laurels in the benefits of the retirement fund. His future is uncertain. One hand offers material promise, the other threatens to wipe him out. His victories are gone, his sense of historic mission lost. Thus, by the compulsion of historical development, without intention, man in his lust to get on has created a society crowded with things which back him into a narrowing corner.[1]

Whether or not one agrees entirely with Snaith's gloomy characterization of the human condition, living today certainly means confronting perpetual and often unprecedented changes. Scientific discoveries, technological innovations, new lifestyles, and shifts in values are constantly making new demands on our attention and adaptability. Unless we can find adequate ways of coping with these challenges, and unless we develop better means of directing, modifying, and even decreasing the speed of change, we may eventually be traumatized by an overload of novel stimuli which Alvin Toffler has called "future shock."

Facing such disturbing prospects, many people today are doubting the traditions of the past, questioning the values of the present, and are uncertain about the promise of the future. Very little may seem certain in a century in which two world wars have been waged, environmental pollution threatens to make the earth uninhabitable, and the outbreak of a third world war could mean the destruction of mankind. Some people cling tenaciously to the traditions and cherished beliefs of their culture, accepting them without question. Others throw over all beliefs, reject the search for certainty, and live as well as they can day-to-day without thinking or bothering to ask questions. Still others claim we must seek radically different alternatives.

To confront such uncertainty and to make some kind of commitment is not easy, but to do so we must reflect and we must doubt. Someone has said that if we wish to dispel doubt, we can only do so by further doubting. Philosophy is systematic and controlled doubting. Through questioning accepted beliefs it aims at achieving clarified and acceptable beliefs. Existentialist Karl Jaspers holds that there can be no genuine philosophy without this radical doubt. Philosophy begins in doubt and confrontation with the human condition; ideally it should end in commitment to philosophical inquiry and more reliable beliefs.

Part One begins with Socrates who taught through example and by questioning. It would be difficult to construct a set of doctrines expounded and accepted by Socrates because he did not record them in writing. But the teachings of Socrates presented by Xenophon and Plato are still provocative and evocative—he provokes us to think about what we take for granted, and evokes in us the desire to achieve more rationally justifiable beliefs.

Socrates exemplifies the confrontation of a rational, morally sensitive person with the contraditions and inconsistencies of the human condition. He acts as a catalyst in achieving clearer and sounder beliefs for himself and others while engaging in dialogue aimed at attaining truth. Socrates also was convinced, as he stated at his trial, that this confrontation performs a necessary social and political function. Beliefs which are rationally examined are less apt to support irrational and pernicious systems of morality and legislation.

Like Socrates, the French philosopher René Descartes considered doubt to be a means to an end. Instead of confronting uncritical common-sense beliefs and social injustice, however, Descartes confronted the authoritarian beliefs and methodology of scholasticism. He saw the necessity of reconciling the doctrines of the Church with the methods and views of the universe that were characteristic of the new science of his time. Despite his methodological scepticism, Descartes' belief in reason and his proofs for the existence of God and soul put him very much in the camp of the scholastics. Yet his willingness to venture, his promotion of his method of doubt, and his arrival at his central certainty, "I think, therefore I am," still serve as landmarks for every explorer in philosophical argument. As one student put it, Descartes may have "copped out by bringing in God," but his thoughts will be viable as long as people are concerned with questions of what can be known with absolute certainty, the nature of the soul, and the relations between man, nature, and God.

Unlike Descartes, Henry David Thoreau was not interested in developing a system of philosophy—he wanted to change attitudes and develop a practical approach to leading the good life. His autobiographical style was in keeping with his Socratic purpose of encouraging individuals to examine and change their lives. Thoreau confronted the quiet desperation of the mass of men; he uncovered the dishonesty, hypocrisy, and sham in political and social life; and he called attention to the encroachment of the authoritarian machinery of government upon the life of the individual. Expressing his views in poetic yet forceful prose, he committed himself to a call to action, a call to awaken people to the need for self-reliance and moral involvement. In his actions and his writings Thoreau raised the questions of moral responsibility, of authority and freedom, and he laid the groundwork for individuals to establish their rights to exist and to develop their resources freely on their own terms.

Leo Tolstoy exemplifies another perspective on the human condition. For a long and agonizing period in his life, Tolstoy was confronted with the problems of death and other "boundary situations." He asked himself the question that Camus later raised in *The Myth of Sisyphus*: Why live if life is meaningless, absurd? Later he found his way to a commitment to primitive Christianity; but during the period described in *My Confession*, Tolstoy adhered to what we may call existential doubt.

Like Socrates and Jesus, Tolstoy asks us to examine our beliefs and to consider our ultimate commitments. But as a follower of Jesus rather than of Socrates and Descartes, Tolstoy would object to the rationalism of the earlier thinkers. Thinking, for him, was not an abstract process that can be done according to strict logical laws, resulting in purely cognitive answers. Thinking is adjoined with feeling; we know the truth of propositions intuitively, not just abstractly. Faith more than reason determines whether or not a life is worth living. The important thing for Tolstoy, was to be committed to his beliefs in an existential sense, to be willing to live and die by his authentic convictions. Tolstoy would agree with Socrates that examining life is of great importance, but to remain content with scepticism would be intolerable, and even immoral. The excerpt from his short story, "The Death of Ivan Ilych" shows Tolstoy at his best in portraying death as a boundary situation, as an integral aspect of the human condition. It also reveals Tolstoy's interest in the concreteness of individual human existence, the profound anxiety and banality of dying and death.

The philosophical writings of the English philosophers A. J. Ayer and John Wisdom, who represent two approaches to "analytic" philosophy, are radically different from Tolstoy's confessions. Like Descartes, they are concerned with methodology, with clarity and distinctness of ideas. Instead of modeling their approach on mathematics, as Descartes did, however, they modeled it on linguistics, believing that a careful study and elucidation of the forms and concepts of technical and ordinary language is a necessary preliminary to philosophical inquiry. If we can clarify the way we talk about the issues of the human condition, we will gain insights into language use—insights helpful in resolving substantive questions regarding the human condition.

The radical empirical temper of Ayer, his analysis, his unflinching confrontation with the confusions of traditional philosophical questions, and his commitment to delineating what is and what is not meaningful discourse is typical of one type of "analytic" philosophy. John Wisdom's interest in the actual workings of ordinary language, his sensitivity to the use of language in its concrete context, and his microscopic focus on the implications of Tolstoy's question regarding the meaning of life is representative of another type of analytic ordinary language philosophy.

Finally with the selection from Erich Fromm's *Sane Society,* we return from the analysis of linguistic meanings to existential experiences. As a psychotherapist and social philosopher, Fromm confronts what he considers to be the major predicament of our times—the sense of alienation that has infected every aspect of contemporary life and threatens the possibility of remaining human and sane in an increasingly insane society. This predicament has arisen, Fromm believes, out of man's increasing separation from nature, from his fellow humans, from the fruits of his labor, and most importantly from himself. Our uniquely human needs, which stem from the conditions of our existence, go unsatisfied and are unsatisfiable within the constraints of capitalism. Today, Fromm argues, it is impossible to be genuinely human and survive. So in the name of humanity Fromm calls for a radical reformation of social institutions to make a more sane society before it is too late.

Each of the thinkers represented in this section saw the human condition in a different light. It inspired awe in Thoreau, anguish in Tolstoy, and anger in Fromm; Socrates and Descartes were assured that the real is rational, and Ayer and Wisdom were challenged to explore the new territory. In some respects, as Snaith asserted, the diminishment of man continues to increase in the modern world. But through the efforts of these thinkers to fathom, understand, and clarify the human condition, we may be able to bring the diminishment into check, adjust to changes in the condition of being human, and replenish our philosophical and spiritual resources.

NOTE

1. William Snaith, *The Irresponsible Arts* (New York: Atheneum Publishers, 1964), pp. 5–7.

I The Committed Philosopher

Socrates

The nature of philosophy may seem quite abstract until one considers such a philosopher as Socrates (469–399 B.C.). He lived and died by his commitment to self-examination, which was to him the essence of philosophizing. Socrates is the paradigm of the committed philosopher. He encountered doubt and questioned authority. He confronted human nature and faced moral conflict. But while confrontation was the beginning, true commitment was the end of his practical vocation as a philosopher.

The current distinction between analytic and speculative philosophy can be traced to Socrates. He was analytic in that he distinguished clearly the meanings of terms and formulated carefully his definitions and assumptions; he was speculative in that he reflected upon the highest ends of moral conduct and attempted to relate the parts of experience within a larger coherent framework of meaning. A study of Socrates' life, methods, and beliefs (such as he admitted to) can therefore present to the beginning student the basic problems that must be grappled with as he or she strives toward a rationally and morally justifiable commitment.

In understanding Socrates' commitments, one should keep in mind that Socrates was convinced that he had an obligation to search for truth himself as well as to sting others into an awareness of the importance of the search. "I am that gadfly which God has attached to the state," he told the Athenians, "and all day long and in all places am always fastening upon you, arousing and persuading and reproaching you."[1] Not that Socrates claimed to know everything. To the contrary, he claimed that he knew nothing. He was astonished, at first, when he was told that the oracle at Delphi, when asked who was the wisest man in Greece, had replied, "Socrates." But finally, after searching throughout Athens for men who could give him convincing answers to the questions he raised, who really *knew* what they were talking about, whether it was politics, poetry, or

20

carpentry, the oracle's meaning became clear to Socrates. As he told his fellow citizens when some of them eventually brought their gadfly to trial:

> The truth is, O men of Athens, that God only is wise; and by his answer he intends to show that the wisdom of men is worth little or nothing; he is not speaking of Socrates, he is only using my name by way of illustration, as if he said, He, O men, is the wisest, who, like Socrates, knows that his wisdom is in truth worth nothing.[2]

SOCRATIC CONVICTIONS

But long before Socrates had to defend his beliefs and his life in a court of law, many Athenians misunderstood his methods and his aim completely. They considered him to be either a dangerous sceptic and atheist, an underminer of the state's traditions and beliefs, or a calculating Sophist who hoped to profit materially from his teachings.

Socrates was none of these. To be sure, he was sceptical in that he doubted that most men knew what they were talking about when they spoke of such things as justice and injustice, beauty and ugliness, truth and falsehood. Socrates felt that he had a moral obligation to confront such men with his doubt. He challenged them to examine the convictions upon which they were acting by asking questions that provoked them to think more deeply about their basic beliefs. For to *be* good, one must *know* precisely what goodness is; virtue *is* knowledge. One has a moral obligation to examine carefully his personal commitments to be sure that they are worthy of the highest human aspiration and conducive to the best possible life. One must discover to what extent he is living up to the potentialities—rational, moral, and aesthetic—with which he has been endowed. The unexamined life, Socrates was convinced, is not worth living.

SOCRATIC METHOD

Only a superficial or malicious observer could have mistaken Socrates' dialectical method, which consisted of his asking questions of his interlocutors and of raising objections to the answers they gave, for a purely sceptical method, the aim of which was to stir up doubt for its own sake or to encourage the suspension of belief. The reliable first-hand reports that we have on Socrates' life and teaching agree that his intention was not to undermine the state but to improve it. He always showed respect for the religious institutions of Athens. While he claimed to be guided by an inner sign, a divine *daemon,* he taught no secret doctrines, sought no disciples, and, unlike some of the earlier Greek philosophers, made no attempt to explain the nature of the universe scientifically. He pursued what he considered to be his divinely appointed mission of helping others to see by the light of reason, and he did this publicly and freely. Xenophon reported,

> Socrates lived ever in the open; for early in the morning he went to the public promenades and training grounds; in the forenoon he was seen in the market; and the rest of the day he passed just where most people were to be met: he was generally talking, and anyone might listen.[3]

His interest was in human not heavenly phenomena. To his admirers it seemed incredible that such a man, so open, conscientious, and dedicated to truth and goodness could be accused, as he later was, of rejecting the gods of Athens and teaching strange deities.

It was perhaps even more incredible to such friends of Socrates as Xenophon and Plato that he could also be accused, as he was in the later charges brought against him, of corrupting the youth of the Athenian city-state. Socrates valued youth. He admired its enthusiasm, its resoluteness, its moral earnestness, and its sense of wonder. He spoke to young men, not as to unequals, but as to fellow searchers after truth. He realized that they were considerably less adept than he in asking and answering the right questions and that they conceived of the search for knowledge to be a far easier undertaking than it actually was. But, nevertheless, Socrates believed that young people were usually much more sincere than their elders in their desire to distinguish appearance from reality, truth from falsehood, and sham learning from authentic wisdom. The example that he set for them to follow seemed irreproachable to Xenophon and Plato. His self-control, his courage, his good humor, and his intellectual honesty made him a captivating figure to his admirers but, at the same time, a constant threat to his enemies, who despised and feared the intellectual and moral discipline for which he stood. "To be sure, he never professed to teach this," Xenophon writes, "but, by letting his own light shine, he led his disciples to hope that they through imitation of him would attain to such excellence."[4]

AIM AND IMPACT OF SOCRATES

Some who at first followed Socrates, later drifted away to settle down to a life of complacent dogmatism and comfortable conformity. Others, such as Critias and Alcibiades, quickly learned the Socratic method of argumentation and applied it, or rather a travesty of it, for their own selfish political ends, thus contributing to the ruin of Athens and the death of Socrates. Such young men, the defenders of Socrates hasten to point out, were not corrupted by Socrates; they became corrupt because they failed to emulate the Socratic example of impartial and critical inquiry. Even some of those who failed to measure up to the high standards that Socrates held up to them recognized that the fault was their own. For example, Alcibiades, his former admirer who went astray, had this to say in praise of Socrates, according to Plato's *Symposium:*

> For he makes me confess that I ought not to live as I do, neglecting the wants of my own soul and busying myself with the concerns of the Athenians. . . . And he is the only person who ever made me ashamed. . . . For I know I cannot answer him or say that I ought not to do as he bids, but when I leave his presence the love of popularity gets the better of me. And therefore I run away and fly from him, and when I see him I am ashamed of what I have confessed to him. Many a time have I wished that he was dead, and yet I know that I should be much more sorry than glad, if he were to die.[5]

Fortunately, Socrates was more successful than Alcibiades suggests in efforts to help young people follow through in examining their convictions. He would have agreed with Nietzsche that we must have, beyond the courage of our convictions, the courage to examine our convictions. The Socratic method submits convictions to rigorous critical scrutiny in order to clarify, test, and revise them. Intellectual and moral growth in the person should, Socrates believed, follow as a consequence of the examination and reappraisal of convictions or beliefs. Socrates attempted to make all of this clear in the defense of his method as reported by Plato in his *Apology.*

NOTES

1.   Plato, "Apology," in *The Dialogues of Plato,* 3rd ed., trans. Benjamin Jowett (Oxford: Clarendon Press, 1892), vol. I, sec. 31.

2.   Ibid., sec. 23.

3.   Xenophon, *Memorabilia,* trans. E. C. Marchant (Cambridge, Mass.: Harvard University Press, 1918), Bk. I, chap. 1, sec. 10, p. 7.

4.   Ibid., Bk. I, chap. 2, sec. 4, p. 15.

5.   Plato, "Symposium," in *Dialogues,* Jowett translation, sec. 216.

Plato's Apology

In 399 B.C. Socrates was brought to trial before a court composed of 501 Athenian citizens. In his defense he spoke as follows:

How you, O Athenians, have been affected by my accusers, I cannot tell; but I know that they almost made me forget who I was—so persuasively did they speak; and yet they have hardly uttered a word of truth. But of the many falsehoods told by them, there was one which quite amazed me;—I mean when they said that you should be upon your guard and not allow yourselves to be deceived by the force of my eloquence. To say this, when they were certain to be detected as soon as I opened my lips and proved myself to be anything but a great speaker, did indeed appear to me most shameless—unless by the force of eloquence they mean the force of truth; for if such is their meaning, I admit that I am eloquent. But in how different a way from theirs! Well, as I was saying, they have scarcely spoken the truth at all; but from me you shall hear the whole truth: not, however, delivered after their manner in a set oration duly ornamented with words and phrases. No, by heaven! but I shall use the words and arguments which occur to me at the moment; for I am confident in the justice of my cause: at my time of life I ought not to be appearing before you, O men of Athens, in the

From Plato, "Apology," in *The Dialogues of Plato,* trans. Benjamin Jowett, 3d ed., Vol. 1 (New York: Oxford University Press, 1892).

character of a juvenile orator—let no one expect it of me. And I must beg of you to grant me a favour:—If I defend myself in my accustomed manner, and you hear me using the words which I have been in the habit of using in the agora, at the tables of the money-changers, or anywhere else, I would ask you not to be surprised, and not to interrupt me on this account. For I am more than seventy years of age, and appearing now for the first time in a court of law, I am quite a stranger to the language of the place; and therefore I would have you regard me as if I were really a stranger, whom you would excuse if he spoke in his native tongue, and after the fashion of his country:—Am I making an unfair request of you? Never mind the manner, which may or may not be good; but think only of the truth of my words, and give heed to that: let the speaker speak truly and the judge decide justly.

And first, I have to reply to the older charges and to my first accusers, and then I will go on to the later ones. For of old I have had many accusers, who have accused me falsely to you during many years; and I am more afraid of them than of Anytus and his associates, who are dangerous, too, in their own way. But far more dangerous are the others, who began when you were children, and took possession of your minds with their falsehoods, telling of one Socrates, a wise man, who speculated about the heaven above, and searched into the earth beneath, and made the worse appear the better cause. The disseminators of this tale are the accusers whom I dread; for their hearers are apt to fancy that such enquirers do not believe in the existence of the gods. And they are many, and their charges against me are of ancient date, and they were made by them in the days when you were more impressible than you are now—in childhood, or it may have been in youth—and the cause when heard went by default, for there was none to answer. And hardest of all, I do not know and cannot tell the names of my accusers; unless in the chance case of a comic poet. All who from envy and malice have persuaded you—some of them having first convinced themselves—all this class of men are most difficult to deal with; for I cannot have them up here, and cross-examine them, and therefore I must simply fight with shadows in my own defence, and argue when there is no one who answers. I will ask you then to assume with me, as I was saying, that my opponents are of two kinds; one recent, the other ancient: and I hope that you will see the propriety of my answering the latter first, for these accusations you heard long before the others, and much oftener.

Well, then, I must make my defence, and endeavour to clear away in a short time, a slander which has lasted a long time. May I succeed, if to succeed be for my good and yours, or likely to avail me in my cause! The task is not an easy one; I quite understand the nature of it. And so leaving the event with God, in obedience to the law I will now make my defence.

I will begin at the beginning, and ask what is the accusation which has given rise to the slander of me, and in fact has encouraged Meletus to prefer this charge against me. Well, what do the slanderers say? They shall be my prosecutors, and I will sum up their words in an affidavit: "Socrates is an evildoer, and a curious person, who searches into things under the earth and in heaven, and he makes the worse appear the better cause; and he teaches the aforesaid doctrines to others." Such is the nature of the accusation: it is just what you have yourselves seen in the comedy of Aristophanes, who has introduced a man whom he calls Socrates, going about and saying that he walks in air, and talking a deal of nonsense concerning matters of which I do not pretend to know either much or little—not that I mean to speak disparagingly of any one who is a student of natural philosophy. I should be very sorry if Meletus could bring so grave a charge against me. But the simple truth is, O Athenians, that I have nothing to do with physical speculations. Very many of those here present are witnesses to the truth of this, and to them I appeal. Speak then, you who have heard me, and tell your neighbours whether any of you have ever known me hold forth in few words or in many upon such matters. . . . You hear their answer. And from what they say of this part of the charge you will be able to judge of the truth of the rest.

As little foundation is there for the report that I am a teacher, and take money; this accusation has no more truth in it than the other. Although, if a man were really able to instruct mankind, to receive money for giving instruction would, in my opinion, be an honour to him. There is Gorgias of Leontium, and Prodicus of Ceos, and Hippias of Elis, who go the round of the cities, and are able to persuade the young men to leave their own citizens by whom they might be taught for nothing, and come to them whom they not only pay, but are thankful if they may be allowed to pay them. There is at this time a Parian philosopher residing in Athens, of whom I have heard; and I came to hear of him in this way:—I came across a man who has spent a world of money on the Sophists, Callias, the son of Hipponicus, and knowing that he had sons, I asked him: "Callias," I said, "if your two sons were foals or calves, there would be no difficulty in finding some one to put over them; we should hire a trainer of horses, or a farmer, probably, who would improve and perfect them in their own proper virtue and excellence; but as they are human beings, whom are you thinking of placing over them? Is there any one who understands human and political virtue? You must have thought about the matter, for you have sons; is there any one?" "There is," he said. "Who is he?" said I; "and of what country? and what does he charge?" "Evenus the Parian," he replied; "he is the man, and his charge is five minae." Happy is Evenus, I said to myself, if he really has this wisdom, and teaches at such a moderate charge. Had I the same, I should have been very proud and conceited; but the truth is that I have no knowledge of the kind.

I dare say, Athenians, that some one among you will reply, "Yes, Socrates, but what is the origin of these accusations which are brought against you; there must have been something strange which you have been doing? All these rumours and this talk about you would never have arisen if you had been like other men: tell us, then, what is the cause of them, for we should be sorry to judge hastily of you." Now, I regard this as a fair challenge, and I will endeavour to explain to you the reason why I am called wise and have such an evil fame. Please to attend then. And although some of you may think that I am joking, I declare that I will tell you the entire truth. Men of Athens, this reputation of mine has come of a certain sort of wisdom which I possess. If you ask me what kind of wisdom, I reply, wisdom such as may perhaps be attained by man, for to that extent I am inclined to believe that I am wise; whereas the persons of whom I was speaking have a superhuman wisdom, which I may fail to describe, because I have it not myself; and he who says that I have, speaks falsely, and is taking away my character. And here, O men of Athens, I must beg you not to interrupt me, even if I seem to say something extravagant. For the word which I will speak is not mine. I will refer you to a witness who is worthy of credit; that witness shall be the god of Delphi—he will tell you about my wisdom, if I have any, and of what sort it is. You must have known Chaerephon; he was early a friend of mine, and also a friend of yours, for he shared in the recent exile of the people, and returned with you. Well, Chaerephon, as you know, was very impetuous in all his doings, and he went to Delphi and boldly asked the oracle to tell him whether —as I was saying, I must beg you not to interrupt—he asked the oracle to tell him whether any one was wiser than I was, and the Pythian prophetess answered, that there was no man wiser. Chaerephon is dead himself; but his brother, who is in court, will confirm the truth of what I am saying.

Why do I mention this? Because I am going to explain to you why I have such an evil name. When I heard the answer, I said to myself, What can the god mean? and what is the interpretation of his riddle? for I know I have no wisdom, small or great. What then can he mean when he says that I am the wisest of men? And yet he is a god, and cannot lie; that would be against his nature. After long consideration, I thought of a method of trying the question. I reflected that if I could only find a man wiser than myself, then I might go to the god with a refutation in my hand. I should say to him, "Here is a man who is wiser than I am; but you said that I was the wisest." Accordingly I went to one who had the reputation of wisdom, and observed him—his name I need not mention; he was a politician whom I selected for examination—and the result was as follows: When I began to talk with him, I could not help thinking that he was not really wise, although he was thought wise by many, and still wiser by himself; and thereupon I tried to explain to him that he thought himself wise, but was not really wise; and the consequence was that he hated me, and his enmity was shared by several who were present and heard me. So I left him, saying to myself, as I went away: Well, although I do not suppose that either of us knows anything really beautiful and good, I am better off than he is,—for he knows nothing, and thinks that he knows; I neither know nor think that I know. In this latter particular, then, I seem to have slightly the advantage of him. Then I went to another who had still higher pretentions to wisdom, and my conclusion was exactly the same. Whereupon I made another enemy of him, and many others besides him.

Then I went to one man after another, being not unconscious of the enmity which I provoked, and I lamented and feared this: but necessity was laid upon me,—the word of God, I thought, ought to be considered first. And I said to myself, Go I must to all who appear to know, and find out the meaning of the oracle. And I swear to you, Athenians, by the dog I swear!—for I must tell you the truth—the result of my mission was just this: I found that the men most in repute were all but the most foolish; and that others less esteemed were really wiser and better. I will tell you the tale of my wanderings and of the "Herculean" labours, as I may call them, which I endured only to find at last the oracle irrefutable. After the politicians, I went to the poets; tragic, dithyrambic, and all sorts. And there, I said to myself, you will be instantly detected; now you will find out that you are more ignorant than they are. Accordingly I took them some of the most elaborate passages in their own writings, and asked what was the meaning of them— thinking that they would teach me something. Will you believe me? I am almost ashamed to confess the truth, but I must say that there is hardly a person present who would not have talked better about their poetry than they did themselves. Then I knew that not by wisdom do poets write poetry, but by a sort of genius and inspiration; they are like diviners or soothsayers who also say many fine things, but do not understand the meaning of them. The poets appeared to me to be much in the same case; and I further observed that upon the strength of their poetry they believed themselves to be the wisest of men in other things in which they were not wise. So I departed, conceiving myself

to be superior to them for the same reason that I was superior to the politicians.

At last I went to the artisans. I was conscious that I knew nothing at all, as I may say, and I was sure that they knew many fine things; and here I was not mistaken, for they did know many things of which I was ignorant, and in this they certainly were wiser than I was. But I observed that even the good artisans fell into the same error as the poets;—because they were good workmen they thought that they also knew all sorts of high matters, and this defect in them overshadowed their wisdom; and therefore I asked myself on behalf of the oracle, whether I would like to be as I was, neither having their knowledge nor their ignorance, or like them in both; and I made answer to myself and to the oracle that I was better off as I was.

This inquisition has led to my having many enemies of the worst and most dangerous kind, and has given occasion also to many calumnies. And I am called wise, for my hearers always imagine that I myself possess the wisdom which I find wanting in others: but the truth is, O men of Athens, that God only is wise; and by his answer he intends to show that the wisdom of men is worth little or nothing; he is not speaking of Socrates, he is only using my name by way of illustration, as if he said, He, O men, is the wisest, who, like Socrates, knows that his wisdom is in truth worth nothing. And so I go about the world obedient to the god, and search and make enquiry into the wisdom of any one, whether citizen or stranger, who appears to be wise; and if he is not wise, then in vindication of the oracle I show him he is not wise; and my occupation quite absorbs me, and I have no time to give either to any public matter of interest or to any concern of my own, but I am in utter poverty by reason of my devotion to the god.

There is another thing:—young men of the richer classes, who have not much to do, come about me of their own accord; they like to hear the pretenders examined, and they often imitate me, and proceed to examine others; there are plenty of persons, as they quickly discover, who think that they know something, but really know little or nothing; and then those who are examined by them instead of being angry with themselves are angry with me: This confounded Socrates, they say; this villainous misleader of youth!—and then if somebody asks them, Why, what evil does he practise or teach? they do not know, and cannot tell; but in order that they may not appear to be at a loss, they repeat the ready-made charges which are used against all philosophers about teaching things up in the clouds and under the earth, and having no gods, and making the worse appear the better cause; for they do not like to confess that their pretence of knowledge has been detected —which is the truth; and as they are numerous and ambitious and energetic, and are drawn up in battle array and have persuasive tongues, they have filled your ears with their loud and inveterate calumnies. And this is the reason why my three accusers, Meletus and Anytus and Lycon, have set upon me; Meletus, who has a quarrel with me on behalf of the poets; Anytus, on behalf of the craftsmen and politicians; Lycon, on behalf of the rhetoricians: and, as I said at the beginning, I cannot expect to get rid of such a mass of calumny all in a moment. And this, O men of Athens, is the truth and the whole truth; I have concealed nothing, I have dissembled nothing. And yet, I know that my plainness of speech makes them hate me, and what is their hatred but a proof that I am speaking the truth? Hence has arisen the prejudice against me; and this is the reason of it, as you will find out either in this or in any future enquiry.

I have said enough in my defence against the first class of my accusers; I turn to the second class. They are headed by Meletus, that good man and true lover of his country, as he calls himself. Against these, too, I must try to make a defence:—Let their affidavit be read: it contains something of this kind: It says that Socrates is a doer of evil, who corrupts the youth; and who does not believe in the gods of the State, but has other new divinities of his own. Such is the charge; and now let us examine the particular counts. He says that I am a doer of evil, and corrupt the youth; but I say, O men of Athens, that Meletus is a doer of evil, in that he pretends to be in earnest when he is only in jest, and is so eager to bring men to trial from a pretended zeal and interest about matters in which he really never had the smallest interest. And the truth of this I will endeavour to prove to you.

Come hither, Meletus, and let me ask a question of you. You think a great deal about the improvement of youth?

Yes, I do.

Tell the judges, then, who is their improver; for you must know, as you have taken the pains to discover their corrupter, and are citing and accusing me before them. Speak, then, and tell the judges who their improver is.—Observe, Meletus, that you are silent, and have nothing to say. But is not this rather disgraceful, and a very considerable proof of what I was saying, that you have no interest in the matter? Speak up, friend, and tell us who their improver is.

The laws.

But that, my good sir, is not my meaning. I want to know who the person is, who, in the first place, knows the laws.

The judges, Socrates, who are present in court.

What, do you mean to say, Meletus, that they are able to instruct and improve youth?

Certainly they are.

What, all of them, or some only and not others?

All of them.

By the goddess. Here, that is good news! There are plenty of improvers, then. And what do you say of the audience,—do they improve them?

Yes, they do.

And the senators?

Yes, the senators improve them.

But perhaps the members of the assembly corrupt them?—or do they improve them?

They improve them.

Then every Athenian improves and elevates them; all with the exception of myself; and I alone am their corrupter? Is that what you affirm?

That is what I stoutly affirm.

I am very unfortunate if you are right. But suppose I ask you a question: How about horses? Does one man do them harm and all the world good? Is not the exact opposite the truth? One man is able to do them good, or at least not many;—the trainer of horses, that is to say, does them good, and others who have to do with them rather injure them? Is not that true, Meletus, of horses, or of any other animals? Most assuredly it is; whether you and Anytus say yes or no. Happy indeed would be the condition of youth if they had one corrupter only, and all the rest of the world were their improvers. But you, Meletus, have sufficiently shown that you never had a thought about the young: your carelessness is seen in your not caring about the very things which you bring against me.

And now, Meletus, I will ask you another question—by Zeus I will: Which is better, to live among bad citizens, or among good ones? Answer, friend, I say; the question is one which may be easily answered. Do not the good do their neighbours good, and the bad do them evil?

Certainly.

And is there any one who would rather be injured than benefited by those who live with him? Answer, my good friend, the law requires you to answer—does any one like to be injured?

Certainly not.

And when you accuse me of corrupting and deteriorating the youth, do you allege that I corrupt them intentionally or unintentionally?

Intentionally, I say.

But you have just admitted that the good do their neighbours good, and the evil do them evil. Now, is that a truth which your superior wisdom has recognized thus early in life, and am I, at my age, in such darkness and ignorance as not to know that if a man with whom I have to live is corrupted by me, I am very likely to be harmed by him; and yet I corrupt him, and intentionally, too—so you say, although neither I nor any other human being is ever likely to be convinced by you. But either I do not corrupt them, or I corrupt them unintentionally; and on either view of the case you lie. If my offence is unintentional, the law has no cognizance of unintentional offences: you ought to have taken me privately, and warned and admonished me; for if I had been better advised, I should have left off doing what I only did unintentionally—no doubt I should; but you would have nothing to say to me and refused to teach me. And now you bring me up in this court, which is a place not of instruction, but of punishment.

It will be very clear to you, Athenians, as I was saying, that Meletus has no care at all, great or small, about the matter. But still I should like to know, Meletus, in what I am affirmed to corrupt the young. I suppose you mean, as I infer from your indictment, that I teach them not to acknowledge the gods which the State acknowledges, but some other new divinities or spiritual agencies in their stead. These are the lessons by which I corrupt the youth, as you say.

Yes, that I say emphatically.

Then, by the gods, Meletus, of whom we are speaking, tell me and the court, in somewhat plainer terms, what you mean! For I do not as yet understand whether you affirm that I teach other men to acknowledge some gods, and therefore that I do believe in gods, and am not an entire atheist—this you do not lay to my charge,—but only you say that they are not the same gods which the city recognizes—the charge is that they are different gods. Or, do you mean that I am an atheist simply, and a teacher of atheism?

I mean the latter—that you are a complete atheist.

What an extraordinary statement! Why do you think so, Meletus? Do you mean that I do not believe in the godhead of the sun or moon, like other men?

I assure you, judges, that he does not: for he says that the sun is stone, and the moon earth.

Friend Meletus, you think that you are accusing Anaxagoras: and you have but a bad opinion of the judges, if you fancy them illiterate to such a degree as not to know that these doctrines are found in the books of Anaxagoras the Clazomenian, which are full of them. And so, forsooth, the youth are said to be taught them by Socrates, when there are not infrequently exhibitions of them at the theatre (price of admission one drachma at the most); and they might pay their money, and laugh at Socrates if he pretends to father these extraordinary views. And so, Meletus, you really think that I do not believe in any god?

I swear by Zeus that you believe absolutely in none at all.

Nobody will believe you, Meletus, and I am pretty sure that you do not believe yourself. I cannot help thinking, that he has written this indictment in a spirit of mere wantonness and youthful bravado. Has he not compounded a riddle, thinking to try me? He said to himself; —I shall see whether the wise Socrates will discover my facetious contradiction, or whether I shall be able to deceive him and the rest of them. For he certainly does appear to me to contradict himself in the indictment as much as if he said that Socrates is guilty of not believing in the gods, and yet of believing in them —but this is not like a person who is in earnest.

I should like you, O men of Athens, to join me in examining what I conceive to be his inconsistency; and do you, Meletus, answer. And I must remind the audience of my request that they would not make a disturbance if I speak in my accustomed manner:

Did ever man, Meletus, believe in the existence of human things, and not of human beings? . . . I wish, men of Athens, that he would answer, and not be always trying to get up an interruption. Did ever any man believe in horsemanship, and not in horses, or in flute-playing, and not in flute-players? No, my friend; I will answer to you and to the court, as you refuse to answer for yourself. There is no man who ever did. But now please to answer the next question: Can a man believe in spiritual and divine agencies, and not in spirits or demigods?

He cannot.

How lucky I am to haxe extracted that answer, by the assistance of the court! But then you swear in the indictment that I teach and believe in divine or spiritual agencies (new or old, no matter for that); at any rate, I believe in spiritual agencies—so you say and swear in the affidavit; and yet if I believe in divine beings, how can I help believing in spirits or demigods;—must I not? To be sure I must; and therefore I may assume that your silence gives consent. Now what are spirits or demigods? are they not either gods or the sons of gods?

Certainly they are.

But this is what I call the facetious riddle invented by you: the demigods or spirits are gods, and you say first that I do not believe in gods, and then again that I do believe in gods; that is, if I believe in demigods. For if the demigods are the illegitimate sons of gods, whether by the nymphs or by any other mothers, of whom they are said to be the sons—what human being will ever believe that there are no gods if they are the sons of gods? You might as well affirm the existence of mules, and deny that of horses and asses. Such nonsense, Meletus, could only have been intended by you to make trial of me. You have put this into the indictment because you had nothing real of which to accuse me. But no one who has a particle of understanding will ever be convinced by you that the same men can believe in divine and superhuman beings, and yet not believe that there are gods and demigods and heroes.

I have said enough in answer to the charge of Meletus: any elaborate defence is unnecessary; but I know only too well how many are the enmities which I have incurred, and this is what will be my destruction if I am destroyed; —not Meletus, nor yet Anytus, but the envy and detraction of the world, which has been the death of many good men, and will probably be the death of many more; there is no danger of my being the last of them.

Some one will say: And are you not ashamed, Socrates, of a course of life which is likely to bring you to an untimely end? To him I may fairly answer: There you are mistaken: a man who is good for anything ought not to calculate the chance of living or dying; he ought only to consider whether in doing anything he is doing right or wrong—acting the part of a good man or a bad. Whereas, upon your view, the son of Thetis above all, who altogether despised danger in comparison with disgrace; and when he was so eager to slay Hector, his goddess mother said to him, that if he avenged his companion Patroclus, and slew Hector, he would die himself—"Fate," she said, in these or the like words, "waits for you next after Hector"; he, receiving this warning, utterly depised danger and death, and instead of fearing them, feared rather to live in dishonour, and not to avenge his friend. "Let me die forthwith," he replies, "and be avenged of my enemy, rather than abide here by the beaked ships, a laughing stock and a burden of the earth." Had Achilles any thought of death and danger? For wherever a man's place is, whether the place which he has chosen or that in which he has been placed by a commander, there he ought to remain in the hour of danger; he should not think of death or of anything but of disgrace. And this, O men of Athens, is a true saying.

Strange, indeed, would be my conduct, O men of Athens, if I, who, when I was ordered by the generals whom you chose to command me at Potidaea and Amphipolis and Delium, remained where they placed me, like any other man, facing death—if now, when, as I conceive and imagine, God orders me to fulfil the philosopher's mission of searching into myself and other men, I were to desert my post through fear of death, or any other fear; that would indeed be strange, and I might justly be arraigned in court for denying the existence of the gods, if I disobeyed the oracle because I was afraid of death, fancying that I was wise when I was not wise. For the fear is indeed the pretence of wisdom, and not real wisdom, being a pretence of knowing the unknown; and no one knows whether death, which men in their fear apprehend to be the greatest evil, may not be the greatest good. Is not this ignorance of a disgraceful sort, the ignorance which is the conceit that a man knows what he does not know? And in this respect only I believe myself to differ from men in general, and may perhaps claim to be wiser than they are:—that whereas I know but little of the world below, I do not suppose that I know: but I do know that injustice and disobedience to a better, whether God or man, is evil and dishonourable, and I will never fear or avoid a possible good rather than a certain evil. And therefore if you let me go now, and are not convinced by Anytus, who said that since I had been prosecuted I must be put to death; (or if not that I ought never to have been prosecuted at all); and that if I escape now, your sons will all be utterly ruined by listening to my words—if you say to me, Socrates, this time we will not mind Anytus, and you shall be let off, but upon one condition, that you are not to enquire and speculate in this way any more, and that if you are caught doing so again you shall die;—if this was the condition on which you let me go, I should reply: Men of Athens, I honour and love you; but I shall obey God rather than you, and while I have life and strength I shall never cease from the practice and teaching of philosophy, exhorting any one whom I meet and saying to him after my manner: You, my friend,—a citizen of the great and mighty and wise city of Athens,— are you not ashamed of heaping up the greatest amount of money and honour and reputation, and caring so little about wisdom and truth and the greatest improvement of the soul, which you never regard or heed at all? And if the person with whom I am arguing, says: Yes, but I do care; then I do not leave him or let him go at once; but I proceed to interrogate and examine him, and if I think that he has no virtue in him, but only says that he has, I reproach him with undervaluing the greater, and overvaluing the less. And I shall repeat the same words to every one whom I meet, young and old, citizen and alien, but especially to the citizens, inasmuch as they are my brethren. For know that this is the command of God; and I believe that no greater good has ever happened in the State than my service to the God. For I do nothing but go about persuading you all, old and young alike, not to take thought for your persons or your properties, but first and chiefly to care about the greatest improvement of the soul. I tell you that virtue is not given by money, but that from virtue comes money and every other good of man, public as well as private. This is my teaching, and if this is the doctrine which corrupts the youth, I am a mischievous person. But if any one says that this is not my teaching, he is speaking an untruth. Wherefore, O men of Athens, I say to you, do as Anytus bids or not as Anytus bids, and either acquit me or not; but whichever you do, understand that I shall never alter my ways, not even if I have to die many times.

Men of Athens, do not interrupt, but hear me; there was an understanding between us that you should hear me to the end: I have something more to say, at which you may be inclined to cry out; but I believe that to hear me will be good for you, and therefore I beg that you will not cry out. I would have you know, that if you kill such an one as I am, you will injure yourselves more than you will injure me. Nothing will injure me, not Meletus nor yet Anytus— they cannot, for a bad man is not permitted to injure a better than himself. I do not deny that Anytus may, perhaps, kill him, or drive him into exile, or deprive him of civil rights; and he may imagine, and others may imagine, that he is inflicting a great injury upon him: but there I do not agree. For the evil of doing as he is doing—the evil of unjustly taking away the life of another—is greater far.

And, now, Athenians, I am not going to argue for my own sake, as you may think, but for yours, that you may not sin against the God by condemning me, who am his gift to you. For if you kill me you will not easily find a successor to me, who, if I may use such a ludicrous figure of speech, am a sort of gadfly, given to the State by God; and the State is a great and noble steed who is tardy in his motions owing to his very size, and requires to be stirred into life. I am that gadfly which God has attached to the State, and all day long and in all places am always fastening upon you, arousing and persuading and reproaching you. You will not easily find another like me, and therefore I would advise you to spare me. I dare say that you may feel out of temper (like a person who is suddenly awakened from sleep), and you think that you might easily strike me dead as Anytus advises, and then you would sleep on for the remainder of your lives, unless God in his care of you sent you another gadfly. When I say that I am given to you by God, the proof of my mission is this:—if I had been like other men, I should not have neglected all my own concerns or patiently seen the neglect of them during all these years, and have been doing yours, coming to you individually like a father or elder brother, exhorting you to regard virtue; such conduct, I say, would be unlike human nature. If I had gained anything, or if my exhortations had been paid, there would have been some sense in my doing so; but now, as you will perceive, not even the impudence of my accusers dares to say that I have ever extracted or sought pay of any one; of that they have no witness. And I have a sufficient witness to the truth of what I say—my poverty.

Some one may wonder why I go about in private giving advice and busying myself with the concerns of others, but do not venture to come forward in public and advise the State. I will tell you why. You have heard me speak at sundry times and in divers places of an oracle or sign which comes to me, and this is the divinity which Meletus ridicules in the indictment. This sign, which is a kind of voice, first began to come to me when I was a child; it always forbids but never commands me to do anything which I am going to do. This is what deters me from being a politician. And rightly, as I think. For I am certain, O men of Athens, that if I had engaged in politics, I should have perished long ago, and done no good either to you or to myself. And do not be offended at my telling you the truth; for the truth is, that no man who goes to war with you or any other multitude, honestly striving against the many lawless and unrighteous deeds which are done in a State, will save his life; he who will fight for the right, if he would live even for a brief space, must have a private station and not a public one.

I can give you convincing evidence of what I say, not words only, but what you value far more—actions. Let me relate to you a passage of my own life which will prove to you that I should never have yielded to injustice from any fear of death and that "as I should have refused to yield" I must have died at once. I will tell you a tale of the courts, not very interesting perhaps, but nevertheless true. The only office of State which I ever held, O men of Athens, was that of senator: the tribe Antiochis, which is my tribe, had the presidency at the trial of the generals who had not taken up the bodies of the slain after the battle of Arginusae; and you proposed to try them in a body, contrary to law, as you all thought afterwards; but at the time I

was the only one of the Prytanes who was opposed to the illegality, and I gave my vote against you; and when the orators threatened to impeach and arrest me, and you called and shouted, I made up my mind that I would run the risk, having law and justice with me, rather than take part in your injustice because I feared imprisonment and death. This happened in the days of the democracy. But when the oligarchy of the Thirty was in power, they sent for me and four others into the rotunda, and bade us bring Leon the Salaminian from Salamis, as they wanted to put him to death. This was a specimen of the sort of commands which they were always giving with the view of implicating as many as possible in their crimes; and then I showed, not in word only but in deed, that, if I may be allowed to use such an expression, I cared not a straw for death, and that my great and only care was lest I should do an unrighteous or unholy thing. For the strong arm of that oppressive power did not frighten me into doing wrong; and when we came out of the rotunda the other four went to Salamis and fetched Leon, but I went quietly home. For which I might have lost my life, had not the power of the Thirty shortly afterwards come to an end. And many will witness to my words.

Now, do you really imagine that I could have survived all these years, if I had led a public life, supposing that like a good man I had always maintained the right and had made justice, as I ought, the first thing? No, indeed, men of Athens, neither I nor any other man. But I have been always the same in all my actions, public as well as private, and never have I yielded any base compliance to those who are slanderously termed my disciples, or to any other. Not that I have any regular disciples. But if any one likes to come and hear me while I am pursuing my mission, whether he be young or old, he is not excluded. Nor do I converse only with those who pay; but any one, whether he be rich or poor, may ask and answer me and listen to my words; and whether he turns out to be a bad man or a good one, neither result can be justly imputed to me; for I never taught or professed to teach him anything. And if any one says that he has ever learned or heard anything from me in private which all the world has not heard, let me tell you that he is lying.

But I shall be asked, Why do people delight in continually conversing with you? I have told you already, Athenians, the whole truth about this matter: they like to hear the cross-examination of the pretenders to wisdom; there is amusement in it. Now, this duty of cross-examining other men has been imposed upon me by God; and has been signified to me by oracles, visions, and in every way in which the will of divine power was ever intimated to any one. This is true, O Athenians; or, if not true, would be soon refuted. If I am or have been corrupting the youth, those of them who are now grown up and have become sensible that I gave them bad advice in the days of their youth should come forward as accusers, and take their revenge; or if they do not like to come themselves, some of their relatives, fathers, brothers, or other kinsmen, should say what evil their families have suffered at my hands. Now is their time. Many of them I see in the court. There is Crito, who is of the same age of the same deme with myself, and there is Critobulus his son, whom I also see. Then again there is Lysanias of Sphettus, who is the father of Aeschines—he is present; and also there is Antiphon of Cephisus, who is the father of Epigenes; and there are the brothers of several who have associated with me. There is Nicostratus the son of Theosdotides, and the brother of Theodotus (now Theodotus himself is dead, and therefore he, at any rate, will not seek to stop him); and there is Paralus the son of Demodocus, who had a brother Theages; and Adeimantus the son of Ariston, whose brother Plato is present; and Aeantodorus, who is the brother of Appollodorus, whom I also see. I might mention a great many others, some of whom Meletus should have produced as witnesses in the course of his speech; and let him still produce them, if he has forgotten—I will make way for him. And let him say, if he has any testimony of the sort which he can produce. Nay, Athenians, the very opposite is the truth. For all these are ready to witness on behalf of the corrupter, of the injurer of their kindred, as Meletus and Anytus call me; not the corrupted youth only—there might have been a motive for that—but their uncorrupted elder relatives. Why should they too support me with their testimony? Why, indeed, except for the sake of truth and justice, and because they know that I am speaking the truth, and that Meletus is a liar.

Well, Athenians, this and the like of this is all the defence which I have to offer. Yet a word more. Perhaps there may be some one who is offended at me, when he calls to mind how he himself on a similar, or even a less serious occasion, prayed and entreated the judges with many tears, and how he produced his children in court, which was a moving spectacle, together with a host of relations and friends; whereas I, who am probably in danger of my life, will do none of these things. The contrast may occur to his mind, and he may be set against me, and vote in anger because he is displeased at me on this account. Now, if there be such a person among you,—mind, I do not say that there is,—to him I may fairly reply: My friend, I am a man, and like other men, a creature of flesh and blood, and not "of wood or stone," as Homer says; and I have a family, yes, and sons, O Athenians, three in number, one almost a man, and two others who are still young; and yet I will not bring any of them hither in order to petition you for an acquittal. And why not? Not from any self-assertion or want of respect for you. Whether I am or am not afraid of death is another question, of which I will not now speak. But, having regard to public opinion, I feel that such conduct would be discreditable to myself, and to you, and to the whole State. One who has reached my years, and who has a name for wisdom, ought not to demean himself. Whether this opinion of me be deserved or not, at any rate the world has decided that Socrates is in some way superior to other men. And if those among you who are said to be superior in wisdom and courage, and any other virtue, demean themselves in this way, how shameful is their conduct! I have seen men of reputation, when they have been condemned, behaving in the strangest manner: they seemed to fancy that they were going to suffer something dreadful if they died, and that they could be immortal if you only allowed them to live; and I think that such are a dishonour to the State, and that any stranger coming in would have said to them that the most eminent men of Athens, to whom the Athenians themselves give honour and command, are no better than women. And I say that these things ought not to be done by those of us who have a reputation; and if they are done, you ought not to permit them; you ought rather to show that you are far more disposed to condemn the man who gets up a doleful scene and makes the city ridiculous, than him who holds his peace.

But, setting aside the question of public opinion, there seems to be something wrong in asking a favour of a judge, and thus procuring an acquittal, instead of informing and convincing him. For his duty is, not to make a present of justice, but to give judgment; and he has sworn that he will judge according to the laws, and not according to his own good pleasure; and we ought not to encourage you, nor should you allow yourselves to be encouraged, in this habit of perjury—there can be no piety in that. Do not then require me to do what I consider dishonourable and impious and wrong, especially now, when I am being tried for impiety on the indictment of Meletus. For if, O men of Athens, by force of persuasion and entreaty I could overpower your oaths, then I should be teaching you to believe that there

are no gods, and in defending should simply convict myself of the charge of not believing in them. But that is not so—far otherwise. For I do believe that there are gods, and in a sense higher than that in which any of my accusers believe in them. And to you and to God I commit my cause, to be determined by you as is best for you and me. . . .

A majority of the jurors then found Socrates guilty: 281 votes against 220. The condemned man was allowed to propose a penalty in lieu of the death penalty proposed by Meletus. Socrates again spoke:

There are many reasons why I am not grieved, O men of Athens, at the vote of condemnation. I expected it, and am only surprised that the votes are so nearly equal; for I had thought that the majority against me would have been far larger; but now, had thirty votes gone over to the other side, I should have escaped Meletus. I may say more; for without the assistance of Anytus and Lycon, any one may see that he would not have had a fifth part of the votes, as the law requires, in which case he would have incurred a fine of a thousand drachmae.

And so he proposes death as the penalty. And what shall I propose on my part, O men of Athens? Clearly that which is my due. And what is my due? What returns shall be made to the man who has never had the wit to be idle during his whole life; but has been careless of what the many care for—wealth, and family interests, and military offices, and speaking in the assembly, and magistracies, and plots, and parties. Reflecting that I was really too honest a man to be a politician and live, I did not go where I could do no good to you or to myself; but where I could do the greatest good privately to every one of you, thither I went, and sought to persuade every man among you that he must look to himself, and seek virtue and wisdom before he looks to his private interests, and look to the State before he looks to the interests of the State; and that this should be the order which he observes in all his actions. What shall be done to such an one? Doubtless some good thing, O men of Athens, if he has his reward; and the good should be of a kind suitable to him. What would be a reward suitable to a poor man who is your benefactor, and who desires leisure that he may instruct you? There can be no reward so fitting as maintenance in the Prytaneum, O men of Athens, a reward which he deserves far more than the citizen who has won the prize at Olympia in the horse or chariot race, whether the chariots were drawn by two horses or by many. For I am in want, and he has enough; and he only gives you the appearance of happiness, and I give you the reality. And if I am to estimate the penalty fairly, I should say that maintenance in the Prytaneum is the just return.

Perhaps you think that I am braving you in what I am saying now, as in what I said before about the tears and prayers. But this is not so. I speak rather because I am convinced that I never intentionally wronged any one, although I cannot convince you—the time has been too short; if there were a law at Athens, as there is in other cities, that a capital cause should not be decided in one day, then I believe that I should have convinced you. But I cannot in a moment refute great slanders; and, as I am convinced that I never wronged another, I will assuredly not wrong myself. I will not say of myself that I serve any evil, or propose any penalty. Why should I? Because I am afraid of the penalty of death which Meletus proposes? When I do not know whether death is a good or an evil, why should I propose a penalty which would certainly be an evil? Shall I say imprisonment? And why should I live in prison, and be the slave of the magistrate of the year—of the Eleven? Or shall the penalty be a fine, and imprisonment until the fine is paid? There is the same objection. I should

have to lie in prison, for money I have none, and cannot pay. And if I say exile (and this may possibly be the penalty which you will affix), I must indeed be blinded by the love of life, if I am so irrational as to expect that when you, who are my own citizens, cannot endure my discourses and words, and have found them so grievous and odious that you will have no more of them, others are likely to endure me. No, indeed, men of Athens, that is not very likely. And what a life should I lead, at my age, wandering from city to city, ever changing my place of exile, and always being driven out! For I am quite sure that wherever I go, there, as here, the young men will flock to me; and if I drive them away, their elders will drive me out at their request; and if I let them come, their fathers and friends will drive me out for their sakes.

Some one will say: Yes, Socrates, but cannot you hold your tongue, and then you may go into a foreign city, and no one will interfere with you? Now, I have great difficulty in making you understand my answer to this. For if I tell you that to do as you say would be a disobedience to the God, and therefore that I cannot hold my tongue, you will not believe that I am serious; and if I say again that daily to discourse about virtue, and of those other things about which you hear me examining myself and others, is the greatest good of man, and that the unexamined life is not worth living, you are still less likely to believe me. Yet I say what is true, although a thing of which it is hard for me to persuade you. Also, I have never been accustomed to think that I deserve to suffer any harm. Had I money I might have estimated the offence at what I was able to pay, and not have been much the worse. But I have none, and therefore I must ask you to proportion the fine to my means. Well, perhaps I could afford a mina, and therefore I propose that penalty: Plato, Crito, Critobulus, and Apollodorus, my friends here, bid me say thirty minae, and they will be the sureties. Let thirty minae be the penalty; for which sum they will be ample security to you. . . .

Another vote was taken and the death penalty was passed. Socrates then made his final statement:

Not much time will be gained, O Athenians, in return for the evil name which you will get from the detractors of the city, who will say that you killed Socrates, a wise man; for they will call me wise, even although I am not wise, when they want to reproach you. If you had waited a little while, your desire would have been fulfilled in the course of nature. For I am far advanced in years, as you may perceive, and not far from death. I am speaking now not to all of you, but only to those who have condemned me to death. And I have another thing to say to them: You think that I was convicted because I had not words of the sort which would have procured my acquittal—I mean, if I had thought fit to leave nothing undone or unsaid. Not so; the deficiency which led to my conviction was not of words—certainly not. But I had not the boldness or impudence or inclination to address you as you would have liked me to do, weeping and wailing and lamenting, and saying and doing many things which you have been accustomed to hear from others, and which, as I maintain, are unworthy of me. I thought at the time that I ought not to do anything common or mean when in danger: nor do I now repent of the style of my defence; I would rather die having spoken after my manner, than speak in your manner and live. For neither in war nor yet at law ought I or any man to use every way of escaping death. Often in battle there can be no doubt that if a man will throw away his arms, and fall on his knees before his pursuers, he may escape death; and in other dangers there are other ways of escaping death, if a man is willing to say and do anything. The difficulty, my friends, is not to avoid death, but to avoid unrighteousness; for that runs faster than death. I am old and move slowly, and the slower runner has overtaken me, and my accusers are keen and quick, and the faster runner, who is unrighteousness, has overtaken them. And now I depart hence condemned by you to suffer the penalty of death,—they too go their ways condemned by the truth to suffer the penalty of villainy and wrong; and I must abide by my award—let them abide by my award—let them abide by theirs. I suppose that these things may be regarded as fated,—and I think that they are well.

And now, O men who have condemned me, I would fain prophesy to you; for I am about to die, and in the hour of death men are gifted with prophetic power. And I prophesy to you who are my murderers, that immediately after my departure punishment far heavier than you have inflicted on me will surely await you. Me you have killed because you wanted to escape the accuser, and not to give an account of your lives. But that will not be as you suppose: far otherwise. For I say that there will be more accusers of you than there are now; accusers whom hitherto I have restrained: and as they are younger they will be more inconsiderate with you, and you will be more offended at them. If you think that by killing men you can prevent some one from censuring your evil lives, you are mistaken; that is not a way of escape which is either possible or honorable; the easiest and the noblest way is not to be disabling others, but to be improving yourselves. This is the prophecy which I utter before my departure to the judges who have condemned me.

Friends, who would have acquitted me, I would like also to talk with you about the thing which has come to pass, while the magistrates are busy, and before I go to the place at which I must die. Stay then a little, for we may as well talk with one another while there is time. You are my friends, and I should like to show you the meaning of this event which has happened to me. O my judges—for you I may truly call judges—I should like to tell you a wonderful circumstance. Hitherto the divine faculty of which the internal oracle is the source has constantly been in the habit of opposing me even about trifles, if I was going to make a slip or error in any matter; and now as you see there has come upon me that which may be thought, and is generally believed to be, the last and worst evil. But the oracle made no sign of opposition, either when I was leaving my house in the morning, or when I was on my way to the court, or while I was speaking, at anything which I was going to say; and yet I have often been stopped in the middle of a speech, but now in nothing I either said or did touching the matter in hand has the oracle opposed me. What do I take to be the explanation of this silence? I will tell you. It is an intimation that what has happened to me is a good, and that those of us who think that death is an evil are in error. For the customary sign would surely have opposed me had I been going to evil and not to good.

Let us reflect in another way, and we shall see that there is great reason to hope that death is a good; for one of two things—either death is a state of nothingness and utter unconsciousness, or, as men say, there is a change and migration of the soul from this world to another. Now, if you suppose that there is no consciousness, but a sleep like the sleep of him who is undisturbed even by dreams, death will be an unspeakable gain. For if a person were to select the night in which his sleep was undisturbed even by dreams, and were to compare with this the other days and nights of his life, and then were to tell us how many days and nights he had passed in the course of his life better and more pleasantly than this one, I think that any man, I will not say a private man, but even the great king will not find many such days or nights, when compared with the others. Now, if death be of such a

nature, I say that to die is gain; for eternity is then only a single night. But if death is the journey to another place, and there, as men say, all the dead abide, what good, O my friends and judges, can be greater than this? If, indeed, when the pilgrim arrives in the world below, he is delivered from the professors of justice in this world, and finds the true judges who are said to give judgment there, Minos and Rhadamanthus and Aeacus and Triptolemus, and other sons of God who were righteous in their own life, that pilgrimage will be worth making. What would not a man give if he might converse with Orpheus and Musaeus and Hesiod and Homer? Nay, if this be true, let me die again and again. I myself, too, shall have a wonderful interest in there meeting and conversing with Palamedes, and Ajax the son of Telamon, and any other ancient hero who has suffered death through an unjust judgment; and there will be no small pleasure, as I think, in comparing my own sufferings with theirs. Above all, I shall then be able to continue my search into true and false knowledge; as in this world, so also in the next; and I shall find out who is wise, and who pretends to be wise, and is not. What would not a man give, O judges, to be able to examine the leader of the great Trojan expedition; or Odysseus or Sisyphus, or numberless others, men and women too! What infinite delight would there be in conversing with them and asking them questions! In another world they do not put a man to death for asking questions: assuredly not. For besides being happier than we are, they will be immortal, if what is said is true.

Wherefore, O judges, be of good cheer about death, and know of a certainty, that no evil can happen to a good man, either in life or after death. He and his are not neglected by the gods; nor has my own approaching end happened by mere chance. But I see clearly that the time had arrived when it was better for me to die and be released from trouble; wherefore the oracle gave no sign. For which reason, also, I am not angry with my condemners, or with my accusers; they have done me no harm, although they did not mean to do me any good; and for this I may gently blame them.

Still, I have a favour to ask of them. When my sons are grown up, I would ask you, O my friends, to punish them; and I would have you trouble them, as I have troubled you, if they seem to care about riches, or anything, more than about virtue; or if they pretend to be something when they are really nothing,—then reprove them, as I have reproved you, for not caring about that for which they ought to care, and thinking that they are something when they are really nothing. And if you do this, both I and my sons will have received justice at your hands.

The hour of departure has arrived, and we go our ways—I to die, and you to live. Which is better God only knows.

2 Doubting One's Way to Certainty

Descartes

Descartes "consecrated Doubt," wrote the nineteenth-century English evolutionist, Thomas Huxley. Descartes, "the father of modern philosophy," had introduced a way of thinking that revolutionized the ideas of his own time and those of generations to come.[1] This way of thinking commenced by entertaining not ideas but doubts. In Huxley's words, "it removed Doubt from the seat of penance among the grievous sins to which it had long been condemned, and enthroned it in that high place among the primary duties, which is assigned to it by the scientific conscience of these latter days."[2]

It would be a mistake, however, to think of René Descartes (1596–1650) as a sceptic of the ancient Greek variety who often seemed to doubt for the sake of doubting and was content to live with uncertainty. Scepticism for Descartes was always a means to an end, a method by which he hoped to attain indubitable truth. "My design," he wrote, "was singly to find ground of assurance, and cast aside the loose earth and sand, that I might reach the rock or the clay."[3]   Before launching his philosophical investigations, he had carefully delineated, as he reports in his *Discourse on Method* (1637), the limits within which he would allow himself to doubt. Within these limits, Descartes provided himself with a "provisory code of Morals," that he believed would keep him from losing his bearings as he proceeded to apply his methodological scepticism to the various fields of knowledge.[4] According to the first of his maxims, Descartes obliged himself to obey the laws and customs of his country, to act with judiciousness and moderation, and to adhere firmly to the religious faith (Catholicism) in which he had been educated. The second maxim required him to be as "firm and resolute" as possible in his actions and not to vacillate in supporting his opinions once he had adopted them. The third maxim stressed that he should always try to conquer himself rather than the world.

Reflecting on the way of life he had chosen, which, as he put it, consisted "in devoting my whole life to the culture of my Reason, and in making the greatest progress I was able in the knowledge of truth, on the principles of the Method which I had prescribed to myself,"[5] Descartes convinced himself that no way could possibly have suited him better. He was filled with intense satisfaction and enthusiasm as he continued to examine himself and probed into the various spheres of knowledge in hope of discovering important new truths. And, like Socrates before him, he believed that the life of the philosopher was divinely sanctioned. "For since God has endowed each of us with some light of Reason by which to distinguish truth from error," he wrote in his *Discourse,* "I could not have believed that I ought for a single moment to rest satisfied with the opinions of another, unless I had resolved to exercise my own judgment in examining these whenever I should be duly qualified for the task."[6]

The method which Descartes formulated and for which he showed such enthusiasm and devotion was basically the rationalistic method of mathematics rather than the empirical method of the natural sciences. Intuition and deduction, rather than observation and induction, were its basic elements. Absolute certainty rather than probable truth was its aim. The method upon which he relied may be summed up in his own words as follows:

1. Never to accept anything for true which I did not clearly know to be such, that is to say, carefully to avoid precipitance and prejudice, and to comprise nothing more in my judgment than what was presented to my mind so clearly and distinctly as to exclude all ground of doubt.
2. To divide each of the difficulties under examination into as many parts as possible, and as might be necessary for its adequate solution.
3. To conduct my thoughts in such order that, by commencing with objects the simplest and easiest to know, I might ascend little and little, and, as it were, step by step, to the knowledge of the more complex; assigning in thought a certain order even to those objects which in their own nature do not stand in a relation of antecedence and sequence.
4. In every case to make enumerations so complete, and reviews so general, that I might be assured that nothing was omitted.[7]

The method thus requires of its practitioners clarity and distinctness of ideas, the utmost care and precision in making deductions, an orderly and analytical procedure, and a coherent and systematic approach. How Descartes applied it to arrive at his basic indubitable premise, the famous *cogito ergo sum* ("I think, therefore I am"), from which he could advance to solve the problems of the nature of mind, the existence of God, and the constitution of the universe will be suggested by the following selections from his *Meditations* and his *Discourse on Method.*

NOTES

1. Thomas H. Huxley, *Methods and Results* (New York: D. Appleton, 1897) p. 169.

2. Ibid., pp. 169–70.

3. René Descartes, *The Discourse on Method,* part III, in *The Method, Meditations, and Philosophy of Descartes,* trans. John Veitch (New York: Tudor Publishing Co., 1901), p. 168.

4. Ibid., pp. 164–67.

5. Ibid., p. 167.

6. Ibid.

7. Ibid., part II, p. 161.

What Can Be Doubted

Several years have now elapsed since I first became aware that I had accepted, even from my youth, many false opinions for true, and that consequently what I afterwards based on such principles was highly doubtful; and from that time I was convinced of the necessity of undertaking once in my life to rid myself of all the opinions I had adopted, and of commencing anew the work of building from the foundation, if I desired to establish a firm and abiding superstructure in the sciences. But as this enterprise appeared to me to be one of great magnitude, I waited until I had attained an age so mature as to leave me no hope that at any stage of life more advanced I should be better able to execute my design. On this account, I have delayed so long that I should henceforth consider I was doing wrong were I still to consume in deliberation any of the time that now remains for action. Today, then, since I have opportunely freed my mind from all cares, [and am happily disturbed by no passions],* and since I am in the secure possession of leisure in a peaceable retirement, I will at length apply myself earnestly and freely to the general overthrow of all my former opinions. But, to this end, it will not be necessary for me to show that the whole of these are false—a point, perhaps, which I shall never reach; but as even now my reason convinces me that I ought not the less carefully to withhold belief from what is not entirely certain and indubitable, than from what is manifestly false, it will be sufficient to justify the rejection of the whole if I shall find in each some ground for doubt. Nor for this purpose will it be necessary even to deal with each belief individually, which would be truly an endless labour; but, as the removal from below of the foundation necessarily involves the downfall of the whole edifice, I will at once approach the criticism of the principles on which all my former beliefs rested.

All that I have, up to this moment, accepted as possessed of the highest truth and certainty, I received either from or through the senses. I observed, however, that these sometimes misled us; and it is the part of prudence not to place absolute confidence in that by which we have even once been deceived.

But it may be said, perhaps, that, although the senses occasionally mislead us respecting minute objects, and such as are so far removed from us as to be beyond the reach of close observation, there are yet many other of their informations (presentations), of the truth of which it is manifestly impossible to doubt; as for example, that I am in this place, seated by the fire, clothed in a winter dressing-gown, that I hold in my hands this piece of paper, with other intimations of the same nature. But how could I deny that I possess these hands and this body, and withal escape being classed

From René Descartes, "Meditation I" in *The Method, Meditations and Philosophy of Descartes*, trans. John Veitch (New York: Tudor Publishing Co., 1901), pp. 219–24.
*Bracketed passages are additions to the original revised French translation.—EDS.

with persons in a state of insanity, whose brains are so disordered and clouded by dark bilious vapours as to cause them pertinaciously to assert that they are monarchs when they are in the greatest poverty; or clothed [in gold] and purple when destitute of any covering; or that their head is made of clay, their body of glass, or that they are gourds? I should certainly be not less insane than they, were I to regulate my procedure according to examples so extravagant.

Though this be true, I must nevertheless here consider that I am a man, and that, consequently, I am in the habit of sleeping, and representing to myself in dreams those same things, or even sometimes others less probable, which the insane think are presented to them in their waking moments. How often have I dreamt that I was in these familiar circumstances,—that I was dressed, and occupied this place by the fire, when I was lying undressed in bed? At the present moment, however, I certainly look upon this paper with eyes wide awake; the head which I now move is not asleep; I extend this hand consciously and with express purpose, and I perceive it; the occurrences in sleep are not so distinct as all this. But I cannot forget that, at other times, I have been deceived in sleep by similar illusions; and, attentively considering those cases, I perceive so clearly that there exist no certain marks by which the state of waking can ever be distinguished from sleep, that I feel greatly astonished; and in amazement I almost persuade myself that I am now dreaming.

Let us suppose, then, that we are dreaming, and that all these particulars—namely, the opening of the eyes, the motion of the head, the forthputting of the hands—are merely illusions; and even that we really possess neither an entire body nor hands such as we see. Nevertheless, it must be admitted at least that the objects which appear to us in sleep are, as it were, painted representations which could not have been formed unless in the likeness of realities; and, therefore, that those general objects, at all events,—namely, eyes, a head, hands, and an entire body—are not simply imaginary, but really existent. For, in truth, painters themselves, even when they study to represent sirens and satyrs by forms the most fantastic and extraordinary, cannot bestow upon them natures absolutely new, but can only make a certain medley of the members of different animals; or if they chance to imagine something so novel that nothing at all similar has ever been seen before, and such as is, therefore, purely fictitious and absolutely false, it is at least certain that the colours of which this is composed are real.

And on the same principle, although these general objects, viz. [a body], eyes, a head, hands, and the like, be imaginary, we are nevertheless absolutely necessitated to admit the reality at least of some other objects still more simple and universal than these, of which, just as of certain real colours, all those images of things, whether true and real, or false and fantastic, that are found in our consciousness, are formed.

To this class of objects seem to belong corporeal nature in general and its extension; the figure of extended things, their quantity or magnitude, and their number, as also the place in, and the time during, which they exist, and other things of the same sort. We will not, therefore, perhaps reason illegitimately if we conclude from this that Physics, Astronomy, Medicine, and all the other sciences that have for their end the consideration of composite objects, are indeed of a doubtful character; but that Arithmetic, Geometry, and the other sciences of the same class, which regard merely the simplest and most general objects, and scarcely inquire whether or not these are really existent, contain somewhat that is certain and indubitable: for whether I am awake or dreaming, it remains true that two and three make five, and that a square has but four sides; nor does it seem possible that truths so apparent can ever fall under a suspicion of falsity [or incertitude].

Nevertheless, the belief that there is a God who is all-powerful, and who created me, such as I am, has, for a long time, obtained steady possession of my mind. How, then, do I know that he has not arranged that there should be neither earth, nor sky, nor any extended thing, nor figure, nor magnitude, nor place, providing at the same time, however, for [the rise in me of the perceptions of all these objects, and] the persuasion that these do not exist otherwise than as I perceive them? And further, as I sometimes think that others are in error respecting matters of which they believe themselves to possess a perfect knowledge, how do I know that I am not also deceived each time I add together two and three, or number the sides of a square, or form some judgment still more simple, if more simple indeed can be imagined? But perhaps Deity has not been willing that I should be thus deceived, for He is said to be supremely good. If, however, it were repugnant to the goodness of Deity to have created me subject to constant deception, it would seem likewise to be contrary to his goodness to allow me to be occasionally deceived; and yet it is clear that this is permitted. Some, indeed, might perhaps be found who would be disposed rather to deny the existence of a Being so powerful than to believe that there is nothing certain. But let us for the present refrain from opposing this opinion, and grant that all which is here said of a Deity is fabulous: nevertheless in whatever way it be supposed that I reached the state in which I exist, whether by fate, or chance, or by an endless series of antecedents and consequents, or by any other means, it is clear (since to be deceived and to err is a certain defect) that the probability of my being so imperfect as to be the constant victim of deception, will be increased exactly in proportion as the power possessed by the cause, to which they assign my origin, is lessened. To these reasonings I have assuredly nothing to reply, but

am constrained at last to avow that there is nothing of all that I formerly believed to be true of which it is impossible to doubt, and that not through thoughtlessness or levity, but from cogent and maturely considered reasons; so that henceforward, if I desire to discover anything certain, I ought not the less carefully to refrain from assenting to those same opinions than to what might be shown to be manifestly false.

But it is not sufficient to have made these observations; care must be taken likewise to keep them in remembrance. For those old and customary opinions perpetually recur—long and familiar usage giving them the right of occupying my mind, even almost against my will, and subduing my belief; nor will I lose the habit of deferring to them and confiding in them so long as I shall consider them to be what in truth they are, viz., opinions to some extent doubtful, as I have already shown, but still highly probable, and such as it is much more reasonable to believe than deny. It is for this reason I am persuaded that I shall not be doing wrong, if, taking an opposite judgment of deliberate design, I become my own deceiver, by supposing, for a time, that all those opinions are entirely false and imaginary, until at length, having thus balanced my old by my new prejudices, my judgment shall no longer be turned aside by perverted usage from the path that may conduct to the perception of truth. For I am assured that, meanwhile, there will arise neither peril nor error from this course, and that I cannot for the present yield too much to distrust, since the end I now seek is not action but knowledge.

I will suppose, then, not that Deity, who is sovereignly good and the fountain of truth, but that some malignant demon, who is at once exceedingly potent and deceitful, has employed all his artifice to deceive me; I will suppose that the sky, the air, the earth, colours, figures, sounds, and all external things, are nothing better than the illusions of dreams, by means of which this being has laid snares for my credulity; I will consider myself as without hands, eyes, flesh, blood, or any of the senses, and as falsely believing that I am possessed of these; I will continue resolutely fixed in this belief, and if indeed by this means it be not in my power to arrive at the knowledge of truth, I shall at least do what is in my power, viz., [suspend my judgment], and guard with settled purpose against giving my assent to what is false, and being imposed upon by this deceiver, whatever be his power and artifice.

But this undertaking is arduous, and a certain indolence insensibly leads me back to my ordinary course of life; and just as the captive, who, perchance, was enjoying in his dreams an imaginary liberty, when he begins to suspect that it is but a vision, dreads awakening, and conspires with the agreeable illusions that the deception may be prolonged; so I, of my own accord, fall back into the train of my former beliefs, and fear to arouse myself from my slumber, lest the time of laborious wakefulness that would succeed this quiet rest, in place of bringing any light of day, should prove inadequate to dispel the darkness that will arise from the difficulties that have now been raised.

What Is Indubitable

I am in doubt as to the propriety of making my first meditations, in the place above mentioned, matter of discourse; for these are so metaphysical, and so uncommon, as not, perhaps, to be acceptable to everyone. And yet, that it may be determined whether the foundations that I have laid are sufficiently secure, I find myself in a measure constrained to advert to them. I had long before remarked that, in relation to practice, it is sometimes necessary to adopt, as if above doubt, opinions which we discern to be highly uncertain, as has been already said; but as I then desired to give my attention solely to the search after truth, I thought that a procedure exactly the opposite was called for, and that I ought to reject as absolutely false all opinions in regard to which I could suppose the least ground for doubt, in order to ascertain whether after that there remained aught in my belief that was wholly indubitable. Accordingly, seeing that our senses sometimes deceive us, I was willing to suppose that there existed nothing really such as they presented to us; and because some men err in reasoning, and fall into paralogisms, even on the simplest matters of Geometry, I, convinced that I was as open to error as any other, rejected as false all the reasonings I had hitherto taken for demonstrations; and finally, when I considered that the very same thoughts (presentations) which we

From René Descartes, "The Discourse on Method," Part IV, in *The Method, Meditations and Philosophy of Descartes,* trans. John Veitch (New York: Tudor Publishing Co., 1901), pp. 170–72.

experience when awake may also be experienced when we are asleep, while there is at that time not one of them true, I supposed that all the objects (presentations) that had ever entered into my mind when awake, had in them no more truth than the illusions of my dreams. But immediately upon this I observed that, whilst I thus wished to think that all was false, it was absolutely necessary that I, who thus thought, should be somewhat; and as I observed that this truth, I THINK, HENCE I AM, was so certain and of such evidence, that no ground of doubt, however extravagant, could be alleged by the Sceptics capable of shaking it, I concluded that I might, without scruple, accept it as the first principle of the philosophy of which I was in search.

In the next place, I attentively examined what I was, and as I observed that I could suppose that I had no body, and that there was no world nor any place in which I might be; but that I could not therefore suppose that I was not; and that, on the contrary, from the very circumstance that I thought to doubt of the truth of all things, it most clearly and certainly followed that I was; while, on the other hand, if I had only ceased to think, although all the other objects which I had ever imagined had been in reality existent, I would have had no reason to believe that I existed; I thence concluded that I was a substance whose whole essence or nature consists only in thinking, and which, that it may exist, has need of no place, nor is dependent on any material thing; so that "I", that is to say, the mind by which I am what I am, is wholly distinct from the body, and is even more easily known than the latter, and is such, that although the latter were not, it would still continue to be all that it is.

After this I inquired in general into what is essential to the truth and certainty of a proposition; for since I had discovered one which I knew to be true, I thought that I must likewise be able to discover the ground of this certitude. And as I observed that in the words I THINK, HENCE I AM, there is nothing at all which gives me assurance of their truth beyond this, that I see very clearly that in order to think it is necessary to exist. I concluded that I might take, as a general rule, the principle, that all the things which we very clearly and distinctly conceive are true, only observing, however, that there is some difficulty in rightly determining the objects which we distinctly conceive.

In the next place, from reflecting on the circumstance that I am doubted, and that consequently my being was not wholly perfect (for I clearly saw that it was a greater perfection to know than to doubt), I was led to inquire whence I had learned to think of something more perfect than myself; and I clearly recognized that I must hold this notion from some Nature which in reality was more perfect. As for the thoughts of many other objects external to me, as of the sky, the earth, light, heat, and a thousand more, I was less at a loss to know whence these came; for since I remarked in them nothing which seemed to render them superior to myself, I could believe that, if these were true, they were dependencies on my own nature, in so far as it possessed a certain perfection, and, if they were false, that I held them from nothing, that is to say, that they were in me because of a certain imperfection of my nature. But this could not be the case with the idea of a Nature more perfect than myself; for to receive it from nothing was a thing manifestly impossible; and, because it is not less repugnant than the more perfect should be an effect of, and dependence on the less perfect, than that something should proceed from nothing, it was equally impossible that I could hold it from myself; accordingly, it but remained that it had been placed in me by a Nature which was in reality more perfect than mine, and which even possessed within itself all the perfections of which I could form any idea: that is to say, in a single word, which was God. And to this I added that, since I knew some perfections which I did not possess, I was not the only being in existence, (I will here, with your permission, freely use the terms of the Schools); but on the contrary, that there was of necessity some other more perfect Being upon whom I was dependent, and from whom I had received all that I possessed; for if I had existed alone, and independently of every other being, so as to have had from myself all the perfection, however little, which I actually possessed, I should have been able, for the same reason, to have had from myself the whole remainder of perfection, of the want of which I was conscious, and thus could of myself have become infinite, eternal, immutable, omniscient, all-powerful, and, in fine, have possessed all the perfections which I could recognize in God. For in order to know the nature of God (whose existence has been established by the preceding reasonings), as far as my own nature permitted, I had only to consider in reference to all the properties of which I found in my mind some idea, whether their possession was a mark of perfection; and I was assured that no one which indicated any imperfection was in him, and that none of the rest was awanting. Thus I perceived that doubt, inconstancy, sadness, and such like, could not be found in God, since I myself would have been happy to be free from them. Besides, I had ideas of many sensible and corporeal things; for although I might suppose that I was dreaming, and that all of which I saw or imagined was false, I could not, nevertheless, deny that the ideas were in reality in my thoughts. But because I had already very clearly recognized in myself that the intelligent nature is distinct from the corporeal, and as I observed that all composition is an evidence of dependency, and that a state of dependency is manifestly a state of imperfection, I therefore determined that it could not be a perfection in God to be compounded of these two natures, and that consequently he was not so compounded; but that if there were any bodies in the world, or even any intelligences, or other natures that were not wholly perfect, their existence depended on his power in such a way that they could not subsist without him for a single moment.

I was disposed straightaway to search for other truths; and when I had represented to myself the object of the geometers, which I conceived to be a continuous body, or a space indefinitely extended in length, breadth, and height or depth, divisible into divers parts which admit of different figures and sizes, and of being moved or transposed in all manner of ways (for all this the geometers suppose to be in the object they contemplate), I went over some of their simplest demonstrations. And, in the first place, I observed that the great certitude which by common consent is accorded to these demonstrations, is founded solely upon this, that they are clearly conceived in accordance with the rules I have already laid down. In the next place, I perceived that there was nothing at all in these demonstrations which could assure me of the existence of their object; thus, for example, supposing a triangle to be given, I distinctly perceived that its three angles were necessarily equal to two right angles, but I did not on that account perceive anything which could assure me that any triangle existed; while, on the contrary, recurring to the examination of the idea of a Perfect Being, I found that the existence of the Being was comprised in the idea in the same way that the equality of its three angles to two right angles is comprised in the idea of a triangle, or as in the idea of a sphere, the equi-

distance of all points on its surface from the center, or even still more clearly; and that consequently, it is at least as certain that God, who is this Perfect Being, is, or exists, as any demonstration of Geometry can be.

But the reason which leads many to persuade themselves that there is a difficulty in knowing this truth, and even also in knowing what their mind really is, is that they never raise their thoughts above sensible objects, and are so accustomed to consider nothing except by way of imagination, which is a mode of thinking limited to material objects, that all that is not imaginable seems to them not intelligible. The truth of this is sufficiently manifest from the single circumstance, that the philosophers of the Schools accept as a maxim that there is nothing in the Understanding which was not previously in the Senses, in which however it is certain that the ideas of God and of the Soul have never been; and it appears to me that they who make use of their imagination to comprehend these ideas do exactly the same thing as if, in order to hear sounds or smell odors, they strove to avail themselves of their eyes; unless indeed that there is this difference, that the sense of sight does not afford us an inferior assurance to those of smell or hearing; in place of which, neither our imagination nor our senses can give us assurance of anything unless our Understanding intervene.

Finally, if there be still persons who are not sufficiently persuaded of the existence of God and of the soul, by the reasons I have adduced, I am desirous that they should know that all the other propositions, of the truth of which they deem themselves perhaps more assured, as that we have a body, and that there exist stars and an earth, and such like, are less certain; for, although we have a moral assurance of these things, which is so strong that there is an appearance of extravagance in doubting of their existence, yet at the same time no one, unless his intellect is impaired, can deny, when the question relates to a metaphysical certitude, that there is sufficient reason to exclude entire assurance, in the observation that when asleep we can in the same way imagine ourselves possessed of another body and that we see other stars and another earth, when there is nothing of the kind. For how do we know that the thoughts which occur in dreaming are false rather than those other which we experience when awake, since the former are often not less vivid and distinct than the latter? And though men of the highest genius study this question as long as they please, I do not believe that they will be able to give any reason which can be sufficient to remove this doubt, unless they presuppose the existence of God. For, in the first place, even the principle which I have already taken as a rule, viz., that all the things which we clearly and distinctly conceive are true, is certain only because God is or exists, and because he is a Perfect Being, and because all that we possess is derived from him; whence it follows that our ideas or notions, which to the extent of their clearness and distinctness are real, and proceed from God, must to that extent be true. Accordingly, whereas we not unfrequently have ideas or notions in which some falsity is contained, this can only be the case with such as are to some extent confused and obscure, and in this proceed from nothing, (participate of negation), that is, exist in us thus confused because we are not wholly perfect. And it is evident that it is not less repugnant that falsity or imperfection, insofar as it is imperfection, should proceed from God, than that truth or perfection should proceed from nothing. But if we did not know that all which we possess of real and true proceeds from a Perfect and Infinite Being, however clear and distinct our ideas might be, we should have no ground on that account for the assurance that they possessed the perfection of being true.

But after the knowledge of God and of the soul has rendered us certain of this rule, we can easily understand that the truth of the thoughts we experience when awake, ought not in the slightest degree to be called in question on account of the illusions of our dreams. For if it happened that an individual, even when asleep, had some very distinct idea, as, for example, if a geometer should discover some new demonstration, the circumstance of his being asleep would not militate against its truth; and as for the most ordinary error of our dreams, which consists in their representing to us various objects in the same way as our external senses, this it not prejudicial, since it leads us very properly to suspect the truth of the ideas of sense; for we are not unfrequently deceived in the same manner when awake; as when persons in the jaundice see all objects yellow, or when the stars or bodies at a great distance appear to us much smaller than they are. For, in fine, whether awake or asleep, we ought never to allow ourselves to be persuaded of the truth of anything unless on the evidence of our Reason. And it must be noted that I say of our REASON, and not of our imagination or of our senses: thus, for example, although we very clearly see the sun, we ought not therefore to determine that it is only of the size which our sense of sight presents; and we may very distinctly imagine the head of a lion joined to the body of a goat, without being therefore shut up to the conclusion that a chimera exists; for it is not a dictate of Reason that what we thus see or imagine is in reality existent; but it plainly tells us that all our ideas or notions contain in them some truth; for otherwise it could not be that God, who is wholly perfect and veracious, should have placed them in us. And because our reasonings are never so clear or so complete during sleep as when we are awake, although sometimes the acts of our imagination are then as lively and distinct, if not more so than in our waking moments, Reason further dictates that, since all our thoughts cannot be true because of our partial imperfection, those possessing truth must infallibly be found in the experience of our waking moments rather than in that of our dreams.

3 Living Intentionally

Thoreau

Like Socrates, Henry David Thoreau (1817–1862) urged us to examine not only our convictions but also the kind of life that these convictions, whether consciously formulated or not, have directed us to follow. How do we spend our lives? In what sorts of activities are we engaged? What are our deepest hopes and our strongest aspirations? To what extent are we able to fulfill these hopes and aspirations?

The vast majority of men, Thoreau believed, live lives of quiet desperation. They find themselves living in a world that is considered to be merely a place of business, where men are preoccupied with buying and selling things, with fitting means to ends and, frequently, with justifying the means used to attain the ends without examining carefully the value of those ends. Practicality and usefulness are appreciated in only the crudest, most materialistic, and selfish sense. Hoarding of material things, exploitation of men and nature, and ruthless competition, in which the least worthy specimens of the human race seem to survive are the inevitable results of this mistaken system of values, which Erich Fromm was later to call the "marketing orientation."

In light of this orientation, it was not surprising to Thoreau that genuine human beings in such a world are made to feel that they are antisocial eccentrics and misfits. "If a man walk in the woods for love of them half of each day, he is in danger of being regarded as a loafer," Thoreau wrote in "Life without Principle," "but if he spends his whole day as a speculator, shearing these woods and making earth bald before her time, he is esteemed an industrious and enterprising citizen. As if a town had no interest in its forests but to cut them down!"[1] Everyone is expected to make a living but not to live, and making a living means, of course, making money. And the ways by which men make money lead them downward, away from any realization of what it really means to be a human being. No matter what you do to make a living, to make money, you are usually being paid "for being something less than a man."[2] Under such a system, inefficient and incompetent human beings often prosper although they do so because they have sold their birthright as free individuals for a mess of pottage.

Unlike the mass of men, Thoreau's ideal man refuses to sell himself, "both his forenoons and afternoons," to the society in which he happens to live. He has learned to be as self-reliant, as self-supporting as possible. He gets down to the real business of living; he lives by loving. He is willing to follow a solitary path, to defend an unpopular cause, and to take a controversial position without fear of losing his livelihood. "A man had better starve at once than lose his innocence in the process of getting his bread."[3] Inwardness, honesty, sincerity, intellectual chastity—these are virtues that the wise man values above anything material. He listens to his heart and to nature rather than to the gossiping of his fellow men. His heightened awareness makes it possible for him to feel enriched by the mere contemplation of the things that ordinary men take for granted—the sun, the clouds, the snow, the trees. Every day wisely lived brings forth its own minor miracles and "it requires more than a day's devotion to know and possess the wealth of a day."[4]

The ultimate commitment by which Thoreau guided his life is sometimes called transcendentalism—a German-inspired idealistic philosophy that put intuition and feeling above reason and sensation as a means for relating the individual to nature and to the cosmos. But Thoreau himself, again like Socrates, made no attempt to construct a system of philosophy or to preach a gospel of salvation. A philosopher is, to him, a *lover* of wisdom, one who attempts to guide his life by the moral principles which are universal to man and to life. Further, he believed that a true philosopher must, on the basis of his convictions, commit himself to action —to solving problems—not just theoretically but practically in the world at large.

Two important and influential actions resulted from Thoreau's adherence to basic principles and "higher laws." The first was his experiment in intentional living in a cabin on Walden Pond near his hometown of Concord, Massachusetts. There he spent over two years simplifying his existence, communing with nature, reflecting on the essential meaning of life, and writing. By achieving, at least for a time, a utopia or ideal life for one, Thoreau blazed a trail for later utopians to follow in returning to a simple, relatively self-sufficient life lived close to nature. In our own time, B. F. Skinner, inspired strongly by Thoreau's example, envisaged in *Walden Two*, a Walden for two, and more, but based on psychological principles quite different from those of Thoreau.

The other of Thoreau's actions which resulted from his philosophical commitment was his defense and practice of civil disobedience, the moral right of the individual to defy the civil authority of the state by refusing to obey a law which does not conform to the individual's conscience.

"Under a government which imprisons any unjustly, the true place for a just man is also in prison."[5] Thoreau did go to jail after refusing to pay a tax to support the federal government which was involved in what Thoreau considered an unjust war against Mexico, while an unjust institution, slavery, was being tolerated. In letting his life be "a counter-friction to stop the machine" of government, Thoreau set an example which later practitioners of civil disobedience (including Mahatma Gandhi and Dr. Martin Luther King, Jr.) followed to achieve moral ends which they considered higher than those of the state under which they lived. "Any man more right than his neighbors," Thoreau insisted, "constitutes a majority of one already."[6]

NOTES

1. "Life Without Principle," *The Writings of Henry David Thoreau* (Boston: Houghton Mifflin & Co., 1906), vol. IV, p. 457.

2. Ibid., p. 457.

3. Ibid., p. 468.

4. Ibid., p. 471.

5. Ibid., p. 370.

6. Ibid.

Life in the Woods

When I wrote the following pages, or rather the bulk of them, I lived alone, in the woods, a mile from any neighbour, in a house which I had built myself, on the shore of Walden Pond, in Concord, Massachusetts, and earned my living by the labour of my hands only. I lived there two years and two months. At present I am a sojourner in civilised life again.

I should not obtrude my affairs so much on the notice of my readers if very particular inquiries had not been made by my townsmen concerning my mode of life, which some would call impertinent, though they do not appear to me at all impertinent, but, considering the circumstances, very natural and pertinent. Some have asked what I got to eat; if I did not feel lonesome; if I was not afraid; and the like. Others have been curious to learn what portion of my income I devoted to charitable purposes; and some, who have large families, how many poor children I maintained. I will therefore ask those of my readers who feel no particular interest in me to pardon me if I undertake to answer some of these questions in this book. In most books, the *I*, or first person, is omitted; in this it will be retained; that, in respect to egotism, is the main difference. We commonly do not remember that it is, after all, always the first person that is speaking. I should not talk so much about myself if there were anybody else whom I knew as well. Unfortunately, I am confined to this theme by the narrowness of my experience. Moreover, I, on my side, require of every writer, first or last, a simple and sincere account of his own life, and not merely what he has heard of other men's lives; some such account as he would send to his kindred from a distant land; for if he has lived sincerely, it must have been in a distant land to me. Perhaps these pages are more particularly addressed to poor students. As for the rest of my readers, they will accept such portions as apply to them. I trust that none will stretch the seams in putting on the coat, for it may do good service to him whom it fits. . . .

Most men, even in this comparatively free country, through mere ignorance and mistake, are so occupied with the factitious cares and superfluously coarse labours of life that its finer fruits cannot be plucked by them. Their fingers, from excessive toil, are too clumsy and tremble too much for that. Actually, the labouring man has not leisure for a true integrity day by day; he cannot afford to sustain the manliest relations to men; his labour would be depreciated in the market. He has no time to be anything but a machine. How can he remember well his ignorance—which his growth requires—who has so often to use his knowledge? We should feed and clothe him gratuitously sometimes, and recruit him with our cordials, before we judge of him. The finest qualities of our nature, like the bloom on fruits, can be preserved only by the most delicate handling. Yet

From Henry David Thoreau, *Walden* (Boston: Houghton Mifflin & Co., 1893).

we do not treat ourselves nor one another thus tenderly....

The mass of men lead lives of quiet desperation. What is called resignation is confirmed desperation. From the desperate city you go into the desperate country, and have to console yourself with the bravery of minks and muskrats. A stereotyped but unconscious despair is concealed even under what are called the games and amusements of mankind. There is no play in them, for this comes after work. But it is a characteristic of wisdom not to do desperate things.

When we consider what, to use the words of the catechism, is the chief end of man, and what are the true necessaries and means of life, it appears as if men had deliberately chosen the common mode of living because they preferred it to any other. Yet they honestly think there is no choice left. But alert and healthy natures remember that the sun rose clear. It is never too late to give up our prejudices. No way of thinking or doing, however ancient, can be trusted without proof. What everybody echoes or in silence passes by as true to-day may turn out to be falsehood to-morrow, mere smoke of opinion, which some had trusted for a cloud that would sprinkle fertilising rain on their fields. What old people say you cannot do you try and find that you can. Old deeds for old people, and new deeds for new. Old people did not know enough once, perchance, to fetch fuel to keep the fire a-going; new people put a little dry wood under a pot, and are whirled round the globe with the speed of birds, in a way to kill old people, as the phrase is. Age is no better, hardly so well, qualified for an instructor as youth, for it has not profited so much as it has lost. One may almost doubt if the wisest man has learned anything of absolute value by living. Practically, the old have no very important advice to give the young, their own experience has been so partial, and their lives have been such miserable failures, for private reasons, as they must believe; and it may be that they have some faith left which belies that experience, and they are only less young than they were. I have lived some thirty years on this planet, and I have yet to hear the first syllable of valuable or even earnest advice from my seniors. They have told me nothing, and probably cannot tell me anything, to the purpose. Here is life, an experiment to a great extent untried by me; but it does not avail me that they have tried it. If I have any experience which I think valuable, I am sure to reflect that this my Mentors said nothing about....

The greater part of what my neighbours call good I believe in my soul to be bad, and if I repent of anything, it is very likely to be my good behaviour. What demon possessed me that I behaved so well? You may say the wisest thing you can, old man,—you who have lived seventy years, not without honour of a kind, —I hear an irresistible voice which invites me away from all that. One generation abandons the enterprises of another like stranded vessels.

I think that we may safely trust a good deal more than we do. We may waive just so much care of ourselves as we honestly bestow elsewhere. Nature is as well adapted to our weakness as to our strength. The incessant anxiety and strain of some is a well-nigh incurable form of disease. We are made to exaggerate the importance of what work we do; and yet how much is not done by us! or, what if we had been taken sick? How vigilant we are! determined not to live by faith if we can avoid it; all the day long on the alert, at night we unwillingly say our prayers and commit ourselves to uncertainties. So thoroughly and sincerely are we compelled to live, reverencing our life, and denying the possibility of change. This is the only way, we say; but there are as many ways as there can be drawn radii from one centre. All change is a miracle to contemplate; but it is a miracle which is taking place every instant. Confucius said, "To know that we know what we know, and that we do not know what we do not know, that is true knowledge." When one man has reduced a fact of the imagination to be a fact to his understanding, I foresee that all men will at length establish their lives on that basis.

Let us consider for a moment what most of the trouble and anxiety which I have referred to is about, and how much it is necessary that we be troubled, or at least, careful. It would be some advantage to live a primitive and frontier life, though in the midst of an outward civilisation, if only to learn what are the gross necessaries of life and what methods have been taken to obtain them; or even to look over the old day-books of the merchants, to see what it was that the men most commonly bought at the stores, what they stored, that is, what are the grossest groceries. For the improvements of ages have had but little influence on the essential laws of man's existence: as our skeletons, probably, are not to be distinguished from those of our ancestors.

By the words, *necessary of life,* I mean whatever, of all that man obtains by his own exertions, has been from the first, or from long use has become, so important to human life that few, if any, whether from savageness, or poverty, or philosophy, ever attempt to do without it. To many creatures there is in this sense but one necessary of life—Food. To the bison of the prairie it is a few inches of palatable grass, with water to drink; unless he seeks the Shelter of the forest or the mountain's shadow. None of the brute creation requires more than Food and Shelter. The necessaries of life for man in this climate may, accurately enough, be distributed under the several heads of Food, Shelter, Clothing, and Fuel; for not till we have secured these are we prepared to entertain the true problems of life with freedom and a prospect of success. Man has invented, not only houses, but clothes and cooked food; and possibly from the accidental discovery of the warmth of fire, and the consequent use of it, at first a luxury, arose the present necessity to sit by it. We ob-

serve cats and dogs acquiring the same second nature. . . .

Most of the luxuries, and many of the so-called comforts of life, are not only not indispensable, but positive hindrances to the elevation of mankind. With respect to luxuries and comforts, the wisest have ever lived a more simple and meagre life than the poor. The ancient philosophers, Chinese, Hindoo, Persian, and Greek, were a class than which none has been poorer in outward riches, none so rich in inward. We know not much about them. It is remarkable that *we* know so much of them as we do. The same is true of the more modern reformers and benefactors of their race. None can be an impartial or wise observer of human life but from the vantage ground of what *we* should call voluntary poverty. Of a life of luxury the fruit is luxury, whether in agriculture, or commerce, or literature, or art. There are nowadays professors of philosophy, but not philosophers. Yet it is admirable to profess because it was once admirable to live. To be a philosopher is not merely to have subtle thoughts, nor even to found a school, but so to love wisdom as to live according to its dictates, a life of simplicity, independence, magnanimity, and trust. It is to solve some of the problems of life, not only theoretically, but practically. . . .

When first I took up my abode in the woods, that is, began to spend my nights as well as days there, which, by accident, was on Independence Day, on the 4th of July, 1845, my house was not finished for winter, but was merely a defence against the rain, without plastering or chimney, the walls being of rough weather-stained boards, with wide chinks, which made it cool at night. The upright white hewn studs and freshly planed door and window-casings gave it a clean and airy look, especially in the morning, when its timbers were saturated with dew, so that I fancied that by noon some sweet gum would exude from them. To my imagination it retained throughout the day more or less of this auroral character, reminding me of a certain house on a mountain which I had visited the year before. This was an airy, an unplastered cabin, fit to entertain a travelling god, and where a goddess might trail her garments. The winds which passed over my dwelling were such as sweep over the ridges of mountains, bearing the broken strains, or celestial parts only, of terrestrial music. The morning wind forever blows, the poem of creation is uninterrupted; but few are the ears that hear it. Olympus is but the outside of the earth everywhere. . . .

I was seated by the shore of a small pond, about a mile and a half south of the village of Concord and somewhat higher than it, in the midst of an extensive wood between that town and Lincoln, and about two miles south of that our only field known to fame, Concord battle ground; but I was so low in the woods that the opposite shore, half a mile off, like the rest, covered with wood, was my most distant horizon. For the first week, whenever I looked out on the pond, it impressed me like a tarn high up on the one side of a mountain, its bottom far above the surface of other lakes, and, as the sun arose, I saw it throwing off its nightly clothing of mist, and here and there, by degrees, its soft ripples or its smooth reflecting surface was revealed, while the mists, like ghosts, were stealthily withdrawing in every direction into the woods, as at the breaking up of some nocturnal conventicle. The very dew seemed to hang upon the trees later into the day than usual, as on the sides of mountains. . . .

I went to the woods because I wished to live deliberately, to front only the essential facts of life, and see if I could not learn what it had to teach, and not, when I came to die, discover that I had not lived. I did not wish to live what was not life, living is so dear; nor did I wish to practise resignation, unless it was quite necessary. I wanted to live deep and suck out all the marrow of life, to live so sturdily and Spartan-like as to put to rout all that was not life, to cut a broad swath and shave close, to

drive life into a corner, and reduce it to its lowest terms, and, if it proved to be mean, why then to get the whole and genuine meanness of it, and publish its meanness to the world; or if it were sublime, to know it by experience, and be able to give a true account of it in my next excursion. For most men, it appears to me, are in a strange uncertainty about it, whether it is of the devil or of God, and have *somewhat hastily* concluded that it is the chief end of man here to "glorify God and enjoy Him forever."

Still we live meanly, like ants; though the fable tells us that we were long ago changed into men; like pygmies we fight with cranes; it is error upon error, and clout upon clout, and our best virtue has for its occasion a superfluous and evitable wretchedness. Our life is frittered away by detail. An honest man has hardly need to count more than his ten fingers, or in extreme cases he may add his ten toes, and lump the rest. Simplicity, simplicity, simplicity! I say, let your affairs be as two or three, and not a hundred or a thousand; instead of a million count half-a-dozen, and keep your accounts on your thumb-nail. In the midst of this chopping sea of civilised life, such are the clouds and storms and quicksands and thousand-and-one items to be allowed for, that a man has to live, if he would not founder and go to the bottom and not make his port at all, by dead reckoning, and he must be a great calculator indeed who succeeds. Simplify, simplify. Instead of three meals a-day, if it be necessary eat but one; instead of a hundred dishes, five; and reduce other things in proportion. . . .

Every morning was a cheerful invitation to make my life of equal simplicity, and I may say innocence, with Nature herself. I have been as sincere a worshipper of Aurora as the Greeks. I got up early and bathed in the pond: that was a religious exercise, and one of the best things which I did. They say that characters were engraven on the bathing tub of king Tching-thang to this effect: "Renew thyself completely each day; do it again, and again, and forever again." I can understand that. Morning brings back the heroic ages. I was as much affected by the faint hum of a mosquito making its invisible and unimaginable tour through my apartment at earliest dawn, when I was sitting with door and windows open, as I could be by any trumpet that ever sang of fame. . . . All poets and heroes, like Memnon, are the children of Aurora, and emit their music at sunrise. To him whose elastic and vigorous thought keeps pace with the sun, the day is a perpetual morning. It matters not what the clocks say or the attitudes and labours of men. Morning is when I am awake and there is a dawn in me. Moral reform is the effort to throw off sleep. Why is it that men give so poor an account of their day if they have not been slumbering? They are not such poor calculators. If they had not been overcome with drowsiness they would have performed something. The millions are awake enough for physical labour; but only one in a million is awake enough for effective intellectual exertion, only one in a hundred millions to a poetic or divine life. To be awake is to be alive. I have never yet met a man who was quite awake. How could I have looked him in the face?

We must learn to reawaken and keep ourselves awake, not by mechanical aids, but by an infinite expectation of the dawn, which does not forsake us in our soundest sleep. I know of no more encouraging fact than the unquestionable ability of man to elevate his life by a conscious endeavour. It is something to be able to paint a particular picture, or to carve a statue, and so to make a few objects beautiful; but it is far more glorious to carve and paint the very atmosphere and medium through which we look, which morally we can do. To affect the quality of the day, that is the highest of arts. Every man is tasked to make his life, even in its details, worthy of the contemplation of his most elevated and critical hour. . . .

Let us spend one day as deliberately as Nature, and not be thrown off the track by every nutshell and mosquito's wing that falls on the rails. Let us rise early and fast, or break fast, gently and without perturbation; let company come and let company go, let the bells ring and the children cry,—determined to make a day of it. . . . Let us settle ourselves, and work and wedge our feet downward through the mud and slush of opinion, and prejudice, and tradition, and delusion, and appearance, that alluvion which covers the globe, through Paris and London, through New York and Boston and Concord, through church and state, through poetry and philosophy and religion, till we come to a hard bottom and rocks in place, which we can call *reality*, and say, This is, and no mistake; and then begin, having a *point d'appui*, below freshet and frost and fire, a place where you might found a wall or a state, or set a lamp-post safely, or perhaps a gauge, not a Nilometer, but a Realometer, that future ages might know how deep a freshet of shams and appearances had gathered from time to time. If you stand right fronting and face to face to a fact, you will see the sun glimmer on both its surfaces, as if it were a cimeter, and feel its sweet edge dividing you through the heart and marrow, and so you will happily conclude your mortal career. Be it life or death, we crave only reality. If we are really dying, let us hear the rattle in our throats and feel cold in the extremities; if we are alive, let us go about our business.

Time is but the stream I go a-fishing in. I drink at it; but while I drink I see the sandy bottom and detect how shallow it is. Its thin current slides away, but eternity remains. I would drink deeper; fish in the sky, whose bottom is pebbly with stars. I cannot count one. I know not the first letter of the alphabet. I have always been regretting that I was not as wise as the day I was born. The intellect is a cleaver; it discerns and rifts its way into the secret of things. I do not wish to be any more busy with my hands than is necessary. My head is hands and feet. I feel all my best faculties concentrated in it. My instinct tells me that my head is an organ for burrowing, as some creatures use their snout and forepaws, and with it I would mine and burrow my way through these hills. I think that the richest vein is somewhere hereabouts; so by the divining rod and thin rising vapours I judge; and here I will begin to mine. . . .

If one listens to the faintest but constant suggestions of his genius, which are certainly true, he sees not to what extremes, or even insanity, it may lead him; and yet that way, as he grows more resolute and faithful, his road lies. The faintest assured objection which one healthy man feels will at length prevail over the arguments and customs of mankind. No man ever followed his genius till it misled him. Though the result were bodily weakness, yet perhaps no one can say that the consequences were to be regretted, for these were a life of conformity to higher principles. If the day and the night are such that you greet them with joy, and life emits a fragrance like flowers and sweet-scented herbs, is more elastic, more starry, more immortal,—that is your success. All nature is your congratulation, and you have cause momentarily to bless yourself. The greatest gains and values are farthest from being appreciated. We easily come to doubt if they exist. We soon forget them. They are the highest reality. Perhaps the facts most astounding and most real are never communicated by man to man. The true harvest of my daily life is somewhat as intangible and indescribable as the tints of morning or evening. It is a little star-dust caught, a segment of the rainbow which I have clutched. . . .

I left the woods for as good a reason as I went there. Perhaps it seemed to me that I had several more lives to live, and could not spare any more time for that one. It is remarkable how easily and insensibly we fall into a particular route, and make a beaten track for ourselves. I had not lived there a week before my feet wore a path from my door to the pondside; and though it is five or six years since I trod it, it is still quite distinct. It is true I fear that others may have fallen into it, and so helped to keep it open. The surface of the earth is soft and impressible by the feet of men; and so with the paths which the mind travels. How worn and dusty, then, must be the highways of the world—how deep the ruts of tradition and conformity! I did not wish to take a cabin passage, but rather to go before the mast and on the deck of the world, for there I could best see the moonlight amid the mountains. I do not wish to go below now.

I learned this, at least, by my experiment: that if one advances confidently in the direction of his dreams, and endeavours to live the life which he has imagined, he will meet with a success unexpected in common hours. He will put some things behind, will pass an invisible boundary; new, universal, and more liberal laws will begin to establish themselves around and within him; or the old laws be expanded, and interpreted in his favour in a more liberal sense, and he will live with the license of a higher order of beings. In proportion as he simplifies his life, the laws of the universe will appear less complex, and solitude will not be solitude, nor poverty poverty, nor weakness weakness. If you have built castles in the air, your work need not be lost; that is where they should be. Now put the foundations under them.

4 Confronting Death in Life

Tolstoy

Up to the point when despair almost drove him to end it, the life of Leo Tolstoy (1828–1910) seemed to have been one of self-fulfillment and satisfaction. His noble birth and inherited wealth had given him the opportunities and leisure to develop his inner resources and talents, as well as a wide range of freedom to explore and observe his outer environment. The brilliance of his intellect, the intensity of his responses, and the fertility of his imagination contributed to his early success as a writer of realistic fiction that was saturated with poetic feeling. His sensual appetites had certainly not gone unsatiated. His passionate idealism had found social objectives upon which to focus, such as the education of the peasants on his family estate. He was adored by his wife and children, admired by his fellow artists, and idolized by his increasingly large reading audience for his greatest literary achievements, the novels *War and Peace* (1864–69) and *Anna Karenina* (1873–77), which were to place him among the literary geniuses of all time.

But instead of finding himself happy at the apex of his career, at fifty Tolstoy found himself completely miserable. In his relentless drive to perfect his literary art, to achieve widespread recognition and perpetual fame, and to reach personal fulfillment in love, marriage, and family life, he had avoided facing certain questions that now could not remain unanswered. Questions about the value of his life and art arose in his mind to plague him. The more he reflected on his predicament as a human being, the more he was confronted with doubt and uncertainty. The questions to which he now required answers were no longer questions related to beauty and ugliness, love and hate, war and peace, but the more fundamental existential questions relating in the most personal way to his own life and death. During this period of his life, which he later described in *My Confession* (1872–82), one day he listed on a sheet of paper the following six "unknown questions" to which he must find answers:

1. Why am I living?
2. What is the cause for my existence and that of everyone else?

3. What purpose has my existence or any other?
4. What does the division which I feel within me into good and evil signify, and for what purpose is it there?
5. How must I live?
6. What is death—how can I save myself?[1]

In the course of pondering such questions, the once happy Russian novelist eventually found the peace of mind he craved by achieving a final transformation in which he became a practicing primitive Christian and a world-famous religious sage. Part of Tolstoy's account of his confrontation with doubt and the conversion that allowed him to vanquish it is given below. It begins after he has just finished describing his marriage and the fifteen years of happy family life that had caused him to postpone his soul-searching.

This remarkable document lends itself to a number of different interpretations. From the psychological point of view, it reveals Tolstoy's strong guilt feelings over his past impulsive acts of violence, greed, and sensuality and his great need to resolve the unconscious conflicts that continued to trouble him. Also revealed is his intense fear of death, which he later expressed so powerfully in his short story "The Death of Ivan Ilych" (1886). From the religious point of view that Tolstoy held, the experiences described have a universal human significance. They are to be understood in light of man's sinful nature and his search for salvation. The need for forgiveness, for atonement, and for peace of soul through a loving and harmonious relationship with a Divine Being are, to Tolstoy, the essential and uniquely human needs. To meet these needs, Tolstoy was willing to renounce his reason and to identify with the mass of sincere but uncritical believers who loved their God and their fellowmen unquestioningly. Eventually he was excommunicated from the Orthodox Church, but this did not bother him. He had found another, more personal faith by which to live and die.

Finally, from the philosophical point of view, Tolstoy's account is of interest because in it he formulates clearly and vividly one of the broadest and most crucial questions with which speculative philosophy has traditionally been concerned: What is the nature of man and the meaning of human existence? Tolstoy suffered his problems and tried to render his thoughts and feelings as concretely as possible. He expressed beautifully the experience of doubt, uncertainty, fear, anxiety, and despair, and acted freely and completely to dispel his doubts by committing himself to a way of believing and acting. Tolstoy thus became, along with Kierkegaard, Nietzsche, and Dostoyevsky, an important nineteenth-century precursor of existentialism and an invaluable illuminator of the human predicament.

NOTE

1. Quoted in Stephan Zweig, *The Living Thoughts of Tolstoy* (Philadelphia, Penn.: David McKay Co., 1939), p. 4.

Doubts about the Meaning of Life

Thus I lived; but, five years ago, a strange state of mind began to grow upon me: I had moments of perplexity, of a stoppage, as it were, of life, as if I did not know how I was to live, what I was to do, and I began to wander, and was a victim to low spirits. But this passed, and I continued to live as before. Later, these periods of perplexity began to return more and more frequently, and invariably took the same form. These stoppages of life always presented themselves to me with the same questions: "Why?" and "What after?"

At first it seemed to me that these were aimless, unmeaning questions; it seemed to me that all they asked about was well known, and that if at any time when I wished to find answers to them I could do so without much trouble—that just at that time I could not be bothered with this, but whenever I should stop to think them over I should find an answer. But these questions presented themselves to my mind with ever-increasing frequency, demanding an answer with still greater and greater persistence, and like dots grouped themselves into one black spot.

It was with me as it happens in the case of every mortal internal ailment—at first appear

From Leo Tolstoy, *My Confession* in *Tolstoi's Works*, trans. Nathan H. Dole (New York: T. Y. Crowell Co., 1899), pp. 12–57 (with omissions).

the insignificant symptoms of indisposition, disregarded by the patient; then these symptoms are repeated more and more frequently, till they merge in uninterrupted suffering. The sufferings increase, and the patient is confronted with the fact that what he took for a mere indisposition has become more important to him than anything else on earth, that it is death!

This is exactly what happened to me. I became aware that this was not a chance indisposition, but something very serious, and that if all these questions continued to recur, I should have to find an answer to them. And I tried to answer them. The questions seemed so foolish, so simple, so childish; but no sooner had I taken hold of them than I was convinced, first, that they were neither childish nor silly, but were concerned with the deepest problems of life; and, in the second place, that I could not decide them—could not decide them, however I put my mind upon them.

Before occupying myself with my Samara estate, with the education of my son, with the writing of books, I was bound to know why I did these things. As long as I do not know the reason "why" I cannot do anything. I cannot live. While thinking about the management of my household and estate, which in these days occupied much of my time, suddenly this question came into my head:

"Well and good, I have now six thousand

desyatins in the government of Samara, and three hundred horses—what then?"

I was perfectly disconcerted, and knew not what to think. Another time, dwelling on the thought of how I should educate my children, I ask myself "*Why?*" Again, when considering by what means the well-being of the people might best be promoted, I suddenly exclaimed, "But what concern have I with it?" When I thought of the fame which my works were gaining me, I said to myself:

"Well, what if I should be more famous than Gogol, Pushkin, Shakespeare, Molière—than all the writers of the world—well, and what then?" . . .

I could find no reply. Such questions will not wait: they demand an immediate answer; without one it is impossible to live; but answer there was none.

I felt that the ground on which I stood was crumbling, that there was nothing for me to stand on, that what I had been living for was nothing, that I had no reason for living . . .

My life had come to a stop. I was able to breathe, to eat, to drink, to sleep, and I could not help breathing, eating, drinking, sleeping; but there was no real life in me because I had not a single desire, the fulfillment of which I could feel to be reasonable. If I wished for anything, I knew beforehand that, were I to satisfy the wish, or were I not to satisfy it, nothing would come of it. Had a fairy appeared and offered me all I desired, I should not have known what to say. If I had, in moments of excitement, I will not say wishes, but the habits of former wishes, at calmer moments I knew that it was a delusion, that I really wished for nothing. I could not even wish to know the truth, because I guessed in what it consisted.

The truth was, that life was meaningless. Every day of life, every step in it, brought me, as it were, nearer the precipice, and I saw clearly that before me there was nothing but ruin. And to stop was impossible; and it was impossible to shut my eyes so as not to see that there was nothing before me but suffering and actual death, absolute annihilation.

Thus, I, a healthy and a happy man, was brought to feel that I could live no longer,—some irresistible force was dragging me onward to escape from life. I do not mean that I wanted to kill myself.

The force that drew me away from life was stronger, fuller, and more universal than any wish; it was a force like that of my previous attachment to life, only in a contrary direction. With all my force I struggled away from life. The idea of suicide came as naturally to me as formerly that of bettering my life. This thought was so attractive to me that I was compelled to practise upon myself a species of self-deception in order to avoid carrying it out too hastily. I was unwilling to act hastily, only because I wanted to employ all my powers in clearing away the confusion of my thoughts; if I should not clear them away, I could at any time kill myself. And here was I, a man fortunately situated, hiding away a cord, to avoid being tempted to hang myself by it to the transom between the closets of my room, where I undressed alone every evening; and I ceased to go hunting with a gun because it offered too easy a way of getting rid of life. I knew not what I wanted; I was afraid of life; I struggled to get away from it, and yet there *was* something I hoped for from it.

Such was the condition I had to come to, at a time when all the circumstances of my life were pre-eminently happy ones, and when I had not reached my fiftieth year. I had a good, loving, and beloved wife, good children, and a large estate, which, without much trouble on my part, was growing and increasing; I was more than ever respected by my friends and acquaintances; I was praised by strangers, and could lay claim to having made my name famous without much self-deception. Moreover, I was not mad or in an unhealthy mental state; on the contrary, I enjoyed a mental and physical strength which I have seldom found in men of my class and pursuits; I could keep up with a peasant in mowing, and could continue mental labor for eight or ten hours at a stretch, without any evil consequences. And in this state of things it came to this,—that I could not live, and as I feared death I was obliged to employ ruses against myself so as not to put an end to my life.

The mental state in which I then was seemed to me summed up in the following: My life was a foolish and wicked joke played on me by some one. Notwithstanding the fact that I did not recognize a "Some one," who may have created me, this conclusion that some one had wickedly and foolishly made a joke of me in bringing me into the world seemed to me the most natural of all conclusions.

It was this that was terrible! And to get free from this horror of what awaited me; I knew that this horror was more horrible than the position itself, but I could not patiently await the end. However persuasive the argument might be that all the same a blood-vessel in the heart would be ruptured or something would burst and all be over, still I could not patiently await the end. The horror of the darkness was too great to bear, and I longed to free myself from it as speedily as possible by a rope or a pistol ball. This was the feeling that, above all, drew me to think of suicide . . .

"But is it possible that I have overlooked something, that I have failed to understand something," I asked myself; "may it not be that this state of despair is common among men?"

And in every branch of human knowledge I sought an explanation of the questions that tormented me; I sought that explanation painfully and long, not out of mere curiosity; I did not seek it indolently, but painfully, obstinately, day and night; I sought it as a perishing man seeks safety, and I found nothing.

I sought it in all branches of knowledge, and not only did I fail, but, moreover, I convinced myself that all those who had searched like myself had likewise found nothing; and not only

had found nothing, but had come, as I had, to the despairing conviction, that the only absolute knowledge man can possess is this,—that life is without meaning.

I sought in all directions, and thanks to a life spent in study, and also to my connections with the learned world, the most accomplished scholars in all the various branches of knowledge were accessible to me, and they did not refuse to open to me all the sources of knowledge both in books and through personal intercourse. I knew all that learning could answer to the question, "What is life?" . . .

I had lost my way in the forest of human knowledge, in the light of the mathematical and experimental sciences which opened out for me clear horizons where there could be no house, and in the darkness of philosophy, plunging me into a greater gloom with every step I took, until I was at last persuaded that there was, and could be, no issue.

When I followed what seemed the bright light of learning, I saw that I had only turned aside from the real question. However alluring and clear were the horizons unfolded before me, however alluring it was to plunge into the infinity of these kinds of knowledge, I saw that the clearer they were the less did I need them, the less did they give me an answer to my question.

Thus my wanderings over the fields of knowledge not only failed to cure me of my despair, but increased it. One branch of knowledge gave no answer at all to the problem of life; another gave a direct answer which confirmed my despair, and showed that the state to which I had come was not the result of my going astray, of any mental disorder, but, on the contrary, it assured me that I was thinking rightly, that I was in agreement with the conclusions of the most powerful intellects among mankind.

I could not be deceived. All is vanity. A misfortune to be born. Death is better than life; life's burden must be got rid of.

My position was terrible. I knew that from the knowledge which reason has given man, I could get nothing but the denial of life, and from faith nothing but the denial of reason, which last was even more impossible than the denial of life. By the knowledge founded on reason it was proved that life is an evil and that men know it to be so, that men may cease to live if they will, but that they have lived and they go on living—I myself lived on, though I had long known that life was meaningless and evil. If I went by faith it resulted that, in order to understand the meaning of life, I should have to abandon reason, the very part of me that required a meaning in life! . . .

When I had come to this conclusion, I understood that it was useless to seek an answer to my question from knowledge founded on reason, and that the answer given by this form of knowledge is only an indication that no answer can be obtained till the question is put differently—till the question be made to include the relation between the finite and the infinite. I also understand that, however unreasonable and monstrous the answers given by faith, they have the advantage of bringing into every question the relation of the finite to the infinite, without which there can be no answer.

However I may put the question, How am I to live? the answer is, "By the law of God."

Will anything real and positive come of my life, and what?

Eternal torment, or eternal bliss.

What meaning is there not to be destroyed by death?

Union with an infinite God, paradise.

In this way I was compelled to admit that, besides the reasoning knowledge, which I once thought the only true knowledge, there was in every living man another kind of knowledge, an unreasoning one,—faith,—which gives a possibility of living . . .

I was now ready to accept any faith that did not require of me a direct denial of reason, for that would be to act a lie; and I studied Buddhism and Mohammedanism in their books, and especially also Christianity, both in its writings and in the lives of its professors around me.

I naturally turned my attention at first to the believers in my own immediate circle, to learned men, to orthodox divines, to the older monks, to the orthodox divines of a new shade of doctrine, the so-called New Christians, who preach salvation through faith in a Redeemer. I seized upon these believers, and asked them what they believed in, and what for them gave a meaning to life.

No arguments were able to convince me of the sincerity of the faith of these men. Only actions, proving their conception of life to have destroyed the fear of poverty, illness, and death, so strong in myself, could have convinced me, and such actions I could not see among the various believers of our class. Such actions I saw, indeed, among the open infidels of my own class in life, but never among the so-called believers of our class.

I understood, then, that the faith of these men was not the faith which I sought; that it was no faith at all, but only one of the Epicurean consolations of life. I understood that this faith, if it could not really console, could at least soothe the repentant mind of a Solomon on his deathbed; but that it could not serve the enormous majority of mankind, who are born, not to be comforted by the labors of others, but to create a life for themselves. For mankind to live, for it to continue to live and be conscious of the meaning of its life, all these milliards must have another and a true conception of faith. It was not, then, the fact that Solomon, Schopenhauer, and I had not killed ourselves, which convinced me that faith existed, but the fact that these milliards have lived and are now living, carrying along with them on the impulse of their life both Solomon and ourselves.

I began to draw nearer to the believers among the poor, the simple, and the ignorant, the pilgrims, the monks, the raskolniks, and the peasants. The doctrines of these men of the people, like those of the pretended believers of my own class, were Christian. Here also much that was superstitious was mingled with the truths of Christianity, but with this difference, that the superstition of the believers of our class was entirely unnecessary to them, and never influenced their lives beyond serving as a kind of Epicurean distraction; while the superstition of the believing laboring class was so interwoven with their lives that it was impossible to conceive them without it—it was a necessary condition of their living at all. The whole life of the believers of our class was in flat contradiction with their faith, and the whole life of the believers of the people was a confirmation of the meaning of life which their faith gave them.

Thus I began to study the lives and the doctrines of the people, and the more I studied the more I became convinced that a true faith was among them, that their faith was for them a necessary thing, and alone gave them a meaning in life and a possibility of living. In direct opposition to what I saw in our circle—where life without faith was possible, and where not one in a thousand professed himself a believer —amongst the people there was not a single unbeliever in a thousand. In direct opposition to what I saw in our circle—where a whole life is spent in idleness, amusement, and dissatisfaction with life—I saw among the people whole lives passed in heavy labor and unrepining content. In direct opposition to what I saw in our circle—men resisting and indignant with the privations and sufferings of their lot—the people unhesitatingly and unresistingly accepting illness and sorrow, in the quiet and firm conviction that all these must be and could not be otherwise, and that all was for the best. In contradiction to the theory that the less learned we are the less we understand the meaning of life, and see in our sufferings and death but an evil joke, these men of the people live, suffer,

and draw near to death, in quiet confidence and oftenest with joy. In contradiction to the fact that an easy death, without terror or despair, is a rare exception in our class, a death which is uneasy, rebellious, and sorrowful is among the people the rarest exception of all.

These people, deprived of all that for us and for Solomon makes the only good in life, and experiencing at the same time the highest happiness, form the great majority of mankind. I looked more widely around me, I studied the lives of the past and contemporary masses of humanity, and I saw that, not two or three, or ten, but hundreds, thousands, millions had so understood the meaning of life that they were able both to live and to die. All these men, infinitely divided by manners, powers of mind, education, and position, all alike in opposition to my ignorance, were well acquainted with the meaning of life and of death, quietly labored, endured privation and suffering, lived and died, and saw in all this, not a vain, but a good thing.

I began to grow attached to these men. The more I learned of their lives, the lives of the living and of the dead of whom I read and heard, the more I liked them, and the easier I felt it so to live. I lived in this way during two years, and then there came a change which had long been preparing in me, and the symptoms of which I had always dimly felt: the life of our circle of rich and learned men, not only became repulsive, but lost all meaning. All our actions, our reasoning, our science and art, all appeared to me in a new light. I understood that it was all child's play, that it was useless to seek a meaning in it. The life of the working classes, of the whole of mankind, of those that create life, appeared to me in its true significance. I understood that this was life itself, and that the meaning given to this life was true, and I accepted it. . . .

When I remembered how these very doctrines had repelled me, how senseless they had seemed when professed by men whose lives were spent in opposition to them, and how these same doctrines had attracted me and seemed reasonable when I saw men living in accordance with them, I understood why I had once rejected them and thought them unmeaning, why I now adopted them and thought them full of meaning. I understood that I had erred, and how I had erred. I had erred, not so much through having thought incorrectly, as through having lived ill. I understood that the truth had been hidden from me, not so much because I had erred in my reasoning, as because I had led the exceptional life of an epicure bent on satisfying the lusts of the flesh. I understood that my question, "What is my life," and the answer, "An evil," were in accordance with the truth of things. The mistake lay in my having applied to life in general an answer which only concerned myself. I had asked what my own life was, and the answer was "An evil and absurdity." Exactly so, my life—a life of indulgence, of sensuality—was an absurdity and an evil, and the answer, "Life is meaningless and evil," therefore, referred only to my own life, and not to human life in general.

I understood the truth which I afterwards found in the Gospel: "That men loved darkness rather than light because their deeds were evil. For every man that doeth evil hateth the light, neither cometh to the light, lest his deeds should be reproved."

I understood that, for the meaning of life to be understood, it was necessary first that life should be something more than evil and meaningless, and afterwards that there should be the light of reason to understand it. I understood why I had so long been circling round this self-evident truth without apprehending it, and that if we would think and speak of the life of mankind, we must think and speak of that life as a whole, and not merely of the life of certain parasites on it.

This truth was always a truth, as $2 + 2 = 4$, but I had not accepted it, because, besides acknowledging $2 + 2 = 4$, I should have been obliged to acknowledge that I was evil. It was

of more importance to me to feel that I was good, more binding on me, than to believe $2 + 2 = 4$. I loved good men, I hated myself, and I accepted truth. Now it was all clear to me. . . .

My conviction of the error into which all knowledge based on reason must fall assisted me in freeing myself from the seductions of idle reasoning. The conviction that a knowledge of truth can be gained only by living, led me to doubt the justness of my own life; but I had only to get out of my own particular groove, and look around me, to observe the simple life of the real working-class, to understand that such a life was the only real one. I understand that, if I wished to understand life and its meaning, I must live, not the life of a parasite, but a real life; and, accepting the meaning given to it by the combined lives of those that really form the great human whole, submit it to a close examination.

At the time I am speaking of, the following was my position:

During the whole of that year, when I was asking myself almost every minute whether I should or should not put an end to it all with a cord or a pistol, during the time my mind was occupied with the thoughts which I have described, my heart was oppressed by a tormenting feeling. This feeling I cannot describe otherwise than as a searching after God.

This search after a God was not an act of my reason, but a feeling, and I say this advisedly, because it was opposed to my way of thinking; it came from the heart. It was a feeling of dread, of orphanhood, of isolation amid things all apart from me, and of hope in a help I knew not from whom.

I remember one day in the early springtime I was alone in the forest listening to the woodland sounds, and thinking only of one thing, the same of which I had constantly thought for two years—I was again seeking for a God.

I said to myself:

"Very good, there is no God, there is none

with a reality apart from my own imaginings, none as real as my own life—there is none such. Nothing, no miracles can prove there is, for miracles only exist in my own unreasonable imagination."

And then I asked myself:

"But my idea of the God whom I seek, whence comes it?"

And again at this thought arose the joyous billows of life. All around me seemed to revive, to have a new meaning. My joy, though, did not last long. Reason continued its work:

"The idea of a God is not God. The idea is what goes on within myself; the idea of God is an idea which I am able to rouse in my mind or not as I choose; it is not what I seek, something without which life could not be."

Then again all seemed to die around and within me, and again I wished to kill myself.

After this I began to retrace the process which had gone on within myself, the hundred times repeated discouragement and revival. I remembered that I had lived only when I believed in a God. As it was before, so it was now; I had only to know God, and I lived; I had only to forget Him, not to believe in Him, and I died.

What was this discouragement and revival? I do not live when I lose faith in the existence of a God; I should long ago have killed myself, if I had not had a dim hope of finding Him. I really live only when I am conscious of Him and seek Him. "What more, then, do I seek?" A voice seemed to cry within me, "This is He, He without whom there is no life. To know God and to live are one. God is life."

Live to seek God, and life will not be without God. And stronger than ever rose up life within and around me, and the light that then shone never left me again.

The Death of Ivan Ilych

Leo Tolstoy

*"The Death of Ivan Ilych" is a story of the life
and death of an ordinary man whose awareness of existence only became extraordinary
when he had to face the fact that he was
dying. Previously he had lived unthinkingly
without examining his values. He had completed his schooling, trained for a profession,
married and lived with an ill-tempered and
spiteful wife, raised children, become successful as a lawyer, and experienced the everyday
joys, disappointments, and uncertainties of
most men. In Tolstoy's words, "Ivan Ilych's life
had been most simple and most ordinary and
therefore most terrible." A major turning point
occurred, however, when Ivan Ilych fell from
a ladder and suffered what at the time appeared to be a minor injury. When the pain
failed to go away he consulted several doctors
but none was able to diagnose his condition
or cure it. Eventually it became apparent to
Ivan Ilych and to his family that he was not
going to recover, that it was rapidly getting
worse rather than better, and finally that there
was no hope. It is at this point that the following selection from Tolstoy's narrative begins.*

Ivan Ilych saw that he was dying, and he was
in continual despair.

In the depth of his heart he knew he was

From Leo Tolstoy, "The Death of Ivan Ilych"
trans. Aylmer Maude in *The Complete Works of
Leo Tolstoy* (New York: D. Estes & Co., 1904–5),
Vol. 18.

dying, but not only was he not accustomed to
the thought, he simply did not and could not
grasp it.

The syllogism he had learnt from Kieze-
wetter's Logic: "Caius is a man, men are mortal,
therefore Caius is mortal," had always seemed
to him correct as applied to Caius, but certainly not as applied to himself. That Caius—
man in the abstract—was mortal, was perfectly
correct, but he was not Caius, not an abstract
man, but a creature quite, quite separate from
all others. He had been little Vanya, with a
mamma and a papa, with Mitya and Volodya,
with the toys, a coachman and a nurse, afterwards with Katenka and with all the joys,
griefs, and delights of childhood, boyhood, and
youth. What did Caius know of the smell of
that striped leather ball Vanya had been so
fond of? Had Caius kissed his mother's hand
like that, and did the silk of her dress rustle so
for Caius? Had he rioted like that at school
when the pastry was bad? Had Caius been in
love like that? Could Caius preside at a session
as he did? "Caius really was mortal, and it was
right for him to die; but for me, little Vanya,
Ivan Ilych, with all my thoughts and emotions,
it's altogether a different matter. It cannot be
that I ought to die. That would be too terrible."

Such was his feeling.

"If I had to die like Caius I should have
known it was so. An inner voice would have
told me so, but there was nothing of the sort
in me and I and all my friends felt that our
case was quite different from that of Caius.

And now here it is!" he said to himself, "It can't be. It's impossible! But here it is. How is this? How is one to understand it?"

He could not understand it, and tried to drive this false, incorrect, morbid thought away and to replace it by other proper and healthy thoughts. But that thought, and not the thought only but the reality itself, seemed to come and confront him.

And to replace that thought he called up a succession of others, hoping to find in them some support. He tried to get back into the former current of thoughts that had once screened the thought of death from him. But strange to say, all that had formerly shut off, hidden, and destroyed, his consciouneess of death, no longer had that effect. Ivan Ilych now spent most of his time in attempting to re-establish that old current. He would say to himself: "I will take up my duties again— after all I used to live by them." And banishing all doubts he would go to the law courts, enter into conversation with his colleagues, and sit carelessly as was his wont, scanning the crowd with a thoughtful look and leaning both his emaciated arms on the arms of his oak chair; bending over as usual to a colleague and drawing his papers nearer he would interchange whispers with him, and then suddenly raising his eyes and sitting erect would pronounce certain words and open the proceedings. But suddenly in the midst of those proceedings the pain in his side, regardless of the stage the proceedings had reached, would begin its own gnawing work. Ivan Ilych would turn his attention to it and try to drive the thought of it away, but without success. *It* would come and stand before him and look at him, and he would be petrified and the light would die out of his eyes, and he would again begin asking himself whether *It* alone was true. And his colleagues and subordinates would see with surprise and distress that he, the brilliant and subtle judge, was becoming confused and making mistakes. He would

shake himself, try to pull himself together, manage somehow to bring the sitting to a close, and return home with the sorrowful consciousness that his judicial labours could not as formerly hide from him what he wanted them to hide, and could not deliver him from *It*. And what was worst of all was that *It* drew his attention to itself not in order to make him take some action but only that he should look at *It*, look it straight in the face: look at it and without doing anything, suffer inexpressibly.

And to save himself from this condition Ivan Ilych looked for consolations—new screens— and new screens were found and for a while seemed to save him, but then they immediately fell to pieces or rather became transparent, as if *It* penetrated them and nothing could veil *It*. . . .

His wife returned late at night. She came in on tiptoe, but he heard her, opened his eyes, and made haste to close them again. She wished to send Gerasim away and to sit with him herself, but he opened his eyes and said: "No, go away."

"Are you in great pain?"

"Always the same."

"Take some opium."

He agreed and took some. She went away.

Till about three in the morning he was in a state of stupefied misery. It seemed to him that he and his pain were being thrust into a narrow, deep black sack, but though they were pushed further and further in they could not be pushed to the bottom. And this, terrible enough in itself, was accompanied by suffering. He was frightened yet wanted to fall through the sack, he struggled but yet co-operated. And suddenly he broke through, fell, and regained consciousness. Gerasim was sitting at the foot of the bed dozing quietly and patiently, while he himself lay with his emaciated stockinged legs resting on Gerasim's shoulders; the same shaded candle was there and the same unceasing pain.

"Go away, Gerasim," he whispered.

"It's all right, sir. I'll stay a while."

"No. Go away."

He removed his legs from Gerasim's shoulders, turned sideways onto his arm, and felt sorry for himself. He only waited till Gerasim had gone into the next room and then restrained himself no longer but wept like a child. He wept on account of his helplessness, his terrible loneliness, the cruelty of man, the cruelty of God, and the absence of God.

"Why hast Thou done all this? Why hast Thou brought me here? Why, why dost Thou torment me so terribly?"

He did not expect an answer and yet wept because there was no answer and could be none. The pain again grew more acute, but he did not stir and did not call. He said to himself: "Go on! Strike me! But what is it for? What have I done to Thee? What is it for?"

Then he grew quiet and not only ceased weeping but even held his breath and became all attention. It was as though he were listening not to an audible voice but to the voice of his soul, to the current of thoughts arising within him.

"What is it you want?" was the first clear conception capable of expression in words, that he heard.

"What do you want? What do you want?" he repeated to himself.

"What do I want? To live and not to suffer," he answered.

And again he listened with such concentrated attention that even his pain did not distract him.

"To live? How?" asked his inner voice.

"Why, to live as I used to—well and pleasantly."

"As you lived before, well and pleasantly?" the voice repeated.

And in imagination he began to recall the best moments of his pleasant life. But strange to say none of those best moments of his pleasant life now seemed at all what they had then seemed—none of them except the first recollections of childhood. There, in childhood, there had been something really pleasant with which it would be possible to live if it could return. But the child who had experienced that happiness existed no longer, it was like a reminiscence of somebody else.

As soon as the period began which had produced the present Ivan Ilych, all that had then seemed joys now melted before his sight and turned into something trivial and often nasty.

And the further he departed from childhood and the nearer he came to the present the more worthless and doubtful were the joys. This began with the School of Law. A little that was really good was still found there—there was light-heartedness, friendship, and hope. But in the upper classes there had already been fewer of such good moments. Then during the first years of his official career, when he was in the service of the Governor, some pleasant moments again occurred: they were the memories of love for a woman. Then all became confused and there was still less of what was good; later on again there was still less that was good, and the further he went the less there was. His marriage, a mere accident, then the disenchantment that followed it, his wife's bad breath and the sensuality and hypocrisy: then that deadly official life and those preoccupations about money, a year of it, and two, and ten, and twenty, and always the same thing. And the longer it lasted the more deadly it became. "It is as if I had been going downhill while I imagined I was going up. And that is really what it was. I was going up in public opinion, but to the same extent life was ebbing away from me. And now it is all done and there is only death."

"Then what does it mean? Why? It can't be that life is so senseless and horrible. But if it really has been so horrible and senseless, why must I die and die in agony? There is something wrong!"

"Maybe I did not live as I ought to have

done," it suddenly occurred to him. "But how could that be, when I did everything properly?" he replied, and immediately dismissed from his mind this, the sole solution of all the riddles of life and death, as something quite impossible.

"Then what do you want now? To live? Live how? Live as you lived in the law courts when the usher proclaimed "The judge is coming!" The judge is coming, the judge!" he repeated to himself. "Here he is, the judge. But I am not guilty!" he exclaimed angrily. "What is it for?" And he ceased crying, but turning his face to the wall continued to ponder on the same question: Why, and for what purpose, is there all this horror? But however much he pondered he found no answer. And whenever the thought occurred to him, as it often did, that it all resulted from his not having lived as he ought to have done, he at once recalled the correctness of his whole life and dismissed so strange an idea.

Another fortnight passed. Ivan Ilych now no longer left his sofa. He would not lie in bed but lay on the sofa, facing the wall nearly all the time. He suffered ever the same unceasing agonies and in his loneliness pondered always on the same insoluble question: "What is this? Can it be that it is Death?" And the inner voice answered: "Yes, it is Death."

"Why these sufferings?" And the voice answered, "For no reason—they just are so." Beyond and besides this there was nothing.

From the very beginning of his illness, ever since he had first been to see the doctor, Ivan Ilych's life had been divided between two contrary and alternating moods: now it was despair and the expectation of this uncomprehended and terrible death, and now hope and an intently interested observation of the functioning of his organs. Now before his eyes there was only a kidney or an intestine that temporarily evaded its duty, and now only that incomprehensible and dreadful death from which it was impossible to escape.

These two states of mind had alternated from the very beginning of his illness, but the further it progressed the more doubtful and fantastic became the conception of the kidney, and the more real the sense of impending death.

He had but to call to mind what he had been three months before and what he was now, to call to mind with what regularity he had been going downhill, for every possibility of hope to be shattered.

Latterly during that loneliness in which he found himself as he lay facing the back of the sofa, a loneliness in the midst of a populous town and surrounded by numerous acquaintances and relations but that yet could not have been more complete anywhere—either at the bottom of the sea or under the earth—during that terrible loneliness Ivan Ilych had lived only in memories of the past. Pictures of his past rose before him one after another. They always began with what was nearest in time and then went back to what was most remote —to his childhood—and rested there. If he thought of the stewed prunes that had been offered him that day, his mind went back to the raw shrivelled French plums of his childhood, their peculiar flavour and the flow of saliva when he sucked their stones, and along with the memory of that taste came a whole series of memories of those days: his nurse, his brother, and their toys. "No, I musn't think of that. . . . It is too painful," Ivan Ilych said to himself, and brought himself back to the present—to the button on the back of the sofa and the creases in its morocco. "Morocco is expensive, but it does not wear well: there had been a quarrel about it. It was a different kind of quarrel and a different kind of morocco that time when we tore father's portfolio and were punished, and mamma brought us some tarts. . . ." And again his thoughts dwelt on his childhood, and again it was painful and he tried to banish them and fix his mind on something else.

Then again together with that chain of memories another series passed through his mind—of how his illness had progressed and grown worse. There also the further back he looked the more life there had been. There had been more of what was good in life and more of life itself. The two merged together. "Just as the pain went on getting worse and worse, so my life grew worse and worse," he thought. "There is one bright spot there at the back, at the beginning of life, and afterwards all becomes blacker and blacker and proceeds more and more rapidly—in inverse ratio to the square of the distance from death," thought Ivan Ilych. And the example of a stone falling downwards with increasing velocity entered his mind. Life, a series of increasing sufferings, flies further and further towards its end—the most terrible suffering. "I am flying. . . ." He shuddered, shifted himself, and tried to resist, but was already aware that resistance was impossible, and again with eyes weary of gazing but unable to cease seeing what was before them, he stared at the back of the sofa and waited—awaiting that dreadful fall and shock and destruction.

"Resistance is impossible!" he said to himself. "If I could only understand what it is all for! But that too is impossible. An explanation would be possible if it could be said that I have not lived as I ought to. But it is impossible to say that," and he remembered all the legality, correctitude, and propriety of his life. "That at any rate can certainly not be admitted," he thought, and his lips smiled ironically as if someone could see that smile and be taken in by it. "There is no explanation! Agony, death . . . What for?"

Another two weeks went by in this way and during that fortnight an event occurred that Ivan Ilych and his wife had desired. Petrish-chev formally proposed. It happened in the evening. The next day Praskovya Fëdorovna came into her husband's room considering how best to inform him of it, but that very night there had been a fresh change for the worse in his condition. She found him still lying on the sofa but in a different position. He lay on his back, groaning and staring fixedly straight in front of him.

She began to remind him of his medicines, but he turned his eyes towards her with such a look that she did not finish what she was saying; so great an animosity, to her in particular, did that look express.

"For Christ's sake let me die in peace!" he said.

She would have gone away, but just then their daughter came in and went up to say good morning. He looked at her as he had done at his wife, and in reply to her inquiry about his health said dryly that he would soon free them all of himself. They were both silent and after sitting with him for a while went away.

"Is it our fault?" Lisa said to her mother. "It's as if we were to blame! I am sorry for papa, but why should we be tortured?"

The doctor came at his usual time. Ivan Ilych answered "Yes" and "No," never taking his angry eyes from him, and at last said: "You know you can do nothing for me, so leave me alone."

"We can ease your sufferings."

"You can't even do that. Let me be."

The doctor went into the drawing-room and told Praskovya Fëdorovna that the case was very serious and that the only resource left was opium to allay her husband's sufferings, which must be terrible.

It was true, as the doctor said, that Ivan Ilych's physical sufferings were terrible, but worse than the physical sufferings were his mental sufferings, which were his chief torture.

His mental sufferings were due to the fact

that that night, as he looked at Gerasim's sleepy, good-natured face with his prominent cheek-bones, the question suddenly occurred to him: "What if my whole life has really been wrong?"

It occurred to him that what had appeared perfectly impossible before, namely that he had not spent his life as he should have done, might after all be true. It occurred to him that his scarcely perceptible attempts to struggle against what was considered good by the most highly placed people, those scarcely noticeable impulses which he had immediately sup-pressed, might have been the real thing, and all the rest false. And his professional duties and the whole arrangement of his life and of his family, and all his social and official interests, might all have been false. He tried to defend all those things to himself and suddenly felt the weakness of what he was defending. There was nothing to defend.

"But if that is so," he said to himself, "and I am leaving this life with the consciousness that I have lost all that was given me and it is impossible to rectify it—what then?"

He lay on his back and began to pass his life in review in quite a new way. In the morn-ing when he saw first his footman, then his wife, then his daughter, and then the doctor, their every word and movement confirmed to him the awful truth that had been revealed to him during the night. In them he saw himself—all that for which he had lived—and saw clearly that it was not real at all, but a terrible and huge deception which had hidden both life and death. This consciousness intensified his physical suffering tenfold. He groaned and tossed about, and pulled at his clothing which choked and stifled him. And he hated them on that account.

He was given a large dose of opium and became unconscious, but at noon his sufferings began again. He drove everybody away and tossed from side to side.

His wife came to him and said:

"Jean, my dear, do this for me. It can't do any harm and often helps. Healthy people often do it."

He opened his eyes wide.

"What? Take communion? Why? It's un-necessary! However..."

She began to cry.

"Yes, do, my dear. I'll send for our priest. He is such a nice man."

"All right. Very well," he muttered.

When the priest came and heard his con-fession, Ivan Ilych was softened and seemed to feel a relief from his doubts and conse-quently from his sufferings, and for a moment there came a ray of hope. He again began to think of the vermiform appendix and the possi-bility of correcting it. He received the sacra-ment with tears in his eyes.

When they laid him down again afterwards he felt a moment's ease, and the hope that he might live awoke in him again. He began to think of the operation that had been suggested to him. "To live! I want to live!" he said to him-self.

His wife came in to congratulate him after his communion, and when uttering the usual conventional words she added:

"You feel better, don't you?"

Without looking at her he said "Yes."

Her dress, her figure, the expression of her face, the tone of her voice, all revealed the same thing. "This is wrong, it is not as it should be. All you have lived for and still live for is false-hood and deception, hiding life and death from you." And as soon as he admitted that thought, his hatred and his agonizing physical suffering again sprang up, and with that suffer-ing a consciousness of the unavoidable, ap-proaching end. And to this was added a new sensation of grinding shooting pain and a feel-ing of suffocation.

The expression of his face when he uttered that "yes" was dreadful. Having uttered it, he looked her straight in the eyes, turned on his face with a rapidity extraordinary in his weak state and shouted:

"Go away! Go away and leave me alone!"

From that moment the screaming began that continued for three days, and was so terrible that one could not hear it through two closed doors without horror. At the moment he answered his wife he realized that he was lost, that there was no return, that the end had come, the very end, and his doubts were still unsolved and remained doubts.

"Oh! Oh! Oh!" he cried in various intonations. He had begun by screaming "I won't!" and continued screaming on the letter *O*.

For three whole days, during which time did not exist for him, he struggled in that black sack into which he was being thrust by an invisible, resistless force. He struggled as a man condemned to death struggles in the hands of the executioner, knowing that he cannot save himself. And every moment he felt that despite all his efforts he was drawing nearer and nearer to what terrified him. He felt that his agony was due to his being thrust into that black hole and still more to his not being able to get right into it. He was hindered from getting into it by his conviction that his life had been a good one. That very justification of his life held him fast and prevented his moving forward, and it caused him most torment of all.

Suddenly some force struck him in the chest and side, making it still harder to breathe, and he fell through the hole and there at the bottom was a light. What had happened to him was like the sensation one sometimes experiences in a railway carriage when one thinks one is going backwards while one is really going forwards and suddenly becomes aware of the real direction.

"Yes, it was all not the right thing," he said to himself, "but that's no matter. It can be done. But what *is* the right thing?" he asked himself, and suddenly grew quiet.

This occurred at the end of the third day, two hours before his death. Just then his schoolboy son had crept softly in and gone up to the bedside. The dying man was still screaming desperately and waving his arms. His hand fell on the boy's head, and the boy caught it, pressed it to his lips, and began to cry.

At that very moment Ivan Ilych fell through and caught sight of the light, and it was revealed to him that though his life had not been what it should have been, this could still be rectified. He asked himself, "What *is* the right thing?" and grew still, listening. Then he felt that someone was kissing his hand. He opened his eyes, looked at his son, and felt sorry for him. His wife came up to him and he glanced at her. She was gazing at him open-mouthed, with undried tears on her nose and cheek and a despairing look on her face. He felt sorry for her too.

"Yes, I am making them wretched," he thought. "They are sorry, but it will be better for them when I die." He wished to say this but had not the strength to utter it. "Besides, why speak? I must act," he thought. With a look at his wife he indicated his son and said: "Take him away . . . sorry for him . . . sorry for you too. . . ." He tried to add, "forgive me," but said "forgo" and waved his hand, knowing that He whose understanding mattered would understand.

And suddenly it grew clear to him that what had been oppressing him and would not leave him was all dropping away at once from two sides, from ten sides, and from all sides. He was sorry for them, he must act so as not to hurt them: release them and free himself from these sufferings. "How good and how simple!" he thought. "And the pain?" he asked himself. "What has become of it? Where are you, pain?"

He turned his attention to it.

"Yes, here it is. Well, what of it? Let the pain be."

"And death . . . where is it?"

He sought his former accustomed fear of death and did not find it. "Where is it? What death?" There was no fear because there was no death.

In place of death there was light.

"So that's what it is!" he suddenly exclaimed aloud. "What joy!"

To him all this happened in a single instant, and the meaning of that instant did not change. For those present his agony continued for another two hours. Something rattled in his throat, his emaciated body twitched, then the gasping and rattle became less and less frequent.

"It is finished!" said someone near him.

He heard these words and repeated them in his soul.

"Death is finished," he said to himself. "It is no more!"

He drew in a breath, stopped in the midst of a sigh, stretched out, and died.

5 Commitment to Clarity

Ayer & Wisdom

It was Karl Kraus who said, "My language is the universal whore whom I have to make into a virgin." The implication is, of course, that it cannot be done; but however we misuse it, language is one major way in which we express our meanings and deal with the human condition. Many philosophers today would insist that we clarify what we mean by "the human condition" and that, whatever we say about it, our statements can in some clear way be shown to be true or false. Because language is so important and because it is the cause of so much confusion, philosophers should value precision of statement over sweeping generalization; clear problems over ambiguous answers. This is the spirit of "analytic philosophy."

Analytic philosophy is not a school of philosophy, but it is an approach to doing philosophy. Today this approach dominates much of the philosophical work being done in most English-speaking countries. Despite the disagreements among the analysts, their common denominator is an interest in the logical criticism of language and in the way in which language can be misleading. Their emphasis is upon precise thinking and clear linguistic expression with regard to the basic concepts of the world, human nature, and society. This view of philosophy, whose central concern is with language and the clarification of meaning, can be traced to the ancient Greek philosophers. Socrates examined the meaning of concepts such as justice and virtue before he would allow the inquiry to begin in earnest.

The philosophical concern with language has often been referred to as a "second-order" interest. "First-order" statements are those belonging to physical or social sciences (e.g., "The causes of the Civil War in the United States were economic"). We formulate second-order statements to talk about and to justify first-order statements. A. J. Ayer's *Language, Truth, and Logic,* published in 1936 (second edition, 1946) expresses this view of the function of philosophy:

> . . . the propositions of philosophy are not factual, but linguistic in character—that is, they do not describe the behavior of physical, or even mental, objects; they express definitions, or the formal consequences of definitions."[1]

The differences among analytic philosophers are often defined by their attitudes toward speculative philosophy, or "metaphysics." A group which met in Vienna in the twenties (the Vienna Circle or "logical positivists") considered it important to demonstrate that all statements which referred to transcendent entities such as "God" or the "Absolute" were without cognitive or factual meaning. This elimination of metaphysical concepts as meaningless was the result of their effort to make philosophy scientific by applying a principle of verification to all propositions, both empirical and normative (e.g., ethical and aesthetic). The early logical positivists in Europe and the logical atomists in Great Britain often relied on artificially constructed languages such as symbolic logic as their model of an adequate and precise language. The movement can be seen as an attempt to adapt the methods of scientific inquiry to issues in philosophy. A. J. Ayer's first book shows the influence of the logical positivists and it was instrumental in introducing logical positivism in England and America.

Characteristic of the logical positivists and Ayer's point of view in the selection below are the following positions:

1. That the aims of philosophy should not be confused with those of the sciences. The function of philosophy is the important second-order activity of the analysis of language. The aims of the physical sciences are accurate descriptions of matters of fact in the world.

2. That meaningful statements are divisible into two mutually exclusive classes: (a) analytic and (b) synthetic statements. (a) Analytic statements merely elucidate the meaning of the words or the syntax of the statement itself; they are empty of factual content; they are necessarily true or false; and they can be known to be true or false *a priori,* independent of the need to make empirical observations. Two examples of analytic statements are: "All bachelors are unmarried males" and "It is snowing or it is not snowing." (b) Synthetic statements are statements which are not empty of factual content; they could possibly be true or false, i.e., their denial does not entail a contradiction; their truth or falsity can only be established with some degree of probability; and they can be known only *a posteriori,* by checking their truth via empirical observations.

3. In order to place a radical limit on statements which are capable of being true, we should adopt a criterion of verifiability, an empirical criterion of meaning by which we can determine whether any statement is cognitively or factually meaningful.

Ayer has attempted to formulate this criterion of verifiability of meaning in order to be able to judge when the requirements of meaningful language are or are not met. For example, Ayer was neither atheist nor agnostic. Theological statements about God are a special case of metaphysical statements, and they should meet the requirements of the verifiability principle. Ayer's conclusion is that statements regarding God are neither true nor false in a literal or factual sense—they are non-sensical. This challenge by Ayer and others has done much to turn attention to the special characteristics of religious language as well as to the analytic character of mathematical propositions, the possibility of ideal languages, and an emotive theory of moral discourse.

Many philosophers, including the English philosopher John Wisdom (b. 1904), were greatly influenced by Ludwig Wittgenstein's work, especially his posthumously published *Philosophical Investigations*. This work portended a change from an almost exclusive concern with logical and linguistic problems associated with the sciences to a concern with the importance of ordinary language. Philosophers broadened their interest to the wider functions of language and to the problems of meaning, its use and usage. For Wisdom, metaphysical questions and arguments are not necessarily beyond the scope of thought and reason, and might even be helpful by calling attention to the pattern of things. Understanding a concept entails examining the situation in which the concept is used because perplexities often occur when expressions or arguments are used out of the context which gives them their meaning.

Wisdom inspects puzzling expressions, the logic of what we say and argue, as one inspects concrete specimens of language use. In his article "Gods," which appeared in 1946, he takes a close look at religious discourse, especially our assertions and arguments about God. The disagreements between the believer and the atheist may be about their interpretations of the same set of facts and may not be disagreements which can be said to be contradictory. Arguments regarding the existence or non-existence of God may mislead us into believing that the resolution of the argument is a matter of straightforward empirical evidence. On the contrary, Wisdom suggests that assertions about God may be more like expressions of appreciation than factual assertions.

In the selection by Wisdom that is presented here, one can see that his central interest is in the nature of philosophy and philosophical questions. His non-speculative and analytical approach is intended to uncover the reasons for our perplexity over certain questions by paying close critical attention to the questions. What is happening when we ask such questions as "What is the meaning of life?" and "What is the meaning of this?" What kind of questions are we asking and what kind of answers would we consider satisfactory?

Philosophy is concerned about language and words but not only about language and words. The interest of the philosopher should be "the illumination of the ultimate structure of facts" by means of a closer analysis of what it is that enables us to say we have or do not have knowledge of these facts. Philosophical difficulties arise out of our misunderstanding and misuse of ordinary language. By analyzing and clarifying linguistic meanings we may avoid fruitless debates over imaginary problems and paradoxes. Philosophy as the vigorous and systematic elucidation of language can be a liberation and therapeutic instrument. But philosophy is not merely linguistic therapy. Philosophical paradoxes, questions which seemingly have no answers, may really be the result of our misapprehension of things due to the misleading nature of ordinary language.

In the first selection, Ayer discusses several of the main themes of the logical positivists: the restricted functions of philosophy in relation to science, the importance of understanding the workings of our language, the different criteria of verifiability, and the kinds of statements rendered non-sensical or meaningless by these criteria of meaning. It should become apparent in reading Ayer's position that the results of his seemingly tedious distinctions are revolutionary for our religious, moral, and aesthetic beliefs. His major point is well taken: a large part of our difficulties in understanding the human condition and the world around us is the result of careless and indiscriminate use of language.

NOTE

1.   A. J. Ayer, *Language, Truth, and Logic* (New York: Dover Publications, 1946), p. 57.

The Elimination of Metaphysics

A. J. Ayer

The traditional disputes of philosophers are, for the most part, as unwarranted as they are unfruitful. The surest way to end them is to establish beyond question what should be the purpose and method of a philosophical enquiry. And this is by no means so difficult a task as the history of philosophy would lead one to suppose. For if there are any questions which science leaves it to philosophy to answer, a straightforward process of elimination must lead to their discovery.

We may begin by criticising the metaphysical thesis that philosophy affords us knowledge of a reality transcending the world of science and common sense. Later on, when we come to define metaphysics and account for its existence, we shall find that it is possible to be a metaphysician without believing in a transcendent reality; for we shall see that many metaphysical utterances are due to the commission of logical errors, rather than to a conscious desire on the part of their authors to go beyond the limits of experience. But it is convenient for us to take the case of those who believe that it is possible to have knowledge of a transcendent reality as a starting-point for our discussion. The arguments which we use to refute them will subsequently be found to apply to the whole of metaphysics.

One way of attacking a metaphysician who claimed to have knowledge of a reality which

From A. J. Ayer, *Language, Truth, and Logic* (New York: Dover Publications, 1950).

transcended the phenomenal world would be to enquire from what premises his propositions were deduced. Must he not begin, as other men do, with the evidence of his senses? And if so, what valid process of reasoning can possibly lead him to the conception of a transcendent reality? Surely from empirical premises nothing whatsoever concerning the properties, or even the existence, of anything super-empirical can legitimately be inferred. But this objection would be met by a denial on the part of the metaphysician that his assertions were ultimately based on the evidence of his senses. He would say that he was endowed with a faculty of intellectual intuition which enabled him to know facts that could not be known through sense-experience. And even if it could be shown that he was relying on empirical premises, and that his venture into a nonempirical world was therefore logically unjustified, it would not follow that the assertions which he made concerning this nonempirical world could not be true. For the fact that a conclusion does not follow from its putative premise is not sufficient to show that it is false. Consequently one cannot overthrow a system of transcendent metaphysics merely by criticising the way in which it comes into being. What is required is rather a criticism of the nature of the actual statements which comprise it. And this is the line of argument which we shall, in fact, pursue. For we shall maintain that no statement which refers to a "reality" transcending the limits of all possible sense-experience can possibly have any literal significance; from which it must follow that the labours of those who have striven to describe such a reality have all been devoted to the production of nonsense. . . .

Our charge against the metaphysician is not that he attempts to employ the understanding in a field where it cannot profitably venture, but that he produces sentences which fail to conform to the conditions under which alone a sentence can be literally significant. Nor are we ourselves obliged to talk nonsense in order to show that all sentences of a certain type are necessarily devoid of literal significance. We need only formulate the criterion which enables us to test whether a sentence expresses a genuine proposition about a matter of fact, and then point out that the sentences under consideration fail to satisfy it. And this we shall now proceed to do. We shall first of all formulate the criterion in somewhat vague terms, and then give the explanations which are necessary to render it precise.

The criterion which we use to test the genuineness of apparent statements of fact is the criterion of verifiability. We say that a sentence is factually significant to any given person, if, and only if, he knows how to verify the proposition which it purports to express—that is, if he knows what observations would lead him, under certain conditions, to accept the proposition as being true, or reject it as being false. If, on the other hand, the putative proposition is of such a character that the assumption of its truth, or falsehood, is consistent with any assumption whatsoever concerning the nature of his future experience, then, as far as he is concerned, it is, if not a tautology, a mere pseudo-proposition. The sentence expressing it may be emotionally significant to him; but it is not literally significant. And with regard to questions the procedure is the same. We enquire in every case what observations would lead us to answer the question, one way or the other; and, if none can be discovered, we must conclude that the sentence under consideration does not, as far as we are concerned, express a genuine question, however strongly its grammatical appearance may suggest that it does.

As the adoption of this procedure is an essential factor in the argument of this book, it needs to be examined in detail.

In the first place, it is necessary to draw a distinction between practical verifiability, and verifiability in principle. Plainly we all understand, in many cases believe, propositions which we have not in fact taken steps to verify. Many of these are propositions which we could verify if we took enough trouble. But there remain a number of significant propositions, concerning matters of fact, which we could not verify even if we chose; simply because we lack the practical means of placing ourselves in the situation where the relevant observations could be made. A simple and familiar example of such a proposition is the proposition that there are mountains on the farther side of the moon.[1] No rocket has yet been invented which would enable me to go and look at the farther side of the moon, so that I am unable to decide the matter by actual observation. But I do know what observations would decide it for me, if, as is theoretically conceivable, I were once in a position to make them. And therefore I say that the proposition is verifiable in principle, if not in practice, and is accordingly significant. On the other hand, such a metaphysical pseudo-proposition as "the Absolute enters into, but is itself incapable of, evolution and progress,"[2] is not even in principle verifiable. For one cannot conceive of an observation which would enable one to determine whether the Absolute did, or did not, enter into evolution and progress. Of course it is possible that the author of such a remark is using English words in a way in which they are not commonly used by English-speaking people, and that he does, in fact, intend to assert something which could be empirically verified. But until he makes us understand how the proposition that he wishes to express would be verified, he fails to communicate anything to us. And if he admits, as I think the author of the remark in question would have admitted, that his words were not intended to express either a tautology or a proposition which was capable, at least in principle, of being verified, then it follows that he has made an utterance which has no literal significance even for himself.

A further distinction which we must make is the distinction between the "strong" and the "weak" sense of the term "verifiable." A proposition is said to be verifiable, in the strong sense of the term, if, and only if, its truth could be conclusively established in experience. But it is verifiable, in the weak sense, if it is possible for experience to render it probable. In which sense are we using the term when we say that a putative proposition is genuine only if it is verifiable?

It seems to me that if we adopt conclusive verifiability as our criterion of significance, as some positivists have proposed, our argument will prove too much. Consider, for example, the case of general propositions of law—such propositions, namely, as "arsenic is poisonous"; "all men are mortal"; "a body tends to expand when it is heated." It is of the very nature of these propositions that their truth cannot be established with certainty by any finite series of observations. But if it is recognised that such general propositions of law are designed to cover an infinite number of cases, then it must be admitted that they cannot, even in principle, be verified conclusively. And then, if we adopt conclusive verifiability as our criterion of significance, we are logically obliged to treat these general propositions of law in the same fashion as we treat the statements of the metaphysician. . . .

Accordingly, we fall back on the weaker sense of verification. We say that the question that must be asked about any putative statement of fact is not, Would any observations make its truth or falsehood logically certain?

but simply, Would any observations be relevant to the determination of its truth or falsehood? And it is only if a negative answer is given to this second question that we conclude that the statement under consideration is nonsensical.

To make our position clearer, we may formulate it in another way. Let us call a proposition which records an actual or possible observation an experiential proposition. Then we may say that it is the mark of a genuine factual proposition, not that it should be equivalent to an experiential proposition, or any finite number of experiential propositions, but simply that some experiential propositions can be deducted from it in conjunction with certain other premises without being deducible from those other premises alone.[3]

This criterion seems liberal enough. In contrast to the principle of conclusive verifiability, it clearly does not deny significance to general propositions or to propositions about the past. Let us see what kinds of assertion it rules out.

A good example of the kind of utterance that is condemned by our criterion as being not even false but nonsensical would be the assertion that the world of sense-experience was altogether unreal. It must, of course, be admitted that our senses do sometimes deceive us. We may, as the result of having certain sensations, expect certain other sensations to be obtainable which are, in fact, not obtainable. But, in all such cases, it is further sense-experience that informs us of the mistakes that arise out of sense-experience. We say that the senses sometimes deceive us, just because the expectations to which our sense-experiences give rise do not always accord with what we subsequently experience. That is, we rely on our senses to substantiate or confute the judgements which are based on our sensations. And therefore the fact that our perceptual judgements are sometimes found to be erroneous has not the slightest tendency to show that the world of sense-experience is unreal. And, indeed, it is plain that no conceivable observation, or series of observations, could have any tendency to show that the world revealed to us by sense-experience was unreal. Consequently, anyone who condemns the sensible world as a world of mere appearance, as opposed to reality, is saying something which, according to our criterion of significance, is literally nonsensical.

An example of a controversy which the application of our criterion obliges us to condemn as fictitious is provided by those who dispute concerning the number of substances that there are in the world. For it is admitted both by monists, who maintain that reality is one substance, and by pluralists, who maintain that reality is many, that it is impossible to imagine any empirical situation which would be relevant to the solution of their dispute. But if we are told that no possible observation could give any probability either to the assertion that reality was one substance or to the assertion that it was many, then we must conclude that neither assertion is significant. We shall see later on that there are genuine logical and empirical questions involved in the dispute between monists and pluralists. But the metaphysical question concerning "substance" is ruled out by our criterion as spurious.

A similar treatment must be accorded to the controversy between realists and idealists, in its metaphysical aspect. A simple illustration, which I have made use of in a similar argument elsewhere,[4] will help to demonstrate this. Let us suppose that a picture is discovered and the suggestion made that it was painted by Goya. There is a definite procedure for dealing with such a question. The experts examine the picture to see in what way it resembles the accredited works of Goya, and to see if it bears any marks which are characteristic of a forgery; they look up contemporary records for evidence of the existence of such a picture, and so on. In the end, they may still disagree, but each one knows what empirical evidence would go to confirm or discredit his opinion. Suppose,

now, that these men have studied philosophy, and some of them proceed to maintain that this picture is a set of ideas in the perceiver's mind, or in God's mind, others that it is objectively real. What possible experience could any of them have which would be relevant to the solution of this dispute one way or the other? In the ordinary sense of the term "real," in which it is opposed to "illusory," the reality of the picture is not in doubt. The disputants have satisfied themselves that the picture is real, in this sense, by obtaining a correlated series of sensations of sight and sensations of touch. Is there any similar process by which they could discover whether the picture was real, in the sense in which the term "real" is opposed to "ideal"? Clearly there is none. But, if that is so, the problem is fictitious according to our criterion. This does not mean that the realist-idealist controversy may be dismissed without further ado. For it can legitimately be regarded as a dispute concerning the analysis of existential propositions, and so as involving a logical problem which, as we shall see, can be definitively solved. What we have just shown is that the question at issue between idealists and realists becomes fictitious when, as is often the case, it is given a metaphysical interpretation.

There is no need for us to give further examples of the operation of our criterion of significance. For our object is merely to show that philosophy, as a genuine branch of knowledge, must be distinguished from metaphysics. We are not now concerned with the historical question how much of what has traditionally passed for philosophy is actually metaphysical. We shall, however, point out later on that the majority of the "great philosophers" of the past were not essentially metaphysicians, and thus reassure those who would otherwise be prevented from adopting our criterion by considerations of piety.

As to the validity of the verification principle, in the form in which we have stated it, a demonstration will be given in the course of this book. For it will be shown that all propositions which have factual content are empirical hypotheses; and that the function of an empirical hypothesis is to provide a rule for the anticipation of experience. And this means that every empirical hypothesis must be relevant to some actual, or possible, experience, so that a statement which is not relevant to any experience is not an empirical hypothesis, and accordingly has no factual content. But this is precisely what the principle of verifiability asserts.

It should be mentioned here that the fact that the utterances of the metaphysician are nonsensical does not follow simply from the fact that they are devoid of factual content. It follows from that fact, together with the fact that they are not *a priori* propositions. And in assuming that they are not *a priori* propositions, we are once again anticipating the conclusions of a later chapter in this book. For it will be shown there that *a priori* propositions, which have always been attractive to philosophers on account of their certainty, owe this certainty to the fact that they are tautologies. We may accordingly define a metaphysical sentence as a sentence which purports to express a genuine proposition, but does, in fact, express neither a tautology nor an empirical hypothesis. And as tautologies and empirical hypotheses form the entire class of significant propositions, we are justified in concluding that all metaphysical assertions are nonsensical. Our next task is to show how they come to be made.

NOTES

1. This example has been used by Professor Schlick to illustrate the same point.

2. A remark taken at random from *Appearance and Reality*, by F. H. Bradley.

3. This is an over-simplified statement, which is not literally correct. (Ayer emended this in 1946.)

4. Vide, "Demonstration of the Impossibility of Metaphysics," *Mind*, 1934, p. 339.

The Meanings of the Questions of Life

John Wisdom

When one asks 'What is the meaning of life?' one begins to wonder whether this large, hazy and bewildering question itself has any meaning. Some people indeed have said boldly that the question has no meaning. I believe this is a mistake. But it is a mistake which is not without excuse. And I hope that by examining the excuse we may begin to remedy the mistake, and so come to see that whether or not life has a meaning it is not senseless to enquire whether it has or not. First, then, what has led some people to think that the whole enquiry is senseless?

There is an old story which runs something like this: A child asked an old man 'What holds up the world? What holds up all things?' The old man answered 'A giant'. The child asked 'And what holds up the giant? You must tell me what holds up the giant'. The old man answered 'An elephant'. The child said, 'And what holds up the elephant?' The old man answered 'A tortoise'. The child said 'You still have not told me what holds up all things. For what holds up the tortoise'. The old man answered 'Run away and don't ask me so many questions'.

From this story we can see how it may happen that a question which looks very like

From John Wisdom, "The Meanings of the Questions of Life," in *Paradox and Discovery* (Oxford: Basil Blackwell, 1965).

sensible meaningful questions may turn out to be a senseless, meaningless one. Again and again when we ask 'What supports this?' it is possible to give a sensible answer. For instance what supports the top-most card in a house of cards? The cards beneath it which are in their turn supported by the cards beneath them. What supports all the cards? The table. What supports the table? The floor and the earth. But the question 'What supports all things, absolutely all things?' is different. It is absurd, it is senseless, like the question 'What is bigger than the largest thing in the world?' And it is easy to see why the question 'What supports all things?' is absurd. Whenever we ask, 'What supports thing A or these things A, B, C', then we can answer this question only by mentioning some thing other than the thing A or things A, B, C about which we asked 'What supports it or them'. We must if we are to answer the question mention something D other than those things which form the subject of our question, and we must say that this thing is what supports them. If we mean by the phrase 'all things' absolutely all things which exist then obviously there is nothing outside that about which we are now asked 'What supports all this?' Consequently any answer to the question will be self-contradictory just as any answer to the question 'What is bigger than the biggest of all things' must be self-contradictory. Such questions are absurd, or, if you like, silly and senseless.

In a like way again and again when we ask 'What is the meaning of this?' we answer in terms of something other than this. For instance imagine that there has been a quarrel in the street. One man is hitting another man on the jaw. A policeman hurries up. 'Now then' he says, 'what is the meaning of all this?' He wants to know what led up to the quarrel, what caused it. It is no good saying to the policeman 'It's a quarrel'. He knows there is a quarrel. What he wants to know is what went before the quarrel, what led up to it. To answer him we must mention something other than the quarrel itself. Again suppose a man is driving a motor car and sees in front of him a road sign, perhaps a red flag, perhaps a skull and cross bones. "What does this mean?' he asks and when he asks this he wants to know what the sign points to. To answer we must mention something other than the sign itself, such as a dangerous corner in the road. Imagine a doctor sees an extraordinary rash on the face of his patient. He is astonished and murmurs to himself 'What is the meaning of this?'. He wants to know what caused the strange symptoms, or what they will lead to, or both. In any case in order to answer his question he must find something which went before or comes after and lies outside that about which he asks 'What does this mean?'. This need to look before or after in order to answer a question of the sort 'What is the meaning of this?' is so common, so characteristic, a feature of such questions that it is natural to think that when it is impossible to answer such a question in this way then the question has no sense. Now what happens when we ask 'What is the meaning of life?'

Perhaps someone here replies, the meaning, the significance of this present life, this life on earth, lies in a life hereafter, a life in heaven. All right. But imagine that some persistent enquirer asks, 'But what I am asking is what is the meaning of all life, life here and life beyond, life now and life hereafter? What is the meaning of all things in earth and heaven?' Are we to say that this question is absurd because there cannot be anything beyond all things while at the same time any answer to 'What is the meaning of all things?' must point to some thing beyond all things?

Imagine that we come into a theatre after a play has started and are obliged to leave before it ends. We may then be puzzled by the part of the play that we are able to see. We may ask 'What does it mean?'. In this case we want to know what went before and what came after in order to understand the part we saw. But sometimes even when we have seen and heard a play from the beginning to the end we are still puzzled and still ask what does the whole thing mean. In this case we are not asking what came before or what came after, we are not asking about anything outside the play itself. We are, if you like, asking a very different sort of question from that we usually put with the words 'What does this mean?' But we are still asking a real question, we are still asking a question which has sense and is not absurd. For our words express a wish to grasp the character, the significance of the whole play. They are a confession that we have not yet done this and they are a request for help in doing it. Is the play a tragedy, a comedy or a tale told by an idiot? The pattern of it is so complex, so bewildering, our grasp of it still so inadequate, that we don't know what to say, still less whether to call it good or bad. But this question is not senseless.

In the same way when we ask 'what is the meaning of all things?' we are not asking a senseless question. In this case, of course, we have not witnessed the whole play, we have only an idea in outline of what went before and what will come after that small part of history which we witness. But with the words 'What is the meaning of it all?' we are trying to find the order in the drama of Time. The question may be beyond us. A child may be able to understand, to grasp a simple play and be unable to understand and grasp a play more complex and more subtle. We do not say on this account that when he asks of the larger more complex play 'What does it mean?' then his question is senseless, nor even that it is senseless for him. He has asked and even answered such a question in simpler cases, he knows the sort of effort, the sort of movement of the mind which such a question calls for, and we do not say that a question is meaningless to him merely because he is not yet able to carry out quite successfully the movement of that sort which is needed in order to answer a complex question of that sort. We do not say that a question in mathematics which is at present rather beyond us is meaningless to us. We know the type of procedure it calls for and may make efforts which bring us nearer and nearer to an answer. We are able to find the meaning which lies not outside but within very complex but still limited wholes whether these are dramas of art or of real life. When we ask 'What is the meaning of all things?' we are bewildered and have not that grasp of the order of things the desire for which we express when we ask that question. But this does not render the question senseless nor make it impossible for us to move towards an answer.

We must however remember that what one calls answering such a question is not giving an answer. I mean we cannot answer such a question in the form: 'The meaning is this'.

Such an idea about what form answering a question must take may lead to a new despair in which we feel we cannot do anything in the way of answering such a question as 'What is the meaning in it all?' merely because we are not able to sum up our results in a phrase or formula.

When we ask what is the meaning of this play or this picture we cannot express the understanding which this question may lead to in the form of a list of just those things in the play or the picture which give it its meaning. No. The meaning eludes such a list. This does not mean that words quite fail us. They may yet help us provided that we do not expect of them more than they can do.

A person who is asked what he finds so hateful or so lovable in another may with words help himself and us in grasping what it is that so moves him. But he will only mislead us and himself if he pretends that his words are a complete account of all that there is in the matter.

It is the same when we ask what is it in all things that makes it all so good, so bad, so grand, so contemptible. We must not anticipate that the answer can be given in a word or in a neat list. But this does not mean that we can do nothing towards answering these questions nor even that words will not help us. Indeed surely the historians, the scientists, the prophets, the dramatists and the poets have said much which will help any man who asks himself: Is the drama of time meaningless as a tale told by an idiot? Or is it not meaningless? And if it is not meaningless is it a comedy or a tragedy, a triumph or a disaster, or is it a mixture in which sweet and bitter are for ever mixed?

6 Uniquely Human Needs

Fromm

"God is Dead" may have described the problem of the nineteenth century for Friedrich Nietzsche, but "man is dead" is, for Erich Fromm, a better description of the problem of the twentieth century. People have lost their sense of vital significance, their reason for being, and as a result they have become alienated from themselves and from each other. As a practicing psychotherapist, social philosopher, and author (*The Sane Society, The Art of Loving, Escape From Freedom, To Have or To Be?*), most of Fromm's thinking has attempted to shed light on the human predicaments of our times.

Self-alienation has not come about accidentally. In *The Sane Society* Fromm traces its roots to the development, under capitalism, of a widespread "marketing orientation" by which people are reduced to mere means to productive ends. They are to be used, exploited, and discarded when they are no longer profitable to their master. Human beings begin to think of themselves and others as things, commodities to be bought and sold. They lose their ability to relate to their work, to their fellow humans, and to themselves in a harmonious and satisfying way. This exploitative attitude to life is supported and justified, Fromm believes, by the philosophy of sociological relativism, which claims that moral standards have no real validity but are relative to individuals and cultures. There is no underlying universal basis for values apart from varying social or individual norms, so no one has a right to claim that his or her way is better than anyone else's way—except that it "works" better or brings more pleasure. Fromm is as much disturbed by this philosophy as was Socrates when he met it in the Greek Sophists.

To this sociological relativism Fromm opposes a normative humanism. He argues in *The Sane Society* that there is in fact a basic human nature from which one can derive universal though not absolute moral norms. He finds this human nature expressed in what he calls uniquely human needs. Man is distinguished in degree and in kind from the other animals by these needs. Until we understand these needs and find ways of meeting them in ourselves and in others, our society will remain sick. The symptoms of our pathological social state are apparent everywhere—in the wars and social upheavals of our time; in the breakdown of law and order in our cities; in the increased suicide rate among young and old; in the soaring divorce rate and alcoholism among the middle-aged; in the political corruption at the highest level; in the emphasis on violence and pornography in the media; and in the shocking deterioration and destruction of our natural environment.

Despite the insanity of our present society, Fromm believes that the cure of our social malady can only be accomplished through overall social reforms, radically transforming our dehumanized sick social organism into a humanized sane society. The problem is not to get individuals to adjust to the society, but rather to create a society which will be better adjusted to the uniquely human needs of the individuals who live in it. Like Plato, Fromm believes that mental health consists of the latter kind of adjustment. As he puts it in *The Sane Society:*

> Whether or not the individual is healthy, is primarily not an individual matter, but depends on the structure of his society. A healthy society furthers man's capacity to love his fellow men, to work creatively, to develop his reason and objectivity, to have a sense of self which is based on the experience of his own productive powers. An unhealthy society is one which creates mutual hostility, distrust, which transforms man into an instrument of use and exploitation for others, which deprives him of a sense of self, except inasmuch as he submits to others or becomes an automaton. Society can have both functions; it can further man's healthy development, and it can hinder it; in fact most societies do both, and the question is only to what degree and in what direction their positive and negative influence is exercised.[1]

Only within a new social order, Fromm believes, will man recover his sense of vitality, freedom, and spontaneity, experiencing the self-actualization that comes from satisfying his uniquely human nature. The major alternatives between which we must choose are not capitalism or communism, but we must choose between the robotism of either a capitalist or communist variety, and a humanistic communitarian socialism. Fromm has taken as his task to probe the causes of the contemporary human condition and of prescribing the social measures which would alleviate if not cure the condition. Until we have taken such measures we will be unable to overcome man's inhumanity to man, which springs not from some innate cruel instinct but from the self-alienation that is so widespread in our society.

Man may still be dead at the present time, but through a "revolution of hope" Fromm believes that he can and will be born again.

NOTE

1. Erich Fromm, *The Sane Society* (New York: Fawcett World Library, 1953), pp. 71–72.

The Human Situation

Man's Needs—as They Stem from the Conditions of His Existence

Man's life is determined by the inescapable alternative between regression and progression, between return to animal existence and arrival at human existence. Any attempt to return is painful, it inevitably leads to suffering and mental sickness, to death either physiologically or mentally (insanity). Every step forward is frightening and painful too, until a certain point has been reached where fear and doubt have only minor proportions. Aside from the physiologically nourished cravings (hunger, thirst, sex), all essential human cravings are determined by this polarity. Man has to solve a problem, he can never rest in the given situation of a passive adaptation to nature. Even the most complete satisfaction of all his instinctive needs does not solve his *human* problem; his most intensive passions and needs are not those rooted in his body, but those rooted in the very peculiarity of his existence.

There lies also the key to humanistic psychoanalysis. Freud, searching for the basic force which motivates human passions and desires, believed he had found it in the libido. But powerful as the sexual drive and all its derivations are, they are by no means the most powerful forces within man and their frustration is not the cause of mental disturbance. The most powerful forces motivating man's be-

From *The Sane Society* by Erich Fromm. Copyright © 1955 by Erich Fromm. Reprinted by permission of Holt, Rinehart and Winston, Publishers.

havior stem from the condition of his existence, the "human situation."

Man cannot live statically because his inner contradictions drive him to seek for an equilibrium, for a new harmony instead of the lost animal harmony with nature. After he has satisfied his animal needs, he is driven by his human needs. While his body tells him what to eat and what to avoid—his conscience ought to tell him which needs to cultivate and satisfy, and which needs to let wither and starve out. But hunger and appetite are functions of the body with which man is born—conscience, while potentially present, requires the guidance of men and principles which develop only during the growth of culture.

All passions and strivings of man are attempts to find an answer to his existence or, as we may also say, they are an attempt to avoid insanity. (It may be said in passing that the real problem of mental life is not why some people become insane, but rather why most avoid insanity.) Both the mentally healthy and the neurotic are driven by the need to find an answer, the only difference being that one answer corresponds more to the total needs of man, and hence is more conducive to the unfolding of his powers and to his happiness than the other. All cultures provide for a patterned system in which certain solutions are predominant, hence certain strivings and satisfactions. Whether we deal with primitive religions, with theistic or non-theistic religions, they are all attempts to give an answer to man's existential problem. The first, as well as the most barbaric cultures have the same function—the difference is only whether the answer given is better or worse. The deviate from the cultural pattern is just as much in search of an answer as his more well-adjusted brother. His answer may be better or worse than the one given by his culture—it is always another answer to the same fundamental question raised by human existence. In this sense all cultures are religious and every neurosis is a private form of religion, provided we mean by religion an attempt to answer the problem of human existence. Indeed, the tremendous energy in the forces producing mental illness, as well as those behind art and religion, could never be understood as an outcome of frustrated or sublimated physiological needs; they are attempts to solve the problem of being born human. All men are idealists and cannot help being idealists, provided we mean by idealism the striving for the satisfaction of needs which are specifically human and transcend the physiological needs of the organism. The difference is only that one idealism is a good and adequate solution, the other a bad and destructive one. The decision as to what is good and bad has to be made on the basis of our knowledge of man's nature and the laws which govern its growth.

What are these needs and passions stemming from the existence of man?

A. RELATEDNESS VS. NARCISSISM

Man is torn away from the primary union with nature, which characterizes animal existence. Having at the same time reason and imagination, he is aware of his aloneness and separateness; of his powerlessness and ignorance; of the accidentalness of his birth and of his death. He could not face this state of being for a second if he could not find new ties with his fellow man which replace the old ones, regulated by instincts. Even if all his physiological needs were satisfied, he would experience his state of aloneness and individuation as a prison from which he had to break out in order to retain his sanity. In fact, the insane person is the one who has completely failed to establish any kind of union, and is imprisoned, even if he is not behind barred windows. The necessity to unite with other living beings, to be related to them, is an imperative need on the fulfillment of which man's sanity depends. This need is behind all phenomena which constitute the whole gamut of intimate human relations, of all passions which are called love in the broadest sense of the word.

There are several ways in which this union can be sought and achieved. Man can attempt to become one with the world by *submission* to a person, to a group, to an institution, to God. In this way he transcends the separateness of his individual existence by becoming part of somebody or something bigger than himself, and experiences his identity in connection with the power to which he has submitted. Another possibility of overcoming separateness lies in the opposite direction: man can try to unite himself with the world by having *power* over it, by making others a part of himself, and thus transcending his individual existence by domination. The common element in both submission and domination is the symbiotic nature of relatedness. Both persons involved have lost their integrity and freedom; they live on each other and from each other, satisfying their craving for closeness, yet suffering from the lack of inner strength and self-reliance which would require freedom and independence, and furthermore constantly threatened by the conscious or unconscious hostility which is bound to arise from the symbiotic relationship. The realization of the submissive (masochistic) or the domineering (sadistic) passion never leads to satisfaction. They have a self-propelling dynamism, and because no amount of submission, or domination (or possession, or fame) is enough to give a sense of identity and union, more and more of it is sought. The ultimate result of these passions is defeat. It cannot be otherwise; while these passions aim at the establishment of a sense of union, they destroy the sense of integrity. The person driven by any one of these passions actually becomes dependent on others; instead of developing his own individual being, he is dependent on those to whom he submits, or whom he dominates.

There is only one passion which satisfies man's need to unite himself with the world, and to acquire at the same time a sense of integrity and individuality, and this is *love*. *Love is union* with somebody, or something, outside oneself, *under the condition of retaining the separateness and integrity of one's own self*. It is an experience of sharing, of communion, which permits the full unfolding of one's own inner activity. The experience of love does away with the necessity of illusions. There is no need to inflate the image of the other person, or of myself, since the reality of active sharing and loving permits me to transcend my individualized existence, and at the same time to experience myself as the bearer of the active powers which constitute the act of loving. What matters is the particular *quality* of loving, not the object. Love is in the experience of human solidarity with our fellow creatures, it is in the erotic love of man and woman, in the love of the mother for the child, and also in the love for oneself, as a human being; it is in the mystical experience of union. In the act of loving, I am one with All, and yet I am myself, a unique, separate, limited, mortal human being. Indeed out of the very polarity between separateness and union, love is born and reborn.

Love is one aspect of what I have called the productive orientation: the active and creative relatedness of man to his fellow man, to himself and to nature. In the realm of *thought,* this productive orientation is expressed in the proper grasp of the world by reason. In the realm of *action,* the productive orientation is expressed in productive work, the prototype of which is art and craftsmanship. In the realm of *feeling,* the productive orientation is expressed in love, which is the experience of union with another person, with all men, and with nature, under the condition of retaining one's sense of integrity and independence. In the experience of love the paradox happens that two people become one, and remain two at the same time. Love in this sense is never restricted to one person. If I can love only one person, and nobody else, if my love for one person makes me more alienated and distant from my fellow man, I may be attached to this person in any number of ways, yet I do not love. If I can say, "I love you," I say, "I love in you all of humanity, all that is alive; I love in you also myself." Self-love, in this sense, is the opposite of selfishness. The latter is actually a greedy concern with oneself which springs from and compensates for the lack of genuine love for oneself. Love, paradoxically, makes me more independent because it makes me stronger and happier—yet it makes me one with the loved person to the extent that individuality seems to be extinguished for the moment. In loving I experience "I am you," you —the loved person, you—the stranger, you— everything alive. In the experience of love lies the only answer to being human, lies sanity.

Productive love always implies a syndrome of attitudes; that of *care, responsibility, respect* and *knowledge.* If I love, I care—that is, I am actively concerned with the other person's growth and happiness; I am not a spectator. I am responsible, that is, I respond to his needs, to those he can express and more so to those he cannot or does not express. I respect him, that is (according to the original meaning of *re-spicere*) I look at him as he is, objectively and not distorted by my wishes and fears. I know him, I have penetrated through his surface to the core of his being and related myself to him from my core, from the center, as against the periphery, of my being.

Productive love when directed toward equals may be called *brotherly love*. In *motherly love* (Hebrew: *rachamim*, from *rechem* = womb) the relationship between the two persons involved is one of inequality; the child is helpless and dependent on the mother. In order to grow, it must become more and more independent, until he does not need mother any more. Thus the mother-child relationship is paradoxical and, in a sense, tragic. It requires the most intense love on the mother's side, and yet this very love must help the child to grow away from the mother, and to become fully independent. It is easy for any mother to love her child before this process of separation has begun—but it is the task in which most fail, to love the child and at the same time to let it go—and to *want* to let it go.

In *erotic love* (Gr. *eros*; Hebrew: *ahawa*, from the root "to glow"), another drive is involved: that for fusion and union with another person. While brotherly love refers to all men and motherly love to the child and all those who are in need of our help, erotic love is directed to one person, normally of the opposite sex, with whom fusion and oneness is desired. Erotic love begins with separateness, and ends in oneness. Motherly love begins with oneness, and leads to separateness. If the need for fusion were realized in motherly love, it would mean destruction of the child as an independent being, since the child needs to emerge from his mother, rather than to remain tied to her. If erotic love lacks brotherly love and is *only* motivated by the wish for fusion, it is sexual desire without love, or the perversion of love as we find it in the sadistic and masochistic forms of "love."

One understands fully man's need to be related only if one considers the outcome of the failure of any kind of relatedness, if one appreciates the meaning of *narcissism*. The only reality the infant can experience is his own body and his needs, physiological needs and the need for warmth and affection. He has not yet the experience of "I" as separate from "thou." He is still in a state of oneness with the world, but a oneness before the awakening of his sense of individuality and reality. The world outside exists only as so much food, or so much warmth to be used for the satisfaction of his own needs, but not as something or somebody who is recognized realistically and objectively. This orientation has been named by Freud that of "primary narcissism." In normal development, this state of narcissism is slowly overcome by a growing awareness of reality outside, and by a correspondingly growing sense of "I" as differentiated from "thou." This change occurs at first on the level of sensory perception, when things and people are perceived as different and specific entities, a recognition which lays the foundation for the possibility of speech; to name things pre-supposes recognizing them as individual and separate entities. It takes much longer until the narcissistic state is overcome emotionally; for the child up to the age of seven or eight years, other people still exist mainly as means for the satisfaction of his needs. They are exchangeable inasmuch as they fulfill the function of satisfying these needs, and it is only around the ages of between eight and nine years that another person is experienced in such a way that the child can begin to love, that is to say, in H. S. Sullivan's formulation, to feel that the needs of another person are as important as his own.

Primary narcissism is a normal phenomenon, conforming with the normal physiological and mental development of the child. But narcissism exists also in later stages of life ("secondary narcissism," according to Freud), if the growing child fails to develop the capacity for love, or loses it again. Narcissism is the essence of all severe psychic pathology. For the narcissistically involved person, there is only one reality, that of his own thought processes, feelings and needs. The world outside is not experienced or perceived *objec-*

tively, i.e., as existing in its own terms, conditions and needs. The most extreme form of narcissism is to be seen in all forms of insanity. The insane person has lost contact with the world; he has withdrawn into himself; he cannot experience reality, either physical or human reality *as it is,* but only as formed and determined by his own inner processes. He either does *not* react to the world outside, or if he does, reacts not in terms of *its* reality, but only in terms of his own processes of thought and feeling. Narcissism is the opposite pole to objectivity, reason and love.

The fact that utter failure to relate oneself to the world is insanity, points to the other fact: that some form of relatedness is the condition for any kind of sane living. But among the various forms of relatedness, only the productive one, love, fulfills the condition of allowing one to retain one's freedom and integrity while being, at the same time, united with one's fellow man.

B. TRANSCENDENCE— CREATIVENESS VS. DESTRUCTIVENESS

Another aspect of the human situation, closely connected with the need for relatedness, is man's situation as a *creature,* and his need to transcend this very state of the passive creature. Man is thrown into this world without his knowledge, consent or will, and he is removed from it again without his consent or will. In this respect he is not different from the animals, from the plants, or from inorganic matter. But being endowed with reason and imagination, he cannot be content with the passive role of the creature, with the role of dice cast out of a cup. He is driven by the urge to transcend the role of the creature, the accidentalness and passivity of his existence, by becoming a "creator."

Man can create life. This is the miraculous quality which he indeed shares with all living beings, but with the difference that he alone is aware of being created and of being a creator. Man can create life, or rather, woman can create life, by giving birth to a child, and by caring for the child until it is sufficiently grown to take care of his own needs. Man—man and woman—can create by planting seeds, by producing material objects, by creating art, by creating ideas, by loving one another. In the act of creation man transcends himself as a creature, raises himself beyond the passivity and accidentalness of his existence into the realm of purposefulness and freedom. In man's need for transcendence lies one of the roots for love, as well as for art, religion and material production.

To create presupposes activity and care. It presupposes love for that which one creates. How then does man solve the problem of transcending himself, if he is not capable of creating, if he cannot love? *There is another answer to this need for transcendence: if I cannot create life, I can destroy it. To destroy life makes me also transcend it.* Indeed, that man can destroy life is just as miraculous a feat as that he can create it, for life is *the* miracle, the inexplicable. In the act of destruction, man sets himself above life; he transcends himself as a creature. Thus, the ultimate choice for man, inasmuch as he is driven to transcend himself, is to create or to destroy, to love or to hate. The enormous power of the will for destruction which we see in the history of man, and which we have witnessed so frightfully in our own time, is rooted in the nature of man, just as the drive to create is rooted in it. To say that man is capable of developing his primary potentiality for love and reason does not imply the naïve belief in man's goodness. Destructiveness is a secondary potentiality, rooted in the very existence of man, and having the same intensity and power as any passion can have. But—and this is the essential point of my argument—it is only the *alternative* to creativeness. Creation and destruction, love and hate, are not two instincts which exist independently. They are both answers to the same need for transcendence, and the will to destroy must rise when the will to create cannot be satisfied. However, the satisfaction of the need to create leads to happiness; destructiveness to suffering, most of all, for the destroyer himself.

C. ROOTEDNESS—
BROTHERLINESS VS. INCEST

Man's birth as man means the beginning of his emergence from his natural home, the beginning of the severance of his natural ties. Yet, this very severance is frightening; if man loses his natural roots, where is he and who is he? He would stand alone, without a home; without roots; he could not bear the isolation and helplessness of this position. He would become insane. He can dispense with the *natural* roots only insofar as he finds new *human* roots and only after he has found them can he feel at home again in this world. Is it surprising, then, to find a deep craving in man not to sever the natural ties, to fight against being torn away from nature, from mother, blood and soil?

The most elementary of the natural ties is the tie of the child to the mother. The child begins life in the mother's womb, and exists there for a much longer time than is the case with most animals; even after birth, the child remains physically helpless, and completely dependent on the mother; this period of helplessness and dependence again is much more protracted than with any animal. In the first years of life no full separation between child and mother has occurred. The satisfaction of all his physiological needs, of his vital need for warmth and affection depend on her; she has not only given birth to him, but she continues to give life to him. Her care is not de-

pendent on anything the child does for her, on any obligation which the child has to fulfill; it is unconditional. She cares because the new creature is her child. The child, in these decisive first years of his life, has the experience of his mother as the fountain of life, as an all-enveloping, protective, nourishing power. Mother is food; she is love; she is warmth; she is earth. To be loved by her means to be alive, to be rooted, to be at home.

Just as birth means to leave the enveloping protection of the womb, growing up means to leave the protective orbit of the mother. Yet even in the mature adult, the longing for this situation as it once existed never ceases completely, in spite of the fact that there is, indeed, a great difference between the adult and the child. The adult has the means to stand on his own feet, to take care of himself, to be responsible for himself and even for others, while the child is not yet capable of doing all this. But considering the increased perplexities of life, the fragmentary nature of our knowledge, the accidentalness of adult existence, the unavoidable errors we make, the situation of the adult is by no means as different from that of the child as it is generally assumed. Every adult is in need of help, of warmth, of protection, in many ways differing and yet in many ways similar to the needs of the child. Is it surprising to find in the average adult a deep longing for the security and rootedness which the relationship to his mother once gave him? Is it not to be expected that he cannot give up this intense longing unless he finds other ways of being rooted?

In psychopathology we find ample evidence for this phenomenon of the refusal to leave the all-enveloping orbit of the mother. In the most extreme form we find the craving to return to the mother's womb. A person completely obsessed by this desire may offer the picture of schizophrenia. He feels and acts like the foetus in the mother's womb; incapable of assuming even the most elementary functions of a small child. In many of the more severe neuroses we find the same craving, but as a repressed desire, manifested only in dreams, symptoms and neurotic behavior, which results from the conflict between the deep desire to stay in the mother's womb and the adult part of the personality which tends to live a normal life. In dreams this craving appears in symbols like being in a dark cave, in a one-man submarine, diving into deep water, etc. In the behavior of such a person, we find a fear of life, and a deep fascination for death (death, in phantasy, being the return to the womb, to Mother Earth).

The less severe form of the fixation to mother is to be found in those cases where a person has permitted himself to be born, as it were, but where he is afraid to take the next step of birth, to be weaned from mother's breasts. People who have become stuck at this stage of birth, have a deep craving to be mothered, nursed, protected by a motherly figure; they are the eternally dependent ones, who are frightened and insecure when motherly protection is withdrawn, but optimistic and active when a loving mother or mother-substitute is provided, either realistically or in phantasy.

These pathological phenomena in individual life have their parallel in the evolution of the human race. The clearest expression of this lies in the fact of the universality of the incest tabu, which we find even in the most primitive societies. The incest tabu is the necessary condition for all human development, not because of its sexual, but because of its affective aspect. Man, in order to be born, in order to progress, has to sever the umbilical cord; he has to overcome the deep craving to remain tied to mother. The incestuous desire has its strength not from the sexual attraction to mother, but from the deep-seated craving to remain in, or to return to the all-enveloping womb, or to the all-nourishing breasts. The incest tabu is nothing else but the two cherubim with fiery swords, guarding the entrance to Paradise and preventing man from returning to the pre-individual existence of oneness with nature. . . .

D. SENSE OF IDENTITY— INDIVIDUALITY VS. HERD CONFORMITY

Man may be defined as the animal that can say "I," that can be aware of himself as a separate entity. The animal being within nature, and not transcending it, has no awareness of himself, has no need for a sense of identity. Man, being torn away from nature, being endowed with reason and imagination, needs to form a concept of himself, needs to say and to feel: "I am I." Because he is not *lived,* but *lives,* because he has lost the original unity with nature, has to make decisions, is aware of himself and of his neighbor as different persons, he must be able to sense himself as the subject of his actions. As with the need for relatedness, rootedness, and transcendence, this need for a sense of identity is so vital and imperative that man could not remain sane if he did not find some way of satisfying it. Man's sense of identity develops in the process of emerging from the "primary bonds" which tie him to mother and nature. The infant, still feeling one with mother, cannot yet say "I," nor has he any need for it. Only after he has conceived of the outer world as being separate and different from himself does he come to the awareness of himself as a distinct being, and one of the last words he learns to use is "I," in reference to himself.

In the development of *the human race* the degree to which man is aware of himself as a separate self depends on the extent to which he has emerged from the clan and the extent to which the process of individuation has developed. The member of a primitive clan might express his sense of identity in the formula "I am we"; he cannot yet conceive of himself as an "individual," existing apart from his group. In the medieval world, the individual was identified with his social role in the feudal hierarchy. The peasant was not a man who happened to be a peasant, the feudal lord not a man who happened to be a feudal lord.

He was a peasant or a lord, and this sense of his unalterable station was an essential part of his sense of identity. When the feudal system broke down, this sense of identity was shaken and the acute question "Who am I?" arose—or more precisely, "How do I know that I am I?" This is the question which was raised, in a philosophical form, by Descartes. He answered the quest for identity by saying, "I doubt— hence I think, I think—hence I am." This answer put all the emphasis on the experience of "I" as the subject of any *thinking* activity, and failed to see that the "I" is experienced also in the process of feeling and creative action.

The development of Western culture went in the direction of creating the basis for the full experience of individuality. By making the individual free politically and economically, by teaching him to think for himself and freeing him from an authoritarian pressure, one hoped to enable him to feel "I" in the sense that he was the center and active subject of his powers and experienced himself as such. But only a minority achieved the new experience of "I." For the majority, individualism was not much more than a façade behind which was hidden the failure to acquire an individual sense of identity.

Many substitutes for a truly individual sense of identity were sought for, and found. Nation, religion, class and occupation serve to furnish a sense of identity. "I am an American." "I am a Protestant," "I am a businessman," are the formulae which help a man experience a sense of identity after the original clan identity has disappeared and before a truly individual sense of identity has been acquired. These different identifications are, in contemporary society, usually employed together. They are in a broad sense status identifications, and they are more efficient if blended with older feudal remnants, as in European countries. In the United States, in which so little is left of feudal relics, and in which there is so much social mobility, these status identifications are naturally less efficient, and the sense of identity is shifted more and more to the experience of conformity.

Inasmuch as I am not different, inasmuch as I am like the others, and recognized by them as "a regular fellow," I can sense myself as "I." I am—"as you desire me"—as Pirandello put it in the title of one of his plays. Instead of the pre-individualistic clan identity, a new herd identity develops, in which the sense of identity rests on the sense of an unquestionable belonging to the crowd. That this uniformity and conformity are often not recognized as such, and are covered by the illusion of individuality, does not alter the facts.

The problem of the sense of identity is not, as it is usually understood, merely a philosophical problem, or a problem only concerning our mind and thought. The need to feel a sense of identity stems from the very condition of human existence, and it is the source of the most intense strivings. Since I cannot remain sane without the sense of "I," I am driven to do almost anything to acquire this sense. Behind the intense passion for status and conformity is this very need, and it is sometimes even stronger than the need for physical survival. What could be more obvious than the fact that people are willing to risk their lives, to give up their love, to surrender their freedom, to sacrifice their own thoughts, for the sake of being one of the herd, of conforming, and thus of acquiring a sense of identity, even though it is an illusory one.

E. THE NEED FOR A FRAME OF ORIENTATION AND DEVOTION— REASON VS. IRRATIONALITY

The fact that man has reason and imagination leads not only to the necessity for having a sense of his own identity, but also for orienting himself in the world intellectually. This need can be compared with the process of physical orientation which develops in the first years of life, and which is completed when the child can walk by himself, touch and handle things, knowing what they are. But when the ability to walk and to speak has been acquired, only the first step in the direction of orientation has been taken. Man finds himself surrounded by many puzzling phenomena and, having reason, he has to make sense of them, has to put them in some context which he can understand and which permits him to deal with them in his thoughts. The further his reason develops, the more adequate becomes his system of orientation, that is, the more it approximates reality. But even if man's frame of orientation is utterly illusory, it satisfies his need for some picture which is meaningful to him. Whether he believes in the power of a totem animal, in a rain god, or in the superiority and destiny of his race, his need for some frame of orientation is satisfied. Quite obviously, the picture of the world which he has depends on the development of his reason and of his knowledge. Although biologically the brain capacity of the human race has remained the same for thousands of generations, it takes a long evolutionary process to arrive at *objectivity,* that is, to acquire the faculty to see the world, nature, other persons and oneself as they are, and not distorted by desires and fears. The more man develops this objectivity, the more he is in touch with reality, the more he matures, the better can he create a human world in which he is at home. Reason is man's faculty for *grasping* the world by thought, in contradiction to intelligence, which is man's ability to *manipulate* the world with the help of thought. Reason is man's instrument for arriving at the truth, intelligence is man's instrument for manipulating the world more successfully; the former is essentially human, the latter belongs to the animal part of man.

Reason is a faculty which must be practiced, in order to develop, and it is indivisible. By this I mean that the faculty for objectivity refers to the knowledge of nature as well as to the knowledge of man, of society and of oneself. If one lives in illusions about one sector of life, one's capacity for reason is restricted or damaged, and thus the use of reason is inhibited with regard to all other sectors. Reason in this respect is like love. Just as love is an orientation which refers to all objects and is incompatible with the restriction to one object, so is reason a human faculty which must embrace the whole of the world with which man is confronted.

The need for a frame of orientation exists on two levels; the first and the more fundamental need is to have *some* frame of orientation, regardless of whether it is true or false. Unless man has such a subjectively satisfactory frame of orientation, he cannot live sanely. On the second level the need is to be in touch with reality by reason, to grasp the world objectively. But the necessity to develop his reason is not as immediate as that to develop some frame of orientation, since what is at stake for man in the latter case is his happiness and serenity, and not his sanity. This becomes very clear if we study the function of *rationalization.* However unreasonable or immoral an action may be, man has an insuperable urge to rationalize it, that is, to prove to himself and to others that his action is determined by reason, common sense, or at least conventional morality. He has little difficulty in acting irrationally, but it is almost impossible for him not to give his action the appearance of reasonable motivation.

If man were only a disembodied intellect, his aim would be achieved by a comprehensive thought system. But since he is an entity endowed with a body as well as a mind, he has to react to the dichotomy of his existence not only in thinking but in the total process of living, in his feelings and actions. Hence any satisfying system of orientation contains not only intellectual elements but elements of feeling and sensing which are expressed in the relationship to an object of devotion.

The answers given to man's need for a system of orientation and an object of devotion differ widely both in content and in form. There are primitive systems such as animism and totemism in which natural objects or ancestors represent answers to man's quest for meaning. There are nontheistic systems like Buddhism, which are usually called religions although in their original form there is no concept of God. There are purely philosophical systems, like Stoicism, and there are the monotheistic religious systems which give an answer to man's quest for meaning in reference to the concept of God.

But whatever their contents, they all respond to man's need to have not only some thought system, but also an object of devotion which gives meaning to his existence and to his position in the world. Only the analysis of the various forms of religion can show which answers are better and which are worse solutions to man's quest for meaning and devotion, "better" or "worse" always considered from the standpoint of man's nature and his development.

RELATED READING

Bacon, Francis. *The Complete Essays*. New York: Washington Square Press, 1963.

Black, Max. *Language and Philosophy*. New York: Cornell University Press, 1949.

Breisach, Ernest. *Introduction to Modern Existentialism*. New York: Grove Press, 1962.

Chase, Stuart. *The Tyranny of Words*. New York: Harcourt, Brace & World, 1938.

Camus, Albert. *The Stranger*. New York: Alfred A. Knopf, 1960.

Commitment and Human Development, in *Humanitas*, vol. VIII (February, 1972).

Doney, Willis, ed. *Descartes: A Collection of Critical Essays*. New York: Doubleday & Co., 1967.

Douglas, Norman. *South Wind*. New York: Bantam Books, 1946.

Durant, Will and Ariel. *Interpretations of Life*. New York: Simon & Schuster, 1970.

Emerson, Ralph Waldo. *Selected Essays, Lectures, and Poems*. New York: Washington Square Press, 1965.

Evans, Bergen. *The Natural History of Nonsense*. New York: Vintage Book, Knopf, 1958.

Erickson, Erik. *Identity, Youth and Crisis*. New York: W. W. Norton & Co., 1968.

Frankl, Viktor. *Man's Search for Meaning*. New York: Washington Square Press, 1963.

Freud, Sigmund. *Civilization and its Discontents*. New York: W. W. Norton & Co., 1961.

Fromm, Erich. *The Art of Loving*. New York: Bantam Books, 1956.

————. *To Have and To Be*. New York: Harper & Row, 1976.

————. *The Revolution of Hope: Toward a Humanized Technology*. New York: Bantam Books, 1968.

Hayakawa, S. I. *Language in Thought and Action*, 3rd ed. New York: Harcourt Brace Jovanovich, 1972.

Harding, Walter, ed. *Henry David Thoreau: A Profile*. New York: Hill & Wang, 1971.

Hendin, Herbert. *The Age of Sensation: A Psychoanalytic Exploration*. New York: W. W. Norton & Co., 1975.

Hesse, Hermann. *My Belief: Essays on Life and Art*. New York: Noonday, Farrar, Straus & Giroux, 1975.

————. *Reflections*. New York: Noonday, Farrar, Straus & Giroux, 1974.

————. *Siddhartha*. New York: New Directions, 1951.

Jaspers, Karl. *Socrates, Buddha, Confucius, Jesus: The Paradigmatic Individuals*. New York: Harcourt, Brace & World, 1962.

Johnson, William A. *The Search for Transcendence*. New York: Harper & Row, 1974.

Kaplan, Abraham. *The New World of Philosophy*. New York: Collier, 1962.

Kaufman, Walter. *Critique of Religion and Philosophy*. New York: Harper & Row, 1958.

Keniston, Kenneth. *The Uncommitted: Alienated Youth in American Society*. New York: Harcourt, Brace & World, 1965.

Kiesler, Charles A. *The Psychology of Commitment*. New York: Academic Press, 1971.

Lavrin, Janko. *Tolstoy: An Approach*. New York: Macmillan, 1946.

Montague, William P. *The Ways of Knowing*. New York: Macmillan, 1925.

Montaigne. *Complete Essays*. New York: Modern Library, Random House, n.d.

May, Rollo. *Man's Search for Himself*. New York: Signet, New American Library, 1953.

Mead, Margaret. *Culture and Commitment: A Study of the Generation Gap*. New York: Doubleday & Co., 1970.

Novak, Michael. *The Experience of Nothingness*. New York: Harper & Row, 1970.

Plato. *The Dialogues of Plato*, trans. Benjamin Jowett. 5 vols. New York: Oxford Books, 1892.

Russell, Bertrand. *Sceptical Essays*. New York: W. W. Norton & Co., 1928.

————. *The Scientific Outlook*. New York: W. W. Norton & Co., 1962.

————. *The Will to Doubt*. New York: Philosophical Library, 1958.

Richardson, Herbert W. and Donald R. Cutler, eds. *Transcendence*. Boston: Beacon Press, 1969.

Roszak, Theodore. *The Making of a Counter Culture*. New York: Doubleday & Co., 1969.

Simmons, Ernest J. *Leo Tolstoy*. Boston: Little, Brown & Co., 1946.

Slater, Philip. *The Pursuit of Loneliness: American Culture at the Breaking Point.* Boston: Beacon Press, 1970.

Schopenhauer, Arthur. *The World as Will and Representation,* trans. E. F. J. Payne. 2 vols. Indian Hills, Col.: The Falcon Wing's Press, 1958.

Taylor, A. E. *Socrates: The Man and His Thought.* New York: Doubleday & Co., 1954.

Voltaire. *Candide,* trans. Tobias Smollett. New York: Washington Square Press, 1966.

Wertheimer, Michael, ed. *Confrontation: Psychology and the Problems of Today.* New York: Scott, Foresman & Co., 1970.

Part 2

CONFRONTATION WITH HUMAN NATURE

Commitment to Human Transformation

Man is the measure of all things.

Protagoras

Man is an imperfected denatured animal intermittently subject to the unpredictable reactions of an unlocated spiritual area.

Rudyard Kipling

Thou hast made him a little lower than the angels.

Psalms

If a man is only a little lower than angels, the angels should reform.

Mary W. Little

Man is a piece of the universe made live.

Ralph Waldo Emerson

The age of chivalry has gone; the age of humanity has come.

Charles Sumner

The creator, the nurturer of civilization is woman; its promulgator and destroyer is man.

Anonymous

You see, dear, it is not true that woman was made from man's rib; she was really made from his funny bone.

J. M. Barrie

Suffer women once to arrive at equality with you, and they will from that moment become your superiors.

Cato the Censor

The nature of man is not what he is born as, but what he is born for.

Aristotle

Earth's noblest thing, a woman perfected.

J. R. Lowell

Age cannot wither her, nor custom stale her infinite variety.

Shakespeare

I am a man; I count nothing human foreign to me.

Terence

Man is the only animal that blushes — or needs to.

Mark Twain

I am not an Athenian, nor a Greek, but a citizen of the world.

Socrates

After all, there is but one race — humanity.

George Moore

Introduction: Human Nature— The Problem

"There's a good deal of human nature in man," quipped the American humorist Artemus Ward. And a sigh of resignation usually accompanies the remark, "You can't change human nature." But is the statement true? What is "human nature?" We may be animals, but we are animals who confront moral choice, authority, beauty, love, religious experience, life, death, and the future. We commit ourselves to the good, freedom, transcendent meaning, and concern for the future of ourselves and others. We are puzzled by questions about our own nature, about the "human condition," and the many conflicting definitions and images of human nature found in anthropology, literature, and philosophy. Philosophical anthropology, or the philosophy of human nature, seeks to interpret the information about human behavior provided by the natural sciences, the social sciences, and the humanities with the purpose of discovering and defining the unique features of human beings which distinguish them from other forms of life.

There is, of course, great disagreement as to the correct definition of human nature. For some philosophers the question itself, What is human nature?, is far too general. It must be broken down into questions whose meaning and verification are clearer and more specific. Many contemporary Anglo-American philosophers have replaced the general question with more specific questions concerning the meaning of terms (such as "mind," "consciousness," and "self"), the distinction between computer operations and human thinking, and the criteria for determining personal identity.

Other philosophers are critical of the question, not because of its generality and vagueness, but because of its implicit assumptions. To ask, What is human nature?, is to make man into an object and to presume that we are to inquire into the nature of man in the same way we inquire into the nature of a mosquito or a chair. The question might be changed to Who is man? so as not to predetermine the answer, and to suggest that any answer must take into account the unique, lived experience of being human. If man is basically a subject in a world of objects, his nature cannot be comprehended fully by any of the sciences developed thus far to deal only with things and objective relations.

The question of the nature of man is being asked today with renewed vigor, partly because man's image of himself is a broken image. Just as our concept of life is being challenged by the study of viruses and the possibility of creating life in a test tube, so our traditional concepts of man are being contested by behavioral psychology, cybernetics, and recent developments in biology. The possibility of our fully understanding and controlling the genetic code raises questions as to the direction man will go when he has full control of his own evolution. The creation of androids and the possible discovery of other forms of life in interplanetary travel raise interesting questions about what we consider human. The very pace of scientific, technological, social, and political change requires adjustments.

Man's self-image was not always as incomplete and disorganized as it seems today. The ancient Greek philosophers tended to view the human as a definite kind of being with a rational and social nature. The species of man was fixed eternally. Aristotle expressed this viewpoint with great assurance in his *Nicomachean Ethics* (see Part Three). Man is a rational animal. In Medieval times, the assurance that human nature had a definite essence was also pervasive. The human was a child of God, and the individual soul was directed toward eternal salvation, reconciling his life on earth with his God-given nature. For the greater part of recorded history, man's view of himself has been that he has a nature. What we are essentially was not in doubt.

For the brooding pessimist Arthur Schopenhauer, the essence of human nature is also not in doubt. The primitive forces of animal appetites and competitiveness in human beings will doom us to lives of egoism, malice, and suffering: human nature is essentially irrational in character. Man has a capacity for thought and social order but these are artificial and in conflict with his more natural instinctive and emotional nature. Our aggressiveness and destructiveness are hidden only by a thin veneer of civility. Although the evil condition of life is rooted in the unconscious will, there is the possibility of release from this enslavement of will in aesthetic contemplation, human compassion, and mystical self-transcendence (see Part Five).

The bio-anthropologist Konrad Lorenz agrees with this view of the inherited animality in human nature, and he attempts to develop a correlation between his studies in biology and a scientifically grounded view of human nature. Lorenz, a Nobel laureate and influential evolutionist, believes that natural selection partially determines not only the form but also the behavior of the organism. His study of geese, for example, indicated that their patterns of behavior are adaptive responses and "inherited." Many of his beliefs regarding the human condition—for example, that civilization is like domestication—are based upon extrapolations of his studies of these lower animals. The tensions, aggression, racism, wars, and violence of the present day are vestiges of the patterns of survival we follow instinctively. Lorenz also suggests that there should be a proper balance between our instinctive nature and the requirements of a culturally evolved social order. These requirements, in turn, reveal other aspects of human nature such as thought, curiosity, rational morality, and invention.

The utopian socialist Edward Bellamy would disagree entirely with Schopenhauer's view of human nature. Bellamy attempts to bridge the gap between the question of man's distinctive nature and the question of his relation to the socio-cultural order. The nineteenth century industrial society, although Christian in professed ideals, fostered the vices of greed and self-seeking—the "virtues" of a capitalist system. Bellamy anticipates a rebirth of the generous and social instincts of the race. These will be released when the oppressive social environment is broken by the advent of socialism and economic equality.

Taking a more orthodox Christian perspective on human nature, Dr. Martin Luther King, Jr. viewed man as *homo religiosus,* in awe of but alienated from God and in desperate need of redemption. Human nature is spiritual as well as physical, "in nature, yet above nature." Our spiritual nature is expressed in our freedom and ability to contemplate the divine order of things, to establish an I-Thou relationship with God, and to experience authentic Christian love. Although human nature is sinful, following the moral laws inherent in God's creation can bring out the moral goodness in each of us.

As an atheist and materialist, Karl Marx rejected all Christian interpretations of human nature. He believed that man was not a child of God but a natural and thoroughly social, historical creature. Although human beings have basic needs, their appetites have been relatively flexible and changing throughout different historical periods. The return of humans to a truly humane existence is possible only through a dialectical, revolutionary transformation of society, promoting the self-realization of man through all aspects of society: labor, property, and control of means of production. Without these fundamental changes human nature will remain alienated. Erich Fromm discusses Marx's concept of alienation and man in the selection from *Marx's Concept of Man.* According to Fromm:

Alienation (or "estrangement") means, for Marx, that man does *not* experience himself as the acting agent in his grasp of the world, but that the world (nature, others, and he himself) remain alien to him. They stand above and against him as objects, even though they may be objects of his own creation. Alienation is essentially experiencing the world and oneself passively, receptively, as the subject separated from the object.[1]

Although Fromm agrees to some extent with Marx's view of society and man, he believes that the transformation should take place through an evolutionary process leading to a humanistic socialist society in which uniquely human needs can be fully satisfied (see Part One). Like Bellamy, King, and Marx, Fromm's view of human nature and alienation leads directly to a critique of society.

For Marx, we humans make our own history and hence we are our own product. History is our act of self-creation. Emphasizing the culturally creative powers of individuals more than any of the above writers, Susanne Langer finds the uniqueness of humanity to lie in the capacity of the species *homo sapiens* to create an "ideal world" of its own. By means of the production and manipulation of symbolic systems, we express this capacity in our language, abstractions, and intersubjective communication. These abilities also make possible the expression of our uniquely human response and feeling through myth, art, religion, science, and history. Our "world" is very much of our own making, and to remake the world in this way is unique to man the symbol maker.

Finally, as Victor Ferkiss points out in discussing the nature of the newly emerging man, technology is also a form of making and self-creation. Man is *homo faber* who, through the use and creation of tools, has more than compensated for his physical weakness relative to other animals; he has acquired the power to recreate his environment and himself. In an age of increasingly automated production, new sources of power, and the multiplication of technologies, some writers are pointing to a new set of symptoms that are characteristic of humans in our post-industrial society. These symptoms belong to the inner life, the psyche, and they indicate a profound change in the human condition. In the age of science and technology, the individual's methods of work, lifestyles, values, and culture are being drastically modified. Although these changes are as important in the history of humanity as the discovery of fire or the development of agriculture, they are so different that no past age can serve as a model. People have limitless possibilities for the recreation or destruction of the environment and for the recreation or destruction of themselves. As humanoids we may be on the verge of radical transformations. Since we are now virtually in control of our own evolution, Ferkiss tries to delineate a new set of values lest the old acquisitive, greedy industrial man returns to put to destructive use the new powers he has created.

These different views on the nature of human nature raise serious questions about who we are and what we will become, about our place in the universe as creatures and as creators. Unlike other animals, human beings seem to have the freedom and power to recreate and to complete themselves. This is what Aristotle meant when he said that the nature of man is not what he is born as, but what he is born for. And to discover this requires much reflection and self-analysis. Perhaps Friedrich Schleiermacher was right when he wrote in his *Soliloquies*, "Mankind is shy of self-analysis, and many people tremble slavishly when they can no longer dodge the question of what they have done, what they have become, and who they really are."[2] But to confront such questions about human nature is to confront the questions which matter most in planning, living, and understanding our lives. "The proper study of mankind is man."

NOTES

1. Erich Fromm, *Marx's Concept of Man* (New York: Ungar, 1961), p. 44.
2. Friedrich Schleiermacher, *Soliloquies,* quoted in Max Rosenberg, *Introduction to Philosophy* (New York: Philosophical Library, 1955), p. 235.

7 Man the Vicious Animal

Schopenhauer & Lorenz

There are two things which make it impossible to believe that this world is the successful work of an all-wise, all-good, and, at the same time, all-powerful Being. Firstly, the misery which abounds in it everywhere; and secondly, the obvious imperfection of its highest product, man, who is a burlesque of what he should be.[1]

Arthur Schopenhauer's (1788–1860) pessimistic appraisal of human nature sprang from a view of life which he claimed any person can verify from experience and justify by rational consideration of the nature of things. Pessimism, for him, was not a matter of temperament or the result of misfortune, but rather it was a philosophical position for which there is much evidence. We only need to look within to discover that we are not fundamentally rational creatures. We are creatures of desires, passions, and appetites. The strongest force in us is our will to live, to survive, to hold on to our existence at any cost. This powerful, instinctive will to live is not just within us; it expresses itself in all things. It is the all-encompassing, omnipresent reality, the universal Will to Live; but to will to live is inevitably to suffer. For when we desire something, we either get the object we desire or we do not. If we do not, we are frustrated. If we do get it, we soon become bored with it and desire something in its place. Life for Schopenhauer was a pendulum swinging between frustration and boredom, with no permanent satisfaction, no lasting happiness possible.

Not only is the goal of happiness unattainable because of the self-defeating nature of desire, but also it is unattainable because of the transitoriness and negativity of its chief object—pleasure. Pleasure to Schopenhauer was negative: the absence of pain. And is not pleasure usually far less gratifying than pain is annoying? And in the long run, do not pleasures pass quickly compared with pains which, as life passes, become more frequent and longer lasting? Furthermore, if one made an impartial and comprehensive survey of the pains and pleasures experienced by the mass of mankind, Schopenhauer thought that one would find that there is a preponderance of pain, of suffering, in the world rather than pleasure and satisfaction. As he put it,

> If we should bring clearly to a man's sight the terrible sufferings and miseries to which his life is constantly exposed, he would be seized with horror; and if we were to conduct the confirmed optimist through the hospitals, infirmaries, and surgical operating rooms, through the prisons, torture chambers, and slave kennels, over battle fields and places of execution; if we were to open to him all the dark abodes of misery, where it hides itself from the glance of cold curiosity, and, finally, allow him to look into the starving dungeons of Ugolino, he too would understand at last the nature of this "best of all possible worlds."[2]

Suffering, then, is the universal, inescapable condition of man. Much of it he brings upon himself because of the insatiable will to live. At all levels of living things, from the microscopic to the human, there is evidence of strife which arises because of the competition for the limited objects of desire. Nature is a war of all against all. Life is never-ceasing strife, as the creatures of the will struggle against each other, destroying and devouring one another. Thus the will to live preys upon itself. Nowhere is there evidence of the presence of an all-good, all-knowing, all-powerful supernatural being who cares and controls what is happening in the world. To the contrary, Schopenhauer felt that there would be far more reason for believing that an entirely evil, indifferent demon created the world to torment mankind.

Turning attention to man, in whom the will to live becomes conscious of itself, Schopenhauer sought to discover the fundamental springs of all human conduct. The first to be analyzed is egoism, which has as its supreme motive one's own welfare. This, in his view, is the most fundamental and powerful motive in human nature. We discover it within ourselves as the omnipotent desire to avoid pain and to possess all pleasures. As egoists, our motto (usually unexpressed) is "all things for me, nothing for others!" Springing out of the will to live, egoism is "colossal; it towers above the world."[3] It is the most direct and obvious motive in human beings, and at the same time, it is the most dangerous and the ugliest motive. It isolates us from others and makes us feel justified in selfishly taking for ourselves what others might need, want, or deserve. "Like a broad trench," Schopenhauer wrote of egoism, "it always lies between one man and another."[4]

The second motive which forms the empirical basis of human conduct, according to Schopenhauer, is malice. Malice is ill-will, spitefulness, which has as its motive another's woe or suffering. Its motto is "injure all people as far as you can." When others do not get what they want, the predominantly malicious person experiences a kind of joy, which at its extreme becomes cruel and diabolical. As Schopenhauer attempted to show in the following discussion of human nature, all the vices in human beings spring either from malice or from egoism. If we went no further than this in probing the roots of human conduct, we could very well view the world, from the aesthetic standpoint, as a den of crooks. It was not surprising to Schopenhauer that so many people become pessimists and even misanthropes.

Even Schopenhauer's world view has a brighter side. Man is not simply a creature motivated by egoism and malice; he also is capable of acting from another inherent motive, compassion. This motive, aiming as it does at the welfare of others, is the only genuinely moral incentive. It is entirely disinterested and unselfish, and it has as its concern the removal of the pain of another. There are, Schopenhauer believed, two degrees of compassion. The first is a kind of passive or negative compassion which requires only that we do no harm to anyone. (From this springs the cardinal virtue of justice.) The second kind of compassion is positive and active, and springs from an empathetic identification with the sufferings of others. Its rule is "Help all people, as far as it lies in your power." From this degree of compassion springs the second cardinal virtue, loving-kindness.

It should be compassion and not conscience that guides our moral conduct, Schopenhauer believed. Much as he admired his great predecessor Immanuel Kant, he rejected Kant's view that conscience, the universal command of duty, should govern our conduct. Kant's "categorical imperative," the absolute inner moral law manifested in rational conscience, to Schopenhauer was an abstraction which could never have the real, extensive, and empirical influence that the motive of compassion could have upon human action. Referring to conscience, Schopenhauer wrote: "The average individual who thinks his conscience such an imposing structure, would be surprised could he see of what it actually consists: probably of about one-fifth, fear of men; one-fifth, fear of the gods; one-fifth, prejudice; one-fifth, vanity; and one-fifth, habit."[5]

Schopenhauer's discussion of man and of ethical conduct thus culminates in praise for boundless compassion for all suffering creatures, animal as well as human. He quotes with approval an old Hindu prayer: "May all living beings remain free from pain."[6] Until we experience compassion, we tend to think in terms of ourselves as individuals differentiated in space and time. But once we see beyond the realm of appearances we see, as Plato saw, that reality transcends our senses and rational categories. We recognize ourselves in others, and others in ourselves. The Hindus long ago recognized this truth: *Tat twam asi* ("That art thou").

Such was the philosophy which Schopenhauer expounded in his *World as Will and Representation.* Man, an insatiable creature, must give up his hope of attaining on earth (or anywhere) happiness as permanent, pleasurable gratification. He must use whatever reason he has to cooly and calmly appraise the unsavory human predicament. Being content to reflect philosophically and to contemplate aesthetically, he will not get caught up in the frustration and boredom which follow from the quest for pleasure. Finally, he will control and overcome the will to live by self-discipline and asceticism (or self-mortification), taking upon himself the sufferings of the world, and allowing himself to experience compassion for all fellow sufferers. Despite the pains and agonies of existence, he will not commit suicide no matter how tempting at times this act may be. He will deny the will to live, renounce it, and, like a good Buddhist, finally transcend it attaining to the blissful extinction of Nirvana—nothingness.

Following Schopenhauer's "Essay on Human Nature" is a selection from *On Aggression* by the Austrian naturalist Konrad Lorenz (b. 1903). Like Schopenhauer, Lorenz believes that aggressive and destructive behavior are inherent in human nature, they are part of our animal heritage; but unlike Schopenhauer he also stresses the importance of the social instincts in determining human behavior. Lorenz also would reject Schopenhauer's overall pessimism in favor of a realistic optimism which sees new hope for man in increased self-knowledge, in the development of an applied science of human behavior, and in the discovery of better ways to channel and sublimate aggressive drives.

The old debate regarding the evolution of human beings has all but disappeared; the issue regarding the violence and aggression exhibited in human nature has not. Is the genesis of human nature, especially the inherited aggressive drives, responsible for the violence in sports, in urban crime, and in international politics today? Or are the aggressiveness and violence in human nature correctable because they are only products of environment and culture? Whether we take the position that nature or nurture is responsible for our most devastating human acts will partly determine the question of whether we can control human nature in the future and channel it into more creative modes. Even if we assume that those who point to our animal past are correct, can we still maintain that modern culture and technology may yet sever human nature from its past?

NOTES

1. Arthur Schopenhauer, "Studies in Pessimism," *Essays,* trans. T. Bailey Saunders, (New York: Wiley Book Company, n. d.), p. 13.

2. Arthur Schopenhauer, *The World as Will and Idea,* trans. R. B. Haldane and A. Kemp, (New York: Doubleday & Co., 1961), pp. 335–336.

3. Arthur Schopenhauer, *On the Basis of Morality,* trans. E. F. J. Payne, (New York: Bobbs-Merrill, 1965), p. 132.

4. Ibid., p. 133.

5. Ibid., p. 127.

6. Ibid., p. 173.

On Human Nature

Arthur Schopenhauer

No one can live among men without feeling drawn again and again to the tempting supposition that moral baseness and intellectual incapacity are closely connected, as though they both sprang direct from one source. That that, however, is not so, I have shown in detail. That it seems to be so is merely due to the fact that both are so often found together; and the circumstance is to be explained by the very frequent occurrence of each of them, so that it may easily happen for both to be compelled to live under one roof. At the same time it is not to be denied that they play into each other's hands to their mutual benefit; and it is this that produces the very unedifying spectacle which only too many men exhibit, and that makes the world to go as it goes. A man who is unintelligent is very likely to show his perfidy, villainy and malice; whereas a clever man understands how to conceal these qualities. And how often, on the other hand, does a perversity of heart prevent a man from seeing truths which his intelligence is quite capable of grasping!

Nevertheless, let no one boast. Just as every man, though he be the greatest genius, has very definite limitations in some one sphere of knowledge, and thus attests his common origin with the essentially perverse and stupid mass of mankind, so also has every man something in his nature which is positively evil. Even the

From *The Essays of Arthur Schopenhauer*, trans. by T. Bailey Saunders, (New York: Wiley Book Company, n.d.).

best, nay the noblest, character will sometimes surprise us by isolated traits of depravity; as though it were to acknowledge his kinship with the human race, in which villainy—nay, cruelty—is to be found in that degree. For it was just in virtue of this evil in him, this bad principle, that of necessity he became a man. And for the same reason the world in general is what my clear mirror of it has shown it to be.

But in spite of all this the difference even between one man and another is incalculably great, and many a one would be horrified to see another as he really is. Oh, for some Asmodeus of morality, to make not only roofs and walls transparent to his favourites, but also to lift the veil of dissimulation, fraud, hypocrisy, pretence, falsehood and deception, which is spread over all things! to show how little true honesty there is in the world, and how often, even where it is least to be expected, behind all the exterior outwork of virtue, secretly and in the innermost recesses, unrighteousness sits at the helm! It is just on this account that so many men of the better kind have four-footed friends: for, to be sure, how is a man to get relief from the endless dissimulation, falsity and malice of mankind, if there were no dogs into whose honest faces he can look without distrust?

For what is our civilised world but a big masquerade? where you meet knights, priests, soldiers, men of learning, barristers, clergymen, philosophers, and I don't know what all! But they are not what they pretend to be; they are only masks, and, as a rule, behind the masks you will find moneymakers. One man, I suppose, puts on the mask of law, which he has borrowed for the purpose from a barrister, only in order to be able to give another man a sound drubbing; a second has chosen the mask of patriotism and the public welfare with a similar intent; a third takes religion or purity of doctrine. For all sorts of purposes men have often put on the mask of philosophy, and even of philanthropy, and I know not what besides. Women have a smaller choice. As a rule they avail themselves of the mask of morality, modesty, domesticity, and humility. Then there are general masks, without any particular character attaching to them like dominoes. They may be met with everywhere; and of this sort is the strict rectitude, the courtesy, the sincere sympathy, the smiling friendship, that people profess. The whole of these masks as a rule are merely, as I have said, a disguise for some industry, commerce, or speculation. It is merchants alone who in this respect constitute any honest class. They are the only people who give themselves out to be what they are; and therefore they go about without any mask at all, and consequently take a humble rank.

It is very necessary that a man should be apprised early in life that it is a masquerade in which he finds himself. For otherwise there are many things which he will fail to understand and put up with, nay, at which he will be completely puzzled. . . . Such for instance is the favour that villainy finds; the neglect that merit, even the rarest and the greatest, suffers at the hands of those of the same profession; the hatred of truth and great capacity; the ignorance of scholars in their own province; and the fact that true wares are almost always despised and the merely specious ones in request. Therefore let even the young be instructed betimes that in this masquerade the apples are of wax, the flowers of silk, the fish of pasteboard, and that all things—yes, all things—are toys and trifles; and that of two men whom he may see earnestly engaged in business, one

is supplying spurious goods and the other paying for them in false coin.

But there are more serious reflections to be made, and worse things to be recorded. Man is at bottom a savage, horrible beast. We know it, if only in the business of taming and restraining him which we call civilisation. Hence it is that we are terrified if now and then his nature breaks out. Wherever and whenever the locks and chains of law and order fall off and give place to anarchy, he shows himself for what he is. But it is unnecessary to wait for anarchy in order to gain enlightenment on this subject. A hundred records, old and new, produce the conviction that in his unrelenting cruelty man is in no way inferior to the tiger and the hyæna. A forcible example is supplied by a publication of the year 1841 entitled *Slavery and the Internal Slave Trade in the United States of North America: being replies to questions transmitted by the British Anti-slavery Society to the American Anti-slavery Society.* This book constitutes one of the heaviest indictments against the human race. No one can put it down without a feeling of horror, and few without tears. For whatever the reader may have ever heard, or imagined, or dreamt, of the unhappy condition of slavery, or indeed of human cruelty in general, it will seem small to him when he reads of the way in which those devils in human form, those bigoted, churchgoing, strictly Sabbatarian rascals—and in particular the Anglican priests among them—treated their innocent black brothers, who by wrong and violence had got into their diabolical clutches.

Other examples are furnished by Tshudi's *Travels in Peru,* in the description which he gives of the treatment of the Peruvian soldiers at the hands of their officers; and by Macleod's *Travels in Eastern Africa,* where the author tells of the coldblooded and truly devilish cruelty with which the Portuguese in Mozambique treat their slaves. But we need not go for examples to the New World, that obverse side of our planet. In the year 1848 it was brought to life that England, not in one, but apparently in a hundred cases within a brief period, a husband had poisoned his wife or *vice versâ*, or both had joined in poisoning their children, or in torturing them slowly to death by starving and ill-treating them, with no other object than to get the money for burying them which they had insured in the Burial Clubs against their death. For this purpose a child was often insured in several, even in as many as twenty clubs at once.

Details of this character belong, indeed, to the blackest pages in the criminal records of humanity. But, when all is said, it is the inward and innate character of man, this god *par excellence* of the Pantheists, from which they and everything like them proceed. In every man there dwells, first and foremost, a colossal egoism, which breaks the bounds of right and justice with the greatest freedom, as everyday life shows on a small scale, and as history on every page of it on a large. Does not the recognised need of a balance of power in Europe, with the anxious way in which it is preserved, demonstrate that man is a beast of prey, who no sooner sees a weaker man near him than he falls upon him without fail? and does not the same hold good of the affairs of ordinary life?

But to the boundless egoism of our nature there is joined more or less in every human breast a fund of hatred, anger, envy, rancour and malice, accumulated like the venom in a serpent's tooth, and waiting only for an opportunity of venting itself, and then, like a demon unchained, of storming and raging. If a man has no great occasion for breaking out, he will end by taking advantage of the smallest, and by working it up into something great by the aid of his imagination; for, however small it may be, it is enough to rouse his anger . . . and then he will carry it as far as he can and may. We see this in daily life, where such outbursts are well known under the name of "venting one's gall on something." It will also have been observed that if such outbursts meet with no opposition the subject of them feels decidedly the better for them afterwards. That anger is not without its pleasure is a truth that was recorded even by Aristotle; and he quotes a passage from Homer, who declares anger to be sweeter than honey. But not in anger alone —in hatred too, which stands to anger like a chronic to an acute disease, a man may indulge with the greatest delight:

Now hatred is by far the longest pleasure,
Men love in haste, but they detest at leisure.

Gobineau in his work *Les Races Humaines* has called man *l'animal méchant par excellence*. People take this very ill, because they feel that it hits them; but he is quite right, for man is the only animal which causes pain to others without any further purpose than just to cause it. Other animals never do it except to satisfy their hunger, or in the rage of combat. If it is said against the tiger that he kills more than he eats, he strangles his prey only for the purpose of eating it; and if he cannot eat it, the only explanation is, as the French phrase has it, that *ses yeux sont plus grand que son estomac*. No animal ever torments another for the mere purpose of tormenting, but man does it, and it is this that constitutes the diabolical feature in his character which is so much worse than the merely animal. I have already spoken of the matter in its broad aspect; but it is manifest even in small things, and every reader has a daily opportunity of observing it. For instance, if two little dogs are playing together—and what a genial and charming sight it is—and a child of three or four years joins them, it is almost inevitable for it to begin hitting them with a whip or stick, and thereby show itself, even at that age, *l'animal méchant par excellence*. The love of teasing and playing tricks, which is common enough, may be traced to the same source. For instance, if a man has expressed his annoyance at any interruption or other petty inconvenience, there will be no lack of people who for that very reason will bring it about: *animal méchant par excellence!* This is so certain that a man should be careful not to express any annoyance at small evils. On the other hand he should also be careful not to express his pleasure at any trifle, for, if he does so, men will act like the jailer who, when he found that his prisoner had performed the laborious task of taming a spider, and took a pleasure in watching it, immediately crushed it under his foot: *l'animal méchant par excellence!* This is why all animals are instinctively afraid of the sight, or even the track of a man, that *animal méchant par excellence!* nor does their instinct play them false; for it is man alone who hunts game for which he has no use and which does him no harm.

It is a fact, then, that in the heart of every man there lies a wild beast which only waits for an opportunity to storm and rage, in its desire to inflict pain on others, or, if they stand in his way, to kill them. It is this which is the source of all the lust of war and battle. In trying to tame and to some extent hold it in check, the intelligence, its appointed keeper, has always enough to do. People may, if they please, call it the radical evil of human nature—a name which will at least serve those with whom a word stands for an explanation. I say, however, that it is the will to live, which, more and more embittered by the constant sufferings of existence, seeks to alleviate its own torment by causing torment in others. But in this way a man gradually develops in himself real cruelty and malice. The observation may also be added that as, according to Kant, matter subsists only through the antagonism of the powers of expansion and contraction, so human society subsists only by the antagonism of hatred, or anger, and fear. For there is a moment in the life of all of us when the malignity of our nature might perhaps make us

murderers, if it were not accompanied by a due admixture of fear to keep it within bounds; and this fear, again, would make a man the sport and laughing stock of every boy, if anger were not lying ready in him, and keeping watch.

But it is *Schadenfreude,* a mischievous delight in the misfortunes of others, which remains the worst trait in human nature. It is a feeling which is closely akin to cruelty, and differs from it, to say the truth, only as theory from practice. In general, it may be said of it that it takes the place which pity ought to take—pity which is its opposite, and the true source of all real justice and charity.

Envy is also apposed to pity, but in another sense; envy, that is to say, is produced by a cause directly antagonistic to that which produces the delight in mischief. The opposition between pity and envy on the one hand, and pity and the delight in mischief on the other, rests, in the main, on the occasions which call them forth. In the case of envy it is only as a direct effect of the cause which excites it that we feel it at all. That is just the reason why envy, although it is a reprehensible feeling, still admits of some excuse, and is, in general, a very human quality; whereas the delight in mischief is diabolical, and its taunts are the laughter of hell.

The delight in mischief, as I have said, takes the place which pity ought to take. Envy, on the contrary, finds a place only where there is no inducement to pity, or rather an inducement to its opposite; and it is just as this opposite that envy arises in the human breast; and so far, therefore, it may still be reckoned a human sentiment. Nay, I am afraid that no one will be found to be entirely free from it. For that a man should feel his own lack of things more bitterly at the sight of another's delight in the enjoyment of them, is natural; nay, it is inevitable; but this should not rouse his hatred of the man who is happier than himself. It is just this hatred, however, in which true envy consists. Least of all should a man be envious, when it is a question, not of the gifts of fortune, or chance, or another's favour, but of the gifts of nature; because everything that is innate in a man rests on a metaphysical basis, and possesses justification of a higher kind; it is, so to speak, given him by Divine grace. But, unhappily, it is just in the case of personal advantages that envy is most irreconcilable. Thus it is that intelligence, or even genius, cannot get on in the world without begging pardon for its existence, wherever it is not in a position to be able, proudly and boldly, to despise the world.

In other words, if envy is aroused only by wealth, rank, or power, it is often kept down by egoism, which perceives that, on occasion, assistance, enjoyment, support, protection, advancement, and so on, may be hoped for from the object of envy or that at least by intercourse with him a man may himself win honour from the reflected light of his superiority; and here, too, there is the hope of one day attaining all those advantages himself. On the other hand, in the envy that is directed to natural gifts and personal advantages, like beauty in women, or intelligence in men, there is no consolation or hope of one kind or the other; so that nothing remains but to indulge a bitter and irreconcilable hatred of the person who possesses these privileges; and hence the only remaining desire is to take vengeance on him.

But here the envious man finds himself in an unfortunate position; for all his blows fall powerless as soon as it is known that they come from him. Accordingly he hides his feelings as carefully as if they were secret sins, and so becomes an inexhaustible inventor of tricks and artifices and devices for concealing and masking his procedure, in order that, unperceived, he may wound the object of his envy. For instance, with an air of the utmost unconcern he will ignore the advantages which are eating his heart out; he will neither see them, nor know them, nor have observed or

even heard of them, and thus make himself a master in the art of dissimulation. With great cunning he will completely overlook the man whose brilliant qualities are gnawing at his heart, and act as though he were quite an unimportant person; he will take no notice of him, and, on occasion, will have even quite forgotten his existence. But at the same time he will before all things endeavour by secret machination carefully to deprive those advantages of any opportunity of showing themselves and becoming known. Then out of his dark corner he will attack these qualities with censure, mockery, ridicule and calumny, like the toad which spurts its poison from a hole. No less will he enthusiastically praise unimportant people, or even indifferent or bad performances in the same sphere. In short, he will becomes a Proteas in stratagem, in order to wound others without showing himself. But what is the use of it? The trained eye recognises him in spite of it all. He betrays himself, if by nothing else, by the way in which he timidly avoids and flies from the object of his envy, who stands the more completely alone, the more brilliant he is; and this is the reason why pretty girls have no friends of their own sex. He betrays himself, too, by the causeless hatred which he shows—a hatred which finds vent in a violent explosion at any circumstance however trivial, though it is often only the product of his imagination. How many such men there are in the world may be recognised by the universal praise of modesty, that is, of a virtue invented on behalf of dull and commonplace people. Nevertheless, it is a virtue which, by exhibiting the necessity for dealing considerately with the wretched plight of these people, is just what calls attention to it.

For our self-consciousness and our pride there can be nothing more flattering than the sight of envy lurking in its retreat and plotting its schemes; but never let a man forget that where there is envy there is hatred, and let him be careful not to make a false friend out of any envious person. Therefore it is important to our safety to lay envy bare; and a man should study to discover its tricks, as it is everywhere to be found and always goes about *incognito;* or as I have said, like a venomous toad it lurks in dark corners. It deserves neither quarter nor sympathy; but as we can never reconcile it let our rule of conduct be to scorn it with a good heart, and as our happiness and glory is torture to it we may rejoice in its sufferings . . .

We have been taking a look at the *depravity* of man, and it is a sight which may well fill us with horror. But now we must cast our eyes on the *misery* of his existence; and when we have done so, and are horrified by that too, we must look back again at his depravity. We shall then find that they hold the balance to each other. We shall perceive the eternal justice of things; for we shall recognise that the world is itself the Last Judgment on it, and we shall begin to understand why it is that everything that lives must pay the penalty of its existence, first in living and then in dying. Thus the evil of the penalty accords with the evil of the sin—*malum pœnæ* with *malum culpæ.* From the same point of view we lose our indignation at that intellectual incapacity of the great majority of mankind which in life so often disgusts us. In this *Sansara,* as the Buddhists call it, human misery, human depravity and human folly correspond with one another perfectly, and they are of like magnitude. But if, on some special inducement, we direct our gaze to one of them, and survey it in particular, it seems to exceed the other two. This, however, is an illusion, and merely the effect of their colossal range.

All things proclaim this *Sansara,* more than all else, the world of mankind; in which, from a moral point of view, villainy and baseness, and from an intellectual point of view, incapacity and stupidity, prevail to a horrifying extent. Nevertheless, there appear in it, although very spasmodically, and always as a fresh surprise, manifestations of honesty, of goodness, nay, even of nobility; and also of great intelligence, of the thinking mind of genius. They never quite vanish, but like single points of light gleam upon us out of the great dark mass. We must accept them as a pledge that this *Sansara* contains a good and redeeming principle, which is capable of breaking through and of filling and freeing the whole of it.

The readers of my *Ethics* know that with me the ultimate foundation of morality is the truth which in the *Vedas* and the *Vedanta* receives its expression in the established, mystical formula, *Tat twam asi (This is thyself),* which is spoken with reference to every living thing, be it man or beast, and is called the *Mahavakya,* the great word.

Actions which proceed in accordance with this principle, such as those of the philanthropist, may indeed be regarded as the beginning of mysticism. Every benefit rendered with a pure intention proclaims that the man who exercises it acts in direct conflict with the world of appearance; for he recognises himself as identical with another individual, who exists in complete separation from him. Accordingly, all disinterested kindness is inexplicable; it is a mystery; and hence in order to explain it a man has to resort to all sorts of fictions.

Man the Aggressor

Konrad Lorenz

Let us imagine that an absolutely unbiased investigator on another planet, perhaps on Mars, is examining human behavior on earth, with the aide of a telescope whose magnification is too small to enable him to discern individuals and follow their separate behavior, but large enough for him to observe occurrences such as migrations of peoples, wars, and similar great historical events. He would never gain the impression that human behavior was dictated by intelligence, still less by responsible morality. If we suppose our extraneous observer to be a being of pure reason, devoid of instincts himself and unaware of the way in which all instincts in general and aggression in particular can miscarry, he would be at a complete loss how to explain history at all. The ever-recurrent phenomena of history do not have reasonable causes. It is a mere commonplace to say that they are caused by what common parlance so aptly terms "human nature." Unreasoning and unreasonable human nature causes two nations to compete, though no economic necessity compels them to do so; it induces two political parties or religions with amazingly similar programs of salvation to fight each other bitterly, and it impels an Alexander or a Napoleon to sacrifice millions

From *On Aggression* by Konrad Lorenz, copyright © 1963 by Dr. Borotha-Schoeler Verlag, Wien, Austria; English translation copyright © 1966 by Konrad Lorenz. Reprinted by permission of Harcourt Brace Jovanovich, Inc. Canadian rights by Methuen & Co., Ltd.

of lives in his attempt to unite the world under his scepter. We have been taught to regard some of the persons who have committed these and similar absurdities with respect, even as "great" men, we are wont to yield to the political wisdom of those in charge, and we are all so accustomed to these phenomena that most of us fail to realize how abjectly stupid and undesirable the historical mass behavior of humanity actually is.

Having realized this, however, we cannot escape the question why reasonable beings do behave so unreasonably. Undeniably, there must be superlatively strong factors which are able to overcome the commands of individual reason so completely and which are so obviously impervious to experience and learning. As Hegel said, "What experience and history teach us is this—that people and governments never have learned anything from history, or acted on principles deduced from it."

All these amazing paradoxes, however, find an unconstrained explanation, falling into place like the pieces of a jigsaw puzzle, if one assumes that human behavior, and particularly human social behavior, far from being determined by reason and cultural tradition alone, is still subject to all the laws prevailing in all phylogenetically adapted instinctive behavior. Of these laws we possess a fair amount of knowledge from studying the instincts of animals. Indeed, if our extramundane observer were a knowledgeable ethologist, he would unavoidably draw the conclusion that man's social organization is very similar to that of rats, which, like humans, are social and peaceful beings within their clans, but veritable devils toward all fellow members of their species not belonging to their own community. If, furthermore, our Martian naturalist knew of the explosive rise in human populations, the ever-increasing destructiveness of weapons, and the division of mankind into a few political camps, he would not expect the future of humanity to be more rosy than that of several hostile clans of rats on a ship almost devoid of food. And this prognosis would even be optimistic, for in the case of rats, reproduction stops automatically when a certain state of overcrowding is reached while man as yet has no workable system for preventing the so-called population explosion. Furthermore, in the case of the rats it is likely that after the wholesale slaughter enough individuals would be left over to propagate the species. In the case of man, this would not be so certain after the use of the hydrogen bomb.

It is a curious paradox that the greatest gifts of man, the unique faculties of conceptual thought and verbal speech which have raised him to a level high above all other creatures and given him mastery over the globe, are not altogether blessings, or at least are blessings that have to be paid for very dearly indeed. All the great dangers threatening humanity with extinction are direct consequences of conceptual thought and verbal speech. They drove man out of the paradise in which he could follow his instincts with impunity and do or not do whatever he pleased. There is much truth in the parable of the tree of knowledge and its fruit, though I want to make an addition to it to make it fit into my own picture of Adam: that apple was thoroughly unripe! Knowledge springing from conceptual thought robbed man of the security provided by his well-adapted instincts long, long before it was sufficient to provide him with an equally safe adaptation. Man is, as Arnold Gehlen has so

truly said, by nature a jeopardized creature.

Conceptual thought and speech changed all man's evolution by achieving something which is equivalent to the inheritance of acquired characters. We have forgotten that the verb "inherit" had a juridic connotation long before it acquired a biological one. When a man invents, let us say, bow and arrow, not only his progeny but his entire community will inherit the knowledge and the use of these tools and possess them just as surely as organs grown on the body. Nor is their loss any more likely than the rudimentation of an organ of equal survival value. Thus, within one or two generations a process of ecological adaptation can be achieved which, in normal phylogeny and without the interference of conceptual thought, would have taken a time of an altogether different, much greater order of magnitude. Small wonder, indeed, if the evolution of social instincts and, what is even more important, social inhibitions could not keep pace with the rapid development forced on human society by the growth of traditional culture, particularly material culture.

Obviously, instinctive behavior mechanisms failed to cope with the new circumstances which culture unavoidably produced even at its very dawn. There is evidence that the first inventors of pebble tools, the African Australopithecines, promptly used their new weapon to kill not only game, but fellow members of their species as well. Peking Man, the Prometheus who learned to preserve fire, used it to roast his brothers: beside the first traces of the regular use of fire lie the mutilated and roasted bones of Sinanthropus pekinensis himself.

One is tempted to believe that every gift bestowed on man by his power of conceptual thought has to be paid for with a dangerous evil as the direct consequence of it. Fortunately for us, this is not so. Besides the faculty of conceptual thought, another constituent characteristic of man played an important role in gaining a deeper understanding of his environment, and this is curiosity. Insatiable curiosity is the root of exploration and experimentation, and these activities, even in their most primitive form, imply a function akin to asking questions. Explorative experimentation is a sort of dialogue with surrounding nature. Asking a question and recording the answer leads to anticipating the latter, and, given conceptual thought, to the linking of cause and effect. From hence it is but a step to consciously foreseeing the consequences of one's actions. Thus, the same human faculties which supplied man with tools and with power dangerous to himself, also gave him the means to prevent their misuse: rational responsibility. I shall now proceed to discuss, one by one, the dangers which humanity incurs by rising above the other animals by virtue of its great, specific gifts. Subsequently I shall try to show in what way the greatest gift of all, rational, responsible morality, functions in banning these dangers. Most important of all, I shall have to expound the functional limitations of morality.

In the chapter on behavior mechanisms functionally analogous to morality, I have spoken of the inhibitions controlling aggression in various social animals, preventing it from injuring or killing fellow members of the species. As I explained, these inhibitions are most important and consequently most highly differentiated in those animals which are capable of killing living creatures of about their own size. A raven can peck out the eye of another with one thrust of its beak, a wolf can rip the jugular vein of another with a single bite. There would be no more ravens and no more wolves if reliable inhibitions did not prevent such actions. Neither a dove nor a hare nor even a chimpanzee is able to kill its own kind with a single peck or bite; in addition, animals with relatively poor defense weapons have a correspondingly great ability to escape quickly, even from specially armed predators

which are more efficient in chasing, catching, and killing than even the strongest of their own species. Since there rarely is, in nature, the possibility of such an animal's seriously injuring one of its own kind, there is no selection pressure at work here to breed in killing inhibitions. The absence of such inhibitions is apparent to the animal keeper, to his own and to his animals' disadvantage, if he does not take seriously the intra-specific fights of completely "harmless" animals. Under the unnatural conditions of captivity, where a defeated animal cannot escape from its victor, it may be killed slowly and cruelly. In my book *King Solomon's Ring*, I have described in the chapter "Morals and Weapons" how the symbol of peace, the dove, can torture one of its own kind to death, without the arousal of any inhibition.

Anthropologists concerned with the habits of Australopithecus have repeatedly stressed that these hunting progenitors of man left humanity with the dangerous heritage of what they term "carnivorous mentality." This statement confuses the concepts of the carnivore and the cannibal, which are to a large extent, mutually exclusive. One can only deplore the fact that man has definitely not got a carnivorous mentality! All his trouble arises from his being a basically harmless, omnivorous creature, lacking in natural weapons with which to kill big prey, and, therefore, also devoid of the built-in safety devices which prevent "professional" carnivores from abusing their killing power to destroy fellow members of their own species. A lion or a wolf may, on extremely rare occasions, kill another by one angry stroke, but, as I have already explained in the chapter on behavior mechanisms functionally analogous to morality, all heavily armed carnivores possess sufficiently reliable inhibitions which prevent the self-destruction of the species.

In human evolution, no inhibitory mechanisms preventing sudden manslaughter were necessary, because quick killing was impossible anyhow; the potential victim had plenty of opportunity to elicit the pity of the aggressor by submissive gestures and appeasing attitudes. No selection pressure arose in the prehistory of mankind to breed inhibitory mechanisms preventing the killing of conspecifics until, all of a sudden, the invention of artificial weapons upset the equilibrium of killing potential and social inhibitions. When it did, man's position was very nearly that of a dove which, by some unnatural trick of nature, has suddenly acquired the beak of a raven. One shudders at the thought of a creature as irascible as all prehuman primates are, swinging a well-sharpened hand-ax. Humanity would indeed have destroyed itself by its first inventions, were it not for the very wonderful fact that inventions and responsibility are both the achievements of the same specifically human faculty of asking questions.

Not that our prehuman ancestor, even at a stage as yet devoid of moral responsibility, was a fiend incarnate; he was by no means poorer in social instincts and inhibitions than a chimpanzee, which, after all, is—his irascibility not withstanding—a social and friendly creature. But whatever his innate norms of social behavior may have been, they were bound to be thrown out of gear by the invention of weapons. If humanity survived, as, after all, it did, it never achieved security from the danger of self-destruction. If moral responsibility and unwillingness to kill indubitably increased, the ease and emotional impunity of killing have increased at the same rate. The distance at which all shooting weapons take effect screens the killer against the stimulus situation which would otherwise activate his killing inhibitions. The deep emotional layers of our personality simply do not register the fact that the crooking of the forefinger to release a shot tears the entrails of another man. No sane man would even go rabbit hunting for pleasure if the necessity of killing his prey with his natural weapons brought home to him the full, emotional realization of what he is actually doing.

The same principle applies, to an even greater degree, to the use of modern remote-control weapons. The man who presses the releasing button is so completely screened against seeing, hearing, or otherwise emotionally realizing the consequences of his action, that he can commit it with impunity—even if he is burdened with the power of imagination. Only thus can it be explained that perfectly good-natured men, who would not even smack a naughty child, proved to be perfectly able to release rockets or to lay carpets of incendiary bombs on sleeping cities, thereby committing hundreds and thousands of children to a horrible death in the flames. The fact that it is good, normal men who did this, is as eerie as any fiendish atrocity of war!

8 Man: Victim of Circumstance or Sinner?

Bellamy & King

Schopenhauer's pessimistic view of human nature would have been objectionable to both of the authors of the following selections, but for different reasons. To Edward Bellamy (1850–1898), journalist, novelist, and influential socialist thinker, Schopenhauer like other pessimists made the mistake of laying blame for social ills on human nature rather than on the oppressive social environment. There is nothing wrong with human nature itself, Bellamy believed, and one does not have to change it; the conditions of human life must be changed, and then the motives of human action will be radically altered.

Martin Luther King, Jr. (1922–1968), a Christian minister and social reformer, would also reject pessimistic evaluations of human nature, pointing to the potentialities of goodness within humanity. However, unlike Bellamy, whom he considered to be overly optimistic, he would attribute humanity's plight not just to faulty social institutions but to the sinfulness which comes from alienation from God and from failure to accept the Christian way of salvation. King considered man as a sinner strayed from the path of righteousness, standing in need of redemption; to Bellamy, man is a victim of unfortunate social circumstances which arise directly from the dominance of the capitalist system.

Martin Luther King, Jr. and Edward Bellamy thus arrived at two quite different philosophies of human nature, but they had several things in common. Both were sons of Baptist ministers and their early lives were steeped in the Judeo-Christian tradition. Both were significant figures in social reform movements of their time: in Bellamy's case through the formation of Nationalist clubs, a new but short-lived political movement; and in King's case by his leadership in the American civil rights movement. Both men were considered radicals by many of their contemporaries

124

although each considered himself to be no more (or less) radical than Jesus Christ. Both favored evolution rather than revolution as the preferred means for bringing about social changes. And finally, both men attacked social and economic inequality as unnecessary social evils and they called for changes consistent with the ideals of justice, freedom, and human dignity.

Edward Bellamy presented his philosophy of man in his utopian novel, *Looking Backward: 2000–1887*. The novel describes the observations and experiences of Julian West, a citizen of the nineteenth century who awakens in twentieth century Boston. The United States, Julian discovers, has been transformed into a socialist paradise and the world is at last free from poverty, suffering, and war. The keys to the new world order had been found in the application of universal economic equality, brought about through social regimentation. The United States, for example, is now run by an industrial army which produces what is needed for the people. Goods are made readily available according to their needs. Private ownership of the means of production has been abolished, and everyone works for the welfare of the whole nation under a labor-credit system which assures economic equality. These changes occurred primarily through economic evolution culminating in a relatively bloodless revolution which had ushered in the new society. Cooperation has replaced competition as the driving force of economic and social affairs. A sense of social solidarity has replaced the old sense of rugged individualism. The kingdom of heaven, a realm of peace, prosperity, and love, has at last been established on earth.

This vision of utopia was to be taken quite seriously by Bellamy. "*Looking Backward*," he wrote, "although in form a fanciful romance, is intended, in all seriousness, as a forecast, in accordance with the principles of evolution, of the next stage in the industrial and social development of humanity, especially in this country."[1]

Bellamy was convinced that he had found the only sane and secure basis for a new social order, and that this basis, economic equality, could and would be instituted once the old capitalistic order had withered away. In his later novel, *Equality* (1897), he further developed his utopian scheme and defended economic equality as the cornerstone of a perfected society. He rejected the objection to his system, raised by the clergy of his time, that social misery was not caused by economic inequality but by human sin and depravity. Sin and depravity are symptoms of social disease, not causes of it. Nor would he admit that the institution of complete economic equality would remove the competitive incentives needed to get people to work. In the old unfair system, the chief incentive to get people to work had been fear and greed; in the new system of economic equality, these motives would be replaced by new motives such as desire to serve others, a motive which previously had been repressed and unrewarded by the capitalistic system.

Bellamy also took issue with several other objections to his idea of economic equality: that it would make everyone alike, it would discourage independence and originality, it would lead to corruption, and it would threaten liberty. On the contrary, for the first time, economic equality would make possible the development of true individuality unhampered by economic insecurity. It would encourage more originality and independence by releasing energies which previously had been dissipated by the struggle for survival in the competitive system. By careful planning and simplified administration, the wastefulness, corruption, and compulsions of the old system would be abolished without any danger of their recurrence. With equality would come security with freedom.

Underlying Bellamy's utopian proposals was an idealistic philosophy of man and nature which he had developed and recorded earlier in an unpublished essay "The Religion of Solidarity." Imbued with the inspiration of transcendentalism, Bellamy had written that "our souls are not islands in the void, but peninsulas forming one continent of life within the universe."[2] To know oneself is to know that one is vitally related to the totality of things which are expressions of the same unitary spiritual reality. "The dual existence of man is at once infinite and infinitesimal and particular."[3] "Telescopic and microscopic are the two windows through which man looks out, the former opening on the infinite, the latter on the infinitesimal."[4] In his religion of solidarity, Bellamy believed he had found the only rational moral philosophy and proof that "unselfishness is not madness." When one discovers that one is an integral part of the larger social reality, one will recognize that "unselfishness is but the sacrifice of the lesser self to the greater self."[5]

To this philosophy Bellamy remained faithful throughout his life. Although he no longer adhered to all of the tenets of the Christian religion by which he had been raised, he always considered his human ideal to be Jesus Christ, and he often referred to his utopian vision as "the Commonwealth of the Golden Rule." His faith remained evangelical in spirit, if not in doctrine.

Martin Luther King, Jr.'s philosophy of human nature was derived from three main sources. The first was the Baptist interpretation of the Judeo-Christian tradition, stressing the individual's personal relationship with God, the joining together of like-minded individuals into a free community of worshippers of the living God, the Bible as the inspired holy word of God, and the revealed truth that Jesus is Christ the Savior. The Gospel or "Good News" is that despite the sinfulness of human nature, there is the possibility of salvation, of being born again as a member of God's kingdom, providing one believes in and practices the teachings of Jesus. In his sermons and in his actions, King attempted to follow these teachings which to him could be summarized in the commandment, "Thou shalt love the Lord thy God with all thy heart, and thy neighbor as thyself."

A second ingredient in King's view of human nature comes from the

writings of the founding fathers of the United States and from later inter-
preters of "the American dream." He quoted often from the Declaration
of Independence, the United States Constitution, and from Thomas Jefferson and Abraham Lincoln. In a time of racism and increasing demand
for equal rights, he reminded his audiences of the contradictions between
what America had guaranteed to all of its citizens—life, liberty, and the
pursuit of happiness—and the indignities and injustices to which many
Black Americans and other minorities were still being subjected. He
demanded that all Americans be given opportunities to actualize their
potentialities freely, and that Black Americans no longer be treated as
second-class citizens.

The third ingredient in King's philosophy of human nature comes from
the life and teachings of Mohatma Gandhi. In working for the liberation
of his fellow Indians from British Imperialism, Gandhi had formulated a
doctrine of "satyagraha," "love-force," or "soul-force" on the basis of which
he had advocated the practice of civil disobedience to unjust laws. This,
in Gandhi's view, was not merely "passive resistance" but rather nonviolent
resistance to social evils through refusing to obey laws which violated
human rights. Gandhi's view of resistance had been developed from various
influences, including Henry David Thoreau's essay on "Civil Disobedience," a work which King also read and praised. Before becoming acquainted with Gandhi's life and teachings, King was somewhat sceptical
of the power of love as a means for solving social problems. The loving,
turn-the-other-cheek approach might work in dealing with individuals, he
then thought, but it probably wouldn't be applicable to conflicts between
racial groups or nations. As he got acquainted with Gandhi's teachings, he
later reported, his "scepticism concerning the power of love gradually
diminished" and he "came to see for the first time that the Christian doctrine of love, operating through the Gandhian method of nonviolence, is
one of the most potent weapons available to an oppressed people in their
struggle for freedom."[6] This commitment, however, was at that time primarily intellectual; it was only later, in the mid-fifties, that he came to see
how the method could be put into practice in the racial struggle of both
North and South.

There were of course many other influences which helped to mold Dr.
King's view of human nature. As the following essay shows, Christianity,
Protestantism, American Idealism, and Indian mysticism helped to shape
King's powerful message. Ideas from these sources were embodied in his
inspirational speeches, sermons, and essays, including his famous "I have a
dream" speech and his "Letter from a Birmingham Jail." In the letter,
which was addressed to Christian ministers who had considered his civil
rights activities to be "unwise and untimely," he justified his stand in a
manner consistent with his overall view of people and their relationship
to God and the Universe. Laws, he argued, were of two kinds: just and
unjust. A just law is in accordance with the moral law or the law of God;

an unjust law contradicts the divine law. "Any law that uplifts human personality is just," he wrote, and "any law that degrades human personality is unjust."[7] He considered segregation statutes to be unjust "because segregation distorts the soul and damages the personality."[8] Further, segregation is sinful because it alienates human from human, and even more destructively it alienates humanity from itself. In light of these convictions, King urged his followers and others to disobey segregation ordinances, but to disobey them openly, nonviolently, and lovingly. His views and actions would undoubtedly cause many to call him an extremist. But as Socrates, Jesus, Martin Luther, and Thomas Jefferson had all been extremists, he felt he was in the best of company. For "after all," he wrote, "maybe the South, the nation, and the world are in dire need of creative extremists."[9]

NOTES

1.   Edward Bellamy, *Looking Backward: 2000–1887* (New York: Modern Library, 1951), p. 273.

2.   Edward Bellamy, "The Religion of Solidarity" in *Edward Bellamy: Selected Writings on Religion and Society* edited by Joseph Schiffman (New York. Liberal Arts Press, 1955), p. 11.

3.   Ibid.

4.   Ibid., p. 24.

5.   Ibid., p. 22.

6.   Martin Luther King, Jr., *Strength to Love* (New York: Pocket Books, 1963), p. 169.

7.   Martin Luther King, Jr., "Letter from a Birmingham Jail" in *Political and Social Philosophy: Traditional and Contemporary Readings* edited by J. Charles King and James A. McGilvray (New York: McGraw-Hill, 1973), p. 465.

8.   Ibid.

9.   Ibid., p. 468.

Human Nature in Utopia

Edward Bellamy

Julian West, the hero of Looking Backward, *hears the following sermon explaining how the world of the future has come about.*

MR. BARTON'S SERMON

'You know the story of that last, greatest, and most bloodless of revolutions. In the time of one generation men laid aside the social traditions and practices of barbarians, and assumed a social order worthy of rational and human beings. Ceasing to be predatory in their habits, they became co-workers, and found in fraternity, at once, the science of wealth and happiness. "What shall I eat and drink, and wherewithal shall I be clothed?" stated as a problem beginning and ending in self, had been an anxious and an endless one. But when once it was conceived, not from the individual, but the fraternal standpoint, "What shall we eat and drink, and wherewithal shall we be clothed?" —its difficulties vanished.

'Poverty with servitude had been the result, for the mass of humanity, of attempting to solve the problem of maintenance from the individual standpoint, but no sooner had the nation become the sole capitalist and employer than not alone did plenty replace poverty, but the last vestige of the serfdom of man to man disappeared from earth. Human slavery, so often

From Edward Bellamy, *Looking Backward: 2000–1887* (Boston: Ticknor & Co., 1888).

vainly scotched, at last was killed. The means of subsistence no longer doled out by men to women, by employer to employed, by rich to poor, was distributed from a common stock as among children at the father's table. It was impossible for a man any longer to use his fellow-men as tools for his own profit. His esteem was the only sort of gain he could thenceforth make out of him. There was no more either arrogance or servility in the relations of human beings to one another. For the first time since the creation every man stood up straight before God. The fear of want and the lust of gain became extinct motives when abundance was assured to all and immoderate possessions made impossible of attainment. There were no more beggars nor almoners. Equity left charity without an occupation. The ten commandments became well-nigh obsolete in a world where there was no temptation to theft, no occasion to lie either for fear or favor, no room for envy where all were equal, and little provocation to violence where men were disarmed of power to injure one another. Humanity's ancient dream of liberty, equality, fraternity, mocked by so many ages, at last was realized.

'As in the old society the generous, the just, the tenderhearted had been placed at a disadvantage by the possession of those qualities, so in the new society the cold-hearted, the greedy, and self-seeking found themselves out of joint with the world. Now that the conditions of life for the first time ceased to operate as a forcing process to develop the brutal qualities of human nature, and the premium which had here-tofore encouraged selfishness was not only re-moved, but placed upon unselfishness, it was for the first time possible to see what unper-verted human nature really was like. The depraved tendencies, which had previously overgrown and obscured the better to so large an extent, now withered like cellar fungi in the open air, and the nobler qualities showed a sudden luxuriance which turned cynics into panegyrists and for the first time in human history tempted mankind to fall in love with itself. Soon was fully revealed, what the divines and philosophers of the old world never would have believed, that human nature in its essen-tial qualities is good, not bad, that men by their natural intention and structure are generous, not selfish, pitiful, not cruel, sympathetic, not arrogant, godlike in aspirations, instinct with divinest impulses of tenderness and self-sacri-fice, images of God indeed, not the travesties upon Him they had seemed. The constant pres-sure, through numberless generations, of condi-tions of life which might have perverted angels, had not been able to essentially alter the natural nobility of the stock, and these conditions once removed, like a bent tree, it had sprung back to its normal uprightness.

'To put the whole matter in the nutshell of a parable, let me compare humanity in the olden time to a rosebush planted in a swamp, watered with black bog-water, breathing miasmatic fogs by day, and chilled with poison dews at night. Innumerable generations of gardeners had done their best to make it bloom, but beyond an occasional half-opened bud with a worm at the heart, their efforts had been unsuccessful. Many, indeed, claimed that the bush was no rosebush at all, but a noxious shrub, fit only to be uprooted and burned. The gardeners, for the most part, however, held that the bush belonged to the rose family, but had some in-eradicable taint about it, which prevented the buds from coming out, and accounted for its generally sickly condition. There were a few,

indeed, who maintained that the stock was good enough, that the trouble was in the bog, and that under more favorable conditions the plant might be expected to do better. But these persons were not regular gardeners, and being condemned by the latter as mere theorists and day dreamers, were, for the most part, so re-garded by the people. Moreover, urged some eminent moral philosophers, even conceding for the sake of the argument that the bush might possibly do better elsewhere, it was a more valuable discipline for the buds to try to bloom in a bog than it would be under more favorable conditions. The buds that succeeded in opening might indeed be very rare, and the flowers pale and scentless, but they represented far more moral effort than if they had bloomed spontaneously in a garden.

'The regular gardeners and the moral philos-ophers had their way. The bush remained rooted in the bog, and the old course of treat-ment went on. Continually new varieties of forcing mixtures were applied to the roots, and more recipes than could be numbered, each declared by its advocates the best and only suitable preparation, were used to kill the ver-min and remove the mildew. This went on a very long time. Occasionally some one claimed to observe a slight improvement in the appear-ance of the bush, but there were quite as many who declared that it did not look so well as it used to. On the whole there could not be said to be any marked change. Finally, during a period of general despondency as to the pros-pects of the bush where it was, the idea of trans-planting it was again mooted, and this time found favor. "Let us try it," was the general voice. "Perhaps it may thrive better elsewhere, and here it is certainly doubtful if it be worth cultivating longer." So it came about that the rosebush of humanity was transplanted, and set in sweet, warm, dry earth, where the sun bathed it, the stars wooed it, and the south wind caressed it. Then it appeared that it was indeed a rosebush. The vermin and the mildew disappeared, and the bush was covered with most beautiful red roses, whose fragrance filled the world.

'It is a pledge of the destiny appointed for us that the Creator has set in our hearts an infinite standard of achievement, judged by which our past attainments seem always insignificant, and the goal never nearer. Had our forefathers conceived a state of society in which men should live together like brethren dwelling in unity, without strifes or envying, violence or overreaching, and where, at the price of a degree of labor not greater than health demands, in their chosen occupations, they should be wholly freed from care for the morrow and left with no more concern for their livelihood than trees which are watered by unfailing streams,—had they conceived such a condition, I say, it would have seemed to them nothing less than paradise. They would have confounded it with their idea of heaven, nor dreamed that there could possibly lie further beyond anything to be desired or striven for.

'But how is it with us who stand on this height which they gazed up to? Already we have well-nigh forgotten, except when it is especially called to our minds by some occasion like the present, that it was not always with men as it is now. It is a strain on our imaginations to conceive the social arrangements of our immediate ancestors. We find them grotesque. The solution of the problem of physical maintenance so as to banish care and crime, so far from seeming to us an ultimate attainment, appears but as a preliminary to anything like real human progress. We have but relieved ourselves of an impertinent and needless harassment which hindered our ancestor from undertaking the real ends of existence. We are merely stripped for the race; no more. We are like a child which has just learned to stand upright and to walk. It is a great event, from the child's point of view, when he first walks. Perhaps he fancies that there can be little beyond that achievement, but a year later he has forgotten that he could not always walk. His horizon did but widen when he rose, and enlarge as he moved. A great event indeed, in one sense, was his first step, but only as a beginning, not as the end. His true career was but then first entered on. The enfranchisement of humanity in the last century, from mental and physical absorption in working and scheming for the mere bodily necessities, may be regarded as a species of second birth of the race, without which its first birth to an existence that was but a burden would forever have remained unjustified, but whereby it is now abundantly vindicated. Since then, humanity has entered on a new phase of spiritual development, an evolution of higher faculties, the very existence of which in human nature our ancestors scarcely suspected. In place of the dreary hopelessness of the nineteenth century, its profound pessimism as to the future of humanity, the animating idea of the present age is an enthusiastic conception of the opportunities of our earthly existence, and the unbounded possibilities of human nature. The betterment of mankind from generation to generation, physically, mentally, morally, is recognized as the one great object supremely worthy of effort and of sacrifice. We believe the race for the first time to have entered on the realization of God's ideal of it, and each generation must now be a step upward.

'Do you ask what we look for when unnumbered generations shall have passed away? I answer, the way stretches far before us, but the end is lost in light. For twofold is the return of man to God "who is our home," the return of the individual by the way of death, and the return of the race by the fulfilment of the evolution, when the divine secret hidden in the germ shall be perfectly unfolded. With a tear for the dark past, turn we then to the dazzling future, and, veiling our eyes, press forward. The long and weary winter of the race is ended. Its summer has begun. Humanity has burst the chrysalis. The heavens are before it.'

What Is Man?

Martin Luther King, Jr.

What is man that thou art mindful of him, and the son of man that thou dost care for him? Yet thou hast made him little less than God, and dost crown him with glory and honor. (Psalm 8:4–5, RSV)

The whole political, social, and economic structure of a society is largely determined by its answer to this vital question. Indeed, the conflict we witness between totalitarianism and democracy is fundamentally centered in this: Is man a person or a pawn? Is he a cog in the wheel of the state or a free, creative being capable of accepting responsibility? This inquiry is as old as ancient man and as new as the morning newspaper. Although there is widespread agreement in asking this question, there is sharp disagreement in answering it.

Those who think of man purely in materialistic terms argue that man is simply an animal, a tiny object in the vast, ever-changing organism called nature, which is wholly unconscious and impersonal. His whole life may be explained in terms of matter in motion. Such a system of thought affirms that the conduct of man is physically determined and that the mind is merely an effect of the brain.

Those who posit the materialistic conception of man are often driven to the dark chambers of pessimism. They often find themselves agreeing with a recent writer that "man is a cosmic accident, a disease on this planet not soon to be cured," or with Jonathan Swift, who wrote, "Man is the most pernicious little race of ominous vermin that nature ever suffered to walk across the face of the earth."

Humanism is another answer frequently given to the question, "What is man?" Believing neither in God nor in the existence of any supernatural power, the humanist affirms that man is the highest form of being which has evolved in the natural universe. Over against the pessimism of materialism, the humanist posits a glowing optimism, exclaiming with Shakespeare's Hamlet:

> What a piece of work is man! How noble in reason! how infinite in faculties! in form, in moving, how express and admirable! in action how like an angel! in apprehension how like a god! the beauty of the world! the paragon of animals!

There are those who, seeking to be a little more realistic about man, wish to reconcile the truths of these opposites, while avoiding the extremes of both. They contend that the truth about man is found neither in the thesis of pessimistic materialism nor the antithesis of optimistic humanism, but in a higher synthesis. Man is neither villain nor hero; he is rather both villain and hero. The realist agrees with Carlyle that "there are depths in man which go down to the lowest hell and heights which

From Martin Luther King, Jr., *Strength to Love* (New York: Harper and Row, 1963). Reprinted by permission of Joan Daves. Copyright © 1963 by Martin Luther King, Jr.

reach the highest heaven, for are not both heaven and hell made out of him, everlasting miracle and mystery that he is?"

Centuries ago the Psalmist looked to the infinite expanse of the solar system. He gazed at the scintillating beauty of the moon and at the stars, hung like swinging lanterns of eternity. As he beheld this huge pattern and this vast cosmic order, the old familiar question came rushing to his mind, "What is man?" His answer breathes with creative truth: "Thou hast made him little less than God, and dost crown him with glory and honor."

His words serve as a basis for our thinking as we seek a realistic Christian view of man.

I

First, the Christian view recognizes that man is a biological being having a physical body. In this sense, he is an animal. So the Psalmist says, "Thou hast made him little less than God." We do not think of God as a being having a body. God is a being of pure spirit, lifted above the categories of time and space; but man, being less than God, is enmeshed in the limitations of time and space. He is in nature and can never disown his kinship with it.

The Psalmist goes on to say that God made man that way. Since this is true, there is nothing essentially wrong with man's created nature, for we read in the Book of Genesis that everything God made is good. There is nothing derogatory in having a body. This assertion is one of the things that distinguish the Christian doctrine of man from the Greek doctrine. Under the impetus of Plato, the Greeks came to feel that the body is inherently evil and that the soul will never reach its full maturity until it is freed from the prison of the body. Christianity, on the other hand, contends that the will, and not the body, is the principle of evil. The body is both sacred and significant in Christian thought.

In any realistic doctrine of man we must be forever concerned about his physical and material well-being. When Jesus said that man cannot live by bread alone, he did not imply that men can live without bread. As Christians we must think not only about "mansions in the sky," but also about the slums and ghettos that cripple the human soul, not merely about streets in heaven "flowing with milk and honey," but also about the millions of people in this world who go to bed hungry at night. Any religion that professes concern regarding the souls of men and fails to be concerned by social conditions that corrupt and economic conditions that cripple the soul, is a do-nothing religion, in need of new blood. Such a religion fails to realize that man is an animal having physical and material needs.

II

But we must not stop here. Some thinkers never get beyond the point of seeing man as an animal. The Marxists, for instance, following a theory of dialectical materialism, contend that man is merely a producing animal who supplies his own needs and whose life is determined largely by economic forces. Others contend that the whole life of man is nothing but a materialistic process with a materialistic meaning.

Can man be explained in such shallow terms? Can we explain the literary genius of Shakespeare, the musical genius of Beethoven, and the artistic genius of Michelangelo in materialistic terms? Can we explain the spiritual genius of Jesus of Nazareth in materialistic terms? Can we explain the mystery and the magic of the human soul in materialistic terms? Oh, no! There is something within man which cannot be explained in chemical and biological terms, for man is more than a tiny vagary of whirling electrons.

This brings us to a second point that must be included in any Christian doctrine of man.

Man is a being of spirit. He moves up "the stairs of his concepts" into a wonder world of thought. Conscience speaks to him, and he is reminded of things divine. This is what the Psalmist means when he says that man has been crowned with glory and honor.

This spiritual quality gives him the unique capacity to live on two levels. He is in nature, yet above nature; he is in space and time, yet above them. He can do creative things that lower animals could never do. Man can think a poem and write it; he can think a symphony and compose it; he can think of a great civilization and produce it. Because of this capacity, he is not bound completely by space and time. He may be a John Bunyan, held within spatial boundaries of Bedford Jail, whose mind transcends the bars and produces *The Pilgrim's Progress*. He may be a Handel, moving into the evening of life, his physical vision almost gone, raising his mental vision to the highest heavens and transcribing the glad thunders and gentle sighings of the great *Messiah*. By his ability to reason, his power of memory, and his gift of imagination, man transcends time and space. As marvelous as are the stars is the mind of man that studies them.

This is what the Bible means when it affirms that man is made in the image of God. The *imago dei* has been interpreted by different thinkers in terms of fellowship, responsiveness, reason, and conscience. An abiding expression of man's higher spiritual nature is his freedom. Man is man because he is free to operate within the framework of his destiny. He is free to deliberate, to make decisions, and to choose between alternatives. He is distinguished from animals by his freedom to do evil or to do good and to walk the high road of beauty or tread the low road of ugly degeneracy.

III

To avoid being victimized by an illusion born of superficiality, it should be said that we err when we assume that because man is made in the image of God, man is basically good. Through his all too prevalent inclination for evil, man has terribly scarred God's image.

We hate to be told that man is a sinner. Nothing so insults modern man's pride. We have tried desperately to find other words— error of nature, absence of good, false concept of mind—to explain the sin of man. Turning to depth psychology, we attempt to dismiss sin as the result of inner conflicts, inhibitions, or a battle between the "id" and the "super-ego." These concepts only serve to remind us that engulfing human nature is a tragic, threefold estrangement by which man is separated from himself, his neighbors, and his God. There is a corruption in man's will.

When we lay our lives bare before the scrutiny of God, we admit that though we know truth, yet we lie; we know how to be just, yet we are unjust; we know we should love, yet we hate; we stand at the juncture of the high road, yet we deliberately choose the low road. "All we like sheep have gone astray."

Man's sinfulness sinks to such devastating depths in his collective life that Reinhold Niebuhr could write a book titled *Moral Man and Immoral Society*. Man collectivized in the group, the tribe, the race, and the nation often sinks to levels of barbarity unthinkable even among lower animals. We see the tragic expression of Immoral Society in the doctrine of white supremacy which plunges millions of black men into the abyss of exploitation and in the horrors of two world wars which have left battlefields drenched with blood, national debts higher than mountains of gold, men psychologically deranged and physically handicapped, and nations of widows and orphans. Man is a sinner in need of God's forgiving grace. This is not deadening pessimism; it is Christian realism.

Despite man's tendency to live on low and degrading planes, something reminds him that he is not made for that. As he trails in the dust, something reminds him that he is made for the stars. As he makes folly his bedfellow, a nagging inner voice tells him that he is born for eternity. God's unbroken hold on us is something that will never permit us to feel right when we do wrong or to feel natural when we do the unnatural.

Jesus told of a young man who left home and wandered into a far country, where in adventure after adventure and sensation after sensation, he sought life. But he never found it; he found only frustration and bewilderment. The farther he moved from his father's house, the closer he came to the house of despair. The more he did what he liked, the less he liked what he did. Instead of leading him to a land flowing with the milk of happiness, the prodigal's journey led him to a pig's trough. This parable is an eternal reminder of the fact that man is made for the Father's house and that every excursion into the far country brings only frustration and homesickness.

Thank God the parable tells us more. The prodigal son was not himself when he left his father's house or when he dreamed that pleasure was the end of life. Only when he made up his mind to go home and be a son again did he really come to himself. There he found a loving father waiting with outstretched arms and a heart filled with unutterable joy. When the soul returns to its true home, there is always joy.

Man has strayed to the far countries of secularism, materialism, sexuality, and racial injustice. His journey has brought a moral and spiritual famine in Western civilization. *But it is not too late to return home.*

The heavenly Father speaks to Western civilization today: "In the far country of colonial-ism more than one billion six hundred million colored brothers have been dominated politically, exploited economically, and deprived of their sense of personal worth. Come to yourself and return to your true home of justice, freedom, and brotherhood, and I will joyously take you in." With an equal urgency God speaks to America: "In the far country of segregation and discrimination, you have oppressed nineteen million of your Negro brothers, binding them economically and driving them into the ghetto, and you have stripped them of their self-respect and self-dignity, making them feel that they are nobodies. Return to your true home of democracy, brotherhood, and fatherhood in God, and I will take you in and give you a new opportunity to be a truly great nation."

As individuals and as a world, may we realize that we are made for that which is high, noble, and good, and that our true home is within the Father's will. Let us choose the road that leads to abundant life.

To every man there openeth
A Way, and Ways, and a Way,
And the High Soul climbs the High Way,
And the Low Soul gropes the Low,
And in between, on the misty flats,
The rest drift to and fro.
But to every man there openeth
A High Way, and a Low,
And every man decideth
The Way his soul shall go.

God grant that we will choose the high way and that everywhere and at all times we shall be known as men who are crowned with glory and honor.

9 Social But Alienated Man

Marx & Fromm

One of the central issues of our times, according to many commentators, is the issue of alienation. "By alienation," writes Erich Fromm, is meant "a mode of experience in which the person feels himself as an alien."[1] The alienated person feels that he is estranged from himself, his life seems devoid of meaning, and it lacks the vital connections to others, to nature, and to a higher realm of meaning (e.g., God) that would make life seem harmonious, satisfying, and full of significance. Another authority on the psychological meaning of alienation, Kenneth Keniston, has delineated different types, including a feeling of being a cosmic outcast (after the realization that "God is dead"); the sense of personal loss that sometimes comes when one has grown beyond or broken away from formerly important relationships; the sense of historical loss that occurs when a culture changes and older values are radically altered or lost; and the feeling of self-estrangement or self-alienation which results from a dissociation between the individual's "conscious self" and his "real self." In reflecting on these and other forms of alienation, Keniston suggested that we keep in mind four fundamental questions about alienation:

1. its *focus*—"alienation from what?"
2. its *replacement*—"what relationship if any has replaced the lost one?"
3. its *mode*—"how is the alienation manifest?"
4. its *agent*—"what is the agent of the alienation?"[2]

In developing his view of man, and of a new social system in which human nature would be fulfilled, Karl Marx (1818–1883), wrestled with each of these questions and presented answers to them.

In 1932, Marx's early writings, the *Economic and Philosophical Manuscripts* (1844) and the *German Ideology* (1846), became readily available.

The relationships between Marx's earlier and later thought have been, and still are, the subject of much debate. Like all influential thinkers, the "real" Marx has been and will be "rediscovered" many times over. The selection below gives the reader some idea of Marx as a humanistic philosopher and his theory of human nature. Human nature is essentially social, and the ways in which people socially organize their physical, environmental, and economic conditions are important for understanding what they are. In his *Thesis on Feuerbach,* Marx states that "the essence of man is no abstraction inherent in each separate individual. In its reality it is the ensemble of social relations."[3] The social and historical dimensions of human nature indicate that nature is not static and fixed, but apart from basic physical needs it is flexible and changing. Marx saw the person in nature, in society, and in history. What humans are and can do during any one historical period depends upon their real material and economic conditions.

An historical age is determined by how the individual deals with the productive forces (i.e., the knowledge, skills, and tools of the period). It is also determined by the relations of production—how these forces are appropriated and organized into class structures, such as freemen and slaves, lords and serfs, bourgeoisie and proletariate. The sum of his relations of production, including the class structure, is the foundation for the legal, political, and cultural forms which express and sublimate this basic social structure.

For Marx, it was not only the case that "the handmill gives you a society with the feudal lord; the steam-mill society with the industrial capitalist." Human consciousness is also an expression of the basic socio-economic organization. Marx used this view of consciousness not only as a theory that attempts to explain the differing philosophies and ideologies throughout history, but also as a basis for a severe criticism of capitalism. Human law, morality, and religion are so many bourgeois prejudices cloaking bourgeois interest. The ruling ideals are those of the ruling class. Since a person's consciousness is based upon the social organization, the organization may blind him to his real needs, his fullest realization.

Marx saw labor as one of the fundamental ways in which humans experience themselves, indeed make themselves, in the world. They reproduce their lives by producing their means of subsistence, but unlike the animals, they consciously and deliberately produce their world. Marx felt that labor, within the capitalist social organization, is the major source of people's separation from themselves, their alienation. Humans cannot overcome the necessity of providing for their physical needs. But in the name of satisfying their physical needs, they, through the capitalist form of social organization, have allowed their labor to be something alien to themselves. As "workers" they do not satisfy their natural needs; the greed of other men, the profit system, is more important. Man has lost control of his labor; his activities are separated from him and they are used to enslave him. What he produces exists independent of his will and power as commodities, and he is reduced to being a tool in a factory.

At the same time, the workers feel alienated from the process or activity of production itself; they neither enjoy nor profit from it in the deepest, most creative sense. In addition, since workers must compete with one another for work and are not allowed to experience the sense of communal interdependence and involvement in the productive process, this leads to two other kinds of alienation, which Marx refers to as "species aliena- tion" and alienation of man from man. "Species alienation" is the feeling of being cut off from the essence of being human, from the sense of unity with the human race, from social solidarity. In a more personal sense, this leads to a feeling of being alienated from his fellow workers, an alienation of man from man.

What has caused these forms of alienation to be so universal? Marx thinks that the answer, in a word, is capitalism—the private ownership of the means of production by a small group who run the industrial apparatus for private profit rather than the common welfare. Echoing Rousseau, Marx believed that humans had been born free but everywhere were in chains, and it was the capitalists who had forged these chains. Although the capitalists themselves are fellow victims of the whole alienating system, and are, like the proletariat, products of powerful historical deter- minants, their expropriation of economic power must be broken and a new communistic system of production and consumption instituted.

At the time Marx was writing, no replacement of the long lost sense of communal production had yet been made, and capitalism still reigned supreme in Western society. He argued that under communism, which would eventually destroy the rapidly deteriorating capitalistic system, workers would regain their sense of relatedness to their products, to the process of production, to their species-life, to their fellow workers, and to themselves. Once capitalism was overthrown by revolution, a dictatorship of the proletariat could begin the process of de-alienation of society, and eventually would emerge a genuine classless society in which the adminis- tration of people would be replaced by the administration of things.

Although Marx and Engels claimed that their brand of socialism was scientific rather than utopian, they themselves could be called utopian in their speculation about the withering away of the state and their vision of a classless society. Previous philosophers, they held, had only interpreted the world, whereas they intended to change it. Utopian schemes had been for the most part mere dreams, with no substantial foundations. As scientific socialists and dialectical materialists, they were going to establish firm foundations for a better society on earth once they had suc- ceeded in destroying the old corrupt system. Humanity would be social- ized, economics would be communized, and man would at last be de- alienated. Alienation is not a permanent part of the human condition; for the return of humans to a humane social existence is possible through a revolutionary social transformation.

Marx's theory of human nature and his theory of revolutionary class struggle come together in his vision of a social organization which allows for a fully developed human being. When the proletariat become aware of their estrangement, they will put an end to their exploitation by capitalists, by bourgeois society. Human emancipation will be economic, political, social, and personal. Society will be the expression of human nature. A capitalist society will no longer determine the entire pattern of human life. The way to change an alienated human is to change an alienating and inhuman society into one in which "the free development of each is the condition for the free development of all." Humans must transform the society in order to find themselves.

In the following essay, Marx's view of man is set forth clearly by Erich Fromm, who has been strongly influenced by Marx in developing his own theory of alienation. A utopian socialist rather than a communist, Fromm believes that a better de-alienating society can be brought about through social reform and evolution rather than through revolution. As a psychoanalyst, he sees alienation as, first of all, a problem in character that arises when a person no longer experiences himself "as the center of his world, as the creator of his own acts." He feels as though he has lost touch with his self-identity. Such a person is out of touch—with himself, with others, and with the world. He sees himself and others as things rather than as living realities. He is what the sociologist Yablonsky terms a robopath—a human being who acts like a machine rather than a person. He externalizes his problems rather than experiences them existentially. He is an idolator, a worshipper of things, rather than a self-directing autonomous agent. In terms of Fromm's view of uniquely human needs, the alienated man is alienated because he is unable, within his culture, to satisfy his needs for rootedness, relatedness, identity, transcendence, and a frame of orientation and devotion. In the *Sane Society*, Fromm analyzed the social processes and institutions which produce human alienation, and he proposed reforms by which they could be rectified. Like Marx, he is convinced that capitalism with its marketing orientation toward things, persons, and ideas must be supplanted by a more equitable and just society, a society in which one does not have to adjust to insane practices in order to be considered sane.

NOTES

1.   Erich Fromm, *The Sane Society* (New York: Fawcett, 1953), p. 111.

2.   See Kenneth Keniston, *The Uncommitted: Alienated Youth in American Society* (New York: Harcourt, Brace & World, 1965).

3.   Karl Marx, *Selected Writings in Sociology and Social Philosophy*, trans. T. B. Bottomore (New York: McGraw-Hill, 1956), p. 68.

Marx's Concept of the Nature of Man

Erich Fromm

1. THE CONCEPT OF HUMAN NATURE

Marx did not believe, as do many contemporary sociologists and psychologists, that there is no such thing as the nature of man; that man at birth is like a blank sheet of paper, on which the culture writes its text. Quite in contrast to this sociological relativism, Marx started out with the idea that man *qua man* is a recognizable and ascertainable entity; that man can be defined as man not only biologically, anatomically and physiologically, but also psychologically.

Of course, Marx was never tempted to assume that "human nature" was identical with that particular expression of human nature prevalent in his own society. In arguing against Bentham, Marx said: "To know what is useful for a dog, one must study dog nature. This nature itself is not to be deducted from the principle of utility. Applying this to man, he that would criticize all human acts, movements, relations, etc., by the principle of utility, *must first deal with human nature in general, and then with human nature as modified in each historical epoch.*"[1] It must be noted that this concept of human nature is not, for Marx—as it was not either for Hegel—an abstraction. It is the *essence* of man—in contrast to the vari-

From: *Marx's Concept of Man* by Erich Fromm. Copyright © 1961, 1966 by Erich Fromm.

ous forms of his historical *existence*—and, as Marx said, "the essence of man is no abstraction inherent in each separate individual."[2] It must also be stated that this sentence from *Capital*, written by the "old Marx," shows the continuity of the concept of man's essence (Wesen) which the young Marx wrote about in the *Economic and Philosophical Manuscripts*. He no longer used the *term* "essence" later on, as being abstract and unhistorical, but he clearly retained the notion of this essence in a more historical version, in the differentiation between "human nature in general" and "human nature as modified" with each historical period.

In line with this distinction between a general human nature and the specific expression of human nature in each culture, Marx distinguishes, as we have already mentioned above, two types of human drives and appetites: the *constant* or fixed ones, such as hunger and the sexual urge, which are an integral part of human nature, and which can be changed only in their form and the direction they take in various cultures, and the *"relative"* appetites, which are not an integral part of human nature but which "owe their origin to certain social structures and certain conditions of production and communication."[3] Marx gives as an example the needs produced by the capitalistic structure of society. "The need for money," he wrote in the *Economic and Philosophical*

Manuscripts, "is therefore the real need created by the modern economy, and the only need which it creates. . . . This is shown subjectively, partly in the fact that the expansion of production and of needs becomes an *ingenious* and always *calculating* subservience to inhuman, depraved, unnatural, and *imaginary* appetites."[4]

Man's potential, for Marx, is a given potential; man is, as it were, the human raw material which, as such, cannot be changed, just as the brain structure has remained the same since the dawn of history. Yet, man *does* change in the course of history; he develops himself; he transforms himself, he is the product of history; since *he* makes his history, he is his own product. History is the history of man's self-realization; it is nothing but the self-creation of man through the process of his work and his production: "the *whole of what is called world history* is nothing but the creation of man by human labor, and the emergence of nature for man; he therefore has the evident and irrefutable proof of his *self-creation,* of his own *origins.*"[5]

2. MAN'S SELF-ACTIVITY

Marx's concept of man is rooted in Hegel's thinking. Hegel begins with the insight that appearance and essence do not coincide. The task of the dialectical thinker is "to distinguish the essential from the apparent process of reality, and to grasp their relations."[6] Or, to put it differently, it is the problem of the relationship between essence and existence. In the process of existence, the essence is realized, and at the same time, existing means a return to the essence. "The world is an estranged and untrue world so long as man does not destroy its dead objectivity and recognize himself and his own life 'behind' the fixed form of things and laws. When he finally wins this *self-consciousness,* he is on his way not only to the truth of himself,

but also of his world. And with the recognition goes the doing. He will try to put this truth into action, and *make* the world what it *essentially* is, namely, the fulfillment of man's self-consciousness."[7] For Hegel, knowledge is not obtained in the position of the subject-object split, in which the object is grasped as something separated from and opposed to the thinker. In order to *know* the world, man has to *make the world his own.* Man and things are in a constant transition from one *suchness* into another; hence "a thing is for itself only when it has posited (*gesetzt*) all its determinates and made them moments of its self-realization, and is thus, in all changing conditions, always 'returning to itself.' "[8] In this process "entering into itself becomes essence." This essence, the unity of being, the identity throughout change is, according to Hegel, a process in which "everything copes with its inherent contradictions and unfolds itself as a result." "The essence is thus as much historical as ontological. The essential potentialities of things realize themselves in the same comprehensive process that establishes their existence. The essence can 'achieve' its existence when the potentialities of things have ripened in and through the conditions of reality. Hegel describes this process as the transition to actuality."[9] In contrast to positivism, for Hegel "facts are facts only if related to that which is not yet fact and yet manifests itself in the given facts as a real possibility. Or, facts are what they are only as moments in a process that leads beyond them to that which is not yet fulfilled in fact."[10]

The culmination of all of Hegel's thinking is the concept of the potentialities inherent in a thing, of the dialectical process in which they manifest themselves, and the idea that this process is one of active movement of these potentialities. This emphasis on the active process within man is already to be found in the ethical system of Spinoza. For Spinoza, all affects were to be divided into passive affects (passions), through which man suffers and does not have an adequate idea of reality, and into active affects (actions) (generosity and fortitude) in which man is free and productive. Goethe, who like Hegel was influenced by Spinoza in many ways, developed the idea of man's productivity into a central point of his philosophical thinking. For him all decaying cultures are characterized by the tendency for pure subjectivity, while all progressive periods try to grasp the world as it is, by one's own subjectivity, but not separate from it.[11] He gives the example of the poet: "as long as he expresses only these few subjective sentences, he can not yet be called a poet, but as soon as he knows *how to appropriate the world for himself, and to express it,* he is a poet. Then he is inexhaustible, and can be ever new, while his purely subjective nature has exhausted itself soon and ceases to have anything to say."[12] "Man", says Goethe, "knows himself only inasmuch as he knows the world; he knows the world only within himself and he is aware of himself only within the world. Each new object truly recognized, opens up a new organ within ourselves."[13] Goethe gave the most poetic and powerful expression to the idea of human productivity in his *Faust.* Neither possession, nor power, nor sensuous satisfaction, Faust teaches, can fulfill man's desire for meaning in his life; he remains in all this separate from the whole, hence unhappy. Only in being productively active can man make sense of his life, and while he thus enjoys life, he is not greedily holding on to it. He has given up the greed for *having,* and is fulfilled by *being;* he is filled because he is empty; he *is* much, because he *has* little.[14] Hegel gave the most systematic and profound expression to the idea of the productive man, of the individual who is he, inasmuch as he is not passive-receptive, but actively related to the world; who is an individual only in this process of grasping the world productively, and thus making it his own. He expressed the idea quite poetically by saying that the subject wanting to bring a content to realization does

so by "translating itself from the night of possibility into the day of actuality." For Hegel the development of all individual powers, capacities and potentialities is possible only by continuous action, never by sheer contemplation or receptivity. For Spinoza, Goethe, Hegel, as well as for Marx, man is alive only inasmuch as he is productive, inasmuch as he grasps the world outside of himself in the act of expressing his own specific human powers, and of grasping the world with these powers. Inasmuch as man is not productive, inasmuch as he is receptive and passive, he is nothing, he is dead. In this productive process, man realizes his own essence, he returns to his own essence, which in theological language is nothing other than his return to God.

For Marx man is characterized by the "principle of movement," and it is significant that he quotes the great mystic Jacob Boehme in connection with this point.[15] The principle of movement must not be understood mechanically but as a drive, creative vitality, energy; human passion for Marx "is the essential power of man striving energetically for its object."

The concept of productivity as against that of receptivity can be understood more easily when we read how Marx applied it to the phenomenon of *love.* "Let us assume *man* to be *man,*" he wrote, "and his relation to the world to be a human one. Then love can only be exchanged for love, trust for trust, etc. If you wish to influence other people you must be a person who really has a stimulating and encouraging effect upon others. Every one of your relations to man and to nature must be a *specific expression* corresponding to the object of your will, of your *real individual life.* If you love without evoking love in return, i.e., if you are not able, by the *manifestation* of yourself as a loving person, to make yourself a *beloved person,* then your love is impotent and a misfortune."[16] Marx expressed also very specifically the central significance of love between man and woman as the immediate relationship of human being to human being. Arguing against a crude communism which proposed the communalization of all sexual relation, Marx wrote: "In the relationship with *woman,* as the prey and the handmaid of communal lust, is expressed the infinite degradation in which man exists for himself; for the secret of this relationship finds its *unequivocal,* incontestable, *open* and revealed expression in the relation of man to woman and in the way in which the *direct* and *natural* species relationship is conceived. The immediate, natural and necessary relation of human being to human being is also the *relation* of *man* to *woman.* In this *natural* species relationship man's relation to nature is directly his relation to man, and his relation to man is directly his relation to nature, to his own *natural* function. Thus, in this relation is *sensuously revealed,* reduced to an observable *fact,* the extent to which human nature has become nature for man and to which nature has become human nature for him. From this relationship man's whole level of development can be assessed. It follows from the character of this relationship how far *man* has become, and has understood himself as, a *species-being,* a *human being.* The relation of man to woman is the *most natural* relation of human being to human being. It indicates, therefore, how far man's *natural* behavior has become *human,* and how far his *human* essence has become a *natural* essence for him, how far his *human nature* has become *nature* for him. It also shows how far man's *needs* have become *human* needs, and consequently how far the other person, as a person, has become one of his needs, and to what extent he is in his individual existence at the same time a social being."[17]

It is of the utmost importance for the understanding of Marx's concept of activity to understand his idea about the relationship between subject and object. Man's senses, as far as they are crude animal senses, have only a restricted meaning. "For a starving man the human form of food does not exist, but only its abstract char-

acter as food. It could just as well exist in the most crude form, and it is impossible to say in what way this feeding activity would differ from that of animals. The needy man, burdened with cares, has no appreciation of the most beautiful spectacle."[18] The senses which man has, so to speak, naturally, need to be formed by the objects outside of them. Any object can only be confirmation of one of my own faculties. "For is it not only the five senses but also the so-called spiritual senses, the practical senses (desiring, loving, etc.) in brief, human sensibility and the human character of the senses *which can only come into being* through the existence of *its* object, through humanized nature."[19] The objects, for Marx, "confirm and realize his [man's] individuality . . . *The manner in which* these objects become his own depends upon the *nature of the object* and the nature of the corresponding faculty; . . . The *distinctive character* of each faculty is precisely its *characteristic* essence and thus also the characteristic mode of its objectification, of its *objectively real,* living *being.* It is therefore not only in thought, but through *all* the senses that man is affirmed in the objective world."[20]

By relating himself to the objective world, through his powers, the world outside becomes real to man, and in fact it is only "love" which makes man truly believe in the reality of the objective world outside himself.[21] Subject and object cannot be separated. "The eye has become a *human* eye when its *object* has become a *human,* social object, created by man and destined for him . . . They [the senses] relate themselves to the thing for the sake of the thing, but the thing itself is an *objective human* relation to itself and to man, and vice versa. Need and enjoyment have thus lost their *egoistic* character, and nature has lost its mere *utility* by the fact that its utilization has become *human* utilization. (In effect, I can only relate myself in a human way to a thing when the thing is related in a human way to man.)"[22]

For Marx, "*Communism* is the *positive* abolition of *private property,*[23] of *human self-alienation,* and thus the real *appropriation* of human nature through and for man. It is, therefore, the return of man himself as a *social,* i.e., really human being, a complete and conscious return which assimilates all the wealth of previous development. Communism as a fully developed naturalism is humanism and as a fully developed humanism is naturalism. It is the *definitive* resolution of the antagonism between man and nature, and between man and man. It is the true solution of the conflict between existence and essence, between objectification and self-affirmation, between freedom and necessity, between individual and species. It is the solution of the riddle of history and knows itself to be this solution."[24] This active relationship to the objective world, Marx calls "productive life." "It is life creating life. In the type of life activity resides the whole character of a species, its species-character; and free, conscious activity is the species-character of human beings."[25] What Marx means by "species-character" is the essence of man; it is that which is universally human, and which is realized in the process of history by man through his productive activity.

From this concept of human self-realization, Marx arrives at a new concept of wealth and poverty, which is different from wealth and poverty in political economy. "It will be seen from this," says Marx, "how, in place of the *wealth* and *poverty* of political economy, we have the *wealthy* man and the plentitude of *human* need. The wealthy man is at the same time one who needs a complex of human manifestations of life, and whose own self-realization exists as an inner necessity, a *need.* Not only the *wealth* but also the *poverty* of man acquires, in a socialist perspective, a *human* and thus a social meaning. Poverty is the passive bond which leads man to experience a need for the greatest wealth, the *other* person. The sway of the objective entity within me; the sensuous outbreak of my life-activity, is the passion which here becomes the *activity* of my being."[26] The same idea was expressed by Marx some years earlier: "The existence of what I truly love [specifically he refers here to freedom of the press] is felt by me as a necessity, as a need, without which my essence cannot be fulfilled, satisfied, complete."[27]

"Just as society at its beginnings finds, through the development of *private property* with its wealth and poverty (both intellectual and material), the materials necessary for this *cultural development,* so the fully constituted society produces man in all the plentitude of his being, the wealthy man endowed with all the senses, as an enduring reality. It is only in a social context that subjectivism and objectivism, spiritualism and materialism, activity and passivity, cease to be antinomies and thus cease to exist as such antinomies. The resolution of the *theoretical* contradictions is possible *only* through *practical* means, only through the practical energy of man. Their resolution is not by any means, therefore, only a problem of knowledge, but is a *real* problem of life which philosophy was unable to solve precisely because it saw there a purely theoretical problem."[28]

Corresponding to his concept of the wealthy man is Marx's view of the difference between the sense of *having* and the sense of *being.* "Private property," he says, "has made us so stupid and partial that an object is only *ours* when we have it, when it exists for us as capital or when it is directly eaten, drunk, worn, inhabited, etc., in short, *utilized* in some way. Although private property itself only conceives these various forms of possession as *means of life,* and the life for which they serve as means is the *life* of *private property*—labor and creation of capital. Thus *all* the physical and intellectual senses have been replaced by the simple alienation of *all* these senses; the sense of *having.* The human being had to be reduced to this absolute poverty in order to be able to give birth to all his inner wealth."[29]

Marx recognized that the science of capitalistic economy, despite its worldly and pleasure-seeking appearance, "is a truly moral science, the most moral of all sciences. Its principal thesis is the renunciation of life and of human needs. The less you eat, drink, buy books, go to the theatre or to balls, or to the public house [*Br.*, pub], and the less you think, love, theorize, sing, paint, fence, etc., the more you will be able to save and the *greater* will become your treasure which neither moth nor rust will corrupt—your *capital*. The less you *are*, the less you express your life, the more you *have*, the greater is your *alienated* life and the greater is the saving of your alienated being. Everything which the economist takes from you in the way of life and humanity, he restores to you in the form of *money* and *wealth*. And everything which you are unable to do, your money can do for you; it can eat, drink, go to the ball and to the theatre. It can acquire art, learning, historical treasures, political power; and it can travel. It *can* appropriate all these things for you, can purchase everything; it is the true *opulence*. But although it can do all this, it only *desires* to create itself, and to buy itself, for everything else is subservient to it. When one owns the master, one also owns the servant, and one has no need of the master's servant. Thus all passions and activities must be submerged in *avarice*. The worker must have just what is necessary for him to want to live, and he must want to live only in order to have this."[30]

The aim of society, for Marx, is not the production of useful things as an aim in itself. One easily forgets, he says, "that the production of too many useful things results in too many *useless* people."[31] The contradictions between prodigality and thrift, luxury and abstinence, wealth and poverty, are only apparent because the truth is that all these antinomies are equivalent. It is particularly important to understand this position of Marx today, when both the Communist, and most of the Socialist parties, with some notable exceptions like the Indian,

also Burmese and a number of European and American socialists, have accepted the principle which underlies all capitalist systems, namely, that maximum production and consumption are the unquestionable goals of society. One must of course not confuse the aim of overcoming the abysmal poverty which interferes with a dignified life, with the aim of an ever-increasing consumption, which has become the supreme value for both Capitalism and Khrushchevism. Marx's position was quite clearly on the side of the conquest of poverty, and equally against consumption as a supreme end.

Independence and *freedom*, for Marx, are based on the act of self-creation. "A being does not regard himself as independent unless he is his own master, and he is only his own master when he owes his existence to himself. A man who lives by the favor of another considers himself a dependent being. But I live completely by another person's favor when I owe to him not only the continuance of my life but also *its creation;* when he is its *source*. My life has necessarily such a cause outside itself if it is not my own creation."[32] Or, as Marx put it, man is independent only ". . . if he affirms his individuality as a total man in each of his relations to the world, seeing, hearing, smelling, tasting, feeling, thinking, willing, loving—in short, if he affirms and expresses all organs of his individuality," if he is not only free *from* but also free *to*.

For Marx the aim of socialism was the emancipation of man, and the emancipation of man was the same as his self-realization in the process of productive relatedness and oneness with man and nature. The aim of socialism was the development of the individual personality. What Marx would have thought of a system such as Soviet communism he expressed very clearly in a statement of what he called "crude communism," and which referred to certain communist ideas and practices of his time. This crude communism "appears in a double form;

the domination of material property looms so large that it aims to destroy everything which is incapable of being possessed by everyone as private property. It wishes to eliminate talent, etc., by *force*. Immediate physical possession seems to it the unique goal of life and existence. The role of *worker* is not abolished but is extended to all men. The relation of private property remains the relation of the community to the world of things. Finally, this tendency to oppose general private property to private property is expressed in an animal form; *marriage* which is incontestably a form of *exclusive private property*) is contrasted with the community of women,[33] in which women become communal and common property. One may say that this idea of the *community of women* is the *open secret* of this entirely crude and unreflective communism. Just as women are to pass from marriage to universal prostitution, so the whole world of wealth (i.e., the objective being of man) is to pass to the relation of universal prostitution with the community. This communism, which negates the *personality* of man in every sphere, is only the logical expression of private property, which *is* this negation. Universal *envy* setting itself up as a power is only a camouflaged form of cupidity which reestablishes itself and satisfies itself in a different way. The thoughts of every individual private property are *at least* directed against any *wealthier* private property, in the form of envy and the desire to reduce everything to a common level; so that this envy and levelling in fact constitute the essence of competition. Crude communism is only the culmination of such envy and levelling-down on the basis of a *preconceived* minimum. How little this abolition of private property represents a genuine appropriation is shown by the abstract negation of the whole world of culture and civilization, and the regression to the *unnatural* simplicity of the poor and wantless individual who has not only not surpassed private property but has not yet even attained to it. The com-

munity is only a community of *work* and of *equality of wages* paid out by the communal capital, by the *community* as universal capitalist. The two sides of the relation are raised to a *supposed* universality; *labor* as a condition in which everyone is placed, and *capital* as the acknowledged universality and power of the community."[34]

Marx's whole concept of the self-realization of man can be fully understood only in connection with his concept of work. First of all, it must be noted that labor and capital were not at all for Marx only economic categories; they were anthropological categories, imbued with a value judgment which is rooted in his humanistic position. Capital, which is that which is accumulated, represents the past; labor, on the other hand is, or ought to be when it is free, the expression of life. "In bourgeois society," says Marx in the *Communist Manifesto*," . . . the past dominates the present. In communist society the present dominates the past. In bourgeois society, capital is independent and has individuality, while the living person is dependent and has no individuality." Here again, Marx follows the thought of Hegel, who understood labor as the "act of man's self-creation." Labor, to Marx, is an activity, not a commodity. Marx originally called man's function "self-activity," not labor, and spoke of the "abolition of labor" as the aim of socialism. Later, when he differentiated between free and alienated labor, he used the term "emancipation of labor."

"Labor is, in the first place, a process in which both man and nature participate, and in which man of his own accord starts, regulates, and controls the material reactions between himself and nature. He opposes himself to nature as one of her own forces, setting in motion arms and legs, head and hands, the natural forces of his body, in order to appropriate nature's productions in a form adapted to his own wants. By thus acting on the external world and changing it, he at the same time changes his own nature. He develops his slumbering powers and compels them to act in obedience to his sway. We are not now dealing with those primitive instinctive forms of labor that remind us of the mere animal. An immeasurable interval of time separates the state of things in which a man brings his labor power to market for sale as a commodity, from that state in which human labor was still in its first instinctive stage. We presuppose labor in a form that stamps it as exclusively human. A spider conducts operations that resemble those of a weaver, and a bee puts to shame many an architect in the construction of her cells. But what distinguishes the worst architect from the best of bees is this, that the architect raises his structure in imagination before he erects it in reality. At the end of every labor process, we get a result that already existed in the imagination of the laborer at its commencement. He not only effects a change of form in the material on which he works, but he also realizes a purpose of his own that gives the law to his modus operandi, and to which he must subordinate his will. And this subordination is no mere momentary act. Besides the exertion of the bodily organs, the process demands that, during the whole operation, the workman's will be steadily in consonance with his purpose. This means close attention. The less he is attracted by the nature of the work, and the mode in which it is carried on, and the less, therefore, he enjoys it as something which gives play to his bodily and mental powers, the more close his attention is forced to be."[35]

Labor is the self-expression of man, an expression of his individual physical and mental powers. In this process of genuine activity man develops himself, becomes himself; work is not only a means to an end—the product—but an end in itself, the meaningful expression of human energy; hence work is enjoyable.

Marx's central criticism of capitalism is not the injustice in the distribution of wealth; it is the perversion of labor into forced, alienated, meaningless labor, hence the transformation of

man into a "crippled monstrosity." Marx's concept of labor as an expression of man's individuality is succinctly expressed in his vision of the complete abolition of the lifelong submersion of a man in one occupation. Since the aim of human development is that of the development of the total, universal man, man must be emancipated from the crippling influence of specialization. In all previous societies, Marx writes, man has been "a hunter, a fisherman, a shepherd, or a critical critic, and must remain so if he does not want to lose his means of livelihood; while in communist society, where nobody has one exclusive sphere of activity but each can become accomplished in any branch he wishes, society regulates the general production and thus makes it possible for me to do one thing today and another tomorrow, to hunt in the morning, fish in the afternoon, rear cattle in the evening, criticize after dinner, just as I have a mind, without ever becoming hunter, fisherman, shepherd or critic."[36]

There is no greater misunderstanding or misrepresentation of Marx than that which is to be found, implicitly or explicitly, in the thought of the Soviet Communists, the reformist socialists, and the capitalist opponents of socialism alike, all of whom assume that Marx wanted only the economic improvement of the working class, and that he wanted to abolish private property so that the worker would own what the capitalist now has. The truth is that for Marx the situation of a worker in a Russian "socialist factory, a British state-owned factory, or an American factory such as General Motors, would appear essentially the same. This, Marx expresses very clearly in the following:

"An enforced *increase in wages* (disregarding the other difficulties, and especially that such an anomaly could only be maintained by force) would be nothing more than a *better remuneration of slaves,* and would not restore, either to the worker or to the work, their human significance and worth.

"Even the *equality of incomes* which Proudhon demands would only change the relation of the present-day worker to his work into a relation of all men to work. Society would then be conceived as an abstract capitalist."[37]

The central theme of Marx is the transformation of alienated, meaningless labor into productive, free labor, not the better payment of alienated labor by a private or "abstract" state capitalism.

NOTES

1.   *Capital I*, l.c., p. 668.

2.   *German Ideology*, l.c., p. 198.

3.   "Heilige Familie," *MEGA V*, p. 359. [My translation—E.F.]

4.   *E.P. MSS.*, p. 141.

5.   *E.P. MSS.*, p. 139.

6.   H. Marcuse, *Reason and Revolution*, Oxford University Press, New York, 1941, p. 146.

7.   Marcuse, l.c., p. 113.

8.   Marcuse, l.c., p. 142. Cf. Hegel, *Science and Logic*, Vol. I, p. 404.

9.   Marcuse, l.c., p. 149.

10.   Marcuse, l.c., p. 152.

11.   Cf. Goethe's conversation with Eckermann, January 29, 1826.

12.   Goethe, conversation with Eckermann on January 29, 1826. [My italics, and translation—E.F.]

13.   Quoted by K. Löwith, *Von Hegel zu Nietzsche*, W. Kohlhammer Verlag, Stuttgart, 1941, p. 24. [My translation—E.F.]

14.   Cf. the detailed description of the productive character orientation in E. Fromm, *Man for Himself*, Rinehart & Co., New York: 1947.

15.   Cf. H. Popitz, "*Der entfremdete Mensch*" (The Alienated Man) Verlag für Recht und Gesellschaft, A.G., Basel, p. 119.

16.   *E.P. MSS.*, p. 168.

17.   *E.P. MSS.*, pp. 126–7.

18.   *E.P. MSS.*, p. 134.

19.   *E.P. MSS.*, p. 134.

20.   *E.P. MSS.*, p. 133.

21.   *MEGA, Vol. III*, p. 191.

22.   *E.P. MSS.*, p. 132. This last statement is one which is almost literally the same as has been made in Zen Buddhist thinking, as well as by Goethe. In fact, the thinking of Goethe, Hegel and Marx is closely related to the thinking of Zen. What is common to them is the idea that man overcomes the subject-object split; the object is an object, yet it ceases to be an object, and in this new approach man becomes one with the object, although he and it remain two. Man, in relating himself to the objective world humanly, overcomes self-alienation.

23.   By "private property" as used here and in other statements, Marx never refers to the private property of things for use (such as a house, a table, etc.) Marx refers to the property of the "propertied classes," that is, of the capitalist who, because he owns the means of production, can hire the property-less individual to work for him, under conditions the latter is forced to accept. "Private property" in Marx's usage, then, always refers to private *property within capitalist class society* and thus is a *social and historical category;* the term does not refer to things for use, as for instance, in a socialist society.

24.   *E.P. MSS.*, p. 127.

25.   *E.P. MSS.*, p. 101.

26.   *E.P. MSS.*, pp. 137–8. This dialectic concept of the wealthy man as being the poor man in need of others is, in many ways, similar to the concept of poverty expressed by Meister Eckhart, in his sermon "Blessed Are the Poor," (Meister Eckhart, transl. by R. B. Blakney, Harper and Bros., New York, 1941).

27.   *MEGA I,* i a p. 184.

28.   *E.P. MSS.*, pp. 134–5.

29.   *E.P. MSS.*, p. 132.

30.   *E.P. MSS.*, pp. 144–5.

31.   *E.P. MSS.*, p. 145.

32.   *E.P. MSS.*, p. 138.

33.   Marx refers here to speculations among certain eccentric communist thinkers of his time who thought that if everything is common property women should be too.

34.   *E.P. MSS.*, pp. 124–6.

35.   *Capital I*, l.c. p. 197–8.

36.   *German Ideology*, l.c. p. 22.

37.   *E.P. MSS.*, p. 107.

10 Man as Symbol Maker

Langer

The classical definition of man as a rational animal has often been attacked not only because it fails to take into account the irrational components of human nature but also because it fails to take into account other uniquely human endowments. The neo-Kantian German philosopher Ernst Cassirer (1874–1945), first in *Philosophy of Symbolic Forms* and later in *An Essay on Man* (1944), developed a theory of human nature that went beyond the undeniable rational components to stress the capacity for symbol creation —the most distinctive and important characteristic of man and human consciousness. Cassirer's philosophy strongly influenced the American philosopher Susanne Langer who popularized it, modified it, and used it as the basis for further reflection in *Philosophy in a New Key* (1942) and *Feeling and Form* (1953).

Human life at the biological level is governed by the rules of all organic life, Cassirer recognized, but as man developed, he discovered "a new method of adapting himself to his environment,"[1] a method of symbolic creation and manipulation that transformed the entire spectrum of human experience. Man is not limited to organic reactions and awareness of signals, but he is able to have highly complex, genuinely human responses to new dimensions of reality through the contemplation and use of symbolic systems. The universe is not merely physical; man lives, and moves, and has his being in a symbolic universe of language, myth, art, and religion, giving order, coherence, and higher significance to human experience. Man does not deal just with things, but rather he deals with things as they appear to be within the network of symbolism. Emotion is a familiar aspect of day to day experience. Rationality is an integral and essential part of human activities.

Although the rational meanings of language, myth, religion, and art must be taken into account, their nature as forms that are symbolic of human feeling and emotion also must be understood. Cassirer asserted that "side by side with conceptual language there is an emotional language; side by side with logical or scientific language there is a language of poetic imagination."[2] We cannot understand human life unless we understand the symbolic thought and symbolic behavior at its uniquely human core. Human nature is more (and sometimes less) than an *animal rationale,* a rational animal; man is also an *animal symbolicum,* a symbolizing animal.

From this point of view, Cassirer undertook to develop a philosophy of symbolic forms based on the presupposition that "if there is any definition or 'essence' of man, this definition can only be understood as a functional one, not a substantial one."[3] For this reason Cassirer did not dwell on the metaphysical or physical nature of man; he focused on man's work, on what he created. For "it is this work, it is the system of human activities, which defines and determines the circle of 'humanity'." In Cassirer's view language, myth, religion, art, science, and history are "the constituents, the various sectors of this circle."[4] If we can develop a philosophical anthropology or coherent philosophy of human nature, we will understand better the fundamental structure underlying each of its symbolic activities and their relationship to one another. There is a common bond, a unity of creative process which holds these activities together in both enclosing (or defining) and expanding human experience.

Using Cassirer's views as a point of departure for further reflection, Susanne Langer devoted much attention to the process of symbolic transformation, especially as it is manifested in art. Instead of focusing on beauty or on some other general category, she developed an aesthetic theory by reflecting on the problem of artistic creation. In *Feeling and Form* she interpreted artistic creation as a process of finding significant forms for the expression of feeling. Expressing feeling does not mean, in her view, revealing the artist's states of mind or manifesting his personality, but it means creating nondiscursive symbols to serve as analogues for the feeling. Music "sounds the way feelings feel" because the pattern of sounds is tonally analogous to the composer's (and the listener's) emotive life. But as the feelings are not expressed through words (discursive symbols) but through sounds (nondiscursive symbols), we should refer not to the music's meaning but rather to its "vital import." This is expressed sensuously through the structure of sounds, the significant form of a musical composition.

Having defined art as "the creation of forms symbolic of feeling,"[5] Langer explained the significance of the various art forms, each of which creates a "purely virtual" (i.e., illusory) object, an image or semblance through which aesthetic feeling can be expressed. Painting expresses the semblance of a virtual three-dimensional space, an illusion of scene. Sculpture makes tactual space visible by creating the semblance of living forms, the import of vital functions; it is essentially "the image of kinetic volume in sensory space."[6] Architecture creates a different semblance of space, that which Langer called "an ethnic domain" or "a virtual place."[7] Such is the nature of the plastic arts.

The "occurrent arts"—music, dance, literature, and drama—were also discussed by Langer as expressive forms which create illusory realms of experience and reveal the emotional significance of things. Since art can reveal to us our innermost life, its importance cannot be overestimated. For without art, our experience would lack coherence or completeness of form. The significance of feeling would not and could not be apparent without aesthetic form. The artist molds the forms that are symbols of feelings and these forms, in turn, mold actual feelings. This is the basis of all aesthetic education. Like John Dewey, Langer opposed the view that art is merely "a cultural veneer" or "a beauty parlor of civilization." She also believed that the arts offer far more than simple diversion, entertainment, and escape from everyday life. Langer saw the world of art as a valuable "school of feeling," a source of exaltation, and a defense against inner and outer chaos.

Although Langer probably is best known for her aesthetic theory and for her detailed analysis of feeling, she has also occasionally made notable contributions to social philosophy. One of these was as an incisive analysis of the fundamental differences between human and animal expression. As an advocate of open society, Langer rejected organismic theories of human nature and stressed social organization as a reflection of man's need for symbolization.

NOTES

1.   Ernst Cassirer, *An Essay on Man* (New Haven, Conn.: Yale University Press, 1953), p. 24.

2.   Ibid., p. 24.

3.   Ibid., p. 68.

4.   Ibid.

5.   Susanne K. Langer, *Philosophical Sketches* (New York: New American Library, 1962), p. 76.

6.   Susanne K. Langer, *Feeling and Form* (New York: Charles Scribner's Sons, 1959), p. 92.

7.   Ibid., p. 95.

Man and Animal:
The City and the Hive

Within the past five or six decades, the human scene has probably changed more radically than ever before in history. The outward changes in our own setting are already an old story: the disappearance of horse-drawn vehicles, riders, children walking to school, and the advent of the long, low, powerful Thing in their stead; the transformation of the mile-wide farm into a ticktacktoe of lots, each sprouting a split-level dream home. These are the obvious changes, more apparent in the country than in the city. The great cities have grown greater, brighter, more mechanized, but their basic patterns seem less shaken by the new power and speed in which the long industrial revolution culminates.

The deepest change, however, is really a change in our picture of mankind, and that is most spectacular where mankind is teeming and concentrated—in the city. Our old picture of human life was a picture of local groups, each speaking its mother tongue, observing some established religion, following its own customs. It might be a civilized community or a savage tribe, but it had its distinct traditions. And in it were subdivisions, usually families, with their more special local ties and human relations.

From Susanne K. Langer, "Man and Animal: The City and the Hive," in *Philosophical Sketches* (Baltimore: Johns Hopkins Press, 1962).

Today, natural tribes and isolated communities have all but disappeared. The ease and speed of travel, the swift economic changes that send people in search of new kinds of work, the two wars that swept over all boundaries, have wiped out most of our traditions. The old family structure is tottering. Society tends to break up into new and smaller units—in fact, into its ultimate units, the human individuals that compose it.

This atomization of society is most obvious in a great cosmopolitan city. The city seems to be composed of millions of unrelated individuals, each scrambling for himself, yet each caught in the stream of all the others.

Discerning eyes saw this a hundred years ago, especially in industrial cities, where individuals from far or near came to do what other individuals from far or near had also come to do—each a cog in the new machine. Most of the cogs had no other relation to each other. And ever since this shake-up in society began, a new picture of society has been in the making—the picture of *human masses*, brought together by some outside force, some imposed function, into a superpersonal unit—masses of people, each representing an atom of "manpower" in a new sort of organism, the industrial state.

The idea of the state as a higher organism —the state as a superindividual—is old. But our conception of such a state is new, because our industrial civilization, which begets our atomized society, is new. The old picture was not one of masses driven by some imposed economic power, or any other outside power. The superindividual was a rational being, directed by a mind within it. The guardians of the state, the rulers, were its mind. Plato described the state as "the man writ large." Hobbes, two thousand years later, called it "Leviathan," the great creature. A city-state like ancient Athens or Sparta might be "a man writ large," but England was too big for that. It was the big fish in the big pond. The mind of Hobbes's fish was perhaps subhuman, but it was still single and sovereign in the organism.

Another couple of centuries later, Rudyard Kipling, faced with a democratic, industrialized civilization, called his allegory of England, "The Mother Hive." Here, a common will, dictated by complicated instincts, replaced even Leviathan's mind; each individual was kept in line by the blind forces of the collective life.

The image of the hive has had a great success as an ideal of collaborative social action. Every modern utopia (except the completely wishful Shangri-La) reflects the beehive ideal. Even a statesman of highest caliber, Jan Smuts, has praised it as a pattern for industrial society. Plato's personified state and Hobbes's sea monster impress us as fantasies, but the hive looks like more than a poetic figure; it seems really to buzz around us.

I think the concept of the state as a collective organism, composed of multitudes of little workers, guided by social forces that none of the little workers can fathom, and accomplishing some greater destiny, is supported by a factor other than our mechanized industry; that other factor is a momentous event in our intellectual history: the spread of the theory of evolution.

First biologists, then psychologists, and finally sociologists and moralists have become nèwly aware that man belongs to the animal kingdom. The impact of the concept of evolution on scientific discovery has been immense, and it has not stopped at laboratory science; it has also produced some less sober and sound inspirations. The concept of continuous animal evolution has made most psychologists belittle the differences between man and his nonhuman relatives, and led some of them, indeed, to think of *Homo sapiens* as just one kind of primate among others, like the others in all essential respects—differing from apes and monkeys not much more than they differ from species to species among themselves. Gradually the notion of the human animal became common currency, questioned only by some religious minds. This in turn has made it natural for social theorists with scientific leanings to model their concepts of human society on animal societies, the anthill and the beehive.

Perhaps it were well, at this point, to say that I myself stand entirely in the scientific camp. I do not argue against any religious or even vitalistic doctrines; such things are not arguable. I speak not *for*, but *from*, a naturalist's point of view, and anyone who does not share it can make his own reservations in judging what I say.

Despite man's zoological status, which I wholeheartedly accept, there is a deep gulf between the highest animal and the most primitive normal human being: a difference in mentality that is fundamental. It stems from the development of one new process in the human brain—a process that seems to be entirely peculiar to that brain: the use of *symbols for ideas.* By "symbols" I mean all kinds of signs that can be used and understood whether the things they refer to are there or not. The word "symbol" has, unfortunately, many different meanings for different people. Some people reserve it for mystic signs, like Rosicrucian symbols; some mean by it *significant images,* such as Keats' "Huge cloudy symbols of a high romance"; some use it quite the opposite way and speak of "mere symbols," meaning empty gestures, signs that have lost their meanings; and some, notably logicians, use the term for mathematical signs, marks that constitute a code, a brief, concise language. In their sense, ordinary words are symbols, too. Ordinary language is a symbolism.

When I say that the distinctive function of the human brain is the use of symbols, I mean any and all of these kinds. They are all different from signs that animals use. Animals interpret signs, too, but only as pointers to actual things and events, cues to action or expectation, threats and promises, landmarks and earmarks in the world. Human beings use such signs, too, but above all they use symbols—especially words—to think and talk about things that are neither present nor expected. The words convey *ideas,* that may or may not have counterparts in actuality. This power of thinking *about* things expresses itself in language, imagination, and speculation—the chief products of human mentality that animals do not share.

Language, the most versatile and indispensable of all symbolisms, has put its stamp on all our mental functions, so that I think they always differ from even their closest analogues in animal life. Language has invaded our feeling and dreaming and action, as well as our reasoning, which is really a product of it. The greatest change wrought by language is the increased scope of awareness in speech-gifted beings. An animal's awareness is always of things in its own place and life. In human awareness, the present, actual situation is often the least part. We have not only memories and expectations; we have *a past* in which we locate our memories, and *a future* that vastly overreaches our own anticipations. Our past is a story, our future a piece of imagination. Likewise our ambient is a place in a wider, symbolically conceived place, the universe. We live in *a world.*

This difference of mentality between man and animal seems to me to make a cleft between them almost as great as the division between animals and plants. There is continuity between the orders, but the division is real nevertheless. Human life differs radically from animal life. By virtue of our incomparably wider awareness, of our power of envisagement of things and events beyond any actual perception, we have acquired needs and aims that animals do not have; and even the most savage human society, having to meet those needs and implement those aims, is not really comparable to any animal society. The two may have some analogous functions, but the essential structure must be different, because man and beast live differently in every way.

Probably the profoundest difference between human and animal needs is made by one piece of human awareness, one fact that is not present to animals, because it is never learned in any direct experience: that is our foreknowledge of death. The fact that we ourselves must die is not a simple and isolated fact. It is built on a wide survey of facts that discloses the structure of history as a succession of overlapping brief lives, the patterns of youth and age, growth and decline; and above all that, it is built on the logical insight that *one's own life is a case in point.* Only a creature that can think symbolically *about* life can conceive of its own death. Our knowledge of death is part of our knowledge of life.

What, then, do we—all of us—know about life?

Every life that we know is generated from other life. Each living thing springs from some other living thing or things. Its birth is a process of new individuation, in a life stream whose beginning we do not know.

Individuation is a word we do not often meet. We hear about individuality, sometimes spoken in praise, sometimes as an excuse for someone's being slightly crazy. We hear and read about "the individual," a being that is forever adjusting, like a problem child, to something called "society." But how does individuality arise? What makes an individual? A fundamental, biological process of *individuation*, that marks the life of every stock, plant or animal. Life is a series of individuations, and these can be of various sorts, and reach various degrees.

Most people would agree, offhand, that every creature lives its life and then dies. This might, indeed, be called a truism. But, like some other truisms, it is not true. The lowest forms of life, such as the amoebae, normally (that is, barring accidents) do not die. When they grow very large and might be expected to lay eggs, or in some other way raise a family, they do no such thing; they divide, and make two small ones ready to grow. Well now, where is the old one? It did not die. But it is gone. Its individuation was only an episode in the life of the stock, a phase, a transient form that changed again. Amoebae are individuated in space—they move and feed as independent, whole organisms—but in time they are not self-identical individuals. They do not generate young ones while they themselves grow old; they grow old and *become* young ones.

All the higher animals, however, are final individuations that end in death. They spring from a common stock, but they do not merge back into it. Each one is an end. Somewhere on its way toward death it usually produces a new life to succeed it, but its own story is finished by death.

That is our pattern, too. Each human individual is a culmination of an inestimably long line—its ancestry—and each is destined to die. The living stock is like a palm tree, a trunk composed of its own past leaves. Each leaf springs from the trunk, unfolds, grows, and dies off; its past is incorporated in the trunk, where new life has usually arisen from it. So there constantly are ends, but the stock lives on, and each leaf has that whole life behind it.

The momentous difference between us and our animal cousins is that they do not know they are going to die. Animals spend their lives avoiding death, until it gets them. They do not know it is going to. Neither do they know that they are part of a greater life, but pass on the torch without knowing. Their aim, then, is simply to keep going, to function, to escape trouble, to live from moment to moment in an endless Now.

Our power of symbolic conception has given us each a glimpse of himself as one final individuation from the great human stock. We do not know when or what the end will be, but we know that there will be one. We also envisage a past and future, a stretch of time so vastly longer than any creature's memory, and a world so much richer than any world of sense, that it makes our time in that world seem infinitesimal. This is the price of the great gift of symbolism.

In the face of such uncomfortable prospects (probably conceived long before the dawn of any religious ideas), human beings have evolved aims different from those of any other creatures. Since we cannot have our fill of existence by going on and on, we want to have *as much life as possible* in our short span. If our individuation must be brief, we want to make it complete; so we are inspired to think, act, dream our desires, create things, express our ideas, and in all sorts of ways make up by concentration what we cannot have by length of days. We seek the greatest possible individuation, or development of personality. In doing this, we have set up a new demand, not for mere continuity of existence, but for *self-realization*. That is a uniquely human aim.

But obviously, the social structure could not arise on this principle alone. Vast numbers of individualists realizing themselves with a vengeance would not make up an ideal society. A small number might try it; there is a place, far away from here, called the Self-Realization Golden World Colony. But most of us have no golden world to colonize. You can only do that south of Los Angeles.

Seriously, however, an ideal is not disposed of by pointing out that it cannot be implemented under existing conditions. It may still be a true ideal; and if it is very important we may have to change the conditions, as we will have to for the ideal of world peace. If complete individuation were really the whole aim of human life, our society would be geared to it much more than it is. It is not the golden world that is wanting, but something else; the complete individualist is notoriously not the happy man, even if good fortune permits his antics.

The fact is that *the greatest possible individuation* is usually taken to mean, "as much as is possible without curtailing the rights of others." But that is not the real measure of how much is possible. The measure is provided in the individual himself, and is as fundamental as his knowledge of death. It is the other part of his insight into nature—his knowledge of life, of the great unbroken stream, the life of the stock from which his individuation stems.

One individual life, however rich, still looks infinitesimal; no matter how much self-realization is concentrated in it, it is a tiny atom—and we don't like to be tiny atoms, not even hydrogen atoms. We need more than fullness of personal life to counter our terrible knowledge of all it implies. And we have more; we have our history, our commitments made for us before we were born, our relatedness to the rest of mankind. The counterpart of individuation from the great life of the stock is our rootedness in that life, our involvement with the whole human race, past and present.

Each person is not only a free, single end, like the green palm leaf that unfolds, grows in a curve of beauty, and dies in its season; he is like the whole palm leaf, the part inside the trunk, too. He is the culmination of his entire ancestry, and *represents* that whole human past. In his brief individuation he is an *expression* of all humanity. That is what makes each person's life sacred and all-important. A single ruined life is the bankruptcy of a long line. This is what I mean by the individual's involvement with all mankind.

All animals are unconsciously involved with their kind. Heredity governs not only their growth, color, and form, but their actions, too. They carry their past about with them in everything they do. But they do not know it. They don't need to, because they never could lose it. Their involvement with the greater life of the race is implicit in their limited selfhood.

Our knowledge that life is finite, and, in fact, precarious and brief, drives us on to greater individuation than animals attain. Our mental talents have largely freed us from that built-in behavior called instinct. The scope of our imagination gives each of us a separate world, and a separate consciousness, and threatens to break the instinctual ties of brotherhood that make all the herrings swim into one net, and all the geese turn their heads at the same moment. Yet we cannot afford to lose the feeling of involvement with our kind; for if we do, personal life shrinks up to nothingness.

The sense of involvement is our social sense. We have it by nature, originally just as animals do, and just as unconsciously. It is the direct feeling of needing our own kind, caring what happens. Social sense is an instinctive sense of being somehow one with all other people—a feeling that reflects the rootedness of our existence in a human past. Human society rests on this feeling. It is often said to rest on the need of collaboration, or on domination of the weak by the strong, or some other circumstance, but I think such theories deal with its modes, and ignore its deeper structure; at the bottom of it is the feeling of involvement, or social sense. If we lose that, no coercion will hold us to our duties, because they do not feel like commitments, and no achievements will matter, because they are doomed to be snuffed out with the individual, without being laid to account in the continuity of life.

Great individual development, such as human beings are driven by their intellectual insights to seek, does of course always threaten to break the bonds of direct social involvement, that give animal life its happy unconscious continuity. When the strain gets hard, we have social turmoil, anarchy, irresponsibility, and in private lives the sense of loneliness and infinite smallness that lands some people in nihilism and cynicism, and leads others to existentialism or less intellectual cults.

It is then that social philosophers look on animal societies as models for human society. There is no revolt, no strike, no competition, no anti-Anything party, in a beehive. As Kipling, fifty years or more ago, represented his British utopia, which he called the Mother Hive, that ideal state had a completely co-operative economy, an army that went into action without a murmur, each man with the same impulse the moment an enemy threatened to intrude, and a populace of such tribal solidarity that it would promptly run out any stranger that tried to become established in the state and disrupt its traditions. Any native individual that could not fit into the whole had to be liquidated; the loss was regrettable, but couldn't be helped, and would be made up.

Yet the beehive really has no possible bearing on human affairs, for it owes its harmonious existence to the fact that its members are *incompletely individuated,* even as animals go. None of them performs all of a creature's essential functions: feeding, food getting, nest building, mating, and procreating. The queen has to be fed and tended; she has only procreative functions. She doesn't even bring up her own children; they have nurses. The drones are born and reared only as her suitors, and when the romance is finished they are killed, like proper romantic heroes. The building, nursing, food getting, and fighting are done by sterile females who cannot procreate, amazons who do all their own housework. So there is not only division of labor, but division of organs, functional and physical incompleteness. This direct involvement of each bee with the whole lets the hive function with an organic rhythm that makes its members appear wonderfully socialized. But they are really not socialized at all, any more than the cells in our tissues are socialized; they are associated, by being unindividuated.

That is as far away from a human ideal as one can get. We need, above all, a world in which we can realize our capacities, develop and act as personalities. That means giving up our instinctive patterns of habit and prejudice, our herd instincts. Yet we need the emotional security of the greater, continuous life—the awareness of our involvement with all mankind. How can we eat that cake, and have it too?

The same mental talent that makes us need so much individuation comes to the rescue of our social involvement: I mean the peculiarly human talent of holding ideas in the mind by means of symbols. Human life, even in the simplest forms we know, is shot through and through with *social symbols*. All fantastic beliefs in a great ancestor are symbolic of the original and permanent life of the stock from which every individual life stems. The totem, the hero, the sacred cow, these are the most elementary social symbols. With a maturer view of the world, and the development of religious ideas, the symbolic image of man is usually taken up into the greater view of a divine world order and a moral law. We are sons of Adam and daughters of Eve. If Adam and Eve were simply some human couple supposed to have lived in the Near East before it was so difficult, this would be an odd way of speaking; we don't ordinarily refer to our neighbor's children as Mr. Brown's boys and Mrs. Brown's girls. But Adam is Man, and Eve is Woman (the names even mean that): and among us transient little mites, every man is Man, every woman is Woman. That is the source of human dignity, the sense of which has to be upheld at all levels of social life.

Most people have some religious ritual that supports their knowledge of a greater life, but even in purely secular affairs we constantly express our faith in the continuity of human existence. Animals provide lairs or nests for their immediate offspring. Man builds for the future—often for nothing else. His earliest great buildings were not mansions, but monuments. And not only physical edifices, but above all laws and institutions are intended for the future, and often justified by showing that they have a precedent, or are in accord with the past. They are conveniences of their day, but symbols of more than their day. They are symbols of society, and of each individual's inalienable membership in society.

What, then, is the measure of our possible individuation, without loss of social sense? It is the power of social symbolism. We can give up our actual, instinctual involvements with our kind just to the extent that we can replace them by symbolic ones. This is the prime function of social symbols, from a handshake, to the assembly of robed judges in a Supreme Court. In protocol and ritual, in the investment of authority, in sanctions and honors, lies our security against loss of involvement with mankind; in such bonds lies our freedom to be individuals.

It has been said that an animal society, like a beehive, is really an organism, and the separate bees its organic parts. I think this statement requires many reservations, but it contains some truth. The hive is an organic structure, a super-individual, something like an organism. A human city, however, is an *organization*. It is above all a symbolic structure, a mental reality. Its citizens are the whole and only individuals. They are not a "living mass," like a swarm of semi-individuated bees. The model of the hive has brought with it the concept of human masses, to be cared for in times of peace, deployed in times of war, educated for use or sacrificed for the higher good of their state. In the specious analogy of animal and human society, the hive and the city, lies, I think, the basic philosophical fallacy of all totalitarian theory, even the most sincere and idealistic—even the thoroughly noble political thought of Plato.

We are like leaves of the palm tree, each deeply embedded in the tree, a part of the trunk, each opening to the light in a final, separate life. Our world is a human world, organized to implement our highest individuation. There may be ten thousand of us working in one factory. There are several millions of us living in a city like New York. But we are not the masses; we are the public.

11 Technological Man

Ferkiss

"No one—not even the most brilliant scientist alive today—really knows where science is taking us. We are aboard a train which is gathering speed, racing down a track on which there are an unknown number of switches leading to unknown destinations. No single scientist is in the engine cab and there may be demons at the switch. Most of society is in the caboose looking backward."[1]

Controlling technology and its impact on people is one of the central concerns of our time. To modern technology we owe our mastery over nature, advances in biomedicine, increases in food production and communication, and the speed and comfort of modern travel. Increasingly and irreversibly we become dependent upon technological advances. It is this very dependence and the unforseen consequences of technological innovation which raise serious questions about where technology is leading us. Is it leading us toward the increase or decrease of human freedom and alienation? Are we headed for a breakdown or strengthening of institutions such as the family and democratic government? What are, and will be, the effects of technological change upon human nature? What are the limits of human adaptability to this change?

In his book *Technological Man: The Myth and the Reality* from which the following selection is taken, Victor Ferkiss assesses technology in relation to recent developments in economics, politics, and Western culture. He evaluates the many critics of technology as well as the prophets who try to envision a new technological society. Social inertia, the tenacity of traditional institutions, still exists in Western societies. The old persists along with the new, the traditional along with the modern, the primitive along with the technological. Ferkiss sees a multiplicity of political forms and the absence of any one political, social, or cultural pattern in the new age. He disagrees with those who argue that humans are losing their individual freedom and identity in an increasingly monolithic culture.

Acceptance of this indictment of technological society leaves only the alternatives of revolt, withdrawal, or despair. But Ferkiss believes the indictment is false. Technology itself may be creating a new phase in human history and man may be evolving into a new form—technological man.

Although technological man is still a myth rather than a reality, the myth provides us with an ideal of man controlling his own development, realizing the need for a new philosophy, displaying a new respect for nature, and knowing himself well enough to develop to his fullest potential. By reaching for this ideal, we may avoid the calamity which might come about if the old competitive and acquisitive industrial man keeps control of the new power which technology gives us.

Ferkiss believes that, since evolution has not ended and humanity can now consciously control its own evolution, man is on the threshold of his own transformation. The power to alter himself is as radical a power for man today as using tools was a radical power for primitive man. Throughout history human freedom was limited by an environment, an economy, and a society that did not readily lend itself to change. Even one's identity was controlled by factors beyond human power. But, as Ferkiss states:

> In the era of absolute technology, freedom and identity must take on new meanings or become meaningless. Other men can change your society, your economy and your physical environment. . . . But perhaps more disturbing is the fact that you can do all these things yourself: you can change your appearance or even your sex, your moods and your memories, you can even decide what you want your children to look like. But if you can be whatever you want to be, how will you distinguish the "real" you from the chosen? Who is it that is doing the choosing?"[2]

NOTES

1. Quoted in Alvin Toffler, *Future Shock* (New York: Bantam Books, 1971); p. 431 from Ralph E. Lapp, *The New Priesthood* (New York: Harper & Row, 1961).

2. Victor C. Ferkiss, *Technological Man: The Myth and the Reality* (New York: New American Library, 1969), p. 31.

Toward the Creation of Technological Man

Technological man is more myth than reality. This is the lesson that even as cursory a survey of modern society as ours clearly points to. Bourgeois man is still in the saddle. Or, to put it more accurately, things are in the saddle, since bourgeois man is increasingly unable to cope with his problems. At the same time, an existential revolution is under way that may destroy the identity of the human race, make society unmanageable and render the planet literally uninhabitable. Bourgeois man is incapable of coping with this revolution. The race's only salvation is in the creation of technological man.

But what does this mean? What can it mean? Will technological man be a new ruling class, performing a new role based on new sources of power? For the most part, no. Science confers power, but ruling classes perform political roles, not scientific roles as such. Technological man will not be a new ruling class in the usual sense of the term. Will technological man then be a new personality type—hyperrational, objective, manipulative? Not noticeably so. The link between certain types of society and certain kinds of dominant personality types is easily oversimplified, and in any event

From Victor Ferkiss, *Technological Man: The Myth and the Reality* (New York: George Braziller, 1969). Reprinted by permission of the publisher.

we have had rationalistic, instrumental, hard-nosed human beings dominating Western society since the beginnings of the modern era; the economic man of the classical economists was such a type. Nor will technological man be a new biological type, created either by manipulation of man's genetic structure or by carrying man-machine symbiosis to the point of altering human integrity. Such a development would mean that technological man had failed to come into existence, and bourgeois civilization had fallen prey to the monsters of its own creation.

Technological man will be man in control of his own development within the context of a meaningful philosophy of the role of technology in human evolution. He will be a new cultural type that will leaven all the leadership echelons of society. Technological man will be man at home with science and technology, for he will dominate them rather than be dominated by them; indeed he will be so at home that the question of who is in charge will never even arise. To state that man should rule technology rather than vice versa is almost a truism, of course. It serves no intellectual function save implicitly to deny the contention of those who argue that man cannot control technology and of those who argue that he should not. But otherwise it is an empty exhortation to virtue, fit more for the political stump than as a basis for serious discussion of human problems. Control technology yes, but in whose interest, in accordance with what norms?

Any useful definition of technological man must therefore include within it some definition of what his outlook on life will be. For to control technology, to control the direction of human evolution, we must have some idea of where we are going and how far, else we will be mere passengers rather than drivers of the chariot of evolution. We are thus forced to try to do two difficult things, simultaneously to predict the future and to develop a new philosophy of society based on the future's needs. But though technological man will create himself and cannot be programmed in advance, the needs that call him forth go far toward defining both his task and the world view he must bring to it.

How can one possibly lay down a future philosophy for general acceptance? Even if such dominant world views as traditional Christianity, orthodox Marxism and classical liberalism have clearly failed to provide a rationale for dealing with the existential revolution, may they not simply be replaced not by a new philosophy but by a variety of conflicting value systems determined by individual histories, whims and tastes? Have we not defined lack of a common value system in the declining period of bourgeois civilization as part of our problem? Will not any new philosophy be intellectually arbitrary, capable of being spread, if at all, only through coercion or an irrational persuasion, which would be self-defeating since a unifying world philosophy for technological man must, above all, be based on shared perceptions and values?

Technological man, by definition, will be possessed of the world view of science and technology, which will themselves provide a standard of value for future civilization. At this point many readers may be tempted to throw up their hands. Those enamored of certain versions of Greek and medieval philosophy

and of traditional religious systems will snort that values are either transcendent in nature or are derived from an analysis of the natural world which is essentially deductive and non-empirical in nature. Others will simply object that part of the whole mission of philosophy from Kant to Wittgenstein has been to show that values cannot be derived from natural philosophy: the belief that the "ought" cannot be derived from the "is" is now an elementary commonplace in every primer in ethics or the social sciences.

But the matter is not so simply resolved. Many leading modern philosophers, such as John Dewey, have argued from what man is to what he should do and be, and many who formally deny that the data of existence provide ethical imperatives sneak their values in through the back door by appeals to common sense as a standard when all is said and done. Various subterfuges are used to get around the problem. Psychologists decide what is proper conduct through application of the concepts of "deviance" and "mental health," which are clearly based on the "is" of common experience. Skinner has been faulted by critics such as Joseph Wood Krutch for assuming in his utopia, *Walden Two*, that the problem of social values could be easily solved, since survival and health are universally acknowledged as values. But what is the alternative to Skinner's position (in essence, that of Aristotle) save to locate values in a transcendent source communicating through mysterious forms of revelation that all men may not accept, in the irrational desires of the individual or in some innate knowledge implanted in the individual brain and available through individual introspection?

Fortunately, we do not have to answer all the fundamental questions about ethics that this discussion raises. The problem is not finding a sanction for values but simply defining them, which though a difficult problem is at least one capable of rational discussion. That is, we can assume we ought to do what is good for us if we can decide the latter. If our doctor tells us smoking will cause cancer this does not prove we should stop smoking. We have the option of preferring an earlier and possibly more painful death. If someone tells us the arms race is suicidal, he does not thereby prove that collectively we should eschew suicide.

In this sense, the "ought" can never be derived from empirically grounded predictions about the consequences of actions. Any preference for pleasure over pain, knowledge over ignorance, health over disease, and survival over destruction is incapable of justification unless we first agree that there is some inherent reason for respecting the order of nature that impels all creatures toward survival, activity and growth. Stated thus, the proposition that science cannot be the source of values is irrefutable.

But what practical consequences does this have for most of mankind? Whether we choose to restrain the suicidal or masochistic is a problem in civil liberties, but few would deny that we should restrain the murderer or torturer. Problems arise from the fact that even if we admit that survival or happiness is desirable these may require different conditions for different people, since what makes me prosperous may make you poor. Not the nature of "goods," but their scarcity, allocation and occasional incompatibility present difficulties. So, too, at a general social level the problem arises of priorities among goods: granted that health and survival are both desirable, what happens if society must risk the health of all, or even just of some, in order to ensure its survival?

But these problems, however complex, may be more amenable to analysis and solution than we assume. Jeremy Bentham's hedonistic calculus may have to be rejected as simplistic, but Bentham did not have the resources of modern science (including the social sciences) to provide data as to what the effects of alternative policies might be, and he lacked computers to manipulate this data. Whether science can help us to reconcile conflicting values is a question that must be decided on the basis of experience and experiment, and the idea that it can help us cannot be dismissed out of hand through essentially irrelevant assumptions about the differences between the descriptive and normative orders. Dewey is certainly right in saying that a culture that permits science to destroy its values without permitting science to create new ones is a culture that destroys itself.

The increasing knowledge of the order of nature provided by contemporary scientific discovery, the increasing power over that nature given to man by his technology and the fact that increases in population have raised the amount and intensity of human interaction to a new plane that bespeaks an evolutionary breakthrough, all combine to present technological man with the outlines of a new philosophy of human existence, a philosophy that can provide general guidelines that he can and must take advantage of if he is to retain control of his civilization.

BASIC ELEMENTS OF A NEW PHILOSOPHY

A basic element in this new philosophy is what might be called the *new naturalism,* which asserts that man is in fact part of nature rather than something apart from it, but that nature is not the rigid, mindless, deterministic machine that earlier eras conceived it to be. The totality of the universe is a dynamic process, a constant movement and becoming. Some scientists have gone so far as to contend that some form of mind exists in even nonliving matter, but such an assumption is not necessary to the belief that the universe is, in a sense, a moving equilibrium of which man is a part.

However, man is not merely a part of nature, but the highest part, an element in a semi-determined system of nature with himself, for all practical purposes, private and undetermined, his mind the most complex thing in the universe. "If this property of complexity could somehow be transformed into visible brightness," writes a leading molecular biologist, "the biological world would become a walking field of light compared to the physical world . . . an earthworm would be a beacon . . . human beings would stand out like blazing suns of complexity, flashing bursts of meaning to each other through the dull night of the physical world between." Man gains in dignity as he is seen as part of physical nature, while his most complex mechanical creations pale into insignificance.

Closely related to the new naturalism is the *new holism,* that is, the realization of how interconnected everything is. From the evolutionary philosophies of the nineteenth century has come the idea of becoming, which destroys the traditional distinctions between being and nonbeing, thus paving the way for the rejection of the Newtonian view of the world as matter in motion, a complex of forces exerted on objects, and of analogies based on leverage and weight and anything else associated with the primitive machinery of the early industrial era. The image of the mechanical universe must give way to the idea of process.

The basic concepts of process and system imply a recognition that no part is meaningful outside the whole, that no part can be defined or understood save in relation to the whole. There are few closed or isolated systems in nature and none in society, save for the desert islands of legend. Gestalt psychologists have always regarded the mind-body relationship as that of an integrated whole, but it is really mind-body-society-nature that is the totality. All men are linked with each other and with their social and physical environments in a fantastically complex moving equilibrium, so that in thinking about social questions we must, in the words of M.I.T. president Julius Stratton, "advance from the anatomy of components to the physiology of the organic whole—which indeed is now the society itself."

But this whole, the universal as well as the social, is a new kind of whole, determined not from outside but from within. For another element in the new world outlook is the *new immanentism.* Eastern philosophies have always stressed the immanent, leading to a pantheism not unlinked to the panpsychism of some modern biologists. But for the Western world, especially the Judaic-Christian tradition, God, the principle of order and change, was primarily outside. Though in theory He was everywhere, He was envisioned as "up there" or "out there." A civilization whose world view was dominated by the physicist and the mechanic could think of the Deity as a cosmic watchmaker, of the universe as in some sense having been created and set down. But the modern world view increasingly rejects this viewpoint as the biological sciences come to the fore. However physicists may look upon the development of the physical universe as a whole, the world of living things is somehow different. Nature here works another way, life is antientropic. "The factory that makes the parts of a flower is inside, and is not a factory but a development. . . . The creative principle of the universe," John Rader Platt writes, "is not an external but an internal one." Nothing is isolated. Life exists within systems. And systems create themselves.

These three principles—the new naturalism, the new holism and the new immanentism—provide the necessary basis for the outlook that must come to dominate human society if man is to survive the existential revolution already under way. Technological man must so internalize these ideas and make them so much a part of his instinctive world view that they inform his personal, political and cultural life. They in turn lead to certain further principles. If man and nature are one, then society and the environment are one. Therefore, meaningful social policies must be ecological in character, that is, they must be based on a recognition that the interrelationship of men to each other and to the total environment means that any decision, any change, affects everything in the total system.

Thus, in a sense, nature has rights as well as man, since its activity and that of man are inextricably intermingled. The new holism, with its emphasis on process, means that not only must every decision be seen in ecological perspective, but it must be recognized that there are no individual decisions any more than there are actually geometric points in the empirical world. Decision-making is part of a seamless process. Man cannot become free by being outside or apart from the process. He is affected by what others do—that is, he is the subject of power—and he exercises power because his actions affect others. For in this holistic process every action of the whole passes through and is modified by the state of every cell or particle. Freedom consists in responding autonomously and authentically to the currents of life and action passing through one; the loss of freedom is not the loss of an impossible complete self-determination—which would necessitate standing outside the universe—but is a synonym for being bypassed and not being allowed to play one's part in shaping the whole.

For the whole shapes itself. This is the meaning of the new immanentism. Order is not imposed from outside in accordance with a predetermined plan of man or nature, it is a structure of interrelationships created by the constant activity of its own elements, which somehow always form a pattern as long as the whole survives. Men's actions, men's ideas and the technological forces that they set in motion are all part of this whole, and their activity leads to further development. Freedom is not outside but within nature, Dewey has said. So, too, freedom does not exist apart from society. Planning is the self-consciousness of the human element in developing patterns of interrelation

—a self-consciousness that alone makes control and therefore freedom possible. Control over the elements in the total system—human and nonhuman—is effected by a constant process of adjustment, pressures and signals. As in nature, cells die or are destroyed; sometimes as in cancer they multiply out of control until checked; often signals are blocked or short-circuited rather than amplified. But there is no need for postulating an overseer who directs from outside; every part of the whole has power and influence, every living particle is a source of direction and life. This diffusion of power runs the risk of becoming a dissipation of responsibility as well unless each participant constantly holds himself responsible not only for the immediate result of his particular acts but also for their ultimate impact upon the shaping of the whole.

Technological man, imbued through education and constant experience with the conviction that this is what the universe is like, will discover techniques and construct guidelines for dealing with the problems created for humanity by the existential revolution. From this basic world view he can derive ethical norms that, channeled through reformed institutional structures, can become the basis for policies that will make survival possible.

What norms can guide technological man in this task? They are not all derived directly from his basic outlook, but are nonetheless compatible with it and rest upon the same sets of data about the universe. The first of these norms is that man is part of nature and therefore cannot be its conquerer, that indeed he owes it some respect. As Albert Schweitzer said, a morality that deals only with the relation of man to man and not of man to nature is only half a morality. Human self-knowledge is impossible in a world in which nature has been destroyed or so altered that it cannot speak to men. "Our goal," in the words of biologist Roger Revelle, chairman of the U.S. Committee for the International Biological Program, "should not be to conquer the natural world but to live in harmony with it."

Secondly, ecological perspective dictates that man's economic and social life demands co-ordination if he is to survive, and his exploitation of natural resources must be determined by what is optimum for the total system. At the same time, the ability of the system to respond demands maximum freedom. Therefore, in purely cultural or individual matters where the linkage of behavior to the system is least direct, maximum freedom should be allowed. What this amounts to is combining economic and physical "planning" with cultural pluralism to the maximum extent possible.

On an even more basic level, man must maintain the distinction between himself and the machines of his creation. Since man is superior in complexity to the physical universe, some presumption exists that this complexity has an evolutionary meaning that should be preserved. Linkages of man to machines and technologies that would make him irrevocably dependent on lower orders of reality would be antievolutionary. The great strength of man throughout his evolutionary history has been the flexibility that has resulted from his variety and his complexity. He has triumphed not merely because of his intelligence but also because of his allied versatility. Human flesh is weak, but man avoided the "error" of the crustaceans in protecting themselves in a way that made future development impossible. The human individual is weak, but man has avoided the dead end of the social insects, who have created a marvelous structure in which the nothingness of the individual and the inability to change are opposite sides of the same coin. Man's destiny lies in continuing to exploit this "openness," rather than entering into a symbiotic relationship with the inorganic machine that, while it might bring immediate increments of power, would inhibit his development by chaining him to a system of lesser potentialities. The possibilities of man as a "soft ma-

chine" are far greater and as yet little explored. Man must stand above his physical technologies if he is to avoid their becoming his shell and the principles of their organization his anthill.

But not only must man stand above the machine, he must be in control of his own evolution. Those who think of man's destiny as a mindless leap forward forget that man is not only the sole creature capable of being conscious of evolution but the only one capable of controlling it, and this control must include the power to slow down and stop evolution if he so desires. Actually, some elements of physical technology may be already peaking, at least as far as their effect on society and man is concerned. If the population explosion is brought under control we may enter what might be called a "steady-state" form, wherein the unplumbed future would lie in biological science, and in man's mind. The final step to man would have been taken.

In such a civilization man will have the task of finally finding himself, of fulfilling his role in the universe by becoming fully man. In the Old Testament, Yahweh reveals essentially nothing of Himself to the Hebrews save that "I am Who I am." Man if he is in any sense akin to divinity has as his role becoming himself, doing his own thing. This means that the conquest of outer space should take second place to furthering man's forward movement to the conquest of "inner space."

How man can best explore himself remains a question. Some see mind-expanding drugs as the way (a minor Hippie organ is called *Inner Space*). Arthur Koestler sees the primitive ape-brain as still existing as a "layer" of man's developed brain, and holds that only through drugs can the savage within us be sufficiently controlled so that we can avoid destroying ourselves, just as the Hippies hold that only thus can the *bourgeoisie* be "turned on." A score of mystic and cultural traditions argue otherwise. But one thing is certain: in a world in which man controls his environment so as to provide for his physical needs and to conquer hunger and disease, the new frontier will be within.

Genetic engineering may have a role to play in perfecting the human body, but the untapped frontiers of knowledge and action lie in the mysterious and versatile computer that is the human brain. Much of what it can do in relation to the body and the external environment by the use of tools we already know through existent technology, but of what it can do directly we may have only an inkling. Newton was the last of the magicians, it has been said; in the world of technological man everyone would be a magician even by Newton's standards. But the basic point is that man's role is not to create a new creature, a new mutation of himself physically, but to exploit this still-unleashed marvel of flesh and bone and synapses that we hardly know.

RELATED READING

Anderson, Alan R., ed. *Minds and Machines.* Englewood Cliffs, N.J.: Prentice-Hall, 1964.

Ardley, Robert. *African Genesis.* New York: Atheneum, 1961.

Barrett, William. *Irrational Man.* New York: Doubleday & Co., 1962.

Bowman, Sylvia E. *The Year 2000: A Critical Biography of Edward Bellamy.* New York: A. B. Bookman Publications, 1958.

Cassirer, Ernst. *Essay on Man: An Introduction to a Philosophy of Human Culture.* New York: Doubleday & Co., 1953.

Clemens, Samuel L. (Mark Twain). *What is Man?* in *The Complete Works of Mark Twain,* Vol. XII, New York: Harper & Row, 1917.

Cook, Joan Marble. *In Defense of Homo Sapiens.* New York: Dell Publishing Co., 1975.

Comfort, Alex. *The Nature of Human Nature.* New York: Harper & Row, 1967.

Dewey, John. *Human Nature and Conduct.* New York: Holt, Rinehart & Winston, 1922.

Ellul, Jacques. *The Technological Society.* New York: Alfred A. Knopf, 1964.

Ettinger, R. C. W. *Man into Superman.* New York: Avon Books, 1972.

Ferkiss, Victor. *The Future of Technological Civilization.* New York: George Braziller, 1974.

Friedman, Maurice. *To Deny Our Nothingness: Contemporary Images of Man.* New York: Dell Publishing Co., 1967.

Josephson, Eric and Mary, eds. *Man Alone: Alienation in Modern Society.* New York: Dell Publishing Co., 1962.

Kelley, W. L. and A. Tallon. *Readings in the Philosophy of Man.* New York: McGraw-Hill Book Co., 1967.

King, Martin Luther, Jr. *The Trumpet of Conscience.* New York: Harper & Row, 1968.

Krutch, Joseph Wood. *The Measure of Man.* Indianapolis: Bobbs-Merrill Co., 1954.

Langer, Susanne K., *Feeling and Form: A Theory of Art*. New York: Charles Scribner's Sons, 1953.

————. *Philosophy in a New Key*. Cambridge, Mass.: Harvard University Press, 1942.

Lamont, Corliss. *The Philosophy of Humanism*, 4th ed. New York: Philosophical Library, 1962.

LaRochefoucauld. *Maxims*. Boston: International Pocket Library, 1917.

Lorenz, Konrad. *Civilized Man's Eight Deadly Sins*. New York: Harcourt Brace Jovanovich, 1974.

Mann, Jesse A. and Gerald F. Kreyche, eds. *Reflections on Man*. New York: Harcourt Brace Jovanovich, 1966.

Marcusse, Herbert. *One-Dimensional Man*. Boston: Beacon Press, 1964.

May, Rollo. *Psychology and the Human Dilemma*. New York: Van Nostrand Reinhold Co., 1967.

Mendel, Arthur P., ed. *Essential Works of Marxism*. New York: Bantam Books, 1961.

Mumford, Lewis. *The Transformations of Man*. New York: Crowell-Collier, 1956.

Nash, Paul. *Models of Man: Explorations in the Western Educational Tradition*. New York: John Wiley & Sons, 1968.

Passmore, John. *The Perfectibility of Man*. New York: Charles Scribner's Sons, 1970.

Platt, John R., ed. *New Views on the Nature of Man*. Chicago, Ill.: University of Chicago Press, 1965.

————. *The Step to Man*. New York: John Wiley & Sons, 1966.

Roszak, Theodore. *The Unfinished Animal*. New York: Harper & Row, 1975.

Schacht, Richard. *Alienation*. New York: Doubleday & Co., 1970.

Shaw, George Bernard. *Man and Superman: A Comedy and a Philosophy*. New York: Bantam Books, 1959.

Teilhard de Chardin, Pierre. *The Phenomenon of Man*. New York: Harper & Row, 1959.

Part 3

CONFRONTATION WITH MORAL CHOICE

Commitment to the Good Life

All good and evil consists in sensation.

Epicurus

Evil is the axis of the universe.

Marquis de Sade

A culture which permits science to destroy traditional values but which distrusts its power to create new ones is destroying itself.

John Dewey

There is no such thing as perpetual tranquillity of mind, while we live here.

Thomas Hobbes

Power is the object of man's pursuit.

C. A. Helvetius

The peace we seek so eagerly has been here all the times.

D. T. Suzuki

The mental situation today compels man, compels every individual, to fight wittingly on behalf of his true essence.

Karl Jaspers

Is not man a miserable creature? Scarcely is it in his power . . . to enjoy a single and entire pleasure, yet he is at pains, by reasoning about it, to curtail it.

Michel de Montaigne

How could anything so good be bad?

Old Vaudeville Song

Question of ultimate ends are not amenable to direct proof.

John Stuart Mill

Life is occupied both in perpetuating itself and in surpassing itself; if all it does is maintain itself, then living is only not dying.

Simone de Beauvoir

The Good is simply what God wills and that we should do.

Emil Brunner

The value of morality is for the first time called into question.

Friedrich Nietzsche

Introduction: Searching for the Good Life

How to live?—that is the essential question for us. Not how to live in the mere material sense only, but in the widest sense. The general problem which comprehends every special problem is the right ruling of conduct in all directions under all circumstances. In what way to treat the body; in what way to treat the mind; in what way to manage our affairs; in what way to bring up a family; in what way to behave as a citizen; in what way to utilize all those sources of happiness which nature supplies—how to use all our faculties to the greatest advantage of ourselves and others—how to live completely.[1]

Today ways of living completely are often referred to as lifestyles. In its broadest sense, lifestyle refers to a person's way of existing. It includes not only the externals of dress, length of hair, and language, but also basic attitudes toward sex, the family, community, livelihood, and artistic taste. The adoption of a new lifestyle may grow out of disillusion and disaffection with the prevalent pattern of a bourgeois, consumer society, or it may arise out of a deep religious conversion as an attempt to revitalize an older ideal of life. In any case, a lifestyle involves the conscious or unconscious acceptance of an ideal of "how to live."

The search for new value alternatives is to be found at the institutional as well as the personal level. Our change oriented society has a powerful influence on the family as a unit and center of value. The mobility of the population and changing social relationships in modern society have profoundly affected the traditional role of parents and the authoritarian functions they often assumed. The increase in experimental communes expresses the need to find alternatives to the values and social structure of traditional familial-social relationships.

The question of what ought to be the aim of human life and society is crucial today for many reasons. The accelerating productive capacities of mankind portend the exhaustion of the earth's energy resources and the resulting ecological disaster. The ever increasing urbanization of our world has led in many places to over-crowding, strain on available services, unemployment, poverty, and violence and crime. A recognition of these possibilities has affirmed values long taken for granted: privacy, freedom from noise, and clean air. In modern times, the question of the good life often takes the form of a question about the quality of life, now and in the future.

Many diverse moral ideals vie for our attention like products in a supermarket. Each seems to offer an ideal of the good, whether it is defined as happiness, pleasure, power, love, self-realization, community, holiness, money, or social service. In part, because of the multiplicity of claims, we tend to be sceptical, and perhaps somewhat cynical, regarding the absolute validity of *any* choice. Discussions of whether there is a *summum bonum*, a highest good which can be claimed to be the ultimate aim of human life, are entered into with a great deal of scepticism. We are confronted with the cultural variability of moral values: good and bad are reducible to that which is approved or disapproved in a given society. In addition, philosophers have suggested that moral statements containing such words as "good," "bad," "right," or "wrong" merely express favorable or unfavorable attitudes on the part of the speaker. Scepticism regarding the view that there is a valid way to settle disagreements about the good seems characteristic of our time.

Perhaps the scepticism is justified. We often debate the alternatives without having a grasp of the meaning of such key notions as good, bad, right, or wrong. Yet rational deliberation also seems required. Many of our moral beliefs and ideals are extremely vague and often incompatible with other values we hold. To form our attitudes and guide our actions by such a bewildering jumble of beliefs is often tantamount to not being guided at all. An unwillingness to choose a lifestyle can be a form of self-deception, a way of hiding behind the momentary security of our prejudices or the comfort of custom and tradition. Perhaps the Socratic creed is correct: the examined life is best. We should make a critical assessment of theories about the good; we should also consider rationally the consequences of our commitments and try to relate theory and practice consistently.

The area of philosophy called "ethics" does this. It is a systematic and critical inquiry into theories regarding the good life and the principles which should guide human conduct. Traditionally, the ultimate purpose of ethics was to establish rational grounds upon which right action and the good are to be determined. However, analytic philosophers have been concerned with clarifying such basic concepts as right, good, conscience, duty, and moral responsibility, and with determining precisely what rules may be appropriate for the resolution of ethical disagreement. Many analytic philosophers refer to their work as "meta-ethics" in contrast to the more traditional "normative ethics."

The following selections represent writers who are committed to normative theories derived from their search for standards of the good and human happiness. Moreover, Part Three conceives of ethics in the ancient Greek sense in which normative questions of the good and the right cannot be separated from broader questions regarding society, politics, knowledge, and the correct characterization of human nature. As Plato, in *The Republic*, was the first thinker to develop systematically these wider questions, a selection from that work is presented first here. Right action depends upon a knowledge of the good, of reality, discoverable by reason. Knowledge of the good as the highest form of knowledge leads us away from the senses and the sensual pleasures. The life of the philosopher-king in *The Republic* suggests the life of the dedicated intellectual in full control of all of his faculties. For Plato, the ethical ideal was the cultivation of the harmonious soul in which the higher rational functions rule the will and the appetites, especially the appetite for pleasure.

Unlike Plato, some philosophers consider pleasure to be the central concern of the good life. For Epicurus, pleasure (the absence of pain) is an end in itself, and prudence, not wisdom in Plato's sense, is the highest virtue. Epicurus' ethical theory was based upon a materialistic view of the universe, also quite different from the idealism of Plato.

Jeremy Bentham was concerned with providing an ethical basis for legal theory and practice. He defined the principle of utility in terms of pleasure and pain. Bentham defined pleasure positively, which places him closer to the hedonism of Aristippus than the refined hedonism of Epicurus. The ideal of social and political reform infused both Bentham's and Mill's ethical writings. However, while following the traditional English hedonistic school, John Stuart Mill made such radical revisions in the doctrine that it constituted a major break with that tradition. In developing his disagreements with traditional hedonism, Mill formulated the foundations for liberalism as a political and social doctrine.

The next selection, by Immanuel Kant, develops a system of ethics in which duty and our internal sense of moral obligation take precedence over pleasure. Our conformity to moral rules, and not our calculation of the utility of our actions, constitutes the highest good—the good will which acts in conformity with that which reason, rational will, dictates. Kant's objections to utilitarian criteria of the good and the right developed into the major rival of utilitarianism. Inclination has no place in the determination of the good life. Reason, not prudence, points to the individual's unique moral obligation to conform to the universal moral laws he or she must accept as an autonomous person. The requirements of a moral life go beyond considerations of pleasure and utility.

Viktor Frankl was in essential agreement with Kant's relegation of pleasure to a peripheral place in the moral life. However, he was concerned with analyzing the psychology of ethical consciousness rather than the logic of ethical judgment. Pleasure itself (or the lack of it) does not determine the meaning of life. Frankl emphasized the fact that we create our own values and ultimately ourselves in the process of making decisions. Commitments are formulated within the concrete situations of our existence. There would be no meanings if we had no "will to meaning."

One of the most popular conceptions of the good life is self-actualization. Aristotle offers an alternative to Kant's ethics of duty. His was a teleological theory of ethics in which the good and the right are determined by the consequences or ends of human action. The standard of the good is to be found in the development of the capacities and dispositions of the individual. Ethics is a highly practical art in which good is defined within the concrete conditions of human life. The end of life is personal happiness, *eudaimonia,* the exercise of human potentialities in accordance with virtue—the self-actualization of the person. Unlike his mentor Plato, Aristotle did not search for the ideal form of the good. Good is to be determined by a close observation of the patterns of human life, desires, and satisfactions. However, he did agree with Plato that the highest good is theoretical wisdom; for intelligence, in the sense of contemplation, is akin to the divine in man.

Abraham Maslow developed a humanistic psychology and ethics which also commend self-realization. The acceptance and expression of the inner self involve a realization of human capacities, strivings, and needs in a proper hierarchy. Religious, aesthetic, and contemplative peak experiences often yield the highest form of self-actualization and aid the individual in his further development toward authentic selfhood. We have a human nature subject to active and passive repressions, but all of us remain "our own projects" to be developed by following a mean between spontaneity and control.

John Dewey's theory was naturalistic, placing man firmly in nature. In this respect, his approach was similar to that of Aristotle; however, he rejected Aristotle's (and Plato's) spectator view of knowledge. Moral choices arise in concrete situations in which there are conflicts of values and alternative solutions to moral problems. His emphasis on deliberation, the use of intelligence, and the idea that human ends are to be clarified and tested by experience point to Dewey's lifelong attempt to use the experimental methods of science for the resolution of moral conflicts. Dewey's comments on the moral life, education, and social issues all reflect his faith in the power of intelligence to imagine a desirable future in the present, and to find the means by which to realize it.

Rosabeth Moss Kanter's discussion of communes, both past and present, can be related to Dewey's experimental ethics and to his own explorations in new forms of education. As Ms. Kanter points out, the communal movement is not just a search for utopia, but it is a search for a lifestyle, a realization of the good through experiments in living. Anarchistic communes (see Kropotkin, Part Four) and communes based on growth centers are two prevalent types of communes today.

Having opened Part Three with Plato's visionary utopian experiment of *The Republic*, it is appropriate to end with a discussion of concrete experiments in utopias of today. Perhaps we have not yet arrived at that final ideal, a completely satisfactory definition of the good. If Dewey is correct, finding a fixed definition is not so important as realizing value possibilities in experience. We may sometimes call ourselves "lords of the earth," yet we often feel vulnerable and helpless to control the accelerating changes we have brought about. The power of our knowledge and techniques is no longer in question—our wisdom is. Spencer's question, "How to live?" is more urgent now than ever before.

NOTE

1.   Quoted in Max Rosenberg, *Introduction to Philosophy* (New York: Philosophical Library, 1955), p. 446.

12   Utopia and the Good Life

Plato

Socrates was one of the first to recognize the importance of clarifying the meaning of moral terms and establishing criteria for their use. Many of Plato's earlier dialogues carry on this tradition; the short works, such as the *Euthyphro, Laches,* and the *Meno,* are inquiries into the basis or grounds (*logoi*) of moral judgments regarding piety, courage, and virtue itself. Like Socrates, Plato believed that through the use of reason and careful dialogue we could arrive at a set of ethical principles that are valid for all deliberative actions and that are conducive to the good. Plato also believed that the good of the individual was impossible to attain apart from the social good. If the good is attainable, it is only within the context of a good society.

The most influential image of a utopia or ideal society in the history of western civilization is presented in *The Republic* of Plato. It is a sketch of a society rather than a fully delineated model. Plato, through his spokesman Socrates, pointed to the model's limitations and possible flaws through the use of detractors, not only in *The Republic* itself, but also in many of his later works. One must not forget that Plato was trying to stimulate thought about the problems he raised, to get his readers to think for themselves, and to get them to realize the importance of the problems. *The Republic* represents Plato's initial, not final, attempt to formulate his utopian ideal—a society in which human beings could live under conditions where goodness and justice were attainable. These problems were Plato's lifelong concern. His last work, *The Laws,* presented a blueprint of another ideal society.

Had Plato, like Marx and Engels, presented his utopian proposal in the form of a manifesto rather than a dialogue, his position might be summarized like this:

1.   The history of society heretofore has been the history of class struggle, political turmoil, continuous violence, and the dictatorship of the

176

worst over the best. Contemporary society is pathological, immoral, and unjust.

2. In order to establish a good society in which all citizens can attain their appropriate good, political power must be given to the only persons that can know (rather than guess, imagine, or feel) what the nature of true goodness and justice is. If virtue is knowledge, then political power and wisdom must be conjoined.

3. These persons are the philosophers, lovers of wisdom like Socrates, who search after knowledge of ideal goodness, beauty, and truth. This class can safely become the guardians of the state and will unselfishly work for the welfare and happiness of all citizens of the state.

4. At present, there may be few such persons, but a group of them can be produced by the proper kind of education. This education will be aimed at forming whole, harmonious, well-integrated human beings. Both bodies and minds will be well molded. The appetites, actions, and reason will be developed in proper proportion so that the appropriate virtues of temperance, courage, and wisdom will be instilled.

5. In order to achieve these aims, the state must have control over education. Beginning with a physical education program for all, education will proceed through several stages including moral and religious training, study of mathematical and scientific subjects, and finally, for the qualified few, study of "dialectics" or philosophy. While all students will start out intellectual equals, as education proceeds a process of selection will be carried forward and will result in the emergence of an elite group who will become the rulers and planners of the society.

6. To assure that these philosophers have the best heredity and the best familial environment, they will be bred through a carefully controlled eugenics program in which the best men will be mated with the best women. For them, the nuclear family will be replaced by communal nurseries and hostels. Private property for this class will be abolished and possessions and children will be considered prized public possessions.

7. The result of these reforms will be a state in which each class—workers, soldiers, and philosophers—performs its appropriate functions: working and providing for the material wants of the society, guarding the society from dangers from within and without, and controlling and planning to promote the healthy and harmonious functioning of the whole society.

Earlier in *The Republic*, Plato stated his central thesis:

Until philosophers are kings, or the kings and princes of this world have the spirit and power of philosophy, and political greatness and wisdom meet in one, and those commoner natures who pursue either to the exclusion of the other are compelled to stand aside, cities will never have rest from their evils,—no, nor the human race, as I believe,—and then only will our State have a possibility of life and behold the light of day.[1]

At the center of the main argument of the work is Plato's belief that since virtue is knowledge, since morality and intelligence should be conjoined, only those who are knowledgeable are virtuous enough to rule. Our search for moral principles is similar to our search for any kind of knowledge. The analogies of the Sun, the Divided Line, and the Cave represent how education may bring one to a full knowledge of truth, beauty, and goodness. "Below the line" and "in the cave or den," we only receive representations in the realm of appearances given by perception, the phenomenal world of sight, individual things, relativity, and change. "Above the line" and the "Sun" represent the realm of real "objects" or universals that can be grasped by intelligence—the supersensible realm of eternal patterns or "forms." We cannot judge something as true or good except by absolute standards which Plato postulated as forms or essences of which sensible things are only copies. The search for knowledge leads us up the line (and out of the cave) away from too much reliance upon our senses toward a conceptual understanding of the intelligible forms by the "eye of the mind." Likewise, the search for the good leads us away from the sensible world of pleasures toward a reflective understanding of timeless ideals. Our actions are right, our conduct is virtuous, and our society is just insofar as we conform to the ideal models of rightness, virtue, and justice. These models or archetypes which together form the ultimate good must be immediately apprehended by the philosopher-rulers before they can initiate political reforms that are in accordance with a higher vision of reality.

The Republic was the first in a long line of works that attempted to imagine a society in which human problems were finally solved and people lived together productively, harmoniously, and happily. Thomas More's *Utopia*, the first work by that name (taken from Latin, *u-topus*, no place, or *eu-topus*, good place), Bellamy's *Looking Backward*, Aldous Huxley's satirical *Brave New World*, and B. F. Skinner's *Walden Two* have all shown the influence of the first great Western utopian thinker. The views set forth in *The Republic* have also been severely criticized, first by Aristotle (*Politics*), who rejected Plato's communalism of the guardians and rulers as unrealistic, and recently by Karl Popper in *The Open Society and Its Enemies*, who argued that Plato's model was a precursor of totalitarianism.

Here we are concerned with Plato's statement and defense of his utopian commitment. Like most other utopians, he believed that through careful planning human intelligence can be applied to achieving a total solution to social problems, that the conditions which produce happiness can be created and sustained, and that we ought to do our utmost as moral agents to bring about a happier life for ourselves and others.

NOTE

1. Plato, *The Republic* in *The Dialogues of Plato*, trans. Benjamin Jowett. (New York: Random House, 1937), Vol. 2, p. 737.

The Way to an Ideal Society

(Speakers are Socrates and Adeimantus.)

I do not wonder that the many refuse to believe; for they have never seen that of which we are now speaking realized; they have seen only a conventional imitation of philosophy, consisting of words artificially brought together, not like these of ours having a natural unity. But a human being who in word and work is perfectly moulded, as far as he can be, into the proportion and likeness of virtue—such a man ruling in a city which bears the same image, they have never yet seen, neither one nor many of them—do you think that they ever did?

No indeed.

No, my friend, and they have seldom, if ever, heard free and noble sentiments; such as men utter when they are earnestly and by every means in their power seeking after truth for the sake of knowledge, while they look coldly on the subtleties of controversy, of which the end is opinion and strife, whether they meet with them in the courts of law or in society.

They are strangers, he said, to the words of which you speak.

And this was what we foresaw, and this was the reason why truth forced us to admit, not without fear and hesitation, that neither cities nor States nor individuals will ever attain per-

fection until the small class of philosophers whom we termed useless but not corrupt are providentially compelled, whether they will or not, to take care of the State, and until a like necessity be laid on the State to obey them; or until kings, or if not kings, the sons of kings or princes, are divinely inspired with a true love of true philosophy. That either or both of these alternatives are impossible, I see no reason to affirm: if they were so, we might indeed be justly ridiculed as dreamers and visionaries. Am I not right?

Quite right.

If then, in the countless ages of the past, or at the present hour in some foreign clime which is far away and beyond our ken, the perfected philosopher is or has been or hereafter shall be compelled by a superior power to have the charge of the State, we are ready to assert to the death, that this our constitution has been, and is—yea, and will be whenever the Muse of Philosophy is queen. There is no impossibility in all this; that there is a difficulty, we acknowledge ourselves.

My opinion agrees with yours, he said.

But do you mean to say that this is not the opinion of the multitude?

I should imagine not, he replied.

O my friend, I said, do not attack the multitude: they will change their minds, if, not in an aggressive spirit, but gently and with the view of soothing them and removing their dislike of overeducation, you show them your philosophers as they really are and describe as you

From Plato, *The Republic,* in *The Dialogues of Plato,* trans. Benjamin Jowett, 3d ed. (New York: Oxford University Press, 1892), Book VI–VII.

(Socrates, Adeimantus.)

were just now doing their character and profession, and then mankind will see that he of whom you are speaking is not such as they supposed—if they view him in this new light, they will surely change their notion of him, and answer in another strain. Who can be at enmity with one who loves them, who that is himself gentle and free from envy will be jealous of one in whom there is no jealousy? Nay, let me answer for you, that in a few this harsh temper may be found but not in the majority of mankind.

I quite agree with you, he said.

And do you not also think, as I do, that the harsh feeling which the many entertain towards philosophy originates in the pretenders, who rush in uninvited, and are always abusing them, and finding fault with them, who make persons instead of things the theme of their conversation? and nothing can be more unbecoming in philosophers than this.

It is most unbecoming.

For he, Adeimantus, whose mind is fixed upon true being, has surely no time to look down upon the affairs of earth, or to be filled with malice and envy, contending against men; his eye is ever directed towards things fixed and immutable, which he sees neither injuring nor injured by one another, but all in order moving according to reason; these he imitates, and to these he will, as far as he can, conform himself. Can a man help imitating that with which he holds reverential converse?

Impossible.

And the philosopher holding converse with the divine order, becomes orderly and divine, as far as the nature of man allows; but like every one else, he will suffer from detraction.

Of course.

And if a necessity be laid upon him of fashioning, not only himself, but human nature generally, whether in States or individuals, into that which he beholds elsewhere, will he, think

you, be an unskilful artificer of justice, temperance, and every civil virtue?

Anything but unskilful.

And if the world perceives that what we are saying about him is the truth, will they be angry with philosophy? Will they disbelieve us, when we tell them that no State can be happy which is not designed by artists who imitate the heavenly pattern?

They will not be angry if they understand, he said. But how will they draw out the plan of which you are speaking?

They will begin by taking the State and the manners of men, from which, as from a tablet, they will rub out the picture, and leave a clean surface. This is no easy task. But whether easy or not, herein will lie the difference between them and every other legislator,—they will have nothing to do either with individual or State, and will inscribe no laws, until they have either found, or themselves made, a clean surface.

They will be very right, he said.

Having effected this, they will proceed to trace an outline of the constitution?

No doubt.

And when they are filling in the work, as I conceive, they will often turn their eyes upwards and downwards: I mean that they will first look at absolute justice and beauty and temperance, and again at the human copy; and will mingle and temper the various elements of life into the image of a man; and thus they will conceive according to that other image, which, when existing among men, Homer calls the form and likeness of God.

Very true, he said.

And one feature they will erase, and another they will put in, until they have made the ways of men, as far as possible, agreeable to the ways of God?

Indeed, he said, in no way could they make a fairer picture.

And now, I said, are we beginning to persuade those whom you described as rushing

(Socrates, Adeimantus.)

at us with might and main, that the painter of constitutions is such an one as we are praising; at whom they were so very indignant because to his hands we committed the State; and are they growing a little calmer at what they have just heard?

Much calmer, if there is any sense in them.

Why, where can they still find any ground for objection? Will they doubt that the philosopher is a lover of truth and being?

They would not be so unreasonable.

Or that his nature, being such as we have delineated, is akin to the highest good?

Neither can they doubt this.

But again, will they tell us that such a nature, placed under favourable circumstances, will not be perfectly good and wise if any ever was? Or will they prefer those whom we have rejected?

Surely not.

Then will they still be angry at our saying, that, until philosophers bear rule, States and individuals will have no rest from evil, nor will this our imaginary State ever be realized?

I think that they will be less angry.

Shall we assume that they are not only less angry but quite gentle, and that they have been converted and for very shame, if for no other reason, cannot refuse to come to terms?

By all means, he said.

Then let us suppose that the reconciliation has been effected. Will any one deny the other point, that there may be sons of kings or princes who are by nature philosophers?

Surely no man, he said.

And when they have come into being will any one say that they must of necessity be destroyed; that they can hardly be saved is not denied even by us; but that in the whole course of ages no single one of them can escape—who will venture to affirm this?

Who indeed!

But, said I, one is enough; let there be one man who has a city obedient to his will, and he might bring into existence the ideal polity about which the world is so incredulous.

Yes, one is enough.

The ruler may impose the laws and institutions which we have been describing, and the citizens may possibly be willing to obey them?

Certainly.

And that others should approve, of what we approve, is no miracle or impossibility?

I think not.

But we have sufficiently shown, in what has preceded, that all this, if only possible, is assuredly for the best.

We have.

And now we say not only that our laws, if they could be enacted, would be for the best, but also that the enactment of them, though difficult, is not impossible.

Very good. . . .

THE ANALOGY OF THE LINE

(Speakers are Socrates and Glaucon.)

I must first come to an understanding with you, and remind you of what I have mentioned in the course of this discussion, and at many other times.

What?

The old story, that there is a many beautiful and a many good, and so of other things which we describe and define; to all of them 'many' is applied.

True, he said.

And there is an absolute beauty and an absolute good, and of other things to which the term 'many' is applied there is an absolute; for they may be brought under a single idea, which is called the essence of each.

Very true.

The many, as we say, are seen but not known, and the ideas are known but not seen.

Exactly.

(Socrates, Glaucon)

And what is the organ with which we see the visible things?

The sight, he said.

And with the hearing, I said, we hear, and with the other senses perceive the other objects of sense?

True.

But have you remarked that sight is by far the most costly and complex piece of workmanship which the artificer of the senses ever contrived?

No, I never have, he said.

Then reflect: has the ear or voice need of any third or additional nature in order that the one may be able to hear and the other to be heard?

Nothing of the sort.

No, indeed, I replied; and the same is true of most, if not all, the other senses—you would not say that any of them requires such an addition?

Certainly not.

But you see that without the addition of some other nature there is no seeing or being seen?

How do you mean?

Sight being, as I conceive, in the eyes, and he who has eyes wanting to see; colour being also present in them, still unless there be a third nature specially adapted to the purpose, the owner of the eyes will see nothing and the colours will be invisible.

Of what nature are you speaking?

Of that which you term light, I replied.

True, he said.

Noble, then, is the bond which links together sight and visibility, and great beyond other bonds by no small difference of nature; for light is their bond, and light is no ignoble thing?

Nay, he said, the reverse of ignoble.

And which, I said, of the gods in heaven would you say was the lord of this element? Whose is that light which makes the eye to see perfectly and the visible to appear?

You mean the sun, as you and all mankind say.

May not the relation of sight to this deity be described as follows?

How?

Neither sight nor the eye in which sight resides is the sun?

No.

Yet of all the organs of sense the eye is the most like the sun?

By far the most like.

And the power which the eye possesses is a sort of effluence which is dispensed from the sun?

Exactly.

Then the sun is not sight, but the author of sight who is recognised by sight.

True, he said.

And this is he whom I call the child of the good, whom the good begat in his own likeness, to be in the visible world, in relation to sight and the things of sight, what the good is in the intellectual world in relation to mind and the things of mind.

Will you be a little more explicit? he said.

Why, you know, I said, that the eyes, when a person directs them towards objects on which the light of day is no longer shining, but the moon and stars only, see dimly, and are nearly blind; they seem to have no clearness of vision in them?

Very true.

But when they are directed towards objects on which the sun shines, they see clearly and there is sight in them?

Certainly.

And the soul is like the eye: when resting upon that on which truth and being shine, the soul perceives and understands and is radiant with intelligence; but when turned towards the twilight of becoming and perishing, then she

(Socrates, Glaucon.)

has opinion only, and goes blinking about, and is first of one opinion and then of another, and seems to have no intelligence?

Just so.

Now, that which imparts truth to the known and the power of knowing to the knower is what I would have you term the idea of good, and this you will deem to be the cause of science, and of truth in so far as the latter becomes the subject of knowledge; beautiful too, as are both truth and knowledge, you will be right in esteeming this other nature as more beautiful than either; and, as in the previous instance, light and sight may be truly said to be like the sun, and yet not to be the sun, so in this other sphere, science and truth may be deemed to be like the good, but not the good; the good has a place of honour yet higher.

What a wonder of beauty that must be, he said, which is the author of science and truth, and yet surpasses them in beauty; for you surely cannot mean to say that pleasure is the good?

God forbid, I replied; but may I ask you to consider the image in another point of view?

In what point of view?

You would say, would you not, that the sun is not only the author of visibility in all visible things, but of generation and nourishment and growth, though he himself is not generation?

Certainly.

In like manner the good may be said to be not only the author of knowledge to all things known, but of their being and essence, and yet the good is not essence, but far exceeds essence in dignity and power.

Glaucon said, with a ludicrous earnestness: By the light of heaven, how amazing!

Yes, I said, and the exaggeration may be set down to you; for you made me utter my fancies.

And pray continue to utter them; at any rate

let us hear if there is anything more to be said about the similitude of the sun.

Yes, I said, there is a great deal more.

Then omit nothing, however slight.

I will do my best, I said; but I should think that a great deal will have to be omitted.

You have to imagine, then, that there are two ruling powers, and that one of them is set over the intellectual world, the other over the visible. I do not say heaven, lest you should fancy that I am playing upon the name (οὐρανός, ὁρατός). May I suppose that you have this distinction of the visible and intelligible fixed in your mind?

I have.

Now take a line which has been cut into two unequal parts, and divide each of them again in the same proportion, and suppose the two main divisions to answer, one to the visible and the other to the intelligible, and then compare the subdivisions in respect of their clearness and want of clearness, and you will find that the first section in the sphere of the visible consists of images. And by images I mean, in the first place, shadows, and in the second place, reflections in water and in solid, smooth and polished bodies and the like. Do you understand?

Yes, I understand.

Imagine, now, the other section, of which this is only the resemblance, to include the animals which we see, and everything that grows or is made.

Very good.

Would you not admit that both the sections of this division have different degrees of truth, and that the copy is to the original as the sphere of opinion is to the sphere of knowledge?

Most undoubtedly.

Next proceed to consider the manner in which the sphere of the intellectual is to be divided.

In what manner?

(Socrates, Glaucon)

Thus:—There are two subdivisions, in the lower of which the soul uses the figures given by the former division as images; the enquiry can only be hypothetical, and instead of going upwards to a principle descends to the other end; in the higher of the two, the soul passes out of hypotheses, and goes up to a principle which is above hypotheses, making no use of images as in the former case, but proceeding only in and through the ideas themselves.

I do not quite understand your meaning, he said.

Then I will try again; you will understand me better when I have made some preliminary remarks. You are aware that students of geometry, arithmetic, and the kindred sciences assume the odd and the even and the figures and three kinds of angles and the like in their several branches of science; these are their hypotheses, which they and every body are supposed to know, and therefore they do not deign to give any account of them either to themselves or others; but they begin with them, and go on until they arrive at last, and in a consistent manner, at their conclusion?

Yes, he said, I know.

And do you not know also that although they make use of the visible forms and reason about them, they are thinking not of these, but of the ideals which they resemble; not of the figures which they draw, but of the absolute square and the absolute diameter, and so on—the forms which they draw or make, and which have shadows and reflections in water of their own, are converted by them into images, but they are really seeking to behold the things themselves, which can only be seen with the eye of the mind?

That is true.

And of this kind I spoke as the intelligible, although in the search after it the soul is compelled to use hypotheses; not ascending to a first principle, because she is unable to rise above the region of hypothesis, but employing the objects of which the shadows below are resemblances in their turn as images, they having in relation to the shadows and reflections of them a greater distinctness, and therefore a higher value.

I understand, he said, that you are speaking of the province of geometry and the sister arts.

And when I speak of the other division of the intelligible, you will understand me to speak of that other sort of knowledge which reason herself attains by the power of dialectic, using the hypotheses not as first principles, but only as hypotheses—that is to say, as steps and points of departure into a world which is above hypotheses, in order that she may soar beyond them to the first principle of the whole; and clinging to this and then to that which depends on this, by successive steps she descends again without the aid of any sensible object, from ideas, through ideas, and in ideas she ends.

I understand you, he replied; not perfectly, for you seem to me to be describing a task which is really tremendous; but, at any rate, I understand you to say that knowledge and being, which the science of dialectic contemplates, are clearer than the notions of the arts, as they are termed, which proceed from hypotheses only: these are also contemplated by the understanding, and not by the senses: yet, because they start from hypotheses and do not ascend to a principle, those who contemplate them appear to you not to exercise the higher reason upon them, although when a first principle is added to them they are cognizable by the higher reason. And the habit which is concerned with geometry and the cognate sciences I suppose that you would term understanding and not reason, as being intermediate between opinion and reason.

You have quite conceived my meaning, I said; and now, corresponding to these four divisions, let there be four faculties in the soul

(Socrates, Glaucon.)

—reason answering to the highest, understanding to the second, faith (or conviction) to the third, and perception of shadows to the last—and let there be a scale of them, and let us suppose that the several faculties have clearness in the same degree that their objects have truth.

I understand, he replied, and give my assent, and accept your arrangement.

THE ALLEGORY OF THE CAVE

And now, I said, let me show in a figure how far our nature is enlightened or unenlightened:—Behold! human beings living in an underground den, which has a mouth open towards the light and reaching all along the den; here they have been from their childhood, and have their legs and necks chained so that they cannot move, and can only see before them, being prevented by the chains from turning round their heads. Above and behind them a fire is blazing at a distance, and between the fire and the prisoners there is a raised way; and you will see, if you look, a low wall built along the way, like the screen which marionette players have in front of them, over which they show the puppets.

I see.

And do you see, I said, men passing along the wall carrying all sorts of vessels, and statues and figures of animals made of wood and stone and various materials, which appear over the wall? Some of them are talking, others silent.

You have shown me a strange image, and they are strange prisoners.

Like ourselves, I replied; and they see only their own shadows, or the shadows of one another, which the fire throws on the opposite wall of the cave?

True, he said; how could they see anything but the shadows if they were never allowed to move their heads?

And of the objects which are being carried in like manner they would only see the shadows?

Yes, he said.

And if they were able to converse with one another, would they not suppose that they were naming what was actually before them?

Very true.

And suppose further that the prison had an echo which came from the other side, would they not be sure to fancy when one of the passers-by spoke that the voice which they heard came from the passing shadow?

No question, he replied.

To them, I said, the truth would be literally nothing but the shadows of the images.

That is certain.

And now look again, and see what will naturally follow if the prisoners are released and disabused of their error. At first, when any of them is liberated and compelled suddenly to stand up and turn his neck round and walk and look towards the light, he will suffer sharp pains; the glare will distress him, and he will be unable to see the realities of which in his former state he had seen the shadows; and then conceive some one saying to him, that what he saw before was an illusion, but that now, when he is approaching nearer to being and his eye is turned towards more real existence, he has a clearer vision,—what will be his reply? And you may further imagine that his instructor is pointing to the objects as they pass and requiring him to name them,—will he not be perplexed? Will he not fancy that the shadows which he formerly saw are truer than the objects which are now shown to him?

Far truer.

And if he is compelled to look straight at the light, will he not have a pain in his eyes which will make him turn away to take refuge in the objects of vision which he can see, and which he will conceive to be in reality clearer than the things which are now being shown to him?

True, he said.

And suppose once more, that he is reluctantly dragged up a steep and rugged ascent, and held fast until he is forced into the presence of the sun himself, is he not likely to be pained and irritated? When he approaches the light his eyes will be dazzled, and he will not be able to see anything at all of what are now called realities.

Not all in a moment, he said.

He will require to grow accustomed to the sight of the upper world. And first he will see the shadows best, next the reflections of men and other objects in the water, and then the objects themselves; then he will gaze upon the light of the moon and the stars and the spangled heaven; and he will see the sky and the stars by night better than the sun or the light of the sun by day?

Certainly.

Last of all he will be able to see the sun, and not mere reflections of him in the water, but he will see him in his own proper place, and not in another; and he will contemplate him as he is.

Certainly.

He will then proceed to argue that this is he who gives the season and the years, and is the guardian of all that is in the visible world, and in a certain way the cause of all things which he and his fellows have been accustomed to behold?

Clearly, he said, he would first see the sun and then reason about him.

And when he remembered his old habitation, and the wisdom of the den and his fellow-prisoners, do you not suppose that he would felicitate himself on the change, and pity them?

Certainly, he would.

And if they were in the habit of conferring honours among themselves on those who were quickest to observe the passing shadows and to remark which of them went before, and which followed after, and which were together; and who were therefore best able to draw conclusions as to the future, do you think that he would care for such honours and glories, or envy the possessors of them? Would he not say with Homer,

'Better to be the poor servant of a poor master.'

and to endure anything, rather than think as they do and live after their manner?

Yes, he said, I think that he would rather suffer anything than entertain these false notions and live in this miserable manner.

Imagine once more, I said, such an one coming suddenly out of the sun to be replaced in his old situation; would he not be certain to have his eyes full of darkness?

To be sure, he said.

And if there were a contest, and he had to compete in measuring the shadows with the prisoners who had never moved out of the den, while his sight was still weak, and before his eyes had become steady (and the time which would be needed to acquire this new habit of sight might be very considerable), would he not be ridiculous? Men would say of him that up he went and down he came without his eyes; and that it was better not even to think of ascending; and if any one tried to loose another and lead him up to the light, let them only catch the offender, and they would put him to death.

No question, he said.

This entire allegory, I said, you may now append, dear Glaucon, to the previous argument; the prison-house is the world of sight, the light of the fire is the sun, and you will not misapprehend me if you interpret the journey upwards to be the ascent of the soul into the intellectual world according to my poor belief,

(Socrates, Glaucon.)

which, at your desire, I have expressed—whether rightly or wrongly God knows. But, whether true or false, my opinion is that in the world of knowledge the idea of good appears last of all, and is seen only with an effort; and, when seen, is also inferred to be the universal author of all things beautiful and right, parent of light and of the lord of light in this visible world, and the immediate source of reason and truth in the intellectual; and that this is the power upon which he who would act rationally either in public or private life must have his eye fixed.

I agree, he said, as far as I am able to understand you.

Moreover, I said, you must not wonder that those who attain to this beatific vision are unwilling to descend to human affairs; for their souls are ever hastening into the upper world where they desire to dwell; which desire of theirs is very natural, if our allegory may be trusted.

Yes, very natural.

And is there anything surprising in one who passes from divine contemplations to the evil state of man, misbehaving himself in a ridiculous manner; if, while his eyes are blinking and before he has become accustomed to the surrounding darkness, he is compelled to fight in courts of law, or in other places, about the images or the shadows of images of justice, and is endeavouring to meet the conceptions of those who have never yet seen absolute justice?

Anything but surprising, he replied.

Any one who has common sense will remember that the bewilderments of the eyes are of two kinds, and arise from two causes, either from coming out of the light or from going into the light, which is true of the mind's eye, quite as much as of the bodily eye; and he who remembers this when he sees any one whose vision is perplexed and weak, will not

be too ready to laugh; he will first ask whether that soul of man has come out of the brighter life, and is unable to see because unaccustomed to the dark, or having turned from darkness to the day is dazzled by excess of light. And he will count the one happy in his condition and state of being, he will pity the other; or, if he have a mind to laugh at the soul which comes from below into the light, there will be more reason in this than in the laugh which greets him who returns from above out of the light into the den.

That, he said, is a very just distinction.

But then, if I am right, certain professors of education must be wrong when they say that they can put a knowledge into the soul which was not there before, like sight into blind eyes.

They undoubtedly say this, he replied.

Whereas, our argument shows that the power and capacity of learning exists in the soul already; and that just as the eye was unable to turn from darkness to light without the whole body, so too, the instrument of knowledge can only by the movement of the whole soul be turned from the world of becoming into that of being, and learn by degrees to endure the sight of being, and of the brightest and best of being, or in other words, of the good.

Very true.

And must there not be some art which will effect conversion in the easiest and quickest manner; not implanting the faculty of sight, for that exists already, but has been turned in the wrong direction, and is looking away from the truth?

Yes, he said, such an art may be presumed.

And whereas the other so-called virtues of the soul seem to be akin to bodily qualities, for even when they are not originally innate they can be implanted later by habit and exercise, the virtue of wisdom more than anything else contains a divine element which always remains, and by this conversion is rendered useful and profitable; or, on the other hand, hurtful and useless. Did you never observe the narrow intelligence flashing from the keen eye of a clever rogue—how eager he is, how clearly his paltry soul sees the way to his end; he is the reverse of blind, but his keen eye-sight is forced into the service of evil, and he is mischievous in proportion to his cleverness?

Very true, he said.

But what if there had been a circumcision of such natures in the days of their youth; and they had been severed from those sensual pleasures, such as eating and drinking, which, like leaden weights, were attached to them at their birth, and which drag them down and turn the vision of their souls upon the things that are below—if, I say, they had been released from these impediments and turned in the opposite direction, the very same faculty in them would have seen the truth as keenly as they see what their eyes are turned to now.

Very likely.

Yes, I said; and there is another thing which is likely, or rather a necessary inference from what has preceded, that neither the uneducated and uninformed of the truth, nor yet those who never make an end of their education, will be able ministers of State; not the former, because they have no single aim of duty which is the rule of all their actions, private as well as public; nor the latter, because they will not act at all except upon compulsion, fancying that they are already dwelling apart in the islands of the blest.

Very true, he replied.

Then, I said, the business of us who are the founders of the State will be to compel the best minds to attain that knowledge which we have already shown to be the greatest of all—they must continue to ascend until they arrive at the good; but when they have as-

cended and seen enough we must not allow them to do as they do now.

What do you mean?

I mean that they remain in the upper world: but this must not be allowed; they must be made to descend again among the prisoners in the den, and partake of their labours and honours, whether they are worth having or not.

But is not this unjust? he said; ought we to give them a worse life, when they might have a better?

You have again forgotten, my friend, I said, the intention of the legislator, who did not aim at making any one class in the State happy above the rest; the happiness was to be in the whole State, and he held the citizens together by persuasion and necessity, making them benefactors of the State, and therefore benefactors of one another; to this end he created them, not to please themselves, but to be his instruments in binding up the State.

True, he said, I had forgotten.

Observe, Glaucon, that there will be no injustice in compelling our philosophers to have a care and providence of others; we shall explain to them that in other States, men of their class are not obliged to share in the toils of politics: and this is reasonable, for they grow up at their own sweet will, and the government would rather not have them. Being self-taught, they cannot be expected to show any gratitude for a culture which they have never received. But we have brought you into the world to be rulers of the hive, kings of yourselves and of the other citizens, and have educated you far better and more perfectly than they have been educated, and you are better able to share in the double duty. Wherefore each of you, when his turn comes, must go down to the general underground abode, and get the habit of seeing in the dark. When you have acquired the habit, you will see ten thousand times better than the inhabi-

(Socrates, Glaucon.)

tants of the den, and you will know what the several images are, and what they represent, because you have seen the beautiful and just and good in their truth. And thus our State which is also yours will be a reality, and not a dream only, and will be administered in a spirit unlike that of other States, in which men fight with one another about shadows only and are distracted in the struggle for power, which in their eyes is a great good. Whereas the truth is that the State in which the rulers are most reluctant to govern is always the best and most quietly governed, and the State in which they are most eager, the worst.

Quite true, he replied.

And will our pupils, when they hear this, refuse to take their turn at the toils of State, when they are allowed to spend the greater part of their time with one another in the heavenly light?

Impossible, he answered; for they are just men, and the commands which we impose upon them are just; there can be no doubt that every one of them will take office as a stern necessity, and not after the fashion of our present rulers of State.

Yes, my friend, I said; and there lies the point. You must contrive for your future rulers another and a better life than that of a ruler, and then you may have a well-ordered State; for only in the State which offers this, will they rule who are truly rich, not in silver and gold, but in virtue and wisdom, which are the true blessings of life. Whereas if they go to the administration of public affairs, poor and hungering after their own private advantage, thinking that hence they are to snatch the chief good, order there can never be; for they will be fighting about office, and the civil and domestic broils which thus arise will be the ruin of the rulers themselves and of the whole State.

Most true, he replied.

And the only life which looks down upon the life of political ambition is that of true philosophy. Do you know of any other?

Indeed, I do not, he said.

And those who govern ought not to be lovers of the task? For if they are, there will be rival lovers, and they will fight.

No question.

Who then are those whom we shall compel to be guardians? Surely they will be the men who are wisest about affairs of State, and by whom the State is best administered, and who at the same time have other honours and another and a better life than that of politics?

They are the men, and I will choose them, he replied.

13   Happiness as the Pursuit of Pleasure

Epicurus, Bentham, & Mill

Hedonism is the belief that pleasure is the only intrinsic good and that it is the supreme end of a good life. Aristippus of Cyrene (c. 435–366 B.C.), at first a disciple of Socrates, believed that the best kinds of pleasures should be the most intense and immediately available kind of pleasures. The experience of pleasurable physical sensations constituted true happiness. Underlying Aristippus' moral position was the belief that by nature all humans seek pleasure, that human desires or actions are determined by pleasure or displeasure. This position is now called *psychological* or *descriptive* hedonism. Aristippus also held that pleasure is the only intrinsic good all humans *ought* to seek; this is referred to as *normative* or *ethical* hedonism.

Cyrenaic hedonism was later evaluated and rejected by Epicurus (341–270 B.C.), who taught that although happiness was indeed the goal of living and that good and evil are meaningful only in reference to pleasure and pain, happiness should be conceived as a state of freedom from pain in body and mind (a state of tranquility which the Greeks called *ataraxia*). To attain this preeminently pleasurable psychological state one must seek lasting pleasures of the mind rather than immediate sense pleasures. Epicurus viewed happiness as the absence of pain rather than the presence of sensuous gratification.

Epicurus also believed that happiness was more a matter of giving up than of getting. Epicurus encouraged his followers to give up many of the things they had previously considered to be essential to the happy life. Because religion usually aroused fear of gods and death, Epicurus felt that it could be an obstacle to happiness. Religion, which can make human beings unhappy by teaching that gods interfere in life and punish after death, must be sacrificed by the determined hedonist.

Political involvement can lead to inner and outer turmoil and was thus eschewed by Epicurus. Passionate love is more often painful and transitory and therefore is not conducive to *ataraxia*. One must, to a large extent, withdraw from the world, from its distractions and disturbances, and "live unknown." The important thing, as Socrates taught, is to know yourself, and that can only be accomplished by sacrificing illusion and replacing ignorance with knowledge. The traditional virtues of courage, temperance, and justice must be measured by their leading to the most pleasant life. The highest virtue is practical wisdom (*phronesis*) or prudence; only when a person is prudent in the assessment of pleasures can he attain a serene life.

One necessary condition of a serene life, for Epicurus, was a true understanding of the laws of nature; believing in myths and stories increases fears and anxieties. By "understanding the laws of nature," Epicurus meant comprehending and appreciating the truth of the theory of nature and the universe as expounded by the Greek philosopher Democritus (fifth century B.C.). According to this theory, the universe is made up of an infinite number of eternally existing atoms—atoms which come together to constitute people and objects. To understand that the universe is so constituted is to see that the gods do not interfere with the actions of persons for good or for evil. The fear that the gods punish you, and the hope that they reward you is wholly unfounded. The fear of death is unfounded, for there is no immortal soul that survives the body. To fear death is, as Epicurus points out in his letter to Menoeceus, to fear nothing; this is foolish and is not conducive to happiness.

The English philosopher Jeremy Bentham (1748–1832) formulated a hedonistic moral philosophy quite different from Epicureanism. Like Epicurus, however, he was both a psychological and an ethical, or normative, hedonist. He believed that human beings by nature seek pleasure, and that pleasure is the supreme end which they ought to seek. Further, he taught that pleasures only differ quantitatively, in amount, strength, or the number of persons involved. One cannot rationally say that one pleasure is better than another or one pain is worse than another unless there is a difference in the *degree* of pleasure or pain that is experienced. Unlike Epicurus, Bentham most often defined happiness as predominance of pleasure over pain. Bentham also presented a more articulate moral philosophy and spelled out its application to specific moral and social issues.

Although Epicurus and Bentham can both be classified as hedonists, Bentham was also interested in a position called utilitarianism. The question as to what is good or desirable is logically distinct from the question as to how we determine whether an act is morally right. For a utilitarian, an act is morally right if, by its performance, it produces or may be expected to produce as much intrinsic good in the world as any other act under the circumstances. Bentham was a utilitarian in this sense as well as a hedonist in that he defined intrinsic good as pleasure.

With hedonism and utilitarianism as tools, Bentham thought he had achieved standards by which institutions, laws, and customs could be judged. A "science of morals" can only be developed if good and evil can be measured in terms of the consequences of actions or policies. A way of measuring and comparing pleasures and pains is needed to determine whether one is a rational hedonist. This measure was provided in Bentham's "hedonistic calculus."

John Stuart Mill (1806–1873), son of philosopher James Mill, was a friend and follower of Jeremy Bentham; and, like Bentham, Mill was concerned with the reform of society and the attainment of happiness for all. However, Mill insisted that pleasures differ in quality as well as quantity, that the happiness of others may come before one's own happiness, and that motives for actions are irrelevant to their rightness or wrongness. Mill's broad use of the term happiness and his principle of "the greatest happiness of the greatest number" developed into an influential social philosophy. Both Bentham and Mill saw that the well-being of society is closely connected with the well-being of the individual. The manner in which Mill perceived this connection was the basis for his liberalism.

Epicurus, Bentham, and Mill all would have agreed with Aristippus' maxim that we should "possess pleasure but not be possessed by it." They all considered the pleasures of the intellect to be superior to the pleasures of mere sensuous gratification. All showed some sense of moral responsibility for others. All agreed with Socrates that "the unexamined life is not worth living." These early theories of hedonism and utilitarianism have also been the basis for the more refined ethical theories in contemporary philosophy.

Letter to Menoeceus

Epicurus

Let no one when young delay to study philosophy, nor when he is old grow weary of his study. For no one can come too early or too late to secure the health of his soul. And the man who says that the age for philosophy has either not yet come or has gone by is like the man who says that the age for happiness is not yet come to him, or has passed away. Wherefore both when young and old a man must study philosophy, that as he grows old he may be young in blessings through the grateful recollection of what has been, and that in youth he may be old as well, since he will know no fear of what is to come. We must then meditate on the things that make our happiness, seeing that when that is with us we have all, but when it is absent we do all to win it.

The things which I used unceasingly to commend to you, these do and practise, considering them to be the first principles of the good life. First of all believe that god is a being immortal and blessed, even as the common idea of a god is engraved on men's minds, and do not assign to him anything alien to his immortality or ill-suited to his blessedness: but believe about him everything that can uphold his blessedness and immortality. For gods there are, since the knowledge of them is by clear vision. But they are not such as the many believe them to be: for indeed they do not consistently represent them as they believe them to be. And the impious man is not he who denies the gods of the many, but he who attaches to the gods the beliefs of the many. For the statements of the many about the gods are not conceptions derived from sensation, but false suppositions, according to which the greatest misfortunes befall the wicked and the greatest blessings the good by the gift of the gods. For men being accustomed always to their own virtues welcome those like themselves, but regard all that is not of their nature as alien.

Become accustomed to the belief that death is nothing to us. For all good and evil consists in sensation, but death is deprivation of sensation. And therefore a right understanding that death is nothing to us makes the mortality of life enjoyable, not because it adds to it an infinite span of time, but because it takes away the craving for immortality. For there is nothing terrible in life for the man who has truly comprehended that there is nothing terrible in not living. So that the man speaks but idly who says that he fears death not because it will be painful when it comes, but because it is painful in anticipation. For that which gives no trouble when it comes, is but an empty pain in anticipation. So death, the most terrifying of ills, is nothing to us, since so

Reprinted by permission from Whitney J. Oates, ed. *The Stoic and Epicurean Philosophers* (New York: Modern Library, Random House, 1940), pp. 30–33. Originally printed in *Epicurus, The Extant Remains,* trans. Cyril Bailey, copyright © 1926 by The Clarendon Press. By permission of the Oxford University Press.

long as we exist death is not with us; but when death comes, then we do not exist. It does not then concern either the living or the dead, since for the former it is not, and the latter are no more.

But the many at one moment shun death as the greatest of evils, at another yearn for it as a respite from the evils in life. But the wise man neither seeks to escape life nor fears the cessation of life, for neither does life offend him nor does the absence of life seem to be any evil. And just as with food he does not seek simply the larger share and nothing else, but rather the most pleasant, so he seeks to enjoy not the longest period of time, but the most pleasant.

And he who counsels the young man to live well, but the old man to make a good end, is foolish, not merely because of the desirability of life, but also because it is the same training which teaches to live well and to die well. Yet much worse still is the man who says it is good not to be born, but

> once born make haste to pass the gates of Death.   [Theognis, 427]

For if he says this from conviction why does he not pass away out of life? For it is open to him to do so, if he had firmly made up his mind to this. But if he speaks in jest, his words are idle among men who cannot receive them.

We must then bear in mind that the future is neither ours, nor yet wholly not ours, so that we may not altogether expect it as sure to come, nor abandon hope of it, as if it will certainly not come.

We must consider that of desires some are natural, others vain, and of the natural some are necessary and others merely natural; and of the necessary some are necessary for happiness, others for the repose of the body, and others for very life. The right understanding of these facts enables us to refer all choice and avoidance to the health of the body and the

soul's freedom from disturbance, since this is the aim of the life of blessedness. For it is to obtain this end that we always act, namely, to avoid pain and fear. And when this is once secured for us, all the tempest of the soul is dispersed, since the living creature has not to wander as though in search of something that is missing, and to look for some other thing by which he can fulfill the good of the soul and the good of the body. For it is then that we have need of pleasure, when we feel pain owing to the absence of pleasure; but when we do not feel pain, we no longer need pleasure. And for this cause we call pleasure the beginning and end of the blessed life. For we recognize pleasure as the first good innate in us, and from pleasure we begin every act of choice and avoidance, and to pleasure we return again, using the feeling as the standard by which we judge every good.

And since pleasure is the first good and natural to us, for this very reason we do not choose every pleasure, but sometimes we pass over many pleasures, when greater discomfort accrues to us as the result of them: and similarly we think many pains better than pleasures, since a greater pleasure comes to us when we have endured pains for a long time. Every pleasure then because of its natural kinship to us is good, yet not every pleasure is to be chosen: even as every pain also is an evil, yet not all are always of a nature to be avoided. Yet by a scale of comparison and by the consideration of advantages and disadvantages we must form our judgment on all these matters. For the good on certain occasions we treat as bad, and conversely the bad as good.

And again independence of desire we think a great good—not that we may at all times enjoy but a few things, but that, if we do not possess many, we may enjoy the few in the genuine persuasion that those have the sweetest pleasure in luxury who least need it, and that all that is natural is easy to be obtained, but that which is superfluous is hard. And so plain savours bring us a pleasure equal to a luxurious diet, when all the pain due to want is removed; and bread and water produce the highest pleasure, when one who needs them puts them to his lips. To grow accustomed therefore to simple and not luxurious diet gives us health to the full, and makes a man alert for the needful employments of life, and when after long intervals we approach luxuries, disposes us better towards them, and fits us to be fearless of fortune.

When, therefore, we maintain that pleasure is the end, we do not mean the pleasures of profligates and those that consist in sensuality, as is supposed by some who are either ignorant or disagree with us or do not understand, but freedom from pain in the body and from trouble in the mind. For it is not continuous drinkings and revellings, nor the satisfaction of lusts, nor the enjoyment of fish and other luxuries of the wealthy table, which produce a pleasant life, but sober reasoning, searching out the motives for all choice and avoidance, and banishing mere opinions, to which are due the greatest disturbance of the spirit.

Of all this the beginning and the greatest good is prudence. Wherefore prudence is a more precious thing even than philosophy: for from prudence are sprung all the other virtues, and it teaches us that it is not possible to live pleasantly without living prudently and honourably and justly, nor, again, to live a life of prudence, honour, and justice without living pleasantly. For the virtues are by nature bound up with the pleasant life, and the pleasant life is inseparable from them. For indeed who, think you, is a better man than he who holds reverent opinions concerning the gods, and is at all times free from fear of death, and has reasoned out the end ordained by nature? He understands that the limit of good things is easy to fulfill and easy to attain, whereas the course of ills is either short in time or slight in pain: he laughs at destiny, whom some have introduced as the mistress of all things. He thinks that with us lies the chief power in determining events, some of which happen by necessity and some by chance, and some are within our control; for while necessity cannot be called to account, he sees that chance is inconstant, but that which is in our control is subject to no master, and to it are naturally attached praise and blame. For, indeed, it were better to follow the myths about the gods than to become a slave to the destiny of the natural philosophers: for the former suggests a hope of placating the gods by worship, whereas the latter involves a necessity which knows no placation. As to chance, he does not regard it as a god as most men do (for in a god's acts there is no disorder), nor as an uncertain cause of all things: for he does not believe that good and evil are given by chance to man for the framing of a blessed life, but that opportunities for great good and great evil are afforded by it. He therefore thinks it better to be unfortunate in reasonable action than to prosper in unreason. For it is better in a man's actions that what is well chosen should fail, rather than that what is ill chosen should be successful owing to chance.

Meditate therefore on these things and things akin to them night and day by yourself, and with a companion like to yourself, and never shall you be disturbed waking or asleep, but you shall live like a god among men. For a man who lives among immortal blessings is not like to a mortal being.

Of the Principle of Utility

Jeremy Bentham

I. Nature has placed mankind under the governance of two sovereign masters, *pain* and *pleasure*. It is for them alone to point out what we ought to do, as well as to determine what we shall do. On the one hand the standard of right and wrong, on the other the chain of causes and effects, are fastened to their throne. They govern us in all we do, in all we say, in all we think: every effort we can make to throw off our subjection, will serve but to demonstrate and confirm it. In words a man may pretend to abjure their empire: but in reality he will remain subject to it all the while. The *principle of utility* recognizes this subjection, and assumes it for the foundation of that system, the object of which is to rear the fabric of felicity by the hands of reason and of law. Systems which attempt to question it, deal in sounds instead of sense, in caprice instead of reason, in darkness instead of light.

But enough of metaphor and declamation: it is not by such means that moral science is to be improved.

II. The principle of utility is the foundation of the present work: it will be proper therefore at the outset to give an explicit and determinate account of what is meant by it. By the principle of utility is meant that principle which approves or disapproves of every

From Jeremy Bentham, *An Introduction to the Principles of Morals and Legislation* (Oxford: Clarendon Press, 1876).

action whatsoever, according to the tendency which it appears to have to augment or diminish the happiness of the party whose interest is in question: or, what is the same thing in other words, to promote or to oppose that happiness. I say of every action whatsoever; and therefore not only of every action of a private individual, but of every measure of government.

III. By utility is meant that property in any object, whereby it tends to produce benefit, advantage, pleasure, good, or happiness, (all this in the present case comes to the same thing) or (what comes again to the same thing) to prevent the happening of mischief, pain, evil, or unhappiness to the party whose interest is considered: if that party be the community in general, then the happiness of the community: if a particular individual, then the happiness of that individual.

IV. The interest of the community is one of the most general expressions that can occur in the phraseology of morals: no wonder that the meaning of it is often lost. When it has a meaning, it is this. The community is a fictitious *body*, composed of the individual persons who are considered as constituting as it were its *members*. The interest of the community then is, what?—the sum of the interests of the several members who compose it.

V. It is in vain to talk of the interest of the community, without understanding what is the interest of the individual. A thing is said to promote the interest, or to be *for* the interest, of an individual, when it tends to add to the sum total of his pleasures: or, what comes to the same thing, to diminish the sum total of his pain.

VI. An action then may be, said to be conformable to the principle of utility, or, for shortness sake, to utility, (meaning with respect to the community at large) when the tendency it has to augment the happiness of the community is greater than any it has to diminish it.

VII. A measure of government (which is but a particular kind of action, performed by a particular person or persons) may be said to be conformable to or dictated by the principle of utility, when in like manner the tendency which it has to augment the happiness of the community is greater than any which it has to diminish it. . . .

Of the Four Sanctions or Sources of Pain and Pleasure

Jeremy Bentham

I. It has been shown that the happiness of the individuals, of whom a community is composed, that is their pleasures and their security, is the end and the sole end which the legislator ought to have in view: the sole standard, in conformity to which each individual ought, as far as depends upon the legislator, to be *made* to fashion his behaviour. But whether it be this or any thing else that is to be *done,* there is nothing by which a man can ultimately be *made* to do it, but either pain or pleasure. Having taken a general view of these two grand objects (*viz.* pleasure, and what comes to the same thing, immunity from pain) in the character of *final* causes; it will be necessary to take a view of pleasure and pain itself, in the character of *efficient* causes or means.

II. There are four distinguishable sources from which pleasure and pain are in use to flow: considered separately, they may be termed the *physical,* the *political,* the *moral,* and the *religious:* and inasmuch as the pleasures and pains belonging to each of them are capable of giving a binding force to any law or rule of conduct, they may all of them be termed *sanctions.**

III. If it be in the present life, and from the ordinary course of nature, not purposely modified by the interposition of the will of any human being, nor by any extraordinary interposition of any superior invisible being, that the pleasure or the pain takes place or is expected, it may be said to issue from or to belong to the *physical sanction.*

IV. If at the hands of a *particular* person or set of persons in the community who under names correspondent to that of *judge,* are chosen for the particular purpose of dispensing it, according to the will of the sovereign or supreme ruling power in the state, it may be said to issue from the *political sanction.*

V. If at the hands of such *chance* persons in the community, as the party in question may happen in the course of his life to have concerns with, according to each man's spontaneous disposition, and not according to any settled or concerted rule, it may be said to issue from the *moral* or *popular sanction.*†

From Jeremy Bentham, *An Introduction to the Principles of Morals and Legislation* (Oxford: Clarendon Press, 1876).

* Sanctio, in Latin, was used to signify the *act of binding,* and, by a common grammatical transition, *any thing which serves to bind a man:* to wit, to the observance of such or such a mode of conduct. A Sanction then is a source of obligatory powers or *motives:* that is, of *pains* and *pleasures;* which, according as they are connected with such or such modes of conduct, operate, and are indeed the only things which can operate, as *motives.*

† Better termed *popular,* as more directly indicative of its constituent cause; as likewise of its relation to the more common phrase *public opinion,* in French *opinion publique,* the name there given to that tutelary power, of which of late so much is

VI. If from the immediate hand of a superior invisible being, either in the present life, or in a future, it may be said to issue from the *religious sanction.*

VII. Pleasures or pains which may be expected to issue from the *physical, political,* or *moral* sanctions, must all of them be expected to be experienced, if ever, in the *present* life: those which may be expected to issue from the *religious* sanction, may be expected to be experienced either in the *present* life or in a *future.*

VIII. Those which can be experienced in the present life, can of course be no others than such as human nature in the course of the present life is susceptible of: and from each of these sources may flow all the pleasures or pains of which, in the course of the present life, human nature is susceptible. With regard to these then (with which alone we have in this place any concern) those of them which belong to any one of those sanctions, differ not ultimately in kind from those which belong to any one of the other three: the only difference there is among them lies in the circumstances that accompany their production. A suffering which befalls a man in the natural and spontaneous course of things, shall be styled, for instance, a *calamity;* in which case, if it be supposed to befall him through any imprudence of his, it may be styled a punishment issuing from the physical sanction. Now this same suffering, if inflicted by the law, will be what is commonly called a *punishment;* if incurred for want of any friendly assistance, which the misconduct, or supposed misconduct, of the sufferer has occasioned to be withholden, a punishment issuing from the *moral* sanction; if through the immediate interposition of a particular providence,

a punishment issuing from the religious sanction.

IX. A man's goods, or his person, are consumed by fire. If this happened to him by what is called an accident, it was a calamity: if by reason of his own imprudence (for instance, from his neglecting to put his candle out) it may be styled a punishment of the physical sanction: if it happened to him by the sentence of the political magistrate, a punishment belonging to the political sanction; that is, what is commonly called a punishment: if for want of any assistance which his *neighbour* withheld from him out of some dislike to his *moral* character, a punishment of the *moral* sanction: if by an immediate act of *God's* displeasure, manifested on account of some *sin* committed by him, or through any distraction of mind, occasioned by the dread of such displeasure, a punishment of the *religious* sanction.

X. As to such of the pleasures and pains belonging to the religious sanction, as regard a future life, of what kind these may be we cannot know. These lie not open to our observation. During the present life they are matter only of expectation: and, whether that expectation be derived from natural or revealed religion, the particular kind of pleasure or pain, if it be different from all those which lie open to our observation, is what we can have no idea of. The best ideas we can obtain of such pains and pleasures are altogether unliquidated in point of quality. In what other respects our ideas of them *may* be liquidated will be considered in another place.

XI. Of these four sanctions the physical is altogether, we may observe, the ground-work of the political and the moral: so is it also of the religious, in as far as the latter bears relation to the present life. It is included in each of those other three. This may operate in any case, (that is, any of the pains or pleasures belonging to it may operate) independently of *them:* none of *them* can operate but by means of this. In a word, the powers of nature may op-

---

said, and by which so much is done. The latter appellation is however unhappy and inexpressive; since if *opinion* is material, it is only in virtue of the influence it exercises over action, through the medium of the affections and the will.

erate of themselves; but neither the magistrate, nor men at large, *can* operate, nor is God in the case in question *supposed* to operate, but through the powers of nature.

XII. For these four objects, which in their nature have so much in common, it seemed of use to find a common name. It seemed of use, in the first place, for the convenience of giving a name to certain pleasures and pains, for which a name equally characteristic could hardly otherwise have been found: in the second place, for the sake of holding up the efficacy of certain moral forces, the influence of which is apt not to be sufficiently attended to. Does the political sanction exert an influence over the conduct of mankind? The moral, the religious sanctions do so too. In every inch of his career are the operations of the political magistrate liable to be aided or impeded by these two foreign powers: who, one or other of them, or both, are sure to be either his rivals or his allies. Does it happen to him to leave them out in his calculations? He will be sure almost to find himself mistaken in the result. Of all this we shall find abundant proofs in the sequel of this work. It behoves him, therefore, to have them continually before his eyes; and that under such a name as exhibits the relation they bear to his own purposes and designs.

How Pleasures and Pains Can Be Measured

Jeremy Bentham

I. Pleasures then, and the avoidance of pains, are the *ends* which the legislator has in view: it behoves him therefore to understand their *value.* Pleasures and pains are the *instruments* he has to work with: it behoves him therefore to understand their force, which is again, in other words, their value.

II. To a person considered *by himself* the value of a pleasure or pain considered *by itself,* will be greater or less, according to the four following circumstances.

1. Its *intensity.*
2. Its *duration.*
3. Its *certainty* or *uncertainty.*
4. Its *propinquity* or *remoteness.*

III. These are the circumstances which are to be considered in estimating a pleasure or a pain considered each of them by itself. But when the value of any pleasure or pain is considered for the purpose of estimating the tendency of any *act* by which it is produced, there are two other circumstances to be taken into the account; these are,

5. Its *fecundity,* or the chance it has of being followed by sensations of the *same* kind:

From Jeremy Bentham, *An Introduction to the Principles of Morals and Legislation* (Oxford: Clarendon Press, 1876).

that is, pleasures, if it be a pleasure: pains, if it be a pain.

6. Its *purity,* or the chance it has of *not* being followed by sensations of the *opposite* kind: that is, pains, if it be a pleasure: pleasures, if it be a pain.

These two last, however, are in strictness scarcely to be deemed properties of pleasure or the pain itself; they are not, therefore, in strictness to be taken into the account of the value of that pleasure or pain. They are in strictness to be deemed properties only of the act, or other event, by which such pleasure or pain has been produced; and accordingly are only to be taken into the account of the tendency of such act or such event.

IV. To a *number* of persons, with reference to each of whom the value of a pleasure or a pain is considered, it will be greater or less, according to seven circumstances: to wit, the six preceding ones; *viz.*

1. Its *intensity.*
2. Its *duration.*
3. Its *certainty* or *uncertainty.*
4. Its *propinquity* or *remoteness.*
5. Its *fecundity.*
6. Its *purity.*

And one other; to wit:

7. Its *extent;* that is, the number of persons

to whom it *extends;* or (in other words) who are affected by it.*

V. To take an exact account then of the general tendency of any act, by which the interests of a community are affected, proceed as follows. Begin with any one person of those whose interests seem most immediately to be affected by it: and take an account,

1. Of the values of each distinguishable *pleasure* which appears to be produced by it in the *first* instance.

2. Of the value of each *pain* which appears to be produced by it in the *first* instance.

3. Of the value of each pleasure which appears to be produced by it *after* the first. This constitutes the *fecundity* of the first *pleasure* and the *impurity* of the first *pain.*

4. Of the value of each *pain* which appears to be produced by it after the first. This constitutes the *fecundity* of the first *pain,* and the *impurity* of the first pleasure.

5. Sum up all the values of all the *pleasures*

* Not long after the publication of the first edition, the following memoriter verses were framed, in the view of lodging more effectually, in the memory, these points, on which the whole fabric of morals and legislation may be seen to rest.

Intense, long, certain, speedy, fruitful, pure—
Such marks in *pleasure* and in *pains* endure.
Such pleasures seek if *private* be thy end:
If it be *public,* wide let them *extend.*
Such *pains* avoid, whichever be thy view:
If pains *must* come, let them *extend* to few.

on the one side, and those of all the pains on the other. The balance, if it be on the side of pleasure, will give the *good* tendency of the act upon the whole, with respect to the interests of that *individual* person; if on the side of pain, the *bad* tendency of it upon the whole.

6. Take an account of the *number* of persons whose interests appear to be concerned; and repeat the above process with respect to each. *Sum up* the numbers expressive of the degrees of *good* tendency, which the act has, with respect to each individual, in regard to whom the tendency of it is *good* upon the whole: do this again with respect to each individual, in regard to whom the tendency of it is *good* upon the whole: do this again with respect to each individual, in regard to whom the tendency of it is *bad* upon the whole. Take the *balance;* which, if on the side of *pleasure,* will give the general *good tendency* of the act, with respect to the total number or community of individuals concerned; if on the side of pain, the general *evil tendency,* with respect to the same community.

VI. It is not to be expected that this process should be strictly pursued previously to every moral judgment, or to every legislative or judicial operation. It may, however, be always kept in view: and as near as the process actually pursued on these occasions approaches to it, so near will such process approach to the character of an exact one.

Utilitarianism and the Good Life

John Stuart Mill

The creed which accepts as the foundation of morals Utility, or the Greatest Happiness Principle, holds that actions are right in proportion as they tend to promote happiness, wrong as they tend to produce the reverse of happiness. By 'happiness' is intended pleasure, and the absence of pain; by 'unhappiness,' pain, and the privation of pleasure. To give a clear view of the moral standard set up by the theory, much more requires to be said; in particular, what things it includes in the ideas of pain and pleasure; and to what extent this is left an open question. But these supplementary explanations do not affect the theory of life on which this theory of morality is grounded—namely, that pleasure, and freedom from pain, are the only things desirable as ends; and that all desirable things (which are as numerous in the utilitarian as in any other scheme) are desirable either for the pleasure inherent in themselves, or as means to the promotion of pleasure and the prevention of pain. . . .

Now, such a theory of life excites in many minds, and among them in some of the most estimable in feeling and purpose, inveterate dislike. To suppose that life has (as they express it) no higher end than pleasure—no better and nobler object of desire and pursuit —they designate as utterly mean and grovel-

From John Stuart Mill, *Utilitarianism* (London: Longmans, Green and Company, 1897).

ing; as a doctrine worthy only of swine, to whom the followers of Epicurus were, at a very early period, contemptuously likened; and modern holders of the doctrine are occasionally made the subject of equally polite comparisons by its German, French, and English assailants.

When thus attacked, the Epicureans have always answered that it is not they, but their accusers, who represent human nature in a degrading light; since the accusation supposes human beings to be capable of no pleasures except those of which swine are capable. If this supposition were true, the charge could not be gainsaid, but would then be no longer an imputation: for if the sources of pleasure were precisely the same to human beings and to swine, the rule of life which is good enough for the one would be good enough for the other. The comparison of the Epicurean life to that of beasts is felt as degrading, precisely because a beast's pleasures do not satisfy a human being's conceptions of happiness. Human beings have faculties more elevated than the animal appetites, and when once made conscious of them, do not regard anything as happiness which does not include their gratification. I do not, indeed, consider the Epicureans to have been by any means faultless in drawing out their scheme of consequences from the utilitarian principle. To do this in any sufficient manner, many Stoic, as well as Christian elements require to be included. But there is no known

Epicurean theory of life which does not assign to the pleasures of the intellect, of the feelings and imagination, and of the moral sentiments, a much higher value as pleasures than to those of mere sensation. It must be admitted, however, that utilitarian writers in general have placed the superiority of mental over bodily pleasures chiefly in the greater permanency, safety, uncostliness, etc., of the former—that is, in their circumstantial advantages rather than in their intrinsic nature. And on all these points utilitarians have fully proved their case; but they might have taken the other, and, as it may be called, higher ground, with entire consistency. It is quite compatible with the principle of utility to recognize the fact, that some *kinds* of pleasure are more desirable and more valuable than others. It would be absurd that while, in estimating all other things, quality is considered as well as quantity, the estimation of pleasures should be supposed to depend on quantity alone. . . .

If I am asked what I mean by difference of quality in pleasures, or what makes one pleasure more valuable than another, merely as a pleasure, except its being greater in amount, there is but one possible answer. Of two pleasures, if there be one to which all or almost all who have experience of both give a decided preference, irrespective of any feeling of moral obligation to prefer it, that is the more desirable pleasure. If one of the two is, by those who are competently acquainted with both, placed so far above the other than they prefer it, even though knowing it to be attended with a greater amount of discontent, and would not resign it for any quantity of the other pleasure which their nature is capable of, we are justified in ascribing to the preferred enjoyment a superiority in quality, so far outweighing quantity as to render it, in comparison, of small account.

Now it is an unquestionable fact that those who are equally acquainted with, and equally capable of appreciating and enjoying, both, do give a most marked preference to the manner of existence which employs their higher faculties. Few human creatures would consent to be changed into any of the lower animals, for a promise of the fullest allowance of a beast's pleasures; no intelligent human being would consent to be a fool, no instructed person would be an ignoramus, no person of feeling and conscience would be selfish and base, even though they should be persuaded that the fool, the dunce, or the rascal is better satisfied with his lot than they are with theirs. They would not resign what they possess more than he, for the most complete satisfaction of all the desires which they have in common with him. If they ever fancy they would, it is only in cases of unhappiness so extreme, that to escape from it they would exchange their lot for almost any other, however undesirable in their own eyes. A being of higher faculties requires more to make him happy, is capable probably of more acute suffering, and certainly accessible to it at more points, than one of an inferior type; but in spite of these liabilities, he can never really wish to sink into what he feels to be a lower grade of existence. We may give what explanation we please of this unwillingness; we may attribute it to pride, a name which is given indiscriminately to some of the most and to some of the least estimable feelings of which mankind are capable; we may refer it to the love of liberty and personal independence, an appeal to which was with the Stoics one of the most effective means for the inculcation of it; to the love of power, or to the love of excitement, both of which do really enter into and contribute to it: but its most appropriate appellation is a sense of dignity, which all human beings possess in one form or other, and in some, though by no means in exact, proportion to their higher faculties, and which is so essential a part of the happiness of those in whom it is strong, that nothing which conflicts with it could be, otherwise than momentarily, an object of desire to them. Whoever supposes that this preference takes place at a sacrifice of happiness—that the superior being, in anything like equal circumstances, is not happier than the inferior—confounds the two very different ideas, of happiness and content. It is indisputable that the being whose capacities of enjoyment are low, has the greatest chance of having them fully satisfied; and a highly-endowed being will always feel that any happiness which he can look for, as the world is constituted, is imperfect. But he can learn to bear its imperfections, if they are at all bearable; and they will not make him envy the being who is indeed unconscious of the imperfections, but only because he feels not at all the good which those imperfections qualify. It is better to be a human being dissatisfied than a pig satisfied; better to be Socrates dissatisfied than a fool satisfied. And if the fool, or the pig, is of a different opinion, it is because they only know their own side of the question. The other party to the comparison knows both sides. . . .

It may be objected, that many who are capable of the higher pleasures, occasionally, under the influence of temptation, postpone them to the lower. But this is quite compatible with a full appreciation of the intrinsic superiority of the higher. Men often, from infirmity of character, make their election for the nearer good, though they know it to be the less valuable; and this no less when the choice is between two bodily pleasures, than when it is between bodily and mental. They pursue sensual indulgences to the injury of health, though perfectly aware that health is the greater good. It may be further objected, that many who begin with youthful enthusiasm for everything noble, as they advance in years sink into indolence and selfishness. But I do not believe that those who undergo this very common change, voluntarily choose the lower description of pleasures in preference to the higher. I believe that before they devote themselves exclusively to the one, they have already become incapable of the other. Capacity for the

nobler feelings is in most natures a very tender plant, easily killed, not only by hostile influences, but by mere want of sustenance; and in the majority of young persons it speedily dies away if the occupations to which their position in life has devoted them, and the society into which it has thrown them, are not favorable to keeping that higher capacity in exercise. Men lose their high aspirations as they lose their intellectual tastes, because they have not time or opportunity for indulging them; and they addict themselves to inferior pleasures, not because they deliberately prefer them, but because they are either the only ones to which they have access, or the only ones which they are any longer capable of enjoying. It may be questioned whether anyone who has remained equally susceptible to both classes of pleasures, ever knowingly and calmly preferred the lower; though many, in all ages, have broken down in an ineffectual attempt to combine both.

From this verdict of the only competent judges, I apprehend there can be no appeal. On a question which is the best worth having of two pleasures, or which of two modes of existence is the most grateful to the feelings, apart from its moral attributes and from its consequences, the judgment of those who are qualified by knowledge of both, or, if they differ, that of the majority among them, must be admitted as final. And there needs to be the less hesitation to accept this judgment respecting the quality of pleasures, since there is no other tribunal to be referred to even on the question of quantity. What means are there of determining which is the acutest of two pains, or the intensest of two pleasurable sensations, except the general suffrage of those who are familiar with both? Neither pains nor pleasures are homogeneous, and pain is always heterogeneous with pleasure. What is there to decide whether a particular pleasure is worth purchasing at the cost of a particular pain, except the feelings and judgment of the experienced? When, therefore, those feelings and judgment declare the pleasures derived from the higher faculties to be preferable *in kind,* apart from the question of intensity, to those of which the animal nature, disjoined from the higher faculties, is susceptible, they are entitled on this subject to the same regard. . . .

I have dwelt on this point, as being a necessary part of a perfectly just conception of Utility, or Happiness, considered as the directive rule of human conduct. But it is by no means an indispensable condition to the acceptance of the utilitarian standard; for that standard is not the agent's own greatest happiness, but the greatest amount of happiness altogether; and if it may possibly be doubted whether a noble character is always the happier for its nobleness, there can be no doubt that it makes other people happier, and that the world in general is immensely a gainer by it. Utilitarianism, therefore, could only attain its end by the general cultivation of nobleness of character, even if each individual were only benefited by the nobleness of others, and his own, so far as happiness is concerned, were a sheer deduction from the benefit. But the bare enunciation of such an absurdity as this last, renders refutation superfluous.

According to the Greatest Happiness Principle, as above explained, the ultimate end, with reference to and for the sake of which all other things are desirable (whether we are considering our own good or that of other people), is an existence exempt as far as possible from pain, and as rich as possible in enjoyments, both in point of quantity and quality; the test of quality, and the rule for measuring it against quantity, being the preference felt by those who, in their opportunities of experience, to which must be added their habits of self-consciousness and self-observation, are best furnished with the means of comparison. This, being, according to the utilitarian opinion, the end of human action is necessarily also the standard of morality; which may accord-

ingly be defined, the rules and precepts for human conduct, by the observance of which an existence such as has been described might be, to the greatest extent possible, secured to all mankind; and not to them only, but, so far as the nature of things admits, to the whole sentient creation. . . .

When, however, it is thus positively asserted to be impossible that human life should be happy, the assertion, if not something like a verbal quibble, is at least an exaggeration. If by happiness be meant a continuity of highly pleasurable excitement, it is evident enough that this is impossible. A state of exalted pleasure lasts only moments, or in some cases, and with some intermissions, hours or days, and is the occasional brilliant flash of enjoyment, not its permanent and steady flame. Of this the philosophers who have taught that happiness is the end of life were as fully aware as those who taunt them. The happiness which they meant was not a life of rapture; but moments of such, in an existence made up of few and transitory pains, many and various pleasures, with a decided predominance of the active over the passive, and having as the foundation of the whole, not to expect more from life than it is capable of bestowing. A life thus composed, to those who have been fortunate enough to obtain it, has always appeared worthy of the name of happiness. And such an existence is even now the lot of many, during some considerable portion of their lives. The present wretched education, and wretched social arrangements, are the only real hinderance to its being attainable by almost all.

The objectors perhaps may doubt whether human beings, if taught to consider happiness as the end of life, would be satisfied with such a moderate share of it. But great numbers of mankind have been satisfied with much less. The main constituents of a satisfied life appear to be two, either of which by itself is often found sufficient for the purpose: tranquillity and excitement. With much tranquillity, many find that they can be content with very little pleasure: with much excitement, many can reconcile themselves to a considerable quantity of pain. There is assuredly no inherent impossibility in enabling even the mass of mankind to unite both; since the two are so far from being incompatible that they are in natural alliance, the prolongation of either being a preparation for, and exciting a wish for, the other. . . . When people who are tolerably fortunate in their outward lot do not find in life sufficient enjoyment to make it valuable to them, the cause generally is, caring for nobody but themselves. To those who have neither public nor private affections, the excitements of life are much curtailed, and in any case dwindle in value as the time approaches when all selfish interests must be terminated by death: while those who leave after them objects of personal affection, and especially those who have also cultivated a fellow-feeling with the collective interests of mankind, retain as lively an interest in life on the eve of death as in the vigor of youth and health. Next to selfishness, the principal cause which makes life unsatisfactory is want of mental cultivation. A cultivated mind—I do not mean that of a philosopher, but any mind to which the fountains of knowledge have been opened, and which has been taught, in any tolerable degree, to exercise its faculties—finds sources of inexhaustible interest in all that surrounds it; in the objects of nature, the achievements of art, the imaginations of poetry, the incidents of history, the ways of mankind past and present, and their prospects in the future. . . .

Let utilitarians never cease to claim the morality of self-devotion as a possession which belongs by as good a right to them, as either to the Stoic or to the Transcendentalist. The utilitarian morality does recognize in human beings the power of sacrificing their own greatest good for the good of others. It only refuses to admit that the sacrifice is itself a good. A sacrifice which does not increase, or tend to increase, the sum total of happiness, it considers as wasted. The only self-renunciation which it applauds, is devotion to the happiness, or to some of the means of happiness, of others; either of mankind collectively, or of individuals within the limits imposed by the collective interests of mankind.

I must again repeat, what the assailants of utilitarianism seldom have the justice to acknowledge, that the happiness which forms the utilitarian standard of what is right in conduct, is not the agent's own happiness, but that of all concerned. As between his own happiness and that of others, utilitarianism requires him to be as strictly impartial as a disinterested and benevolent spectator. In the golden rule of Jesus of Nazareth, we read the complete spirit of the ethics of utility. To do as one would be done by, and to love one's neighbor as oneself, constitute the ideal perfection of utilitarian morality. As the means of making the nearest approach to this ideal, utility would enjoin, first, that laws and social arrangements should place the happiness, or (as speaking practically it may be called) the interest, of every individual, as nearly as possible in harmony with the interest of the whole; and secondly, that education and opinion, which have so vast a power over human character, should so use that power as to establish in the mind of every individual an indissoluble association between his own happiness and the good of the whole; especially between his own happiness and the practice of such modes of conduct, negative and positive, as regard for the universal happiness prescribes: so that not only he may be unable to conceive the possibility of happiness to himself, consistently with conduct opposed to the general good, but also that a direct impulse to promote the general good may be in every individual one of the habitual motives of action, and the sentiments connected therewith may fill a large and prominent place in every human being's sentient existence. If the impugners of the utilitarian morality represented it to their own minds in this its true character, I know not what recommendation possessed by any other morality they could possibly affirm to be wanting to it: what more beautiful or more exalted developments of human nature any other ethical system can be supposed to foster, or what springs of action, not accessible to the utilitarian, such systems rely on for giving effect to their mandates. . . .

They say it is exacting too much to require that people shall always act from the inducement of promoting the general interests of society. But this is to mistake the very meaning of a standard of morals, and confound the rule of action with the motive of it. It is the business of ethics to tell us what are our duties, or by what test we may know them; but no system of ethics requires that the sole motive of all we do shall be a feeling of duty; on the contrary, ninety-nine hundredths of all our actions are done from other motives, and rightly so done; if the rule of duty does not condemn them. It is the more unjust to utilitarianism that this particular misapprehension should be made a ground of objection to it, inasmuch as utilitarian moralists have gone beyond almost all others in affirming that the motive has nothing to do with the morality of the action, though much with the worth of the agent. He who saves a fellow creature from drowning does what is morally right, whether his motive be duty, or the hope of being paid for his trouble; he who betrays the friend that trusts him, is guilty of a crime, even if his object be to serve another friend to whom he is under greater obligations. But to speak only of actions done from the motive of duty, and in direct obedience to principle: it is a misapprehension of the utilitarian mode of thought, to conceive it as implying that people should fix their minds upon so wide a generality as the world, or society at large. The great majority of good actions are intended not for the benefit of the world, but for that of individuals, of which the good of the world is made up; and the thoughts of the most virtuous man need not on these occasions travel beyond the particular persons concerned, except so far as is necessary to assure himself that in benefiting them he is not violating the rights—that is, the legitimate and authorized expectations—of anyone else. . . .

The principle of utility either has, or there is no reason why it might not have, all the sanctions which belong to any other system of morals. Those sanctions are either external or internal. Of the external sanctions it is not necessary to speak at any length. They are, the hope of favor and the fear of displeasure from our fellow creatures or from the Ruler of the Universe, along with whatever we may have of sympathy or affection for them, or of love and awe of Him, inclining us to do His will independently of selfish consequences. There is evidently no reason why all these motives for observance should not attach themselves to the utilitarian morality, as completely and as powerfully as to any other. Indeed, those of them which refer to our fellow creatures are sure to do so, in proportion to the amount of general intelligence; for whether there be any other ground of moral obligation than the general happiness or not, men do desire happiness; and however imperfect may be their own practice, they desire and commend all conduct in others towards themselves, by which they think their happiness is promoted. With regard to the religious motive, if men believe, as most profess to do, in the goodness of God, those who think that conduciveness to the general happiness is the essence, or even only the criterion of good, must necessarily believe that it is also that which God approves. The whole force therefore of external reward and punishment, whether physical or moral, and whether proceeding from God or from our fellow men, together with all that the capacities of human nature admit, of disinterested devotion to either, become available to enforce the utilitarian morality, in proportion as that morality is recognized; and the more powerfully, the more the appliances of education and general cultivation are bent to the purpose.

So far as to external sanctions. The internal sanction of duty, whatever our standard of duty may be, is one and the same—a feeling in our own mind; a pain, more or less intense, attendant on violation of duty, which in properly cultivated moral natures rises, in the more serious cases, into shrinking from it as an impossibility. This feeling, when disinterested, and connecting itself with the pure idea of duty, and not with some particular form of it, or with any of the merely accessory circumstances, is the essence of Conscience; though in that complex phenomenon as it actually exists, the simple fact is in general all encrusted over with collateral associations, derived from sympathy, from love, and still more from fear; from all the forms of religious feeling; from the recollections of childhood and of all our past life; from self-esteem, desire of the esteem of others, and occasionally even self-abasement. . . .

It is not necessary, for the present purpose, to decide whether the feeling of duty is innate or implanted. Assuming it to be innate, it is an open question to what objects it naturally attaches itself; for the philosophic supporters of that theory are now agreed that the intuitive perception is of principles of morality, and not of the details. If there be anything innate in the matter, I see no reason why the feeling which is innate should not be that of regard to the pleasures and pains of others. If there is any principle of morals which is intuitively obligatory, I should say it must be that. If so, the intuitive ethics would coincide with the utilitarian, and there would be no further quarrel between them. Even as it is, the intuitive moralists, though they believe that there are other intuitive moral obligations, do already believe this to be one; for they unanimously hold that a large *portion* of morality turns upon the consideration due to the interests of our fellow

creatures. Therefore, if the belief in the transcendental origin of moral obligation gives any additional efficacy to the internal sanction, it appears to me that the utilitarian principle has already the benefit of it.

On the other hand, if, as is my own belief, the moral feelings are not innate, but acquired, they are not for that reason the less natural. It is natural to man to speak, to reason, to build cities, to cultivate the ground, though these are acquired faculties. The moral feelings are not indeed a part of our nature, in the sense of being in any perceptible degree present in all of us; but this, unhappily, is a fact admitted by those who believe the most strenuously in their transcendental origin. Like the other acquired capacities above referred to, the moral faculty, if not a part of our nature, is a natural outgrowth from it; capable, like them, in a certain small degree, of springing up spontaneously; and susceptible of being brought by cultivation to a high degree of development. Unhappily it is also susceptible, by a sufficient use of the external sanctions and of the force of early impressions, of being cultivated in almost any direction: so that there is hardly anything so absurd or so mischievous that it may not, by means of these influences, be made to act on the human mind with all the authority of conscience. To doubt that the same potency might be given by the same means to the principle of utility, even if it had no foundation in human nature, would be flying in the face of all experience.

But moral associations which are wholly of artificial creation, when intellectual culture goes on, yield by degrees to the dissolving force of analysis: and if the feeling of duty, when associated with utility, would appear equally arbitrary; if there were no leading department of our nature, no powerful class of sentiments, with which that association would harmonize, which would make us feel it congenial, and incline us not only to foster it in others (for which we have abundant interested motives), but also to cherish it in ourselves; if there were not, in short, a natural basis of sentiment for utilitarian morality, it might well happen that this association also, even after it had been implanted by education, might be analyzed away.

But there *is* this basis of powerful natural sentiment; and this it is which, when once the general happiness is recognized as the ethical standard, will constitute the strength of the utilitarian morality. This firm foundation is that of the social feelings of mankind; the desire to be in unity with our fellow creatures, which is already a powerful principle in human nature, and happily one of those which tend to become stronger, even without express inculcation, from the influences of advancing civilisation.

The deeply-rooted conception which every individual even now has of himself as a social being, tends to make him feel it one of his natural wants that there should be harmony between his feeling and aims and those of his fellow creatures. If differences of opinion and of mental culture make it impossible for him to share many of their actual feelings—perhaps make him denounce and defy those feelings—

he still needs to be conscious that his real aim and theirs do not conflict; that he is not opposing himself to what they really wish for, namely, their own good, but is, on the contrary, promoting it. This feeling in most individuals is much inferior in strength to their selfish feelings, and is often wanting altogether. But to those who have it, it possesses all the characters of a natural feeling. It does not present itself to their minds as a superstition of education, or a law despotically imposed by the power of society, but as an attribute which it would not be well for them to be without. This conviction is the ultimate sanction of the greatest-happiness morality. This it is which makes any mind, of well-developed feelings, work with, and not against, the outward motives to care for others, afforded by what I have called the external sanctions; and when those sanctions are wanting, or act in an opposite direction, constitutes in itself a powerful internal binding force, in proportion to the sensitiveness and thoughtfulness of the character; since few but those whose mind is a moral blank, could bear to lay out their course of life on the plan of paying no regard to others except so far as their own private interest compels.

14 Beyond Pleasure and Happiness

Kant & Frankl

Schopenhauer's pessimistic arguments against living a life of pleasure have already been presented, but long before Schopenhauer the belief that the good life should have as its focal point the pursuit of pleasures was the subject of philosophical scrutiny. Both Socrates and Plato placed rational enlightenment above all sensuous delights. Aristotle considered pleasure to be a byproduct of successful functioning, and thus an important part of the good life, but not the supreme end of life or the highest form of self-realization. Other Greek philosophers, the Cynics and the Stoics, totally rejected hedonism and delivered strictures against it.

The anti-hedonistic strain in Greek and Roman philosophy could be considered minor, however, compared with the dominant ascetic emphasis of Christian philosophy, which worshipped a suffering God who had commanded his followers to reject earthly pleasures for heavenly rewards. This Christian tradition played an important role in molding the attitudes and views of the German philosopher Immanuel Kant (1724–1804), the greatest proponent of duty in the history of ethics. In a series of works, the most famous of which is *The Critique of Pure Reason,* Kant assessed the cognitive powers of reason, explored the nature and limits of scientific knowledge, and made way for the establishment of a firm basis for man's most cherished beliefs—the beliefs in God, freedom, and immortality.

Our knowledge of the natural world comes from a highly complex rational structuring of our experience by inner *a priori* forms of thought. Some of these forms of thought are "the categories of understanding" by which we classify and comprehend the sensations which present themselves to our minds. These rational concepts such as "cause" and "substance" would be empty were there no sensations to which they referred. Conversely, without these concepts to give them order, coherence, and significance, sensations would be blind. What our knowledge of nature gives us is a structured appearance of things and not "things in themselves," i.e., things apart from the knowing process. Scientific knowledge involves rational and empirical factors and is a cooperative affair in which both the mind and the object make a contribution. The world as we know it carries the stamp of our concepts.

Since scientific knowledge is limited in its scope to what the mind structures, we can pass from epistemology to ethics. Kant sought an underlying *a priori* basis for moral obligation, not in "pure reason" but in "practical reason," reason which regulates our actions. For utilitarians, reason functions as a tool useful in the pursuit of pleasure or happiness. For Kant, reason represented the capacity, founded upon an internal sense of moral obligation, to recognize universal laws. An act is right to perform and we should perform it because we see that it is right. This concept of duty as the exclusive moral motive is central to Kant, and acting in accordance with self-imposed unconditional principles dictated by practical reason is the key to understanding his ethical theory. The criterion of right actions and the moral worth of the agent are not dependent upon the consequences of the action (happiness, pleasure) or the inclination to do the action, but on the agent's intent to obey the moral law which one accepts by one's own autonomous will. To be rational is to act in accordance with general rules consistently capable of being followed by all rational beings. The "good will" is thus the supreme good; the reward of virtue is not pleasure but the dignity and freedom that comes from being a dutiful moral agent.

Like Socrates, Kant searched out the rational assumptions from which moral actions spring. He was more interested in understanding the absolutely binding decrees of a rational, universally valid conscience than the varying preferences of an empirical, culturally influenced conscience. "Conscience," he stated in one of his lectures, "is an instinct to pass judgment upon ourselves in accordance with moral laws."[1] This judgment, Kant pointed out, is judgment not in the logical but in the judicial sense. Like a judge, conscience passes judgment; it does not merely form a judgment. Our sense of obligation to do our duty is categorical or absolutely binding, not hypothetical or relative to inclination or circumstances. The poet who called duty "stern daughter of the voice of God" was close to Kant's view of conscience and duty, especially if we substitute "reason" for the word "God" in the above passage.

Within this context, Kant viewed pleasure as a relatively minor part of the good life. Except for the good will, it is only a partial, qualified good. We may have the inclination to seek pleasure, but that does not mean that we are justified in seeking pleasure above everything else. A man of good will may deserve happiness, including pleasurable satisfaction, but he may never achieve it in his lifetime. In fact, the greatest good or *summum bonum*, were it achieved, would consist of perfect virtue adjoined with perfect happiness. But whether or not our present circumstances are happy, we should regard the absolute good will as our supreme guiding principle of action which should take precedence over all other considerations including our inclinations and pleasures. Having this view, Kant would have regarded hedonism as a limited and lax moral philosophy. He certainly would have rejected as irrational and immoral Mill's belief that "the motive has nothing to do with the morality of the action, though much with the worth of the agent."

From quite a different philosophical perspective, the contemporary psychotherapist Viktor Frankl rejects pleasure as the highest good in life and lays heavy stress on moral commitment and responsibility. Because he was able to discover a meaning in suffering, Frankl survived a Nazi death camp and lived to develop logotherapy, a search for meaning (*logos*), which unlike psychoanalysis focuses more on the future rather than on the past. Frankl's viewpoint is somewhat Kantian in stressing the primacy of the will, the essence of which is neither a will to power (Nietzsche) nor a will to pleasure (Freud) but a will to meaning. But his philosophy differs from that of Kant in that he does not claim to have discovered an *a priori* moral law, a categorical imperative in the Kantian sense. As an existentialist, Frankl gives full account of the disturbing feelings of boredom, emptiness, and anguish which manifest themselves as an "existential vacuum." He would agree with Albert Camus that the most serious philosophical problem is the problem of suicide. Unless we can discover some meaning in life, why not die rather than continue to live?

When Frankl speaks of searching for the meaning of life, he does not intend that we should search for some general, abstract principle or value which will imbue existence with new and vital significance. Rather he means that we must accept the responsibility for finding our own unique meaning in life through our own specific vocation or mission. We must be committed to concrete tasks rather than to abstract principles. Instead of always questioning life, we must realize that life sometimes is questioning us: "What meaning do I have to life?" rather than "What meaning does life have to me?"

Each of us, Frankl holds, must accept full and deep responsibility for the decisions by which we make our lives. We are responsible for choosing and for our failure to choose; for as Sartre reminded us, "not to choose is to choose not to choose." There is no escape from freedom and responsibility. Frankl formulates his own "categorical imperative of logotherapy" which he prefers to Kant's absolutist formulation. "So live as if you were living already for the second time and if you had acted the first time as wrongly as you are about to act now!"[2] Reference to this maxim and reflection on it will, Frankl thinks, help us to realize the past repercussions and the present possibilities of our everyday actions. It can make us freer by making us more responsible.

Just as there is no single meaning to life which everyone can discover, so there is no one way of discovering individual human meaning. Some may find a meaning to life through action, through creating a value, while others may discover it receptively, that is, by experiencing a value that someone else has created. Still others may only be able to realize value by suffering.

While it is relatively easy to understand and appreciate how meaning can be achieved through action and experience, it is extremely difficult to accept that some people can only achieve it through suffering. This is why Frankl and other logotherapists devote so much attention to the problem of suffering, for if meaning cannot be discovered in the painful, even agonizing, aspects of human existence, much of life would ultimately be devoid of purpose and significance. Pain, not pleasure, offers the supreme challenge to moral philosophy.

Kant had little to say about pain or suffering, and as a critical rationalist he probably would have found incomprehensible and unhealthy the current preoccupation with death and violence. Suicide was, in his view, abominable "in that it degrades man's inner worth below that of the animal creation," and he pointed out that as a rule "those who labour for their happiness are more liable to suicide; having tasted the refinements of pleasure, and being deprived of them, they give way to grief, sorrow, and melancholy."[3] It is unacceptable morally because the maxim by which it is committed cannot be universalized.

As different as their views are on many points, Kant and Frankl provided strong and defensible alternatives to easy as well as informed hedonism.

The pursuit of pleasures remains an important goal perhaps for the majority of mankind. However, from the ancient Cynics to the contemporary existentialists, it has had its detractors. They, like John Savage in the pleasure-crazed Brave New World, have demanded the right to be unhappy, to suffer, to create meaning.

NOTES

1.   Immanuel Kant, *Lectures on Ethics,* trans. Louis Infield (New York: Harper & Row, 1963), p. 129.

2.   Viktor Frankl, *Man's Search for Meaning* (New York: Washington Square Press, 1963), p. 173.

3.   Kant, *Lectures on Ethics,* p. 154.

The Moral Life

Immanuel Kant

Nothing can possibly be conceived in the world, or even out of it, which can be called good without qualification, except a Good Will. Intelligence, wit, judgment, and the other *talents* of the mind, however they may be named, or courage, resolution, perseverance, as qualities of temperament, are undoubtedly good and desirable in many respects; but these gifts of nature may also become extremely bad and mischievous if the will which is to make use of them, and which, therefore, constitutes what is called *character,* is not good. It is the same with the *gifts of fortune*. Power, riches, honour, even health, and the general well-being and contentment with one's condition which is called *happiness,* inspire pride, and often presumption, if there is not a good will to correct the influence of these on the mind, and with this also to rectify the whole principle of acting, and adapt it to its end. The sight of a being who is not adorned with a single feature of a pure and good will, enjoying unbroken prosperity, can never give pleasure to an impartial rational spectator. Thus a good will appears to constitute the indispensable condition even of being worthy of happiness.

There are even some qualities which are of service to this good will itself, and may facilitate its action, yet which have no intrinsic uncondi-

From Immanuel Kant, *Fundamental Principles of the Metaphysics of Morals,* trans. Thomas K. Abbott in *Kant's Ethics or Practical Philosophy* (London: Longmans, Green, Reader and Dyer, 1873).

tional value, but always presuppose a good will, and this qualifies the esteem that we justly have for them, and does not permit us to regard them as absolutely good. Moderation in the affections and passions, self-control and calm deliberation are not only good in many respects, but even seem to constitute part of the intrinsic worth of the person; but they are far from deserving to be called good without qualification, although they have been so unconditionally praised by the ancients. For without the principles of a good will, they may become extremely bad, and the coolness of a villain not only makes him far more dangerous, but also directly makes him more abominable in our eyes than he would have been without it.

A good will is good not because of what it performs or effects, not by its aptness for the attainment of some proposed end, but simply by virtue of the volition, that is, it is good in itself, and considered by itself is to be esteemed much higher than all that can be brought about by it in favour of any inclination, nay, even of the sum total of all inclinations. Even if it should happen that, owing to special disfavour of fortune, or the niggardly provision of a step-motherly nature, this will should wholly lack power to accomplish its purpose, if with its greatest efforts it should yet achieve nothing, and there should remain only the good will (not, to be sure, a mere wish, but the summoning of all means in our power), then, like a jewel, it would still shine by its own light, as a thing which has its whole value in itself. Its usefulness or fruitlessness can neither add to nor take away anything from this value. It would be, as it were, only the setting to enable us to handle it the more conveniently in common commerce, or to attract to it the attention of those who are not yet connoisseurs, but not to recommend it to true connoisseurs, or to determine its value. . . .

We have then to develop the notion of a will which deserves to be highly esteemed for itself, and is good without a view to anything further, a notion which exists already in the sound natural understanding, requiring rather to be cleared up than to be taught, and which in estimating the value of our actions always takes the first place, and constitutes the condition of all the rest. In order to do this we will take the notion of duty, which includes that of a good will, although implying certain subjective restrictions and hindrances. These, however, far from concealing it, or rendering it unrecognisable, rather bring it out by contrast, and make it shine forth so much the brighter.

I omit here all actions which are already recognised as inconsistent with duty, although they may be useful for this or that purpose, for with these the question whether they are done *from duty* cannot arise at all, since they even conflict with it. I also set aside those actions which really conform to duty, but to which men have *no* direct *inclination*, performing them because they are impelled thereto by some other inclination. For in this case we can readily distinguish whether the action which agrees with duty is done *from duty*, or from a selfish view. It is much harder to make this distinction when the action accords with duty, and the subject has besides a *direct* inclination to it. For example, it is always a matter of duty that a dealer should not overcharge an inexperienced purchaser, and wherever there is much commerce the prudent tradesman does not overcharge, but keeps a fixed price for everyone, so that a child buys of him as well as any other. Men are thus *honestly*

served; but this is not enough to make us believe that the tradesman has so acted from duty and from principles of honesty: his own advantage required it; it is out of the question in this case to suppose that he might besides have a direct inclination in favour of the buyers, so that as it were, from love he should give no advantage to one over another. Accordingly the action was done neither from duty nor from direct inclination, but merely with a selfish view.

On the other hand, it is a duty to maintain one's life; and, in addition, everyone has also a direct inclination to do so. But on this account the often anxious care which most men take for it has no intrinsic worth, and their maxim has no moral import. They preserve their life *as duty requires*, no doubt, but not *because duty requires*. On the other hand, if adversity and hopeless sorrow have completely taken away the relish for life; if the unfortunate one, strong in mind, indignant at his fate rather than desponding or dejected, wishes for death, and yet preserves his life without loving it—not from inclination or fear, but from duty—then his maxim has a moral worth.

To be beneficent when we can is a duty; and besides this, there are many minds so sympathetically constituted that, without any other motive of vanity or self-interest, they find a pleasure in spreading joy around them, and can take delight in the satisfaction of others so far as it is their own work. But I maintain that in such a case an action of this kind, however proper, however amiable it may be, has nevertheless no true moral worth, but is on a level with other inclinations, *e.g.*, the inclination to honour, which, if it is happily directed to that which is in fact of public utility and accordant with duty, and consequently honourable, deserves praise and encouragement, but not esteem. For the maxim lacks the moral import, namely, that such actions be done *from duty*, not from inclination. Put the case that the mind of that philanthropist were clouded by sorrow of his own, extinguishing all sympathy with the lot of others, and that while he still has the power to benefit others in distress, he is not touched by their trouble because he is absorbed with his own; and now suppose that he tears himself out of this dead insensibility, and performs the action without any inclination to it, but simply from duty, then first has his action its genuine moral worth. Further still; if nature has put little sympathy in the heart of this or that man; if he, supposed to be an upright man, is by temperament cold and indifferent to the sufferings of others, perhaps because in respect of his own he is provided with the special gift of patience and fortitude, and supposes, or even requires, that others should have the same—and such a man would certainly not be the meanest product of nature —but if nature had not specially framed him for a philanthropist, would he not still find in himself a source from whence to give himself a far higher worth than that of a good-natured temperament could be? Unquestionably. It is just in this that the moral worth of the character is brought out which is incomparably the highest of all, namely, that he is beneficent, not from inclination, but from duty. . . .

The second proposition is: That an action done from duty derives its moral worth, *not from the purpose* which is to be attained by it, but from the maxim by which it is determined, and therefore does not depend on the realization of the object of the action, but merely on the *principle of volition* by which the action has taken place, without regard to any object of desire. It is clear from what precedes that the purposes which we may have in view in our actions, or their effects regarded as ends and springs of the will, cannot give to actions any unconditional or moral worth. In what, then, can their worth lie, if it is not to consist in the will and in reference to its expected effect? It cannot lie anywhere but in the *principle of the will* without regard to the ends which can be attained by the action. . . .

The third proposition, which is a consequence of the two preceding, I would express thus: *Duty is the necessity of acting from respect for the law.* I may have *inclination* for an object as the effect of my proposed action, but I cannot have *respect* for it, just for this reason, that it is an effect and not an energy of will. Similarly, I cannot have respect for inclination, whether my own or another's; I can at most, if my own, approve it; if another's, sometimes even love it; *i.e.,* look on it as favourable to my own interest. It is only what is connected with my will as a principle, by no means as an effect—what does not subserve my inclination, but overpowers it, or at least in case of choice excludes it from its calculation—in other words, simply the law of itself, which can be an object of respect, and hence a command. Now an action done from duty must wholly exclude the influence of inclination, and with it every object of the will, so that nothing remains which can determine the will except objectively the *law,* and subjectively *pure respect* for this practical law, and consequently the maxim that I should follow this law even to the thwarting of all my inclinations.

Thus the moral worth of an action does not lie in the effect expected from it, nor in any principle of action which requires to borrow its motive from this expected effect. For all these effects—agreeableness of one's condition, and even the promotion of the happiness of others—could have been also brought about by other causes, so that for this there would have been no need of the will of a rational being; whereas it is in this alone that the supreme and unconditional good can be found. The pre-eminent good which we call moral can therefore consist in nothing else than *the conception of law* in itself, *which certainly is only possible in a rational being,* in so far as this conception, and not the expected effect, determines the will. This is a good which is already present in the person who acts accordingly, and we have not to wait for it to appear first in the result.

But what sort of law can that be, the conception of which must determine the will, even without paying any regard to the effect expected from it, in order that this will may be called good absolutely and without qualification? As I have deprived the will of every impulse which could arise to it from obedience to any law, there remains nothing but the universal conformity of its actions to law in general, which alone is to serve the will as a principle, *i.e.*, I am never to act otherwise than so *that I could also will that my maxim should become a universal law.* Here now, it is simple conformity to law in general, without assuming any particular law applicable to certain actions, that serves the will as its principle, and must so serve it, if duty is not to be a vain delusion and a chimerical notion. The common reason of men in its practical judgments perfectly coincides with this, and always has in view the principle here suggested. Let the question be, for example: May I when in distress make a promise with the intention not to keep it? I readily distinguish here between the two significations which the question may have: Whether it is prudent, or whether it is right, to make a false promise. The former may undoubtedly often be the case. I see clearly indeed that it is not enough to extricate myself from a present difficulty by means of this subterfuge, but it must be well considered whether there may not hereafter spring from this lie much greater inconvenience than that from which I now free myself, and as, with all my supposed *cunning*, the consequences cannot be so easily foreseen but that credit once lost may be much more injurious to me than any mischief which I seek to avoid at present, it should be considered whether it would not be more *prudent* to act herein according to a universal maxim, and to make it a habit to promise nothing except with the intention of keeping it. But it is soon clear to me that such a maxim will still only be based on the fear of consequences. Now it is a wholly different thing to be truthful from duty, and to be so from apprehension of injurious consequences. In the first case, the very notion of the action already implies a law for me; in the second case, I must first look about elsewhere to see what results may be combined with it which would affect myself. For to deviate from the principle of duty is beyond all doubt wicked; but to be unfaithful to my maxim of prudence may often be very advantageous to me, although to abide by it is certainly safer. The shortest way, however, and an unerring one, to discover the answer to this question whether a lying promise is consistent with duty, is to ask myself, Should I be content that my maxim (to extricate myself from difficulty by a false promise) should hold good as a universal law, for myself as well as for others? and should I be able to say to myself, "Every one may make a deceitful promise when he finds himself in a difficulty from which he cannot otherwise extricate himself"? Then I presently become aware that while I can will the lie, I can by no means will that lying should be a universal law. For with such a law there would be no promises at all, since it would be in vain to allege my intention in regard to my future actions to those who would not believe this allegation, or if they over-hastily did so, would pay me back in my own coin. Hence my maxim, as soon as it should be made a universal law, would necessarily destroy itself....

The conception of an objective principle, in so far as it is obligatory for a will, is called a command (of reason), and the formula of the command is called an Imperative.

All imperatives are expressed by the word *ought* (or *shall*), and thereby indicate the relation of an objective law of reason to a will, which from its subjective constitution is not necessarily determined by it (an obligation). They say that something would be good to do or to forbear, but they say it to a will which does not always do a thing because it is conceived to be good to do it. That is practically *good,* however, which determines the will by means of the conceptions of reason, and consequently not from subjective causes, but objectively, that is on principles which are valid for every rational being as such. It is distinguished from the *pleasant,* as that which influences the will only by means of sensation from merely subjective causes, valid only for the sense of this or that one, and not as a principle of reason, which holds for every one . . .

Now all *imperatives* command either *hypothetically* or *categorically.* The former represent the practical necessity of a possible action as means to something else that is willed (or at least which one might possibly will). The categorical imperative would be that which represented an action as necessary of itself without reference to another end, *i.e.,* as objectively necessary.

Since every practical law represents a possible action as good, and on this account, for a subject who is practically determinable by reason, necessary, all imperatives are formulae determining an action which is necessary according to the principle of a will good in some respects. If now the action is good only as a means *to something else,* then the imperative is *hypothetical;* if it is conceived as good *in itself* and consequently as being necessarily the principle of a will which of itself conforms to reason, then it is *categorical.* . . .

When I conceive a hypothetical imperative in general, I do not know beforehand what it will contain until I am given the condition. But when I conceive a categorical imperative I know at once what it contains. For as the imperative contains besides the law only the necessity that the maxims shall conform to this law, while the law contains no conditions restricting it, there remains nothing but the general statement that the maxim of the action should conform to a universal law, and it is this conformity alone that the imperative properly represents as necessary.

There is therefore but one categorical imperative, namely this: *Act only on that maxim whereby thou canst at the same time will that it should become a universal law.*

Now if all imperatives of duty can be deduced from this one imperative as from their principle, then although it should remain undecided whether what is called duty is not merely a vain notion, yet at least we shall be able to show what we understand by it and what this notion means.

Since the universality of the law according to which effects are produced constitutes what is properly called *nature* in the most general sense (as to form), that is the existence of things as far as it is determined by general laws, the imperative of duty may be expressed thus: *Act as if the maxim of thy action were to become by thy will a Universal Law of Nature.*

We will now enumerate a few duties, adopting the usual divisions of them into duties to ourselves and to others. . . .

1. A man reduced to despair by a series of misfortunes feels wearied of life, but is still so far in possession of his reason that he can ask himself whether it would not be contrary to his duty to himself to take his own life. Now he inquires whether the maxim of his action could become a universal law of nature. His maxim is: From self-love I adopt it as a principle to shorten my life when its longer duration is likely to bring more evil than satisfaction. It is asked then simply whether this principle founded on self-love can become a universal law of nature. Now we see at once that a system of nature of which it should be a law to destroy life by means of the very feeling whose special nature it is to impel to the improvement of life would contradict itself, and therefore could not exist as a system of nature; hence that maxim cannot possibly exist as a universal law of nature, and consequently would be wholly inconsistent with the supreme principle of all duty.

2. Another finds himself forced by necessity to borrow money. He knows that he will not be

able to repay it, but sees also that nothing will be lent to him, unless he promises stoutly to repay it in a definite time. He desires to make this promise, but he has still so much conscience as to ask himself: Is it not unlawful and inconsistent with duty to get out of a difficulty in this way? Suppose, however, that he resolves to do so, then the maxim of his action would be expressed thus: When I think myself in want of money, I will borrow money and promise to repay it, although I know that I never can do so. Now this principle of self-love or of one's own advantage may perhaps be consistent with my whole future welfare; but the question now is, Is it right? I change then the suggestion of self-love into a universal law, and state the question thus: How would it be if my maxim were a universal law? Then I see at once that it could never hold as a universal law of nature, but would necessarily contradict itself. For supposing it to be a universal law that everyone when he thinks himself in a difficulty should be able to promise whatever he pleases, with the purpose of not keeping his promise, the promise itself would become impossible, as well as the end that one might have in view in it, since no one would consider that anything was promised to him, but would ridicule all such statements as vain pretences.

3. A third finds in himself a talent which with the help of some culture might make him a useful man in many respects. But he finds himself in comfortable circumstances, and prefers to indulge in pleasure rather than to take pains in enlarging and improving his happy natural capacities. He asks, however, whether his maxim of neglect of his natural gifts, besides agreeing with his inclination to indulgence, agrees also with what is called duty. He sees then that a system of nature could indeed subsist with such a universal law although men (like the South Sea islanders) should let their talents rust, and resolve to devote their lives merely to idleness, amusement, and propagation of their species—in a word, to enjoyment;

but he cannot possibly *will* that this should be a universal law of nature, or be implanted in us as such by a natural instinct. For, as a rational being, he necessarily wills that his faculties be developed, since they serve him, and have been given him, for all sorts of possible purposes.

4. A fourth, who is in prosperity, while he sees that others have to contend with great wretchedness and that he could help them, thinks: What concern is it of mine? Let everyone be as happy as heaven pleases, or as he can make himself; I will take nothing from him nor even envy him, only I do not wish to contribute anything to his welfare or to his assistance in distress! Now no doubt if such a mode of thinking were a universal law, the human race might very well subsist, and doubtless even better than in a state in which everyone talks of sympathy and good-will, or even takes care occasionally to put it into practice, but on the other side, also cheats when he can, betrays the rights of men, or otherwise violates them. But although it is possible that a universal law of nature might exist in accordance with that maxim, it is impossible to *will* that such a principle should have the universal validity of a law of nature. For a will which resolved this would contradict itself, inasmuch as many cases might occur in which one would have need of the love and sympathy of others, and in which, by such a law of nature, sprung from his own will, he would deprive himself of all hope of the aid he desires.

These are a few of the many actual duties, or at least what we regard as such, which obviously fall into two classes on the one principle that we have laid down. We must be *able to will* that a maxim of our action should be a universal law. This is the canon of the moral appreciation of the action generally. Some actions are of such a character that their maxim cannot without contradiction be even *conceived* as a universal law of nature, far from it being possible that we should *will* that it *should* be so. In others this intrinsic impossibility is not found, but still it is impossible to *will* that their maxim should be raised to the universality of a law of nature, since such a will would contradict itself. It is easily seen that the former violate strict or rigorous (inflexible) duty; the latter only laxer (meritorious) duty. Thus it has been completely shown by these examples how all duties depend as regards the nature of the obligation (not the object of the action) on the same principle. . . .

Supposing . . . that there were something *whose existence* has *in itself* an absolute worth, something which, being *an end in itself*, could be a source of definite laws, then in this and this alone would lie the source of a possible categorical imperative, *i.e.*, a practical law.

Now I say: man and generally any rational being *exists* as an end in himself, *not merely as a means* to be arbitrarily used by this or that will, but in all his actions, whether they concern himself or other rational beings, must be always regarded at the same time as an end. All objects of the inclinations have only a conditional worth, for if the inclinations and the wants founded on them did not exist, then their object would be without value. But the inclinations themselves being sources of want, are so far from having an absolute worth for which they should be desired, that on the contrary it must be the universal wish of every rational being to be wholly free from them. Thus the worth of any object which is *to be acquired* by our action is always conditional. Beings whose existence depends not on our will but on nature's, have nevertheless, if they are irrational beings, only a relative value as means, and are therefore called *things;* rational beings, on the contrary, are called *persons,* because their very nature points them out as ends in themselves, that is as something which must not be used merely as means, and so far therefore restricts freedom of action (and is an object of respect). These, therefore, are not merely subjective ends whose existence has a worth *for us* as an effect of our action, but *ob-jective ends,* that is things whose existence is an end in itself: an end moreover for which no other can be substituted, which they should subserve *merely* as means, for otherwise nothing whatever would possess *absolute worth;* but if all worth were conditioned and therefore contingent, then there would be no supreme practical principle of reason whatever.

If then there is a supreme practical principle or, in respect of the human will, a categorical imperative, it must be one which, drawn from the conception of that which is necessarily an end for every one because it is *an end in itself,* constitutes an *objective* principle of will, and can therefore serve as a universal practical law. The foundation of this principle is: *rational nature exists as an end in itself*. Man necessarily conceives his own existence as being so: so far then this is a *subjective* principle of human actions. But every other rational being regards its existence similarly, just on the same rational principle that holds for me: so that it is at the same time an objective principle, from which as a supreme practical law all laws of the will must be capable of being deduced. Accordingly the practical imperative will be as follows: *So act as to treat humanity, whether in thine own person or in that of any other, in every case as an end withal, never as means only. . . .*

The principle: So act in regard to every rational being (thyself and others), that he may always have place in thy maxim as an end in himself, is accordingly essentially identical with this other: Act upon a maxim which, at the same time, involves its own universal validity for every rational being. For that in using means for every end I should limit my maxim by the condition of its holding good as a law for every subject, this comes to the same thing as that the fundamental principle of all maxims of action must be that the subject of all ends, *i.e.,* the rational being himself, be never employed merely as means, but as the supreme condition restricting the use of all means, that is in every case as an end likewise. . . .

Happiness Not the End

Viktor E. Frankl

In the foregoing we have dealt with the question of meaning as it applies to the meaning of the universe. Now we shall take up a consideration of the many cases where patients ask what is the meaning of their individual, their personal lives. There is a characteristic twist a good many patients give to this question, which inexorably leads them to ethical nihilism. The patient will flatly assert that, after all, the whole meaning of life is pleasure. In the course of his argument he will cite it as an indisputable finding that all human activity is governed by the striving for happiness, that all psychic processes are determined exclusively by the pleasure principle. This theory of the dominant role of the pleasure principle in the whole of the psychic life is, as is well known, one of the basic tenets of psychoanalysis; the reality principle is not actually opposed to the pleasure principle, but is a mere extension of the pleasure principle, and serves its purposes.

Now, to our mind the pleasure principle is an artificial creation of psychology. Pleasure is not the goal of our aspirations, but the consequence of attaining them. Kant long ago pointed this out. Commenting on the hedonist ethics, eudemonism, Scheler has remarked that pleasure does not loom up before us as the goal of an ethical act; rather, an ethical act

From *The Doctor and the Soul: From Psychotherapy to Logotherapy,* by Viktor E. Frankl, translated by Richard and Clara Winston. Copyright © 1955, 1965 by Alfred A. Knopf, Inc. Reprinted by permission of the publisher.

carries pleasure on its back. The theory of the pleasure principle overlooks the intentional quality of all psychic activity. In general, men do not want pleasure; they simply want what they want. Human volition has any number of ends, of the most varied sorts, whereas pleasure would always take the same form, whether secured by ethical or unethical behavior. Hence it is evident that adopting the pleasure principle would, on the moral plane, lead to a leveling of all potential-human aims. It would become impossible to differentiate one action from another, since all would have the same purpose in view. A sum of money disbursed on good food or given in alms could be said to have served the same purpose: in either case the money went to remove unpleasurable feelings within the spender.

Define conduct in these terms and you devaluate every genuine moral impulse in man. In reality, an impulse of sympathy is already moral in itself, even before it is embodied in an act which allegedly has only the negative significance of eliminating unpleasure. For the same situation which in one person may arouse sympathy may stimulate a sadistic malicious joy in another, who gloats over someone's misfortune and in this manner experiences positive pleasure. If it were true that, for example, we read a good book only for the sake of the pleasurable sensation we feel during the reading, we might with equal justification spend our money on good cake. In reality, life is little concerned with pleasure or unpleasure. For the spectator in the theater it does not matter so much that he see a comedy or a tragedy; what allures him is the content, the intrinsic value of the play. Certainly no one will maintain that the unpleasure sensations which are aroused in the spectators who behold tragic events upon the stage are the real aim of their attendance at the theater. In that case, all theatergoers would have to be classed as disguised masochists.

But the argument that pleasure is the final goal of all (not merely the final effect of certain isolated) aspirations can be most effectively countered by reversing it. If, for example, it were true that Napoleon fought his battles only in order to experience the pleasure sensations of victory (the same pleasure sensations which the ordinary soldier might obtain by stuffing his belly, swilling, and whoring), then the reverse must also be true; that the "ultimate aim" of Napoleon's last disastrous battles, the "final purpose" of his defeats, could only have been the unpleasurable sensations which followed these defeats as surely as the pleasurable sensations followed the victories.

When we set up pleasure as the whole meaning of life, we insure that in the final analysis life shall inevitably seem meaningless. Pleasure cannot possibly lend meaning to life. For what is pleasure? A condition. The materialist —and hedonism is generally linked up with materialism—would even say pleasure is nothing but a state of the cells of the brain. And for the sake of inducing such a state, is it worth living, experiencing, suffering, and doing deeds? Suppose a man condemned to death is asked, a few hours before his execution, to choose the menu for his last meal. He might then reply: Is there any sense, in the face of death, in enjoying the pleasures of the palate? Since the organism will be a cadaver two hours later, does it matter whether it did or did not have one more opportunity to experience that state of the brain cells which is called pleasure? Yet all life is confronted with death, which should cancel out this element of pleasure.

Anyone holding this hapless view of life as nothing but a pursuit of pleasure would have to doubt every moment of such a life, if he were to be consistent. He would be in the same frame of mind as a certain patient who was hospitalized after an attempted suicide. The patient in question described to me the following experience: In order to carry out his plan for suicide, he needed to get to an outlying part of the city. The street-cars were no longer running, and he therefore decided to take a cab. "Then I thought it over," he said, "wondering whether I ought to spend the few marks. Right away I could not help smiling at wanting to save a few marks when I would be dead so soon."

Life itself teaches most people that "we are not here to enjoy ourselves." Those who have not yet learned this lesson might be edified by the statistics of a Russian experimental psychologist who showed that the normal man in an average day experiences incomparably more unpleasure sensations than pleasure sensations. How unsatisfying the pleasure principle is in theory as well as practice is evident from a commonplace experience. If we ask a person why he does not do something that to us seems advisable, and the only "reason" he gives is: "I don't feel like it; it would give me no pleasure," we feel that this reply is distinctly unsatisfactory. It is apparent that the reply is insufficient because we can never admit pleasure or unpleasure as an argument for or against the advisability of any action.

The pleasure principle would remain untenable as a moral maxim even if it were actually what Freud claims it to be in his *Beyond the Pleasure Principle:* namely, a derivative from the general tendency of organic life to return to the peace of the inorganic. Freud thought he could prove the kinship of all pleasure-striving with what he named the death instinct. To our mind it is quite conceivable that all these psychological and biological primary tendencies might be reduced further, perhaps to a universal principle of tension reduction which operates to reduce all tensions in every realm of being. Physics recognizes a similar law in its theory of entropy as leading to a final phase of the cosmos. Nirvana might be considered the psychological correlate of entropy; reduction of all psychic tensions by liberation from unpleasure sensations might then be viewed as the microcosmic equivalent of macrocosmic entropy. Nirvana, that is, may be entropy "seen from within." The principle of tension reduction itself, however, would represent the opposite of a principle of individuation which would endeavor to preserve all being as individuated being, as otherness. The very existence of such a polarity suggests that such formulations of universal principles, such findings of cosmic laws lead us up a blind alley, as far as ethics is concerned. For these phenomena have little bearing on our subjective and moral lives. What commands us to identify ourselves with all these principles and tendencies? To what extent is our ethical system to assent to such principles, even if we discover them in our own psychic life? We might equally well take the stand that our moral task is to oppose the rule of such forces with all our strength.

The nature of our education, heavily weighted as it is on the side of materialism, has left most of us with an exaggerated respect for the findings of the so-called exact sciences. We accept without question the picture of the world presented by physics. But how real, for example, is the entropy with which physics threatens us—how real is this universal doom, or this cosmic catastrophe which physics predicts, and in the light of which all the efforts of ourselves and our posterity seem to dwindle to nought? Are we not rather taught by "inner experience," by ordinary living unbiased by theories, that our natural pleasure in a beautiful sunset is in a way "more real" than, say, astronomical calculations of the time when the earth will crash into the sun? Can anything be given to us more directly than our own personal experience, our own deep feeling of our humanity as responsibility? "The most certain science is conscience," someone once remarked, and no theory of the physiological nature of life, nor the assertion that joy is a strictly organized dance of molecules or atoms or electrons within the gray matter of the brain, has ever been so compelling and convincing. Similarly, a man who is enjoying supreme artistic pleasure or the happiness of love never doubts for a moment that his life is meaningful.

Joy, however, may make life meaningful only if it itself has meaning. Its meaning cannot lie within itself. In fact it lies outside of itself. For joy is always directed toward an object. Scheler has already shown that joy is an intentional emotion—in contrast to mere pleasure, which he reckons among non-intentional emotions in a category he calls "conditional" emotions. Pleasure, that is, is an emotional condition. Here we are again reminded of Erwin Straus's concept of the "presentist" mode of life. In that mode a person remains in the conditional state of pleasure (say, in intoxication) without reaching out to the realm of objects —which in this case would be the realm of values. Only when the emotions work in terms of values can the individual feel pure "joy." This is the explanation of why joy can never be an end in itself; it itself, as joy, cannot be purposed as a goal. How well Kierkegaard expressed this in his maxim that the door to happiness opens outward. Anyone who tries to push this door open thereby causes it to close still more. The man who is desperately anxious to be happy thereby cuts off his own path to happiness. Thus in the end all striving for happiness—for the supposed "ultimate" in human life—proves to be in itself impossible. . . .

ON THE MEANING OF SUFFERING

We have said that man's being consists of being conscious and being responsible. His responsibility is always responsibility for the actualization of values: not only "eternal" values, but also "situational values" (Scheler). Opportunities for the actualization of values change from person to person just as much as they change from hour to hour. The requirement that values be actualized—a requirement that radiates from the world of values into the lives of men—thus becomes a concrete demand for every single hour and a personal summons to every single person. The possibilities that every person has exclusively for himself are just as specific as the possibilities presented by every historical situation in its peculiar singularity. Thus the various values merge to form a concrete task for the individual. That merging gives them the uniqueness whereby every man feels himself personally and validly addressed. Until he learns what constitutes the singularity and uniqueness of his own existence, he cannot experience the fulfillment of his life task as something binding upon him.

In discussing the question of the meaning of life we have set up three categories of values. While the values of the first category are actualized by doing, experiential values are realized by the passive receiving of the world (nature, art) into the ego. Attitudinal values, however, are actualized wherever the individual is faced with something unalterable, something imposed by destiny. From the manner in which a person takes these things upon himself, assimilates these difficulties into his own psyche, there flows an incalculable multitude of value-potentialities. This means that *human life can be fulfilled not only in creating and enjoying, but also in suffering!*

Those who worship the superficial cult of success obviously will not understand such conclusions. But when we pause and consider our everyday judgments upon human existence, we see that we ascribe value and dignity to many things independently of the success or failure which may attend them. Great artists, in particular, have understood and described this phenomenon of inner fulfillment in spite of outward failure. An example that comes readily to mind is Tolstoy's story *The Death of Ivan Ilyich*. The story concerns a respectable government official, the abysmal meaninglessness of whose life only dawns upon him when he is faced with unexpected death. But with insight into this meaninglessness the man grows far beyond himself in the last hours of his life; he attains an inner greatness which retroactively hallows all of his previous life—in spite of its apparent futility—and makes it meaningful. Life, that is, can receive its ultimate meaning not only as the result of death (the man who is a hero), but in the very process of death. Not only the sacrifice of one's life can give life meaning; life can reach nobility even as it founders on the rocks.

The untenability of the cult of success becomes obvious as soon as we consider the moral problem of sacrifice. Insofar as a sacrifice is "calculated," performed after careful reckoning of the prospects of its bringing about a desired end, it loses all ethical significance. Real sacrifice occurs only when we run the risk of having sacrificed in vain. Would anyone maintain that a person who plunges into the water to save someone has acted less ethically, or unethically, because both are drowned? Do we not rather presuppose this risk when we assign a high ethical standing to the rescuer's action? Consider what a high ethical rating we place upon the life of a man who has fought vainly but heroically—and has died heroically but not vainly.

Lack of success does not signify lack of meaning. This also becomes obvious when we look back upon our own past and consider, say, the times we have been in love. Let anyone honestly ask himself whether he would be prepared to strike his unhappy love affairs, with all their self-doubt and suffering, out of the record of his life. Almost certainly he would not. The fullness of suffering did not seem to him lack of fulfillment. On the contrary, the suffering matured him; he grew as a result of it; his ill-fated love gave him more than many an erotic success might have given him.

In general, people are inclined to overestimate the positive or negative aspects, or the pleasant or unpleasant tone of their experiences. In giving an exaggerated importance to these aspects, they are apt to cultivate an unjustified self-pity in respect to fate. We have already discussed the numerous senses in which man is "not in this world for enjoyment." We have pointed out that pleasure is incapable of giving meaning to man's life. If this is so, lack of pleasure in life does not detract from its meaning. Once again art comes to our aid with examples: we have only to recall how irrelevant with regard to artistic merit is the question of whether a melody is in the major or minor modes. Not only are the unfinished symphonies among the finest, as we have mentioned in another connection; so also are the *"pathétiques."*

We have said that in creating, man actualizes creative values; in experiencing, experiential values; and in suffering, attitudinal values. Beyond that, however, suffering has a meaning in itself. In suffering from something we move inwardly away from it, we establish a distance between our personality and this something. As long as we are still suffering from a condition that ought not to be, we remain in a state of tension between what actually is on the one hand and what ought to be on the other hand. And only while in this state of tension can we continue to envision the ideal. As we have already seen, this even applies to the person who has despaired of himself; by the very fact of his despair he has cast off some of the blame attaching to himself, since he is evaluating his own reality in terms of an ideality and the fact that he can at all envision values (even though unrealized ones) implies a certain value in himself. He could not sit in judgment upon himself if he did not already possess the worth and dignity of a judge—of a man who has perceived what ought to be as against what at the moment is. Suffering therefore establishes a fruitful, one might say a revolutionary, tension in that it makes for emotional awareness of what ought not to be. To the degree that a person identifies himself with things as they are, he eliminates his distance from them and forfeits the fruitful tension between what is and what ought to be.

Thus there is revealed in man's emotions a deep wisdom superior to all reason, which in fact runs counter to the gospel of rationalistic utility. Consider, for instance, the effects of grief and repentance. From the utilitarian point of view both necessarily appear to be meaningless. To mourn for anything irrevocably lost must seem useless and foolish from the point of view of "sound common sense," and this holds also for repenting an irredeemable wrong. But for the inner biography of man, grief and repentance do have meaning. Grieving for a person whom we have loved and lost in a sense continues his life, and repentance permits the culprit to rise again, as it were, freed of guilt. The loved person whom we grieve for has been lost objectively, in empirical time, but he is preserved subjectively, in inner time. Grief brings him into the mind's present. And repentance, as Scheler has shown, has the power to wipe out a wrong; though the wrong cannot be undone, the culprit himself undergoes a moral rebirth. This opportunity to make past events fruitful for one's inner history does not stand in opposition to man's responsibility, but in a dialectical relationship. For guilt presupposes responsibility. Man is responsible in view of the fact that he cannot retrace a single step; the smallest as well as the biggest decision remains a final one. None of his acts of commission or omission can be wiped off the slate as if they had never been. Nevertheless, in repenting man may inwardly break with an act, and in living out this repentance —which is an inner event—he can undo the outer event on a spiritual, moral plane. Only to the most superficial view is there any contradiction between these two statements.

Schopenhauer, as is well known, complained

that human life dangles between trouble and boredom. In reality both have their profound meaning. Boredom is a continual reminder. What leads to boredom? Inactivity. But activity does not exist for the purpose of our escaping boredom; rather, boredom exists so that we will escape inactivity and do justice to the meaning of our life. The struggle of life keeps us in "suspense" because the meaning of life depends upon whether or not we fulfill the demands placed upon us by our tasks. This suspense is therefore different in nature from the type engendered by a neurotic passion for sensation or a hysterical hunger for stimulus.

The meaning of "trouble" is also that it is a reminder. On the biological plane, as we know, pain is a meaningful watcher and warder. In the psycho-spiritual realm it has a similar function. Suffering is intended to guard man from apathy, from psychic *rigor mortis*. As long as we suffer we remain psychically alive. In fact, we mature in suffering, grow because of it—it makes us richer and stronger. Repentance, as we have seen, has the power to undo, and the significance of undoing, an outer event in the moral sense, within the biography of the individual; grief has the power to perpetuate, and the significance of perpetuating, the past in the present. Both thus serve to correct the past, so to speak. In so doing they solve a problem—as diversion and narcotization cannot do. The person who tries to "take his mind off" a misfortune or narcotize his feelings solves no problem, comes to no terms with misfortune; all he does is get rid of a mere aftereffect of the misfortune: the sensation of unpleasure. By diversion or narcotization he makes himself "ignore" what has happened—he no longer knows it. He tries to escape reality. He takes refuge, say, in intoxication. But this is to commit a subjectivistic, in fact a psychologistic, error: the error of acting as if "silencing" the feeling by narcotization also makes an end of the object of the emotion; as if what has been banished to non-consciousness were thereby banished to unreality. But the act of looking at something does not create that thing; neither does the act of looking away annihilate it. And so the suppression of an impulse of grief does not annul the thing that is grieved over. Mourners, in fact, ordinarily rebel against, say, taking a sedative instead of weeping all through the night. To the trite suggestion that he take a sleeping-powder the grief-stricken person commonly retorts that his sleeping better will not awaken the lost one whom he mourns. Death—that paradigm of the irreversible event—is not wiped off the slate by being pushed out of consciousness, any more than when the mourner himself takes refuge in absolute non-consciousness—the non-consciousness and the non-responsibility of his own death.

As contrasted with narcotization, intoxication has positive aspects. The essence of intoxication is a turning away from the objective world and a turning toward a subjective world. Narcotization, on the other hand, leads only to non-consciousness of unhappiness, to "happiness" in Schopenhauer's negative sense, to a nirvana mood. Narcotization is spiritual anesthesia. But just as surgical anesthesia can induce death, so spiritual anesthesia can lead to a kind of spiritual death. Consistent suppression of intrinsically meaningful emotional impulses because of their possible unpleasurable tone ends in the killing of a person's inner life. A sense of the meaning of emotional experiences is deeply rooted in human beings, as the following example indicates. There is a type of melancholia in which sadness is conspicuous by its absence. Instead, the patients complain that they cannot feel sad enough, that they cannot cry out their melancholy, that they are emotionally cold and inwardly dead. Such patients are suffering from what we call *melancholia anæsthetica*. Anyone acquainted with such cases knows that greater despair can scarcely exist than the despair of such persons because they are unable to be sad. This paradox again makes it plain that the pleasure principle is a mere construct but not a phenomenological fact. Out of his emotional *"logique du cœur"* man is actually always striving, whether his emotions be joyful or sad, to remain psychically "alive" and not to sink into apathy. The paradox that the sufferer from *melancholia anæsthetica* should suffer from his incapacity to suffer is therefore only a paradox for psychopathology. For existential analysis it is no paradox at all, since existential analysis recognizes the meaning of suffering, installs suffering in a place of honor in life. Suffering and trouble belong to life as much as fate and death. None of these can be subtracted from life without destroying its meaning. To subtract trouble, death, fate, and suffering from life would mean stripping life of its form and shape. Only under the hammer blows of fate, in the white heat of suffering, does life gain shape and form.

The destiny a person suffers therefore has a twofold meaning: to be shaped where possible, and to be endured where necessary. Let us also remember that "inactive," passive enduring still retains the immanent meaning of all suffering. On the other hand, man must be on his guard against the temptation to lay down his arms prematurely, too soon accepting a state of things as destined and bowing his head before a merely imaginary fate. Only when he no longer has any possibility of actualizing creative values, when there is really no means at hand for shaping fate—then is the time for attitudinal values to be actualized; then alone does it have meaning for him to "take his cross." The very essence of an attitudinal value inheres in the manner in which a person resigns himself to the inevitable; in order therefore for attitudinal values to be truly actualized, it is important that the fate he resigns himself to must be actually inevitable. It must be what Brod has called "noble misfortune" as against the "ignoble misfortune," the latter being some-

thing which is either avoidable, or for which the person himself is to blame.[*]

One way or another, then, every situation holds out the opportunity for the actualization of values—either creative or attitudinal values. "There is no predicament that we cannot ennoble either by doing or enduring," says Goethe. We might say that even in enduring there is a kind of doing implicit, provided that the enduring is of the right kind, that what must be endured is a fated situation that cannot be either altered by doing or avoided by not doing. This "right" enduring is the kind which constitutes a moral achievement; only such unavoidable suffering is meaningful suffering. This moral achievement implicit in suffering is something that the ordinary person in his simple, straightforward way knows quite well. He can well understand, for example, the following incident:

Some years ago when prizes were to be awarded to British Boy Scouts for highest accomplishments, the coveted awards went to three boys hospitalized for incurable diseases who nevertheless remained brave and cheerful and steadfastly endured their suffering. Their record of suffering was recognized as greater in accomplishment than the records in athletics, etc., of so many other Boy Scouts.

"Life is not anything; it is only the opportunity for something." This maxim of Hebbel's seems to cover the subject. For the alternatives are either to shape fate (that is, one's unalter-

---

[*] The difference between evitable or blameworthy destiny ("ignoble misfortune") on the one hand and inevitable, immutable destiny ("noble misfortune") on the other hand (to suffer the latter alone provides opportunities for the realization of attitudinal values) has its parallel in the distinction mountaineers make between subjective and objective dangers. For the mountaineer it is not discreditable to succumb to objective perils (such as a falling rock), while it is considered shameful to be halted by a subjective failure (such as faulty equipment, lack of skill, or .inadequate climbing-experience).

able situation) and so realize creative values, or, if this should really prove to be impossible, to take such an attitude toward fate that, in the sense of attitudinal values, there is achievement in suffering. It sounds like a tautology to say that illnesses give people the "opportunity" for "suffering." But if we understand "opportunity" and "suffering" in the above sense, the matter ceases to be obvious. It is above all not obvious because a fundamental distinction must be made between sickness—including psychic illness—and suffering. On the one hand, people can be sick without "suffering" in the proper sense. On the other hand, there is a suffering beyond all sickness, a fundamental human suffering, the suffering which belongs to human life by the very nature and meaning of life. Consequently, cases may arise where existential analysis is called upon to make a person capable of suffering—whereas psychoanalysis, for instance, aims only at making him capable of pleasure or capable of doing. For there are situations in which man can fulfill himself only in genuine suffering, and in no other way. And just as men can miss the "opportunity for something" which life means, so can they miss their opportunity for genuine suffering, with its opening for the actualizing of attitudinal values. In the light of this we can agree with Dostoevsky when he said that he feared only one thing: that he might not be worthy of his torment. And we can now appreciate what an accomplishment there is in the suffering of patients who appear to be struggling—to be worthy of their torment.

An extraordinarily brilliant young man was abruptly forced to give up his active professional life. An abscess of the spinal cord caused by tubercular affection had produced symptoms of paralysis in the legs. An operation (laminectomy) was considered. Friends of the patient consulted one of the foremost neurosurgeons of Europe. He was pessimistic about the prognosis and refused to undertake the operation. This decision was reported in a letter to another of the sick man's friends, who was caring for him at her country house. The unsuspecting servant girl handed the letter to her mistress while the latter was breakfasting with her sick guest. What followed is described by the patient in a letter of his from which we take the following passages: ". . . In the situation Eva could not help letting me read the letter. And so I was informed of my death sentence, which was obvious from the surgeon's remarks.—I recall the movie about the *Titanic*, which I saw many years ago. What I particularly recall is the scene in which the paralyzed cripple, played by Fritz Kortner, reciting the Lord's Prayer, ushers a small group of fellow victims toward death, while the ship sinks and the water rises higher and higher around their bodies. I came out of the movie deeply shaken. What a gift of fate it must be, I thought at the time, consciously to go toward one's death. And now here was fate granting me that! I get this last chance to test my fighting spirit, only this is a fight where the question of victory is ruled out at the start. Rather, it's a last exertion of simple strength, a last gymnastic drill, as it were. . . . I want to bear the pain without narcotics as long as it is at all possible. . . . 'A fight for a lost cause?' In terms of our philosophy, that phrase has to be stricken off the books. The fighting alone is what counts. . . . There cannot be any lost causes. . . . In the evening we played Bruckner's *Fourth*, the *Romantic Symphony*. I was filled with emotion of love for all mankind, a sense of cosmic vastness.—For the rest, I work away at mathematics and don't give way to sentimentality."

At another time illness and the approach of death may draw forth the ultimate capacities from a man who has hitherto wasted his life in "metaphysical frivolity" (Scheler) and let his own potentialities lie fallow. A young woman who had led an utterly pampered existence was one day unexpectedly thrown into a concentration camp. There she fell ill and was visibly wasting away. A few days before she died she said these very words: "Actually I am grateful to my fate for having treated me so harshly. In my former middle-class existence I certainly had things a great deal too easy. I never was very serious about my literary ambitions." She saw death coming and looked it squarely in the eye. From her bed in the infirmary she could catch a glimpse of a chestnut tree in blossom outside the window. She spoke of this tree often, though from where the sick woman's head lay just one twig with two blossoms was visible. "This tree is my only friend in solitude," the woman said. "I converse with it." Was this a hallucination? Was she delirious? Did she think the tree was "answering" her? What strange dialogue was this; what had the flowering tree "said" to the dying woman? "It says:

'I am here, I am here—I am life, eternal life.' "

Viktor von Weizsäcker once remarked that the patient, as the sufferer, is superior to the doctor. Certainly I had that feeling when I left this patient. A doctor who is sensitive to the imponderables of a situation will always feel a kind of shame when attending a patient with an incurable disease, or a dying person. For the doctor himself is helpless, incapable of wresting this victim from death. But the patient has become a hero who is meeting his fate and holding his own by accepting it in tranquil suffering. That is, upon a metaphysical plane, a true achievement—while the doctor in the physical world, in his physician's realm, has his hands tied, is a failure.

15 Self-Actualization and the Good Life

Aristotle & Maslow

Self-actualization as the key to the good life is associated with the psychology of Abraham Maslow (1908–1970), but the ethical concept goes back to the Greeks, to Socrates, Plato, and Aristotle. Socrates believed that one must attain knowledge in order to be virtuous or to achieve excellence, and in achieving this rational and moral end one's highest potentialities as a human being are actualized. Plato showed how this concept can be applied not only to individual self-realization but to the realization of a just or good society. Aristotle (384–322 B.C.), Plato's greatest disciple, found much of his master's teaching acceptable. He agreed that man is a purposive being and a socio-political animal who cannot find his most complete and fullest self-actualization outside of the state. He agreed, as he points out at the end of the following selection, that philosophical contemplation is the highest form of happiness.

However, Aristotle's orientation to philosophy was more empirical, more analytic, less mystical, and less idealistic than that of Plato. He disagreed with Plato's utopianism and with the communalistic proposals outlined in *The Republic*. He also de-emphasized Plato's vision of the good as an absolute independent of the world of individuals. Aristotle's study of biology, psychology, and politics led him to define the good as the attainment of goals at which human beings naturally aim. The rules humans obey stem from their own experience and reason.

In approaching the problems of ethics, Aristotle began by pointing out that all human beings are striving to achieve various ends or purposes. Some of these ends are desired because they lead to other ends; they are instrumental or extrinsic goods (e.g., wealth). Other ends are desired, however, not because they lead to something else, but because they are what they are; they are intrinsically valuable ends (e.g., health). At the apex of these various means and ends must stand a supreme end or good for the sake of which man ultimately strives. What is this good? Before answering this question, Aristotle pointed out that in order for anything to qualify as the supreme good, it must have three characteristics. It must be *final*, that is, *the* end which is desired for itself and not because it leads to another higher end. It must be achievable by action and attainable by human beings, otherwise it would not be considered to be the end motivating so much human effort. In addition, the supreme good must be self-sufficient, i.e., something which when isolated would make life desirable and complete in itself.

Happiness obviously meets all of these criteria, but to say that happiness is the chief good is, Aristotle admitted, platitudinous. Happiness must be defined; its various kinds must be distinguished; and the conditions which bring it about must be set forth. To do all of this, Aristotle returned to a consideration of the nature of man. Man's unique function, he believed, was a rational activity of soul. This being the fundamental fact about human nature, happiness is an activity of soul which accords with virtue, and the highest kind of happiness is that which accords with the best and most complete kind of virtue. Aristotle also recognized that just as "one swallow does not make a summer, nor does one day," a person cannot be regarded as happy if his happiness is not relatively long lasting throughout his life.

If we are thinking of the happiest, most self-actualized man, we must also think of him as being endowed generously with external goods, possessed of friends, riches, and political power, and the lucky recipient of "good birth, goodly children, and beauty." Aristotle found it unlikely that an ugly, ill-born, solitary, childless man could be happy.

Against this background, Aristotle developed his ethics. He first distinguished between the rational and the irrational psyche or soul, and distinguished two functions of the rational part, practical reason (*phronesis*) and theoretical or contemplative reason. Practical reason controls the irrational drives, while theoretical reason is for the discovery of truth. He then discussed the practical moral virtues, which are the result of behavior governed by a golden mean, a way of moderation between extremes or vices of excess and defect. Higher than these moral virtues are the intellectual virtues which are developed from theoretical reason. Without the rational development of "practical wisdom," our conduct would not be intelligent, and without the rational development of "philosophical wisdom," we would not be able to pursue and discover truth. Aristotle's conclusion was that there are various forms of the good or happy life, such as the life of pleasure, honor, and contemplation. However, the life devoted to intellectual contemplation is the best. For this kind of happiness is the most final and self-sufficient, the end through which man achieves his most god-like self-actualization.

Abraham Maslow, in *Toward a Psychology of Being,* stressed the importance of understanding human capacities and purposive strivings in order to promote growth and self-actualization. "Capacities clamor to be used," and they must be well used if satisfaction is to be achieved and if growth is to be fostered. If a person does not use his capacity to think, to exert himself, to love, that capacity will atrophy and eventually reduce his total self-actualization. Growth will be thwarted rather than furthered.

Since Maslow considers capacities to be needs also, it is important to recall his hierarchical classification of human needs. The lowest material needs are for food, shelter, and clothing. Above these are the needs for security, for belongingness, for esteem, and for freedom to develop one's capacities. To Maslow these higher, nonmaterial needs are just as "basic" as the lower, physical needs.

While Maslow is as concerned as Aristotle was with understanding growth in terms of its inner vital purpose, he points out the pains and obstacles standing in its way. Human beings find it difficult to break with the past and look to the future. They cling to comfort and fear the risks entailed in growth. They sometimes yield to homeostatic tendencies in themselves rather than nurturing growth tendencies. Also, they may live in a society or culture that is growth-inhibiting. However, Maslow believes that since the sources of growth are within us we are largely responsible for the extent to which we grow or atrophy. Society can influence or condition our capacity to grow by providing or withholding the necessary means for self-actualization, but it cannot determine that capacity.

As he develops the latter point, Maslow sounds more like Erich Fromm than Aristotle. One culture is better than another in so far as it better meets the basic human needs, thereby making a higher level of self-actualization possible. He also agrees with Fromm that the goals of self-actualization are not achieved by adjusting to a given culture unless that culture is such that it can permit the full satisfaction of the fully functioning person.

Like Aristotle, Maslow places a high premium on the self-actualized person's ability to transcend space and time in his contemplative moments. In such moments, which Maslow calls peak experiences, the process of becoming stops and one experiences the intrinsic value of being. But Maslow's concept of the "peak experience" goes far beyond the kind of purely rational contemplation Aristotle considered to be the apogee of self-actualization. Peak experiences can be precipitated by intellectual insights but they can also be caused by aesthetic or sensuous encounters. They are moments of total absorption, exalted fulfillment, perfect rapture. They are revelations of the supreme value of existence, little deaths and rebirths in life. In a later work, *Religions, Values and Peak Experiences,* Maslow argues that it is likely that "the peak experience may be the model of the religious revelation or the religious illumination."[1] Holistic perception of the universe, rapt attention, detachment, ego-transcendence, disorientation in space and time, wonder, resolution of conflicts—these are some of the features which religious and peak experience have in common. Maslow is careful to point out, however, that in his view, religious experience like other kinds of peak experiences can be understood and interpreted naturalistically. It is not necessary to posit the existence of some supernatural being or of some "God above God" (Tillich) in order to explain their nature and significance.

Maslow's ideal of the self-actualized, fully functioning person is probably far more appealing to young people today than Aristotle's god-like philosopher discovering and contemplating truths about the nature of reality. Maslow's ideal person seems god-like in that he is so much more realistic, tolerant, spontaneous, detached, free, appreciative, democratic, and creative than is the ordinary person.[2] Such "peakers" may be as rare as Aristotelian "contemplators," but a utopian society made up of such individuals represents an ideal happiness toward which many people today would aspire.

NOTES

1.   Abraham Maslow, *Religions, Values and Peak Experiences* (New York: Viking Press, 1964), p. 20.

2.   Ibid., p. 26.

Happiness and the Golden Mean

Aristotle

Since happiness is an activity of soul in accordance with perfect virtue; we must consider the nature of virtue; for perhaps we shall thus see better the nature of happiness. The true student of politics, too, is thought to have studied virtue above all things; for he wishes to make his fellow citizens good and obedient to the laws. As an example of this we have the lawgivers of the Cretans and the Spartans, and any others of the kind that there may have been. And if this inquiry belongs to political science, clearly the pursuit of it will be in accordance with our original plan. But clearly the virtue we must study is human virtue; for the good we were seeking was human good and the happiness human happiness. By human virtue we mean not that of the body but that of the soul; and happiness also we call an activity of soul. But if this is so, clearly the student of politics must know somehow the facts about soul, as the man who is to heal the eyes or the body as a whole must know about the eyes or the body; and all the more since politics is more prized and better than medicine; but even among doctors the best educated spend much labour on acquiring knowledge of the body. The student of politics, then, must study the soul, and must study it with these objects in

From "Nichomachean Ethics" translated by W. D. Ross, from *The Oxford Translation of Aristotle* edited by W. D. Ross, Vol. IX (1952). By permission of Oxford University Press.

view, and do so just to the extent which is sufficient for the questions we are discussing; for further precision is perhaps something more laborious than our purposes require.

Some things are said about it, adequately enough, even in the discussions outside our school, and we must use these; e.g. that one element in the soul is irrational and one has a rational principle. Whether these are separated as the parts of the body or of anything divisible are, or are distinct by definition but by nature inseparable, like convex and concave in the circumference of a circle, does not affect the present question.

Of the irrational element one division seems to be widely distributed, and vegetative in its nature, I mean that which causes nutrition and growth; for it is this kind of power of the soul that one must assign to all nurslings and to embryos, and this same power to full-grown creatures; this is more reasonable than to assign some different power to them. Now the excellence of this seems to be common to all species and not specifically human . . . let us leave the nutritive faculty alone, since it has by its nature no share in human excellence.

There seems to be also another irrational element in the soul—one which in a sense, however, shares in a rational principle. For we praise the rational principle of the continent man and of the incontinent, and the part of their soul that has such a principle, since it urges them aright and towards the best objects; but there is found in them also another element naturally opposed to the rational principle, which fights against and resists that principle. For exactly as paralyzed limbs when we intend to move them to the right turn on the contrary to the left, so is it with the soul; the impulses of incontinent people move in contrary directions. But while in the body we see that which moves astray, in the soul we do not. No doubt, however, we must none the less suppose that in the soul too there is something contrary to the rational principle, resisting and opposing it. In what sense it is distinct from the other elements does not concern us. Now even this seems to have a share in a rational principle, as we said; at any rate in the continent man it obeys the rational principle— and presumably in the temperate and brave man it is still more obedient; for in him it speaks, on all matters, with the same voice as the rational principle.

Therefore the irrational element also appears to be twofold. For the vegetative element in no way shares in a rational principle, but the appetitive, and in general the desiring element in a sense shares in it, in so far as it listens to and obeys it; this is the sense in which we speak of 'taking account' of one's father or one's friends, not that in which we speak of 'accounting' for a mathematical property. That the irrational element is in some sense persuaded by a rational principle is indicated also by the giving of advice and by all reproof and exhortation. And if this element also must be said to have a rational principle, that which has a rational principle (as well as that which has not) will be twofold, one subdivision having it in the strict sense and in itself, and the other having a tendency to obey as one does one's father.

Virtue too is distinguished into kinds in accordance with this difference; for we say that some of the virtues are intellectual and others moral, philosophic wisdom and understanding and practical wisdom being intellectual, liberality and temperance moral. For in speaking about a man's character we do not say that he is wise or has understanding but that he is good-tempered or temperate; yet we praise the wise man also with respect to his state of mind; and of states of mind we call those which merit praise virtues.

Virtue, then, being of two kinds, intellectual and moral, intellectual virtue in the main owes both its birth and its growth to teaching (for which reason it requires experience and time), while moral virtue comes about as a result of habit, whence also its name *ethike* is one that is formed by a slight variation from the word *ethos* (habit). From this it is also plain that none of the moral virtues arises in us by nature; for nothing that exists by nature can form a habit contrary to its nature. For instance the stone which by nature moves downwards cannot be habituated to move upwards, not even if one tries to train it by throwing it up ten thousand times; nor can fire be habituated to move downwards, nor can anything else that by nature behaves in one way be trained to behave in another. Neither by nature, then, nor contrary to nature do the virtues arise in us; rather we are adapted by nature to receive them, and are made perfect by habit.

Again, of all the things that come to us by nature we first acquire the potentiality and later exhibit the activity (this is plain in the case of the senses; for it was not by often seeing or often hearing that we got these senses, but on the contrary we had them before we used them, and did not come to have them by using them); but the virtues we get by first exercising them, as also happens in the case of the arts as well. For the things we have to learn before we can do them, we learn by doing them, e.g. men become builders by building and lyre-players by playing the lyre; so too we become just by doing just acts, temperate by doing temperate acts, brave by doing brave acts. . . .

We must, however, not only describe virtue as a state of character, but also say what sort of state it is. We may remark, then, that every virtue or excellence both brings into good condition the thing of which it is the excellence and makes the work of that thing be done well; e.g. the excellence of the eye makes both the eye and its work good; for it is by the excellence of the eye that we see well. Similarly the excellence of the horse makes a horse both good in itself and good at running and at carrying its rider and at awaiting the attack of the enemy. Therefore, if this is true in every case, the virtue of man also will be the state of character which makes a man good and which makes him do his own work well.

How this is to happen we have stated already, but it will be made plain also by the following consideration of the specific nature of virtue. In everything that is continuous and divisible it is possible to take more, less, or an equal amount, and that either in terms of the thing itself or relatively to us; and the equal is an intermediate between excess and defect. By the intermediate in the object I mean that which is equidistant from each of the extremes, which is one and the same for all men; by the intermediate relatively to us that which is neither too much nor too little—and this is not one, nor the same for all. For instance, if ten is many and two is few, six is the intermediate, taken in terms of the object; for it exceeds and is exceeded by an equal amount; this is intermediate according to arithmetical proportion. But the intermediate relatively to us is not to be taken so; if ten pounds are too much for a particular person to eat and two too little, it does not follow that the trainer will order six pounds; for this also is perhaps too much for the person who is to take it, or too little—too little for Milo, too much for the beginner in athletic exercises. The same is true of running

and wrestling. Thus a master of any art avoids excess and defect, but seeks the intermediate and chooses this—the intermediate not in the object but relatively to us. . . .

Virtue, then, is a state of character concerned with choice, lying in a mean, i.e. the mean relative to us, this being determined by a rational principle, and by that principle by which the man of practical wisdom would determine it. Now it is a mean between two vices, that which depends on excess and that which depends on defect; and again it is a mean because the vices respectively fall short of or exceed what is right in both passions and actions, while virtue both finds and chooses that which is intermediate. Hence in respect of its substance and the definition which states its essence virtue is a mean, with regard to what is best and right an extreme.

But not every action nor every passion admits of a mean; for some have names that already imply badness, e.g., spite, shamelessness, envy, and in the case of actions adultery, theft, murder; for all of these and suchlike things imply by their names that they are themselves bad, and not the excesses or deficiencies of them. It is not possible, then, ever to be right with regard to them; one must always be wrong. Nor does goodness or badness with regard to such things depend on committing adultery with the right woman, at the right time, and in the right way, but simply to do any of them is to go wrong. It would be equally absurd, then, to expect that in unjust, cowardly, and voluptuous action there should be a mean, an excess, and a deficiency; for at that rate there would be a mean of excess and of deficiency, an excess of excess, and a deficiency of deficiency. But as there is no excess and deficiency of temperance and courage because what is intermediate is in a sense an extreme, so too of the actions we have mentioned there is no mean nor any excess and deficiency, but however they are done they are wrong; for in general there is neither a mean of excess and deficiency, nor excess and deficiency of a mean.

We must, however, not only make this general statement, but also apply it to the individual facts. For among statements about conduct those which are general apply more widely, but those which are particular are more genuine, since conduct has to do with individual cases, and our statements must harmonize with the facts in these cases. We may take these cases from our table. With regard to feelings of fear and confidence courage is the mean; of the people who exceed, he who exceeds in fearlessness has no name (many of the states have no name), while the man who exceeds in confidence is rash, and he who exceeds in fear and falls short in confidence is a coward. With regard to pleasures and pains— not all of them, and not so much with regard to the pains—the mean is temperance, the excess self-indulgence. Persons deficient with regard to the pleasures are not often found; hence such persons also have received no name. But let us call them 'insensible.'

With regard to giving and taking of money the mean is liberality, the excess and the defect prodigality and meanness. In these actions people exceed and fall short in contrary ways; the prodigal exceeds in spending and falls short in taking, while the mean man exceeds in taking and falls short in spending. . . . With regard to money there are also other dispositions—a mean, magnificence (for the magnificent man differs from the liberal man; the former deals with large sums, the latter with small ones), an excess, tastelessness and vulgarity, and a deficiency, niggardliness . . .

With regard to honour and dishonour the mean is proper pride, the excess is known as a sort of 'empty vanity,' and the deficiency is undue humility; and as we said liberality was related to magnificence, differing from it by dealing with small sums, so there is a state similarly related to proper pride, being concerned with small honours while that is concerned with great. For it is possible to desire honour as one ought, and more than one ought, and less, and the man who exceeds in his desires is called ambitious, the man who falls short unambitious, while the intermediate person has no name. The dispositions also are nameless, except that that of the ambitious man is called ambition. Hence the people who are at the extremes lay claim to the middle place; and we ourselves sometimes call the intermediate person ambitious and sometimes unambitious, and sometimes praise the ambitious man and sometimes the unambitious. The reason of our doing this will be stated in what follows; but now let us speak of the remaining states according to the method which has been indicated.

With regard to anger also there is an excess, a deficiency, and a mean. Although they can scarcely be said to have names, yet since we call the intermediate person good-tempered let us call the mean good temper; of the persons at the extremes let the one who exceeds be called irascible, and his vice irascibility, and the man who falls short an inirascible sort of person, and the deficiency inirascibility. . . .

If happiness is activity in accordance with virtue, it is reasonable that it should be in accordance with the highest virtue; and this will be that of the best thing in us. Whether it be reason or something else that is this element which is thought to be our natural ruler and guide and to take thought of things noble and divine, whether it be itself also divine or only the most divine element in us, the activity of this in accordance with its proper virtue will be perfect happiness. That this activity is contemplative we have already said.

Now this would seem to be in agreement both with what we said before and with the truth. For, firstly, this activity is the best (since not only is reason the best thing in us, but the objects of reason are the best of knowable objects); and, secondly, it is the most continuous, since we can contemplate truth more continuously than we can *do* anything. And we think happiness has pleasure mingled with it, but the activity of philosophic wisdom is admittedly the pleasantest of virtuous activities; at all events the pursuit of it is thought to offer pleasures marvelous for their purity and their enduringness, and it is to be expected that those who know will pass their time more pleasantly than those who inquire. And the self-sufficiency that is spoken of must belong most to the contemplative activity. For while a philosopher, as well as a just man or one possessing any other virtue, needs the necessaries of life, when they are sufficiently equipped with things of that sort the just man needs people towards whom and with whom he shall act justly, and the temperate man, the brave man, and each of the others is in the same case, but the philosopher, even when by himself, can contemplate truth, and the better the wiser he is; he can perhaps do so better if he has fellow-workers, but still he is the most self-sufficient. And this activity alone would seem to be loved for its own sake; for nothing arises from it apart from the contemplating, while from practical activities we gain more or less apart from the action. And happiness is thought to depend on leisure; for we are busy that we may have leisure, and make war that we may live in peace. Now the activity of the practical virtues is exhibited in political or military affairs, but the actions concerned with these seem to be unleisurely. Warlike actions are completely so (for no one chooses to be at war, or provokes war, for the sake of being at war; any one would seem absolutely murderous if he were to make enemies of his friends in order to bring about battle and slaughter); but the action of the statesman is also unleisurely, and—apart from the political action itself—aims at despotic power and honours, or at all events happiness, for him and his fellow citizens—a happiness different from political action, and evidently sought as being different. So if among virtuous actions political and military actions are distinguished by nobility and greatness, and these are unleisurely and aim at an end and are not desirable for their sake, but the activity of reason, which is contemplative, seems both to be superior in serious worth and to aim at no end beyond itself, and to have its pleasure proper to itself (and this augments the activity), and the self-sufficiency, leisureliness, unweariedness (so far as this is possible for man), and all the other attributes ascribed to the supremely happy man are evidently those connected with this activity, it follows that this will be the complete happiness of man, if it be allowed a complete term of life (for none of the attributes of happiness is *in*complete).

But such a life would be too high for man; for it is not in so far as he is man that he will live so, but in so far as something divine is present in him; and by so much as this is superior to our composite nature is its activity superior to that which is the exercise of the other kind of virtue. If reason is divine, then, in comparison with man, the life according to it is divine in comparison with human life. But we must not follow those who advise us, being men, to think of human things, and, being mortal, of mortal things, but must, so far as we can, make ourselves immortal, and strain every nerve to live in accordance with the best thing in us; for even if it be small in bulk, much more does it in power and worth surpass everything. This would seem, too, to be each man himself, since it is the authoritative and better part of him. It would be strange, then, if he were to choose not the life of his self but that of something else. And what we said before will apply now; that which is proper to each thing is by nature best and most pleasant for each thing; for man, therefore, the life according to reason is best and pleasantest, since reason more than anything else *is* man. This life therefore is also the happiest.

Growth and Self-Actualization

Abraham Maslow

When the philosophy of man (his nature, his goals, his potentialities, his fulfillment) changes, then everything changes, not only the philosophy of politics, of economics, of ethics and values, of interpersonal relations and of history itself, but also the philosophy of education, of psychotherapy and of personal growth, the theory of how to help men become what they can and deeply need to become.

We are now in the middle of such a change in the conception of man's capacities, potentialities and goals. A new vision is emerging of the possibilities of man and of his destiny, and its implications are many, not only for our conceptions of education, but also for science, politics, literature, economics, religion, and even our conceptions of the non-human world.

I think it is now possible to begin to delineate this view of human nature as a total, single, comprehensive system of psychology even though much of it has arisen as a reaction *against* the limitations (as philosophies of human nature) of the two most comprehensive psychologies now available—behaviorism (or associationism) and classical, Freudian psychoanalysis. Finding a single label for it is still a difficult task, perhaps a premature one. In the past I have called it the "holistic-dynamic" psychology to express my conviction about its major roots. Some have called it "organismic" fol-

From *Toward a Psychology of Being*, 2nd ed. by Abraham H. Maslow, 1968, Litton Educational Publishing, Inc., reprinted by permission of D. Van Nostrand Company.

lowing Goldstein. Sutich and others are calling it the Self-psychology or Humanistic psychology. We shall see. My own guess is that, in a few decades, if it remains suitably eclectic and comprehensive, it will be called simply "psychology."

I think I can be of most service by speaking primarily for myself and out of my own work rather than as an "official" delegate of this large group of thinkers, even though I am sure that the areas of agreement among them are very large. A selection of works of this "third force" is listed in the bibliographies. Because of the limited space I have, I will present here only some of the major propositions of this point of view. I should warn you that at many points I am way out ahead of the data. Some of these propositions are more based on private conviction than on publicly demonstrated facts. However, they are all in principle confirmable or disconfirmable.

1. We have, each one of us, an essential inner nature which is instinctoid, intrinsic, given, "natural," i.e., with an appreciable hereditary determinant, and which tends strongly to persist.

It makes sense to speak here of the hereditary, constitutional and very early acquired roots of the *individual* self, even though this biological determination of self is only partial, and far too complex to describe simply. In any case, this is "raw material" rather than finished product, to be reacted to by the person, by his significant others, by his environment, etc.

I include in this essential inner nature instinctoid basic needs, capacities, talents, anatomical equipment, physiological or temperamental balances, prenatal and natal injuries, and traumata to the neonate. This inner core shows itself as natural inclinations, propensities or inner bent. Whether defense and coping mechanisms, "style of life," and other characterological traits, all shaped in the first few years of life, should be included is still a matter for discussion. This raw material very quickly starts growing into a self as it meets the world outside and begins to have transaction with it.

2. These are potentialities, not final actualizations. Therefore they have a life history and must be seen developmentally. They are actualized, shaped or stifled mostly (but not altogether) by extra-psychic determinants (culture, family, environment, learning, etc.). Very early in life these goalless urges and tendencies become attached to objects ("sentiments") by canalization but also by arbitrarily learned associations.

3. This inner core, even though it is biologically based and "instinctoid," is weak in certain senses rather than strong. It is easily overcome, suppressed or repressed. It may even be killed off permanently. Humans no longer have instincts in the animal sense, powerful, unmistakable inner voices which tell them unequivocally what to do, when, where, how and with whom. All that we have left are instinct-remnants. And furthermore, these are weak, subtle and delicate, very easily drowned out by learning, by cultural expectations, by fear, by disapproval, etc. They are *hard* to know, rather than easy. Authentic selfhood can be defined in part as being able to hear these impulse-voices within oneself, i.e., to know what one really wants or doesn't want, what one is fit for and what one is *not* fit for, etc. It appears that there are wide individual differences in the strength of these impulse-voices.

4. Each person's inner nature has some characteristics which all other selves have (species-wide) and some which are unique to the person (idiosyncratic). The need for love characterizes every human being that is born (although it can disappear later under certain circumstances). Musical genius however is given to very few, and these differ markedly from each other in style, e.g., Mozart and Debussy.

5. It is possible to study this inner nature scientifically and objectively (that is, with the right kind of "science") and to discover what it is like (*discover*—not invent or construct). It is also possible to do this subjectively, by inner search and by psychotherapy, and the two enterprises supplement and support each other. An expanded humanistic philosophy of science must include these experiential techniques.

6. Many aspects of this inner, deeper nature are either (a) actively repressed, as Freud has described, because they are feared or disapproved of or are ego-alien, or (b) "forgotten" (neglected, unused, overlooked, unverbalized or suppressed), as Schachter has described. Much of the inner, deeper nature is therefore unconscious. This can be true not only for impulses (drives, instincts, needs) as Freud has stressed, but also for capacities, emotions, judgments, attitudes, definitions, perceptions, etc. Active repression takes effort and uses up energy. There are many specific techniques of maintaining active unconsciousness, such as denial, projection, reaction-formation, etc. However, repression does not kill what is repressed. The repressed remains as one active determinant of thought and behavior.

Both active and passive repressions seem to begin early in life, mostly as a response to parental and cultural disapprovals.

However, there is some clinical evidence that repression may arise also from intra-psychic, extra-cultural sources in the young child, or at puberty, i.e., out of fear of being overwhelmed by its own impulses, of becoming disintegrated, of "falling apart," exploding, etc.

It is theoretically possible that the child may spontaneously form attitudes of fear and disapproval toward its own impulses and may then defend himself against them in various ways. Society need not be the only repressing force, if this is true. There may also be intrapsychic repressing and controlling forces. These we may call "intrinsic counter-cathexes."

It is best to distinguish unconscious drives and needs from unconscious ways of cognizing because the latter are often easier to bring to consciousness and therefore to modify. Primary process cognition (Freud) or archaic thinking Jung) is more recoverable by, e.g., creative art education, dance education, and other nonverbal educational techniques.

7. Even though "weak," this inner nature rarely disappears or dies, in the usual person, in the U.S. (such disappearance or dying is possible early in the life history, however). It persists underground, unconsciously, even though denied and repressed. Like the voice of the intellect (which is part of it), it speaks softly but it *will* be heard, even if in a distorted form. That is, it has a dynamic force of its own, pressing always for open, uninhibited expression. Effort must be used in its suppression or repression from which fatigue can result. This force is one main aspect of the "will to health," the urge to grow, the pressure to self-actualization, the quest for one's identity. It is this that makes psychotherapy, education and self-improvement possible in principle.

8. However, this inner core, or self, grows into adulthood only partly by (objective or subjective) discovery, uncovering and acceptance of what is "there" beforehand. Partly it is also a creation of the person himself. Life is a continual series of choices for the individual in which a main determinant of choice is the person as he already is (including his goals for himself, his courage or fear, his feeling of responsibility, his ego-strength or "will power," etc.). We can no longer think of the person as "fully determined" where this phrase implies "determined only by forces external to the person." The person, insofar as he *is* a real person, is his own main determinant. Every person is, in part, "his own project" and makes himself.

9. If this essential core (inner nature) of the person is frustrated, denied or suppressed, sickness results, sometimes in obvious forms, sometimes in subtle and devious forms, sometimes immediately, sometimes later. These psychological illnesses include many more than those listed by the American Psychiatric Association. For instance, the character disorders and disturbances are now seen as far more important for the fate of the world than the classical neuroses or even the psychoses. From this new point of view, new kinds of illness are most dangerous, e.g., "the diminished or stunted person," i.e., the loss of any of the defining characteristics of humanness, or personhood, the failure to grow to one's potential, valuelessness, etc.

That is, general-illness of the personality is seen as any falling short of growth, or of self-actualization, or of full-humanness. And the main source of illness (although not the only one) is seen as frustrations (of the basic needs, of the B-values, of idiosyncratic potentials, of expression of the self, and of the tendency of the person to grow in his own style and at his own pace) especially in the early years of life. That is, frustration of the basic needs is not the only source of illness or of human diminution.

10. This inner nature, as much as we know of it so far, is definitely not primarily "evil," but is rather what we adults in our culture call "good," or else it is neutral. The most accurate way to express this is to say that it is "prior to good and evil." There is little question about this if we speak of the inner nature of the infant and child. The statement is much more complex if we speak of the "infant" as he still exists in the adult. And it gets still more complex if the individual is seen from the point of view of B-psychology rather than D-psychology.

This conclusion is supported by all the truth-revealing and uncovering techniques that have anything to do with human nature: psychotherapy, objective science, subjective science, education and art. For instance, in the long run, uncovering therapy lessens malice, fear, greed, etc., and increases love, courage, creativeness, kindness, altruism, etc., leading us to the conclusion that the latter are "deeper," more natural, and more intrinsically human than the former, i.e., that what we call "bad" behavior is lessened or removed by uncovering, while what we call "good" behavior is strengthened and fostered by uncovering.

11. We must differentiate the Freudian type of superego from intrinsic conscience and intrinsic guilt. The former is in principle a taking into the self of the disapprovals and approvals of persons other than the person himself, fathers, mothers, teachers, etc. Guilt then is recognition of disapproval by others.

Intrinsic guilt is the consequence of betrayal of one's own inner nature or self, a turning off the path to self-actualization, and is essentially justified self-disapproval. It is therefore not as culturally relative as is Freudian guilt. It is "true" or "deserved" or "right and just" or "correct" because it is a discrepancy from something profoundly real within the person rather than from accidental, arbitrary or purely relative localisms. Seen in this way it is good, even *necessary*, for a person's development to have intrinsic guilt when he deserves to. It is not just a symptom to be avoided at any cost but is rather an inner guide for growth toward actualization of the real self, and of its potentialities.

12. "Evil" behavior has mostly referred to unwarranted hostility, cruelty, destructiveness, "mean" aggressiveness. This we do not know enough about. To the degree that this quality of hostility is instinctoid, mankind has one kind of future. To the degree that it is reactive (a response to bad treatment), mankind has a very different kind of future. My opinion is that the weight of the evidence so far indicates that indiscriminately *destructive* hostility is reactive, because uncovering therapy reduces it, and changes its quality into "healthy" self-affirmation, forcefulness, selective hostility, self-defense, righteous indignation, etc. In any case, the *ability* to be aggressive and angry is found in all self-actualizing people, who are able to let it flow forth freely when the external situation "calls for" it.

The situation in children is far more complex. At the very least, we know that the healthy child is also able to be justifiably angry, self-protecting and self-affirming, i.e., reactive aggression. Presumably, then, a child should learn not only how to control his anger, but also how and when to express it.

Behavior that our culture calls evil can also come from ignorance and from childish misinterpretations and beliefs (whether in the child or in the repressed or "forgotten" child-in-the-adult). For instance, sibling rivalry is traceable to the child's wish for the exclusive love of his parents. Only as he matures is he in principle capable of learning that his mother's love for a sibling is compatible with her continued love for him. Thus out of a childish version of love, not in itself reprehensible, can come unloving behavior.

In any case, much that our or any other culture calls evil need not be considered evil in fact, from the more universal, species-wide point of view outlined in this book. If humanness is accepted and loved, then many local, ethnocentric problems simply disappear. To take only one example, seeing sex as intrinsically evil is sheer nonsense from a humanistic point of view.

The commonly seen hatred or resentment of or jealousy of goodness, truth, beauty, health or intelligence ("counter-values") is largely (though not altogether) determined by threat of loss of self-esteem, as the liar is threatened by the honest man, the homely girl by the beautiful girl, or the coward by the hero. Every superior person confronts us with our own shortcomings.

Still deeper than this, however, is the ultimate existential question of the fairness and justice of fate. The person with a disease may be jealous of the healthy man who is no more deserving than he.

Evil behaviors seem to most psychologists to be reactive as in these examples, rather than instinctive. This implies that though "bad" behavior is very deeply rooted in human nature and can never be abolished altogether, it may yet be expected to lessen as the personality matures and as the society improves.

13. Many people still think of "the unconscious," of regression, and of primary process cognition as necessarily unhealthy, or dangerous or bad. Psychotherapeutic experience is slowly teaching us otherwise. Our depths can also be good, or beautiful or desirable. This is also becoming clear from the general findings from investigations of the sources of love, creativeness, play, humor, art, etc. Their roots are deep in the inner, deeper self, i.e., in the unconscious. To recover them and to be able to enjoy and use them we must be able to "regress."

14. No psychological health is possible unless this essential core of the person is fundamentally accepted, loved and respected by others and by himself (the converse is not necessarily true, i.e., that if the core is respected, etc., then psychological health must result, since other prerequisite conditions must also be satisfied).

The psychological health of the chronologically immature is called healthy growth. The psychological health of the adult is called variously, self-fulfillment, emotional maturity, individuation, productiveness, self-actualization, authenticity, full-humanness, etc.

Healthy growth is conceptually subordinate, for it is usually defined now as "growth toward self-actualization," etc. Some psychologists speak simply in terms of one overarching goal or end, or tendency of human development, considering all immature growth phenomena to be only steps along the path to self-actualization (Goldstein, Rogers).

Self-actualization is defined in various ways but a solid core of agreement is perceptible. All definitions accept or imply, (a) acceptance and expression of the inner core or self, i.e., actualization of these latent capacities, and potentialities, "full functioning," availability of the human and personal essence. (b) They all imply minimal presence of ill health, neurosis, psychosis, of loss or diminution of the basic human and personal capacities.

15. For all these reasons, it is at this time best to bring out and encourage, or at the very least, to recognize this inner nature, rather than to suppress or repress it. Pure spontaneity consists of free, uninhibited, uncontrolled, trusting, unpremeditated expression of the self, i.e., of the psychic forces, with minimal interference by consciousness. Control, will, caution, self-criticism, measure, deliberateness are the brakes upon this expression made intrinsically necessary by the laws of the social and natural worlds outside the psychic world, and secondarily, made necessary by fear of the psyche itself (intrinsic counter-cathexis). Speaking in a very broad way, controls upon the psyche which come from *fear of the psyche* are largely neurotic or *psychotic*, or not intrinsically or theoretically necessary. (The healthy psyche is not terrible or horrible and therefore doesn't have to be feared, as it has been for thousands of years. Of course, the *unhealthy* psyche is another story.) This kind of control is usually lessened by psychological health, by deep psychotherapy, or by any *deeper* self-knowledge and self-acceptance. There are also, however, controls upon the psyche which do not come out of fear, but out of the necessities for keeping it integrated, organized and unified (intrinsic counter-cathexes). And there are also "controls," probably in another sense, which are necessary as capacities are actualized, and as

higher forms of expression are sought for, e.g., acquisition of skills through hard work by the artist, the intellectual, the athlete. But these controls are eventually transcended and become aspects of spontaneity, as they become self. I propose that we call these desirable and necessary controls "Apollonizing controls" because they do not call into question the desirability of the gratification, but rather *enhance* pleasure by organizing, estheticizing, pacing, styling and savoring the gratification, e.g., as in sex, eating, drinking, etc. The contrast is with repressive or suppressive controls.

The balance between spontaneity and control varies, then, as the health of the psyche and the health of the world vary. Pure spontaneity is not long possible because we live in a world which runs by its own, non-psychic laws. It *is* possible in dreams, fantasies, love, imagination, sex, the first stages of creativity, artistic work, intellectual play, free association, etc. Pure control is not permanently possible, for then the psyche dies. Education must be directed then *both* toward cultivation of controls and cultivation of spontaneity and expression. In our culture and at this point in history, it is necessary to redress the balance in favor of spontaneity, the ability to be expressive, passive, unwilled, trusting in processes other than will and control, unpremeditated, creative, etc. But it must be recognized that there have been and will be other cultures and other areas in which the balance was or will be in the other direction. . . .

16 Experimental Morality and Alternate Lifestyles

Dewey & Kanter

Early in his career, the American philosopher John Dewey (1859–1952) recognized the necessity for an overall reconstruction of social and educational institutions. In his later writings he stressed the urgency of the crisis and the need for its intelligent resolution. Traditional mores and theories about the standards and principles by which people judge life and make moral decisions were in trouble. The root of the crisis was the incompatibility of traditional values and ideals with the changed circumstances of human existence brought about by the scientific and industrial revolutions. Dewey suggested that an approach to morality be patterned after scientific attitudes and methods but directing inquiry into human and essentially moral problems. This would begin to heal the breach between people's outmoded beliefs about values and their largely unguided contemporary experience.

Dewey believed that a major obstacle to the needed reconstruction was traditional philosophy and the way in which it presented moral problems and their solutions. One of his major criticisms of traditional philosophers was that they had been too enamored with the search for fixed truths. They believed that only the immutable truth could be the proper object of human knowledge. Many ancient philosophers believed that the world presented to us by sense perception and ordinary experience could not yield certain knowledge. The world as grasped by theoretical understanding, as contrasted with the world of opinion and practice, became the aim of the philosopher.

This spectator view of knowledge carried with it a distinction between knowing, as a pure intellectual activity, and doing. This was generalized into a separation of the theoretical and the practical and it depreciated doing, making, and action. It did not see human thought as a purposive and reflective activity by which people relate to and change their environment. Instead of emphasizing the practical and experimental and ameliorating the hazards and precariousness of human existence, it emphasized changing the inner soul and focused upon an ideal, much more perfect world. This emphasis had given us consolation and some good literature, but it had diverted us from our real task.

Dewey was against this approach to morality. Reason is not a searchlight by which, if we focus correctly, the eternal verities will be grasped. Thinking is a human instrument for our interaction with our physical and social environment. Human values and moral problems come into play when some practical choice is made involving human conduct, desires, and satisfactions. Human aims are not to be taken as fixed ends in advance of inquiry into, and intelligent deliberation about, concrete moral situations. Nor are the ends of human action separable from the means for carrying them out. Dewey believed that we ought to assess the various roads to human improvement rather than argue about the validity of this or that description of the final destination. The value of science is not any one conclusion or theory but its adoption of an open-ended procedure and method; the important thing in morals is not a conclusion or definition about the good, but the adoption of a procedure for intelligent deliberation. The good life is one in which we avoid making moral choices by instinct or habit and are intelligently guided by changing needs and circumstances.

Since the Renaissance and the rise of science, the traditional view of moral values as belonging to a higher and more spiritual realm had been on the defensive. The new science seemed to have stripped the world of the qualities that made it beautiful and good and had ruled out everything but a world composed of particles acting according to mechanical laws. There was no place for value in a world of fact.

Dewey's reaction to this was not to lament the loneliness of individuals in a meaningless universe nor to portray them as heroically asserting values despite their ultimate meaninglessness. Rather he denied this picture of both science and human morality; he denied the separation of human beings and nature. He tried to reconcile the two by looking for one method that would deal with both factors in human existence. Since values are a part of human experience, we should use our intelligence to judge the conditions and results of human satisfactions and, accordingly, our future desires, affections, and enjoyments.

That the structure of society, habits, living conditions, and daily life have been radically transformed by the scientific and technological revolutions is even more obvious to us than it was to Dewey. Human behavior and the context of moral decisions have been profoundly influenced and altered by, for example, such recent developments in medicine as birth control methods, new ways of prolonging life, and organ transplants. These developments affect the way in which we live (and die) in our environment. Despite all of these outward changes, institutions and concepts of the good remain relatively the same. Thus there is a cultural and moral lag between inner thoughts and the conditions of outward behavior. The scientific attitude should be used to create new attitudes and beliefs about morals rather than to remain largely subordinate to instincts or the inertia of institutions.

It is within this context of Dewey's thought that the phrase "learning through doing" becomes more than a cliché. It formulates in brief the practical maxim of the experimental method, which "refers not to random and aimless action but to action directed by ideas and knowledge."

Dewey was careful to point out that his proposal that the experimental method be taken over from science into social affairs—into education, political organization, and morality—did not mean that he was proposing a sharp break with the past or a rejection of all customs and established institutions. Such a break, he believed, could lead to chaos rather than creative reconstruction. One must first intelligently examine the consequences of traditions, customs, and established institutions, then evaluate them and consider in what ways they may be changed to generate more satisfactory consequences (i.e., conducive to growth). He would agree with Frazier, the planner in B. F. Skinner's *Walden Two*, that "a constantly experimental attitude toward everything—that's all we need."

Following the selection from Dewey is a brief account by Rosabeth Moss Kanter of the recent commune movement. Before it peaked and receded in the early seventies, this movement represented a dramatic and far-reaching effort to accomplish some of the goals that Dewey proposed. As social experiments, most of the communes may have been too vaguely conceived and poorly administered, and the majority may have failed miserably for a variety of reasons; but they were conscientious attempts at intentional living and intensive explorations in alternative lifestyles. Perhaps there is something to be learned from those experiments that were undertaken with a boldness of invention, a willingness to venture, and the courage of commitment to experimentation rather than to dogma.

Reconstruction in Moral Conceptions

John Dewey

Morals is not a catalogue of acts nor a set of rules to be applied like drugstore prescriptions or cook-book recipes. The need in morals is for specific methods of inquiry and of contrivance: Methods of inquiry to locate difficulties and evils; methods of contrivance to form plans to be used as working hypotheses in dealing with them. And the pragmatic import of the logic of individualized situations, each having its own irreplaceable good and principle, is to transfer the attention of theory from preoccupation with general conceptions to the problem of developing effective methods of inquiry.

Two ethical consequences of great moment should be remarked. The belief in fixed values has bred a division of ends into intrinsic and instrumental, of those that are really worth while in themselves and those that are of importance only as means to intrinsic goods. Indeed, it is often thought to be the very beginning of wisdom, of moral discrimination, to make this distinction. Dialectically, the distinction is interesting and seems harmless. But carried into practice it has an import that is tragic. Historically, it has been the source and justification of a hard and fast difference be-

From John Dewey, *Reconstruction in Philosophy.* Original edition, copyright 1920 by Henry Holt and Co. Enlarged edition, copyright 1948 by Beacon Press. Reprinted by permission of Beacon Press.

tween ideal goods on one side and material goods on the other. At present those who would be liberal conceive intrinsic goods as esthetic in nature rather than as exclusively religious or as intellectually contemplative. But the effect is the same. So-called intrinsic goods, whether religious or esthetic, are divorced from those interests of daily life which because of their constancy and urgency form the preoccupation of the great mass. Aristotle used this distinction to declare that slaves and the working class though they are necessary *for* the state—the commonweal—are not constituents *of* it. That which is regarded as *merely* instrumental must approach drudgery; it cannot command either intellectual, artistic or moral attention and respect. Anything becomes *unworthy* whenever it is thought of as intrinsically lacking worth. So men of "ideal" interests have chosen for the most part the way of neglect and escape. The urgency and pressure of "lower" ends have been covered up by polite conventions. Or, they have been relegated to a baser class of mortals in order that the few might be free to attend to the goods that are really or intrinsically worth while. This withdrawal, in the name of higher ends, has left, for mankind at large and especially for energetic "practical" people the lower activities in complete command.

No one can possibly estimate how much of the obnoxious materialism and brutality of our economic life is due to the fact that economic ends have been regarded as *merely* instrumental. When they are recognized to be as intrinsic and final in their place as any others, then it will be seen that they are capable of idealization, and that if life is to be worth while, they must acquire ideal and intrinsic value. Esthetic, religious and other "ideal" ends are now thin and meagre or else idle and luxurious because of the separation from "instrumental" or economic ends. Only in connection with the latter can they be woven into the texture of daily life and made substantial and pervasive. The vanity and irresponsibility of values that are merely final and not also in turn means to the enrichment of other occupations of life ought to be obvious. But now the doctrine of "higher" ends gives aid, comfort and support to every socially isolated and socially irresponsible scholar, specialist, esthete and religionist. It protects the vanity and irresponsibility of his calling from observation by others and by himself. The moral deficiency of the calling is transformed into a cause of admiration and gratulation.

The other generic change lies in doing away once for all with the traditional distinction between moral goods, like the virtues, and natural goods like health, economic security, art, science and the like. The point of view under discussion is not the only one which has deplored this rigid distinction and endeavored to abolish it. Some schools have even gone so far as to regard moral excellencies, qualities of character as of value only because they promote natural goods. But the experimental logic when carried into morals makes every quality that is judged to be good according as it contributes to amelioration of existing ills. And in so doing, it enforces the moral meaning of natural science. When all is said and done in criticism of present social deficiencies, one may well wonder whether the root difficulty does not lie in the separation of natural and moral science. When physics, chemistry, biology, medicine, contribute to the detection of concrete human woes and to the development of

plans for remedying them and relieving the human estate, they become moral; they become part of the apparatus of moral inquiry or science. The latter then loses its peculiar flavor of the didactic and pedantic; its ultra-moralistic and hortatory tone. It loses its thinness and shrillness as well as its vagueness. It gains agencies that are efficacious. But the gain is not confined to the side of moral science. Natural science loses its divorce from humanity; it becomes itself humanistic in quality. It is something to be pursued not in a technical and specialized way for what is called truth for its own sake, but with the sense of its social bearing, its intellectual indispensableness. It is technical only in the sense that it provides the technique of social and moral engineering.

When the consciousness of science is fully impregnated with the consciousness of human value, the greatest dualism which now weighs humanity down, the split between the material, the mechanical, the scientific and the moral and ideal will be destroyed. Human forces that now waver because of this division will be unified and reinforced. As long as ends are not thought of as individualized according to specific needs and opportunities, the mind will be content with abstractions, and the adequate stimulus to the moral or social use of natural science and historical data will be lacking. But when attention is concentrated upon the diversified concretes, recourse to all intellectual materials needed to clear up the special cases will be imperative. At the same time that morals are made to focus in intelligence, things intellectual are moralized. The vexatious and wasteful conflict between naturalism and humanism is terminated.

These general considerations may be amplified. First: Inquiry, discovery take the same place in morals that they have come to occupy in sciences of nature. Validation, demonstration become experimental, a matter of consequences. Reason, always an honorific term in ethics becomes actualized in the methods by which the needs and conditions, the obstacles and resources, of situations are scrutinized in detail, and intelligent plans of improvement are worked out. Remote and abstract generalities promote jumping at conclusions, "anticipations of nature." Bad consequences are then deplored as due to natural perversity and untoward fate. But shifting the issue to analysis of a specific situation makes inquiry obligatory and alert observation of consequences imperative. No past decision nor old principle can ever be wholly relied upon to justify a course of action. No amount of pains taken in forming a purpose in a definite case is final; the consequences of its adoption must be carefully noted, and a purpose held only as a working hypothesis until results confirm its rightness. Mistakes are no longer either mere unavoidable accidents to be mourned or moral sins to be expiated and forgiven. They are lessons in wrong methods of using intelligence and instructions as to a better course in the future. They are indications of the need of revision, development, readjustment. Ends grow, standards of judgment are improved. Man is under just as much obligation to develop his most advanced standards and ideals as to use conscientiously those which he already possesses. Moral life is protected from falling into formalism and rigid repetition. It is rendered flexible, vital, growing.

In the second place, every case where moral action is required becomes of equal moral importance and urgency with every other. If the need and deficiencies of a specific situation indicate improvement of health as the end and good, then for that situation health is the ultimate and supreme good. It is no means to something else. It is a final and intrinsic value. The same thing is true of improvement of economic status, of making a living, of attending to business and family demands—all of the things which under the sanction of fixed ends have been rendered of secondary and merely instrumental value, and so relatively base and unimportant. Anything that in a given situation is an end and good at all is of equal worth, rank

and dignity with every other good of any other situation, and deserves the same intelligent attention.

We note thirdly the effect in destroying the roots of Phariseeism. We are so accustomed to thinking of this as deliberate hypocrisy that we overlook its intellectual premises. The conception which looks for the end of action within the circumstances of the actual situation will not have the same measure of judgment for all cases. When one factor of the situation is a person of trained mind and large resources, more will be expected than with a person of backward mind and uncultured experience. The absurdity of applying the same standard of moral judgment to savage peoples that is used with civilized will be apparent. No individual or group will be judged by whether they come up to or fall short of some fixed result, but by the direction in which they are moving. The bad man is the man who no matter how good he *has* been is beginning to deteriorate, or grow less good. The good man is the man who no matter how morally unworthy he *has* been is moving to become better. Such a conception makes one severe in judging himself and humane in judging others. It excludes that arrogance which always accompanies judgment based on degree of approximation to fixed ends.

In the fourth place, the process of growth, of improvement and progress, rather than the static outcome and result, becomes the significant thing. Not health as an end fixed once and for all, but the needed improvement in health—a continual process—is the end and good. The end is no longer a terminus or limit to be reached. It is the active process of transforming the existent situation. Not perfection as a final goal, but the ever-enduring process of perfecting, maturing, refining is the aim in living. Honesty, industry, temperance, justice, like health, wealth and learning, are not goods to be possessed as they would be if they expressed fixed ends to be attained. They are directions of change in the quality of experience. Growth itself is the only moral "end."

Although the bearing of this idea upon the problem of evil and the controversy between optimism and pessimism is too vast to be here discussed, it may be worth while to touch upon it superficially. The problem of evil ceases to be a theological and metaphysical one, and is perceived to be the practical problem of reducing, alleviating, as far as may be removing, the evils of life. Philosophy is no longer under obligation to find ingenious methods for proving that evils are only apparent, not real, or to elaborate schemes for explaining them away or, worse yet, for justifying them. It assumes another obligation:—That of contributing in however humble a way to methods that will assist us in discovering the causes of humanity's ills. Pessimism is a paralyzing doctrine. In declaring that the world is evil wholesale, it makes futile all efforts to discover the remediable causes of specific evils and thereby destroys at the root every attempt to make the world better and happier. Wholesale optimism, which has been the consequence of the attempt to explain evil away, is, however, equally an incubus.

After all, the optimism that says that the world is already the best possible of all worlds might be regarded as the most cynical of pessimisms. If this is the best possible, what would a world which was fundamentally bad be like? Meliorism is the belief that the specific conditions which exist at one moment, be they comparatively bad or comparatively good, in any event may be bettered. It encourages intelligence to study the positive means of good and the obstructions to their realization, and to put forth endeavor for the improvement of conditions. It arouses confidence and a reasonable hopefulness as optimism does not. For the latter in declaring that good is already realized in ultimate reality tends to make us gloss over the evils that concretely exist. It becomes too readily the creed of those who live at ease, in comfort, of those who have been successful in obtaining this world's rewards. Too readily optimism makes the men who hold it callous

and blind to the sufferings of the less fortunate, or ready to find the cause of troubles of others in their personal viciousness. It thus co-operates with pessimism, in spite of the extreme nominal differences between the two, in benumbing sympathetic insight and intelligent effort in reform. It beckons men away from the world of relativity and change into the calm of the absolute and eternal.

The import of many of these changes in moral attitude focuses in the idea of happiness. Happiness has often been made the object of the moralists' contempt. Yet the most ascetic moralist has usually restored the idea of happiness under some other name, such as bliss. Goodness without happiness; valor and virtue without satisfaction, ends without conscious enjoyment—these things are as intolerable practically as they are self-contradictory in conception. Happiness is not, however, a bare possession; it is not a fixed attainment. Such a happiness is either the unworthy selfishness which moralists have so bitterly condemned, or it is, even if labelled bliss, an insipid tedium, a millennium of ease in relief from all struggle and labor. It could satisfy only the most delicate of molly-coddles. Happiness is found only in success; but success means succeeding, getting forward, moving in advance. It is an active process, not a passive outcome. Accordingly it includes the overcoming of obstacles, the elimination of sources of defect and ill. Esthetic sensitiveness and enjoyment are a large constituent in any worthy happiness. But the esthetic appreciation which is totally separated from renewal of spirit, from re-creation of mind and purification of emotion is a weak and sickly thing, destined to speedy death from starvation. That the renewal and re-creation come unconsciously not by set intention but makes them the more genuine. . . .

If a few words are added upon the topic of education, it is only for the sake of suggesting that the educative process is all one with the moral process, since the latter is a continuous passage of experience from worse to better. Education has been traditionally thought of as preparation: as learning, acquiring certain things because they will later be useful. The end is remote, and education is getting ready, is a preliminary to something more important to happen later on. Childhood is only a preparation for adult life, and adult life for another life. Always the future, not the present, has been the significant thing in education: Acquisition of knowledge and skill for future use and enjoyment; formation of habits required later in life in business, good citizenship and pursuit of science. Education is thought of also as something needed by some human beings merely because of their dependence upon others. We are born ignorant, unversed, unskilled, immature, and consequently in a state of social dependence. Instruction, training, moral discipline are processes by which the mature, the adult, gradually raise the helpless to the point where they can look out for themselves. The business of childhood is to grow into the independence of adulthood by means of the guidance of those who have already attained it. Thus the process of education as the main business of life ends when the young have arrived at emancipation from social dependence.

These two ideas, generally assumed but rarely explicitly reasoned out, contravene the conception that growing, or the continuous reconstruction of experience, is the only end. If at whatever period we choose to take a person, he is still in process of growth, then education is not, save as a by-product, a preparation for something coming later. Getting from the present the degree and kind of growth there is in it is education. This is a constant function, independent of age. The best thing that can be said about any special process of education, like that of the formal school period, is that it renders its subject capable of further education: more sensitive to conditions of growth and more able to take advantage of them. Acquisition of skill, possession of knowledge, attainment of culture are not ends: they are marks of growth and means to its continuing.

The contrast usually assumed between the period of education as one of social dependence and of maturity as one of social independence does harm. We repeat over and over that man is a social animal, and then confine the significance of this statement to the sphere in which sociality usually seems least evident, politics. The heart of the sociality of man is in education. The idea of education as preparation and of adulthood as a fixed limit of growth are two sides of the same obnoxious untruth. If the moral business of the adult as well as the young is a growing and developing experience, then the instruction that comes from social dependencies and interdependencies are as important for the adult as for the child. Moral independence for the adult means arrest of growth, isolation means induration. We exaggerate the intellectual dependence of childhood so that children are too much kept in leading strings, and then we exaggerate the independence of adult life from intimacy of contacts and communication with others. When the identity of the moral process with the processes of specific growth is realized, the more conscious and formal education of childhood will be seen to be the most economical and efficient means of social advance and reorganization, and it will also be evident that the test of all the institutions of adult life is their effect in furthering continued education. Government, business, art, religion, all social institutions have a meaning, a purpose. That purpose is to set free and to develop the capacities of human individuals without respect to race, sex, class or economic status. And this is all one with saying that the test of their value is the extent to which they educate every individual into the full stature of his possibility. Democracy has many meanings, but if it has a moral meaning, it is found in resolving that the supreme test of all political institutions and industrial arrangements shall be the contribution they make to the all-around growth of every member of society.

Communes

Rosabeth Moss Kanter

"The things that make up community are terribly subtle; it's the little things . . . Someone getting his hair cut on the porch . . . Babysitting at home; someone calls to ask if you need relief. That awareness and caring . . . We got a weaving frame to have communal weaves . . . I make dinner with a crew once a week and remember who's a vegetarian and needs a special meal. Expanded consciousness of others . . . Nothing big and spectacular. The scenes that move me are the little things about our life together."

"Life together" is the experience of communal living expressed by one founder of a new 30-member commune in Vermont. Like others, she is participating in a renewed search for utopia and community, brotherhood and sharing, warmth and intimacy, participation and involvement, purpose and meaning. Today's utopians want to return to fundamentals. They want to put people back in touch with each other, nature and themselves.

This quest for togetherness is behind the proliferation of communal-living experiments. The ventures vary widely. There are small urban groups that share living quarters and raise their families together but hold outside jobs, and there are rural farming communes that combine work and living. Some are formal organizations with their own business enterprises, such as the Bruderhof communities,

From "Communes" by Rosabeth Moss Kanter in *Psychology Today,* July, 1970.

which manufacture Community Playthings. Others are loose aggregates without chosen names.

They have been started by political radicals, return-to-the-land homesteaders, intellectuals, pacifists, hippies and drop-outs, ex-drug addicts, behavioral psychologists following B. F. Skinner's *Walden Two,* humanistic psychologists interested in environments for self-actualization, Quakers in South America, ex-monks in New Hampshire, and Hasidic Jews in Boston. Estimates of the number of communal experiments today run to the hundreds. There are intercommunity magazines, newsletters, information clearinghouses and conferences to share experiences, help build new utopias and bring potential communards together.

NOW

Today's communal movement is a reawakening of the search for utopia in America that started as early as 1680, when religious sects first retreated to the wilderness to live in community. While experiments in communal living have always been part of the American landscape, only a few dozen survived for more than a few years. Building community has been difficult, and today's communes are heirs to the problems.

I have studied 19th-Century American communities, comparing 21 that lasted with nine that didn't, and have gathered information from 20 contemporary communes and from growth-and-learning communities. I then compared successful 19th-Century utopias with today's anarchist communes and growth-center communities and found that while the growth centers tend to incorporate important features of the 19th-Century groups that were successful, many of the anarchist communes do not.

FAMILY

Today's communes seek a family warmth and intimacy, to become extended families. A 50-person hippie commune in California, for example, called itself "the Lynch family"; a New Mexico commune "The Chosen Family"; a New York City group simply "The Family."

For some communes becoming a family means collective child-rearing, shared responsibility for raising children. Children and adults in a Vermont commune have their own separate rooms, and the children consider all the adults in the community their "parents." Other communes experiment sexually to change the man-woman relationship from monogamy to group marriage.

The desire is to create intense involvement in the group—feelings of connectedness, belonging and the warmth of many attachments. How did the successful utopias of the past achieve this?

Intimacy was a daily fact of life for successful 19th-Century communities. The group was an ever-present part of the member's day, for his fellows were his work-mates as well as his neighbors, and people ate and slept together in central buildings. Many successful communities saw themselves as families and addressed leaders in parental terms—Father Noyes in Oneida, Father Rapp in Harmony.

Exclusive couples and biological families were discouraged through celibacy, free love or group marriage. In Oneida's system of complex marriage, for example, each member had sexual access to every other member, with his or her consent and under the general supervision of community leaders. A man interested in a liaison would approach a woman through a third party; she had the right to refuse his attentions. Couples showing an excess of special love would be broken up or forced into relationships with others.

Successful 19th-Century communities tended to separate biological families and place children in dwelling units apart from their parents, creating instead a "family of the whole." In Oneida children were raised communally from soon after weaning. The heads of the children's department raised the children; they were called "papa" and "mother." Children visited their own parents individually once or twice a week but accepted the community's family life as the focus of their existence.

They also celebrated their togetherness joyfully in group rituals such as singing, religious services and observance of anniversaries, holidays and other festive occasions.

GROUP

Many members look to today's communities for personal growth through small-group processes in which members honestly and openly criticize and support one another. T-group interaction or mutual criticism in its various forms can be a primary and essential part of a community's goals. In the Synanon groups, community was first embodied in self-help group sessions for drug addicts and only later grew into the desire to establish a total way of life.

Other communes use group process to work out disagreements, to regenerate commitment, and to create a sense of intimate involvement. A Vermont commune reached a crisis when so many problems accumulated that people asked: *Just what are we doing here anyway?*

An extended encounter group was held and the sense of common purpose reaffirmed.

Successful 19th-Century communities used a variety of group techniques, including confession, self-criticism, and mutual-criticism sessions, to solidify the group and deal with deviance and discontent before they became disruptive. The individual could bare his soul to the group, express his weaknesses, failings, doubts, problems, inner secrets. Disagreements between members could be discussed openly. These T-group-like sessions also showed that the content of each person's inner world was important to the community. Oneidans periodically submitted themselves for criticism by a committee of six to 12 judges and were expected to receive the criticism in silence and acquiesce to it in writing. Excessive introspection was considered a sin, and no matter was too private for mutual criticism.

The Llano Colony, a 20th-Century, socialist utopia, had a weekly "psychology" meeting that one observer described as a combination of "revival, pep meeting, and confessional."

Possibly because they developed such strong group ties, successful 19th-Century groups stayed together in the face of outside persecution, financial shakiness, and natural disasters. Unsuccessful utopias of the past, on the other hand, did not tend to build these kinds of group relations.

PROPERTY

The desire for sharing, participation and cooperation in today's communes extends to property and work. One ideal is to create economically self-sufficient communities, with all property owned in common. The desire for self-sufficiency and control over their own financial destinies leads many communes to form around farms, to attempt to provide for their maintenance needs themselves, to live in simple dwellings and to work the land.

Many of today's communards believe that money and private property create barriers between people. Money should be thrown into a common pot and property should belong to anyone who uses it. This acceptance of common ownership is reflected in the answer of a small child in a Cambridge commune, questioned about who owned a cat. He said, *The cat is everyone's.*

Many urban communes where members work at outside jobs try to operate with common exchequers. The commune has the responsibility to provide for everyone economically. In Synanon's new Tomales Bay city, as in all Synanon houses, goods and facilities are community-owned. Members receive small amounts of "walking-around money."

A common-work community is another important goal of today's groups. Some have their own businesses—agriculture, crafts, toy manufacturing (the Bruderhof), advertising specialties and gas stations (Synanon), schools, film and other media. In the Bruderhof groups, members work at assigned jobs in the household or school or factory, sharing kitchen and dining-room chores. Other communes without money-making enterprises may still expect strong participation in community upkeep.

In most successful 19th-Century utopias, property was jointly owned and shared, goods equally distributed to all members, and private property abolished. The successful groups all required members to sign over their property and financial holdings to the community on admission. At one point in Harmony's history the leader, George Rapp, even burned the contribution record book.

The successful groups tended to have their own means of support. Generally all members worked within the community. Oneidans, for example, first supported themselves by farming. Because of financial difficulties, they later engaged in manufacturing enterprises ranging from steel traps to silverware. A business board of individual department heads and other interested members regulated the industries. Work was a community-wide affair where possible, and jobs were rotated among members.

Such work arrangements required central coordination; how a member spent his time was a matter of community policy. In unsuccessful communities like Brook Farm, individual members made their own decisions about when and how long to work. The Shakers, on the other hand, instituted a minute-by-minute routine with bells ringing to mark the time.

These property and work arrangements were conducive to a strong community commitment and help account for the successful groups' longevity.

BELIEVERS

Often today's communities are founded to implement elaborate philosophies or world views communicated through charismatic leaders. Synanon coalesced 11 years ago around the visions of Chuck Dederich, who formed the community (now numbering in the thousands) on a $33 unemployment check. His personal example and teachings continue to guide the community. Mel Lyman is the central presence for Fort Hill. A number of communes consider their leaders manifestations of Christ, great prophets, or seers.

Many successful 19th-Century communities had charismatic figures; they were considered godlike, if not actually manifestations of God, and were viewed with awe by members, treated with deference and respect, and accorded special privileges and immunities. In successful communities when the charismatic died his teachings lived on. The Shakers continued to coalesce around Mother Ann Lee after her death, and today the Bruderhof still are translating the teachings of their founder from the German.

The emphasis on a value-based and value-oriented life required an ideological commitment or a set of vows for admission, a striking contrast with some of the unsuccessful communities. New Harmony, for example, merely advertised for anyone interested in joining a communal experiment.

TWO KINDS

Today's communities differ as widely in structure, values and ideology among themselves as the 19th-Century ones did. One set of present-day utopias, religious communities such as the Bruderhof and the Hutterian Brethren, have their roots in the traditional communities of the past. But two distinct kinds of groups are emerging as the *now* forms: small anarchistic communes and communities formed around growth centers, of which Esalen, Kairos, Cumbres are examples.

Some of today's communes are small and anarchistic, consisting of 12, 20, to 30 persons. They seek intimacy and involvement, but refuse to structure community life. Everyone does his own thing at his own time. They are concerned with flexibility and mobility, not with permanence. They reject the control of other groups. Many tend to share living arrangements in which members continue to work outside instead of developing self-sufficient communities. Their lack of solid financial bases is a great problem. In addition they report that many jobs within the commune remain undone, many conflicts never get ironed out, and "family feeling" develops only with difficulty.

I find little definable pattern, rule, or group structure in many of today's anarchist communes. In a Maryland commune of 12, one pays nothing to join. Private property remains private, although members report that it is shared freely. Most members have outside jobs and contribute $30 a month each for food and utilities. All work within the community is voluntary. There are no leadership positions. Decisions are made individually.

Some of these communes do try to develop the intimate, T-group-like sessions of the 19th-Century utopias. But the anarchist groups have a tendency not to do this on a regular or formal basis.

Today's anarchist communes tend to lack integrating philosophies. Many begin with only a vague desire for closer personal relationships and group living in the most general sense.

A member of one short-lived commune talked about its failure: "We weren't ready to define who we were; we certainly weren't prepared to define who we weren't—it was still just a matter of intuition. We had come together for various reasons—not overtly for a common idea or ideal. . . . The different people managed to work together side by side for awhile, but there really was no shared vision."

Anarchist communes tend to be open to all comers at the start. In strong contrast with the successful 19th-Century communities, some anarchist communes do not make a member/non-member distinction. A member of a rural California commune that dissolved after a year saw this as one of their problems: "We were entirely open. We did not say no—we felt that this would make a more dynamic group. But we got a lot of sick people. . . . Most people came here just to get out of the city. . . . they had no commitment."

The prospects for most of today's anarchistic communes are dim; they lack the commitment-building practices of the successful communities of the 19th Century.

Today's growth-and-learning centers on the other hand offer greater prospects for success in longevity, economic viability and personal fulfillment. These groups tend to be highly organized, by comparison with their anarchistic cousins. In their own ways they implement many of the practices of successful 19th-Century groups.

These 100 or so growth centers—many of them outgrowths of the encounter-group movement—provide temporary communities in which their guests find intimacy and expressive involvement. For their staffs they are permanent communities of total involvement.

Growth-and-learning communities are centered around small-group interaction that generates strong group ties and family feeling. Encounter groups are part of the community life. Lama, in New Mexico, has a group meeting every evening for personal growth and the release of interpersonal tensions. The Synanon game is in many ways the Synanon community's most central activity.

At some communities, family feeling is extended; the community encourages sexual experimentation and acting on physical feelings. While some members may be married, they are not bound by monogamy. Finally, in these communities there is often an abundance of group rituals—from Tai Chi exercises (a Chinese moving meditation that resembles dance) to mixed-media celebrations of important events.

The growth-and-learning communities also tend to have explicit sets of values, integrating philosophies that members must share—from the principles of zazen to humanistic psychology. Members are expected to grow in the community spirit and, as at Synanon, character is the only status.

Some communities have communal living arrangements with minimum privacy. They tend to have stringent entrance requirements: potential members must meet community standards and often must serve long apprenticeships to be accepted.

In the growth-and-learning communities work tends to be communal; a member may lead a workshop, then clean the kitchen, sharing responsibility as a growth experience. Discipline through work is a theme at Zen learning centers; a new Synanon member's first job often is to scrub toilets.

These communities also tend to have fixed daily routines and schedules with tasks assigned in advance.

COMPARISON OF 9 SUCCESSFUL AND 21 UNSUCCESSFUL COMMUNITIES GROUP RELATIONS

	Successful:	*Unsuccessful:*
	Percentage that adhered to the practice	
Communal family structure:		
Free love or celibacy	100%	29%
Parent-child separation	48%	15%
Biological families not living together	33%	5%
Ritual:		
Songs about the community	63%	14%
Group singing	100%	73%
Special community occasions celebrated	83%	50%
Mutual criticism:		
Regular confession	44%	0
Mutual-criticism sessions	44%	26%
Daily group meetings	56%	6%
PROPERTY & WORK		
Communistic sharing:		
Property signed over to community at admission	100%	45%
Community-as-whole owned land	89%	76%
Community-owned buildings	89%	71%
Community-owned furniture, tools	100%	79%
Community-owned clothing, personal effects	67%	28%
Communal labor:		
No compensation for labor	100%	41%
No charge for community services	100%	47%
Job rotation	50%	44%
Communal work efforts	100%	50%
Fixed daily routine	100%	54%
Detailed specification of routine	67%	13%

Like the successful utopias of the past, the growth communities have their charismatic figures, from the late Fritz Perls and William Schutz at Esalen to Cesareo Pelaez at Cumbres in New Hampshire.

Growth-and-learning communities, in short, tend to create family-like feeling, to use mutual criticism, to provide a strong sense of participation and responsibility, to affirm their bonds through ritual, to organize work communally, to have stringent entrance requirements, and to develop strong values symbolized by charismatic leaders.

In the light of history, the small anarchistic commune does not seem to be stable or enduring, while the growth-and-learning community appears to have much greater prospects. Yet in today's world—a mobile, change-oriented society that is increasingly wary of long-range commitments—there may be room for both kinds of groups. The small, dissolvable, unstructured commune may meet its members' needs for a temporary home and family. The more permanent growth-and-learning center is a place for enduring commitment for those who want a rooted way of life in community.

RELATED READING

Albert, Ethel, et al. *Great Traditions in Ethics: An Introduction,* 3rd ed. New York: Van Nostrand Reinhold Co., 1975.

Allport, Gordon. *Becoming: Basic Considerations for a Psychology of Personality.* New Haven, Conn.: Yale University Press, 1960.

Ayer, A. J. *Language, Truth and Logic.* New York: Dover Publications, 1936.

Barnes, Hazel. *An Existential Ethics.* New York: Alfred A. Knopf, 1967.

Brandt, Richard B. *Ethical Theory.* Englewood Cliffs, N.J.: Prentice-Hall, 1959.

Crossman, R. H S. *Plato Today,* 2nd ed. New York: Oxford, 1959.

De Beauvoir, Simone. *The Ethics of Ambiguity.* New York: Citadel Press, 1964.

Dewey, John. *The Quest for Certainty.* New York: G. P. Putnam's Sons, 1960.

Dewitt, N. W. *Epicurus and His Philosophy.* Minneapolis, Minn.: University of Minnesota Press, 1954.

Field, G. C. *Plato and His Contemporaries,* 3rd ed. New York: Barnes & Noble, 1967.

Frankl, Victor E. *Man's Search for Meaning.* New York: Washington Square Press, 1963.

Goble, Frank. *The Third Force: The Psychology of Abraham Maslow.* New York: Pocket Books, 1970.

Guthrie, W. K. C. *The Greek Philosophers.* New York: Harper & Row, 1960.

Hill, Thomas H. *Contemporary Ethical Theories.* New York: Macmillan, 1959.

Hook, Sidney. *John Dewey: An Intellectual Portrait.* New York: John Day Co., 1939.

Hospers, John. *Human Conduct: An Introduction to the Problem of Ethics.* New York: Harcourt Brace Jovanovich, 1961.

Houriet, Robert. *Getting Back Together.* New York: Avon Books, 1971.

Huysmans, J. K. *Against Nature.* Baltimore, Md.: Penguin Books, 1959.

Kant, Immanuel. *Lectures on Ethics.* New York: Harper & Row, 1963.

Klinke, Willibald. *Kant for Everyman.* New York: Macmillan, 1962.

Kurtz, Paul, ed. *Moral Problems in Contemporary Society: Essays in Ethics.* Englewood Cliffs, N.J.: Prentice-Hall, 1969.

Levinson, R. B. *In Defense of Plato.* Cambridge, Mass.: Harvard University Press, 1950.

LuBac, Henri de. *Teilhard de Chardin: The Man and His Meaning.* New York: New American Library, 1967.

Lucretius. *On Nature,* trans. by R. M. Geer. New York: Bobbs-Merrill Co., 1965.

Maslow, Abraham. *Religions, Values, and Peak Experiences.* New York: Viking Press, 1964.

Mill, John Stuart. *Autobiography.* New York: Columbia University Press, 1944.

———. *The Essential Works of John Stuart Mill.* Max Lerner, ed. New York: Bantam Books, 1961.

Mumford, Lewis. *The Conduct of Life*. New York: Harcourt Brace Jovanovich, 1951.

Omar Khayyam. *Rubáiyát*, trans. by Edward Fitzgerald. New York: Thomas Y. Crowell Co.

Paton, H. J. *The Categorical Imperative: A Study in Kant's Moral Philosophy*. New York: Harper & Row, 1967.

Popper, Karl. *The Open Society and Its Enemies*. Princeton, N.J.: Princeton University Press, 1950.

Rader, Melvin. *Ethics and the Human Community*. New York: Holt, Rinehart & Winston, 1966.

Roberts, Ron E. *The New Communes: Coming Together in America*. Englewood Cliffs, N.J.: Prentice-Hall, 1971.

Ross, W. D. *Aristotle*. London: Methuen, 1923.

Russell, Bertrand. *The Conquest of Happiness*. New York: New American Library, 1951.

Shinn, Roger L. *Restless Adventure: Essays on Contemporary Expressions of Existentialism*. New York: Charles Scribner's Sons, 1968.

Spanos, William V. *A Casebook on Existentialism*. New York: Thomas Y. Crowell Co., 1966.

Spiro, Melford E. *Kibbutz: Venture in Utopia*. New York: Schocken Books, 1956.

Taylor, A. E. *Plato: The Man and His Work*. New York: Barnes & Noble, 1957.

Thorson, Thomas L. (ed.) *Plato: Totalitarian or Democrat?* Englewood Cliffs, N.J.: Prentice-Hall, 1963.

Titus, Harold H. *Ethics for Today*. New York: American Book Company, 1957.

Part 4

CONFRONTATION WITH AUTHORITY

Commitment to Freedom

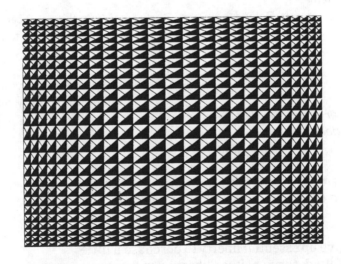

. . . That this nation, under God, shall have a new birth of
freedom.

Abraham Lincoln

Eternal vigilance is the price of liberty.

J. P. Curran

And ye shall know the truth and the truth
shall make you free.

Jesus Christ

I would rather sit on a pumpkin, and have it all to
myself, than to be crowded on a velvet cushion.

Henry David Thoreau

In a free country there is much clamour, with little suffering;
in a despotic state there is little complaint, with much
grievance.

Lazare Carnot

O liberty! How many crimes are
committed in thy name!

Mme. Jeanne Roland

Liberty is the only thing you cannot have
unless you are willing to give it to others.

William Allen White

No amount of political freedom will
satisfy the hungry masses.

Lenin

*The people never give up their liberties
but under some delusion.*

Edmund Burke

Give me the liberty to know, to think, to believe, and to utter
freely according to conscience, above all other liberties.

John Milton

Those who give up essential liberty to purchase a little
temporary safety deserve neither liberty nor safety.

Benjamin Franklin

Since the general civilization of mankind I believe there are more
instances of the abridgement of the freedom of the people by gradual
and silent encroachments of those in power than by violent and sudden
usurpations.

James Madison

Introduction:
What Price Freedom?

The exercise of authority may often be so coercive and our assertions of freedom so bold that the two will be in conflict. Because of the importance of this conflict, the following selections throw a series of spotlights on various aspects of the difficult and complex concepts of "authority" and "freedom." Socrates' *Apology* can be read as a powerful indictment of all authority, institutions, or persons that would in theory or in fact curtail human freedom or stymie individual spontaneity and self-actualization. But what is freedom? Is there no justification for limits or for having conditions imposed upon the actions of individuals? Can we conceive of freedom without restrictions? If there are restrictions, what are they and by whom (and by what authority) are these limits to be imposed? "Freedom" has had a wide use as a moral and socio-political concept in the history of liberal Western thought. Most often it has referred to "freedom from" coercion or constraint by another, especially from the power of outside social and political forces.

Dostoyevsky's magnificent vision of the Grand Inquisitor suggests that humanity apparently cannot rise above its craving for authority, miracle, and mystery. As a person who had temporarily lost his freedom in punishment by state authorities for activities considered subversive, Dostoyevsky fully appreciated the extent to which external sanctions or enforcing agencies could impinge upon and transform the values of the persons confronting them. As a creative genius, he highly valued freedom of art, thought, and action. Yet is the author on the side of Christ or the Grand Inquisitor? Does he favor freedom or authority? Are the alternatives this simple? Authority can assuage guilt; it can impose upon life a pattern and thus a meaning; it can arouse a sense of awe in human beings and silence dissent by force. Through its ability to accumulate and hoard power, it can develop ways of controlling human beings which eventually can make them love the calamity of tyranny and loathe the opportunity of freedom. Yet Dostoyevsky, the Christian, identifies Christ as the liberator of mankind and as the champion of freedom. A person may become genuinely free only through a subservient and harmonious relationship to Christ.

Despite Socrates' commitment to freedom of thought and speech in the *Apology*, he also represents a typical ancient Greek viewpoint with his deep conviction that we are social animals and therefore we can attain freedom only under a government of law. In the *Crito* he accepts his sentence and goes to his death, not because he believes his sentence is just, but because it is lawful. His acceptance of death was in accord with his inner divine moral law and gave him a way out without breaking the externally imposed laws of Athens.

The anarchist Kropotkin had a different view of the state, the law, and individual freedom. He rejected authoritarian government, affirming voluntary institutions as being more consistent with his conception of human nature. His vision of a libertarian society is intended to reaffirm the lost virtues of a more natural state in which persons are naturally cooperative.

Albert Camus was also concerned with freedom without constraint, but from a moral and cosmic perspective. Despite the belief that life is meaningless or absurd, that the universe provides no justification for the deepest of human concerns, the inner freedom which allows for the affirmation of human choice and purpose in face of this absurdity is the only way out. The heroic and exhilarating revolt in freedom against the hopeless human condition is our only dignity: "revolt gives life its value."

John Stuart Mill, in the selection from his essay *On Liberty*, refocuses our attention on the justification of the exercise of social and political authority over the individual. He also appreciated the values of individuality and personal initiative but, as a socialist and utilitarian, he recognized that these values could only be nurtured and protected under a government that had as its aim the realization of the greatest happiness of the greatest number in society. Mill, therefore, tried to strike a balance between individualism and collectivism, with the scales tipped toward individualism where, he believed, freedom rests.

The dialogue presented in this section between the psychologists B. F. Skinner and Carl Rogers brings out Skinner's refusal to accept a view of freedom which is characteristic of our Western tradition. For the determinist Skinner, the concept of the person as an autonomous agent is dead; for Rogers, this concept is very much alive and more crucial than ever as we approach a viable science of human behavior. The implications of these two different views upon our concepts of punishment, responsibility, education, and government are developed in this important exchange. For Rogers, the increasingly important choice of goals and values for science still depends upon the concept of the person as a self-directing agent.

What of the future of freedom? In answer to this question, Huxley's *Brave New World* acquires the qualities of prophecy and nightmare. As more and more people grow weary or fearful of their freedom, Huxley raises the question of whether humans are not becoming more willing to exchange it for the promise of security, certainty, and comfort offered by advocates of strong authority and technological or behavioral control. The possibility of the replacement of more efficient, scientific planners for the Grand Inquisitor makes the issue of authority and freedom even more critical for our age.

Dostoyevsky's Grand Inquisitor and Huxley's World Controller both cast equally long threatening shadows across the domain of freedom in modern times. As the poet Schiller said, "the iron chain and the silken cord are both equally bonds."

17 Flight from Freedom

Dostoyevsky

Through the characters in his fiction, the Russian novelist Feodor Dostoyevsky (1821–1881) portrays with remarkable clarity and power many of the basic conflicts within the human psyche. He depicts those that arise between passion and reason, raw impulse and ideal aspiration, self-hatred and self-love, desire to withdraw from others and need to unite with them. Believing that these and other such conflicts are inherent in human nature, Dostoyevsky thinks that they must be taken into account in any discussion of freedom.

The hero or anti-hero of *Notes from Underground* (1864) exemplifies man's complexity and self-contradiction. He points out that man is more than a mere rational animal. He also possesses some irrational and antirational elements that he must give vent to and satisfy in order to fulfill himself. Reason analyzes, dissects, reflects, and appraises. These functions are useful and necessary in solving many human problems, but reason often fails to take into account those aspects of human nature which are self-contradictory and mysterious. Freedom entails more than willing what is rational and doing it; it also entails willing and doing the irrational. For what purpose would a man voluntarily choose not to follow reason? For the sake of passion, from depravity, or simply for no purpose at all, says the Underground Man. The human psyche does not feel obliged to obey the laws of thought, such as the law of noncontradiction. Unconscious impulses, which well up from the depths of a human being, are nonrational but nonetheless real. Dostoyevsky would not agree with Socrates' view that no man intentionally does wrong. More often than not man sees the right and refuses to choose it; instead, he willfully goes toward the evil, the self-destructive, even the diabolical.

Reflection on the nature of man and on what it means to be human leads Dostoyevsky's hero (and Dostoyevsky himself) to stress, against the views of all optimists, rationalists, and scientific-minded utopian socialists, the unfathomed, unexplored, murky depths of human nature. Because of his inherent nature, man desires more than sheer enjoyment, well-being, perfect utopian bliss. Man also craves and needs suffering, not only to satisfy the irrational aspects of human nature, but also in order to contrast it with enjoyment, in order to learn, to teach, and, ultimately, to transcend human existence, to sanctify life, and to redeem it. "Man is sometimes extraordinarily, passionately in love with suffering, and that is a fact," says the Underground man.[1] Christianity owes a good part of its appeal to its presenting to man a suffering man-god who holds out to man salvation, not through science and reason but through suffering.

In light of such considerations, Dostoyevsky believes that the goal of human aspiration and the ultimate good for man should be more than a utopian anthill in which each human ant does its bit for the welfare of the whole. To attain such a goal—and with increased scientific knowledge it does seem more and more feasible—may not be desirable. Perhaps, says Dostoyevsky's Underground Man, the value of the goal that man strives for lies in the process of his striving for it, not in his attaining it. Attaining utopia would bring boredom, frustration, and despair to man, not the satiation of desire and the fulfillment of human potentialities and aspirations.

Also concerned with the problem of freedom, another of Dostoyevsky's characters, Shigalov in *The Possessed* (1871), proposes a system of world organization that he believes is based on the realities of human nature.[2] Mankind is divided into two unequal categories, one-tenth being granted individual freedom and ruling the remaining nine-tenths who have lost all freedom and individuality. Through conditioning and a series of mutations the larger group has beeen gradually transformed into a happy human herd living in primeval innocence and paradisiacal happiness. Although he cannot conceive of any better workable solution to social problems, Shigalov is in despair over the outcome of his utopian speculation. Having started out envisaging a social order in which there would be unrestricted freedom, he has ended up proposing an anti-utopia of unrestrained despotism.

In his final and greatest novel, *The Brothers Karamazov* (1880), Dostoyevsky again confronts his readers with the problem of freedom. Here he does so in the form of a legend, "The Grand Inquisitor," which is narrated by one of the novel's heroes, the atheistic Ivan Karamazov, to his saintly brother Alyosha.

NOTES

1. Feodor Dostoyevsky, *Notes from Underground*, in *White Nights and Other Stories*, trans. Constance Garnett (New York: Macmillan, 1923), p. 77.
2. See Feodor Dostoyevsky, *The Possessed*, trans. Constance Garnett (Greenwich, Conn.: Fawcett Publications, Inc., 1966), Part II, Chap. 7.

The Legend of the Grand Inquisitor

"My story is laid in Spain, in Seville, in the most terrible time of the Inquisition, when fires were lighted every day to the glory of God, and 'in the splendid *auto da fé* the wicked heretics were burnt.' Oh, of course, this was not the coming in which He will appear according to His promise at the end of time in all His heavenly glory, and which will be sudden 'as lightning flashing from east to west.' No, He visited His children only for a moment, and there where the flames were crackling round the heretics. In His infinite mercy He came once more among men in that human shape in which He walked among men for three years fifteen centuries ago. He came down to the 'hot pavement' of the southern town in which on the day before almost a hundred heretics had, *ad majorem gloriam Dei,* been burnt by the cardinal, the Grand Inquisitor, in a magnificent *auto da fé*, in the presence of the king, the court, the knights, the cardinals, the most charming ladies of the court, and the whole population of Seville.

"He came softly, unobserved, and yet, strange to say, everyone recognized Him. That might be one of the best passages in the poem. I mean, why they recognized Him. The people are irresistibly drawn to Him, they surround Him, they flock about Him, follow Him. He moves silently in their midst with a gentle smile of infinite compassion. The sun of love burns in His heart, light and power shine from His eyes, and their radiance, shed on the people, stirs their hearts with responsive love. He holds out His hands to them, blesses them, and a healing virtue comes from contact with Him, even with His garments. An old man in the crowd, blind from childhood, cries out, 'O Lord, heal me and I shall see thee!' and, as it were, scales fall from his eyes and the blind man sees Him. The crowd weeps and kisses the earth under His feet. Children throw flowers before Him, sing, and cry hosannah. 'It is He— it is He!' all repeat. 'It must be He, it can be no one but Him!' He stops at the steps of the Seville cathedral at the moment when the weeping mourners are bringing in a little open white coffin. In it lies a child of seven, the only daughter of a prominent citizen. The dead child lies hidden in flowers. 'He will raise your child,' the crowd shouts to the weeping mother. The priest, coming to meet the coffin, looks perplexed, and frowns, but the mother of the dead child throws herself at His feet with a wail. 'If it is Thou, raise my child!' she cries, holding out her hands to Him. The procession halts, the coffin is laid on the steps at His feet. He looks with compassion, and His lips once more softly pronounce, 'Maiden, arise!' and the

From Feodor Dostoyevsky, *The Brothers Karamazov*, trans. Constance Garnett (New York: Random House, 1937), bk. V, chap. 5 ("The Grand Inquisitor"), pp. 305–25.

maiden arises. The little girl sits up in the coffin and looks around, smiling with wide-open wondering eyes, holding a bunch of white roses they had put in her hand.

"There are cries, sobs, confusion among the people, and at that moment the cardinal himself, the Grand Inquisitor, passes by the cathedral. He is an old man, almost ninety, tall and erect, with a withered face and sunken eyes, in which there is still a gleam of light. He is not dressed in his gorgeous cardinal's robes, as he was the day before, when he was burning the enemies of the Roman Church—at that moment he was wearing his coarse, old, monk's cassock. At a distance behind him come his gloomy assistants and slaves and the 'holy guard.' He stops at the sight of the crowd and watches it from a distance. He sees everything; he sees them set the coffin down at His feet, sees the child rise up, and his face darkens. He knits his thick grey brows and his eyes gleam with a sinister fire. He holds out his finger and bids the guards take Him. And such is his power, so completely are the people cowed into submission and trembling obedience to him, that the crowd immediately makes way for the guards, and in the midst of deathlike silence they lay hands on Him and lead Him away. The crowd instantly bows down to the earth, like one man, before the old inquisitor. He blesses the people in silence and passes on. The guards lead their prisoner to the close, gloomy vaulted prison in the ancient palace of the Holy Inquisition and shut Him in it. The day passes and is followed by the dark, burning 'breathless' night of Seville. The air is 'fragrant with laurel and lemon.' In the pitch darkness the iron door of the prison is suddenly opened and the Grand Inquisitor himself comes in with a light in his hand. He is alone; the door is closed at once behind him. He stands in the doorway and for a minute or two gazes into His face. At last he goes up slowly, sets the light on the table and speaks.

" 'Is it Thou? Thou?' but receiving no answer, he adds at once, 'Don't answer, be silent. What canst Thou say, indeed? I know too well what Thou wouldst say. And Thou hast no right to add anything to what Thou hadst said of old. Why, then, art Thou come to hinder us? For Thou hast come to hinder us, and Thou knowest that. But dost Thou know what will be tomorrow? I know not who Thou art and care not to know whether it is Thou or only a semblance of Him, but tomorrow I shall condemn Thee and burn Thee at the stake as the worst of heretics. And the very people who have today kissed Thy feet, tomorrow at the faintest sign from me will rush to heap up the embers of Thy fire. Knowest Thou that? Yes, maybe Thou knowest it,' he added with thoughtful penetration, never for a moment taking his eyes off the Prisoner."

"I don't quite understand, Ivan. What does it mean?" Alyosha, who had been listening in silence, said with a smile. "Is it simply a wild fantasy, or a mistake on the part of the old man —some impossible *quid pro quo?*"

"Take it as the last," said Ivan, laughing, "if you are so corrupted by modern realism and can't stand anything fantastic. If you like it to be a case of mistaken identity, let it be so. It is true," he went on, laughing, "the old man was ninety, and he might well be crazy over his set idea. He might have been struck by the appearance of the Prisoner. It might, in fact, be simply his ravings, the delusion of an old man of ninety, over-excited by the *auto da fé* of a hundred heretics the day before. But does it matter to us after all whether it was a mistake of identity or a wild fantasy? All that matters is that the old man should speak out, should speak openly of what he had thought in silence for ninety years."

"And the Prisoner too is silent? Does He look at him and not say a word?"

"That's inevitable in any case," Ivan laughed again. "The old man has told Him He hasn't the right to add anything to what He has said of old. One may say it is the most fundamental feature of Roman Catholicism, in my opinion at least. 'All has been given by Thee to the Pope,' they say, 'and all, therefore, is still in the Pope's hands, and there is no need for Thee to come now at all. Thou must not meddle for the time, at least.' That's how they speak and write too —the Jesuits, at any rate. I have read it myself in the works of their theologians. 'Hast Thou the right to reveal to us one of the mysteries of that world from which Thou has come?' my old man asks Him, and answers the question for Him. 'No, Thou hast not; that Thou mayest not add to what has been said of old, and mayest not take from men the freedom which Thou didst exalt when Thou wast on earth. Whatsoever Thou revealest anew will encroach on men's freedom of faith; for it will be manifest as a miracle, and the freedom of their faith was clearer to Thee than anything in those days fifteen hundred years ago. Didst Thou not often say then, "I will make you free"? But now Thou hast seen these "free" men,' the old man adds suddenly with a pensive smile. 'Yes, we've paid dearly for it,' he goes on, looking sternly at Him, 'but now it is ended and over for good. Dost Thou not believe that it's over for good? Thou lookest meekly at me and deignest not even to be wroth with me. But let me tell Thee that now, today, people are more persuaded than ever that they have perfect freedom, yet they have brought their freedom to us and laid it humbly at our feet. But that has been our doing. Was this what Thou didst? Was this Thy freedom?'"

"I don't understand again," Alyosha broke in. "Is he ironical, is he jesting?"

"Not a bit of it! He claims it as a merit for himself and his Church that at last they have vanquished freedom and have done so to make men happy. 'For now' (he is speaking of the Inquisition, of course) 'for the first time it has become possible to think of the happiness of men. Man was created a rebel; and how can rebels be happy? Thou was warned,' he says to Him. 'Thou hast had no lack of admonitions and warnings, but Thou didst not listen to those warnings; Thou didst reject the only way by which men might be made happy. But, fortunately, departing Thou didst hand on the work to us. Thou hast promised, Thou hast established by Thy word, Thou hast given to us the right to bind and to unbind, and now, of course, Thou canst not think of taking it away. Why, then, hast Thou come to hinder us?'"

"And what's the meaning of 'no lack of admonitions and warnings'?" asked Alyosha.

"Why, that's the chief part of what the old man must say."

"'The wise and dread spirit, the spirit of self-destruction and non-existence,' the old man goes on, 'the great spirit talked with Thee in the wilderness, and we are told in the books that he "tempted" Thee. Is that so? And could anything truer be said than what he revealed to Thee in three questions and what Thou didst reject, and what in the books is called "the temptation"? And yet if there has ever been on earth a real stupendous miracle, it took place on that day, on the day of the three temptations. The statement of those three questions was itself the miracle. If it were possible to imagine simply for the sake of argument that those three questions of the dread spirit had perished utterly from the books, and that we had to restore them and to invent them anew, and to do so had gathered together all the wise men of the earth—rulers, chief priests, learned men, philosophers, poets—and had set them the task to invent three questions, such as would not only fit the occasion, but express in three words, three human phrases, the whole future history of the world and of humanity —dost Thou believe that all the wisdom of the earth united could have invented anything in depth and force equal to the three questions which were actually put to Thee then by the wise and mighty spirit in the wilderness? From those questions alone, from the miracle of their statement, we can see that we have here to do not with the fleeting human intelligence, but with the absolute and eternal. For in those three questions the whole subsequent history of mankind is, as it were, brought together into one whole, and foretold, and in them are united all the unsolved historical contradictions of human nature. At the time it could not be so clear, since the future was unknown; but now that fifteen hundred years have passed, we see that everything in those three questions was so justly divined and foretold, and has been so truly fulfilled, that nothing can be added to them or taken from them.

" 'Judge Thyself who was right—Thou or he who questioned Thee then? Remember the first question; its meaning, in other words, was this: "Thou wouldst go into the world, and art going with empty hands, with some promise of freedom which men in their simplicity and their natural unruliness cannot even understand, which they fear and dread—for nothing has ever been more insupportable for a man and a human society than freedom. But seest Thou these stones in this parched and barren wilderness? Turn them into bread, and mankind will run after Thee like a flock of sheep, grateful and obedient, though for ever trembling, lest Thou withdraw Thy hand and deny them Thy bread." But Thou wouldst not deprive man of freedom and didst reject the offer, thinking, what is that freedom worth, if obedience is bought with bread? Thou didst reply that man lives not by bread alone. But does Thou know that for the sake of that earthly bread the spirit of the earth will rise up against Thee and will strive with Thee and overcome Thee, and all will follow him, crying, "Who can compare with this beast? He has given us fire from heaven!" Dost Thou know that the ages will pass, and humanity will proclaim by the lips of their sages that there is no crime, and therefore no sin; there is only hunger? "Feed men, and then ask of them virtue!" that's what they'll write on the banner, which they will raise against Thee, and with which they will destroy Thy temple. Where Thy temple stood

will rise a new building; the terrible tower of Babel will be built again, and though, like the one of old, it will not be finished, yet Thou mightest have prevented that new tower and have cut short the sufferings of men for a thousand years; for they will come back to us after a thousand years of agony with their tower. They will seek us again, hidden underground in the catacombs, for we shall be again persecuted and tortured. They will find us and cry to us, "Feed us, for those who have promised us fire from heaven haven't given it!" And then we shall finish building their tower, for he finishes the building who feeds them. And we alone shall feed them in Thy name, declaring falsely that it is in Thy name. Oh, never, never can they feed themselves without us! No science will give them bread so long as they remain free. In the end they will lay their freedom at our feet, and say to us, "Make us your slaves, but feed us." They will understand themselves, at last, that freedom and bread enough for all are inconceivable together, for never, never will they be able to share between them! They will be convinced, too, that they can never be free, for they are weak, vicious, worthless and rebellious. Thou didst promise them the bread of Heaven, but, I repeat again, can it compare with earthly bread in the eyes of the weak, ever sinful and ignoble race of man? And if for the sake of the bread of Heaven thousands and tens of thousands shall follow Thee, what is to become of the millions and tens of thousands of millions of creatures who will not have the strength to forego the earthly bread for the sake of the heavenly? Or dost Thou care only for the tens of thousands of the great and strong, while the millions, numerous as the sands of the sea, who are weak but love Thee, must exist only for the sake of the great and strong? No, we care for the weak too. They are sinful and rebellious, but in the end they too will become obedient. They will marvel at us and look on us as gods, because we are ready to endure the freedom which they have found so dreadful and to rule over them—so awful it will seem to them to be free. But we shall tell them that we are Thy servants and rule them in Thy name. We shall deceive them again, for we will not let Thee come to us again. That deception will be our suffering, for we shall be forced to lie.

" 'This is the significance of the first question in the wilderness, and this is what Thou hast rejected for the sake of that freedom which Thou hast exalted above everything. Yet in this question lies hid the great secret of this world. Choosing "bread," Thou wouldst have satisfied the universal and everlasting craving of humanity—to find some one to worship. So long as man remains free he strives for nothing so incessantly and so painfully as to find some one to worship. But man seeks to worship what is established beyond dispute, so that all men would agree at once to worship it. For these pitiful creatures are concerned not only to find what one or the other can worship, but to find something that all would believe in and worship; what is essential is that all may be *together* in it. This craving for *community* of worship is the chief misery of every man individually and of all humanity from the beginning of time. For the sake of common worship they've slain each other with the sword. They have set up gods and challenged one another, "Put away your gods and come and worship ours, or we will kill you and your gods!" And so it will be to the end of the world, even when gods disappear from the earth; they will fall down before idols just the same. Thou didst know, Thou couldst not but have known, this fundamental secret of human nature, but Thou didst reject the one infallible banner which was offered Thee to make all men bow down to Thee alone—the banner of earthly bread; and Thou hast rejected it for the sake of freedom and the bread of Heaven. Behold what Thou didst further. And all again in the name of freedom! I tell Thee that man is tormented by no greater anxiety than to find some one

quickly to whom he can hand over that gift of freedom with which the ill-fated creature is born. But only one who can appease their conscience can take over their freedom. In bread there was offered Thee an invincible banner; give bread, and man will worship Thee, for nothing is more certain than bread. But if some one else gains possession of his conscience—oh! then he will cast away Thy bread and follow after him who has ensnared his conscience. In that Thou wast right. For the secret of man's being is not only to live but to have something to live for. Without a stable conception of the object of life, man would not consent to go on living, and would rather destroy himself than remain on earth, though he had bread in abundance. That is true. But what happened? Instead of taking men's freedom from them, Thou didst make it greater than ever! Didst Thou forget that man prefers peace, and even death, to freedom of choice in the knowledge of good and evil? Nothing is more seductive for man than his freedom of conscience, but nothing is a greater cause of suffering. And behold, instead of giving a firm foundation for setting the conscience of man at rest for ever, Thou didst choose all that is exceptional, vague and enigmatic; Thou didst choose what was utterly beyond the strength of men, acting as though Thou didst not love them at all—Thou who didst come to give Thy life for them! Instead of taking possession of men's freedom, Thou didst increase it, and burdened the spiritual kingdom of mankind with its sufferings forever. Thou didst desire man's free love, that he should follow Thee freely, enticed and taken captive by Thee. In place of the rigid ancient law, man must hereafter with free heart decide for himself what is good and what is evil, having only Thy image before him as his guide. But didst Thou not know he would at last reject even Thy image and Thy truth, if he is weighed down with the fearful burden of free choice? They will cry aloud at last that the truth is not in Thee, for they could not have been left in greater confusion and suffering than Thou hast caused, laying upon them so many cares and unanswerable problems.

" 'So that, in truth, Thou didst Thyself lay the foundation for the destruction of Thy kingdom, and no one is more to blame for it. Yet what was offered Thee? There are three powers, three powers alone, able to conquer and to hold captive for ever the conscience of these impotent rebels for their happiness— those forces are miracle, mystery and authority. Thou hast rejected all three and hast set the example for doing so. When the wise and dread spirit set Thee on the pinnacle of the temple and said to Thee, "If Thou wouldst know whether Thou art the Son of God then cast Thyself down, for it is written: the angels shall hold him up lest he fall and bruise himself, and Thou shalt know then whether Thou art the Son of God and shall prove then how great is Thy faith in Thy Father." But Thou didst refuse and wouldst not cast Thyself down. Oh! of course, Thou didst proudly and well, like God; but the weak, unruly race of men, are they gods? Oh, Thou didst know then that in taking one step, in making one movement to cast Thyself down, Thou wouldst be tempting God and have lost all Thy faith in Him, and wouldst have been dashed to pieces against that earth which Thou didst come to save. And the wise spirit that tempted Thee would have rejoiced. But I ask again, are there many like Thee? And couldst Thou believe for one moment that men, too, could face such a temptation? Is the nature of men such, that they can reject miracle, and at the great moments of their life, the moments of their deepest, most agonising spiritual difficulties, cling only to the free verdict of the heart? Oh, Thou didst know that Thy deed would be recorded in books, would be handed down to remote times and the utmost ends of the earth, and Thou didst hope that man, following Thee, would cling to God and not ask for a miracle. But Thou didst not know that when man rejects miracle he rejects God too; for man seeks not so much God as the miraculous. And as man cannot bear to be without the miraculous, he will create new miracles of his own for himself, and will worship deeds of sorcery and witchcraft, though he might be a hundred times over a rebel, heretic and infidel. Thou didst not come down from the Cross when they shouted to Thee, mocking and reviling Thee, "Come down from the cross and we will believe that Thou art He." Thou didst not come down, for again Thou wouldst not enslave man by a miracle, and didst crave faith given freely, not based on miracle. Thou didst crave for free love and not the base raptures of the slave before the might that has overawed him for ever. But Thou didst think too highly of men therein, for they are slaves, of course, though rebellious by nature. Look round and judge; fifteen centuries have passed, look upon them. Whom hast Thou raised up to Thyself? I swear, man is weaker and baser by nature than Thou hast believed him! Can he, can he do what Thou didst? By showing him so much respect, Thou didst, as it were, cease to feel for him, for Thou didst ask far too much from him—Thou who hast loved him more than Thyself! Respecting him less, Thou wouldst have asked less of him. That would have been more like love, for his burden would have been lighter. He is weak and vile. What though he is everywhere now rebelling against our power, and proud of his rebellion? It is the pride of a child and a schoolboy. There are little children rioting and barring out the teacher at school. But their childish delight will end; it will cost them dear. They will cast down temples and drench the earth with blood. But they will see at last, the foolish children, that, though they are rebels, they are impotent rebels, unable to keep up their own rebellion. Bathed in their foolish tears, they will recognise at last that He who created them rebels must have meant to mock at them. They will say this in despair, and their utterance will be a blasphemy which will make them more unhappy still, for man's nature cannot bear blasphemy, and in the end always avenges it on itself. And so unrest, confusion and unhappiness—that is the present lot of man after Thou didst bear so much for their freedom! Thy great prophet tells in vision and in image, that he saw all those who took part in the first resurrection and that they were of each tribe twelve thousand. But if there were so many of them, they must have been not men but gods. They had borne Thy cross, they had endured scores of years in the barren, hungry wilderness, living upon locusts and roots—and Thou mayest indeed point with pride at those children of freedom, of free love, of free and splendid sacrifice for Thy name. But remember that they were only some thousands; and what of the rest? And how are the other weak ones to blame, because they could not endure what the strong have endured? How is the weak soul to blame that it is unable to receive such terrible gifts? Canst Thou have simply come to the elect and for the elect? But if so, it is a mystery and we cannot understand it. And if it is a mystery, we too have a right to preach a mystery, and to teach them that it's not the free judgment of their hearts, not love that matters, but a mystery which they must follow blindly, even against their conscience. So we have done. We have corrected Thy work and have founded it upon *miracle, mystery* and *authority*. And men rejoiced that they were again led like sheep, and that the terrible gift that had brought them such suffering, was, at last, lifted from their hearts. Were we right teaching them this? Speak. Did we not love mankind, so meekly acknowledging their feebleness, lovingly lightening their burden, and permitting their weak nature even sin with our sanction? Why hast Thou come now to hinder us? And why dost Thou look silently and searchingly at me with Thy mild eyes? Be angry. I don't want Thy love, for I love Thee not. And what use is it for me to hide anything from Thee? Don't I know to Whom I am

speaking? All that I can say is known to Thee already. And is it for me to conceal from Thee our mystery? Perhaps it is Thy will to hear it from my lips. Listen, then. We are not working with Thee, but with *him*—that is our mystery. It's long—eight centuries—since we have been on *his* side and not on Thine. Just eight centuries ago, we took from him what Thou didst reject with scorn, that last gift he offered Thee, showing Thee all the kingdoms of the earth. We took from him Rome and the sword of Caesar, and proclaimed ourselves sole rulers of the earth, though hitherto we have not been able to complete our work. But whose fault is that? Oh, the work is only beginning, but it has much to suffer, but we shall triumph and shall be Caesars, and then we shall plan the universal happiness of man. But Thou mightest have taken even then the sword of Caesar. Why didst Thou reject that last gift? Hadst Thou accepted that last counsel of the mighty spirit, Thou wouldst have accomplished all that man seeks on earth—that is, some one to worship, some one to keep his conscience, and some means of uniting all in one unanimous and harmonious antheap, for the craving for universal unity is the third and last anguish of men. Mankind as a whole has always striven to organise a universal state. There have been many great nations with great histories, but the more highly they were developed the more unhappy they were, for they felt more acutely than other people the craving for worldwide union. The great conquerors, Timours and Ghenghis-Khan, whirled like hurricanes over the face of the earth striving to subdue its people, and they too were but the unconscious expression of the same craving for universal unity. Hadst Thou taken the world and Caesar's purple, Thou wouldst have founded the universal state and have given universal peace. For who can rule men if not he who holds their conscience and their bread in his hands? We have taken the sword of Caesar, and in taking it, of course, have rejected Thee and followed *him*. Oh, ages are yet to come of the confusion of free thought, of their science and cannibalism. For having begun to build their tower of Babel without us, they will end, of course, with cannibalism. But then the beast will crawl to us and lick our feet and spatter them with tears of blood. And we shall sit upon the beast and raise the cup, and on it will be written, "Mystery." But then, and only then, the reign of peace and happiness will come for men. Thou art proud of Thine elect, but Thou hast only the elect, while we give rest to all. And besides, how many of those elect, those mighty ones who could become elect, have grown weary waiting for Thee, and have transferred and will transfer the powers of their spirit and the warmth of their heart to the other camp, and end by raising their *free* banner against Thee. Thou didst Thyself lift up that banner. But with us all will be happy and will no more rebel nor destroy one another as under Thy freedom. Oh, we shall persuade them that they will only become free when they renounce their freedom to us and submit to us. And shall we be right or shall we be lying? They will be convinced that we are right, for they will remember the horrors of slavery and confusion to which Thy freedom brought them. Freedom, free thought and science, will lead them into such straits and will bring them face to face with such marvels and insoluble mysteries, that some of them, the fierce and rebellious, will destroy themselves, others, rebellious but weak, will destroy one another, while the rest, weak and unhappy, will crawl fawning to our feet and whine to us: "Yes, you were right, you alone possess His mystery, and we come back to you, save us from ourselves!"

" 'Receiving bread from us, they will see clearly that we take the bread made by their hands from them, to give it to them, without any miracle. They will see that we do not change the stones to bread, but in truth they will be more thankful for taking it from our hands than for the bread itself! For they will remember only too well that in old days, without our help, even the bread they made turned to stones in their hands, while since they have come back to us, the very stones have turned to bread in their hands. Too, too well they know the value of complete submission! And until men know that, they will be unhappy. Who is most to blame for their not knowing it, speak? Who scattered the flock and sent it astray on unknown paths? But the flock will come together again and will submit once more, and then it will be once for all. Then we shall give them the quiet humble happiness of weak creatures such as they are by nature. Oh, we shall persuade them at last not to be proud, for Thou didst lift them up and thereby taught them to be proud. We shall show them that they are weak, that they are only pitiful children, but that childlike happiness is the sweetest of all. They will become timid and will look to us and huddle close to us in fear, as chicks to the hen. They will marvel at us and will be awestricken before us, and will be proud at our being so powerful and clever, that we have been able to subdue such a turbulent flock of thousands of millions. They will tremble impotently before our wrath, their minds will grow fearful, they will be just as ready at a sign from us to pass to laughter and rejoicing, to happy mirth and childish song. Yes, we shall set them to work, but in their leisure hours we shall make their life like a child's game, with children's songs and innocent dance. Oh, we shall allow them even sin, they are weak and helpless, and they will love us like children because we allow them to sin. We shall tell them that every sin will be expiated, if it is done with our permission, that we allow them to sin because we love them, and the punishment for these sins we take upon ourselves. And we shall take it upon ourselves, and they will adore us as their saviours, who have taken on themselves their sins before God. And they will have no secrets from us.

We shall allow or forbid them to live with their wives and mistresses, to have or not to have children—according to whether they have been obedient or disobedient—and they will submit to us gladly and cheerfully. The most painful secrets of their conscience, all, all they will bring to us, and we shall have an answer for all. And they will be glad to believe our answer, for it will save them from the great anxiety and terrible agony they endure at present in making a free decision for themselves. And all will be happy, all the millions of creatures except the hundred thousand who rule over them. For only we, we who guard the mystery, shall be unhappy. There will be thousands of millions of happy babes, and a hundred thousand sufferers who have taken upon themselves the curse of the knowledge of good and evil. Peacefully they will die, peacefully they will expire in Thy name, and beyond the grave they will find nothing but death. But we shall keep the secret, and for their happiness we shall allure them with the reward of heaven and eternity. Though if there were anything in the other world, it certainly would not be for such as they. It is prophesied that Thou wilt come again in victory, Thou wilt come with Thy chosen, the proud and strong, but we will say that they have only saved themselves, but we have saved all. We are told that the harlot who sits upon the beast, and holds in her hands the *mystery*, shall be put to shame, that the weak will rise up again, and will rend her royal purple and will strip naked her loathsome body. But then I will stand up and point out to Thee the thousand millions of happy children who have known no sin. And we who have taken their sins upon us for their happiness will stand up before Thee and say: "Judge us if Thou canst and darest." Know that I too have been in the wilderness, I too have lived on roots and locusts, I too prized the freedom with which Thou hast blessed men, and I too was striving to stand among Thy elect, among the strong and powerful, thirsting "to make up the

number." But I awakened and would not serve madness. I turned back and joined the ranks of those *who have corrected Thy work*. I left the proud and went back to the humble, for the happiness of the humble. What I say to Thee will come to pass, and our dominion will be built up. I repeat, tomorrow Thou shalt see that obedient flock who at a sign from me will hasten to heap up the hot cinders about the pile on which I shall burn Thee for coming to hinder us. For if any one has ever deserved our fires, it is Thou. Tomorrow I shall burn Thee. Dixi.'"

Ivan stopped. He was carried away as he talked and spoke with excitement; when he had finished, he suddenly smiled.

Alyosha had listened in silence; towards the end he was greatly moved and seemed several times on the point of interrupting, but restrained himself. Now his words came with a rush.

"But . . . that's absurd!" he cried, flushing. "Your poem is in praise of Jesus, not in blame of Him—as you meant it to be. And who will believe you about freedom? Is that the way to understand it? That's not the idea of it in the Orthodox Church . . . That's Rome, and not even the whole of Rome, it's false—those are the worst of the Catholics, the Inquisitors, the Jesuits. . . . And there could not be such a fantastic creature as your Inquisitor. What are these sins of mankind they take on themselves? Who are these keepers of the mystery who have taken some curse upon themselves for the happiness of mankind? When have they been seen? We know the Jesuits, they are spoken ill of, but surely they are not what you describe? They are not that at all, not at all. . . . They are simply the Romish army for the earthly sovereignty of the world in the future, with the Pontiff of Rome for Emperor . . . that's their ideal, but there's no sort of mystery or lofty melancholy about it. . . . It's simple lust of power, of filthy earthly gain, of domination—something like a universal serfdom with them as masters—that's all they stand for. They don't even believe in God perhaps. Your suffering inquisitor is a mere fantasy."

"Stay, stay," laughed Ivan, "how hot you are! A fantasy you say, let it be so! Of course it's a fantasy. But allow me to say: do you really think that the Roman Catholic movement of the last centuries is actually nothing but the lust of power, of filthy earthly gain? Is that Father Païssy's teaching?"

"No, no, on the contrary, Father Païssy did once say something rather the same as you . . . but of course it's not the same, not a bit the same," Alyosha hastily corrected himself.

"A precious admission, in spite of your 'not a bit the same.' I ask you why your Jesuits and Inquisitors have united simply for vile material gain? Why can there not be among them one martyr oppressed by great sorrow and loving humanity? You see, only suppose that there was one such man among all those who desire nothing but filthy material gain—if there's only one like my old inquisitor, who had himself eaten roots in the desert and made frenzied efforts to subdue his flesh to make himself free and perfect. But yet all his life he loved humanity, and suddenly his eyes were opened, and he saw that it is no great moral blessedness to attain perfection and freedom, if at the same time one gains the conviction that millions of God's creatures have been created as a mockery, that they will never be capable of using their freedom, that these poor rebels can never turn into giants to complete the tower, that it was not for such geese that the great idealist dreamt his dream of harmony. Seeing all that he turned back and joined—the clever people. Surely that could have happened?"

"Joined whom, what clever people?" cried Alyosha, completely carried away. "They have no such great cleverness and no mysteries and secrets. . . . Perhaps nothing but Atheism, that's all their secret. Your inquisitor does not believe in God, that's his secret!"

"What if it is so! At last you have guessed it. It's perfectly true that that's the whole secret, but isn't that suffering, at least for a man like that, who has wasted his whole life in the desert and yet could not shake off his incurable love of humanity? In his old age he reached the clear conviction that nothing but the advice of the great dread spirit could build up any tolerable sort of life for the feeble, unruly, 'incomplete, empirical creatures created in jest.' And so, convinced of this, he sees that he must follow the counsel of the wise spirit, the dread spirit of death and destruction, and therefore accept lying and deception, and lead men consciously to death and destruction, and yet deceive them all the way so that they may not notice where they are being led, that the poor blind creatures may at least on the way think themselves happy. And note, the deception is in the name of Him in Whose ideal the old man had so fervently believed all his life long. Is not that tragic? And if only one such stood at the head of the whole army 'filled with the lust of power only for the sake of filthy gain'—would not one such be enough to make a tragedy? More than that, one such standing at the head is enough to create the actual leading idea of the Roman Church with all its armies and Jesuits, its highest idea. I tell you frankly that I firmly believe that there has always been such a man among those who stood at the head of the movement. Who knows, there may have been some such even among the Roman Popes. Who knows, perhaps the spirit of that accursed old man who loves mankind so obstinately in his own way, is to be found even now in a whole multitude of such old men, existing not by chance but by agreement, as a secret league formed long ago for the guarding of the mystery, to guard it from the weak and the unhappy, so as to make them happy. No doubt it is so, and so it must be indeed. I fancy that even among the Masons there's something of the same mystery at the bottom, and that that's why the Catholics so detest the Masons as their rivals breaking up the unity of the idea, while it is so essential that there should be one flock and one shepherd. . . . But from the way I defend my idea I might be an author impatient of your criticism. Enough of it."

"You are perhaps a Mason yourself!" broke suddenly from Alyosha. "You don't believe in God," he added, speaking this time very sorrowfully. He fancied besides that his brother was looking at him ironically. "How does your poem end?" he asked, suddenly looking down. "Or was it the end?"

"I meant it to end like this. When the Inquisitor ceased speaking he waited some time for his Prisoner to answer him. His silence weighed down upon him. He saw that the Prisoner had listened intently all the time, looking gently in his face and evidently not wishing to reply. The old man longed for Him to say something, however bitter and terrible. But He suddenly approached the old man in silence and softly kissed him on his bloodless aged lips. That was all his answer. The old man shuddered. His lips moved. He went to the door, opened it, and said to Him: 'Go, and come no more. . . . come not at all, never, never!' And he let Him out into the dark alleys of the town. The Prisoner went away."

"And the old man?"

"The kiss glows in his heart, but the old man adheres to his idea."

"And you with him, you too?" cried Alyosha, mournfully.

Ivan laughed.

"Why, it's all nonsense, Alyosha. It's only a senseless poem of a senseless student, who could never write two lines of verse. Why do you take it so seriously? Surely you don't suppose I am going straight off to the Jesuits, to join the men who are correcting His work? Good Lord, it's no business of mine. I told you, all I want is to live on to thirty, and then . . . dash the cup to the ground!"

"But the little sticky leaves, and the precious tombs, and the blue sky, and the woman you love! How will you live, how will you love them?" Alyosha cried sorrowfully. "With such a hell in your heart and your head, how can you? No, that's just what you are going away for, to join them . . . if not, you will kill yourself, you can't endure it."

"There is a strength to endure everything," Ivan said with a cold smile.

"What strength?"

"The strength of the Karamazov—the strength of the Karamazov baseness."

"To sink into debauchery, to stifle your soul with corruption, yes?"

"Possibly even that . . . only perhaps till I am thirty I shall escape it, and then."

"How will you escape it? By what will you escape it? That's impossible with your ideas."

"In the Karamazov way, again."

" 'Everything is lawful,' you mean? Everything is lawful, is that it?"

Ivan scowled, and all at once turned strangely pale.

"Ah, you've caught up yesterday's phrase, which so offended Miusov—and which Dmitri pounced upon so naively and paraphrased!" he smiled queerly.

"Yes, if you like, 'everything is lawful' since the word has been said. I won't deny it. And Mitya's version isn't bad."

Alyosha looked at him in silence.

"I thought that going away from here I have you at least," Ivan said suddenly, with unexpected feeling; "but now I see that there is no place for me even in your heart, my dear hermit. The formula, 'all is lawful,' I won't renounce—will you renounce me for that, yes?"

Alyosha got up, went to him and softly kissed him on the lips.

"That's plagiarism," cried Ivan, highly delighted "You stole that from my poem. Thank you though. Get up, Alyosha, it's time we were going, both of us." . . .

18 Freedom under Law

Socrates

Plato's *Apology* highlighted Socrates' conviction that we should examine our beliefs critically. "For I am and always have been one of those natures who must be guided by reason," Socrates declared in the *Crito*. Socrates was committed to acting wisely; he voluntarily suffered death rather than do what he reasoned to be wrong. Plato wrote the *Crito* as part of the continuing story of the martyrdom of his beloved teacher, Socrates.

As Plato presents the story, Socrates was concerned mainly with problems of human values and conduct. Plato's dialogues, most of which use Socrates as the main character, explore these problems. They reveal philosophy as the search for enlightenment regarding the fundamental purpose of human existence. Separately, each dialogue is a search for definitions of such notions as justice, piety, and courage. Together, the dialogues are Plato's way of leading us to find our way to philosophy, to love wisdom.

Socrates remained convinced that once the debris of vague and unquestioned moral concepts was cleared away, men could discover the goods that are worth seeking and the rules that ought to govern human action. Knowledge is the necessary prerequisite to right living and conduct, because it enables a person to discern between what has value and what has not. Human virtue or excellence comes not by chance or by blindly following the opinions of others, but by knowing the principles that regulate and control the appetites and passions of men. The function of reason and philosophic dialogue is to seek those standards that will hold up against the shifting beliefs and scepticism of man.

The example of Socrates' life indicates that merely declaring the examined life as an ideal is not enough; the test is in pursuing the ideal. Many of our most important beliefs are highly personal convictions. To be willing to clarify, criticize, and modify these is to be willing to risk radical change in outlook and direction. It may also involve incurring the ridicule of the society in which we live. Philosophizing in the Socratic sense is a task that takes a great deal of intellectual discipline, uncompromising honesty, and courage. Socrates lived in an age when it was dangerous to be a philosopher, yet he was committed to living such a life and living it freely.

As the following dialogue between Socrates and his friend Crito makes clear, even in prison Socrates was convinced he was a free man. For, he had chosen not to recant his beliefs at his trial, not to accept exile as an alternative to death, and not to escape from prison with the help of his friends. But no man, Socrates held, should voluntarily do evil, and to have accepted any of these value alternatives would have meant ignorantly placing immediate self-interest above what reason and the law dictated.

Socrates' rational commitment, therefore, was voluntarily to remain in prison and die a physical death rather than to escape and live a death in life. His entire life had been a testimony to his belief that the unexamined life was not worth living, and therefore had been a preparation for knowing how to face death. To philosophize is to learn not only how to live, but also how to die. The real problem then is not just to live but to learn to live well, that is, to learn how to make one's conduct conform to the laws of reason. Socrates was convinced that to achieve such a life would be to achieve genuine freedom. The paradox that conformity to law is also the highest and most real freedom was clearly recognized by Socrates. He also believed that it is better to suffer an injustice than to inflict one.

Like Jesus, Socrates believed he was on a divine mission, and was guided by a conscience. Socrates, however, came not to save the world by faith but to enlighten it by reason. He did not consider himself a god, but a lover of wisdom. He shared Jesus' belief that if one really knows the truth, one will be free. And like Jesus, he stood for freedom of choice, for responsibility and individual conscience against the forces of injustice and tyranny represented by the awesome figure of a Grand Inquisitor who proposed to enslave mankind rather than to liberate it. Miracle, mystery, and authority would not have been substitutes acceptable to Socrates for reason, evidence, and inquiry. The life and death of Socrates, like that of Jesus, bears witness to the power of choice, of commitment, of freedom.

Crito*

Plato

PERSONS OF THE DIALOGUE: *Socrates, Crito*
SCENE: *The Prison of Socrates*

SOCRATES: Why have you come at this hour, Crito? It must be quite early?

CRITO: Yes, certainly.

SOCRATES: What is the exact time?

CRITO: The dawn is breaking.

SOCRATES: I wonder that the keeper of the prison would let you in.

CRITO: He knows me, because I often come, Socrates; moreover, I have done him a kindness.

SOCRATES: And are you only just arrived?

CRITO: No, I came some time ago.

SOCRATES: Then why did you sit and say nothing, instead of awakening me?

* The *Crito*, which depicts the scene in the jail where Socrates is awaiting the day of his execution, is given here complete. But a full vindication of the death of Socrates cannot be had unless many other dialogues of Plato are read and related to one another. Especially, this includes the *Apology*, which presents Socrates' defense of himself at his trial, and the *Phaedo*, which contains an extended discussion between Socrates and his friends concerning the nature of the philosopher, the soul, and the possibility of immortality. This latter dialogue ends with a moving description (given in Part Five) of the last few minutes in the life of Socrates. For Plato, the death of Socrates represented the culmination of a life of philosophical commitment to the good.
From Plato, "Crito" in *The Dialogues of Plato*, trans. Benjamin Jowett, 3d ed. (New York: Oxford University Press, 1892).

CRITO: I should not have liked myself, Socrates, to be in such great trouble and unrest as you are—indeed I should not; I have been watching with amazement your peaceful slumbers; and for that reason I did not awake you, because I wished to minimize the pain. I have always thought you to be of a happy disposition; but never did I see anything like the easy, tranquil manner in which you bear this calamity.

SOCRATES: Why, Crito, when a man has reached my age he ought not to be repining at the approach of death.

CRITO: And yet other old men find themselves in similar misfortunes, and age does not prevent them from repining.

SOCRATES: That is true. But you have not told me why you come at this early hour.

CRITO: I come to bring you a message which is sad and painful; not, as I believe, to yourself, but to all of us who are your friends, and saddest of all to me.

SOCRATES: What? Has the ship come from Delos, on the arrival of which I am to die?

CRITO: No, the ship has not actually arrived, but she will probably be here today, as persons who have come from Sunium tell me that they left her there; and therefore tomorrow, Socrates, will be the last day of your life.

SOCRATES: Very well, Crito; if such is the will of God, I am willing; but my belief is that there will be a delay of a day.

CRITO: Why do you think so?

SOCRATES: I will tell you. I am to die on the day after the arrival of the ship.

CRITO: Yes; that is what the authorities say.

SOCRATES: But I do not think that the ship will be here until tomorrow; this I infer from a vision which I had last night, or rather only just now, when you fortunately allowed me to sleep.

CRITO: And what was the nature of the vision?

SOCRATES: There appeared to me the likeness of a woman, fair and comely, clothed in bright raiment, who called to me and said: O Socrates,
"The third day hence to fertile Phthia shalt thou go."[1]

CRITO: What a singular dream, Socrates!

SOCRATES: There can be no doubt about the meaning, Crito, I think.

CRITO: Yes; the meaning is only too clear. But, oh! my beloved Socrates, let me entreat you once more to take my advice and escape. For if you die I shall not only lose a friend who can never be replaced, but there is another evil: people who do not know you and me will believe that I might have saved you if I had been willing to give money, but that I did not care. Now, can there be a worse disgrace than this—that I should be thought to value money more than the life of a friend? For the many will not be persuaded that I wanted you to escape, and that you refused.

SOCRATES: But why, my dear Crito, should we care about the opinion of the many? Good men, and they are the only persons who are worth considering, will think of these things truly as they occurred.

CRITO: But you see, Socrates, that the opinion of the many must be regarded, for what is now happening shows that they can do the greatest evil to any one who has lost their good opinion.

SOCRATES: I only wish it were so, Crito; and that the many could do the greatest evil; for then they would also be able to do the greatest good—and what a fine thing this would be! But in reality they can do neither; for they cannot make a man either wise or foolish; and whatever they do is the result of chance.

CRITO: Well, I will not dispute with you; but please to tell me, Socrates, whether you are not acting out of regard to me and your other friends: are you not afraid that if you escape from prison we may get into trouble with the informers for having stolen you away, and lose either the whole or a great part of our property; or that even a worse evil may happen to us? Now, if you fear on our account, be at ease; for in order to save you, we ought surely to run this, or even a greater risk; be persuaded, then, and do as I say.

SOCRATES: Yes, Crito, that is one fear which you mention, but by no means the only one.

CRITO: Fear not—there are persons who are willing to get you out of prison at no great cost; and as for the informers, they are far from being exorbitant in their demands—a little money will satisfy them. My means, which are certainly ample, are at your service, and if you have a scruple about spending all mine, here are strangers who will give you the use of theirs; and one of them, Simmias the Theban, has brought a large sum of money for this very purpose; and Cebes and many others are prepared to spend their money in helping you to escape. I say, therefore, do not hesitate on our account, and do not say, as you did in the court, that you will have a difficulty in knowing what to do with yourself anywhere else. For men will love you in other places to which you may go, and not in Athens only; there are friends of mine in Thessaly, if you like to go to them, who will value and protect you, and no Thessalian will give you any trouble. Nor can I think that you are at all justified, Socrates, in betraying your own life when you might be saved; in acting thus you are playing into the hands of your enemies, who are hurrying on your destruction. And further I should say that you are deserting your own children; for you might bring them up and educate them; instead of which you go away and leave them, and they will have to take their chance; and if they do not meet with the usual fate of orphans, there will be small thanks to you. No man should bring children into the world who is unwilling to persevere to the end in their nurture and education. But you appear to be choosing the easier part, not the better and manlier, which would have been more becoming in one who professes to care for virtue in all his actions, like yourself. And, indeed, I am ashamed not only of you, but of us who are your friends, when I reflect that the whole business will be attributed entirely to our want of courage. The trial need never have come on, or might have been managed differently; and this last act, or crowning folly, will seem to have occurred through our negligence and cowardice, who might have saved you, if we had been good for anything; and you might have saved yourself, for there was no difficulty at all. See now, Socrates how sad and discreditable are the consequences, both to us and you. Make up your mind, then, or rather have your mind already made up, for the time of deliberation is over, and there is only one thing to be done, which must be done this very night, and if we delay at all will be no longer practicable or possible; I beseech you thererore, Socrates, be persuaded by me, and do as I say.

SOCRATES: Dear Crito, your zeal is invaluable, if a right one; but if wrong, the greater the zeal the greater the danger; and therefore we ought to consider whether I shall or shall not do as you say. For I am and always have been one of those natures who must be guided by reason, whatever the reason may be which upon reflection appears to me to be the best; and now that this chance has befallen me, I cannot repudiate my own words: the principles which I have hitherto honoured and revered I still honour, and unless we can at once find other and better principles, I am certain not to agree with you; no, not even if the power of the multitude could inflict many more imprisonments, confiscations, deaths, frightening us like children with hobgoblin terrors. What will be the fairest way of considering the question? Shall I return to your old argument about the opinions of men?—we were saying that some of them are to be regarded, and others not. Now, were we right in maintaining this before I was condemned? And has the argument which was once good now proved to be talk for the sake of talking— mere childish nonsense? That is what I want to consider with your help, Crito:— whether, under my present circumstances, the argument appears to be in any way different or not; and is to be allowed by me or disallowed. That argument, which, as I believe, is maintained by many persons of authority, was to the effect, as I was saying, that the opinions of some men are to be regarded, and of other men not to be regarded. Now you, Crito, are not going to die tomorrow—at least, there is no human probability of this—and therefore you are disinterested and not liable to be deceived by the circumstances in which you are placed. Tell me, then, whether I am right in saying that some opinions, and the opinions of some men only, are to be valued, and that other opinions, and the opinions of other men, are not to be valued. I ask you whether I was right in maintaining this?

CRITO: Certainly.

SOCRATES: The good are to be regarded, and not the bad?

CRITO: Yes.

SOCRATES: And the opinions of the wise are

good, and the opinions of the unwise are evil?

CRITO: Certainly.

SOCRATES: And what was said about another matter? Is the pupil who devotes himself to the practice of gymnastic supposed to attend to the praise and blame and opinion of every man, or of one man only—his physician or trainer, whoever he may be?

CRITO: Of one man only.

SOCRATES: And he ought to fear the censure and welcome the praise of that one only, and not of the many?

CRITO: Clearly so.

SOCRATES: And he ought to act and train, and eat and drink in the way which seems good to his single master who has understanding, rather than according to the opinion of all other men put together?

CRITO: True.

SOCRATES: And if he disobeys and disregards the opinion and approval of the one, and regards the opinion of the many who have no understanding, will he not suffer evil?

CRITO: Certainly he will.

SOCRATES: And what will the evil be, whither tending and what affecting, in the disobedient person?

CRITO: Clearly, affecting the body; that is what is destroyed by the evil.

SOCRATES: Very good; and is not this true, Crito, of other things which we need not separately enumerate? In questions of just and unjust, fair and foul, good and evil, which are the subjects of our present consultation, ought we to follow the opinion of the many and to fear them; or the opinion of the one man who has understanding? ought we not to fear and reverence him more than all the rest of the world: and if we desert him shall we not destroy and injure that principle in us which may be assumed to be improved by justice and deteriorated by injustice;— there is such a principle?

CRITO: Certainly there is, Socrates.

SOCRATES: Take a parallel instance:—if, acting under the advice of those who have no understanding, we destroy that which is improved by health and is deteriorated by disease, would life be worth having? And that which has been destroyed is—the body?

CRITO: Yes.

SOCRATES: Could we live, having an evil and corrupted body?

CRITO: Certainly not.

SOCRATES: And will life be worth having, if that higher part of man be destroyed, which is improved by justice and depraved by injustice? Do we suppose that principle, whatever it may be in man, which has to do with justice and injustice, to be inferior to the body?

CRITO: Certainly not.

SOCRATES: More honourable than the body?

CRITO: Far more.

SOCRATES: Then, my friend, we must not regard what the many say of us: but what he, the one man who has understanding of just and unjust, will say, and what the truth will say. And therefore you begin in error when you advise that we should regard the opinion of the many about just and unjust, good and evil, honourable and dishonourable,— "Well," some one will say, "But the many can kill us."

CRITO: Yes, Socrates; that will clearly be the answer.

SOCRATES: And it is true: but still I find with surprise that the old argument is unshaken as ever. And I should like to know whether I may say the same of another proposition —that not life, but a good life, is to be chiefly valued?

CRITO: Yes, that also remains unshaken.

SOCRATES: And a good life is equivalent to a just and honourable one—that holds also?

CRITO: Yes, it does.

SOCRATES: From these premises I proceed to argue the question whether I ought or ought not to try to escape without the consent of the Athenians: and if I am clearly right in escaping, then I will make the attempt; but if not, I will abstain. The other considerations which you mention, of money and loss of character and the duty of educating one's children, are, I fear, only the doctrines of the multitude, who would be as ready to restore people to life, if they were able, as they are to put them to death—and with as little reason. But now, since the argument has thus far prevailed, the only question which remains to be considered is, whether we shall do rightly either in escaping or in suffering others to aid in our escape and paying them in money and thanks, or whether in reality we shall not do rightly; and if the latter, then death or any other calamity which may ensue on my remaining here must not be allowed to enter into the calculation.

CRITO: I think that you are right Socrates; how then shall we proceed?

SOCRATES: Let us consider the matter together, and do you either refute me if you can, and I will be convinced; or else cease, my dear friend, from repeating to me that I ought to escape against the wishes of the Athenians: for I highly value your attempts to persuade me to do so, but I may not be persuaded against my own better judgment. And now please to consider my first position, and try how you can best answer me.

CRITO: I will.

SOCRATES: Are we to say that we are never intentionally to do wrong, or that in one way we ought and in another way we ought not to do wrong, or is doing wrong always evil and dishonourable, as I was just now saying, and as has been already acknowledged by us? Are all our former admissions which were made within a few days to be thrown away? And have we, at our age, been earnestly discoursing with one another all our life long only to discover that we are no better than children? Or, in spite of the opinion of the many, and in spite of consequences whether better or worse, shall we insist on the truth of what was then said, that injustice is always an evil and dishonour to him who acts unjustly? Shall we say so or not?

CRITO: Yes.

SOCRATES: Then we must do no wrong?

CRITO: Certainly not.

SOCRATES: Nor when injured injure in return, as the many imagine; for we must injure no one at all?

CRITO: Clearly not.

SOCRATES: Again, Crito, may we do evil?

CRITO: Surely, not, Socrates.

SOCRATES: And what of doing evil in return for evil, which is the morality of the many— is that just or not?

CRITO: Not just.

SOCRATES: For doing evil to another is the same as injuring him?

CRITO: Very true.

SOCRATES: Then we ought not to retaliate or render evil for evil to any one, whatever evil we may have suffered from him. But I would have you consider, Crito, whether you really mean what you are saying. For this opinion has never been held, and never will be held, by any considerable number of persons; and those who are agreed and those who are not agreed upon this point have no common ground, and can only despise one another when they see how widely they differ. Tell me, then, whether you agree with and assent to my first principle, that neither injury nor retaliation nor warding off evil by evil is ever right. And shall that be the premise of our argument? Or do you decline and dissent from this? For so I have ever thought, and continue to think; but, if you are of another opinion, let me hear what you have to say. If, however, you remain of the same mind as formerly, I will proceed to the next step.

CRITO: You may proceed, for I have not changed my mind.

SOCRATES: Then I will go on to the next point, which may be put in the form of a question:—Ought a man to do what he admits to be right, or ought he to betray the right?

CRITO: He ought to do what he thinks is right.

SOCRATES: But if this is true, what is the application? In leaving the prison against the will of the Athenians, do I wrong any? or rather do I not wrong those whom I ought least to wrong? Do I not desert the principles which were acknowledged by us to be just—what do you say?

CRITO: I cannot tell, Socrates; for I do not know.

SOCRATES: Then consider the matter in this way:—Imagine that I am about to play truant (you may call the proceeding by any name which you like), and the laws and the government come and interrogate me: "Tell us, Socrates," they say; "what are you about? are you not going by an act of yours to overturn us—the laws, and the whole state, as far as in you lies? Do you imagine that a state can subsist and not be overthrown, in which the decisions of law have no power, but are set aside and trampled upon by individuals?" What will be our answer, Crito, to these and the like words? Any one, and especially a rhetorician, will have a good deal to say on behalf of the law which requires a sentence to be carried out. He will argue that this law should not be set aside; and shall we reply, "Yes; but the state has injured us and given an unjust sentence." Suppose I say that?

CRITO: Very good, Socrates.

SOCRATES: "And was that our agreement with you?" the law would answer; "or were you to abide by the sentence of the state?" And if I were to express my astonishment at their words, the law would probably add: "Answer, Socrates, instead of opening your eyes —you are in the habit of asking and answering questions. Tell us,—What complaint have you to make against us which justifies you in attempting to destroy us and the state? In the first place did we not bring you into existence? Your father married your mother by our aid and begat you. Say whether you have any objection to urge against those of us who regulate marriage?" None, I should reply. "Or against those of us who after birth regulate the nurture and education of children, in which you also were trained? Were not the laws, which have the charge of education, right in commanding your father to train you in music and gymnastic?" Right, I should reply. "Well, then, since you were brought into the world and nurtured and educated by us, can you deny in the first place that you are our child and slave, as your fathers were before you? And if this is true, you are not on equal terms with us; nor can you think that you have a right to do to us what we are doing to you. Would you have any right to strike or revile or do any other evil to your father or your master, if you had one, because you have been struck or reviled by him, or received some other evil at his hands?—you would not say this? And because we think right to destroy you, do you think that you have any right to destroy us in return, and your country as far as in you lies? Will you, O professor of true virtue, pretend that you are justified in this? Has a philosopher like you failed to discover that our country is more to be valued and higher and holier far than mother or father or any ancestor, and more to be regarded in the eyes of the gods and of men of understanding? also to be soothed, and gently and reverently entreated when angry, even more than a father, and either to be persuaded, or if not persuaded, to be obeyed? And when we are punished by her, whether with imprisonment or stripes, the punishment is to be endured in silence; and if she lead us to wounds or death in battle, thither we follow as is right; neither may any one yield or retreat or leave his rank, but whether in battle or in a court of law, or in any other place, he must do what his city and his country order him; or he must change their view of what is just: and if he may do no violence to his father or mother, much less may he do violence to his country." What answer shall we make to this, Crito? Do the laws speak truly, or do they not?

CRITO: I think that they do.

SOCRATES: Then the laws will say: "Consider, Socrates, if we are speaking truly that in your present attempt you are going to do us an injury. For, having brought you into the world, and nurtured and educated you, and given you and every other citizen a share in every good which we had to give, we further proclaim to any Athenian by the liberty which we allow him, that if he does not like us when he has become of age and has seen the ways of the city, and made our acquaintance, he may go where he pleases and take his goods with him. None of us laws will forbid him or interfere with him. Any one who does not like us and the city, and who wants to emigrate to a colony or to any other city, may go where he likes, retaining his property. But he who has experience of the manner in which we order justice and administer the State, and still remains, has entered into an implied contract that he will do as we command him. And he who disobeys us is, as we maintain, thrice wrong; first, because in disobeying us he is disobeying his parents; secondly, because we are the authors of his education; thirdly, because he has made an agreement with us that he will duly obey our commands; and he neither obeys them nor convinces us that our commands are unjust; and we do not rudely impose them, but give him the alternative of obeying or convincing us;— that is what we offer, and he does neither.

"These are the sort of accusations to which, as we were saying, you, Socrates, will be exposed if you accomplish your intentions; you, above all other Athenians." Suppose now I ask, why I rather than anybody else? they will justly retort upon me that I above all other men have acknowledged the agreement. "There is clear proof," they will say, "Socrates, that we and the city were not displeasing to you. Of all Athenians you have been the most constant resident in the city, which, as you never leave, you may be supposed to love. For you never went out of the city either to see the games, except once when you went to the Isthmus, or to any other place unless when you were on military service; nor did you travel as other men do. Nor had you any curiosity to know other States or their laws: your affections did not go beyond us and our State; we were your special favourites, and you acquiesced in our government of you; and here in this city you begat your children, which is a proof of your satisfaction. Moreover, you might in the course of the trial, if you had liked, have fixed the penalty at banishment; the State which refuses to let you go now would have to let you go then. But you pretended that you preferred death to exile, and that you were not unwilling to die. And now you have forgotten these fine sentiments, and pay no respect to us, the laws, of whom you are the destroyer; and are doing what only a miserable slave would do, running away and turning your back upon the compacts and agreements which you made as a citizen. And, first of all, answer this very question: Are we right in saying that you agreed to be governed according to us in deed, and now in word only? Is that true or not?" How shall we answer, Crito? Must we not assent?

CRITO: We cannot help it, Socrates.

SOCRATES: Then will they not say: "You, Socrates, are breaking the covenants and agreements which you made with us at your leisure, not in any haste or under any compulsion or deception, but after you have had seventy years to think of them, during which time you were at liberty to leave the city, if we were not to your mind, or if our covenants appeared to you to be unfair. You had your choice, and might have gone either to Lacedaemon or Crete, both which States are often praised by you for their good government, or to some other Hellenic or foreign State. Whereas you, above all other Athenians, seemed to be so fond of the State, or, in other words, of us, her laws (and who would care about a State which has no laws?), that you never stirred out of her; the halt, the blind, the maimed were not more stationary in her than you were. And now you run away and forsake your agreements. Not so, Socrates, if you will take our advice; do not make yourself ridiculous by escaping out of the city.

"For just consider, if you transgress and err in this sort of way, what good will you do either to yourself or to your friends? That your friends will be driven into exile and deprived of citizenship, or will lose their property, is tolerably certain; and you yourself, if you fly to one of the neighboring cities, as, for example, Thebes or Megara, both of which are well governed, will come to them as an enemy, Socrates, and their government will be against you, and all patriotic citizens will cast an evil eye upon you as a subverter of the laws, and you will confirm in the minds of the judges the justice of their own condemnation of you. For he who is a corrupter of the laws is more than likely to be a corrupter of the young and foolish portion of mankind. Will you then flee from well-ordered cities and virtuous men? and is existence worth having on these terms? Or will you go to them ·without shame, and talk to them, Socrates? And what will you say to them? What you say here about virtue and justice and institutions and laws being the best things among men? Would that be decent of you? Surely not. But if you go away from well-governed States to Crito's friends in Thessaly, where there is great disorder and licence, they will be charmed to hear the tale of your escape from prison, set off with ludicrous particulars of the manner in which you were wrapped in a goatskin or some other disguise, and metamorphosed as the manner is of runaways; but will there be no one to remind you that in your old age you were not ashamed to violate the most sacred laws from a miserable desire of a little more life? Perhaps not, if you keep them in a good temper; but if they are out of temper you will hear many degrading things; you will live, but how?—as the flatterer of all men, and the servant of all men; and doing what?—eating and drinking in Thessaly, having gone abroad in order that you may get a dinner. And where will be your fine sentiments about justice and virtue? Say that you wish to live for the sake of your children—you want to bring them up and educate them—will you take them into Thessaly and deprive them of Athenian citizenship? Is this the benefit which you will confer upon them? Or are you under the impression that they will be better cared for and educated here if you are still alive, although absent from them; for your friends will take care of them? Do you fancy that if you are an inhabitant of Thessaly they will take care of them, and if you are an inhabitant of the other world that they will not take care of them? Nay; but if they who call themselves friends are good for anything, they will—to be sure they will.

"Listen, then, Socrates, to us who have brought you up. Think not of life and children first, and of justice afterwards, but of justice first, that you may be justified before the princes of the world below. For neither will you nor any that belong to you be happier or holier or juster in this life, or happier in another, if you do as Crito bids. Now you depart in innocence, a sufferer and not a doer of evil; a victim, not of the laws but of men. But if you go forth, returning evil for evil; and injury for injury, breaking the covenants and agreements which you have made with us, and wronging those whom you ought least of all to wrong, that is to say, yourself, your friends, your country, and us, we shall be angry with you while you live, and our brethren, the laws in the world below, will receive you as an enemy; for they will know that you have done your best to destroy us. Listen, then, to us and not to Crito."

This, dear Crito, is the voice which I seem to hear murmuring in my ears, like the sound of the flute in the ears of the mystic; that voice, I say, is humming in my ears, and prevents me from hearing any other. And I know that anything more which you may say will be vain. Yet speak, if you have anything to say.

CRITO: I have nothing to say, Socrates.

SOCRATES: Leave me, then, Crito, to fulfill the will of God, and to follow whither he leads.

NOTE

1. Homer, II. ix. 363.

19 Beyond Law and Order

Kropotkin & Camus

The anarchist, geographer, and Russian aristocrat Peter Kropotkin (1842–1921) would have been strongly opposed to the respect and reverence Socrates expressed for laws in the *Crito*. Observing the inhuman conditions in the Russian Siberian penal system, he knew what the state's laws could do. Kropotkin would have agreed with Thoreau, that government is best that governs least, or not at all. (Anarchism is not the same as anarchy. It literally means "no government" or un-rule, and of its many varieties from peasant anarchism to pacifist anarchism there are several radically different attitudes toward the use of violence in bringing about an anarchistic society.)

In Kropotkin's view, the strength of anarchism is in the fact that, like all socialisms, it springs not from an academic philosophy but from the people. "All power to the people!" is the rallying cry of the dedicated anarchist. For anarchism is the expression of a strong faith in the wisdom of people to set up counter defenses to the tyranny of a law and the order that is imposed by a dominant minority. Anarchism, in Kropotkin's view, is "the creative constructive force of the masses." This force, to be sure, must be guided and objectified into institutions to provide for social stability and sustained satisfaction of human needs. But under anarchism, social institutions such as the family, education, and administration will not be the impersonal bureaucratic repressive institutions which they have become under an exploitive regime based on competition and survival of the fittest. Having as their basis voluntary cooperation and mutual aid, the new liberalized institutions of anarchism will be integral and vital parts of a decentralized government that is truly by, of, and for the people.

Taking justification from their ends (setting up a new social order—open, democratic, free), anarchists have often not hesitated to use force as a means of rebellion. Those truly imbued with the anarchist spirit will not be content to stop where other socialists have stopped, with the overthrow of capitalism and the abolition of the exploitation of the working class. They would continue until they destroy the real core of capitalism—"the State and its principal supports—centralization of authority, law, always made by a minority for its own profit, and a form of justice whose chief aim is to protect authority and capitalism."[1] Anarchism will lift "its sacrilegious arm" and knock down the very pillars—law, authority, and the state—which support the temple of capitalism.

In reviewing previous conceptions of the origin and value of laws, Kropotkin found no reason for the sense of respect and reverence which they inspire in a large portion of mankind. Law is not, in his view, "truth expressed in an objective form."[2] Certainly law and morality are not identical. There is no divine origin to law nor does it have any kind of metaphysical basis. Law has developed as other social phenomena have developed—from human motive and ingenuity. On the true origin of law, Kropotkin wrote:

> All laws have a double origin, and it is precisely this double origin which distinguishes them from customs established by usage and representing the principles of morality existing in a particular society at a particular epoch. Law confirms these customs: it crystalizes them; but at the same time it takes advantages of these generally approved customs, in order to introduce in disguise, under their sanction, some new institution that is entirely to the advantage of the military and governing minorities. For instance, Law introduces, or gives sanction to, slavery, caste, paternal, priestly, and military authority; or else it smuggles in serfdom, and, later on, subjection to the State. By this means, Law has always succeeded in imposing a yoke on man without his perceiving it, a yoke that he has never been able to throw off save by means of revolution.[3]

Like the laws that are its underpinnings, the state also, in Kropotkin's opinion, merits none of the respect or reverential obedience it often elicits. The state certainly is not, as it has sometimes been called, "the affirmation of justice on earth" or "the instrument and the bearer of progress." Kropotkin held to believe the maxim "without state—no society" would be to believe sheer nonsense. The state is a social invention that developed during a definite and determinable historical era. It developed simultaneously with capitalism, to which it is necessarily linked. The state, for Kropotkin, is "a society of mutual insurance between the landlord, the military commander, the judge, the priest, and later the capitalist, in order to support each other's authority over the people and for exploiting the poverty of the masses and getting rich themselves."[4]

Adhering to this view of the state, Kropotkin could not conceive of how capitalism could be abolished while the state is maintained. Whether by evolution or by revolution, gradually or suddenly, a new form of economic organization and self-sufficiency must be brought about and with it the development of a new form of local political organization. The new organization would be more popular, more decentralized, and freer than any representative government ever could be. With economic freedom would come political freedom and "liberation from the yoke of the state by means of free agreement, territorial, professional and functional."[5]

Social sanctions would be sufficient to restrain those who might abuse their liberties, and a voluntary society in which "from each according to his means, to each according to his needs" would become feasible.

Albert Camus, the French writer, journalist, and Nobel Prize winner, was concerned with freedom in most of his plays, short stories, and essays. In *The Myth of Sisyphus* (1942) and *The Rebel* (1951), he extolled the person who has the courage to say no to tyranny, whether it be tyranny of religious, political, or psychological force. The rebel by his very act of rebellion is giving overt testimony not only to the freedom by which he asserts his right, but also to the fuller freedom which he demands for himself and others. In the past, when tyrannies were less efficient in suppressing unorthodox works and artistic or scientific creativity, writers could perhaps remain detached and silent. Today, however, in an age of improved methods of thought control and behavioral engineering, to be silent or neutral under tyranny, according to Camus, is often as dangerous as to oppose it. "One has to take a stand, be either for or against."[6]

Camus also gave serious thought to how rebellion applies to the artist. "The era of chair-bound artists is over."[7] "Commit thyself" must be the new artistic maxim, and not "Art for art's sake." While Camus stressed the importance of artistic commitment, he also stressed the importance of maintaining artistic detachment, or what the English psychologist Edward Bullough called "aesthetic distance." The artist must throw himself into the historical arena, sharing in the misfortunes of his time and seeking to alleviate them; otherwise he can never "insert his art into its time." But he must also withdraw sufficiently from the action if he is to evaluate and recreate it. "Every work presupposes a content of reality and a creator who shapes the container," Camus pointed out.[8] The artist, then, cannot understand the content of action unless he has been a part of it—that is, unless he has been involved in and committed to it—yet he cannot give it form unless he has been able to tear himself away from it long enough to see it, in Spinoza's phrase, "under the form of eternity."

It is a symptom of the sickness and derangement of our times, Camus believed, that the artist has to be reminded that he is, after all, only another human being. Like the ordinary man, he longs for solitude, justice, help, pleasure, friendship, love, admiration, freedom, and hope. Hope to Camus was particularly important; for by means of hope he was able to reject nihilism, concentrate on the idea of fecundity, and remain committed to his role of artist. In the very process of negating, of criticizing and defying the world in which he lived, Camus noted that to negate is also to affirm. Even when he was depicting the sordidness and absurdity of life, he recognized that he was also paying "homage to the wretched and magnificent life of ours."[9]

Camus also realized that he was paying homage to the value that he prized above all others in art and in life, the value of freedom. "The aim of art, the aim of life can only be to increase the sum of freedom and responsibility to be found in every man and in the world."[10] An artist who uses his art as a means of expressing his hatred of life and his contempt for human beings is like the artist who uses his works as disguised tracts for converting his readers to a cause to which the artist is committed. Neither kind of artist will succeed in creating works with lasting value as their works will add nothing to the understanding and appreciation of freedom. In the contemporary world, Camus was convinced, "the force of resistance, together with the value of freedom gives us new reasons for living."[11]

Finding reasons for living is essential, Camus believed, if one is to live creatively, productively, and authentically. In fact, if one cannot discover a reason for living, why live at all? *The Myth of Sisyphus* begins with Camus' statement that the chief philosophical problem is that of suicide. As an atheist, one must face the possibility that life is meaningless, that one's most cherished efforts will come to naught, and that all of us will be isolated in the end.

Other writers admired Apollo for his wisdom, Dionysius for his passion, Prometheus for his defiance, Atlas for his strength, but Camus admired Sisyphus, a man who because of a transgression had been doomed in his afterlife to push an enormous stone up a hill, never reaching the top before it would fall back of its own weight. Camus admired Sisyphus for undertaking what he knew would be a hopeless and absurd task—a task he would have to do over and over again despite his continual defeat. Camus believed that "crushing truths perish from being acknowledged." Sisyphus was superior to his fate, Camus argued, because he was conscious and scornful of it. Even if he could do nothing about his fate, he could accept it, become involved in it, even rejoice in it. In rebellion, human beings may transcend the despair of the universe's indifference to them. In fact, from his examination of the nature of the absurd, Camus became convinced that true happiness and a deepened sense of the absurd are inseparable. This is why he imagines Sisyphus, though damned, to be happy.

NOTES

1. Irving Horowitz, ed., *The Anarchists* (New York: Dell Publishing Co., (1964), p. 150.
2. Ibid.
3. Ibid., p. 151.
4. Ibid., p. 159.
5. Ibid., p. 160.
6. Albert Camus, "The Artist and His Time" in *The Myth of Sisyphus and Other Essays* (New York: Vintage Books, 1955), p. 207.
7. Ibid., p. 212.
8. Albert Camus, *Resistance, Rebellion and Death* (New York: Modern Library, 1963), p. 182.
9. Ibid., p. 183.
10. Ibid., p. 184.
11. Ibid., p. 185.

Law and Authority

Peter Kropotkin

"When ignorance reigns in society and disorder in the minds of men, laws are multiplied, legislation is expected to do everything, and each fresh law being a fresh miscalculation, men are continually led to demand from it what can proceed only from themselves, from their own education and their own morality." It is no revolutionist who says this, not even a reformer. It is the jurist, Dalloy, author of the collection of French law known as *Repertoire de la Législation*. And yet, though these lines were written by a man who was himself a maker and admirer of law, they perfectly represent the abnormal condition of our society.

In existing States a fresh law is looked upon as a remedy for evil. Instead of themselves altering what is bad, people begin by demanding a *law* to alter it. If the road between two villages is impassable, the peasant says:—"There should be a law about parish roads." If a park-keeper takes advantage of the want of spirit in those who follow him with servile observance and insults one of them, the insulted man says, "There should be a law to enjoin more politeness upon park-keepers." If there is stagnation in agriculture or commerce, the husbandman, cattle-breeder, or corn speculator argues. "It is protective legislation that we require." Down to the old clothesman there is not one who does not de-

From *Kropotkin's Revolutionary Pamphlets*, ed. Roger N. Baldwin (New York: Vanguard Press, 1927). Originally published in London, Freedom Press, 1886.

mand a law to protect his own little trade. If the employer lowers wages or increases the hours of labor, the politician in embryo exclaims, "We must have a law to put all that to rights." In short, a law everywhere and for everything! A law about fashions, a law about mad dogs, a law about virtue, a law to put a stop to all the vices and all the evils which result from human indolence and cowardice.

We are so perverted by an education which from infancy seeks to kill in us the spirit of revolt, and to develop that of submission to authority; we are so perverted by this existence under the ferrule of a law, which regulates every event in life—our birth, our education, our development, our love, our friendship—that, if this state of things continues, we shall lose all initiative, all habit of thinking for ourselves. Our society seems no longer able to understand that it is possible to exist otherwise than under the reign of law, elaborated by a representative government and administered by a handful of rulers. And even when it has gone so far as to emancipate itself from the thralldom, its first care has been to reconstitute it immediately. "The Year I of Liberty" has never lasted more than a day, for after proclaiming it men put themselves the very next morning under the yoke of law and authority.

Indeed, for some thousands of years, those who govern us have done nothing but ring the changes upon "Respect for law, obedience to authority." This is the moral atmosphere in which parents bring up their children, and school only serves to confirm the impression. Cleverly assorted scraps of spurious science are inculcated upon the children to prove necessity of law; obedience to the law is made a religion; moral goodness and the law of the masters are fused into one and the same divinity. The historical hero of the schoolroom is the man who obeys the law, and defends it against rebels.

Later when we enter upon public life, society and literature, impressing us day by day and hour by hour as the water drop hollows the stone, continue to inculate the same prejudice. Books of history, of political science, of social economy, are stuffed with this respect for law. Even the physical sciences have been pressed into the service by introducing artificial modes of expresesion, borrowed from theology and arbitrary power, into knowledge which is purely the result of observation. Thus our intelligence is successfully befogged, and always to maintain our respect for law. The same work is done by newspapers. They have not an article which does not preach respect for law, even where the third page proves every day the imbecility of that law, and shows how it is dragged through every variety of mud and filth by those charged with its administration. Servility before the law has become a virtue, and I doubt if there was ever even a revolutionist who did not begin in his youth as the defender of law against what are generally called "abuses," although these last are inevitable consequences of the law itself.

Art pipes in unison with would-be science. The hero of the sculptor, the painter, the musician, shields Law beneath his buckler, and with flashing eyes and distended nostrils stands ever ready to strike down the man who would lay hands upon her. Temples are raised to her; revolutionists themselves hesitate to touch the high priests consecrated to her service, and when revolution is about to sweep away some ancient institution, it is still by law that it endeavors to sanctify the deed.

The confused mass of rules of conduct called law, which has been bequeathed to us by slavery, serfdom, feudalism, and royalty, has taken the place of those stone monsters, before whom human victims used to be immolated, and whom slavish savages dared not even touch lest they should be slain by the thunderbolts of heaven.

This new worship has been established with especial success since the rise to supreme power of the middle class—since the great French Revolution. Under the ancient régime, men spoke little of laws; unless, indeed, it were, with Montesquieu, Rousseau and Voltaire, to oppose them to royal caprice. Obedience to the good pleasure of the king and his lackeys was compulsory on pain of hanging or imprisonment. But during and after the revolutions, when the lawyers rose to power, they did their best to strengthen the principle upon which their ascendancy depended. The middle class at once accepted it as a dyke to dam up the popular torrent. The priestly crew hastened to sanctify it, to save their bark from foundering amid the breakers. Finally the people received it as an improvement upon the arbitrary authority and violence of the past.

To understand this, we must transport ourselves in imagination into the eighteenth century. Our hearts must have ached at the story of the atrocities committed by the all-powerful nobles of that time upon the men and women of the people before we can understand what must have been the magic influence upon the peasant's mind of the words, "Equality before the law, obedience to the law without distinction of birth or fortune." He who until then had been treated more cruelly than a beast, he who had never had any rights, he who had never obtained justice against the most revolting actions on the part of a noble, unless in revenge he killed him and was hanged—he saw himself recognized by this maxim, at least in theory, at least with regard to his personal rights, as the equal of his lord. Whatever this law might be, it promised to affect lord and peasant alike; it proclaimed the equality of rich and poor before the judge. The promise was a lie, and today we know it; but at that period it was an advance, a homage to justice, as hypocrisy is a homage rendered to truth. This is the reason that when the saviors of the menaced middle class (the Robespierres and the Dantons) took their stand upon the writings of the Rousseaus and the Voltaires, and proclaimed "respect for law, the same for every man," the people accepted the compromise; for their revolutionary impetus had already spent its force in the contest with a foe whose ranks drew closer day by day; they bowed their neck beneath the yoke of law to save themselves from the arbitrary power of their lords.

The middle class has ever since continued to make the most of this maxim, which with another principle, that of representative government, sums up the whole philosophy of the bourgeois age, the nineteenth century. It has preached this doctrine in its schools, it has propagated it in its writings, it has moulded its art and science to the same purpose, it has thrust its beliefs into every hole and corner— like a pious Englishwoman, who slips tracts under the door—and it has done all this so successfully that today we behold the issue in the detestable fact that men who long for freedom begin the attempt to obtain it by entreating their masters to be kind enough to protect them by modifying the laws which these masters themselves have created!

But times and tempers are changed. Rebels are everywhere to be found who no longer wish to obey the law without knowing whence it comes, and what are its uses, and whither arises the obligation to submit to it, and the reverence with which it is encompassed. The rebels of our day are criticizing the very foundations of society which have hitherto been held sacred, and first and foremost amongst them that fetish, law.

The critics analyze the sources of law, and find there either a god, product of the terrors of the savage, and stupid, paltry and malicious as the priests who vouch for its supernatural origin, or else, bloodshed, conquest by fire and sword. They study the characteristics of law, and instead of perpetual growth corresponding to that of the human race, they find its distinctive trait to be immobility, a tendency to crystallize what should be modified and developed day by day. They ask how law has been maintained, and in its service they see the atrocities of Byzantinism, the cruelties of the Inquisition, the tortures of the middle ages, living flesh torn by the lash of the executioner, chains, clubs, axes, the gloomy dungeons of prisons, agony, curses and tears. In our own days they see, as before, the axe, the cord, the rifle, the prison; on the one hand, the brutalized prisoner, reduced to the condition of a caged beast by the debasement of his whole moral being, and on the other, the judge, stripped of every feeling which does honor to human nature, living like a visionary in a world of legal fictions, revelling in the infliction of imprisonment and death, without even suspecting, in the cold malignity of his madness, the abyss of degradation into which he has himself fallen before the eyes of those whom he condemns.

They see a race of law-makers legislating without knowing what their laws are about; today voting a law on the sanitation of towns, without the faintest notion of hygiene, tomorrow making regulations for the armament of troops, without so much as understanding a gun; making laws about teaching and education without ever having given a lesson of any sort, or even an honest education to their own children; legislating at random in all directions, but never forgetting the penalties to be meted out to ragamuffins, the prison and the galleys, which are to be the portion of men a thousand times less immoral than these legislators themselves.

Finally, they see the jailer on the way to lose

all human feeling, the detective trained as a blood-hound, the police spy despising himself; "informing," metamorphosed into a virtue; corruption, erected into a system; all the vices, all the evil qualities of mankind countenanced and cultivated to insure the triumph of law.

All this we see, and, therefore, instead of inanely repeating the old formula, "Respect the law," we say, "Despise law and all its attributes!" In place of the cowardly phrase, "Obey the law," our cry is "Revolt against all laws!"

Only compare the misdeeds accomplished in the name of each law with the good it has been able to effect, and weigh carefully both good and evil, and you will see if we are right.

The millions of laws which exist for the regulation of humanity appear upon investigation to be divided into three principal categories: protection of property, protection of persons, protection of government. And by analyzing each of these three categories, we arrive at the same logical and necessary conclusion: *the uselessness and hurtfulness of law.*

Socialists know what is meant by protection of property. Laws on property are not made to guarantee either to the individual or to society the enjoyment of the produce of their own labor. On the contrary, they are made to rob the producer of a part of what he has created, and to secure to certain other people that portion of the produce which they have stolen either from the producer or from society as a whole. When, for example, the law establishes Mr. So-and-So's right to a house, it is not establishing his right to a cottage he has built for himself, or to a house he has erected with the help of some of his friends. In that case no one would have disputed his right. On the contrary, the law is establishing his right to a house which is *not* the product of his labor; first of all because he has had it built for him by others to whom he has not paid the full value of their work, and next because that house represents a social value which he could

not have produced for himself. The law is establishing his right to what belongs to everybody in general and to nobody in particular. The same house built in the midst of Siberia would not have the value it possesses in a large town, and, as we know, that value arises from the labor of something like fifty generations of men who have built the town, beautified it, supplied it with water and gas, fine promenades, colleges, theatres, shops, railways and roads leading in all directions. Thus, by recognizing the right of Mr. So-and-So to a particular house in Paris, London or Rouen, the law is unjustly appropriating to him a certain portion of the produce of the labor of mankind in general. And it is precisely because this appropriation and all other forms of property bearing the same character are a crying injustice, that a whole arsenal of laws and a whole army of soldiers, policemen and judges are needed to maintain it against the good sense and just feeling inherent in humanity.

Half our laws,—the civil code in each country,—serves no other purpose than to maintain this appropriation, this monopoly for the benefit of certain individuals against the whole of mankind. Three-fourths of the causes decided by the tribunals are nothing but quarrels between monopolists—two robbers disputing over their booty. And a great many of our criminal laws have the same object in view, their end being to keep the workman in a subordinate position towards his employer, and thus afford security for exploitation.

As for guaranteeing the product of his labor to the producer, there are no laws which even attempt such a thing. It is so simple and natural, so much a part of the manners and customs of mankind, that law has not given it so much as a thought. Open brigandage, sword in hand, is no feature of our age. Neither does one workman ever come and dispute the produce of his labor with another. If they have a misunderstanding they settle it by calling in a third person, without having recourse to law. The only person who exacts from another what that other has produced, is the proprietor, who comes in and deducts the lion's share. As for humanity in general, it everywhere respects the right of each to what he has created, without the interposition of any special laws.

As all the laws about property which make up thick volumes of codes and are the delight of our lawyers have no other object than to protect the unjust appropriation of human labor by certain monopolists, there is no reason for their existence, and, on the day of the revolution, social revolutionists are thoroughly determined to put an end to them. Indeed, a bonfire might be made with perfect justice of all laws bearing upon the so-called rights of property, all title-deeds, all registers, in a word, of all that is in any way connected with an institution which will soon be looked upon as a blot in the history of humanity, as humiliating as the slavery and serfdom of past ages.

The remarks just made upon laws concerning property are quite as applicable to the second category of laws; those for the maintenance of government, i.e., constitutional law.

It again is a complete arsenal of laws, decrees, ordinances, orders in council, and what not, all serving to protect the diverse forms of representative government, delegated or usurped, beneath which humanity is writhing. We know very well—anarchists have often enough pointed out in their perpetual criticism of the various forms of government—that the mission of all governments, monarchical, constitutional, or republican, is to protect and maintain by force the privileges of the classes in possession, the aristocracy, clergy and traders. A good third of our laws—and each country possesses some tens of thousands of them—the fundamental laws on taxes, excise duties, the organization of ministerial departments and their offices, of the army, the police, the church, etc., have no other end than to maintain, patch up, and develop the administrative machine. And this machine in its turn serves almost entirely to protect the privileges of the possessing classes. Analyze all these laws, observe them in action day by day, and you will discover that not one is worth preserving.

About such laws there can be no two opinions. Not only anarchists, but more or less revolutionary radicals also, are agreed that the only use to be made of laws concerning the organization of government is to fling them into the fire.

The third category of law still remains to be considered; that relating to the protection of the person and the detection and prevention of "crime." This is the most important because most prejudices attach to it; because, if law enjoys a certain amount of consideration, it is in consequence of the belief that this species of law is absolutely indispensable to the maintenance of security in our societies. These are laws developed from the nucleus of customs useful to human communities, which have been turned to account by rulers to sanctify their own domination. The authority of the chiefs of tribes, of rich families in towns, and of the king, depended upon their judicial functions, and even down to the present day, whenever the necessity of government is spoken of, its function as supreme judge is the thing implied. "Without a government men would tear one another to pieces," argues the village orator. "The ultimate end of all government is to secure twelve honest jurymen to every accused person," said Burke.

Well, in spite of all the prejudices existing on this subject, it is quite time that anarchists should boldly declare this category of laws as useless and injurious as the preceding ones.

First of all, as to so-called crimes—assaults upon persons—it is well known that two-thirds, and often as many as three-fourths, of such "crimes" are instigated by the desire to obtain possession of someone's wealth. This immense class of so-called crimes and misdemeanors will disappear on the day on which private property ceases to exist. "But," it will be said, "there will always be brutes who will attempt the lives of their fellow citizens, who will lay their hands to a knife in every quarrel, and revenge the slightest offense by murder, if there are no laws to restrain and punishments to withhold them." This refrain is repeated every time the right of society *to punish* is called in question.

Yet there is one fact concerning this head which at the present time is thoroughly established; the severity of punishment does not diminish the amount of crime. Hang, and, if you like, quarter murderers, and the number of murders will not decrease by one. On the other hand, abolish the penalty of death, and there will not be one murder more; there will be fewer. Statistics prove it. But if the harvest is good, and bread cheap, and the weather fine, the number of murders immediately decreases. This again is proved by statistics. The amount of crime always augments and diminishes in proportion to the price of provisions and the state of the weather. Not that all murderers are actuated by hunger. That is not the case. But when the harvest is good, and provisions are at an obtainable price, and when the sun shines, men, lighter-hearted and less miserable than usual, do not give way to gloomy passions, do not from trivial motives plunge a knife into the bosom of a fellow creature.

Moreover, it is also a well known fact that the fear of punishment has never stopped a single murderer. He who kills his neighbor from revenge or misery does not reason much about consequences; and there have been few murderers who were not firmly convinced that they should escape prosecution.

Without speaking of a society in which a man will receive a better education, in which the development of all his faculties, and the possibility of exercising them, will procure him so many enjoyments that he will not seek to poison them by remorse—even in our society, even with those said products of misery whom we see today in the public houses of great cities —on the day when no punishment is inflicted

upon murderers, the number of murders will not be augmented by a single case. And it is extremely probable that it will be, on the contrary, diminished by all those cases which are due at present to habitual criminals, who have been brutalized in prisons.

We are continually being told of the benefits conferred by law, and the beneficial effect of penalties, but have the speakers ever attempted to strike a balance between the benefits attributed to laws and penalties, and the degrading effect of these penalties upon humanity? Only calculate all the evil passions awakened in mankind by the atrocious punishments formerly inflicted in our streets! Man is the cruelest animal upon earth. And who has pampered and developed the cruel instincts unknown, even among monkeys, if it is not the king, the judge, and the priests, armed with law, who caused flesh to be torn off in strips, boiling pitch to be poured into wounds, limbs to be dislocated, bones to be crushed, men to be sawn asunder to maintain their authority? Only estimate the torrent of depravity let loose in human society by the "informing" which is countenanced by judges, and paid in hard cash by governments, under pretext of assisting in the discovery of "crime." Only go into the jails and study what man becomes when he is deprived of freedom and shut up with other depraved beings, steeped in the vice and corruption which oozes from the very walls of our existing prisons. Only remember that the more these prisons are reformed, the more detestable they become. Our model modern penitentiaries are a hundred-fold more abominable than the dungeons of the middle ages. Finally, consider what corruption, what depravity of mind is kept up among men by the idea of obedience, the very essence of law; of chastisement; of authority having the right to punish, to judge irrespective of our conscience and the esteem of our friends; of the necessity for executioners, jailers, and informers—in a word, by all the attributes of law and authority. Consider all this, and you will assuredly agree with us in saying that a law inflicting penalties is an abomination which should cease to exist.

Peoples without political organization, and therefore less depraved than ourselves, have perfectly understood that the man who is called "criminal" is simply unfortunate; that the remedy is not to flog him, to chain him up, or to kill him on the scaffold or in prison, but to help him by the most brotherly care, by treatment based on equality, by the usages of life among honest men. In the next revolution we hope that this cry will go forth:

"Burn the guillotines; demolish the prisons; drive away the judges, policemen and informers—the impurest race upon the face of the earth; treat as a brother the man who has been led by passion to do ill to his fellow; above all, take from the ignoble products of middle-class idleness the possibility of displaying their vices in attractive colors; and be sure that but few crimes will mar our society."

The main supports of crime are idleness, law and authority; laws about property, laws about government, laws about penalties and misdemeanors; and authority, which takes upon itself to manufacture these laws and to apply them.

No more laws! No more judges! Liberty, equality, and practical human sympathy are the only effectual barriers we can oppose to the anti-social instincts of certain among us.

Absurd Freedom

Albert Camus

Now the main thing is done, I hold certain facts from which I cannot separate. What I know, what is certain, what I cannot deny, what I cannot reject—this is what counts. I can negate everything of that part of me that lives on vague nostalgias, except this desire for unity, this longing to solve, this need for clarity and cohesion. I can refute everything in this world surrounding me that offends or enraptures me, except this chaos, this sovereign chance and this divine equivalence which springs from anarchy. I don't know whether this world has a meaning that transcends it. But I know that I do not know that meaning and that it is impossible for me just now to know it. What can a meaning outside my condition mean to me? I can understand only in human terms. What I touch, what resists me—that is what I understand. And these two certainties—my appetite for the absolute and for unity and the impossibility of reducing this world to a rational and reasonable principle—I also know that I cannot reconcile them. What other truth can I admit without lying, without bringing in a hope I lack and which means nothing within the limits of my condition?

If I were a tree among trees, a cat among animals, this life would have a meaning, or rather this problem would not arise, for I should belong to this world. I should *be* this

From *The Myth of Sisyphus and Other Essays*, by Albert Camus, translated by Justin O'Brien. Copyright © 1955 by Albert A. Knopf, Inc. Reprinted by permission of the publisher.

world to which I am now opposed by my whole consciousness and my whole insistence upon familiarity. This ridiculous reason is what sets me in opposition to all creation. I cannot cross it out with a stroke of the pen. What I believe to be true I must therefore preserve. What seems to me so obvious, even against me, I must support. And what constitutes the basis of that conflict, of that break between the world and my mind, but the awareness of it? If therefore I want to preserve it, I can through a constant awareness, ever revived, ever alert. This is what, for the moment, I must remember. At this moment the absurd, so obvious and yet so hard to win, returns to a man's life and finds its home there. At this moment, too, the mind can leave the arid, dried-up path of lucid effort. That path now emerges in daily life. It encounters the world of the anonymous impersonal pronoun "one," but henceforth man enters in with his revolt and his lucidity. He has forgotten how to hope. This hell of the present is his Kingdom at last. All problems recover their sharp edge. Abstract evidence retreats before the poetry of forms and colors. Spiritual conflicts become embodied and return to the abject and magnificent shelter of man's heart. None of them is settled. But all are transfigured. Is one going to die, escape by the leap, rebuild a mansion of ideas and forms to one's own scale? Is one, on the contrary, going to take up the heart-rending and marvelous wager of the absurd? Let's make a final effort in this regard and draw all our conclusions.

The body, affection, creation, action, human nobility will then resume their places in this mad world. At last man will again find there the wine of the absurd and the bread of indifference on which he feeds his greatness.

Let us insist again on the method: it is a matter of persisting. At a certain point on his path the absurd man is tempted. History is not lacking in either religions or prophets, even without gods. He is asked to leap. All he can reply is that he doesn't fully understand, that it is not obvious. Indeed, he does not want to do anything but what he fully understands. He is assured that this is the sin of pride, but he does not understand the notion of sin; that perhaps hell is in store, but he has not enough imagination to visualize that strange future; that he is losing immortal life, but that seems to him an idle consideration. An attempt is made to get him to admit his guilt. He feels innocent. To tell the truth, that is all he feels— his irreparable innocence. This is what allows him everything. Hence, what he demands of himself is to live *solely* with what he knows, to accommodate himself to what is, and to bring in nothing that is not certain. He is told that nothing is. But this at least is a certainty. And it is with this that he is concerrned: he wants to find out if it is possible to live *without appeal*.

Now I can broach the notion of suicide. It has already been felt what solution might be given. At this point the problem is reversed. It was previously a question of finding out whether or not life had to have a meaning to be lived. It now becomes clear, on the contrary, that it will be lived all the better if it has no meaning. Living an experience, a particular fate, is accepting it fully. Now, no one will live this fate, knowing it to be absurd, unless he does everything to keep before him that absurd brought to light by consciousness. Negating one of the terms of the opposition on which he lives amounts to escaping it. To abolish conscious revolt is to elude the problem. The theme of permanent revolution is thus carried into individual experience. Living is keeping the absurd alive. Keeping it alive is, above all, contemplating it. Unlike Eurydice, the absurd dies only when we turn away from it. One of the only coherent philosophical positions is thus revolt. It is a constant confrontation between man and his own obscurity. It is an insistence upon an impossible transparency. It challenges the world anew every second. Just as danger provided man the unique opportunity of seizing awareness, so metaphysical revolt extends awareness to the whole of experience. It is that constant presence of man in his own eyes. It is not aspiration, for it is devoid of hope. That revolt is the certainty of a crushing fate, without the resignation that ought to accompany it.

This is where it is seen to what a degree absurd experience is remote from suicide. It may be thought that suicide follows revolt— but wrongly. For it does not represent the logical outcome of revolt. It is just the contrary by the consent it presupposes. Suicide, like the leap, is acceptance at its extreme. Everything is over and man returns to his essential history. His future, his unique and dreadful future—he sees and rushes toward it. In its way, suicide settles the absurd. It engulfs the absurd in the same death. But I know that in order to keep alive, the absurd cannot be settled. It escapes suicide to the extent that it is simultaneously awareness and rejection of death. It is, at the extreme limit of the condemned man's last thought, that shoelace that despite everything he sees a few yards away, on the very brink of his dizzying fall. The contrary of suicide, in fact, is the man condemned to death.

That revolt gives life its value. Spread out over the whole length of a life, it restores its majesty to that life. To a man devoid of blinders, there is no finer sight than that of the intelligence at grips with a reality that transcends it. The sight of human pride is unequaled. No disparagement is of any use. That discipline that the mind imposes on itself, that will conjured up out of nothing, that face-to-face struggle have something exceptional about them. To impoverish that reality whose inhumanity constitutes man's majesty is tantamount to impoverishing him himself. I understand then why the doctrines that explain everything to me also debilitate me at the same time. They relieve me of the weight of my own life, and yet I must carry it alone. At this juncture, I cannot conceive that a skeptical metaphysics can be joined to an ethics of renunciation.

Consciousness and revolt, these rejections are the contrary of renunciation. Everything that is indomitable and passionate in a human heart quickens them, on the contrary, with its own life. It is essential to die unreconciled and not of one's own free will. Suicide is a repudiation. The absurd man can only drain everything to the bitter end, and deplete himself. The absurd is his extreme tension, which he maintains constantly by solitary effort, for he knows that in that consciousness and in that day-to-day revolt he gives proof of his only truth, which is defiance. This is a first consequence.

If I remain in that prearranged position which consists in drawing all the conclusions (and nothing else) involved in a newly discovered notion, I am faced with a second paradox. In order to remain faithful to that method, I have nothing to do with the problem of metaphysical liberty. Knowing whether or not man is free doesn't interest me. I can experience only my own freedom. As to it, I can have no general notions, but merely a few clear insights. The problem of "freedom as such" has no meaning. For it is linked in quite a different way with the problem of God. Knowing

whether or not man is free involves knowing whether he can have a master. The absurdity peculiar to this problem comes from the fact that the very notion that makes the problem of freedom possible also takes away all its meaning. For in the presence of God there is less a problem of freedom than a problem of evil. You know the alternative: either we are not free and God the all-powerful is responsible for evil. Or we are free and responsible but God is not all-powerful. All the scholastic subtleties have neither added anything to nor subtracted anything from the acuteness of this paradox.

This is why I cannot get lost in the glorification or the mere definition of a notion which eludes me and loses its meaning as soon as it goes beyond the frame of reference of my individual experience. I cannot understand what kind of freedom would be given me by a higher being. I have lost the sense of hierarchy. The only conception of freedom I can have is that of the prisoner or the individual in the midst of the State. The only one I know is freedom of thought and action. Now if the absurd cancels all my chances of eternal freedom, it restores and magnifies, on the other hand, my freedom of action. That privation of hope and future means an increase in man's availability.

Before encountering the absurd, the everyday man lives with aims, a concern for the future or for justification (with regard to whom or what is not the question). He weighs his chances, he counts on "someday," his retirement or the labor of his sons. He still thinks that something in his life can be directed. In truth, he acts as if he were free, even if all the facts make a point of contradicting that liberty. But after the absurd, everything is upset. That idea that "I am," my way of acting as if everything has a meaning (even if, on occasion, I said that nothing has)—all that is given the lie in vertiginous fashion by the absurdity of a possible death. Thinking of the future, establishing aims for oneself, having preferences—all this presupposes a belief in freedom, even if one occasionally ascertains that one doesn't feel it. But at that moment I am well aware that that higher liberty, that freedom *to be*, which alone can serve as basis for a truth, does not exist. Death is there as the only reality. After death the chips are down. I am not even free, either, to perpetuate myself, but a slave, and, above all, a slave without hope of an eternal revolution, without recourse to contempt. And who without revolution and without contempt can remain a slave? What freedom can exist in the fullest sense without assurance of eternity?

But at the same time the absurd man realizes that hitherto he was bound to that postulate of freedom on the illusion of which he was living. In a certain sense, that hampered him. To the extent to which he imagined a purpose to his life, he adapted himself to the demands of a purpose to be achieved and became the slave of his liberty. Thus I could not act otherwise than as the father (or the engineer or the leader of a nation, or the post-office sub-clerk) that I am preparing to be. I think I can choose to be that rather than something else. I think so unconsciously, to be sure. But at the same time I strengthen my postulate with the beliefs of those around me, with the presumptions of my human environment (others are so sure of being free, and that cheerful mood is so contagious!). However far one may remain from any presumption, moral or social, one is partly influenced by them and even, for the best among them (there are good and bad presumptions), one adapts one's life to them. Thus the absurd man realizes that he was not really free. To speak clearly, to the extent to which I hope, to which I worry about a truth that might be individual to me, about a way of being or creating, to the extent to which I arrange my life and prove thereby that I accept its having a meaning, I create for myself

barriers between which I confine my life. I do like so many bureaucrats of the mind and heart who only fill me with disgust and whose only vice, I now see clearly, is to take man's freedom seriously.

The absurd enlightens me on this point: there is no future. Henceforth this is the reason for my inner freedom. I shall use two comparisons here. Mystics, to begin with, find freedom in giving themselves. By losing themselves in their god, by accepting his rules, they become secretly free. In spontaneously accepted slavery they recover a deeper independence. But what does that freedom mean? It may be said, above all, that they *feel* free with regard to themselves, and not so much free as liberated. Likewise, completely turned toward death (taken here as the most obvious absurdity), the absurd man feels released from everything outside that passionate attention crystallizing in him. He enjoys a freedom with regard to common rules. It can be seen at this point that the initial themes of existential philosophy keep their entire value. The return to consciousness, the escape from everyday sleep represent the first steps of absurd freedom. But it is existential *preaching* that is alluded to, and with it that spiritual leap which basically escapes consciousness. In the same way (this is my second comparison) the slaves of antiquity did not belong to themselves. But they knew that freedom which consists in not feeling responsible.[1] Death, too, has patrician hands which, while crushing, also liberate.

Losing oneself in that bottomless certainty, feeling henceforth sufficiently remote from one's own life to increase it and take a broad view of it—this involves the principle of a liberation. Such new independence has a definite time limit, like any freedom of action. It does not write a check on eternity. But it takes the place of the illusions of *freedom*, which all stopped with death. The divine availability of the condemned man before whom the prison doors open in a certain early dawn, that unbelievable disinterestedness with regard to everything except for the pure flame of life—it is clear that death and the absurd are here the principles of the only reasonable freedom: that which a human heart can experience and live. This is a second consequence. The absurd man thus catches sight of a burning and frigid, transparent and limited universe in which nothing is possible but everything is given, and beyond which all is collapse and nothingness. He can then decide to accept such a universe and draw from it his strength, his refusal to hope, and the unyielding evidence of a life without consolation.

But what does life mean in such a universe? Nothing else for the moment but indifference to the future and a desire to use up everything that is given. Belief in the meaning of life always implies a scale of values, a choice, our preferences. Belief in the absurd, according to our definitions, teaches the contrary. But this is worth examining.

Knowing whether or not one can live *without appeal* is all that interests me. I do not want to get out of my depth. This aspect of life being given me, can I adapt myself to it? Now, faced with this particular concern, belief in the absurd is tantamount to substituting the quantity of experiences for the quality. If I convince myself that this life has no other aspect than that of the absurd, if I feel that its whole equilibrium depends on that perpetual opposition between my conscious revolt and the darkness in which it struggles, if I admit that my freedom has no meaning except in relation to its limited fate, then I must say that what counts is not the best living but the most living. It is not up to me to wonder if this is vulgar or revolting, elegant or deplorable. Once and for all, value judgments are discarded here in favor of factual judgments. I have merely to draw the conclusions from what I can see and to risk nothing that is hypothetical. Supposing that living in this way were not honorable, then true

propriety would command me to be dishonorable.

The most living, in the broadest sense, that rule means nothing. It calls for definition. It seems to begin with the fact that the notion of quantity has not been sufficiently explored. For it can account for a large share of human experience. A man's rule of conduct and his scale of values have no meaning except through the quantity and variety of experiences he has been in a position to accumulate. Now, the conditions of modern life impose on the majority of men the same quantity of experiences and consequently the same profound experience. To be sure, there must also be taken into consideration the individual's spontaneous contribution, the "given" element in him. But I cannot judge of that, and let me repeat that my rule here is to get along with the immediate evidence. I see, then, that the individual character of a common code of ethics lies not so much in the ideal importance of its basic principles as in the norm of an experience that it is possible to measure. To stretch a point somewhat, the Greeks had the code of their leisure just as we have the code of our eight-hour day. But already many men among the most tragic cause us to foresee that a longer experience changes this table of values. They make us imagine that adventurer of the everyday who through mere quantity of experiences would break all records (I am purposely using this sports expression) and would thus win his own code of ethics.[2] Yet let's avoid romanticism and just ask ourselves what such an attitude may mean to a man with his mind made up to take up his bet and to observe strictly what he takes to be the rules of the game.

Breaking all the records is first and foremost being faced with the world as often as possible. How can that be done without contradictions and without playing on words? For on the one hand the absurd teaches that all experiences are unimportant, and on the other it urges toward the greatest quantity of experiences.

How, then, can one fail to do as so many of those men I was speaking of earlier—choose the form of life that brings us the most possible of that human matter, thereby introducing a scale of values that on the other hand one claims to reject?

But again it is the absurd and its contradictory life that teaches us. For the mistake is thinking that that quantity of experiences depends on the circumstances of our life when it depends solely on us. Here we have to be oversimple. To two men living the same number of years, the world always provides the same sum of experiences. It is up to us to be conscious of them. Being aware of one's life, one's revolt, one's freedom, and to the maximum, is living, and to the maximum. Where lucidity dominates, the scale of values becomes useless. Let's be even more simple. Let us say that the sole obstacle, the sole deficiency to be made good, is constituted by premature death. Thus it is that no depth, no emotion, no passion, and no sacrifice could render equal in the eyes of the absurd man (even if he wished it so) a conscious life of forty years and a lucidity spread over sixty years.[3] Madness and death are his irreparables. Man does not choose. The absurd and the extra life it involves *therefore do not depend on man's will,* but on its contrary, which is death.[4] Weighing words carefully, it is altogether a question of luck. One just has to be able to consent to this. There will never be any substitute for twenty years of life and experience.

By what is an odd inconsistency in such an alert race, the Greeks claimed that those who died young were beloved of the gods. And that is true only if you are willing to believe that entering the ridiculous world of the gods is forever losing the purest of joys, which is feeling, and feeling on this earth. The present and the succession of presents before a constantly conscious soul is the ideal of the absurd man. But the word "ideal" rings false in this connection. It is not even his vocation, but merely the third

consequence of his reasoning. Having started from an anguished awareness of the inhuman, the meditation on the absurd returns at the end of its itinerary to the very heart of the passionate flames of human revolt.[5]

Thus I draw from the absurd three consequences, which are my revolt, my freedom, and my passion. By the mere activity of consciousness I transform into a rule of life what was an invitation to death—and I refuse suicide. I know, to be sure, the dull resonance that vibrates throughout these days. Yet I have but a word to say: that it is necessary. When Nietzsche writes: "It clearly seems that the chief thing in heaven and on earth is to *obey* at length and in a single direction: in the long run there results something for which it is worth the trouble of living on this earth as, for example, virtue, art, music, the dance, reason, the mind—something that transfigures, something delicate, mad, or divine," he elucidates the rule of a really distinguished code of ethics. But he also points the way of the absurd man. Obeying the flame is both the easiest and the hardest thing to do. However, it is good for man to judge himself occasionally. He is alone in being able to do so.

"Prayer," says Alain, "is when night descends over thought." "But the mind must meet the night," reply the mystics and the existentials. Yes, indeed, but not that night that is born under closed eyelids and through the mere will of man—dark, impenetrable night that the mind calls up in order to plunge into it. If it must encounter a night, let it be rather that of despair, which remains lucid—polar night, vigil of the mind, whence will arise perhaps that white and virginal brightness which outlines every object in the light of the intelligence. At that degree, equivalence encounters passionate understanding. Then it is no longer even a question of judging the existential leap. It resumes its place amid the age-old fresco of human attitudes. For the spectator, if he is conscious, that leap is still absurd. In so far as it thinks it solves the paradox, it reinstates it intact. On this score, it is stirring. On this score, everything resumes its place and the absurd world is reborn in all its splendor and diversity.

But it is bad to stop, hard to be satisfied with a single way of seeing, to go without contradiction, perhaps the most subtle of all spiritual forces. The preceding merely defines a way of thinking. But the point is to live.

NOTES

1.   I am concerned here with a factual comparison, not with an apology of humility. The absurd man is the contrary of the reconciled man.

2.   Quantity sometimes constitutes quality. If I can believe the latest restatements of scientific theory, all matter is constituted by centers of energy. Their greater or lesser quantity makes its specificity more or less remarkable. A billion ions and one ion differ not only in quantity but also in quality. It is easy to find an analogy in human experience.

3.   Same reflection on a notion as different as the idea of eternal nothingness. It neither adds anything to nor subtracts anything from reality. In psychological experience of nothingness, it is by the consideration of what will happen in two thousand years that our own nothingness truly takes on meaning. In one of its aspects, eternal nothingness is made up precisely of the sum of lives to come which will not be ours.

4.   The will is only the agent here: it tends to maintain consciousness. It provides a discipline of life, and that is appreciable.

5.   What matters is coherence. We start out here from acceptance of the world. But Oriental thought teaches that one can indulge in the same effort of logic by choosing *against* the world. That is just as legitimate and gives this essay its perspectives and its limits. But when the negation of the world is pursued just as rigorously, one often achieves (in certain Vedantic schools) similar results regarding, for instance, the indifference of works. In a book of great importance, *Le Choix*, Jean Grenier establishes in this way a veritable "philosophy of indifference."

20 Why Freedom Pays

Mill

A liberal thinker, John Stuart Mill (1806–1873) was opposed to forms of political tyranny that restrict freedom of thought, discussion, and action. He was also opposed to the "tyranny of the majority," which he felt was characteristic of his times. Under this kind of tyranny, which can flourish under the pretense of democratic government, society itself becomes a tyrant; collective opinions exert tremendous pressures upon individuals to conform, and those who dissent suffer from powerful social sanctions that make them feel isolated, rejected, and ostracized. Those moral standards that are approved by the majority are not to be questioned by individuals, since such questioning undermines the customary and traditional values that support the social order. Customary beliefs, not philosophically examined ideas, must guide human behavior. Those who question such beliefs are often seen as threats to the status quo and as enemies of the people.

Such substitutes for rational inquiry, Mill believes, result in placing prejudice above reasoning, dogmatism above research, and in bestowing infallibility upon individuals and institutions whose interest may be in applying sanctions, including physical punishment, upon dissenting persons. Consequently, often the highest exemplars of human virtue suffer gross social injustice. Socrates is condemned as a corrupter of youth and forced to drink hemlock; Jesus is accused of blasphemy and crucified. Despite their unjust fates, such individuals nevertheless usually do succeed in rendering great service to the society that mistreats and condemns them. Mill is convinced that "to discover to the world something which deeply concerns it, and of which it was previously ignorant; to prove to it that it had been mistaken on some vital point of temporal or spiritual interest, is as important a service as a human being can render to his fellow creatures."[1]

This service to society is often overlooked, ignored, or underestimated. In fact, some excuse their own lack of courage or lack of interest in preserving and furthering freedom of expression by repeating the dictum that truth always triumphs over persecution in the long run or, as Dr. Samuel Johnson believed, that truth even requires persecution in order to triumph. Mill rejects such beliefs as contrary to experience, citing numerous historical instances of truths that were put down by persecution.[2] Men can be as zealous to perpetuate error as truth, and, in Mill's view, "it is a piece of idle sentimentality that truth, merely as truth, has any inherent power denied to error of prevailing against the dungeon and the stake."[3] In our own time, heretics are seldom put to death in civilized countries, but they are often victims of methods no less effective and insidious. Under the pretense of maintaining a so-called healthy society, whether communist, fascist, or capitalist, dissent is often stigmatized and silenced, thus destroying the possibility of critical judgment and social change.

Not only heretics suffer from restrictions on freedom of thought and discussion, Mill points out; ordinary men do, too. A "closed society" eventually cramps everyone's mental development, atrophies creative faculties, and poisons human aspirations at their source. A few great intellects may rise above the mental stagnation but an intellectually active people can never emerge. Only in the free exchange of ideas can men develop their intellectual resources and awaken a desire to realize more fully their potentialities as unique individuals.

Individuality, in Mill's view, is one of the basic elements of well-being. Unless a person is free to follow his own interests, to develop his own lifestyle, and to act spontaneously when and howsoever he chooses—insofar as his actions do not harm others or restrict their individuality—a person is not genuinely free. In fact, to grow more free is to grow more individualized and to become more of a unique person. Uniformity, standardization, and conformity may sometimes make life easier and more efficient to manage and, in certain situations, may even be necessary, but they are nonetheless enemies of individuality and must be guarded against if life is to become richer, more diversified, and challenging. For, in Mill's words, "whatever crushes individuality is despotism."[4]

Mill believes that, even from a purely selfish point of view, we should encourage others to develop their individuality as freely and fully as possible. First of all, as more people develop their individuality, there are more fulfilled and thus more happy people in the world manifesting more happiness in which others can share. Furthermore, individuality is the principle of innovation and originality. Without it, beliefs would become ossified and practices mechanical. Traditions would remain unchallenged. Life would become a bore. Mankind would be robbed of its geniuses, the most individual and creative of all people, for they "can only breathe freely in an atmosphere of freedom."[5]

For these and other reasons he elaborated upon in *On Liberty*, Mill believes that all wise men and women will encourage individuality and not merely tolerate but appreciate eccentricity. Only in this way can the despotism of custom be overthrown and cult of conformity be dispersed. Mill catalogues a mass of influences he considers hostile to individuality in his time and foresees their strengthening rather than weakening in the future. The growth of government bureaucracies, the leveling down of classes, the extension of education to the masses, the expansion of public services, the industrial system with its regimentation of people and its standardization of products, and the increased influence of mass media are some of the major influences that Mill mentions as having strengthened "the tyranny of opinion."[6] "In this age," Mill writes in the midst of the Victorian age in England, "the mere example of non-conformity, the mere refusal to bend a knee to custom, is itself a service."[7] Eccentricity is not a sign of decadence in a society, Mill concludes, but is symptomatic of a free, tolerant, and vigorous environment in which geniuses can be spawned and the greatest happiness of the greatest number of individuals becomes a realizable ideal.

NOTES

1.   John Stuart Mill, *On Liberty* (New York: John W. Lovell, n.d.), chap. 2, pp. 48–49.

2.   Ibid., chap. 2, p. 50.

3.   Ibid.

4.   Ibid., chap. 3, p. 107.

5.   Ibid., p. 109.

6.   Ibid., pp. 112–13.

7.   Ibid., p. 112.

On Liberty

The object of this Essay is to assert one very simple principle, as entitled to govern absolutely the dealings of society with the individual in the way of compulsion and control, whether the means used be physical force in the form of legal penalties, or the moral coercion of public opinion. That principle is, that the sole end for which mankind are warranted, individually or collectively, in interfering with the liberty of action of any of their number, is self-protection. That the only purpose for which power can be rightfully exercised over any-member of a civilised community, against his will, is to prevent harm to others. His own good, either physical or moral, is not a sufficient warrant. He cannot rightfully be compelled to do or forbear because it will be better for him to do so, because it will make him happier, because, in the opinions of others, to do so would be wise, or even right. These are good reasons for remonstrating with him, or reasoning with him, or persuading him, or entreating him, but not for compelling him, or visiting him with any evil in case he do otherwise. To justify that, the conduct from which it is desired to deter him must be calculated to produce evil to someone else. The only part of the conduct of anyone, for which he is amenable to society, is that which concerns others. In the part which merely concerns himself, his independence is, of right,

absolute. Over himself, over his own body and mind, the individual is sovereign.

It is, perhaps, hardly necessary to say that this doctrine is meant to apply only to human beings in the maturity of their faculties. We are not speaking of children, or of young persons below the age which the law may fix as that of manhood or womanhood. Those who are still in a state to require being taken care of by others, must be protected against their own actions as well as against external injury. For the same reason, we may leave out of consideration those backward states of society in which the race itself may be considered as in its nonage. The early difficulties in the way of spontaneous progress are so great, that there is seldom any choice of means for overcoming them; and a ruler full of the spirit of improvement is warranted in the use of any expedients that will attain an end, perhaps otherwise unattainable. Despotism is a legitimate mode of government in dealing with barbarians, provided the end be their improvement, and the means justified by actually effecting that end. Liberty, as a principle, has no application to any state of things anterior to the time when mankind have become capable of being improved by free and equal discussion. Until then, there is nothing for them but implicit obedience to an Akbar or a Charlemagne, if they are so fortunate to find one. But as soon as mankind have attained the capacity of being guided to their own improvement by conviction or persuasion (a period long since reached in all nations with whom we need here

From John Stuart Mill, *On Liberty* (New York: John W. Lovell, n.d.), chaps. 1–2, pp. 20–93 (with omissions).

concern ourselves), compulsion, either in the direct form or in that of pains and penalties for non-compliance, is no longer admissible as a means to their own good, and justifiable only for the security of others.

It is proper to state that I forego any advantage which could be derived to my argument from the idea of abstract right, as a thing independent of utility. I regard utility as the ultimate appeal on all ethical questions; but it must be utility in the largest sense, grounded on the permanent interests of a man as a progressive being. Those interests, I contend, authorize the subjection of individual spontaneity to external control, only in respect to those actions of each which concern the interest of other people. If any one does an act hurtful to others, there is a *prima facie* case for punishing him, by law, or, where legal penalties are not safely applicable, by general disapprobation. There are also many positive acts for the benefit of others, which he may rightfully be compelled to perform; such as to give evidence in a court of justice; to bear his fair share in the common defence, or in any other joint work necessary to the interest of the society of which he enjoys the protection; and to perform certain acts of individual beneficence, such as saving a fellow-creature's life, or interposing to protect the defenceless against ill-usage, things which whenever it is obviously a man's duty to do, he may rightfully be made responsible to society for not doing. A person may cause evil to others not only by his actions but by his inaction, and in either case he is justly accountable to them for the injury. The latter case, it is true, requires a much more cautious exercise of compulsion than the former. To make any one answerable for doing evil to others is the rule; to make him answerable for not preventing evil is, comparatively speaking, the exception. Yet there are many cases clear enough and grave enough to justify that exception. In all things which regard the external relations of the individual, he is *de jure* amenable to those whose interests are

concerned, and, if need be, to society as their protector. There are often good reasons for not holding him to the responsibility; but these reasons must arise from the special expediencies of the case: either because it is a kind of case in which he is on the whole likely to act better, when left to his own discretion, than when controlled in any way in which society have it in their power to control him; or because the attempt to exercise control would produce other evils, greater than those which it would prevent. When such reasons as these preclude the enforcement of responsibility, the conscience of the agent himself should step into the vacant judgment seat, and protect those interests of others who have no external protection; judging himself all the more rigidly, because the case does not admit of his being made accountable to the judgment of his fellow-creatures.

But there is a sphere of action in which society, as distinguished from the individual, has, if any, only an indirect interest; comprehending all that portion of a person's life and conduct which affects only himself, or if it also affects others, only with their free, voluntary, and undeceived consent and participation. When I say only himself, I mean directly, and in the first instance; for whatever affects himself, may affect others through himself; and the objection which may be grounded on this contingency, will receive consideration in the sequel. This, then, is the appropriate region of human liberty. It comprises, first, the inward domain of consciousness; demanding liberty of conscience in the most comprehensive sense; liberty of thought and feeling; absolute freedom of opinion and sentiment on all subjects, practical or speculative, scientific, moral, or theological. The liberty of expressing and publishing opinions may seem to fall under a different principle, since it belongs to that part of the conduct of an individual which concerns other people; but, being almost of as much importance as the liberty of thought itself, and resting in great part on the same reasons, is practically inseparable from it. Secondly, the principle requires liberty of tastes and pursuits; of framing the plan of our life to suit our character; of doing as we like, subject to such consequences as may follow: without impediment from our fellow-creatures, so long as what we do does not harm them, even though they should think our conduct foolish, perverse, or wrong. Thirdly, from this liberty of each individual, follows the liberty, within the same limits, of combination among individuals; freedom to unite, for any purpose not involving harm to others: the persons combining being supposed to be of full age, and not forced or deceived.

No society in which these liberties are not, on the whole, respected, is free, whatever may be its form of government; and none is completely free in which they do not exist absolute and unqualified. The only freedom which deserves the name, is that of pursuing our own good in our own way, so long as we do not attempt to deprive others of theirs, or impede their efforts to obtain it. Each is the proper guardian of his own health, whether bodily, *or* mental and spiritual. Mankind are greater gainers by suffering each other to live as seems good to themselves, than by compelling each to live as seems good to the rest. . . .

Apart from the peculiar tenets of individual thinkers, there is also in the world at large an increasing inclination to stretch unduly the powers of society over the individual, both by the force of opinion, and even by that of legislation; and as the tendency of all the changes taking place in the world is to strengthen society, and diminish the power of the individual, this encroachment is not one of the evils which tend spontaneously to disappear, but, on the contrary, to grow more and more formidable. The disposition of mankind, whether as rulers or as fellow-citizens, to impose their own opinions and inclinations as a rule of conduct on others, is so energetically supported by some of the best and by some of the worst feelings incident to human nature, that it is hardly ever kept upon restraint by anything but want of power; and as the power is not declining, but growing, unless a strong barrier of moral conviction can be raised against the mischief, we must expect, in the present circumstances of the world to see it increase.

It will be convenient for the argument, if, instead of at once entering upon the general thesis, we confine ourselves in the first instance to a single branch of it, on which the principle here stated is, if not fully, yet to a certain point, recognised by the current opinions. This one branch is the Liberty of Thought: from which it is impossible to separate the cognate liberty of speaking and of writing. Although these liberties, to some considerable amount, form part of the political morality of all countries which profess religious toleration and free institutions, the grounds, both philosophical and practical, on which they rest, are perhaps not so familiar to the general mind, nor so thoroughly appreciated by many even of the leaders of opinion, as might have been expected. Those grounds, when rightly understood, are of much wider application than to only one division of the subject, and a thorough consideration of this part of the question will be found the best introduction to the remainder. Those to whom nothing which I am about to say will be new, may therefore, I hope, excuse me, if on a subject which for now three centuries has been so often discussed, I venture on one discussion more. . . .

The time, it is to be hoped, is gone by, when any defence would be necessary of the "liberty of the press" as one of the securities against corrupt or tyrannical government. No argument, we may suppose, can now be needed, against permitting a legislature or an executive, not identified in interest with the people, to prescribe opinions to them, and determine what doctrines or what arguments they shall be allowed to hear. This aspect of the question, besides, has been so often and so triumphantly enforced by preceding writers, that it needs not be specially insisted on in this place. Though the law of England, on the subject of the press, is as servile to this day as it was in the time of the Tudors, there is little danger of its being actually put in force against political discussion, except during some temporary panic, when fear of insurrection drives ministers and judges from their propriety; and, speaking generally, it is not, in constitutional countries, to be apprehended, that the government, whether completely responsible to the people or not, will often attempt to control the expression of opinion, except when in doing so it makes itself the organ of the general intolerance of the public. Let us suppose, therefore, that the government is entirely at one with the people, and never thinks of exerting any power of coercion unless in agreement with what it conceives to be their voice. But I deny the right of the people to exercise such coercion, either by themselves or by their government. The power itself is illegitimate. The best government has no more title to it than the worst. It is as noxious, or more noxious, when exerted in accordance with public opinion, than when in opposition to it. If all mankind minus one were of one opinion, and only one person were of the contrary opinion, mankind would be no more justified in silencing that one person, than he, if he had the power, would be justified in silencing mankind. Were an opinion a personal possession of no value except to the owner; if to be obstructed in the enjoyment of it were simply a private injury, it would make some difference whether the injury was inflicted only on a few persons or on many. But the peculiar evil of silencing the expression of an opinion is, that it is robbing the human race: posterity as well as the existing generation; those who dissent from the opinion, still more than those who hold it. If the opinion is right, they are deprived of the opportunity of exchanging error for truth: if wrong, they lose, what is almost as great a benefit, the clearer perception and livelier impression of truth, produced by its collision with error.

It is necessary to consider separately these two hypotheses, each of which has a distinct branch of the argument corresponding to it. We can never be sure that the opinion we are endeavouring to stifle is a false opinion; and if we were sure, stifling it would be an evil still.

First, the opinion which it is attempted to suppress by authority may possibly be true. Those who desire to suppress it, of course deny its truth; but they are not infallible. They have no authority to decide the question for all mankind, and exclude every other person from the means of judging. To refuse a hearing to an opinion, because they are sure that it is false, is to assume that *their* certainty is the same thing as *absolute* certainty. All silencing of discussion is an assumption of infallibility. Its condemnation may be allowed to rest on this common argument, not the worse for being common.

Unfortunately for the good sense of mankind, the fact of their fallibility is far from carrying the weight in their practical judgment which is always allowed to it in theory; for while every one well knows himself to be fallible, few think it necessary to take any precautions against their own fallibility, or admit the supposition that any opinion, of which they feel very certain, may be one of the examples of the error to which they acknowledge themselves to be liable. Absolute princes, or others who are accustomed to unlimited deference, usually feel this complete confidence in their own opinions on nearly all subjects. People more happily situated, who sometimes hear their opinions disputed, and are not wholly unused to be set right when they are wrong, place the same unbounded reliance only on such of their opinions as are shared by all who surround them, or to whom they habitually defer; for in proportion to a man's want of confidence in his own solitary judgment, does he usually repose, with implicit trust, on the infallibility of "the world" in general. And the world, to each individual, means the part of it with which he comes in contact: his party, his sect, his church, his class of society; the man may be called, by comparison, almost liberal and large-minded to whom it means anything so comprehensive as his own country or his own age. Nor is his faith in this collective authority at all shaken by his being aware that other ages, countries, sects, churches, classes, and parties have thought, and even now think, the exact reverse. He devolves upon his own world the responsibility of being in the right against the dissentient worlds of other people; and it never troubles him that mere accident has decided which of these numerous worlds is the object of his reliance, and that the same causes which make him a Churchman in London, would have made him a Buddhist or a Confucian in Pekin. Yet it is as evident in itself, as any amount of argument can make it, that ages are no more infallible than individuals; every age having held many opinions which subsequent ages have deemed not only false but absurd; and it is as certain that many opinions now general will be rejected by future ages, as it is that many, once general, are rejected by the present.

The objection likely to be made to this argument would probably take some such form as the following. There is no greater assumption of infallibility in forbidding the propagation of error, than in any other thing which is done by public authority on its own judgment and responsibility. Judgment is given to men that they may use it. Because it may be used erroneously, are men to be told that they ought not to use it at all? To prohibit what they think pernicious, is not claiming exemption from error, but fulfilling the duty incumbent on them, although fallible, of acting on their conscientious conviction. If we were never to act on our opinions, because those opinions may be wrong, we should leave all our interest uncared for, and all our duties unperformed. An objection which applies to all conduct can be no valid objection to conduct in particular. It is the duty of governments and of individuals, to form the truest opinions they can; to form them carefully, and never impose them upon others unless they are quite sure of being right. But when they are sure (such reasoners may say), it is not conscientiousness but cowardice to shrink from acting on their opinions, and allow doctrines from which they honestly think dangerous to the welfare of mankind, either in this life or in another, to be scattered abroad without restraint, because other people, in less enlightened times, have persecuted opinions now believed to be true. Let us take care, it may be said, not to make the same mistake; but governments and nations have made mistakes in other things, which are not denied to be fit subjects for the exercise of authority: they have laid on bad taxes, made unjust wars. Ought we therefore to lay on no taxes, and, under whatever provocation, make no wars: Men, and governments, must act to the best of their ability. There is no such thing as absolute certainty, but there is assurance sufficient for the purposes of human life. We may, and must, assume our opinion to be true for the guidance of our own conduct: and it is assuming no more when we forbid bad men to pervert society by the propagation of opinions which we regard as false and pernicious.

I answer, that it is assuming very much more. There is the greatest difference between presuming an opinion to be true, because, with every opportunity for contesting it, it has not been refuted, and assuming its truth for the purpose of not permitting its refutation. Complete liberty of contradicting and disproving our opinion is the very condition which justifies us in assuming its truth for purposes of action; and on no other terms can a being with human faculties have any rational assurance of being right.

When we consider either the history of opinion, or the ordinary conduct of human life, to what is it to be ascribed that the one and the other are no worse than they are? Not certainly to the inherent force of the human understanding; for, on any matter not self-evident, there are ninety-nine persons totally incapable of judging of it for one who is capable; and the capacity of the hundredth person is only comparative for the majority of the eminent men of every past generation held many opinions now known to be erroneous, and did or approved numerous things which no one will now justify. Why is it, then, that there is on the whole a preponderance among mankind of rational opinions and rational conduct? If there really is this preponderance—which there must be unless human affairs are, and have always been, in almost desperate state—it is owing to a quality of the human mind, the source of everything respectable in man either as an intellectual or as a moral being, namely, that his errors are corrigible. He is capable of rectifying his mistakes, by discussion and experience. Not by experience alone. There must be discussion, to show how experience is to be interpreted. Wrong opinions and practices gradually yield to fact and argument; but facts and arguments, to produce any effect on the mind, must be brought before it. Very few facts are able to tell their own story, without comments to bring out their meaning. The whole strength and value, then, of human judgment, depending on the one property, that it can be set right when it is wrong, reliance can be placed on it only when the means of setting it right are kept constantly at hand. In the case of any person whose judgment is really deserving of confidence, how has it become so? Because he has kept his mind open to criticism of his opinions and conduct. Because it has been his practice to listen to all that could be said against him; to profit by as much of it as was just, and expound to himself, and upon occasion to others, the fallacy of what was fallacious. Because he has felt, that the only way in which a human being can make some approach to knowing the whole of a sub-

ject, is by hearing what can be said about it by persons of every variety of opinion, and studying all modes in which it can be looked at by every character of mind. No wise man ever acquired his wisdom in any mode but this; nor is it in the nature of human intellect to become wise in any other manner. The steady habit of correcting and completing his own opinion by collating it with those of others, so far from causing doubt and hesitation in carrying it into practice, is the only stable foundation for a just reliance on it: for, being cognisant of all that can, at least obviously, be said against him, and having taken up his position against all gainsayers—knowing that he has sought for objections and difficulties, instead of avoiding them, and has shut out no light which can be thrown upon the subject from any quarter—he has a right to think his judgment better than that of any person or any multitude, who have not gone through a similar process. . . .

Let us now pass to the second division of the argument, and dismissing the supposition that any of the received opinions may be false, let us assume them to be true, and examine into the worth of the manner in which they are likely to be held, when their truth is not freely and openly canvassed. However unwillingly a person who has a strong opinion may admit the possibility that his opinion may be false, he ought to be moved by the consideration that, however true it may be, if it is not fully, frequently, and fearlessly discussed, it will be held as a dead dogma, not a living truth.

There is a class of persons (happily not quite so numerous as formerly) who think it enough if a person assents undoubtingly to what they think true, though he has no knowledge whatever of the grounds of the opinion, and could not make a tenable defence of it against the most superficial objections. Such persons, if they can once get their creed taught from authority, naturally think that no good, and some harm, comes of its being allowed to be questioned. Where their influence prevails, they make it nearly impossible for the received opinion to be rejected wisely and considerately, though it may still be rejected rashly and ignorantly; for to shut out discussion entirely is seldom possible, and when it once gets in, beliefs not grounded on convictions are apt to give way before the slightest semblance of an argument. Waiving, however, this possibility—assuming that the true opinion abides in the mind, but abides as a prejudice, a belief independent of, and proof against, argument—this is not the way in which truth ought to be held by a rational being. This is not knowing the truth. Truth, thus held, is but one superstition the more, accidently clinging to the words which enunciate a truth.

If the intellect and judgment of mankind ought to be cultivated, a thing which Protestants at least do not deny, on what can these faculties be more appropriately exercised by any one, than on the things which concern him so much that it is considered necessary for him to hold opinions on them? If the cultivation of the understanding consists in one thing more than in another, it is surely in learning the grounds of one's own opinions. Whatever people believe, on subjects on which it is of the first importance to believe rightly, they ought to be able to defend against at least the common objections. But, some one may say, "Let them be *taught* the grounds of their opinions. It does not follow that opinions must be merely parroted because they are never heard controverted. Persons who learn geometry do not simply commit the theorems to memory, but understand and learn likewise the demonstrations; and it would be absurd to say that they remain ignorant of the grounds of geometrical truths, because they never hear any one deny, and attempt to disprove them." Undoubtedly: and such teaching suffices on a subject like mathematics, where there is nothing at all to be said on the wrong side of the question. The peculiarity of the evidence of mathematical truths is that all the argument is on one side.

There are no objections, and no answers to objections. But on every subject on which difference of opinion is possible, the truth depends on a balance to be struck between two sets of conflicting reasons. Even in natural philosophy, there is always some other explanation possible of the same facts: some geocentric theory instead of heliocentric, some phlogiston instead of oxygen; and it has to be shown why that other theory cannot be the true one; and until this is shown, and until we know how it is shown, we do not understand the grounds of our opinion. But when we turn to subjects infinitely more complicated, to morals, religion, politics, social relations, and the business of life, three-fourths of the arguments for every disputed opinion consists in dispelling the appearances which favour some opinion different from it. The greatest orator, save one, of antiquity, has left it on record that he always studied his adversary's case with as great, if not still greater, intensity than even his own. What Cicero practised as the means of forensic success requires to be imitated by all who study any subject in order to arrive at the truth. He who knows only his own side of the case, knows little of that. His reasons may be good, and no one may have been able to refute them. But if he is equally unable to refute the reasons on the opposite side; if he does not so much as know what they are, he has no ground for preferring either opinion. The rational position for him would be suspension of judgment, and unless he contents himself with that, he is either led by authority, or adopts, like the generality of the world, the side to which he feels most inclination. Nor is it enough that he should hear the arguments of adversaries from his own teachers, presented as they state them, and accompanied by what they offer as refutations. That is not the way to do justice to the arguments, or bring them into real contact with his own mind. He must be able to hear them from persons who actually believe them; who defend them in earnest, and do their very most for

them. He must know them in their most plausible and persuasive form; he must feel the
whole force of the difficulty which the true
view of the subject has to encounter and dis-
pose of; else he will never really possess himself
of the portion of truth which meets and re-
moves that difficulty. Ninety-nine in a hundred
of what are called educated men are in this condition; even of those who can argue fluently for
their opinions. Their conclusion may be true,
but it might be false for anything they know:
they have never thrown themselves into the
mental position of those who think differently
from them, and considered what such persons
may have to say; and consequently they do not,
in any proper sense of the word, know the doctrine which they themselves profess. They do
not know those parts of it which explain and
justify the remainder; the considerations which
show that a fact which seemingly conflicts with
another is reconcilable with it, or that, of two
apparently strong reasons, one and not the other
ought to be preferred. All that part of the truth
which turns the scale, and decides the judgment
of a completely informed mind, they are strangers to; nor is it ever really known, but to those
who have attended equally and impartially to
both sides, and endeavoured to see the reasons
of both in the strongest light. So essential is this
discipline to a real understanding of moral and
human subjects, that if opponents of all important truths do not exist, it is indispensable to
imagine them, and supply them with the strongest arguments which the most skillful devil's
advocate can conjure up. . . .

It still remains to speak of one of the principal causes which make diversity of opinion
advantageous, and will continue to do so until
mankind shall have entered a stage of intellectual advancement which at present seems at an
incalculable distance. We have hitherto considered only two possibilities: that the received
opinion may be false, and some other opinion,
consequently, true; or that, the received opinion
being true, a conflict with the opposite error is
essential to a clear apprehension and deep

feeling of its truth. But there is a commoner
case than either of these; when the conflicting
doctrines, instead of being one true and the
other false, share the truth between them; and
the nonconforming opinion is needed to supply
the remainder of the truth, of which the received doctrine embodies only a part. Popular
opinions, on subjects not palpable to sense, are
often true, but seldom or never the whole truth.
They are a part of the truth; sometimes a
greater, sometimes a smaller part, but exaggerated, distorted, and disjointed from the
truths by which they ought to be accompanied
and limited. Heretical opinions, on the other
hand, are generally some of these suppressed
and neglected truths, bursting the bonds which
kept them down, and either seeking reconciliation with the truth contained in the common
opinion, or fronting it as enemies, and setting
themselves up, with similar exclusiveness, as
the whole truth. The latter case is hitherto the
most frequent, as in the human mind, one-sid-
edness has always been the rule, and many-
sidedness the exception. Hence, even in revolutions of opinion, one part of the truth usually
sets while another rises. Even progress, which
ought to superadd, for the most part only substitutes one partial and incomplete truth for
another; improvement consisting chiefly in this,
that the new fragment of truth is more wanted,
more adapted to the needs of the time, than
that which it displaces. Such being the partial
character of prevailing opinions, even when
resting on a true foundation; every opinion
which embodies somewhat of the portion of
truth which the common opinion omits, ought
to be considered precious, with whatever
amount of error and confusion that truth may
be blended. No sober judge of human affairs
will feel bound to be indignant because those
who force on our notice truths which we should
otherwise have overlooked, overlook some of
those which we see. Rather, he will think that
so long as popular truth is one-sided, it is more
desirable than otherwise that unpopular truth
should have one-sided assertors too; such being

usually the most energetic, and the most likely to compel reluctant attention to the fragment of wisdom which they proclaim as if it were the whole.

Thus, in the eighteenth century, when nearly all the instructed, and all those of the uninstructed who were led by them, were lost in admiration of what is called civilisation, and of the marvels of modern science, literature, and philosophy, and while greatly overrating the amount of unlikeness between the men of modern and those of ancient times, indulged the belief that the whole of the difference was in their own favour; with what a salutary shock did the paradoxes of Rousseau explode like bombshells in the midst, dislocating the compact mass of one-sided opinion, and forcing its elements to recombine in a better form and with additional ingredients. Not that the current opinions were on the whole farther from the truth than to it; they contained more of positive truth, and very much less of error. Nevertheless there lay in Rousseau's doctrine, and has floated down the stream of opinion along with it, a considerable amount of exactly those truths which the popular opinion wanted; and these are the deposit which was left behind when the flood subsided. The superior worth of simplicity of life, the enervating and demoralising effect of the trammels and hypocrisies of artificial society, are ideas which have never been entirely absent from cultivated minds since Rousseau wrote; and they will in time produce their due effect, though at present needing to be asserted as much as ever, and to be asserted by deeds, for words, on this subject have nearly exhausted their power.

In politics, again, it is almost a commonplace, that a party of order or stability, and a party of progress or reform, are both necessary elements of a healthy state of political life; until the one or the other shall have so enlarged its mental grasp as to be a party equally of order and of progress, knowing and distinguishing what is fit to be preserved from what ought to be swept away. Each of these modes of thinking derives its utility from the deficiencies of the other; but it is in a great measure the opposition of the other that keeps each within the limits of reason and sanity. Unless opinions favourable to democracy and to aristocracy, to property and to equality, to co-operation and to competition, to luxury and to abstinence, to sociality and individuality, to liberty and discipline, and all the other standing antagonisms of practical life, are expressed with equal freedom, and enforced and defended with equal talent and energy, there is no chance of both elements obtaining their due; one scale is sure to go up, and the other down. Truth, in the great practical concerns of life, is so much a question of the reconciling and combining of opposites that very few have minds sufficiently capacious and impartial to make the adjustments with an approach to correctness, and it has to be made by the rough process of a struggle between combatants fighting under hostile banners. On any of the great open questions just enumerated, if either of the two opinions has a better claim than the other, not merely to be tolerated, but to be encouraged and countenanced, it is the one which happens at the particular time and place to be in a minority. That is the opinion which, for the time being, represents the neglected interests, the side of human well-being which is in danger of obtaining less than its share. I am aware that there is not, in this country, any intolerance of differences of opinion on most of these topics. They are adduced to show, by admitted and multiplied examples, the universality of the fact, that only through diversity of opinion is there, in the existing state of human intellect, a chance of fair play to all sides of the truth. When there are persons to be found who form an exception to the apparent unanimity of the world on any subject, even if the world is in the right, it is always probable that dissentients have something worth hearing to say for themselves, and that truth would lose something by their silence. . . .

21 Freedom and Control

Rogers & Skinner

Carl Rogers and B. F. Skinner are American psychologists who differ radically in their views on human nature, on the means for attaining the good life, and on freedom. Whereas Rogers is a client-centered therapist who has spent his professional life studying and aiding in the solution of human psychological problems, Skinner is a behaviorist who has devoted much of his time to studying and conditioning the behavior of laboratory animals. Rogers looks within and tries to understand the subjective processes by which one becomes a person; Skinner denies the usefulness of the concept of "personal consciousness" and looks outside to the environment, the external factors which impinge upon the organism, for explaining, predicting, and conditioning animal and human behavior. In studying human behavior, Rogers is primarily interested in establishing better means of communication; Skinner, on the other hand, is primarily interested in establishing better means of control. And, as the following debate between the two psychologists shows, Rogers is deeply committed to a belief in the freedom of human beings, while Skinner rejects the notion of freedom altogether.

Despite these and other differences, Rogers and Skinner have a good deal in common. Both are humanists, focusing attention on the importance of human beings and their values. Both are searching for order, uniformity, and lawfulness as they try to understand human experience and behavior. Both are interested in the role that the social sciences are playing and will increasingly play in the understanding, prediction, and control of man— now and in the future.

In discussing his views on the good life, Rogers stresses that it is a dynamic process rather than a static end to be achieved. "It is a direction not a destination."[1] This direction is one freely chosen by the total organism and has several universal characteristics. Among the characteristics Rogers discusses are an increasing openness to experience, ability to live in the moment, self-confidence, and ability to function more fully.[2] As a client grows in therapy and begins to develop these characteristics, his feeling of freedom increases, that is, he is able to *choose* the direction in which he wants to move, the most deeply satisfying and rewarding direction. From the client's inner subjective point of view, he at last feels free to choose what he *wants* to do. This increased feeling of freedom is proportional to his sense of creativeness. To be creative, Rogers says, is to be one's own judge of the merits of activities and products, and to maintain perpetually "the ability to toy with elements and concepts."[3]

Underlying Rogers' discussion is his view that human nature is basically creative and trustworthy. Like Bellamy, he believes that removing the obstacles and defenses which obstruct the inherent constructive tendencies in human beings will lead to their positive and productive growth. Rogers rejects the view that man is basically irrational and vicious. Learned defensiveness rather than inherent destructiveness accounts for the socially undesirable and personally self-defeating behavior of most human beings. When the person's defenses are gradually eliminated through nondirective client-centered therapy, the person enters into the process of living "with greater range, greater variety, greater richness."[4] To Rogers, "the deeply exciting thing about human beings is that when the individual is inwardly free, he chooses as the good life this process of becoming."[5]

Skinner's approach to the good life is from a much broader social context. What is needed is more behavioral engineers to control people for their own best interest, not more client-centered therapists to liberate them. Skinner agrees with Marx's idea that a new and improved social order is desperately needed; however, his solution is not to revolt against control, but to move toward more rational control and conditioning. Skinner does not ask, Should we allow ourselves to be controlled? We are already controlled by a complex of institutional and environmental factors. He asks, How can we scientifically design a culture to do a better and more efficient job in controlling the conditions under which people live?

Government, industry, education, religion, the family, and other social institutions use modes of control that are, to varying degrees, successful in molding and controlling human behavior. Skinner believes that some modes of control, such as punishment, are inefficient and undesirable because they lead to countercontrols that block the achievement of their intended ends. These should be discarded in favor of methods that use positive rather than negative reinforcement of behavior. Behavior that is reinforced is strengthened. This can be done either by removing aversive, i.e., unwanted stimuli (negative reinforcement), or by rewarding it with attractive, i.e., wanted stimuli (positive reinforcement). Skinner approves of and advises only the latter in satisfactorily controlling human behavior.

Skinner's view of human nature results from a scientific study of human behavior. There is nothing spontaneous or mysterious about human behavior that makes it different from the behavior of other organisms and thus places it outside the domain of scientific methods and principles. To think of man as an autonomous agent who can do what he pleases is to ignore the factors that determine preferences and to posit a freedom of choice that is indefensible against the overwhelming evidence that all behavior is caused. If freedom and dignity must be discarded to make way for predictability and control, then the sooner we discard them the better.

Skinner has devoted a great deal of attention not only to a systematic and intensive study of operant conditioning, but also to the technology of teaching and to problems relating to cultural design and behavioral engineering. He has also shown a keen interest in utopian speculation, planning, and experimentation. This interest is coupled with an awareness that utopias have usually failed in the past and that, at present, the design of a fully utopian cultural pattern may be premature. This does not mean, however, that he thinks we should stop trying to achieve it. At the very least, there can be a piecemeal improvement of cultural practices. The science of behavior is a science in the making. The possibility of a utopia is in direct proportion to the development of this science.

Skinner's vision of a totally planned society is presented in *Walden Two* (1948). Named in honor of Henry David Thoreau's original utopian experiment, Walden Two is a community of a thousand members planned and instituted by T. E. Frazier, a behavioral engineer. The affairs of the community are overseen by a Board of Planners and are carried out by the managers, workers, and scientists, all of whom work on a labor-credit system. There is communal ownership of property and collective sharing of the rights and responsibilities of membership. The cohesive community is virtually self-sufficient. Marriage of couples still exists but, as children are raised in community nurseries and cared for by all members of the utopia, the nuclear family has been replaced by the communal family. Leisure time is plentiful and filled with creative, educational activities. Religion is virtually nonexistent. Moral training is completed by the time a child is six, due to refined techniques of positive reinforcement. In such a carefully controlled community, democracy is considered superfluous because it rests upon the false assumption that man can choose freely and ignores the fact that, in actuality, the state determines man. Totalitarianism is no less inadequate: it fails to be experimental, employs terror and brute force as means of control, and overpropagandizes. What is needed to achieve an ideal society, Frazier insists, is "a constantly experimental attitude" and the courage to develop and consistently apply a science of behavior for the good of mankind.

In a new preface to *Walden Two* written twenty years after its initial publication, Skinner reaffirmed his commitment to the ideal of a planned community similar to the one he had described in his earlier book. An adequate and precise science of behavior will point the way to a transformation of man's cultural environment and thus man himself. Then we shall see at last, Skinner believes, "what man can make of man."

Whatever may be made of man in the future, Skinner stated quite clearly in his most controversial book, *Beyond Freedom and Dignity* (1971), that he would welcome the abolition of "autonomous man," which is, in his view, "a device used to explain what we cannot explain in any other way."[6] We must get rid of such a conception of man before we can begin to understand, predict, and control human behavior. "Only then," Skinner believes, "can we turn from the inferred to the observed, from the miraculous to the natural, from the inaccessible to the manipulable."[7]

The following debate took place, at Skinner's invitation, at the Convention of the American Psychological Association in 1956. As Rogers wrote later, the subject of the debate was a problem "which one day will be seen as a profoundly momentous decision for society."[8]

NOTES

1. Carl R. Rogers, *On Becoming a Person* (Boston: Houghton Mifflin, 1961), p. 186.

2. Ibid., p. 191.

3. Ibid., p. 354.

4. Ibid., p. 195.

5. Ibid., p. 196.

6. B. F. Skinner, *Beyond Freedom and Dignity* (New York: Alfred A. Knopf, 1971), p. 190.

7. Ibid.

8. Rogers, *On Becoming a Person*, p. 364.

Some Issues Concerning the Control of Human Behavior: A Symposium

SKINNER

Science is steadily increasing our power to influence, change, mold—in a word, control—human behavior. It has extended our "understanding" (whatever that may be) so that we deal more successfully with people in nonscientific ways, but it has also identified conditions or variables which can be used to predict and control behavior in a new, and increasingly rigorous, technology. The broad disciplines of government and economics offer examples of this, but there is special cogency in those contributions of anthropology, sociology, and psychology which deal with individual behavior. Carl Rogers has listed some of the achievements to date in a recent paper.[1]

Those of his examples which show or imply the control of the single organism are primarily due, as we should expect, to psychology. It is the experimental study of behavior which carries us beyond awkward or inaccessible "principles," "factors," and so on, to variables which can be directly manipulated.

It is also, and for more or less the same reasons, the conception of human behavior emerging from an experimental analysis which most

From Carl Rogers and B. F. Skinner, "Some Issues Concerning the Control of Human Behavior: A Symposium," in *Science*, Vol. 124, November 30, 1956, pp. 1057–66.

directly challenges traditional views. Psychologists themselves often do not seem to be aware of how far they have moved in this direction. But the change is not passing unnoticed by others. Until only recently it was customary to deny the possibility of a rigorous science of human behavior by arguing, either that a lawful science was impossible because man was a free agent, or that merely statistical predictions would always leave room for personal freedom. But those who used to take this line have become most vociferous in expressing their alarm at the way these obstacles are being surmounted.

Now, the control of human behavior has always been unpopular. Any undisguised effort to control usually arouses emotional reactions. We hesitate to admit, even to ourselves, that we are engaged in control, and we may refuse to control, even when this would be helpful, for fear of criticism. Those who have explicitly avowed an interest in control have been roughly treated by history. Machiavelli is the great prototype. As Macaulay said of him, "Out of his surname they coined an epithet for a knave and out of his Christian name a synonym for the devil." There were obvious reasons. The control that Machiavelli analyzed and recommended, like most political control, used techniques that were aversive to the controllee. The threats and punishments of the bully, like those of the government operating on the same plan, are not designed—whatever their success—to endear themselves to those who are controlled. Even when the techniques themselves are not aversive, control is usually exercised for the selfish purposes of the controller and, hence, has indirectly punishing effects upon others.

Man's natural inclination to revolt against selfish control has been exploited to good purpose in what we call the philosophy and literature of democracy. The doctrine of the rights of man has been effective in arousing individuals to concerted action against governmental and religious tyranny. The literature which has had this effect has greatly extended the number of terms in our language which express reactions to the control of men. But the ubiquity and ease of expression of this attitude spells trouble for any science which may give birth to a powerful technology of behavior. Intelligent men and women, dominated by the humanistic philosophy of the past two centuries, cannot view with equanimity what Andrew Hacker has called "the specter of predictable man."[2] Even the statistical or actuarial prediction of human events, such as the number of fatalities to be expected on a holiday weekend, strikes many people as uncanny and evil, while the prediction and control of individual behavior is regarded as little less than the work of the devil. I am not so much concerned here with the political or economic consequences for psychology, although research following certain channels may well suffer harmful effects. We ourselves, as intelligent men and women, and as exponents of Western thoughts, share these attitudes. They have already interfered with the free exercise of a scientific analysis, and their influence threatens to assume more serious proportions.

Three broad areas of human behavior supply good examples. The first of these—*personal control*—may be taken to include person-to-person relationships in the family, among friends, in social and work groups, and in counseling and psychotherapy. Other fields are *education* and *government*. A few examples from each will show how nonscientific preconceptions are affecting our current thinking about human behavior.

PERSONAL CONTROL

People living together in groups come to control one another with a technique which is not inappropriately called "ethical." When an individual behaves in a fashion acceptable to the group, he receives admiration, approval, affection, and many other reinforcements which increase the likelihood that he will continue to behave in that fashion. When his behavior is not acceptable, he is criticized, censured, blamed, or otherwise punished. In the first case the group calls him "good"; in the second, "bad." This practice is so thoroughly ingrained in our culture that we often fail to see that it is a technique of control. Yet we are almost always engaged in such control, even though the reinforcements and punishments are often subtle.

The practice of admiration is an important part of a culture, because behavior which is otherwise inclined to be weak can be set up and maintained with its help. The individual is especially likely to be praised, admired, or loved when he acts for the group in the face of greater danger, for example, or sacrifices himself or his possessions, or submits to prolonged hardship, or suffers martyrdom. These actions are not admirable in any absolute sense, but they require admiration if they are to be strong. Similarly, we admire people who behave in original or exceptional ways, not because such behavior is itself admirable, but because we do not know how to encourage original or exceptional behavior in any other way. The group acclaims independent, unaided behavior in part because it is easier to reinforce than to help.

As long as this technique of control is misunderstood, we cannot judge correctly an environment in which there is less need for hero-ism, hardship, or independent action. We are likely to argue that such an environment is itself less admirable or produces less admirable people. In the old days, for example, young scholars often lived in undesirable quarters, ate unappetizing or inadequate food, performed unprofitable tasks for a living or to pay for necessary books and materials or publication. Older scholars and other members of the group offered compensating reinforcement in the form of approval and admiration for these sacrifices. When the modern graduate student receives a generous scholarship, enjoys good living condi-tions, and has his research and publication subsidized, the grounds for evaluation seem to be pulled from under us. Such a student no longer *needs* admiration to carry him over a series of obstacles (no matter how much he may need it for other reasons), and, in missing certain familiar objects of admiration, we are likely to conclude that such *conditions* are less admirable. Obstacles to scholarly work may serve as a useful measure of motivation—and we may go wrong unless some substitute is found but we can scarcely defend a deliberate harassment of the student for this purpose. The productivity of any set of conditions can be evaluated only when we have freed our-selves of the attitudes which have been gen-erated in us as members of an ethical group.

A similar difficulty arises from our use of punishment in the form of censure or blame. The concept of responsibility and the related concepts of foreknowledge and choice are used to justify techniques of control using punish-ment. Was So-and-So aware of the probable consequences of his action, and was the action deliberate? If so, we are justified in punishing him. But what does this mean? It appears to be a question concerning the efficacy of the contingent relations between behavior and punishing consequences. We punish behavior because it is objectionable to us or the group, but in a minor refinement of rather recent origin

we have come to withhold punishment when it cannot be expected to have any effect. If the objectionable consequences of an act were ac-cidental and not likely to occur again, there is no point in punishing. We say that the individ-ual was not "aware of the consequences of his action" or that the consequences were not "in-tentional." If the action could not have been avoided—if the individual "had no choice"—punishment is also withheld, as it is if the in-dividual is incapable of being changed by pun-ishment because he is of "unsound mind." In all these cases—different as they are—the indi-vidual is held "not responsible" and goes un-punished.

Just as we say that it is "not fair" to punish a man for something he could not help doing, so we call it "unfair" when one is rewarded be-yond his due or for something he could not help doing. In other words, we also object to wasting *reinforcers* where they are not needed or will do no good. We make the same point with the words *just* and *right*. Thus we have no right to punish the irresponsible, and a man has no right to reinforcers he does not earn or deserve. But concepts of choice, responsibility, justice, and so on, provide a most inadequate analysis of efficient reinforcing and punishing contin-gencies because they carry a heavy semantic cargo of a quite different sort, which obscures any attempt to clarify controlling practices or to improve techniques. In particular, they fail to prepare us for techniques based on other than aversive techniques of control. Most peo-ple would object to forcing prisoners to serve as subjects of dangerous medical experiments, but few object when they are induced to serve by the offer of return privileges—even when the reinforcing effect of these privileges has been created by forcible deprivation. In the tra-ditional scheme the right to refuse guarantees the individual against coercion or an unfair bargain. But to what extent *can* a prisoner re-fuse under such circumstances?

We need not go so far afield to make the

point. We can observe our own attitude toward personal freedom in the way we resent any interference with what we want to do. Suppose we want to buy a car of a particular sort. Then we may object, for example, if our wife urges us to buy a less expensive model and to put the difference into a new refrigerator. Or we may resent it if our neighbor questions our need for such a car or our ability to pay for it. We would certainly resent it if it were illegal to buy such a car (remember Prohibition); and if we find we cannot actually afford it, we may resent governmental control of the price through tariffs and taxes. We resent it if we discover that we cannot get the car because the manufacturer is holding the model in deliberately short supply in order to push a model we do not want. In all this we assert our democratic right to buy the car of our choice. We are well prepared to do so and to resent any restriction on our freedom.

But why do we not ask *why* it is the car of our choice and resent the forces which made it so? Perhaps our favorite toy as a child was a car, of a very different model, but nevertheless bearing the name of the car we now want. Perhaps our favorite TV program is sponsored by the manufacturer of that car. Perhaps we have seen pictures of many beautiful or prestigeful persons driving it—in pleasant or glamorous places. Perhaps the car has been designed with respect to our motivational patterns: the device on the hood is a phallic symbol; or the horsepower has been stepped up to please our competitive spirit in enabling us to pass other cars swiftly (or, as the advertisements say, "safely"). The concept of freedom that has emerged as part of the cultural practice of our group makes little or no provision for recognizing or dealing with these kinds of control. Concepts like "responsibility" and "rights" are scarcely applicable. We are prepared to deal with coercive measures, but we have no traditional recourse with respect to other measures which in the long run (and especially with the help of sci-

ence) may be much more powerful and dangerous.

EDUCATION

The techniques of education were once frankly aversive. The teacher was usually older and stronger than his pupils and was able to "make them learn." This meant that they were not actually taught but were surrounded by a threatening world from which they could escape only by learning. Usually they were left to their own resources in discovering how to do so. Claude Coleman has published a grimly amusing reminder of these older practices.[3] He tells of a schoolteacher who published a careful account of his services during 51 years of teaching, during which he administered: ". . . 911,527 blows with a cane; 124,010 with a rod; 20,989 with a ruler; 136,715 with the hand; 10,295 over the mouth; 7,905 boxes on the ear; [and] 1,115,800 slaps on the head. . . ."

Progressive education was a humanitarian effort to substitute positive reinforcement for such aversive measures, but in the search for useful human values in the classroom it has never fully replaced the variables it abandoned. Viewed as a branch of behavioral technology, education remains relatively inefficient. We supplement it, and rationalize it, by admiring the pupil who learns *for himself;* and we often attribute the learning process, or knowledge itself, to something *inside* the individual. We admire behavior which seems to have inner sources. Thus we admire one who *recites* a poem more than one who simply *reads* it. We admire one who *knows* the answer more than one who *knows where to look it up.* We admire the *writer* rather than the *reader.* We admire the arithmetician who can do a problem in his head rather than with a slide rule or calculating machine, or in "original" ways rather than by a direct application of rules. In general we feel that any aid or "crutch"—except those aids to which we are now thoroughly accustomed—

reduces the credit due. In Plato's *Phaedrus*, Thamus, the king, attacks the invention of the alphabet on similar grounds! He is afraid "it will produce forgetfulness in the minds of those who learn to use it, because they will not practice their memories. . . ." In other words, he holds it more admirable to remember than to use a memorandum. He also objects that pupils "will read many things without instruction . . . [and] will therefore seem to know many things when they are for the most part ignorant." In the same vein we are today sometimes contemptuous of book learning, but, as educators, we can scarcely afford to adopt this view without reservation.

By admiring the student for knowledge and blaming him for ignorance, we escape some of the responsibility of teaching him. We resist any analysis of the educational process which threatens the notion of inner wisdom or questions the contention that the fault of ignorance lies with the student. More powerful techniques which bring about the same changes in behavior by manipulating *external* variables are decried as brainwashing or thought control. We are quite unprepared to judge *effective* educational measures. As long as only a few pupils learn much of what is taught, we do not worry about uniformity or regimentation. We do not fear the feeble technique; but we should view with dismay a system under which every student learned everything listed in a syllabus —although such a condition is far from unthinkable. Similarly, we do not fear a system which is so defective that the student must *work* for an education; but we are loath to give credit for anything learned without effort— although this could well be taken as an ideal result—and we flatly refuse to give credit if the student already knows what a school teaches.

A world in which people are wise and good without trying, without "having to be," without "choosing to be," could conceivably be a far better world for everyone. In such a world we should not have to "give anyone credit"—we should not need to admire anyone—for being wise and good. From our present point of view we cannot believe that such a world would be admirable. We do not even permit ourselves to imagine what it would be like.

GOVERNMENT

Government has always been the special field of aversive control. The state is frequently defined in terms of the power to punish, and jurisprudence leans heavily upon the associated notion of personal responsibility. Yet it is becoming increasingly difficult to reconcile current practice and theory with these earlier views. In criminology, for example, there is a strong tendency to drop the notion of responsibility in favor of some such alternative as capacity or controllability. But no matter how strongly the facts, or even practical expedience, support such a change, it is difficult to make the change in a legal system designed on a different plan. When governments resort to other techniques (for example, positive reinforcement), the concept of responsibility is no longer relevant and the theory of government is no longer applicable.

The conflict is illustrated by two decisions of the Supreme Court in the 1930's which dealt with, and disagreed on, the definition of control or coercion.[4] The Agricultural Adjustment Act proposed that the Secretary of Agriculture make "rental or benefit payments" to those farmers who agreed to reduce production. The government agreed that the Act would be unconstitutional if the farmer had been *compelled* to reduce production but was not, since he was merely *invited* to do so. Justice Roberts[5] expressed the contrary majority view of the court that "The power to confer or withhold unlimited benefits is the power to coerce or destroy." This recognition of positive reinforcement was withdrawn a few years later in another case in which Justice Cardozo[6] wrote "To hold that motive or temptation is equivalent to coercion is to plunge the law in endless difficulties." We may agree with him, without implying that the proposition is therefore wrong. Sooner or later the law must be prepared to deal with all possible techniques of governmental control.

The uneasiness with which we view government (in the broadest possible sense) when it does not use punishment is shown by the reception of my utopian novel, *Walden Two*.[7] This was essentially a proposal to apply a behavioral technology to the construction of a workable, effective, and productive pattern of government. It was greeted with wrathful violence. *Life* magazine called it "a travesty on the good life," and "a menace . . . a triumph of mortmain or the dead hand not envisaged since the days of Sparta . . . a slur upon a name, a corruption of an impulse." Joseph Wood Krutch devoted a substantial part of his book, *The Measure of Man*,[8] to attacking my views and those of the protagonist, Frazier, in the same vein, and Morris Viteles has recently criticized the book in a similar manner in *Science*.[9]—Perhaps the reaction is best expressed in quotation from *The Quest for Utopia* by Negley and Patrick:[10]

"Halfway through this contemporary utopia, the reader may feel sure, as we did, that this is a beautifully ironic satire on what has been called 'behavioral engineering.' The longer one stays in this better world of the psychologist, however, the plainer it becomes that the inspiration is not satiric, but messianic. This is indeed the behaviorally engineered society, and while it was to be expected that sooner or later the principle of psychological conditioning would be made the basis of a serious construction of utopia—Brown anticipated it in *Limanora*—yet not even the effective satire of Huxley is adequate preparation for the shocking horror of the idea when positively presented. Of all the dictatorships espoused by utopists, this is the most profound, and incipient dictators might well find in this utopia a guidebook of political practice."

One would scarcely guess that the authors are talking about a world in which there is food, clothing, and shelter for all, where everyone chooses his own work and works on the average only four hours a day, where music and the arts flourish, where personal relationships develop under the most favorable circumstances, where education prepares every child for the social and intellectual life which lies before him, where—in short—people are truly happy, secure, productive, creative, and forward-looking. What is wrong with it? Only one thing: someone "planned it that way." If these critics had come upon a society in some remote corner of the world which boasted similar advantages, they would undoubtedly have hailed it as providing a pattern we all might well follow—provided that it was clearly the result of a natural process of cultural evolution. Any evidence that intelligence had been used in arriving at this version of the good life would, in their eyes, be a serious flaw. No matter if the planner of *Walden Two* diverts none of the proceeds of the community to his own use, no matter if he has no current control or is, indeed, unknown to most of the other members of the community (he planned that, too), somewhere back of it all he occupies the position of prime mover. And this, to the child of the democratic tradition, spoils it all.

The dangers inherent in the control of human behavior are very real. The possibility of the misuse of scientific knowledge must always be faced. We cannot escape by denying the power of a science of behavior or arresting its development. It is no help to cling to familiar philosophies of human behavior simply because they are more reassuring. As I have pointed out elsewhere,[11] the new techniques emerging from a science of behavior must be subject to the explicit countercontrol which has already been applied to earlier and cruder forms. Brute force and deception, for example, are now fairly generally suppressed by ethical practices and by explicit governmental and religious agencies. A similar countercontrol of scientific knowledge in the interests of the group is a feasible and promising possibility. Although we cannot say how devious the course of its evolution may be, a cultural pattern of control and countercountrol will presumably emerge which will be most widely supported because it is most widely reinforcing.

If we cannot foresee all the details of this (as we obviously cannot), it is important to remember that this is true of the critics of science as well. The dire consequences of new techniques of control, the hidden menace in original cultural designs—these need some proof. It is only another example of my present point that the need for proof is so often overlooked. Man has got himself into some pretty fixes, and it is easy to believe that he will do so again. But there is a more optimistic possibility. The slow growth of the methods of science, now for the first time being applied to human affairs, *may* mean a new and exciting phase of human life to which historical analogies will not apply and in which earlier political slogans will not be appropriate. If we are to use the knowledge that a science of behavior is now making available with any hope of success, we must look at human nature as it is brought into focus through the methods of science rather than as it has been presented to us in a series of historical accidents.

If the advent of a powerful science of behavior causes trouble, it will not be because science itself is inimical to human welfare but because older conceptions have not yielded easily or gracefully. We expect resistance to new techniques of control from those who have heavy investments in the old, but we have no reason to help them preserve a series of principles that are not ends in themselves but rather outmoded means to an end. What is needed is a new conception of human behavior which is compatible with the implications of a scientific analysis. All men control and are controlled. The question of government in the broadest possible sense is not how freedom is to be preserved but what kinds of control are to be used and to what ends. Control must be analyzed and considered in its proper proportions. No one, I am sure, wishes to develop new master-slave relationships or bend the will of the people to despotic rulers in new ways. These are patterns of control appropriate to a world without science. They may well be the first to go when the experimental analysis of behavior comes into its own in the design of cultural practices.

ROGERS

There are, I believe, a number of matters in connection with this important topic on which the authors of this article, and probably a large majority of psychologists, are in agreement. These matters then are not issues as far as we are concerned, and I should like to mention them briefly in order to put them to one side.

POINTS OF AGREEMENT

I am sure we agree that men—as individuals and as societies—have always endeavored to understand, predict, influence, and control human behavior—their own behavior and that of others.

I believe we agree that the behavioral sciences are making and will continue to make increasingly rapid progress in the understanding of behavior, and that as a consequence the capacity to predict and to control behavior is developing with equal rapidity.

I believe we agree that to deny these advances, or to claim that man's behavior cannot be a field of science, is unrealistic. Even though this is not an issue for us, we should recognize that many intelligent men still hold strongly to the view that the actions of men are free in some sense such that scientific knowledge of man's behavior is impossible. Thus Reinhold Niebuhr, the noted theologian, heaps scorn on the concept of psychology as a science of man's behavior and even says, "In any event, no scientific investigation of past behavior can become the basis of predictions of future behavior."[12] So, while this is not an issue for psychologists, we should at least notice in passing that it is an issue for many people.

I believe we are in agreement that the tremendous potential power of a science which permits the production and control of behavior may be misused, and that the possibility of such misuse constitutes a serious threat.

Consequently Skinner and I are in agreement that the whole question of the scientific control of human behavior is a matter with which psychologists and the general public should concern themselves. As Robert Oppenheimer told the American Psychological Association last year[13] the problems that psychologists will pose for society by their growing ability to control behavior will be much more grave than the problems posed by the ability of physicists to control the reactions of matter. I am not sure whether psychologists generally recognize this. My impression is that by and large they hold a laissez-faire attitude. Obviously Skinner and I do not hold this laissez-faire view, or we would not have written this article.

POINTS AT ISSUE

With these several points of basic and important agreement, are there then any issues that remain on which there are differences? I believe there are. They can be stated very briefly: Who will be controlled? Who will exercise control? What type of control will be exercised? Most important of all, toward what end or what purpose, or in the pursuit of what value, will control be exercised?

It is on questions of this sort that there exist ambiguities, misunderstandings, and probably deep differences. These differences exist among psychologists, among members of the general public in this country, and among various world cultures. Without any hope of achieving a final resolution of these questions, we can, I believe, put these issues in clearer form.

SOME MEANINGS

To avoid ambiguity and faulty communication, I would like to clarify the meanings of some of the terms we are using.

Behavioral science is a term that might be defined from several angles but in the context of this discussion it refers primarily to knowledge that the existence of certain describable conditions in the human being and/or in his environment is followed by certain describable consequences in his actions.

Prediction means the prior identification of behaviors which then occur. Because it is important in some things I wish to say later, I would point out that one may predict a highly specific behavior, such as an eye blink, or one may predict a class of behaviors. One might correctly predict "avoidant behavior," for example, without being able to specify whether the individual will run away or simply close his eyes.

The word *control* is a very slippery one, which can be used with any one of several meanings. I would like to specify three that seem most important for our present purposes. *Control* may mean: (i) The setting of conditions by B for A, A having no voice in the matter, such that certain predictable behaviors then occur in A. I refer to this as external control. (ii) The setting of conditions by B for A, A giving some degree of consent to these conditions, such that certain predictable behaviors then occur in A. I refer to this as the influence of B on A. (iii) The setting of conditions by A such that certain predictable behaviors then occur in himself. I refer to this as internal control. It will be noted that Skinner lumps together the first two meanings, external control and influence, under the concept of control. I find this confusing.

USUAL CONCEPT OF CONTROL OF HUMAN BEHAVIOR

With the underbrush thus cleared away (I hope), let us review very briefly the various elements that are involved in the usual concept of the control of human behavior as mediated by the behavioral sciences. I am drawing here on the previous writings of Skinner, on his present statements, on the writings of others who have considered in either friendly or antagonistic fashion the meanings that would be involved in such control. I have not excluded the science fiction writers, as reported recently by Vandenberg,[14] since they often show an awareness of the issues involved, even though the methods described are as yet fictional. These then are the elements that seem common to these different concepts of the application of science to human behavior.

1. There must first be some sort of decision about goals. Usually desirable goals are assumed, but sometimes, as in George Orwell's book *1984,* the goal that is selected is an aggrandizement of individual power with which most of us would disagree. In a recent paper Skinner suggests that one possible set of goals to be assigned to the behavioral technology is this: "Let men be happy, informed, skillful, well-behaved and productive."[15] In the first draft of his part of this article, which he was kind enough to show me, he did not mention such definite goals as these, but desired "improved" educational practices, "wiser" use of knowledge in government, and the like. In the final version of his article he avoids even these value-laden terms, and his implicit goal is the very general one that scientific control of behavior is desirable, because it would perhaps bring "a far better world for everyone."

Thus the first step in thinking about the control of human behavior is the choice of goals, whether specific or general. It is necessary to come to terms in some way with the issue, "For what purpose?"

2. A second element is that, whether the end selected is highly specific or is a very general one such as wanting "a better world," we proceed by the methods of science to discover the means to these ends. We continue through further experimentation and investigation to discover more effective means. The method of science is self-correcting in thus arriving at increasingly effective ways of achieving the purpose we have in mind.

3. The third aspect of such control is that as the conditions or methods are discovered by which to reach the goal, some person or some group establishes these conditions and uses these methods, having in one way or another obtained the power to do so.

4. The fourth element is the exposure of individuals to the prescribed conditions, and this leads, with a high degree of probability, to behavior which is in line with the goals desired. Individuals are now happy, if that has been the goal, or well-behaved, or submissive, or whatever it has been decided to make them.

5. The fifth element is that if the process I have described is put in motion then there is a continuing social organization which will continue to produce the types of behavior that have been valued.

SOME FLAWS

Are there any flaws in this way of viewing the control of human behavior? I believe there are. In fact the only element in this description with which I find myself in agreement is the second. It seems to me quite incontrovertibly true that the scientific method is an excellent way to discover the means by which to achieve our goals. Beyond that, I feel many sharp differences, which I will try to spell out.

I believe that in Skinner's presentation here

and in his previous writings, there is a serious underestimation of the problem of power. To hope that the power which is being made available by the behavioral sciences will be exercised by the scientist, or by a benevolent group, seems to me a hope little supported by either recent or distant history. It seems far more likely that behavioral scientists, holding their present attitudes, will be in the position of the German rocket scientists specializing in guided missiles. First they worked devotedly for Hitler to destroy the U.S.S.R. and the United States. Now, depending on who captured them, they work devotedly for the U.S.S.R. in the interest of destroying the United States, or devotedly for the United States in the interest of destroying the U.S.S.R. If behavioral scientists are concerned solely with advancing their science, it seems most probable that they will serve the purposes of whatever individual or group has the power.

But the major flaw I see in this review of what is involved in the scientific control of human behavior is the denial, misunderstanding, or gross underestimation of the place of ends, goals or values in their relationship to science. This error (as it seems to me) has so many implications that I would like to devote some space to it.

Ends and Values in Relation to Science

In sharp contradiction to some views that have been advanced, I would like to propose a two-pronged thesis: (i) In any scientific endeavor —whether "pure" or applied science—there is a prior subjective choice of the purpose or value which that scientific work is perceived as serving. (ii) This subjective value choice which brings the scientific endeavor into being must always lie outside of that endeavor and can never become a part of the science involved in that endeavor.

Let me illustrate the first point from Skinner himself. It is clear that in his earlier writing it is recognized that a prior value choice is necessary, and it is specified as the goal that men are to become happy, well-behaved, productive, and so on. I am pleased that Skinner has retreated from the goals he then chose, because to me they seem to be stultifying values. I can only feel that he was choosing these goals for others, not for himself. I would hate to see Skinner become "well-behaved," as that term would be defined for him by behavioral scientists. His recent article in the *American Psychologist*[16] shows that he certainly does not want to be "productive" as that value is defined by most psychologists. And the most awful fate I can imagine for him would be to have him constantly "happy." It is the fact that he is very unhappy about many things which makes me prize him.

In the first draft of his part of this article, he also included such prior value choices, saying for example, "We must decide how we are to use the knowledge which a science of human behavior is now making available." Now he has dropped all mention of such choices, and if I understand him correctly, he believes that science can proceed without them. He has suggested this view in another recent paper, stating that "We must continue to experiment in cultural design . . . testing the consequences as we go. Eventually the practices which make for the greatest biological and psychological strength of the group will presumably survive."[17]

I would point out, however, that to choose to experiment is a value choice. Even to move in the direction of perfectly random experimentation is a value choice. To test the consequences of an experiment is possible only if we have first made a subjective choice of a criterion value. And implicit in his statement is a valuing of biological and psychological strength. So even when trying to avoid such choice, it seems inescapable that a prior subjective value choice is necessary for any scientific endeavor, or for any application of scientific knowledge.

I wish to make it clear that I am not saying that values cannot be included as a subject of science. It is not true that science deals only with certain classes of "facts" and that these classes do not include values. It is a bit more complex than that, as a simple illustration or two may make clear.

If I value knowledge of the "three R's" as a goal of education, the methods of science can give me increasingly accurate information on how this goal may be achieved. If I value problem-solving ability as a goal of education, the scientific method can give me the same kind of help.

Now, if I wish to determine whether problem-solving ability is "better" than knowledge of the three R's, then scientific method can also study those two values but *only*—and this is very important—in terms of some other value which I have subjectively chosen. I may value college success. Then I can determine whether problem-solving ability or knowledge of the three R's is most closely associated with that value. I may value personal integration or vocational success or responsible citizenship. I can determine whether problem-solving ability or knowledge of the three R's is "better" for achieving any one of these values. But the value or purpose that gives meaning to a particular scientific endeavor must always lie outside of that endeavor.

Although our concern in this symposium is largely with applied science, what I have been saying seems equally true of so-called "pure" science. In pure science the usual prior subjective value choice is the discovery of truth. But this is a subjective choice, and science can never say whether it is the best choice, save in the light of some other value. Geneticists in the U.S.S.R., for example, had to make a subjective choice of whether it was better to pursue truth or to discover facts which upheld a governmental dogma. Which choice is "better"? We could

make a scientific investigation of those alternatives but only in the light of some other subjectively chosen value. If, for example, we value the survival of a culture, then we could begin to investigate with the methods of science the question of whether pursuit of truth or support of governmental dogma is most closely associated with cultural survival.

My point then is that any endeavor in science, pure or applied, is carried on in the pursuit of a purpose or value that is subjectively chosen by persons. It is important that this choice be made explicit, since the particular value which is being sought can never be tested or evaluated, confirmed or denied, by the scientific endeavor to which it gives birth. The initial purpose or value always and necessarily lies outside the scope of the scientific effort which it sets in motion.

Among other things this means that if we choose some particular goal or series of goals for human beings and then set out on a large scale to control human behavior to the end of achieving those goals, we are locked in the rigidity of our initial choice, because such a scientific endeavor can never transcend itself to select new goals. Only subjective human persons can do that. Thus if we chose as our goal the state of happiness for human beings (a goal deservedly ridiculed by Aldous Huxley in *Brave New World*), and if we involved all of society in a successful scientific program by which people become happy, we would be locked in a colossal rigidity in which no one would be free to question this goal, because our scientific operations could not transcend themselves to question their guiding purposes. And without laboring this point, I would remark that colossal rigidity, whether in dinosaurs or dictatorships, has a very poor record of evolutionary survival.

If, however, a part of our scheme is to set free some "planners" who do not have to be happy, who are not controlled, and who are therefore free to choose other values, this has several meanings. It means that the purpose we have chosen as our goal is not a sufficient and a satisfying one for human beings but must be supplemented. It also means that if it is necessary to set up an elite group which is free, then this shows all too clearly that the great majority are only the slaves—no matter by what high-sounding name we call them—of those who select the goals.

Perhaps, however, the thought is that a continuing scientific endeavor will evolve its own goals; that the initial findings will alter the directions, and subsequent findings will alter them still further, and that science somehow develops its own purpose. Although he does not clearly say so, this appears to be the pattern Skinner has in mind. It is surely a reasonable description, but it overlooks one element in this continuing development, which is that subjective personal choice enters in at every point at which the direction changes. The findings of a science, the results of an experiment, do not and never can tell us what next scientific purpose to pursue. Even in the purest of science, the scientist must decide what the findings mean and must subjectively choose what next step will be most profitable in the pursuit of his purpose. And if we are speaking of the application of scientific knowledge, then it is distressingly clear that the increasing scientific knowledge of the structure of the atom carries with it no necessary choice as to the purpose to which this knowledge will be put. This is a subjective personal choice which must be made by many individuals.

Thus I return to the proposition with which I began this section of my remarks—and which I now repeat in different words. Science has its meaning as the objective pursuit of a purpose which has been subjectively chosen by a person or persons. This purpose or value can never be investigated by the particular scientific experiment or investigation to which it has given birth and meaning. Consequently, any discussion of the control of human beings by the be-havioral sciences must first and most deeply concern itself with the subjectively chosen purposes which such an application of science is intended to implement.

IS THE SITUATION HOPELESS?

The thoughtful reader may recognize that, although my remarks up to this point have introduced some modifications in the conception of the process by which human behavior will be controlled, these remarks may have made such control seem, if anything, even more inevitable. We might sum it up this way: Behavioral science is clearly moving forward; the increasing power for control which it gives will be held by someone or some groups; such an individual or group will surely choose the values or goals to be achieved; and most of us will then be increasingly controlled by means so subtle that we will not even be aware of them as controls. Thus, whether a council of wise psychologists (if this is not a contradiction in terms), or a Stalin, or a Big Brother has the power, and whether the goal is happiness, or productivity, or resolution of the Oedipus complex, or submission, or love of Big Brother, we will inevitably find ourselves moving toward the chosen goal and probably thinking that we ourselves desire it. Thus, if this line of reasoning is correct, it appears that some form of *Walden Two* or of *1984* (and at a deep philosophic level they seem indistinguishable) is coming. The fact that it would surely arrive piecemeal, rather than all at once, does not greatly change the fundamental issues. In any event, as Skinner has indicated in his writings, we would then look back upon the concepts of human freedom, the capacity for choice, the responsibility for choice, and the worth of the human individual as historical curiosities which once existed by cultural accident as values in a prescientific civilization.

I believe that any person observant of trends must regard something like the foregoing sequence as a real possibility. It is not simply a fantasy. Something of that sort may even be the most likely future. But is it an inevitable future? I want to devote the remainder of my remarks to an alternative possibility.

ALTERNATIVE SET OF VALUES

Suppose we start with a set of ends, values, purposes, quite different from the type of goals we have been considering. Suppose we do this quite openly, setting them forth as a possible value choice to be accepted or rejected. Suppose we select a set of values that focuses on fluid elements of process rather than static attributes. We might then value: man as a process of becoming, as a process of achieving worth and dignity through the development of his potentialities; the individual human being as a self-actualizing process, moving on to more challenging and enriching experiences; the process by which the individual creatively adapts to an ever-new and changing world; the process by which knowledge transcends itself, as, for example, the theory of relativity transcended Newtonian physics, itself to be transcended in some future day by a new perception.

If we select values such as these we turn to our science and technology of behavior with a very different set of questions. We will want to know such things as these: Can science aid in the discovery of new modes of richly rewarding living? more meaningful and satisfying modes of interpersonal relationships? Can science inform us on how the human race can become a more intelligent participant in its own evolution—its physical, psychological and social evolution? Can science inform us on ways of releasing the creative capacity of individuals, which seem so necessary if we are to survive in this fantastically expanding atomic age? Oppenheimer has pointed out[18] that knowledge, which used to double in millennia or centuries, now doubles in a generation or a

decade. It appears that we must discover the utmost in release of creativity if we are to be able to adapt effectively. In short, can science discover the methods by which man can most readily become a continually developing and self-transcending process, in his behavior, his thinking, his knowledge? Can science predict and release an essentially "unpredictable" freedom?

It is one of the virtues of science as a method that it is as able to advance and implement goals and purposes of this sort as it is to serve static values, such as states of being well-informed, happy, obedient. Indeed we have some evidence of this.

SMALL EXAMPLE

I will perhaps be forgiven if I document some of the possibilities along this line by turning to psychotherapy, the field I know best.

Psychotherapy, as Meerloo[19] and others have pointed out, can be one of the most subtle tools for the control of A by B. The therapist can subtly mold individuals in imitation of himself. He can cause an individual to become a submissive and conforming being. When certain therapeutic principles are used in extreme fashion, we call it brainwashing, an instance of the disintegration of the personality and a reformulation of the person along lines desired by the controlling individual. So the principles of therapy can be used as an effective means of external control of human personality and behavior. Can psychotherapy be anything else?

Here I find the developments going on in client-centered psychotherapy[20] an exciting hint of what a behavioral science can do in achieving the kinds of values I have stated. Quite aside from being a somewhat new orientation in psychotherapy, this development has important implications regarding the relation of a behavioral science to the control of human behavior. Let me describe our experience as it relates to the issues of this discussion.

In client-centered therapy, we are deeply engaged in the prediction and influencing of behavior, or even the control of behavior. As therapists, we institute certain attitudinal conditions, and the client has relatively little voice in the establishment of these conditions. We predict that if these conditions are instituted, certain behavioral consequences will ensue in the client. Up to this point this is largely external control, no different from what Skinner has described, and no different from what I have discussed in the preceding sections of this article. But here any similarity ceases.

The conditions we have chosen to establish predict such behavioral consequences as these: that the client will become self-directing, less rigid, more open to the evidence of his senses, better organized and integrated, more similar to the ideal which he has chosen for himself. In other words, we have established by external control conditions which we predict will be followed by internal control by the individual, in pursuit of internally chosen goals. We have set the conditions which predict various classes of behaviors—self-directing behaviors, sensitivity to realities within and without, flexible adaptiveness—which are by their very nature unpredictable in their specifics. Our recent research[21] indicates that our predictions are to a significant degree corroborated, and our commitment to the scientific method causes us to believe that more effective means of achieving these goals may be realized.

Research exists in other fields—industry, education, group dynamics—which seems to support our own findings. I believe it may be conservatively stated that scientific progress has been made in identifying those conditions in an interpersonal relationship which, if they exist in B, are followed in A by greater maturity in behavior, less dependence on others, an increase in expressiveness as a person, an increase in variability, flexibility and effectiveness of adaptation, an increase in self-responsibility and self-direction. And, quite in contrast to the concern expressed by some, we do not find that the creatively adaptive behavior which results from such self-directed variability of expression is a "happy accident" which occurs in "chaos." Rather, the individual who is open to his experience, and self-directing, is harmonious not chaotic, ingenious rather than random, as he orders his responses imaginatively toward the achievement of his own purposes. His creative actions are no more a "happy accident" than was Einstein's development of the theory of relativity.

Thus we find ourselves in fundamental agreement with John Dewey's statement: "Science has made its way by releasing, not by suppressing, the elements of variation, of invention and innovation, of novel creation in individuals."[22] Progress in personal life and in group living is, we believe, made in the same way.

POSSIBLE CONCEPT OF THE CONTROL OF HUMAN BEHAVIOR

It is quite clear that the point of view I am expressing is in sharp contrast to the usual conception of the relationship of the behavioral sciences to the control of human behavior. In order to make this contrast even more blunt, I will state this possibility in paragraphs parallel to those used before.

1. It is possible for us to choose to value man as a self-actualizing process of becoming; to value creativity, and the process by which knowledge becomes self-transcending.
2. We can proceed, by the methods of science, to discover the conditions which necessarily precede these processes and, through continuing experimentation, to discover better means of achieving these purposes.
3. It is possible for individuals or groups to set these conditions, with a minimum of power or control. According to present knowledge, the only authority necessary is the authority to establish certain qualities of interpersonal relationship.

4. Exposed to these conditions, present knowledge suggests that individuals become more self-responsible, make progress in self-actualization, become more flexible, and become more creatively adaptive.

5. Thus such an initial choice would inaugurate the beginnings of a social system or subsystem in which values, knowledge, adaptive skills, and even the concept of science would be continually changing and self-transcending. The emphasis would be upon man as a process of becoming.

I believe it is clear that such a view as I have been describing does not lead to any definable utopia. It would be impossible to predict its final outcome. It involves a step-by-step development, based on a continuing subjective choice of purposes, which are implemented by the behavioral sciences. It is in the direction of the "open society," as that term has been defined by Popper,[23] where individuals carry responsibility for personal decisions. It is at the opposite pole from his concept of the closed society, of which *Walden Two* would be an example.

I trust it is also evident that the whole emphasis is on process, not on end-states of being. I am suggesting that it is by choosing to value certain qualitative elements of the process of becoming that we can find a pathway toward the open society.

THE CHOICE

It is my hope that we have helped to clarify the range of choice which will lie before us and our children in regard to the behavioral sciences. We can choose to use our growing knowledge to enslave people in ways never dreamed of before, depersonalizing them, controlling them by means so carefully selected that they will perhaps never be aware of their loss of personhood. We can choose to utilize our scientific knowledge to make men happy,

well-behaved, and productive, as Skinner earlier suggested. Or we can insure that each person learns all the syllabus which we select and set before him, as Skinner now suggests. Or at the other end of the spectrum of choice we can choose to use the behavioral sciences in ways which will free, not control; which will bring about constructive variability, not conformity; which will develop creativity, not contentment; which will facilitate each person in his self-directed process of becoming; which will aid individuals, groups, and even the concept of science to become self-transcending in freshly adaptive ways of meeting life and its problems. The choice is up to us, and, the human race being what it is, we are likely to stumble about, making at times some nearly disastrous value choices and at other times highly constructives ones.

I am aware that to some, this setting forth of a choice is unrealistic, because a choice of values is regarded as not possible. Skinner has stated: "Man's vaunted creative powers . . . his capacity to choose and our right to hold him responsible for his choice—none of these is conspicuous in this new self-portrait (provided by science). Man, we once believed, was free to express himself in art, music, and literature, to inquire into nature, to seek salvation in his own way. He could initiate action and make spontaneous and capricious changes of course. . . . But science insists that action is initiated by forces impinging upon the individual, and that caprice is only another name for behavior for which we have not yet found a cause."[24]

I can understand this point of view, but I believe that it avoids looking at the great paradox of behavioral science. Behavior, when it is examined scientifically, is surely best understood as determined by prior causation. This is one great fact of science. But responsible personal choice, which is the most essential element in being a person, which is the core experience in psychotherapy, which exists prior to any scientific endeavor, is an equally prominent fact in our lives. To deny the experience of responsible choice is, to me, as restricted a view as to deny the possibility of a behavioral science. That these two important elements of our experience appear to be in contradiction has perhaps the same significance as the contradiction between the wave theory and the corpuscular theory of light, both of which can be shown to be true, even though incompatible. We cannot profitably deny our subjective life, any more than we can deny the objective description of that life.

In conclusion then, it is my contention that science cannot come into being without a personal choice of the values we wish to achieve. And these values we choose to implement will forever lie outside of the science which implements them; the goals we select, the purposes we wish to follow, must always be outside of the science which achieves them. To me this has the encouraging meaning that the human person, with his capacity of subjective choice, can and will always exist, separate from and prior to any of his scientific undertakings. Unless as individuals and groups we choose to relinquish our capacity of subjective choice, we will always remain persons, not simply pawns of a self-created science.

SKINNER

I cannot quite agree that the practice of science *requires* a prior decision about goals or a prior choice of values. The metallurgist can study the properties of steel and the engineer can design a bridge without raising the question of whether a bridge is to be built. But such questions are certainly frequently raised and tentatively answered. Rogers wants to call the answers "subjective choices of values." To me, such an expression suggests that we have had to abandon more rigorous scientific practices in order to talk about our own behavior. In the experimental analysis of other organisms

I would use other terms, and I shall try to do so here. Any list of values is a list of reinforcers—conditioned or otherwise. We are so constituted that under certain circumstances food, water, sexual contact, and so on, will make any behavior which produces them more likely to occur again. Other things may acquire this power. We do not need to say that an organism chooses to eat rather than to starve. If you answer that it is a very different thing when a man chooses to starve, I am only too happy to agree. If it were not so, we should have cleared up the question of choice long ago. An organism can be reinforced by—can be made to "choose"—almost any given state of affairs.

Rogers is concerned with choices that involve multiple and usually conflicting consequences. I have dealt with some of these elsewhere[25] in an analysis of self-control. Shall I eat these delicious strawberries today if I will then suffer an annoying rash tomorrow? The decision I am to make used to be assigned to the province of ethics. But we are now studying similar combinations of positive and negative consequences, as well as collateral conditions which affect the result, in the laboratory. Even a pigeon can be taught some measure of self-control! And this work helps us to understand the operation of certain formulas—among them value judgments—which folk-wisdom, religion, and psychotherapy have advanced in the interests of self-discipline. The observable effect of any statement of value is to alter the relative effectiveness of reinforcers. We may no longer enjoy the strawberries for thinking about the rash. If rashes are made sufficiently shameful, illegal, sinful, maladjusted, or unwise, we may glow with satisfaction as we push the strawberries aside in a grandiose avoidance response which would bring a smile to the lips of Murray Sidman.

People behave in ways which, as we say, conform to ethical, governmental, or religious patterns because they are reinforced for doing so. The resulting behavior may have far-reaching consequences for the survival of the pattern to which it conforms. And whether we like it or not, survival is the ultimate criterion. This is where, it seems to me, science can help—not in choosing a goal, but in enabling us to predict the survival value of cultural practices. Man has too long tried to get the kind of world he wants by glorifying some brand of immediate reinforcement. As science points up more and more of the remoter consequences, he may begin to work to strengthen behavior, not in a slavish devotion to a chosen value, but with respect to the ultimate survival of mankind. Do not ask me why I want mankind to survive. I can tell you why only in the sense in which the physiologist can tell you why I want to breathe. Once the relation between a given step and the survival of my group has been pointed out, I will take that step. And it is the business of science to point out just such relations.

The values I have occasionally recommended (and Rogers has not led me to recant) are transitional. Other things being equal, I am betting on the group whose practices make for healthy, happy, secure, productive, and creative people. And I insist that the values recommended by Rogers are transitional, too, for I can ask him the same kind of question. Man as a process of becoming—*what?* Self-actualization—for what? Inner control is no more a goal than external.

What Rogers seems to me to be proposing, both here and elsewhere,[26] is this: Let us use our increasing power of control to create individuals who will not need and perhaps will no longer respond to control. Let us solve the problem of our power by renouncing it. At first blush this seems as implausible as a benevolent despot. Yet power has occasionally been foresworn. A nation has burned its Reichstag, rich men have given away their wealth, beautiful women have become ugly hermits in the desert, and psychotherapists have become nondirective. When this happens, I look to other possible reinforcements for a plausible explana-

tion. A people relinquish democratic power when a tyrant promises them the earth. Rich men give away wealth to escape the accusing finger of their fellowmen. A woman destroys her beauty in the hope of salvation. And a psychotherapist relinquishes control because he can thus help his client more effectively.

The solution that Rogers is suggesting is thus understandable. But is he correctly interpreting the result? What evidence is there that a client ever becomes truly *self*-directing? What evidence is there that he ever makes a truly *inner* choice of ideal or goal? Even though the therapist does not do the choosing, even though he encourages "self-actualization"—he is not out of control as long as he holds himself ready to step in when occasion demands—when, for example, the client chooses the goal of becoming a more accomplished liar or murdering his boss. But supposing the therapist does withdraw completely or is no longer necessary—what about all the other forces acting upon the client? Is the self-chosen goal independent of his early ethical and religious training? of the folk-wisdom of his group? of the opinions and attitudes of others who are important to him? Surely not. The therapeutic situation is only a small part of the world of the client. From the therapist's point of view it may appear to be possible to relinquish control. But the control passes, not to a "self," but to forces in other parts of the client's world. The solution of the therapist's problem of power cannot be our solution, for we must consider *all* the forces acting upon the individual.

The child who must be prodded and nagged is something less than a fully developed human being. We want to see him hurrying to his appointment, not because each step is taken in response to verbal reminders from his mother, but because certain temporal contingencies, in which dawdling has been punished and hurrying reinforced, have worked a change in his behavior. Call this a state of better organization, a greater sensitivity to reality, or what you will. The plain fact is that the child passes from a temporary verbal control exercised by his parents to control by certain inexorable features of the environment. I should suppose that something of the same sort happens in successful psychotherapy. Rogers seems to me to be saying this: Let us put an end, as quickly as possible, to any pattern of master-and-slave, to any direct obedience to command, to the submissive following of suggestions. Let the individual be free to adjust himself to more rewarding features of the world about him. In the end, let his teachers and counselors "wither away," like the Marxist state. I not only agree with this as a useful ideal, I have constructed a fanciful world to demonstrate its advantages. It saddens me to hear Rogers say that "at a deep philosophic level" *Walden Two* and George Orwell's *1984* "seem indistinguishable." They could scarcely be more unlike—at any level. The book *1984* is a picture of immediate aversive control for vicious selfish purposes. The founder of *Walden Two,* on the other hand, has built a community in which neither he nor any other person exerts any *current* control. His achievement lay in his original *plan,* and when he boasts of this ("It is enough to satisfy the thirstiest tyrant") we do not fear him but only pity him for his weakness.

Another critic of *Walden Two,* Andrew Hacker[27] has discussed this point in considering the bearing of mass conditioning upon the liberal notion of autonomous man. In drawing certain parallels between the Grand Inquisitor passage in Dostoevsky's *Brothers Karamazov,* Huxley's *Brave New World,* and *Walden Two,* he attempts to set up a distinction to be drawn in any society between conditioners and conditioned. He assumes that "the conditioner can be said to be autonomous in the traditional liberal sense," But then he notes: "Of course the conditioner has been conditioned. But he has not been conditioned by the conscious manipulation of another *person*." But how does this affect the resulting behavior? Can we not soon forget the origins of the "artificial" diamond which is identical with the real thing? Whether it is an "accidental" cultural pattern, such as is said to have produced the founder of *Walden Two,* or the engineered environment which is about to produce his successors, we are dealing with sets of conditions generating human behavior which will ultimately be measured by their contribution to the strength of the group. We look to the future, not the past, for the test of "goodness" or acceptability.

If we are worthy of our democratic heritage we shall, of course, be ready to resist any tyrannical use of science for immediate or selfish purposes. But if we value the achievements and goals of democracy we must not refuse to apply science to the design and construction of cultural patterns, even though we may then find ourselves in some sense in the position of controllers. Fear of control, generalized beyond any warrant, has led to a misinterpretation of valid practices and the blind rejection of intelligent planning for a better way of life. In terms which I trust Rogers will approve, in conquering this fear we shall become more mature and better organized and shall, thus, more fully actualize ourselves as human beings.

NOTES

1. C. R. Rogers, *Teachers College Record* 57, 316 (1956).

2. A. Hacker, *Antioch Rev.* 14, 195 (1954).

3. C. Coleman, *Bull. Am. Assoc. Univ. Professors* 39, 457 (1953).

4. P. A. Freund *et al., Constitutional Law: Cases and Other Problems,* vol. I, p. 233 (Little, Brown, Boston, 1954).

5. Ibid.

6. Ibid., p. 244.

7. B. F. Skinner, *Walden Two* (Macmillan, New York, 1948).

8. J. W. Krutch, *The Measure of Man* (Bobbs-Merrill, Indianapolis, 1953).

9. M. Viteles, *Science* 122, 1167 (1955).

10.   G. Negley and J. M. Patrick, *The Quest for Utopia* (Schuman, New York, 1952).

11.   B. F. Skinner, *Trans. N.Y. Acad. Sci.* 17, 547 (1955).

12.   R. Niebuhr, *The Self and the Dramas of History* (Scribner, New York, 1955), p. 47.

13.   R. Oppenheimer, *Am. Psychol.* 11, 127 (1956).

14.   S. G. Vandenberg, *Am. Psychol.* 11, 339 (1956).

15.   B. F. Skinner, *Am. Scholar* 25, 47 (1955–56).

16.   ——, *Am. Psychol.* 11, 221 (1956).

17.   B. F. Skinner, *Trans. N.Y. Acad. Sci.* 17, 549 (1955).

18.   R. Oppenheimer, *Roosevelt University Occasional Papers* 2 (1956).

19.   J. A. M. Meerloo, *J. Nervous Mental Disease* 122, 353 (1955).

20.   C. R. Rogers, *Client-Centered Therapy* (Houghton Mifflin, Boston, 1951).

21.   —— and R. Dymond, Eds., *Psychotherapy and Personality Change* (Univ. of Chicago Press, Chicago, 1954).

22.   J. Ratner, Ed., *Intelligence in the Modern World: John Dewey's Philosophy* (Modern Library, New York, 1939), p. 359.

23.   K. R. Popper, *The Open Society and Its Enemies* (Rutledge and Kegan Paul, London, 1945).

24.   B. F. Skinner, *Am. Scholar* 25, 52–53 (1955–56).

25.   B. F. Skinner, *Science and Human Behavior* (Macmillan, New York, 1953).

26.   C. R. Rogers, *Teachers College Record* 57, 316 (1956).

27.   A. Hacker, *J. Politics* 17, 590 (1955).

22 Freedom, Utopia, and Dystopia

Huxley

Brave New World by Aldous Huxley (1894–1963) can be read and interpreted on several levels. Some read it as a work of science fiction, a fantasy about the world of the distant future in which everyone (with the exception of a few social deviants) has been made scientifically happy. Genetic engineering, sleep-teaching (*hypnopaedia*), Neo-Pavlovian conditioning, and a wonder drug (*soma*) are among the scientific and technological "advancements" which have made such a "brave new world" possible.

Another perspective, which was the intention of the author, is that it is a satire of an increasingly sensate age, which began in Europe and in America in the 1920s and has continued to become more evident. The stress on pleasure seeking, the decline of religion, the loosening of moral standards, the belief that science and technology can solve all problems (including the problems of suffering and death), and the belief that a utopia can be established on earth—these were some of the tendencies in Huxley's time which he satirized.

A third interpretation of the novel is that it is a symbolic form expressing feeling. This view stresses Huxley's intuitive awareness of the essential problems arising from the nature of man and the good life. Can a person be completely happy experiencing no conflicts, confronting no agonizing moral choices, and having all desires satisfied by a pampering planned environment? In order to remain free, must one relinquish the attempt to achieve a completely happy existence? These are some of the deeper questions raised by Huxley, and he frequently returned to them in later essays and novels. His intention is clearly suggested by his use of a quotation from the Russian existentialist Nikolai Berdyaev (1874–1948) to the effect that it is now apparent that utopias are more realizable than was previously believed; in fact, we now face the question as to whether or not we can

345

prevent their realization. Berdyaev expressed a hope that we would soon, before it is too late, discover the means for avoiding utopia and return to a nonutopian society, one which is less perfect and more free.

Huxley, taking this as his point of departure, presented us with a vision of a perfected society which had been founded on the principles that the highest ends of social organization are "Community, Identity, and Stability," the values which were stressed and perpetuated in the Brave New World Society. They were achieved by allowing the state to control every aspect of every individual's life—production, consumption, leisure, and reproduction. Through scientific means, children were "decanted" in state "hatcheries," and sex was practiced in this world of the future only for pleasure; free love had become a substitute for religious ecstasy in order to promote a sense of social solidarity. There was a rigid class system consisting of a highly intelligent Alpha group down to the lowest menial slaving class of Epsilons. The supreme authorities and planners in the World State were ten world controllers, one of whom, Mustapha Mond, appears in the following selection.

The plot of *Brave New World* revolves around an outsider, John Savage, who has been brought into the utopian society from a more primitive world, the Savage Reservation, as a novelty and a diversion. Not being a product of the new World State, John Savage saw the defects in the system, refused to conform to its values, and held fast to his more natural and, for him, higher values, even at the risk of suffering and death. To John Savage, Brave New World was not a utopia but a dystopia, not a heaven on earth but a hell. Huxley later admitted that in the novel he had given the Savage only two alternatives, going back to a primitive society in which he would have to live a less than human life, or remaining in and conforming to a society in which genuinely human values had been lost in the quest for security. It was as though he had to choose "between insanity on the one hand and lunacy on the other."[1] Were he to rewrite the book, Huxley stated, he would have given the Savage a third option, that of living in a decentralized, anarchist commune in which science and technology would be completely subservient to higher human needs and the mystical consciousness would be cultivated. (In a later novel, *Island*, published shortly before Huxley's death, he presented his vision of this more utopian society.)

It is apparent from Huxley's later comments on *Brave New World*, especially his extensive commentary on it in *Brave New World Revisited*, that he was frightened by his own dystopian vision. He had set the action of the novel in the twenty-sixth century when time is marked B.F. and A.F. (before and after Ford, the pioneer of mass production), but even in his own lifetime Huxley saw plenty of evidence that the dystopia was fast coming about. The techniques of a new totalitarianism were evident in bureaucratic tendencies toward over-organization and behavioral engineering; advances were being made in the science of genetics; new forms of chemical and psychological persuasion were being perfected; God had been declared dead.

Before it became too late to check the erosion of freedom in the modern world, Huxley urged a concerted attempt at an "education for freedom" which would begin "by stating facts and enunciating values."[2] He urged opposition to the threats to freedom which were "of many different kinds —demographic, social, political, psychological."[3] Needed in addition to this education for freedom were "social organization for freedom, birth control for freedom, legislation for freedom."[4] Huxley was convinced that freedom was of supreme value; "without freedom, human beings cannot become fully human."[5]

The following episode from *Brave New World* is comparable to Dostoyevsky's Legend of the Grand Inquisitor, although the times and characters are different. Issues in both cases are the same: security or freedom; conformity or individuality; satiation or suffering; pleasure or self-actualization. The Grand Inquisitor, in defending his position, had said that nothing was more insupportable for a man or a human society than freedom. Huxley's answer was: "Nothing, except the absence of freedom." In *Brave New World Revisited* he showed how new and more competent controllers could find new and better means for enforcing their authority, for performing miracles, and for instilling a sense of mysterious infallibility to their decrees. The Grand Inquisitor did very well for his day and time, Huxley admitted, but today and tomorrow, with the help of new "breakthroughs" in mind manipulation and genetic intervention, scientifically grounded dictatorships can be made to work and to last. In the meantime, however, Huxley suggested that we must resist the forces that take us in the direction of a new world neither brave nor free. The truly free man, like John Savage, will be willing to pay the price, no matter how painful, to preserve his freedom of choice, even if the choice is between liberty and death.

NOTES

1. Aldous Huxley, *Brave New World* (New York: Harper & Row, 1932), p. viii.
2. Aldous Huxley, *Brave New World Revisited* (New York: Harper & Row, 1958), p. 94.
3. Ibid., p. 106.
4. Ibid.
5. Ibid., p. 116.

The Savage and the Controller

The room into which the three were ushered was the Controller's study.

"His fordship will be down in a moment." The Gamma butler left them to themselves.

Helmholtz laughed aloud.

"It's more like a caffeine-solution party than a trial," he said, and let himself fall into the most luxurious of the pneumatic arm-chairs. "Cheer up, Bernard," he added, catching sight of his friend's green unhappy face. But Bernard would not be cheered; without answering, without even looking at Helmholtz, he went and sat down on the most uncomfortable chair in the room, carefully chosen in the obscure hope of somehow deprecating the wrath of the higher powers.

The Savage meanwhile wandered restlessly round the room, peering with a vague superficial inquisitiveness at the books in the shelves, at the sound-track rolls and reading machine bobbins in their numbered pigeon-holes. On the table under the window lay a massive volume bound in limp black leather-surrogate, and stamped with large golden T's. He picked it up and opened it. MY LIFE AND WORK, BY OUR FORD. The book had been published at Detroit by the Society for the Propagation of Fordian Knowledge. Idly he turned the pages, read a sentence here, a paragraph there, and had just come to the conclusion that the book didn't interest him, when the door opened, and

From Aldous Huxley, *Brave New World*, copyright 1932, 1960 by Aldous Huxley. By permission of Harper & Row, Publishers, Inc.

the Resident World Controller for Western Europe walked briskly into the room.

Mustapha Mond shook hands with all three of them; but it was to the Savage that he addressed himself. "So you don't much like civilization, Mr. Savage," he said.

The Savage looked at him. He had been prepared to lie, to bluster, to remain sullenly unresponsive; but, reassured by the good-humoured intelligence of the Controller's face, he decided to tell the truth, straightforwardly. "No." He shook his head.

Bernard started and looked horrified. What would the Controller think? To be labelled as the friend of a man who said that he didn't like civilization—said it openly and, of all people, to the Controller—it was terrible. "But John," he began. A look from Mustapha Mond reduced him to an abject silence.

"Of course," the Savage went on to admit, "there are some very nice things. All that music in the air, for instance . . ."

"Sometimes a thousand twangling instruments will hum about my ears and sometimes voices."

The Savage's face lit up with a sudden pleasure. "Have you read it too?" he asked. "I thought nobody knew about that book here, in England."

"Almost nobody. I'm one of the very few. It's prohibited, you see. But as I make the laws here, I can also break them. With impunity, Mr. Marx," he added, turning to Bernard "Which I'm afraid you *can't* do."

Bernard sank into a yet more hopeless misery.

"But why is it prohibited?" asked the Savage. In the excitement of meeting a man who had read Shakespeare, he had momentarily forgotten everything else.

The Controller shrugged his shoulders. "Because it's old; that's the chief reason. We haven't any use for old things here."

"Even when they're beautiful?"

"Particularly when they're beautiful. Beauty's attractive, and we don't want people to be attracted by old things. We want them to like the new ones."

"But the new ones are so stupid and horrible. Those plays, where there's nothing but helicopters flying about and you *feel* the people kissing." He made a grimace. "Goats and monkeys!" Only in Othello's words could he find an adequate vehicle for his contempt and hatred.

"Nice tame animals, anyhow," the Controller murmured parenthetically.

"Why don't you let them see *Othello* instead?"

"I've told you; it's old. Besides, they couldn't understand it."

Yes, that was true. He remembered how Helmholtz had laughed at *Romeo and Juliet.* "Well then," he said, after a pause, "something new that's like *Othello,* and that they could understand."

"That's what we've all been wanting to write," said Helmholtz, breaking a long silence.

"And it's what you never will write," said the Controller. "Because, if it were really like *Othello* nobody could understand it, however new it might be. And if were new, it couldn't possibly be like *Othello.*"

"Why not?"

"Yes, why not?" Helmholtz repeated. He too was forgetting the unpleasant realities of the situation. Green with anxiety and apprehension, only Bernard remembered them; the others ignored him. "Why not?"

"Because our world is not the same as Othello's world. You can't make flivvers without steel—and you can't make tragedies without social instability. The world's stable now. People are happy; they get what they want, and they never want what they can't get. They're well off; they're safe; they're never ill; they're not afraid of death; they're blissfully ignorant of passion and old age; they're plagued with no mothers or fathers; they've got no wives, or children, or lovers to feel strongly about; they're so conditioned that they practically can't help behaving as they ought to behave. And if anything should go wrong, there's *soma.* Which you go and chuck out of the window in the name of liberty, Mr. Savage. *Liberty!*" He laughed. "Expecting Deltas to know what liberty is! And now expecting them to understand *Othello!* My good boy!"

The Savage was silent for a little. "All the same," he insisted obstinately, "*Othello's* good, *Othello's* better than those feelies."

"Of course it is," the Controller agreed. "But that's the price we have to pay for stability. You've got to choose between happiness and what people used to call high art. We've sacrificed the high art. We have the feelies and the scent organ instead."

"But they don't mean anything."

"They mean themselves; they mean a lot of agreeable sensations to the audience."

"But they're . . . they're told by an idiot."

The Controller laughed. "You're not being very polite to your friend, Mr. Watson. One of our most distinguished Emotional Engineers..."

"But he's right," said Helmholtz gloomily. "Because it *is* idiotic. Writing when there's nothing to say . . ."

"Precisely. But that requires the most enormous ingenuity. You're making flivvers out of the absolute minimum of steel—works of art out of practically nothing but pure sensation."

The Savage shook his head. "It all seems to me quite horrible."

"Of course it does. Actual happiness always looks pretty squalid in comparison with the over-compensations for misery. And, of course, stability isn't nearly so spectacular as instability. And being contented has none of the glamour of a good fight against misfortune, none of the picturesqueness of a struggle with temptation, or a fatal overthrow by passion or doubt. Happiness is never grand."

"I suppose not," said the Savage after a silence. "But need it be quite so bad as those twins?" He passed his hand over his eyes as though he were trying to wipe away the remembered image of those long rows of identical midgets at the assembling tables, those queued-up twin-herds at the entrance to the Brentford monorail station, those human maggots swarming round Linda's bed of death, the endlessly repeated face of his assailants. He looked at his bandaged left hand and shuddered. "Horrible!"

"But how useful! I see you don't like our Bokanovsky Groups; but, I assure you, they're the foundation on which everything else is built. They're the gyroscope that stabilizes the rocket plane of state on its unswerving course." The deep voice thrillingly vibrated; the gesticulating hand implied all space and the onrush of the irresistible machine. Mustapha Mond's oratory was almost up to synthetic standards.

"I was wondering," said the Savage, "why you had them at all—seeing that you can get whatever you want out of those bottles. Why don't you make everybody an Alpha Double Plus while you're about it?"

Mustapha Mond laughed. "Because we have no wish to have our throats cut," he answered. "We believe in happiness and stability. A society of Alphas couldn't fail to be unstable and miserable. Imagine a factory staffed by Alphas—that is to say by separate and unrelated individuals of good heredity and conditioned so as to be capable (within limits) of making a free choice and assuming responsibilities. Imagine it!" he repeated.

The Savage tried to imagine it, not very successfully.

"It's an absurdity. An Alpha-decanted, Alpha-conditioned man would go mad if he had to do Epsilon Semi-Moron work—go mad, or start smashing things up. Alphas can be completely socialized—but only on condition that you make them do Alpha work. Only an Epsilon can be expected to make Epsilon sacrifices, for the good reason that for him they aren't sacrifices; they're the line of least resistance. His conditioning has laid down rails along which he's got to run. He can't help himself; he's foredoomed. Even after decanting, he's still inside a bottle—an invisible bottle of infantile and embryonic fixations. Each one of us, of course," the Controller meditatively continued, "goes through life inside a bottle. But if we happen to be Alphas, our bottles are, relatively speaking, enormous. We should suffer acutely if we were confined in a narrower space. You cannot pour upper-caste champagne-surrogate into lower-caste bottles. It's obvious theoretically. But it has also been proved in actual practice. The result of the Cyprus experiment was convincing."

"What was that?" asked the Savage.

Mustapha Mond smiled. "Well, you can call it an experiment in rebottling if you like. It began in A.F. 473. The Controllers had the island of Cyprus cleared of all its existing inhabitants and re-colonized with a specially prepared batch of twenty-two thousand Alphas. All agricultural and industrial equipment was handed over to them and they were left to manage their own affairs. The result exactly fulfilled all the theoretical predictions. The land wasn't properly worked; there were strikes in all the factories; the laws were set at naught, orders disobeyed; all the people detailed for a spell of low-grade work were perpetually intriguing for high-grade jobs, and all the people with high-grade jobs were counter-intriguing at all costs to stay where they were. Within six years they were having a first-class civil war. When nineteen out of the twenty-two thousand had been killed, the survivors unanimously petitioned the World Controllers to resume the government of the island. Which they did. And that was the end of the only society of Alphas that the world has ever seen."

The Savage sighed, profoundly.

"The optimum population," said Mustapha Mond, "is modelled on the iceberg—eight-ninths below the water line, one-ninth above."

"And they're happy below the water line?"

"Happier than above it. Happier than your friend here, for example." He pointed.

"In spite of that awful work?"

"Awful? *They* don't find it so. On the contrary, they like it. It's light, it's childishly simple. No strain on the mind or the muscles. Seven and a half hours of mild, unexhausting labour, and then the *soma* ration and games and unrestricted copulation and the feelies. What more can they ask for? True," he added, "they might ask for shorter hours. And of course we could give them shorter hours. Technically, it would be perfectly simply to reduce all lower-caste working hours to three or four a day. But would they be any the happier for that? No, they wouldn't. The experiment was tried, more than a century and a half ago. The whole of Ireland was put on to the four-hour day. What was the result? Unrest and a large increase in the consumption of *soma;* that was all. Those three and a half hours of extra leisure were so far from being a source of happiness, that people felt constrained to take a holiday from them. The Inventions Office is stuffed with plans for labour-saving processes. Thousands of them." Mustapha Mond made a lavish gesture. "And why don't we put them into execution? For the sake of the labourers; it would be sheer cruelty to afflict them with excessive leisure. It's the same with agriculture. We could synthesize every morsel of food, if we wanted to. But we don't. We prefer to keep a third of the population on the land. For their own sakes—because it takes *longer* to get food out

of the land than out of a factory. Besides, we have our stability to think of. We don't want to change. Every change is a menace to stability. That's another reason why we're so chary of applying new inventions. Every discovery in pure science is potentially subversive; even science must sometimes be treated as a possible enemy. Yes, even science."

Science? The Savage frowned. He knew the word. But what it exactly signified he could not say. Shakespeare and the old men of the pueblo had never mentioned science, and from Linda he had only gathered the vaguest hints: science was something you made helicopters with, something that caused you to laugh at the Corn Dances, something that prevented you from being wrinkled and losing your teeth. He made a desperate effort to take the Controller's meaning.

"Yes," Mustapha Mond was saying, "that's another item in the cost of stability. It isn't only art that's incompatible with happiness; it's also science. Science is dangerous; we have to keep it most carefully chained and muzzled."

"What?" said Helmholtz, in astonishment. "But we're always saying that science is everything. It's a hypnopædic platitude."

"Three times a week between thirteen and seventeen," put in Bernard.

"And all the science propaganda we do at the College . . ."

"Yes, but what sort of science?" asked Mustapha Mond sarcastically. "You've had no scientific training, so you can't judge. I was a pretty good physicist in my time. Too good—good enough to realize that all our science is just a cookery book, with an orthodox theory of cooking that nobody's allowed to question, and a list or recipes that mustn't be added to except by special permission from the head cook. I'm the head cook now. But I was an inquisitive young scullion once. I started doing a bit of cooking on my own. Unorthodox cooking, illicit cooking. A bit of real science, in fact." He was silent.

"What happened?" asked Helmholtz Watson.

The Controller sighed. "Very nearly what's going to happen to you young men. I was on the point of being sent to an island."

The words galvanized Bernard into violent and unseemly activity. "Send *me* to an island?" He jumped up, ran across the room, and stood gesticulating in front of the Controller. "You can't send *me*. I haven't done anything. It was the others. I swear it was the others." He pointed accusingly to Helmholtz and the Savage. "Oh, please don't send me to Iceland. I promise I'll do what I ought to do. Give me another chance. Please give me another chance." The tears began to flow. "I tell you, it's their fault," he sobbed. "And not to Iceland. Oh please, your fordship, please . . ." And in a paroxysm of abjection he threw himself on his knees before the Controller. Mustapha Mond tried to make him get up; but Bernard persisted in his grovelling; the stream of words poured out inexhaustibly. In the end the Controller had to ring for his fourth secretary.

"Bring three men," he ordered, "and take Mr. Marx into a bedroom. Give him a good *soma* vaporization and then put him to bed and leave him."

The fourth secretary went out and returned with three green-uniformed twin footmen. Still shouting and sobbing, Bernard was carried out.

"One would think he was going to have his throat cut," said the Controller, as the door closed. "Whereas, if he had the smallest sense, he'd understand that his punishment is really a reward. He's being sent to an island. That's to say, he's being sent to a place where he'll meet the most interesting set of men and women to be found anywhere in the world. All the people who, for one reason or another, have got too self-consciously individual to fit into community-life. All the people who aren't satisfied with orthodoxy, who've got independent ideas of their own. Every one, in a word, who's any one. I almost envy you, Mr. Watson."

Helmholtz laughed. "Then why aren't you on an island yourself?"

"Because, finally, I preferred this," the Controller answered. "I was given the choice: to be sent to an island, where I could have got on with my pure science, or to be taken on to the Controllers' Council with the prospect of succeeding in due course to an actual Controllership. I chose this and let the science go." After a little silence, "Sometimes," he added, "I rather regret the science. Happiness is a hard master—particularly other people's happiness. A much harder master, if one isn't conditioned to accept it unquestioningly, than truth." He sighed, fell silent again, then continued in a brisker tone, "Well, duty's duty. One can't consult one's own preference. I'm interested in truth, I like science. But truth's a menace, science is a public danger. As dangerous as it's been beneficial. It has given us the stablest equilibrium in history. China's was hopelessly insecure by comparison; even the primitive matriarchies weren't steadier than we are. Thanks, I repeat, to science. But we can't allow science to undo its own good work. That's why we so carefully limit the scope of its researches —that's why I almost got sent to an island. We don't allow it to deal with any but the most immediate problems of the moment. All other enquiries are most sedulously discouraged. It's curious," he went on after a little pause, "to read what people in the time of Our Ford used to write about scientific progress. They seemed to have imagined that it could be allowed to go on indefinitely, regardless of everything else. Knowledge was the highest good, truth the supreme value; all the rest was secondary and subordinate. True, ideas were beginning to change even then. Our Ford himself did a great deal to shift the emphasis from truth and beauty to comfort and happiness. Mass production demanded the shift. Universal happiness keeps the wheels steadily turning; truth and beauty can't. And, of course, whenever the masses seized political power, then it was happiness rather than truth and beauty that mattered. Still, in spite of everything, unrestricted scientific research was still permitted. People still went on talking about truth and beauty as though they were the sovereign goods. Right up to the time of the Nine Years' War. *That* made them change their tune all right. What's the point of truth or beauty or knowledge when the anthrax bombs are popping all around you? That was when science first began to be controlled—after the Nine Years' War. People were ready to have even their appetites controlled then. Anything for a quiet life. We've gone on controlling ever since. It hasn't been very good for truth, of course. But it's been very good for happiness. One can't have something for nothing. Happiness has got to be paid for. You're paying for it, Mr. Watson—paying because you happen to be too much interested in beauty. I was too much interested in truth; I paid too."

"But *you* didn't go to an island," said the Savage, breaking a long silence.

The Controller smiled. "That's how I paid. By choosing to serve happiness. Other people's —not mine. It's lucky," he added, after a pause, that there are such a lot of islands in the world. I don't know what we should do without them. Put you all in the lethal chamber, I suppose. By the way, Mr. Watson, would you like a tropical climate? The Marquesas, for example; or Samoa? Or something rather more bracing?"

Helmholtz rose from his pneumatic chair. "I should like a thoroughly bad climate," he answered. "I believe one would write better if the climate were bad. If there were a lot of wind and storms, for example . . ."

The Controller nodded his approbation. "I like your spirit, Mr. Watson. I like it very much indeed. As much as I officially disapprove of it." He smiled. "What about the Falkland Islands?"

"Yes, I think that will do," Helmholtz answered. "And now, if you don't mind, I'll go and see how poor Bernard's getting on."

"Art, science—you seem to have paid a fairly high price for your happiness," said the Savage, when they were alone. "Anything else?"

"Well, religion, of course," replied the Controller. "There used to be something called God —before the Nine Years' War. But I was forgetting; you know all about God, I suppose."

"Well . . ." The Savage hesitated. He would have liked to say something about solitude, about night, about the mesa lying pale under the moon, about the precipice, the plunge into shadowy darkness, about death. He would have liked to speak; but there were no words. Not even in Shakespeare.

The Controller, meanwhile, had crossed to the other side of the room and was unlocking a large safe set into the wall between the bookshelves. The heavy door swung open. Rummaging in the darkness within, "It's a subject," he said, "that has always had a great interest for me." He pulled out a thick black volume. "You've never read this, for example."

The Savage took it. "*The Holy Bible, containing the Old and New Testaments,*" he read aloud from the title-page.

"Nor this." It was a small book and had lost its cover.

"*The Imitation of Christ.*"

"Nor this." He handed out another volume.

"*The Varieties of Religious Experience. By William James.*"

"And I've got plenty more," Mustapha Mond continued, resuming his seat. "A whole collection of pornographic old books. God in the safe and Ford on the shelves." He pointed with a laugh to his avowed library—to the shelves of books, the rack full of reading-machine bobbins and sound-track rolls.

"But if you know about God, why don't you tell them?" asked the Savage indignantly. "Why don't you give them these books about God?"

"For the same reason as we don't give them *Othello*: they're old; they're about God hundreds of years ago. Not about God now."

"But God doesn't change."

"Men do, though."

"What difference does that make?"

"All the difference in the world," said Mustapha Mond. He got up again and walked to the safe. "There was a man called Cardinal Newman," he said. "A cardinal," he exclaimed parenthetically, "was a kind of Arch-Community-Songster."

"'I Pandulph, of fair Milan, cardinal.' I've read about them in Shakespeare."

"Of course you have. Well, as I was saying, there was a man called Cardinal Newman. Ah, here's the book." He pulled it out. "And while I'm about it I'll take this one too. It's by a man called Maine de Biran. He was a philosopher, if you know what that was."

"A man who dreams of fewer things than there are in heaven and earth," said the Savage promptly.

"Quite so. I'll read you one of the things he *did* dream of in a moment. Meanwhile, listen to what this old Arch-Community-Songster said." He opened the book at the place marked by a slip of paper and began to read. "'We are not our own any more than what we possess is our own. We did not make ourselves, we cannot be supreme over ourselves. We are not our own masters. We are God's property. Is it not our happiness thus to view the matter? Is it any happiness or any comfort, to consider that we *are* our own? It may be thought so by the young and prosperous. These may think it a great thing to have everything, as they suppose, their own way—to depend on no one—to have to think of nothing out of sight, to be without the irksomeness of continual acknowledgment, continual prayer, continual reference of what they do to the will of another. But as time goes on, they, as all men, will find that independence was not made for man—that it is an unnatural state—will do for a while, but will not carry us on safely to the end...'" Mustapha Mond paused, put down the first book and, picking up the other, turned over the pages. "Take this, for example," he said, and in his deep voice once more began to read: "'A man grows old; he feels in himself that radical sense of weakness, of listlessness, of discomfort, which accompanies the advance of age; and, feeling thus, imagines himself merely sick, lulling his fears with the notion that this distressing condition is due to some particular cause, from which, as from an illness, he hopes to recover. Vain imaginings! That sickness is old age; and a horrible disease it is. They say that it is the fear of death and of what comes after death that makes men turn to religion as they advance in years. But my own experience has given me the conviction that, quite apart from any such terrors or imaginings, the religious sentiment tends to develop as we grow older; to develop because, as the passions grow calm, as the fancy and sensibilities are less excited and less excitable, our reason becomes less troubled in its working, less obscured by the images, desires and distractions, in which it used to be absorbed; whereupon God emerges as from behind a cloud; our soul feels, sees, turns towards the source of all light; turns naturally and inevitably; for now that all that gave to the world of sensations its life and charms has begun to leak away from us, now that phenomenal existence is no more bolstered up by impressions from within or from without, we feel the need to lean on something that abides, something that will never play us false—a reality, an absolute and everlasting truth. Yes, we inevitably turn to God; for this religious sentiment is of its nature so pure, so delightful to the soul that experiences it, that it makes up to us for all our other losses.'" Mustapha Mond shut the book and leaned back in his chair. "One of the numerous things in heaven and earth that these philosophers didn't dream about was this" (he waved his hand), "us, the modern world. 'You can only be independent of God while you've got youth and prosperity; independence won't take you safely to the end.' Well, we've now got youth and prosperity right up to the end. What follows? Evidently, that we can be independent of God. 'The religious sentiment will compensate us for all our losses.' But there aren't any losses for us to compensate; religious sentiment is superfluous. And why should we go hunting for a substitute for youthful desires, when youthful desires never fail? A substitute for distractions, when we go on enjoying all the old fooleries to the very last? What need have we of repose when our minds and bodies continue to delight in activity? of consolation, when we have *soma?* of something immovable, when there is the social order?"

"Then you think there is no God?"

"No, I think there quite probably is one."

"Then why? . . ."

Mustapha Mond checked him. "But he manifests himself in different ways to different men. In premodern times he manifested himself as the being that's described in these books. Now . . ."

"How does he manifest himself now?" asked the Savage.

"Well, he manifests himself as an absence; as though he weren't there at all."

"That's your fault."

"Call it the fault of civilization. God isn't compatible with machinery and scientific medicine and universal happiness. You must make your choice. Our civilization has chosen machinery and medicine and happiness. That's why I have to keep these books locked up in the safe. They're smut. People would be shocked if . . ."

The Savage interrupted him. "But isn't it *natural* to feel there's a God?"

"You might as well ask if it's natural to do up one's trousers with zippers," said the Controller sarcastically. "You remind me of another of those fellows called Bradley. He defined philosophy as the finding of bad reason for what one believes by instinct. As if one believed anything by instinct! One believes things because one has been conditioned to believe them. Finding bad reasons for what one believes for other bad reasons—that's philosophy. People believe in God because they've been conditioned to believe in God."

"But all the same," insisted the Savage, "it is natural to believe in God when you're alone—quite alone, in the night, thinking about death . . ."

"But people never are alone now," said Mustapha Mond. "We make them hate solitude; and we arrange their lives so that it's almost impossible for them ever to have it."

The Savage nodded gloomily. At Malpais he had suffered because they had shut him out from the communal activities of the pueblo, in civilized London he was suffering because he could never escape from those communal activities, never be quietly alone.

"Do you remember that bit in *King Lear?*" said the Savage at last. " 'The gods are just and of our pleasant vices make instruments to plague us; the dark and vicious place where thee he got cost him his eyes,' and Edmund answers—you remember, he's wounded, he's dying—'Thou hast spoken right; 'tis true. The wheel has come full circle; I am here.' What about that now? Doesn't there seem to be a God managing things, punishing, rewarding?"

"Well, does there?" questioned the Controller in his turn. "You can indulge in any number of pleasant vices with a freemartin and run no risks of having your eyes put out by your son's mistress. 'The wheel has come full circle; I am here.' But where would Edmund be nowadays? Sitting in a pneumatic chair, with his arm round a girl's waist, sucking away at his sex-hormone chewing-gum and looking at the feelies. The gods are just. No doubt. But their code of law is dictated, in the last resort, by the people who organize society; Providence takes its cue from men."

"Are you sure?" asked the Savage. "Are you quite sure that the Edmund in that pneumatic chair hasn't been just as heavily punished as the Edmund who's wounded and bleeding to death? The gods are just. Haven't they used his pleasant vices as an instrument to degrade him?"

"Degrade him from what position? As a

happy, hard-working, goods-consuming citizen he's perfect. Of course, if you choose some other standard than ours, then perhaps you might say he was degraded. But you've got to stick to one set of postulates. You can't play Electro-magnetic Golf according to the rules of Centrifugal Bumble-puppy."

"But value dwells not in particular will," said the Savage. "It holds his estimate and dignity as well wherein 'tis precious of itself as in the prizer."

"Come, come," protested Mustapha Mond, "that's going rather far, isn't it?"

"If you allowed yourselves to think of God, you wouldn't allow yourselves to be degraded by pleasant vices. You'd have a reason for bearing things patiently, for doing things with courage. I've seen it with the Indians."

"I'm sure you have," said Mustapha Mond. "But then we aren't Indians. There isn't any need for a civilized man to bear anything that's seriously unpleasant. And as for doing things—Ford forbid that he should get the idea into his head. It would upset the whole social order if men started doing things on their own."

"What about self-denial, then? If you had a God, you'd have a reason for self-denial."

"But industrial civilization is only possible when there's no self-denial. Self-indulgence up to the very limits imposed by hygiene and economics. Otherwise the wheels stop turning."

"You'd have a reason for chastity!" said the Savage, blushing a little as he spoke the words.

"But chastity means passion, chastity means neurasthenia. And passion and neurasthenia mean instability. And instability means the end of civilization. You can't have a lasting civilization without plenty of pleasant vices."

"But God's the reason for everything noble and fine and heroic. If you had a God . . ."

"My dear young friend," said Mustapha Mond, "civilization has absolutely no need of nobility or heroism. These things are symptoms of political inefficiency. In a properly organized society like ours, nobody has any opportunities for being noble or heroic. Conditions have got to be thoroughly unstable before the occasion can arise. Where there are wars, where there are divided allegiances, where there are temptations to be resisted, objects of love to be fought for or defended—there, obviously, nobility and heroism have some sense. But there aren't any wars nowadays. The greatest care is taken to prevent you from loving any one too much. There's no such thing as a divided allegiance; you're so conditioned that you can't help doing what you ought to do. And what you ought to do is on the whole so pleasant, so many of the natural impulses are allowed free play, that there really aren't any temptations to resist. And if ever, by some unlucky chance, anything unpleasant should somehow happen, why, there's always *soma* to give you a holiday from the facts. And there's always *soma* to calm your anger, to reconcile you to your enemies, to make you patient and long-suffering. In the past you could only accomplish these things by making a great effort and after years of hard moral training. Now, you swallow two or three half-gramme tablets, and there you are. Anybody can be virtuous now. You can carry at least half your mortality about in a bottle. Christianity without tears—that's what *soma* is."

"But the tears are necessary. Don't you remember what Othello said? 'If after every tempest came such calms, may the winds blow till they have wakened death.' There's a story one of the old Indians used to tell us, about the Girl of Mátaski. The young men who wanted to marry her had to do a morning's hoeing in her garden. It seemed easy; but there were flies and mosquitoes, magic ones. Most of the young men simply couldn't stand the biting and stinging. But the one that could—he got the girl."

"Charming! But in civilized countries," said the Controller, "you can have girls without hoeing for them; and there aren't any flies or mosquitoes to sting you. We got rid of them all centuries ago."

The Savage nodded, frowning. "You got rid of them. Yes, that's just like you. Getting rid of everything unpleasant instead of learning to put up with it. Whether 'tis better in the mind to suffer the slings and arrows of outrageous fortune, or to take arms against a sea of troubles and by opposing end them . . . But you don't do either. Neither suffer nor oppose. You just abolish the slings and arrows. It's too easy."

He was suddenly silent, thinking of his mother. In her room on the thirty-seventh floor, Linda had floated in a sea of singing lights and perfumed caresses—floated away, out of space, out of time, out of the prison of her memories, her habits, her aged and bloated body. And Tomakin, ex-Director of Hatcheries and Conditioning, Tomakin was still on holiday—on holiday from humiliation and pain, in a world where he could not hear those words, that derisive laughter, could not see that hideous face, feel those moist and flabby arms round his neck, in a beautiful world . . .

"What you need," the Savage went on, "is something *with* tears for a change. Nothing costs enough here."

("Twelve and a half million dollars," Henry Foster had protested when the Savage told him that. "Twelve and a half million—that's what the new Conditioning Centre cost. Not a cent less.")

"Exposing what is mortal and unsure to all that fortune, death and danger dare, even for an eggshell. Isn't there something in that?" he asked, looking up at Mustapha Mond. "Quite apart from God—though of course God would be a reason for it. Isn't there something in living dangerously?"

"There's a great deal in it," the Controller replied. "Men and women must have their adrenals stimulated from time to time."

"What?" questioned the Savage, uncomprehending.

"It's one of the conditions of perfect health. That's why we've made the V.P.S. treatments compulsory."

"V.P.S.?"

"Violent Passion Surrogate. Regularly once a month. We flood the whole system with adrenin. It's the complete physiological equivalent of fear and rage. All the tonic effects of murdering Desdemona and being murdered by Othello, without any of the inconveniences."

"But I like the inconveniences."

"We don't," said the Controller. "We prefer to do things comfortably."

"But I don't want comfort. I want God, I want poetry, I want real danger, I want freedom, I want goodness. I want sin."

"In fact," said Mustapha Mond, "you're claiming the right to be unhappy."

"All right then," said the Savage defiantly, "I'm claiming the right to be unhappy."

"Not to mention the right to grow old and ugly and impotent; the right to have syphilis and cancer; the right to have too little to eat; the right to be lousy; the right to live in constant apprehension of what may happen tomorrow; the right to catch typhoid; the right to be tortured by unspeakable pains of every kind." There was a long silence.

"I claim them all," said the Savage at last.

Mustapha Mond shrugged his shoulders. "You're welcome," he said.

RELATED READING

Adler, Mortimer J. *The Idea of Freedom: A Dialectical Examination of the Conceptions of Freedom,* 2 vols. Westport, Conn.: Greenwood Press, 1961.

Anschutz, R. P. *The Philosophy of John Stuart Mill.* Oxford: Clarendon Press, 1953.

Apter, David E., and James Joll. *Anarchism Today.* New York: Doubleday & Co., 1972.

Bart, Alan. *The Price of Liberty.* New York: Viking Press, 1961.

Bury, John. *A History of Freedom of Thought.* New York: Oxford University Press, 1913.

Camus, Albert. *The Rebel: An Essay on Man in Revolt.* New York: Vintage, 1956.

Clark, Mary T. *The Problem of Freedom.* Englewood Cliffs, N.J.: Prentice-Hall, 1973.

Cohen, Morris R. *The Faith of a Liberal.* New York: Holt, Rinehart & Winston, 1961.

Dewey, John. *Freedom and Culture.* New York: G. P. Putnam's Sons, 1939.

Douglas, Jack D., ed. *Freedom and Tyranny: Social Problems in a Technological Society.* New York: Alfred A. Knopf, 1970.

Ebenstein, William. *Today's Isms,* 3rd ed. Englewood Cliffs, N.J.: Prentice-Hall, 1961.

Edman, Irwin. *Foundations of Freedom: The Growth of the Democratic Idea.* New York: Reynal and Hitchcock, 1941.

Fromm, Erich. *Escape from Freedom.* New York: Holt, Rinehart & Winston, 1947.

―――. *The Revolution of Hope: Toward a Humanized Technology.* New York: Bantam Books, 1968.

Harris, Robert T. *Social Ethics.* New York: J. B. Lippincott Co., 1962.

Highet, Gilbert. *Man's Unconquerable Mind.* New York: Columbia University Press, 1960.

Hook, Sidney. *The Hero in History.* New York: Humanities Press, 1967

―――. *Political Power and Personal Freedom.* New York: Criterion Books, 1959.

―――. *The Paradoxes of Freedom.* Los Angeles: University of California Press, 1964.

Horowitz, Irving. *The Anarchists.* New York: Dell Publishing Co., 1964.

Kaufman, Walter, ed. *Existentialism from Dostoevsky to Sartre.* New York: Meridian Books, 1956.

Kinkade, Kathleen. *A Walden Two Experiment: The First Five Years of Twin Oaks Community.* New York: William Morrow & Co., 1973.

Kirk, Russell. *The Conservative Mind from Burke to Santayana.* Chicago: Henry Regnery Co., 1953.

Kostelanetz, Richard, ed. *Beyond Left and Right: Radical Thought for Our Times.* New York: William Morrow & Co., 1968.

Meiklejohn, Alexander. *Political Freedom.* New York: Galaxy Books, 1965.

Muller, Herbert J. *Issues of Freedom.* New York: Harper & Row, 1960.

Rand, Ayn. *Capitalism: The Unknown Ideal.* New York: Signet, 1967.

Reich, Charles. *The Greening of America.* New York: Random House, 1970.

Robinson, Paul A. *The Freudian Left: Wilhelm Reich, Geza Roheim, Herbert Marcuse.* New York: Harper & Row, 1969.

Rogers, Carl. *On Becoming a Person.* Boston: Houghton Mifflin, 1961.

Skinner, B. F. *About Behaviorism.* New York: Alfred A. Knopf, 1974.

———. *Beyond Freedom and Dignity.* New York: Alfred A. Knopf, 1971.

———. *Science and Human Behavior.* New York: Macmillan, 1953.

———. *Walden Two.* New York: Macmillan, 1948.

Van Over, Raymond, ed. *The Psychology of Freedom.* New York: Fawcett, 1974.

Wagar, W. Warren. *The City of Man.* Baltimore, Md.: Penguin Books, 1970.

Weldon, T. D. *The Vocabulary of Politics.* Baltimore, Md.: Penguin Books, 1953.

Wellek, Rene. *Dostoevsky, A Collection of Critical Essays.* Englewood Cliffs, N.J.: Prentice-Hall, 1962.

Yablonsky, Lewis. *Robopaths.* Indianapolis, Ind.: Bobbs-Merrill Co., 1972.

Part 5

CONFRONTATION WITH RELIGIOUS EXPERIENCE

Commitment to Search for Transcendence

To see a World in a Grain of Sand
And a Heaven in a Wild Flower
Hold Infinity in the palm of your
hand And Eternity in an hour.
                    William Blake

Religion is morality tinged with emotion.
                    Matthew Arnold

Religion is what the individual does with his
own solitariness . . . if you are never solitary, you
are never religious.
                    Alfred North Whitehead

We are deprived of Truth by the energy with which
we immerse ourselves in a truth.
                    Karl Barth

Neither faith nor doubt can be eliminated from man as man.
                    Paul Tillich

*Words have a power, a terrible power, of intruding
between man and God.*
                    St. Ignatius

Religion — the opiate of the people.
                    Karl Marx

He who cleaveth firmly unto God is
already directed in the right way.
                    The Koran

Men overlook traces of divinity by reason of their
incredulity.
                    Heraclitus

Religious phenomena are to be understood only as
the model of the neurotic symptoms of the individual.
                    Sigmund Freud

When it comes to the question of life itself we cannot wait for
the ultimate solution to be offered by the intellect.
                    D. T. Suzuki

Introduction: Religion Revisited

What is religion? The attempt to answer this question has spawned a variety of often conflicting metaphors, definitions, and theories. Religion has been likened to a crutch, a security blanket, an opiate, an illusion, a storm shelter, a lookout post, a launching pad, a placebo, a window on the cosmos, the Ground of Being, "that voice of deepest human experience" (Matthew Arnold), and "a daughter of Hope and Fear, explaining to ignorance the nature of the Unknowable" (Ambrose Bierce). The essence of religion has been found in "morality tinged with emotion," an aspiration for self-transcendence, an ultimate concern or an ultimate commitment, union with Absolute Spirit, contemplation of eternal Goodness, Beauty and Truth, and confrontation with the Awe-ful, the Numinous, the Holy, and the Divine.

Whatever the definition of religion, religions make a promise: that an authentic encounter with the divine will transform human life and open the person to a totally new way of experiencing the world. People who have had such an encounter sometimes have radically different conceptions of themselves and of reality. The commitment to God can be so momentous that religious commitments have often become models for the "total commitment."

However, "commitment to God" is inadequate in characterizing the complex phenomenon called "religion." In trying to formulate a definition of religion that includes Greek polytheism, the many forms of Christianity, Buddhism, and Hinduism, it is difficult if not impossible to find a common characteristic universally expressive of the unique nature of religion. We can look for a definition in its external manifestations, such as its institutions, ceremonies, forms of worship, and rituals. We can also look for a definition in terms of its attitudes, beliefs, emotions, and its special feelings of awe and reverence. One such definition, which emphasizes the internal, is the one given by the American philosopher Josiah Royce. Royce defined religion as consisting of three interconnecting components.

These three elements, then, go to constitute any religion. A religion must teach some moral code, must in some way inspire a strong feeling of devotion to that code, and in so doing must show something in the nature of things that answers to that code or that serves to reinforce the feeling. A religion is therefore practical, emotional, and theoretical; it teaches us to do, to feel, and to believe, and it teaches the belief as a means to its teaching of the action and of the feeling.[1]

Any one of these components alone is insufficient to define religion. A feeling is not religious merely because it is strong or "elevated." Believing in God or the supernatural is not enough. A mere moral code is not religion either, although every religion does involve some form of moral command. All three factors, interrelated through personal commitment, are required. There must be a moral code, an emotional content which inspires devotion, and a view of reality that supports the other two factors, according to Royce.

There is still considerable disagreement regarding the basic features of the concept of religion. There is less disagreement regarding the definition of "the philosophy of religion." The philosophy of religion is not itself a religion, nor must it entail a religious faith or commitment. It deals with the origin, nature, and function of religion and analyzes such central concepts as God, worship, creation, and revelation. Recently, there has been interest in analyzing religious language and assessing the special claims made regarding religious knowledge. Although religion is directly expressed in the worship, meditation, and practices of particular sects, it also has a doctrinal aspect. Its theoretical component, which is usually embodied in its doctrinal theology, accompanies and supports the experiential and moral components of religion. Historically, the major interest of the philosopher of religion has been in this theoretical component, and in analyzing religious beliefs about the divine, man's relation to it, and human destiny.

At the center of philosophical questions about religion are the rational arguments for the existence of God. In the following selection, these arguments are presented in their "classic" form by the great thirteenth-century Catholic theologian Saint Thomas Aquinas. They formed only a small portion of Saint Thomas' elaborate ideational structure, *The Summa Theologica,* in which he attempted to survey, criticize, and systematize the science, philosophy, and religion of his day.

In the second selection, these arguments are restated and clarified by Fulton J. Sheen, a contemporary theologian and exponent of Thomism. In developing the philosophical basis of religion, Archbishop Sheen, like Saint Thomas, assumed that the ultimate modes of reality, or of "the transcendentals," are being, truth, and goodness. From this point, he proceeds to develop arguments for God's existence which, he believes, give a secure rational basis for believing in a supernatural being.

These traditional arguments for the existence of God have been vehemently attacked by many agnostics, atheists, and sceptics, including those represented in the following two selections. The agnosticism of Bertrand Russell was born not only out of his rational criticism of these arguments but also out of his moral revulsion regarding the teaching and behavior of religious believers throughout history. He concentrates his attacks against the argument from first cause, the argument from design, and one of the moral arguments for the existence of Deity.

Ernest Nagel went beyond the agnosticism and scepticism of Russell. His atheistic naturalism was the background for his criticism of the traditional arguments. In addition, he attacked the ontological argument and the argument from mystical experience. Naturalists such as Russell and Nagel do not ascribe to the supernaturalistic world view that is characteristic of most of the world's major religions. Religion is a phenomenon which can be explained within the framework of human nature and society.

The next three selections on mysticism focus not upon doctrines and beliefs, but upon an experience, a mode of consciousness. Mystics have claimed that direct knowledge of a higher consciousness or spiritual reality transported them beyond the bounds of ordinary sensory evidence and rational argument. The history of religion, East and West, is filled with accounts of this consciousness and the way in which it has changed peoples' lives. Although religions encompass a wide variety of practices, beliefs, and attitudes, mystical experiences are a part of the vitality of religion and religious life, whether in the Nirvana of.the Buddhist, the encounter with the Oneness of all things of the Hindu mystic, or the Christian's joyful bliss in experiencing "the peace of God which passeth all understanding."

A mystical experience has been the most profound event in some people's lives. Yet understanding that experience presents several problems. The diversity of the accounts of mystical experiences in different parts of the world challenges us to devise an adequate description. Is the content of mystical experience wholly determined by the culture in which it occurs? How are we to evaluate the claims that some mystics make about their experiences? For example, some mystics claim that the existence of God is not an inference from some set of empirical facts, but is shown through experience of Him in mystical ecstasy and absorption into His divine nature. To what extent can we take the reported experience as evidence for anything beyond the fact that the mystic has had the experience? Can we devise valid criteria for testing the truth claims of these experiences? These questions are raised by the following selections from the teaching of the Buddha and the Zen scholar, and they are discussed by Walter Stace in his article on mysticism and reason.

Often associated with religion, but not necessarily connected with the belief in God, is the belief in life after death and the immortality of the soul. Plato was one of the first philosophers to outline a distinction between body and mind (or soul) and to attempt to prove the immortality of the soul. The body belongs to the world perceived by the senses, it is changing and impermanent; the soul is related to the unchanging realities of a higher permanent world (see Part Three).

Curt Ducasse's article on the possibility of life after death tries to remove the ambiguities regarding the question itself. Arguing against the opponents of the idea of life after death and using material from psychical research, he proceeds to present anew a case for believing in survival after death.

Finally, the selection from William James returns to the issue of the intellectual belief in God, or the religious hypothesis. Since the question of the existence of God cannot be conclusively settled by rational argument, we have the right to will to believe, and to avail ourselves of the benefits which result from a commitment to the religious hypothesis.

NOTE

1. Josiah Royce, *The Religious Aspects of Philosophy* (Boston: Houghton Mifflin, 1885), p. 4.

23 God's Existence—Provable

Aquinas & Sheen

> The foundation upon which all religious faith rests is God. Without a Supreme Being all religion would be a delusion and a snare. There can be no intelligent discussion of religions until the existence of God has been clearly and definitely established.[1]

The authenticity of religious belief does not rest on the ability of the believer to prove rationally the existence of God to himself or to others. It may well be that the mass of believers know or care little about rational proofs of God's existence, and certainly whether or not one can come forth with reasons for believing in God does not affect the *reality* of God's existence.

However, *discussion* of religion, debate as to whether one can support and defend one's religious beliefs by empirical and rational considerations, is another matter. There will always be those who agree with the view that "to the person who does not believe in God, no proof is possible; and to the person who believes in God, no proof is necessary." If we assume that man is a rational animal who by nature desires to know, it is natural and desirable to investigate the possibilities of finding reasons for religious as well as for other beliefs.

Rational arguments for the existence of a God can be found in ancient Greek philosophy, particularly in the works of Plato and Aristotle. Aristotle, for example, in his *Metaphysics,* argued that there must be an Unmoved Mover to account for the motion throughout the universe. Like Plato, he saw evidence of purposiveness and design inherent in the nature of things which seemed to imply a cosmic purposer if not a divine creator. With the triumph of Christianity in the West, defenders of the faith, feeling the need for rational arguments to support their religious beliefs, drew materials from the Greeks and other sources. The most influential list of the arguments for God's existence was formulated by the greatest Catholic theologian of the Middle Ages, Saint Thomas Aquinas (1225?–1274).

Saint Thomas spent a lifetime synthesizing and harmonizing a view of the universe that was first set forth by Aristotle. This view was based on reason and on the Church's doctrines derived from divine revelation. So successful was he in his achievement that even today Catholic theologians such as Archbishop Fulton J. Sheen rely upon his works for the rational justification of faith. Of course, Saint Thomas did not expect that people's beliefs in God would depend upon the arguments he presented, nor did he deny that people can know of God's existence in ways other than rational proofs. He was careful to make the distinction between mere intellectual assent to these proofs and a genuine and complete Christian commitment based on a deep love of God. However, if one needs proofs these arguments should be sufficiently convincing to the intellect.

Profoundly influenced by the work of Saint Thomas, whom he sometimes refers to as "the Angelic Doctor," Fulton J. Sheen relies upon him at most points in providing metaphysical arguments for God's existence. While one can study religion historically, psychologically, and metaphysically, Sheen holds that the latter is the most fundamental approach. The metaphysical approach has to do primarily not with the origin, development, or effects of religious beliefs but with their rational ground and foundation. Sheen holds "that everything in this world, whether inert or living, moral or amoral, spiritual or temporal, can be said *to be, to be true,* and *to be good.*"[2] Being, truth, and goodness are the ultimate modes of classification, which Saint Thomas and the other Scholastic philosophers called the transcendentals. Sheen begins his arguments for God's existence by relating human experience to these fundamental realities.

It is important to realize, after reading Sheen's account of the rational proofs of God's existence, that neither he nor other Thomistic thinkers would be satisfied to stop at the rational level of religious experience. He and they do not hesitate to make use of revelation and faith, in so far as these do no violence to reason, in amplifying the deeper and wider meaning of Being, Truth, and Goodness. In Sheen's view, "faith no more destroys reason, than a telescope destroys the vision."[3] To him faith is a new kind of daylight by which previously unclear realities can be seen more sharply and completely. Faith, he holds, is not "a leap in the dark, an hypothesis, a chance, a wish or a will to believe." It is rather "the assent of the intellect to a truth on the authority of God revealing."[4] Faith, in this sense, must be present to achieve full understanding of Being, Truth, and Goodness. As another theologian put it, "you must believe before you can understand."

Although Sheen and other Thomists believe that religious experience must lie at the basis of genuine religious commitment, religious experience to them does not mean "a nonintellectual approach to God in which feeling is primary." Religious experience certainly involves an affective or emotional response, but it is basically an intellectual rather than an emotional approach to Being, Truth, and Goodness. In his *Philosophy of Religion,* Sheen pointed out that "the only God attained by a purely affective approach is a subjective God, born of one's own feelings."[5] As feelings vary, so would conceptions of God.

> God will vary from man to man, and from experience to experience, which means there is no God except the one man makes to his own feelings and experiences. Feeling good does not mean being good, and feeling God does not mean discovering His existence. To appeal to emotions on questions where reason is relevant, is to end in illusion and subjectivism.[6]

Thus Sheen would reject the usual modern views that put affective or feeling elements in religious experience first. In his view, as the emotional state is dependent in man on the rational, the rational must take precedence. "Once given the rational, then there is an organic repercussion on the emotional." It is necessary, therefore, to know God not just in the immediate sense of intellectual knowledge which, following Saint Thomas, Sheen calls confused intellectual knowledge. It is necessary to attain perfect, developed, or "reflex knowledge" of God that will withstand analysis and criticism. At this level, we go beyond the immediate rational recognition that God is the Governor of the universe, and we get to know His nature and attributes. To attain this higher kind of knowledge is the purpose, Sheen says, of Saint Thomas's rational proofs. And "it is therefore not valid to object that the five proofs of Saint Thomas are too dry and abstract."[7]

NOTES

1.   John A. O'Brien, *Truths Men Live By* (New York: Macmillan, 1946), p. 1.

2.   Fulton J. Sheen, *Religion Without God* (New York: Garden City Books, 1954), p. 321.

3.   Ibid., p. 338.

4.   Ibid.

5.   Fulton J. Sheen, *Philosophy of Religion* (New York: Appleton-Century-Crofts, 1948), p. 238.

6.   Ibid.

7.   Sheen, *Religion Without God,* p. 240.

The Five Ways

Saint Thomas Aquinas

The existence of God can be proved in five ways.

The first and more manifest way is the argument from motion. It is certain, and evident to our senses, that in the world some things are in motion. Now whatever is moved is moved by another, for nothing can be moved except it is in potentiality to that towards which it is moved; whereas a thing moves inasmuch as it is in act. For motion is nothing else than the reduction of something from potentiality to actuality. But nothing can be reduced from potentiality to actuality, except by something in a state of actuality. Thus that which is actually hot, as fire, makes wood, which is potentially hot, to be actually hot, and thereby moves and changes it. Now it is not possible that the same thing should be at once in actuality and potentiality in the same respect, but only in different respects. For what is actually hot cannot simultaneously be potentially hot; but it is simultaneously potentially cold. It is therefore impossible that in the same respect and in the same way a thing should be both mover and moved, i.e., that it should move itself. Therefore, whatever is moved must be moved by another. If that by which it is moved be itself moved, then this also must needs be moved by another, and that by another again. But this cannot go on to infinity, because then there

From *The Basic Writings of St. Thomas Aquinas,* edited by Anton G. Pegis, (New York: Random House, Inc., 1945).

would be no first mover, and, consequently, no other mover, seeing that subsequent movers move only inasmuch as they are moved by the first mover; as the staff moves only because it is moved by the hand. Therefore it is necessary to arrive at a first mover, moved by no other; and this everyone understands to be God.

The second way is from the nature of efficient cause. In the world of sensible things we find there is an order of efficient causes. There is no case known (neither is it, indeed, possible) in which a thing is found to be the efficient cause of itself; for so it would be prior to itself, which is impossible. Now in efficient causes it is not possible to go to infinity, because in all efficient causes following in order, the first is the cause of the intermediate cause, and the intermediate is the cause of the ultimate cause, whether the intermediate cause be several, or one only. Now to take away the cause is to take away the effect. Therefore, if there be no first cause among efficient causes, there will be no ultimate, nor any intermediate, cause. But if in efficient causes it is possible to go on to infinity, there will be no first efficient cause, neither will there be an ultimate effect, nor any intermediate efficient causes; all of which is plainly false. Therefore it is necessary to admit a first efficient cause, to which everyone gives the name of God.

The third way is taken from possibility and necessity, and runs thus. We find in nature things that are possible to be and not to be, since they are found to be generated, and to be corrupted, and consequently, it is possible for them to be and not to be. But it is impossible for these always to exist, for that which can not-be at some time is not. Therefore, if everything can not-be, then at one time there was nothing in existence. Now if this were true, even now there would be nothing in existence, because that which does not exist begins to exist only through something already existing. Therefore, if at one time nothing was in existence, it would have been impossible for anything to have begun to exist; and thus even now nothing would be in existence—which is absurd. Therefore, not all beings are merely possible, but here must exist something the existence of which is necessary. But every necessary thing either has its necessity caused by another, or not. Now it is impossible to go on to infinity in necessary things which have their necessity caused by another, as has been already proved in regard to efficient causes. Therefore we cannot but admit the existence of some being having of itself its own necessity, and not receiving it from another, but rather causing in others their necessity. This all men speak of as God.

The fourth way is taken from the gradation to be found in things. Among beings there are some more and some less good, true, noble, and the like. But *more* and *less* are predicated of different things according as they resemble in their different ways something which is the maximum, as a thing is said to be hotter according as it more nearly resembles that which is hottest; so that there is something which is truest, something best, something noblest, and, consequently, something which is most being, for those things that are greatest in truth are greatest in being. . . . Now the maximum in any genus is the cause of all in that genus, as fire, which is the maximum of heat, is the cause of all hot things. . . . Therefore there must also be something which is to all beings the cause of their being, goodness, and every other perfection and this we call God.

The fifth way is taken from the governance of the world. We see that things which lack knowledge, such as natural bodies, act for an end, and this is evident from their acting always, or nearly always, in the same way, so as to obtain the best result. Hence it is plain that they achieve their end, not fortuitously, but designedly. Now whatever lacks knowledge cannot move towards an end, unless it be directed by some being endowed with knowledge and intelligence; as the arrow is directed by the archer. Therefore some intelligent being exists by whom all natural things are directed to their end; and this being we call God.

Proofs of God's Existence

Fulton J. Sheen

There are three fundamental cravings in the human heart, to which all others are resolvable. They are the craving for *being* or life, *truth* and *love*. The first of these, the inclination toward the preservation and the perfection of life is the basis of the others. A human being will sacrifice all other possessions, wealth, pleasures, honors and the like providing that he can cling on to that which he treasures last of all—life. The very tendency to put out our hand before us as we walk in the dark is a proof that we are willing to lose even our members provided we can conserve our existence.

The second fundamental craving is the desire to know and possess truth. The first question a child asks when he comes into this world is the question: Why? Every babe is an incipient philosopher. He tears his toys to pieces to find out what makes the wheels go round, and then later on, when he grows to man's estate he tears apart the wheels of the universe by a mental process to determine why its wheels go round, in other words, to know its causes. Man has an appetite for truth as he has for food, and truth is just as satisfying to the mind, even more so, than food is for the body.

The third fundamental craving is the desire to love and to be loved. From the first day when

Copyright 1928 by Longmans Green and Co. From the book *Religion Without God* by Fulton J. Sheen. Reprinted by permission of the publisher, Longmans, Green and Co., a division of David McKay Co., Inc.

God said "It is not good for man to be alone," even unto the end, man will hunger and thirst for love. Companions and friends will be sought out to whom he can unpack his heart with words, and above all, life-long friends who will measure up to the test of friendship—one in whose presence he can keep silence.

What makes a man then? A soul which is life, which seeks truth, which seeks love. Being, Truth, and Love. That is man.

But do we carry within ourselves the fulfillment of these appetites? We possess a modicum of life, a modicum of truth, a modicum of love, but do we possess life, truth, and love in their entirety? The richness of our life is borrowed; the children of parents do not always live in the family circle, but obeying the law of nature, leave them who gave them life, to establish their own fireside. Is not our life an approaching death? Does not each tick of the clock bring us nearer the grave; does not the very food we eat burn up our body and hasten the end of our earthly life? "Our hearts like muffled drums are beating funeral marches to the grave." "From hour to hour we ripe and ripe; then from hour to hour we rot and rot." In a word, is not death mingled with life?

And while truth is a condition of our nature, we cannot say that we possess truth in its entirety. Are we not under the necessity of being taught; does not the multitude of religions, political doctrines and social theories prove we are but vaguely and dimly possessing truth? If but our sight were lost in our cradle much of the knowledge of truth would be shut off from us. Are we not always searching after the secrets of life and yet never fully understanding nor comprehending them? In a word—is not truth mingled with error; is not knowledge mingled with falsity? Have not the great geniuses of all times confessed that after years of study they were still ignorant of truth, and that they seemed to stand merely on the shore of truth with its infinite expanse stretching before them? How often too, study in old age corrects the prejudices of youth, and how often those who have come to mock have remained to pray. We do not possess the fullness of truth. Love too is a condition of our nature, and yet who can say that he has never had sorrow? Are not broken friendships, ruined homes, sad hearts eloquent proofs that man does not possess the fullness of love? How often do we not feel that love reaches its satiety; that it loses its bloom and its freshness; that often it turns to hate. And even when it does remain fresh and delicate, it ends and nothing that ends is perfect. A day must come when the last cake is crumbled at life's great feast and the last embrace passed from friend to friend. We do not possess the fullness of love.

Though we are men, though we possess the three conditions by which man is man, we find imperfections in these three conditions. Life is mingled with death, truth with error, love with hate. Our life then is not in creatures, our truth then is not in the spoken word, our love then is not in what we see. Life cannot exist with death, truth with error, love with hate.

But where we are to find Supreme Life, Supreme Truth, Supreme Love? Where find the source of daylight that is in this room? Not under the chair, for there there is light mingled with darkness. Not under the table, for there also there is light mingled with darkness. Where find its source then? I must go outside of this room, out to something which is pure light without any admixture of darkness, namely to the sun. There is the reason for all the light that surrounds me. So too, if I am to find the source of the Life, the Truth and the Love in this world, I must go out beyond this world, out beyond a life which is mingled with its shadow death, out beyond a truth which is mingled with its shadow error, and out beyond a love which is mingled with its shadow hate. I must go out to that which is Perfect Life, Perfect Truth, and Perfect Love—to God.

"There is a quest that haunts me
In the nights when I am alone;
The need to ride, where the ways divide
The Known from the Unknown.
I mount what thought is near me,
And soon I reach the place,
The tenuous rim where the Seen grows dim
And the Sightless hides its face.

I have ridden the wind,
I have ridden the sea,
I have ridden the moon and stars,
I have sat my feet in the stirrup seat
Of a comet coursing Mars,
And everywhere thro' the earth and air
My thought speeds, lightning shod,
It comes to a place where checking pace
It cries, 'Beyond lies God!' "

Beyond lies God—Perfect Life: *I am the Life;* Perfect Truth: *I am the Truth;* Perfect Love: *God is Love. Ens, Verum, Bonum*—Life, Truth and Love.

Now we are in a position to understand why Being, Truth, and Love are the transcendental attributes of everything in this world. As reflections or participations of that which is Perfect, they can exist only in virtue of different kinds of Causality. There is a thing before me. I may ask: what is it? The answer is: a statue of the Madonna. In Metaphysics the Madonna, the form, or the model, is called the Formal Cause. Again, I may ask: who made it? The answer is Raphael. In Metaphysics, Raphael would be called the Efficient Cause. Finally, I might ask: why was it made? The answer might be: to glorify the Mother of God. This motive, or intention or end, in Metaphysics is called the Final Cause.°

Now the transcendentals are related to these causalities. In other words, everything that is, *is* because God is its Efficient Cause; everything is true, because God is its Formal Cause; everything is good because God is its Final Cause.

Speaking of God as Efficient Cause St. Thomas writes: "It must be said that every being in any way existing is from God. For whatever is found in anything by participation, must be caused in it by that to which it belongs essentially, as iron becomes ignited by fire. Subsisting being must be one; if whiteness were self-subsisting, it would be one since whiteness is multiplied by its recipients. Therefore all beings apart from God are not their own being, but are beings by participation. It must be then that all things which are diversified by the diverse participation of being, so as to be more or less perfect, are caused by one first Being, Who possesses being most completely. Hence Plato said (Parmen. XXVI) that unity must come before multitude; and Aristotle said (Metap. II, text 4) that whatever is greatest in being and greatest in truth is the cause of all being and every truth just as whatever is the greatest in heat is the cause of all heat.

"Since to be caused does not enter into the essence of being as such, it is possible for us to find a being uncaused. . . . But the reason why an efficient cause is required is not merely because the effect is not necessary, but because the effect might not be if the cause were not."

But God is not only Efficient Cause, in virtue of which things possess existence; He is also Formal Cause in virtue of which things are true. There is an Intelligence to which reality is *essentially* conformed, other than the purely human intellect. Although ontological truth is for us proximately and immediately the conformity of reality with our own conceptions, it is primarily and fundamentally the essential conformity of all reality with the Divine Mind. God has created all things according to the archetypal ideas existing in His Mind, and the essence of everything for that reason is an imitation or reflection of these exemplar ideas. That is why St. Thomas holds there would be truth even though every human mind were annihilated, for there would still be the Divine Mind with which all things are in conformity.

St. Thomas puts this doctrine in these words: "Truth is found in the intellect according as it apprehends a thing as it is; and in things according as they have been conformable to an intellect. This is to the greatest degree found in God. For His own being is not only conformed to His intellect, but it is the very act of His intellect; and His act of understanding is the measure and cause of every other being and of every other intellect, and He Himself is His own existence and act of understanding. Whence it follows not only that Truth is in Him, but He is Truth itself, and the Sovereign and First Truth."

Since God is the Formal Cause of all Truth, because all things are made according to His Exemplar ideas, as the house conforms to archetypal ideas in the mind of the architect, it follows that we see all truth in the Eternal Truth. We can say that we see all bodies in the sun, not because we see them in the solar disc itself, but because we could not see them except by means of the light of the sun. Although there is a proximate ground for truth without taking God into consideration, there is really no ultimate ground for it without Him. As one object may be reflected many times in a mirror, so too, the Divine Truth may be imaged imperfectly in all creatures. That is why there is a unanimous accord among all men in judgments relative to first principles and their legitimate conclusions; all these are ultimately resolvable into

° Here we ignore the material cause as we are interested only in Supreme Causalities, and not the matter from which things are made.

the Supreme Truth which is God and by Whom all things are true.

There still remains the question, why things are good, and the answer to this, in its metaphysical and ultimate basis, must be that things are good because God is their Final Cause, and His intention or purpose in making things was the manifestation of His Goodness. "Everything is called good," writes St. Thomas, "from the Divine Goodness, as from the first exemplary effective and final principle of all goodness."

"Nevertheless, everything is called good by reason of the similitude of the Divine Goodness, belonging to it, which is formally its own goodness, whereby it is denominated good. And so of all things there is one Goodness and yet many things which are good."

Everything tends toward its perfection by the very fact that it tends toward its end, because everything is good in the measure of its own achievement. Matter tends toward its perfection through physical laws; living beings tend to theirs by instincts, and man by reason. As the arrow would never speed toward its target unless there was an archer, neither would things tend to their perfection unless there was some Supreme Archer. And in the measure that each tends toward the *good,* it approaches the Divine, for every being resembles God inasmuch as it is good.

God's Will is the Cause of all things, or in other words, since in God, Will and Goodness are identical, God's Goodness is the Cause of all things. God has no need of time for His Life for He is Eternal; He has no need of Space for He is Spiritual; "Since then, the Divine Being is undetermined, and contains in Himself the full perfection of Being, it cannot be that He acts by a necessity of His Nature." If He does act, it is not because of indigence, or need, but because of Perfect Liberality. "He who wills to take a bitter draught, in doing so wills nothing else than health; and this alone moves his will. It is different with one who takes a draught that is pleasant, which anyone may will to do, not only for the sake of health, but also for its own sake. Hence, although God wills things apart from Himself only for the sake of the end, which is His own goodness, it does not follow that anything else moves His Will, except His goodness. So, as He understands things apart from Himself, by understanding His own essence, so He wills things apart from Himself, by willing His own goodness." "God's Will is the Cause of all things. It must needs be therefore that a thing has existence, and is good only inasmuch as it is willed by God." "We love things because goodness in things calls forth our love; but God is not drawn toward things because things possess goodness, but rather they possess goodness because He willed them." And since God willed creatures from all eternity it is true to say that He loved creatures from all eternity. He did not begin to love man when man was made, as He did not begin to know man when man was made. He knew and loved man when man existed only as an idea in His Mind from all eternity. God's love is eternal and infinite. Our love is temporal and finite. Our love is like the estuary of a stream which flows strongly and abundantly as long as it is confined within narrow banks, but becomes feeble and shallow when its banks widen. The more we love, the less we love; i.e., the greater the extension of our affection, the lesser the intensity. As the circumference of our love widens it becomes farther and farther away from the centre of its flame. But this is not true of God. Though all enjoy sunlight, yet one does not receive less of it than the other. Though God loves all, He loves each one infinitely, and even though thousands sit down on the green grass for the banquet, each one rises "with his fill."

Being, Truth, and Love—three names for God Who is the Efficient, Formal and Final Cause of this universe. These three: Power, Law and Goodness are found written across the face of this universe; Power, because God is the Omnipotence that acts; *Potentia ut exequens;* Law because God is the Wisdom that directs: *Sapientia ut dirigens;* Goodness because God is the Will that orders: *Voluntas ut imperans. Ex Ipso,* because *from Him* all things have received their being; *Per Ipsum,* because *through Him,* all things have been ordered according to law; *In Ipso* because *to Him* all things tend and strive as their ultimate end.

Reason then can know God through the visible things of the earth, and the conclusion of reason is not just the *idea of God,* but God, and God is not an abstract mathematical entity, not a temporal-spatial quality, but the Perfect Being, Truth, and Love of Which all earthly existence, and earthly truth and earthly love is but a dim far-off echo and feeble reflection. And if we would transpose these philosophical terms to the concrete and still know what God is in the realm of the human experience, we need but sound the depths of the human heart. If we receive but a two-billionth part of the light and heat that streams from the sun, may it not be that we receive an equally small fraction of that which is Perfect Life, Perfect Truth and Perfect Love? If human life at its best is a joy, then what must be Perfect Life! If a feeble truth which we but dimly grasp can so possess our minds as to give us a peace which no earthly treasure can give, then what must be Perfect Truth! If a human heart in its purest quest for love can so thrill and exalt and cast us into an ecstasy, then what must be the Heart of Hearts! *If the spark is so bright, what must be the Flame!*

24 God's Existence—Unprovable

Russell & Nagel

When Bertrand Russell's lecture, "Why I am not a Christian," was first presented, it must have shocked many members of his audience. He attempted to demolish, and even to ridicule, traditional rational arguments for the existence of God; he criticized the moral character of Christ, placing him below the Buddha and Socrates in wisdom and virtue; he delivered a parting attack on the church as an obstacle to progress and enlightenment; and he concluded with a call to action against the superstition associated with religious belief. Russell's lecture became one of his most popular "unpopular essays."

To the end of his long and eventful life, Russell (1872–1970) retained his sceptical attitude and his willingness to take up and to defend unpopular causes—agnosticism, pacifism, trial marriage—causes which despite the public stigma had survived his scrutiny and succeeded in arousing his enthusiasm. Even in his eighties he did not hesitate to participate in a protest against nuclear armaments, leading to his arrest and to another brief stay in jail. By rational arguments he always attempted to defend his positions, even while his critics were accusing him of irrational conduct, submission to remote control, or, toward the end of his life, senility. Like Socrates (however, lacking the modesty of Socrates) Russell spoke in the name of rational thought, which he saw as "the light of the world and the chief glory of man." He tracked down inconsistency in belief and confusion in ideas with the keen and relentless fanaticism of a logician. With the moral fervor of an idealist, he condemned individuals and institutions that were, in his opinion, tyrannical or which stood in the way of scientific inquiry and advancement. "No institution inspired by fear," he said, "can further life."

In the Prologue to his *Autobiography*, Russell wrote that three main concerns governed his entire life: his desire for love, his quest for knowledge, and his pity for human suffering. Religious aspiration played little or no role in his long and eventful life. Whereas William James advocated "the will to believe" when faced with "forced options" which could not be decided on purely rational grounds, Russell advocated "the will to doubt." Russell believed in rationality as the highest ideal for man. He held that one's beliefs should always be based on rational and empirical evidence, evidence which is open to critical scrutiny and public verification (i.e., evidence which can be dealt with by scientific methods).

To achieve and maintain the kind of rational doubt which Russell advocated would necessitate the attainment of a philosophical as well as a scientific temper. A contemplative habit of mind must be developed. The value of "useless knowledge"—the kind of knowledge which is enjoyable for its own sake—must be appreciated along with knowledge that is more narrowly useful or practical. An ability to face the prospects of suffering and death without irrational fear but with Stoical courage must be cultivated. One must learn to look beyond the immediate to the ultimate; beyond the present disappointments to the (relatively) permanent satisfactions of love, knowledge, and beauty; and beyond the narrowly personal to the impersonal perspective. Russell expressed this positive attitude toward life and the universe in his famous essay "A Free Man's Worship." His conviction was that despite the fact that from a cosmic point of view all human efforts eventually must come to nothing, it is nevertheless possible for man "to preserve a mind free from the wanton tyranny that rules his outward life."

Like Russell, Ernest Nagel, a contemporary American philosopher (b. 1901), has made extensive and important contributions in the areas of logic and the philosophy of science. Nagel's view goes beyond the agnosticism and scepticism of Russell to deny the existence of any realm transcending nature. He has been a leading exponent of "naturalism." Naturalism accepts the methods of the sciences as providing the only reliable way to obtain knowledge. Nature itself is all we need to explain the nature of things, and a secular, utilitarian ethics can be the basis for an adequate moral code for mankind.

In the following selection, Nagel argues against most of the classical proofs for the existence of God and expresses his scepticism regarding special avenues to religious truth claimed by some religious thinkers. Nagel is careful to state that his atheism is philosophical and directed against the concept of God and the religious view of the origin and nature of the world characteristic of theism; he refers to theism as a "theological proposition." His own view of religion emphasizes the social and communal aspects of religion; the profession of creeds is only a minor aspect of religion. He also denies that religious experience provides evidence for the existence of a deity.

The Existence of God Questioned

Bertrand Russell

THE EXISTENCE OF GOD

To come to this question of the existence of God: it is a large and serious question, and if I were to attempt to deal with it in any adequate manner I should have to keep you here until Kingdom Come, so that you will have to excuse me if I deal with it in a somewhat summary fashion. You know, of course, that the Catholic Church has laid it down as a dogma that the existence of God can be proved by the unaided reason. That is a somewhat curious dogma, but it is one of their dogmas. They had to introduce it because at one time the freethinkers adopted the habit of saying that there were such and such arguments which mere reason might urge against the existence of God, but of course they knew as a matter of faith that God did exist. The arguments and the reasons were set out at great length, and the Catholic Church felt that they must stop it. Therefore they laid it down that the existence of God can be proved by the unaided reason and they had to set up what they considered were arguments to prove it. There are, of course, a number of them, but I shall take only a few.

THE FIRST-CAUSE ARGUMENT

Perhaps the simplest and easiest to understand is the argument of the First Cause. (It is main-

From Bertrand Russell, *Why I Am Not a Christian*, copyright 1957 by Allen & Unwin. Reprinted by permission of Simon & Schuster, Inc. and George Allen & Unwin Ltd.

tained that everything we see in this world has a cause, and as you go back in the chain of causes further and further you must come to a First Cause, and to that First Cause you give the name of God.) That argument, I suppose, does not carry very much weight nowadays, because, in the first place, cause is not quite what it used to be. The philosophers and the men of science have got going on cause, and it has not anything like the vitality it used to have; but, apart from that, you can see that the argument that there must be a First Cause is one that cannot have any validity. I may say that when I was a young man and was debating these questions very seriously in my mind, I for a long time accepted the argument of the First Cause, until one day, at the age of eighteen, I read John Stuart Mill's Autobiography, and I there found this sentence: "My father taught me that the question 'Who made me?' cannot be answered, since it immediately suggests the further question 'Who made God?'" That very simple sentence showed me, as I still think, the fallacy in the argument of the First Cause. If everything must have a cause, then God must have a cause. If there can be anything without a cause, it may just as well be the world as God, so that there cannot be any validity in that argument. It is exactly of the same nature as the Hindu's view, that the world rested upon an elephant and the elephant rested upon a tortoise; and when they said, "How about the tortoise?" the Indian said, "Suppose we change the subject." The argument is really no better than that. There is no reason why the world could not have come into being without a cause; nor, on the other hand, is there any reason why it should not have always existed. There is no reason to suppose that the world had a beginning at all. The idea that things must have a beginning is really due to the poverty of our imagination. Therefore, perhaps, I need not waste any more time upon the argument about the First Cause.

THE NATURAL-LAW ARGUMENT

Then there is a very common argument from natural law. That was a favorite argument all through the eighteenth century, especially under the influence of Sir Isaac Newton and his cosmogony. People observed the planets going around the sun according to the law of gravitation, and they thought that God had given a behest to these planets to move in that particular fashion, and that was why they did so. That was, of course, a convenient and simple explanation that saved them the trouble of looking any further for explanations of the law of gravitation. Nowadays we explain the law of gravitation in a somewhat complicated fashion that Einstein has introduced. I do not propose to give you a lecture on the law of gravitation, as interpreted by Einstein, because that again would take some time; at any rate, you no longer have the sort of natural law that you had in the Newtonian system, where, for some reason that nobody could understand, nature behaved in a uniform fashion. We now find that a great many things we thought were natural laws are really human conventions. You know that even in the remotest depths of stellar space there are still three feet to a yard. That is, no doubt, a very remarkable fact, but you would hardly call it a law of nature. And a great many things that have been regarded as laws of nature are of that kind. On the other hand, where you can get down to any knowledge of what atoms actually do, you will find they are much less subject to law than people thought, and that the laws at which you arrive are statistical averages of just the sort that would emerge from chance. There is, as we all know, a law that if you throw dice you will get double sixes only about once in thirty-six times, and we do not regard that as evidence that the fall of the dice is regulated by design; on the contrary, if the double sixes came every time we should think that there was design. The laws of nature are of that sort as regards a great many of them. They are statistical averages such as would emerge from the laws of chance and that makes this whole business of natural law much less impressive than it formerly was. Quite apart from that, which represents the momentary state of science that may change tomorrow, the whole idea that natural laws imply a lawgiver is due to a confusion between natural and human laws. Human laws are behests commanding you to behave a certain way, in which way you may choose to behave, or you may choose not to behave; but natural laws are a description of how things do in fact behave, and being a mere description of what they in fact do, you cannot argue that there must be somebody who told them to do that, because even supposing that there were, you are then faced with the question "Why did God issue just those natural laws and no others?" If you say that he did it simply from his own good pleasure, and without any reason, you then find that there is something which is not subject to law, and so your train of natural law is interrupted. If you say, as more orthodox theologians do, that in all the laws which God issues he had a reason for giving those laws rather than others—the reason, of course, being to create the best universe, although you would never think it to look at it—if there were a reason for the laws which God gave, then God himself was subject to law, and therefore you do not get any advantage by introducing God as an intermediary. You have really a law outside and anterior to the divine edicts, and

God does not serve your purpose, because he is not the ultimate lawgiver. In short, this whole argument about natural law no longer has anything like the strength that it used to have. I am traveling on in time in my review of the arguments. The arguments that are used for the existence of God change their character as time goes on. They were at first hard intellectual arguments embodying certain quite definite fallacies. As we come to modern times they become less respectable intellectually and more and more affected by a kind of moralizing vagueness.

THE ARGUMENT FROM DESIGN

The next step in this process brings us to the argument from design. You all know the argument from design: everything in the world is made just so that we can manage to live in the world, and if the world was ever so little different, we could not manage to live in it. That is the argument from design. It sometimes takes a rather curious form; for instance, it is argued that rabbits have white tails in order to be easy to shoot. I do not know how rabbits would view that application. It is an easy argument to parody. You all know Voltaire's remark, that obviously the nose was designed to be such as to fit spectacles. That sort of parody has turned out to be not nearly so wide of the mark as it might have seemed in the eighteenth century, because since the time of Darwin we understand much better why living creatures are adapted to their environment. It is not that their environment was made to be suitable to them but that they grew to be suitable to it, and that is the basis of adaptation. There is no evidence of design about it.

When you come to look into this argument from design, it is a most astonishing thing that people can believe that this world, with all the things that are in it, with all its defects, should be the best that omnipotence and omniscience have been able to produce in millions of years. I really cannot believe it. Do you think that, if you were granted omnipotence and omniscience and millions of years in which to perfect your world, you could produce nothing better than the Ku Klux Klan or the Fascists? Moreover, if you accept the ordinary laws of science, you have to suppose that human life and life in general on this planet will die out in due course: it is a stage in the decay of the solar system; at a certain stage of decay you get the sort of conditions of temperature and so forth which are suitable to protoplasm, and there is life for a short time in the life of the whole solar system. You see in the moon the sort of thing to which the earth is tending—something dead, cold, and lifeless.

I am told that that sort of view is depressing, and people will sometimes tell you that if they believed that, they would not be able to go on living. Do not believe it; is is all nonsense. Nobody really worries much about what is going to happen millions of years hence. Even if they think they are worrying much about that, they are really deceiving themselves. They are worried about something much more mundane, or it may merely be a bad digestion; but nobody is really seriously rendered unhappy by the thought of something that is going to happen to this world millions and millions of years hence. Therefore, although it is of course a gloomy view to suppose that life will die out—at least I suppose we may say so, although sometimes when I contemplate the things that people do with their lives I think it is almost a consolation—it is not such as to render life miserable. It merely makes you turn your attention to other things.

THE MORAL ARGUMENTS
FOR DEITY

Now we reach one stage further in what I shall call the intellectual descent that the Theists have made in their argumentations, and we come to what are called the moral arguments for the existence of God. You all know, of course, that there used to be in the old days three intellectual arguments for the existence of God, all of which were disposed of by Immanuel Kant in the *Critique of Pure Reason;* but no sooner had he disposed of those arguments than he invented a new one, a moral argument, and that quite convinced him. He was like many people: in intellectual matters he was skeptical, but in moral matters he believed implicitly in the maxims that he had imbibed at his mother's knee. That illustrates what the psychoanalysts so much emphasize—the immensely stronger hold upon us that our very early associations have than those of later times.

Kant, as I say, invented a new moral argument for the existence of God, and that in varying forms was extremely popular during the nineteenth century. It has all sorts of forms. One form is to say that there would be no right or wrong unless God existed. I am not for the moment concerned with whether there is a difference between right and wrong, or whether there is not: that is another question. The point I am concerned with is that, if you are quite sure there is a difference between right and wrong, you are then in this situation: Is that difference due to God's fiat or is it not? If it is due to God's fiat, then for God himself there is no difference between right and wrong, and it is no longer a significant statement to say that God is good. If you are going to say, as theologians do, that God is good, you must then say that right and wrong have some meaning which is independent of God's fiat, because God's fiats are good and not bad independently of the mere fact that he made them. If you are going to say that, you will then have to say that it is not only through God that right and wrong came into being, but that they are in their essence logically anterior to God. You could, of course, if you liked, say that there was a su-

perior deity who gave orders to the God who made this world, or could take up the line that some of the gnostics took up—a line which I often thought was a very plausible one—that as a matter of fact this world that we know was made by the devil at a moment when God was not looking. There is a good deal to be said for that, and I am not concerned to refute it.

THE ARGUMENT FOR THE REMEDYING OF INJUSTICE

Then there is another very curious form of moral argument, which is this: they say that the existence of God is required in order to bring justice into the world. In the part of this universe that we know there is great injustice, and often the good suffer, and often the wicked prosper, and one hardly knows which of those is the more annoying; but if you are going to have justice in the universe as a whole you have to suppose a future life to redress the balance of life here on earth. So they say that there must be a God, and there must be heaven and hell in order that in the long run there may be justice. That is a very curious argument. If you looked at the matter from a scientific point of view, you would say, "After all, I know only this world. I do not know about the rest of the universe, but so far as one can argue at all on probabilities one would say that probably this world is a fair sample, and if there is injustice here the odds are that there is injustice elsewhere also." Supposing you got a crate of oranges that you opened, and you found all the top layer of oranges bad, you would not argue, "The underneath ones must be good, so as to redress the balance." You would say, "Probably the whole lot is a bad consignment"; and that is really what a scientific person would argue about the universe. He would say, "Here we find in this world a great deal of injustice, and so far as that goes that is a reason for supposing that justice does not rule in the world; and therefore so far as it goes it affords a moral argument against deity and not in favor of one." Of course I know that the sort of intellectual arguments that I have been talking to you about are not what really moves people. What really moves people to believe in God is not any intellectual argument at all. Most people believe in God because they have been taught from early infancy to do it, and that is the main reason.

Then I think that the next most powerful reason is the wish for safety, a sort of feeling that there is a big brother who will look after you. That plays a very profound part in influencing people's desire for a belief in God.

A Defense of Atheism

Ernest Nagel

The essays in this book are devoted in the main to the exposition of the major creeds of humanity. It is a natural expectation that this final paper, even though its theme is so radically different from nearly all of the others, will show how atheism belongs to the great tradition of religious thought. Needless to say, this expectation is difficult to satisfy, and did anyone succeed in doing so he would indeed be performing the neatest conjuring trick of the week. But the expectation nevertheless does cause me some embarrassment, which is only slightly relieved by an anecdote Bertrand Russell reports in his recent book, *Portraits from Memory*. Russell was imprisoned during the First World War for pacifistic activities. On entering the prison he was asked a number of customary questions about himself for the prison records. One question was about his religion. Russell explained that he was an agnostic. "Never heard of it," the warden declared. "How do you spell it?" When Russell told him, the warden observed "Well, there are many religions, but I suppose they all worship the same God." Russell adds that this remark kept him cheerful for about a week. Perhaps philosophical atheism is also a religion.

Ernest Nagel, "Philosophical Concepts of Atheism," *Basic Beliefs: The Religious Philosophies of Mankind,* ed. Johnson E. Fairchild (New York: Sheridan House, Inc., 1959), pp. 167–86 (with omissions). Reprinted by permission.

1.

I must begin by stating what sense I am attaching to the word "atheism," and how I am construing the theme of this paper. I shall understand by "atheism" a critique and a denial of the major claims of all varieties of theism. And by theism I shall mean the view which holds, as one writer has expressed it, "that the heavens and the earth and all that they contain owe their existence and continuance in existence to the wisdom and will of a supreme, self-consistent, omnipotent, omniscient, righteous, and benevolent being, who is distinct from, and independent of, what he has created." Several things immediately follow from these definitions.

In the first place, atheism is not necessarily an irreligious concept, for theism is just one among many views concerning the nature and origin of the world. The denial of theism is logically compatible with a religious outlook upon life, and is in fact characteristic of some of the great historical religions. For as readers of this volume will know, early Buddhism is a religion which does not subscribe to any doctrine about a god; and there are pantheistic religions and philosophies which, because they deny that God is a being separate from and independent of the world, are not theistic in the sense of the word explained above.

The second point to note is that atheism is not to be identified with sheer unbelief, or with disbelief in some particular creed of a religious group. Thus, a child who has received no religious instruction and has never heard about God, is not an atheist—for he is not denying any theistic claims. Similarly in the case of an adult who, if he has withdrawn from the faith of his fathers without reflection or because of frank indifference to any theological issue, is also not an atheist—for such an adult is not challenging theism and is not professing any views on the subject. Moreover, though the term "atheist" has been used historically as an abusive label for those who do not happen to subscribe to some regnant orthodoxy (for example, the ancient Romans called the early Christians atheists, because the latter denied the Roman divinities), or for those who engage in conduct regarded as immoral it is not in this sense that I am discussing atheism.

One final word of preliminary explanation. I propose to examine some *philosophic* concepts of atheism, and I am not interested in the slightest in the many considerations atheists have advanced against the evidences for some particular religious and theological doctrine—for example, against the truth of the Christian story. What I mean by "philosophical" in the present context is that the views I shall consider are directed against any form of theism, in a comprehensive account of the world believed to be wholly intelligible without the adoption of a theistic hypothesis.

Theism as I conceive it is a theological proposition, not a statement of a position that belongs primarily to religion. On my view, religion as a historical and social phenomenon is primarily an institutionalized *cultus* or practice, which possesses identifiable social functions and which expresses certain attitudes men take toward their world. Although it is doubtful whether men ever engage in religious practices or assume religious attitudes without some more or less explicit interpretation of their ritual or some rationale for their attitude, it is

still the case that it is possible to distinguish religion as a social and personal phenomenon from the theological doctrines which may be developed as justifications for religious practices. Indeed, in some of the great religions of the world the profession of a creed plays a relatively minor role. In short, religion is a form of social communion, a participation in certain kinds of ritual (whether it be a dance, worship, prayer, or the like), and a form of experience (sometimes, though not invariably, directed to a personal confrontation with divine and holy things). Theology is an articulated and, at its best, a rational attempt at understanding these feelings and practices, in the light of their relation to other parts of human experience, and in terms of some hypothesis concerning the nature of things entire.

2.

As I see it, atheistic philosophies fall into two major groups: 1. those which hold that the theistic doctrine is meaningful, but reject it either on the ground that, (a) the positive evidence for it is insufficient, or (b) the negative evidence is quite overwhelming; and 2. those who hold the theistic thesis is not even meaningful, and reject it (a) as just nonsense or (b) as literally meaningless but interpreting it as a symbolic rendering of human ideals, thus reading the theistic thesis in a sense that most believers in theism would disavow. It will not be possible in the limited space at my disposal to discuss the second category of atheistic critiques; and in any event, most of the traditional atheistic critiques of theism belong to the first group.

But before turning to the philosophical examination of the major classical arguments for theism, it is well to note that such philosophical critiques do not quite convey the passion with which atheists have often carried on their analyses of theistic views. For historically, atheism has been, and indeed continues to be, a form of social and political protest, directed as much against institutionalized religion as against theistic doctrine. Atheism has been, in effect, a moral revulsion against the undoubted abuses of the secular power exercised by religious leaders and religious institutions.

Religious authorities have opposed the correction of glaring injustices, and encouraged politically and socially reactionary policies. Religious institutions have been havens of obscurantist thought and centers for the dissemination of intolerance. Religious creeds have been used to set limits to free inquiry, to perpetuate inhumane treatment of the ill and the underprivileged, and to support moral doctrines insensitive to human suffering.

These indictments may not tell the whole story about the historical significance of religion; but they are at least an important part of the story. The refutation of theism has thus seemed to many as an indispensable step not only towards liberating men's minds from superstition, but also towards achieving a more equitable reordering of society. And no account of even the more philosophical aspects of atheistic thought is adequate, which does not give proper recognition to the powerful social motives that actuate many atheistic arguments.

But however this may be, I want now to discuss three classical arguments for the existence of God, arguments which have constituted at least a partial basis for theistic commitments. As long as theism is defended simply as dogma, asserted as a matter of direct revelation or as the deliverance of authority, belief in the dogma is impregnable to rational argument. In fact, however, reasons are frequently advanced in support of the theistic creed, and these reasons have been the subject of acute philosophical critiques.

One of the oldest intellectual defenses of theism is the cosmological argument, also known as the argument from a first cause. Briefly put,

the argument runs as follows. Every event must have a cause. Hence an event A must have as cause some event B, which in turn must have a cause C, and so on. But if there is no end to this backward progression of causes, the progression will be infinite; and in the opinion of those who use this argument, an infinite series of actual events is unintelligible and absurd. Hence there must be a first cause, and this first cause is God, the initiator of all change in the universe.

The argument is an ancient one, and is especially effective when stated within the framework of assumptions of Aristotelian physics; and it has impressed many generations of exceptionally keen minds. The argument is nonetheless a weak reed on which to rest the theistic thesis. Let us waive any question concerning the validity of the principle that every event has a cause, for though the question is important its discussion would lead us far afield. However, if the principle is assumed, it is surely incongruous to postulate a first cause as a way of escaping from the coils of an infinite series. For if everything must have a cause, why does not God require one for His own existence? The standard answer is that He does not need any, because He is self-caused. But if God can be self-caused, why cannot the world be self-caused? Why do we require a God transcending the world to bring the world into existence and initiate changes in it? On the other hand, the supposed inconceivability and absurdity of an infinite series of regressive causes will be admitted by no one who has competent familiarity with the modern mathematical analysis of infinity. The cosmological argument does not stand up under scrutiny.

The second "proof" of God's existence is usually called the ontological argument. It too has a long history going back to early Christian days, though it acquired great prominence only in medieval times. The argument can be stated in several ways, one of which is the following. Since God is conceived to be omnipotent, he is a perfect being. A perfect being is defined as one whose essence or nature lacks no attributes (or properties) whatsoever, one whose nature is complete in every respect. But it is evident that we have an idea of a perfect being, for we have just defined the idea; and since this is so, the argument continues, God who is the perfect being must exist. Why must he? Because his existence follows from his defined nature. For if God lacked the attribute of existence, he would be lacking at least one attribute, and would therefore not be perfect. To sum up, since we have an idea of God as a perfect being, God must exist.

There are several ways of approaching this argument, but I shall consider only one. The argument was exploded by the eighteenth-century philosopher Immanuel Kant. The substance of Kant's criticism is that it is just a confusion to say that existence is an attribute, and that though the *word* "existence" may occur as the grammatical predicate in a sentence, no attribute is being predicted of a thing when we say that the thing exists or has existence. Thus, to use Kant's example, when we think of $100 we are thinking of the nature of this sum of money; but the nature of $100 remains the same whether we have $100 in our pocket or not. Accordingly, we are confounding grammar with logic if we suppose that some characteristic is being attributed to the nature of $100 when we say that a hundred dollar bill exists in someone's pocket.

To make the point clearer, consider another example. When we say that a lion has a tawny color, we are predicating a certain attribute of the animal, and similarly when we say that the lion is fierce or is hungry. But when we say the lion exists, all that we are saying is that something is (or has the nature of) a lion; we are not specifying an attribute which belongs to the nature of anything that is a lion. In short, the word "existence" does not signify any attribute, and in consequence no attribute that belongs to the nature of anything. Accord-

ingly, it does not follow from the assumption that we have an idea of a perfect being that such a being exists. For the idea of a perfect being does not involve the attribute of existence as a constituent of that idea, since there is no such attribute. The ontological argument thus has a serious leak, and it can hold no water.

3.

The two arguments discussed thus far are purely dialectical, and attempt to establish God's existence without any appeal to empirical data. The next argument, called the argument from design, is different in character, for it is based on what purports to be empirical evidence. I wish to examine two forms of this argument.

One variant of it calls attention to the remarkable way in which different things and processes in the world are integrated with each other, and concludes that this mutual "fitness" of things can be explained only by the assumption of a divine architect who planned the world and everything in it. For example, living organisms can maintain themselves in a variety of environments, and do so in virtue of their delicate mechanisms which adapt the organisms to all sort of environmental changes. There is thus an intricate pattern of means and ends throughout the animate world. But the existence of this pattern is unintelligible, so the argument runs, except on the hypothesis that the pattern has been deliberately instituted by a Supreme Designer. If we find a watch in some deserted spot, we do not think it came into existence by chance, and we do not hesitate to conclude that an intelligent creature designed and made it. But the world and all its contents exhibit mechanisms and mutual adjustments that are far more complicated and subtle than are those of a watch. Must we not therefore conclude that these things too have a Creator?

The conclusion of this argument is based on

an inference from analogy: the watch and the world are alike in possessing a congruence of parts and an adjustment of means to ends; the watch has a watch-maker; hence the world has a world-maker. But is the analogy a good one? Let us once more waive some important issues, in particular the issue whether the universe is the unified system such as the watch admittedly is. And let us concentrate on the question, what is the ground for our assurance that watches do not come into existence except through the operations of intelligent manufacturers. The answer is plain. We have never run across a watch which has not been deliberately made by someone. But the situation is nothing like this in the case of the innumerable animate and inanimate systems with which we are familiar. Even in the case of living organisms, though they are generated by their parent organisms, the parents do not "make" their progeny in the same sense in which watch-makers make watches. And once this point is clear, the inference from the existence of living organisms to the existence of a supreme designer no longer appears credible.

Moreover, the argument loses all its force if the facts which the hypothesis of a divine designer is supposed to explain can be understood on the basis of a better supported assumption. And indeed, such an alternative explanation is one of the achievements of Darwinian biology. For Darwin showed that one can account for the variety of biological species, as well as for their adaptations to their environments, without invoking a divine creator and acts of special creation. The Darwinian theory explains the diversity of biological species in terms of chance variations in the structure of organisms, and of a mechanism of selection which retains those variant forms that possess some advantages for survival. The evidence for these assumptions is considerable; and developments subsequent to Darwin have only strengthened the case for a thoroughly naturalistic explanation of the facts of biological adaptation. In any

event, this version of the argument from design has nothing to recommend it.

A second form of this argument has been recently revived in the speculations of some modern physicists. No one who is familiar with the facts can fail to be impressed by the success with which the use of mathematical methods has enabled us to obtain intellectual mastery of many parts of nature. But some thinkers have therefore concluded that since the book of nature is ostensibly written in mathematical language, nature must be the creation of a divine mathematician. However, the argument is most dubious. For it rests, among other things, on the assumption that mathematical tools can be successfully used only if the events of nature exhibit some special kind of order, and on the further assumption that if the structure of things were different from what they are mathematical language would be inadequate for describing such structure. But it can be shown that no matter what the world were like—even if it impressed us as being utterly chaotic— it would still possess some order, and would in principle be amenable to a mathematical description. In point of fact, it makes no sense to say that there is absolutely no pattern in any conceivable subject matter. To be sure, there are differences in complexities of structure, and if the patterns of events were sufficiently complex we might not be able to unravel them. But however that may be, the success of mathematical physics in giving us some understanding of the world around us does not yield the conclusion that only a mathematician could have devised the patterns of order we have discovered in nature.

4.

The inconclusiveness of the three classical arguments for the existence of God was already made evident by Kant, in a manner substantially not different from the above discussion. . . .

One further type of argument, pervasive in much Protestant theological literature, deserves brief mention. Arguments of this type take their point of departure from the psychology of religious and mystical experience. Those who have undergone such experiences, often report that during the experience they feel themselves to be in the presence of the divine and holy, that they lose their sense of self-identity and become merged with some fundamental reality, or that they enjoy a feeling of total dependence upon some ultimate power. The overwhelming sense of transcending one's finitude which characterizes such vivid periods of life, and of coalescing with some ultimate source of all existence, is then taken to be compelling evidence for the existence of a supreme being. In a variant form of this argument, other theologians have identified God as the object which satisfies the commonly experienced need for integrating one's scattered and conflicting impulses into a coherent unity, or as the subject which is of ultimate concern to us. In short, a proof of God's existence is found in the occurrence of certain distinctive experiences.

It would be flying in the face of well-attested facts were one to deny that such experiences frequently occur. But do these facts constitute evidence for the conclusion based on them?

Does the fact, for example, that an individual experiences a profound sense of direct contact with an alleged transcendent ground of all reality, constitute competent evidence for the experience? If well-established canons for evaluating evidence are accepted, the answer is surely negative. No one will dispute that many men do have vivid experiences in which such things as ghosts or pink elephants appear before them; but only the hopelessly credulous will without further ado count such experiences as establishing the existence of ghosts and pink elephants. To establish the existence of such things, evidence is required that is obtained under controlled conditions and that can be confirmed by independent inquirers. Again, though a man's report that he is suffering pain may be taken at face value, one cannot take at face value the claim, were he to make it, that it is the food he ate which is the cause (or a contributory cause) of his felt pain—not even if the man were to report a vivid feeling of abdominal disturbance. And similarly, an overwhelming feeling of being in the presence of the Divine is evidence enough for admitting the genuineness of such feeling; it is no evidence for the claim that a supreme being with a substantial existence independent of the experience is the cause of the experience. . . .

25 The Inward Way Out

The Buddha, Suzuki, & Stace

Buddhism, one of the most profound answers to the search for the meaning of life, originated in the attempt of a young Hindu to come to grips with human suffering and to find an escape from it. Gautama Siddhartha Sakyamuni was a happy and wealthy Nepalese prince who lived in the sixth century B.C. and was protected from a realization of the painful aspects of human existence until, according to legend, while out taking rides he saw for the first time a decrepit old man, a disease-ridden body, and a decaying corpse. These three sights, along with the sight of a shaven-headed monk, brought on in the compassionate, intelligent young man what today would be called an existential crisis.

As a result, he renounced his luxurious life, left his family and possessions, and began to practice a life of rigorous asceticism in hopes of achieving liberation from the horror of existence. His agonizing confrontation with human suffering and his impassioned quest for liberation from selfish human cravings convinced Gautama that "what is dear to one brings hurt and misery, suffering, grief and despair which comes from what is dear." After a long and arduous period of self-mortification and meditation, he finally succeeded, while seated under the Bo tree, in achieving enlightenment. He was then able to diagnose the malady of the human condition and to prescribe the treatment that, he believed, would eventually cure it.

Gautama, now the Buddha or the Enlightened One, was concerned not with theory, but with practice. His cure for human suffering, summed up in his Four Noble Truths and the Eightfold Noble Way, is presented in the following sermon. Escape from selfish craving, which he believed lay at the root of human suffering, must be the focal point of all striving. To devote time to metaphysical speculations or controversy about religious dogmas when the basic moral problem of achieving salvation from suffering remains unsolved would be as foolish as to try to determine the cause of a fire in one's house when one should first be concerned with escaping from the threatening flames.

An agnostic himself, the Buddha apparently conceived of himself neither as a god nor as a holy guru, but rather as an experienced guide who, having achieved enlightenment, could help his fellow men and women with the urgent task of escaping from life's "existential predicament," the inevitability of suffering. In doing this, the Buddha turned his back on both asceticism and sensuous indulgence to practice and teach "the Middle Way." This path went between the dangerous extremes where one would be lost either in self-renunciation or in self-indulgence. This was the only way, he taught, which led safely to liberation from selfish craving and to the final extinction of all desiring, to the goal of Nirvana.

After the death of the Buddha, the meaning of Nirvana, the Buddhist salvation from suffering, and the ways of achieving it became subjects of controversy. Eventually, two different schools of Buddhism emerged and flourished: *Hinayana* ("Little Vehicle") or *Theravada* ("Way of the Elders") Buddhism, and *Mahayana* ("Greater Vehicle") Buddhism. Reflecting different cultural contexts and interpretations, many variations within these major divisions later developed. Despite the wide variety of doctrine and practice, however, the universal elements of Buddhism remained essentially the same: the belief in the Founder, the Way, and the Order of Monks.

Whether Buddhism is regarded as a philosophy or religion, much of its continuing appeal rests upon the experience that its founder had under the Bo tree and which he transmitted, through his example and teaching, to his followers. Buddha later said that this experience came about only after a long, agonizing, and frustrating effort. It was not, however, the result of any kind of vigorous ascetic discipline nor was it a miraculous gift. It was also ineffable—that is to say, ultimately indescribable in words —and it was supremely significant, genuine, real, and achievable by others following the way of the guide who had achieved or "seen" it. Finally, it was a supremely valuable experience, the only truly worthwhile experience a human being can have. If one does have such an experience, the meaning of life becomes clear and one can live and act accordingly.

The result of this realization, the Buddhist believes, will not be either pessimism or quietism (do-nothingism). Rather, it will be a peace of mind and serenity of spirit, a willingness to cooperate with the good and renounce the evil, and a deep and all-encompassing sense of compassion with all those beings, both animal and human, who perpetually suffer.

In Zen Buddhism, an unusual form that Mahayana Buddhism took when it spread from China into Japan during the twelfth century, the enlightenment which is sought through sitting (za-zen) and meditation on enigmatic problems (ko-ans) is called *satori*. One of the best attempts to suggest to Westerners what is meant by satori is given below in an essay by D. T. Suzuki (1870–1966). Since the awareness which is satori is a unique mystical experience, it cannot be described adequately or defined with any precision. But through those who have experienced and reported upon it, we know that it is the supreme moment of the Zen process which "begins with a breakthrough, small or large, to that Void of all attributes of which the intuition can become directly aware."[1]

The impact of Zen on Japanese culture—on painting, poetry, drama, gardens, tea ceremony, and architecture—has been enormous, and some commentators believe that this unique form of Buddhism is so rooted in its Japanese milieu that it cannot be extracted, to be practiced or comprehended apart from it.

The experience of the Buddha under the Bo tree has often been considered the prime example of the truly mystical experience. Walter Stace (1886–1967) attempted to define the mystical experience and to assess its significance. He maintained that the mystical experience is universal, and the differences reported by mystics are only superficial. The intensified consciousness, the feeling of blessedness, the sense of oneness with the divine, and the ineffability of the experience are characteristic of the mystical vision in any time or place. Stace attempted to give concrete examples of the mystical experience and to cite others who have studied its features. He raised the paradoxes of mysticism that produce conflicts with reason and logic. The paradoxes cannot be eliminated, he concluded, especially the one that arises from the conviction that the mystical experience is neither subjective nor objective, but transcendental. For those who have not had such experiences, this article raises many questions regarding the extent to which these experiences should be taken as evidence for the reality the mystic declares is their source and verification.

---

[1] D. T. Suzuki, *The Field of Zen* (New York: Harper & Row, 1970), ix.

The Gospel of the Buddha

ENLIGHTENMENT

Bôdhisattva having put to flight Mâra, gave himself up to meditation. All the miseries of the world, the evils produced by evil deeds and the sufferings arising therefrom passed before his mental eye, and he thought:

"Surely if living creatures saw the results of all their evil deeds, they would turn away from them in disgust. But selfhood blinds them, and they cling to their obnoxious desires.

"They crave for pleasure and they cause pain; when death destroys their individuality, they find no peace; their thirst for existence abides and their selfhood reappears in new births.

"Thus they continue to move in the coil and can find no escape from the hell of their own making. And how empty are their pleasures, how vain are their endeavors! Hollow like the plantain-tree and without contents like the bubble.

"The world is full of sin and sorrow, because it is full of error. Men go astray because they think that delusion is better than truth. Rather than truth they follow error, which is pleasant to look at in the beginning but causes anxiety, tribulation, and misery."

And Bôdhisattva began to expound the dharma. The dharma is the truth. The dharma

The Gospel of Buddha According to Old Records, 5th ed., ed. Paul Carus (Chicago: The Open Court Publishing Co., 1897), pp. 30–43 (with omissions).

is the sacred law. The dharma is religion. The dharma alone can deliver us from error, sin, and sorrow.

Pondering on the origin of birth and death, the Enlightened One recognised that ignorance was the root of all evil; and these are the links in the development of life, called the twelve nidânas:

"In the beginning there is existence blind and without knowledge; and in this sea of ignorance there are appetences formative and organising. From appetences, formative and organising, rises awareness or feelings. Feelings beget organisms that live as individual beings. These organisms develop the six fields, that is, the five senses and the mind. The six fields come in contact with things. Contact begets sensation. Sensation creates the thirst of individualised being. The thirst of being creates a cleaving to things. The cleaving produces the growth and continuation of selfhood. Selfhood continues in renewed births. The renewed births of selfhood are the cause of suffering, old age, sickness, and death. They produce lamentation, anxiety, and despair.

"The cause of all sorrow lies at the very beginning; it is hidden in the ignorance from which life grows. Remove ignorance and you will destroy the wrong appetences that rise from ignorance; destroy these appetences and you will wipe out the wrong perception that rises from them. Destroy wrong perception and there is an end of errors in individualised beings. Destroy errors in individualised beings and the illusions of the six fields will disappear. Destroy illusions and the contact with things will cease to beget misconception. Destroy misconception and you do away with thirst. Destroy thirst and you will be free of all morbid cleaving. Remove the cleaving and you destroy the selfishness of selfhood. If the selfishness of selfhood is destroyed you will be above birth, old age, disease, and death, and you escape all suffering."

The Enlightened One saw the four noble truths which point out the path that leads to Nirvâna or the extinction of self:

"The first noble truth is the existence of sorrow. Birth is sorrowful, growth is sorrowful, illness is sorrowful, and death is sorrowful. Sad it is to be joined with that which we do not like. Sadder still is the separation from that which we love, and painful is the craving for that which cannot be obtained.

"The second noble truth is the cause of suffering. The cause of suffering is lust. The surrounding world affects sensation and begets a craving thirst, which clamors for immediate satisfaction. The illusion of self originates and manifests itself in a cleaving to things. The desire to live for the enjoyment of self entangles us in the net of sorrow. Pleasures are the bait and the result is pain.

"The third noble truth is the cessation of sorrow. He who conquers self will be free from lust. He no longer craves, and the flame of desire finds no material to feed upon. Thus it will be extinguished.

"The fourth noble truth is the eightfold path that leads to the cessation of sorrow. There is salvation for him whose self disappears before Truth, whose will is bent upon what he ought to do, whose sole desire is the performance of his duty. He who is wise will enter this path and make an end of sorrow.

"The eightfold path is (1) right comprehension; (2) right resolutions; (3) right speech; (4) right acts; (5) right way of earning a liveli-

hood; (6) right efforts; (7) right thoughts; and (8) the right state of a peaceful mind."

This is the dharma. This is the truth. This is religion. And the Enlightened One uttered this stanza:

Long have I wandered! Long!
Bound by the chain of desire
Through many births,
Seeking thus long in vain,
Whence comes this restlessness in man?
Whence his egotism, his anguish?
And hard to bear is samsâra
When pain and death encompass us.
Found! it is found!
Author of selfhood,
No longer shalt thou build a house for me.
Broken are the beams of sin;
The ridge-pole of care is shattered,
Into Nirvâna my mind has passed,
The end of cravings has been reached at last.

There is self and there is truth. Where self is, truth is not. Where truth is, self is not. Self is the fleeting error of samsâra; it is individual separateness and that egotism which begets envy and hatred. Self is the yearning for pleasure and the lust after vanity. Truth is the correct comprehension of things; it is the permanent and everlasting, the real in all existence, the bliss of righteousness.

The existence of self is an illusion, and there is no wrong in this world, no vice, no sin, except what flows from the assertion of self.

The attainment of truth is possible only when self is recognised as an illusion. Righteousness can be practised only when we have freed our mind from the passions of egotism. Perfect peace can dwell only where all vanity has disappeared.

Blessed is he who has understood the dharma. Blessed is he who does no harm to his fellow-beings. Blessed is he who overcomes sin and is free from passion. To the highest bliss has he attained who has conquered all selfishness and vanity. He has become Buddha, the Perfect One, the Blessed One, the Holy One. . . .

Now the Blessed One thought: "To whom shall I preach the doctrine first? My old teachers are dead. They would have received the good news with joy. But my five disciples are still alive. I shall go to them, and to them shall I first proclaim the gospel of deliverance."

At that time the five bhikshus dwelt in the Deer Park at Benares, and the Blessed One not thinking of their unkindness in having left him at a time when he was most in need of their sympathy and help, but mindful only of the services which they had ministered unto him, and pitying them for the austerities which they practised in vain, rose and journeyed to their abode. . . .

THE SERMON AT BENARES

The five bhikshus saw their old teacher approach and agreed among themselves not to salute him, nor to address him as a master, but by his name only. "For," so they said, "he has broken his vow and has abandoned holiness. He is no bhikshu but Gautama, and Gautama has become a man who lives in abundance and indulges in the pleasures of worldliness."

But when the Blessed One approached in a dignified manner, they involuntarily rose from their seats and greeted him in spite of their resolution. Still they called him by his name and addressed him as "friend."

When they had thus received the Blessed One, he said: "Do not call the Tathâgata by his name nor address him 'friend,' for he is Buddha, the Holy One. Buddha looks equally with a kind heart on all living beings and they therefore call him 'Father.' To disrespect a father is wrong; to despise him, is sin.

"The Tathâgata," Buddha continued, "does not seek salvation in austerities, but for that reason you must not think that he indulges in worldly pleasures, nor does he live in abundance. The Tathâgata has found the middle path.

"Neither abstinence from fish or flesh, nor going naked, nor shaving the head, nor wearing matted hair, nor dressing in a rough garment, nor covering oneself with dirt, nor sacrificing to Agni, will cleanse a man who is not free from delusions.

"Reading the Vêdas, making offerings to priests, or sacrifices to the gods, self-mortification by heat or cold, and many such penances performed for the sake of immortality, these do not cleanse the man who is not free from delusions.

"Anger, drunkenness, obstinacy, bigotry, deception, envy, self-praise, disparaging others, superciliousness, and evil intentions constitute uncleanness; not verily the eating of flesh.

"Let me teach you, O bhikshus, the middle path, which keeps aloof from both extremes. By suffering, the emaciated devotee produces confusion and sickly thoughts in his mind. Mortification is not conducive even to worldly knowledge; how much less to a triumph over the senses!

"He who fills his lamp with water will not dispel the darkness, and he who tries to light a fire with rotten wood will fail.

"Mortifications are painful, vain, and profitless. And how can any one be free from self by leading a wretched life if he does not succeed in quenching the fires of lust.

"All mortification is vain so long as self remains, so long as self continues to lust after either worldly or heavenly pleasures. But he in whom self has become extinct is free from lust; he will desire neither worldly nor heavenly pleasures, and the satisfaction of his natural wants will not defile him. Let him eat and drink according to the needs of the body.

"Water surrounds the lotus-flower, but does not wet its petals.

"On the other hand, sensuality of all kind is enervating. The sensual man is a slave of his passions, and pleasure-seeking is degrading and vulgar.

"But to satisfy the necessities of life is not evil. To keep the body in good health is a duty, for otherwise we shall not be able to trim the lamp of wisdom, and keep our mind strong and clear.

"This is the middle path, O bhikshus, that keeps aloof from both extremes."

And the Blessed One spoke kindly to his disciples, pitying them for their errors, and pointing out the uselessness of their endeavors, and the ice of ill-will that chilled their hearts melted away under the gentle warmth of the Master's persuasion.

Now the Blessed One set the wheel of the most excellent law a-rolling, and he began to preach to the five bhikshus, opening to them the gate of immortality, and showing them the bliss of Nirvâna.

And when the Blessed One began his sermon, a rapture thrilled through all the universes.

The dêvas left their heavenly abodes to listen to the sweetness of the truth; the saints that had parted from life crowded around the great teacher to receive the glad tidings; even the animals of the earth felt the bliss that rested upon the words of the Tathâgata; and all the creatures of the host of sentient beings, gods, men, and beasts, hearing the message of deliverance, received and understood it in their own language.

Buddha said:

"The spokes of the wheel are the rules of pure conduct; justice is the uniformity of their length; wisdom is the tire; modesty and thoughtfulness are the hub in which the immovable axle of truth is fixed.

"He who recognises the existence of suffering, its cause, its remedy, and its cessation has fathomed the four noble truths. He will walk in the right path.

"Right views will be the torch to light his way. Right aims will be his guide. Right words will be his dwelling-place on the road. His gait will be straight, for it is right behavior. His refreshments will be the right way of earning his livelihood. Right efforts will be his steps: right thoughts his breath; and peace will follow in his footprints."

And the Blessed One explained the instability of the ego.

"Whatsoever is originated will be dissolved again. All worry about the self is vain; the ego is like a mirage, and all the tribulations that touch it will pass away. They will vanish like a nightmare when the sleeper awakes.

"He who has awakened is freed from fear; he has become Buddha; he knows the vanity of all his cares, his ambitions, and also of his pains.

"It easily happens that a man, when taking a bath, steps upon a wet rope and imagines that it is a snake. Horror will overcome him, and he will shake from fear, anticipating in his mind all the agonies caused by the serpent's venomous bite. What a relief does this man experience when he sees that the rope is no snake. The cause of his fright lies in his error, his ignorance, his illusion. If the true nature of the rope is recognised, his tranquillity of mind will come back to him; he will feel relieved; he will be joyful and happy.

"This is the state of mind of one who has recognised that there is no self, that the cause of all his troubles, cares, and vanities is a mirage, a shadow, a dream.

"Happy is he who has overcome all selfishness; happy is he who has attained peace; happy is he who has found the truth.

"The truth is noble and sweet; the truth can deliver from evil. There is no saviour in the world except the truth.

"Have confidence in the truth, although you may not be able to comprehend it, although you may suppose its sweetness to be bitter, although you may shrink from it at first. Trust in the truth.

"The truth is best as it is. No one can alter it; neither can any one improve it. Have faith in the truth and live it.

"Errors lead astray; illusions beget miseries. They intoxicate like strong drinks; but they fade away soon and leave you sick and disgusted.

"Self is a fever; self is a transient vision, a dream; but truth is wholesome, truth is sublime, truth is everlasting. There is no immortality except in truth. For truth alone abideth forever."

And when the doctrine was propounded, the venerable Kaundinya, the oldest one among the five bhikshus, discerned the truth with his mental eye, and he said: "Truly, O Buddha, our Lord, thou hast found the truth."

And the dêvas and saints and all the good spirits of the departed generations that had listened to the sermon of the Tathâgata, joyfully received the doctrine and shouted: "Truly, the Blessed One has founded the kingdom of righteousness. The Blessed One has moved the earth; he has set the wheel of Truth rolling, which by no one in the universe, be he god or man, can ever be turned back. The kingdom of Truth will be preached upon earth; it will spread; and righteousness, good-will, and peace will reign among mankind."

The Meaning of Satori

D. T. Suzuki

Satori is a Japanese term, *wu* in Chinese. The Sanskrit *bodhi* and *buddha* come from the same root, *bud,* "to be aware of", "to wake". *Buddha* is thus "the awakened one", "the enlightened one", while *bodhi* is "enlightenment". "Buddhism" means the teaching of the enlightened one, that is to say, Buddhism is the doctrine of enlightenment. What Buddha teaches, therefore, is the realisation of bodhi, which is satori. Satori is the centre of all Buddhist teachings. Some may think satori is characteristic of Mahayana Buddhism, but it is not so. Earlier Buddhists also talk about this, the realization of *bodhi;* and as long as they talk about *bodhi* at all they must be said to base their doctrine on the experience of satori.

We have to distinguish between *prajna* and *vijnana.* We can divide knowledge into two categories: intuitive knowledge which is *prajna* whereas discursive knowledge is *vijnana.* To distinguish further: *prajna* grasps reality in its oneness, in its totality; *vijnana* analyses it into subject and object. Here is a flower; we can take this flower as representing the universe itself. We talk about the petals, pollen, stamen and stalk; that is physical analysis. Or we can analyse it chemically into so much hydrogen, oxygen, etc. Chemists analyse a flower, enumerate all its elements and say that the aggregate of all those elements makes up the flower. But they have not exhausted the flower; they

From D. T. Suzuki, *The Field of Zen,* ed. with Foreword by Christmas Humphreys (New York: Doubleday, 1970). By permission of The Buddhist Society, London.

have simply analysed it. That is the *vijnana* way of understanding a flower. The *prajna* way is to understand it just as it is without analysis or chopping it into pieces. It is to grasp it in its oneness, in its totality, in its suchness (*sono mame* in Japanese.)

We are generally attracted to analytical knowledge or discriminative understanding, and we divide reality into several pieces. We dissect it and by dissecting it we kill reality. When we have finished our analysis we have murdered reality, and this dead reality we think is our understanding of it. When we see reality dead, after analysing it, we say that we understand it, but what we understand is not reality itself but its corpse after it has been mutilated by our intellect and senses. We fail to see that this result of dissection is not reality itself, and when we take this analysis as a basis of our understanding it is inevitable that we go astray, far away from the truth. Because in this way we shall never reach the final solution of the problem of reality.

Prajna grasps this reality in its oneness, in its totality, in its suchness. *Prajna* does not divide reality into any form of dichotomy; it does not dissect it either metaphysically or physically or chemically. The dividing of reality is the function of *vijnana* which is very useful in a practical way, but *prajna* is different.

Vijnana can never reach infinity. When we write the numbers 1, 2, 3, etc., we never come to an end, for the series goes on to infinity. By adding together all those individual numbers we try to reach the total of the numbers, but as numbers are endless this totality can never be reached. *Prajna,* on the other hand, intuits the whole totality instead of moving through 1, 2, 3 to infinity; it grasps things as a whole. It does not appeal to discrimination; it grasps reality from inside, as it were. Discursive *vijnana* tries to grasp reality objectively, that is, by addition objectively one after another. But this objective method can never reach its end because things are infinite, and we can never exhaust them objectively. Subjectively, however, we turn that position upside down and get to the inside. By looking at this flower objectively we can never reach its essence or life, but when we turn that position inside out, enter into the flower, and become the flower itself, we live through the process of growth: I am the shoot, I am the stem, I am the bud, and finally I am the flower and the flower is me. That is the *prajna* way of comprehending the flower.

In Japan there is a seventeen syllable poem called *haiku,* and one composed by a modern woman-poet reads in literal translation:

Oh, Morning Glory!
Bucket taken captive,
I beg for water.

The following was the incident that led her to compose it. One early morning the poet came outdoors to draw water from the well, and saw the morning glory winding round the bamboo pole attached to the bucket. The morning glory in full bloom looks its best in the early morning after a dewy night. It is bright, refreshing, vivifying; it reflects heavenly glory not yet tarnished by things earthly. She was so struck with its untainted beauty that she remained silent for a little while; she was so absorbed in the flower that she lost the power of speech. It took a few seconds at least before she could exclaim: "Oh, Morning Glory!" Physically, the interval was a space of a second or two or perhaps more; but metaphysically, it was eternity as beauty itself is. Psychologically, the poet was the unconscious itself in which there was no dichotomisation of any kind.

The poet was the morning glory and the morning glory was the poet. There was self-identity of flower and poet. It was only when she became conscious of herself seeing the flower that she cried: "Oh, Morning Glory!" When she said that, consciousness revived in her. But she did not like to disturb the flower, because although it is not difficult to unwind the flower from the bamboo pole she feared that to touch the flower with human hands would be the desecration of the beauty. So she went to a neighbour and asked for water.

When you analyse that poem you can picture to yourself how she stood before the flower, losing herself. There was then no flower, no human poet; just a "something" which was neither flower nor poet. But when she recovered her consciousness, there was the flower, there was herself. There was an object which was designated as morning glory and there was one who spoke—a bifurcation of subject-object. Before the bifurcation there was nothing to which she could give expression, she herself was non-existent. When she uttered, "Oh, Morning Glory!" the flower was created and along with it herself, but before that bifurcation, that dualisation of subject and object, there was nothing. And yet there was a "something" which could divide itself into subject-object, and this "something" which had not yet divided itself, not become subject to bifurcation, to discriminative understanding (i.e., before *vijnana* asserted itself)—this is *prajna.* For *prajna* is subject and at the same time object; it divides itself into subject-object and also stands by itself, but that standing by itself is not to be understood on the level of duality. Standing by itself, being absolute in its complete totality or oneness—that is the moment which the poet realised, and that is satori. Satori consists in not staying in that oneness, not remaining with itself, but in awakening from it and being just about to divide itself into subject and object. Satori is the staying in oneness and yet rising from it and dividing itself into subject-object. First, there is "something" which has not divided itself into subject-object; this is oneness as it is. Then this "something," becoming conscious of itself, divides itself into flower and poet. The becoming conscious is the dividing. Poet now sees flower and flower sees poet, there is mutual seeing. When this seeing each other, not just from one side alone but from the other side as well, when this kind of seeing actually takes place, there is a state of satori.

When I talk like this it takes time. There is something which has not divided itself but which then becomes conscious of itself, and this leads to an utterance, and so on. But in actual satori there is no time interval, hence no consciousness of the bifurcation. The oneness dividing itself into subject-object and yet retaining its oneness at the very moment that there is the awakening of a consciousness—this is satori.

From the human point of view we talk of *prajna* and *vijnana* as the integral understanding and the discriminative understanding of reality respectively. We speak of these things in order to satisfy our human understanding. Animals and plants do not divide themselves; they just live and act, but humans have awakened this consciousness. By the awakening of consciousness we become conscious of this and that, and this universe of infinite diversity arises. Because of this awakening we discriminate, and because of discrimination we talk of *prajna* and *vijnana* and make these distinctions, which is characteristic of human beings. To satisfy this demand we talk about having satori, or the awakening of this self-identity consciousness.

When the poet saw the flower, that very moment before she spoke even a word there was an intuitive apprehension of something which eludes our ordinary intuition. This *sui generis* intuition is what I would call *prajna*-intuition. The moment grasped by *prajna*-intuition is satori. That is what made Buddha the

Enlightened one. Thus, to attain satori, *prajna*-intuition is to be awakened.

That is more or less a metaphysical explanation of satori, but psychologically satori may be said to take place this way. Our consciousness contains all things; but there must be at least two things whereby consciousness is possible. Consciousness takes place when two things stand opposing one another. In our ordinary life, consciousness is kept too busy with all things going on in it and has not time to reflect within itself. Consciousness has thus no opportunity to become conscious of itself. It is so deeply involved in action, it is in fact action itself. Satori never takes place as long as consciousness is kept turning outwardly, as it were. Satori is born of self-consciousness. Consciousness must be made to look within itself before it is awakened to satori.

To get satori, all things which crowd into our daily-life consciousness must be wiped off clean. This is the function of *samadhi*, which Indian philosophers emphasize so much. "Entering into *samadhi*" is to attain uniformity of consciousness, i.e. to wipe consciousness clean, though practically speaking, this wiping clean is something almost impossible. But we must try to do it in order to attain this state of uniformity, which, according to early Buddhist thinkers, is a perfect state of mental equilibrium, for here there are no passions, no intellectual functions, but only a perfectly balanced state of indifference. When this takes place it is known as *samadhi*, or entering into the fourth stage of *dhyana* or *jhana*, as described in most early Buddhist sutras. This is not, however, a state of satori. *Samadhi* is not enough, which is no more than the unification of consciousness. There must be an awakening from this state of unification or uniformity. The awakening is becoming aware of consciousness in its own activities. When consciousness starts to move, begins to divide itself into subject-object and says: I am sorry, or glad, or I hear, and so on—this very moment as it moves on is caught up in satori. But as soon as you say "I have caught it" it is no more there. Therefore, satori is not something you can take hold of and show to others, saying, "See, it is here!"

Consciousness is something which never ceases to be active though we may be quite unconscious of it, and what we call perfect uniformity is not a state of sheer quietness, that is, of death. As consciousness thus goes on unceasingly, no one can stop it for inspection. Satori must take place while consciousness is going through stages or instant points of becoming. Satori is realised along with the becoming, which knows no stoppage. Satori is no particular experience like other experiences of our daily life. Particular experiences are experiences of particular events while the satori experience is the one that runs through all experiences. It is for this reason that satori cannot be singled out of other experiences and pronounced, "See, here is my satori!" It is always elusive and alluring. It can never be separated from our everyday life, it is for ever there, inevitably there. Becoming, not only in its each particularisable moment but through its never-terminating totality is the body of satori.

The nature of human understanding and reasoning is to divide reality into the dichotomy of this and that, of "A" and "not-A" and then to take reality so divided as really reality. We do not seem to understand reality in any other way. This being so, as long as we are depending on "the understanding," there will be no grasping of reality, no intuitive taking hold of reality, and satori is no other than this intuitive taking hold of reality. There is no reality beside becoming, becoming is reality and reality is becoming. Therefore, the satori intuition of reality consists in identifying oneself with becoming, to take becoming as it goes on becoming. We are not to cut becoming into pieces, and, picking up each separate piece which drops from "becoming," to say to people, "Here is reality." While making this announcement we will find that becoming is no more there; reality is flown away into the realm of the irrevocable past.

This is illustrated by a Zen story. A woodman went to the mountains and saw a strange animal on the other side of the tree which he was cutting. He thought: "I might kill that animal." The animal then spoke to the woodman and said: "Are you going to kill me?" Having his mind read, the woodman got angry and wondered what to do. The animal said: "Now you are thinking what to do with me." Whatever thought the woodman had, the animal intuited, and told him so. Finally, the woodman said: "I will stop thinking about the animal and go on cutting wood." While he was so engaged the top of the axe flew off and killed the animal.

This illustrates that when you are not thinking of it there is satori. When you try to realise satori, the more you struggle the farther it is away. You cannot help pursuing satori, but so long as you make that special effort satori will never be gained. But you cannot forget about it altogether. If you expect satori to come to you of its own accord, you will not get it.

To realise satori is very difficult, as the Buddha found. When he wished to be liberated from the bondage of birth and death he began to study philosophy, but this did not avail him, so he turned to asceticism. This made him so weak that he could not move, so he took milk and decided to go on with his search for liberation. Reasoning did not do any good and pursuing moral perfection did not help him either. Yet the urge to solve this problem was still there. He could go no farther, yet he could not retreat, so he had to stay where he was, but even that would not do. This state of spiritual crisis means that you cannot go on, nor retreat, nor stay where you are. When this dilemma is genuine, there prevails a state of consciousness ready for satori. When we really come to this stage (but we frequently think that what is not real is real), when we find ourselves at this critical moment, something is sure to rise from the depths of reality, from the depths of our own being. When this comes up there is satori. Then you understand all things and are at peace with the world as well as with yourself.

Mysticism and Human Reason

W. T. Stace

Anyone who is acquainted with the mystical literature of the world will know that great mystics invariably express themselves in the language of paradox and contradiction; and it is to this aspect of mysticism that I especially want to draw your attention tonight. But before I do so I would like to make a few introductory remarks about mysticism in general. Mysticism is not a regional or local phenomenon. It is universal. By this I mean that it is found in every country, in every age, in every culture, and in association with every one of the great world-religions. I do not speak here of primitive cultures and primitive religions. No doubt mysticism expresses itself in them in primitive ways. But I am only speaking about advanced cultures and advanced religions. For instance, those ancient inspired documents, the Upanishads, which go back in time from 2,500 to 3,000 years, and which are the fountain-heads both of the Hindu religion and of the Vedanta philosophy, are a direct report of mystical experience. Buddhism, too, is a mystical religion throughout. It is founded upon the mystical experience of Gautama Buddha. In the East, in India, the word "mysticism" or any word corresponding to it is not generally used. It is called "enlightenment" or "illumination." But the enlightenment experience of the East

From W. T. Stace, "Mysticism and Human Reason," University of Arizona Bulletin Series, Vol. XXVI, No. 3, May 1955. Copyright by University of Arizona Press, 1955: Riecker Memorial Lecture No. 1.

is basically the same as what is called the mystical experience in the West. In the Mohammedan religion the Sufis were the great representatives of mysticism. Mysticism appears in China in connection with Taoism. The Tao is a mystical conception. Judaism produced notable mystics. The history of Christianity is rich with the names of great mystics and some of these names are household words: Meister Eckhart, Saint Teresa, St. John of the Cross, and many others. Even outside the boundaries of any institutional religion, in the ancient Greco-Roman pagan world, not attached, perhaps, to any particular religion, Plotinus was one of the supremely great mystics.

Now, of course, as between these mysticisms in the various cultures, there are certain differences. For instance, Hindu mysticism is not quite the same as Christian mysticism. But I believe that the resemblances, the common elements, the elements which are universally found in all these mysticisms, are far more striking than the differences. I should say that the differences are superficial, while the common, basic, universal elements in all mysticism are fundamental. Should you ask me: "What are those common elements which appear in mysticism in all these different cultures and religions?" I can, perhaps, very briefly, summarize them.

In the first place, the absolutely basic, fundamental characteristic of all mystical experience is that it is called "the unitary consciousness," or, as it is sometimes called, "the unifying vision." We may contrast the mystical consciousness with our ordinary, everyday, rational consciousness. Our ordinary, everyday consciousness is characterized by multiplicity. I mean that both the senses and the intellect, which constitute our everyday consciousness, are in contact with and are aware of a vast number, a plurality, a multiplicity of different things. In our ordinary consciousness we discriminate between one thing and another. But the mystical consciousness transcends all differences and all multiplicity. In it there is no multiplicity and no division of difference. "Here," says Eckhart "all is one, and one is all." He goes on to say that in that supreme vision there are "no contrasts." "Contrast" is Eckhart's word for the difference between one thing and another, for instance between yellow and green. He even goes so far as to say that in that experience there are no contrasts, i.e., differences, between grass, wood, and stone, but that all these "are one."

Closely connected with, and perhaps as a result of this characteristic of transcending all multiplicity, discrimination, and division are other characteristics common to mystical experience in all religions. It is non-sensuous, non-intellectual, and non-conceptual. And since all words except proper names stand for concepts, this means mystical experience is beyond all words, incapable of being expressed in any language; "ineffable" is the usual word. Another characteristic is that what is experienced is beyond space and beyond time. It is timeless; and timelessness is eternity. And therefore the mystical consciousness, even though it lasts only for a very short while, perhaps only a moment, is nevertheless eternal. For that moment gathers into itself all eternity. It is an eternal moment.

Another universal characteristic is that mystical consciousness is blessedness—it is the peace which passeth all understanding. One might quote at length from the utterances of great mystics in all religions to prove that these are the common characteristics. I have time for only one quotation which I choose because it happens to include most of them in a few sentences. In the Mandukya Upanishad it is written:

> It is neither inward experience nor outward experience. It is neither intellectual knowledge nor inferential knowledge. It is beyond the senses, beyond the understanding, beyond all expression. It is the pure unitary consciousness wherein awareness of the world and of multiplicity is completely obliterated. It is ineffable peace. It is the supreme good. It is the One without a second.

One other common element I must mention. The mystic everywhere, except perhaps in Buddhism, which is a rather doubtful case here, invariably feels an absolute certainty that he is in direct touch with, and not only in direct touch with, but has entered into actual union with, the Divine Being. Plotinus expressed this by saying that "the man"—the mystic, that is—"is merged with the Supreme, sunken into it, one with it." And William James in his famous book, *Varieties of Religious Experience,* has an excellent brief chapter on mysticism, and in that he uses these words:

> This overcoming of all barriers between the individual and the Absolute is the great mystic achievement. In mystic states we become one with the Absolute. This is the everlasting and triumphant mystic tradition, hardly altered by differences of climate, culture, or creed. In Hinduism, in Neo-Platonism, in Sufism, in Christian mysticism, we find the same recurring note, so that there is about mystic utterances an eternal unanimity which ought to make the critic stop and think.

Now, of course, this mystical experience, basically the same in all cultures as it is, might nevertheless be nothing but a beautiful dream. It is possible that it is a purely subjective state of the mystic's own mind, and that he is under an illusion when he thinks that he is in contact with some great being objective and outside himself. The only logical argument, the only piece of evidence which can be used to show that it is more than a beautiful dream, that it does actually reveal contact with an objective, divine being is this remarkable agreement, as regards basic features, of the different mysticisms in all the cultures of the world. Of course one may be convinced by faith, or intuition, or feeling. But I am speaking here of logical argument or evidence.

Regarding this I will quote you a few words written by Professor C. D. Broad of Cambridge, England. He says this:

> I am prepared to admit that although the experiences have differed considerably at different times and places, there are probably certain characteristics which are common to all of them, and which suffice to distinguish them from all other kinds of experience. In view of this, I think it more likely than not that in mystical experience men come into contact with some Reality or some aspect of Reality which they do not come into contact with in any other way.[1]

The reason I read this very guarded statement—you see, he doesn't speak of this aspect of Reality as God—the reason I read this is because Broad happens to be a very remarkable kind of witness in such a matter. He says, in the same book which I am quoting, that he has no religious beliefs. He says also that he has never had anything which could be called a mystical or even a religious experience. But he claims that he has absolutely no bias, either for religion or against it. He thus claims to be entirely impartial. His is certainly a critical mind, inclined to be skeptical, certainly not inclined to accept any moonshine. Any of my philosophical colleagues who are acquainted, as they all are, with Broad's writings, will bear out the fact that this is a correct description of Broad. You will see that the evidence which he himself quoted for supposing that mystical experience is something more than a beautiful subjective dream is precisely the unanimity, the universal character of certain basic characteristics of it.

I consider that Broad's opinion is a reasonable one, and I shall adopt it, going, however, just one little step—or is it a little step?—further than Broad. For this aspect of reality, or this reality, with which the mystic is in contact, I shall use, as he does not, the name "God." I use this word partly because it is the word that the mystics themselves use, but also because, whatever it is, the experience possesses the kind of qualities or characteristics that we think of as divine qualities: supreme value, blessedness, supreme goodness, love, and so on. But I do not wish to be understood as saying more than I actually am saying. I mean by the word "God" only what I have just said, namely, a reality which is possessed of divine qualities. I do not wish that there should be included in the connotation of the term the many superstitions and anthropomorphic meanings which have often clustered around it.

I turn now to what is the essential subject of my lecture, the paradoxes of mysticism. There are many such paradoxes. Their general character is this: that whatever is affirmed of God must be at the same time and in one and the same breath categorically denied. Whatever is said of the Divine Being, the opposite, the contradictory, must also be said. There are many such paradoxes, but I am going to speak tonight only about one, which is perhaps the most startling of them. This may be expressed by saying that God is both being and nonbeing. If you like, you can say it means that God both exists and does not exist; or again that God is beyond both existence and nonexistence. There is thus both a positive and negative aspect. There is the positive divine and the negative divine. As to the positive divine, it is hardly necessary for me to say much about it because it is well known to everyone. It is the content of popular religion everywhere. We begin, I suppose, by saying that God exists. "Exist" is a positive word. We go on to say that he is a mind, a spirit, a person. These, too, are positive conceptions. Finally, we say that God is love, justice, mercy, power, knowledge, wisdom, and so on. All these are positive terms. And you will recognize that statements of this kind about the Divine Being are the content of ordinary, everyday, popular religious thought. This is true not only of Christianity but, I think, of all the great religions of the world, with the possible exception of Buddhism which is often called an atheistic religion. I don't think that there is really very much disagreement between the great world religions in regard to these basic attributes of God. There may be some difference of emphasis. No doubt it is the case that in Christianity the emphasis is upon God as love. In Hinduism the emphasis is on God as bliss. In Islam perhaps the emphasis is on God as power, and so on.

If we turn now to the negative divine, we pass into a region which is not so well known. This is usually especially associated with mystical religion. It may be expressed by saying that, just as for the positive divine God is being, here God is non-being. Even more striking words than this are used by the great mystics. God is "Nothing." He is "empty." He is "the Void." He is "the bottomless abyss of nothingness." And sometimes metaphors are used. Darkness as the absence of light, and silence as the absence of sound, are negative. Therefore God is spoken of as the great darkness, the great silence.

I am going to document these statements by referring very briefly (I cannot give very much of the evidence in a short lecture) to some of the great mystic utterances in the different religions of the world. I want to show that this is universal.

To begin with Christianity: Meister Eckhart, as you know, was a great Roman Catholic mystic of the 13th century. In one place he says: "God is as void as if he were not."

Elsewhere he says: "Thou shalt worship God as he is, a non-God, a non-form, a non-person." One of his followers wrote this of him: "Wise Meister Eckhart speaks to us about Nothingness. He who does not understand this, in him has never shone the divine light." Using the metaphor of darkness, Eckhart says: "The end of all things is the hidden darkness of the eternal Godhead." He also refers on many occasions to God as "the nameless nothing." Another well-known Christian mystic, Tauler, uses the same kind of language. He, too, refers to God as "the nameless nothing." Albertus Magnus writes this: "We first deny of God all bodily and sensible attributes, and then all intelligible attributes, and lastly, that being which would place him among created things." Notice that being, existence, is here said to be the mark of created things.

Turning to Judaism we find that Jewish mystics often referred to Jehovah as "the mystical Nothing." And again, "in depths of His nothingness" is a common phrase. One of the Hassidic mystics wrote: "There are those who worship God with their human intellects, and others whose gaze is fixed on Nothing. He who is granted this supreme experience loses the reality of his intellect, but when he returns from such contemplation to the intellect, he finds it full of divine and inflowing splendor."

Turning to Buddhism we find a rather difficult case for our exposition because it is often said that Buddhism is an atheistic religion. This is true with some reservations. It is true that you do not find the Western concept of God in Buddhism. And it therefore might be said that it is obvious that Buddhism can have neither a positive nor a negative conception of God. This, however, is really not a justifiable conclusion. I can't go into the matter in any great detail here. On the whole, the concept of Nirvana is what corresponds in Buddhism to the Christian and Jewish concept of God. Nirvana, the experience of Nirvana, is, I think, what we would recognize as the divine experience, the experience of the divine element in the world. It is not important that the word God is not used. If Nirvana corresponds to the concept of the concept of the divine, then one can say that the concept of Nirvana has both the positive and negative aspects. Positively, it is bliss unspeakable. Negatively, it is the Void. This conception of the Void which you see that Eckhart also uses, is basic to Buddhism. Ultimate reality is the Void.

I find that in Hinduism this positive-negative paradox is more fully developed, more clear than it is in Christianity, Judaism, or Buddhism. In Hinduism it may be said that this paradox has three aspects. Brahman is the name used in the Upanishads and generally in Hindu thought for the ultimate, supreme God. The first aspect of the paradox is that Brahman both has qualities and yet is without any qualities at all. On the positive side the qualities of Brahman are the usual divine qualities to which I have already referred. On the negative side he is "unqualified." This is often expressed in the Upanishads by using a string of negative terms. For example, it is said that Brahman "is soundless, formless, shapeless, intangible, tasteless, odorless, mindless." Notice this last word, "mindless." This quotation is similar in meaning to the one which I read from Albertus Magnus. First we deny all physical qualities. He is "soundless, formless, shapeless, intangible, odorless, and tasteless." Next we deny all "intelligible," i.e. psychological or spiritual attributes. He is "mindless." But the negative of the paradox, the denial of all qualities, is summed up in a very famous verse in the Upanishads. Brahman is here, as often, referred to as the Self. The verse says: "That Self is to be described as not this, not that." One of the earlier translators worded it thus: "That Self is to be described by 'No! No!'." The force of this "No! No!" is clear. Whatever attribute you suggest, whatever predicate you suggest, whatever quality you suggest, of Brahman, the answer always is "No." Is he matter? No. Is he mind?

No. Is he good? No. Is he evil? No. And so throughout every word that you can possibly choose.

The second aspect of the paradox in Hinduism is that Brahman is both personal and impersonal. His personality is carried by the very word "Self." He is the Self. He is personal and as such is wise, just, good, and so on. But he is also wholly impersonal. The word "mindless" contains this implication. For a person must necessarily be a mind. Also he is specifically referred to as "the impersonal Brahman." And sometimes the word "he" and sometimes the word "it" is used of Brahman. "He" conveys the notion of personality, "it" the notion of impersonality.

The third and final aspect of the paradox in Hinduism is that Brahman is both dynamic and static. Dynamic means that he is active, static means that he is actionless. On the positive side God is dynamic. He is the creative energy of the world, the creator. Also he acts in the world, guides and controls the world. On the static side it is specifically stated in the Upanishads that he is wholly actionless.[2] And the entire paradox is summed up in the following verse from the Upanishads:

That One, though never stirring, is swifter than thought; though standing still, it overtakes those who run. It moves and it moves not.

In this phrase, "It moves and it moves not," you have the whole paradox of the dynamic and static character of God summed up in six words.

Perhaps you will say, "Well, this is just poetic language. Everybody knows that poets like pleasant sounding phrases. And they like a balance of clauses. 'It moves and it moves not' sounds very well but it is mere words." I think you are quite mistaken if you take that interpretation. This is a literal statement of the paradox of the dynamic and the static.

Now I am persuaded that this entire paradox, and particularly that of the dynamic and the static character of the divine being, is not peculiar to Hinduism but is a universal characteristic of the religious consciousness everywhere, although in Hinduism it is more explicit, more baldly stated, than in other religions. In other religions it is present but tends to be veiled. Let us look at Christianity, for example. No one will deny that the Christian God is active. He is the creator of the world; he guides and controls it. But where, you will ask me, do you find evidence that the Christian God is static, inactive? It is true that you must look under the surface to find this. It is implied, implicit rather than explicit, in the concept of God as *unchangeable and immutable*. The changelessness, the immutability of God, is not only a Christian idea. It is a universal intuition of the religious consciousness found in all religions. "In him is no shadow of turning," and there is a well-known hymn which begins with the words:

O strength and stay upholding all creation
Who ever dost thyself *unmoved abide.*

The last two words convey the idea of the motionless, actionless character of God. We hardly realize when we speak of God as "immutable" and yet as the Creator of the world that we are uttering a paradox. There is, in fact, a contradiction between God as active and God as unchanging, because that which acts necessarily changes—changes from that state in which the action is not done to that state in which the action is done. Therefore, that which is wholly unchanging is also wholly inactive. The same idea also appears in poetry. T. S. Eliot twice to my knowledge in his poems uses the phrase, "The still point of the turning world." The literal meaning of this is obvious. It refers to the planet, the periphery and the outer parts of which are turning, while the axis in the middle is motionless. But the mystical meaning is also clear. It means that this world is a world of flux and change and becoming, but at the center of it, in the heart of things, there is silence, stillness, motionlessness.

So much, then, for the exposition of this paradox. But the human intellect, when it comes to a logical contradiction, necessarily attempts to get rid of it, attempts to explain away the contradiction. It tries to show that although there is an apparent contradiction, there is not really one. To get rid of a contradiction is essential to the very nature of our logical and rationalistic intellect.

Mystics themselves often show this characteristic since they are rational beings. I will give you two examples of attempts by religious thinkers to explain this paradox of the positive and negative divine logically, to make it comprehensible to the logical intellect. One logical way of getting rid of a contradiction is to separate the contradictory predicates and to declare that they apply to two different things. For example, if we speak of a square circle, this is a contradiction. If I say this desk top in front of me is both square and circular, this is a contradiction. But if I say the concept "square" applies to one thing and the concept "circular" to something else, if I say "this thing over here is square, and that thing over there is circular," then of course the contradiction disappears. This method of getting rid of the contradiction of the positive and negative has been used by mystics themselves. The great Hindu philosopher Sankara, who lived in the eighth century A.D. and who wrote a great commentary upon the Upanishads and endeavored to systematize the Vedanta philosophy, was very clearly and well aware of this contradiction about which I have been speaking. He attempted a solution by saying that there are really two Brahmans. One of them, which he called the Higher Brahman, is void, empty, qualityless, impersonal, actionless, negative. The other Brahman, which he calls the Lower Brahman, carries the usual divine attributes—that is, he is the creator of the universe, he is personal, wise, just and so on. He is, in fact, the God of popular religion. Sankara held, however, that the ultimate ground of the world is the Higher Brahman, and the Lower Brahman merely issues forth from this ultimate ground as its first manifestation. Thus the contradiction is got rid of because the Higher Brahman carries the inactive, the negative character, while the Lower Brahman carries the positive attributes.

One may be quite sure that this is the wrong solution because the religious intuition is peremptory that God is one and not two, and this is especially the case in Hinduism since everywhere Brahman is spoken of as the One, and more emphatically as "the One without a second."

It is extremely instructive and interesting to see that exactly the same solution of this paradox is offered by the Christian mystic, Meister Eckhart, of course in complete independence of Sankara. Eckhart makes a distinction between God and the Godhead. It is the Godhead, according to him, which is void, empty, and negative. God has the usual positive, divine attributes. As before, one must say that this is the wrong solution. But Eckhart, in a sense, withdraws it himself. For he identifies the Godhead with God the Father, and God with God the Son. And in accordance with the doctrine of the Trinity these two are one in spite of their duality. Yet Eckhart, like Sankara, declares that it is the void Godhead which is the ultimate ground of all things.

My own belief is that all attempts to rationalize the paradox, to make it logically acceptable, are futile because the paradoxes of religion and of mysticism are irresoluble by the human intellect. My view is that they never have been, they never can be, and they never will be resolved, or made logical. That is to say, these paradoxes and contradictions are inherent in the mystical experience and cannot be got rid of by any human logic or ingenuity. This, in my opinion, is an aspect of what is

sometimes called the mystery of God or the incomprehensibility of God. This mystery of God is not something which we can get rid of, something which we could understand by being a little more clever or a little more learned. It is ultimate, it is an ultimate and irremovable character of the divine. When you say that God is incomprehensible, one thing you mean is just that these contradictions break out in our intellect and cannot be resolved, no matter how clever or how good a logician you may be. And I think that this view is in the end the view of the mystics themselves, including Eckhart, in spite of his apparent attempt to explain the paradox.

In order to show that this is in fact the view of the mystics themselves in all religions, I will read to you from a Christian mystic, a Hindu, and a Buddhist. The Christian example again is Eckhart. Rudolph Otto writes that "Eckhart establishes a polar unity between rest and motion within the Godhead itself. The eternally resting Godhead is also the wheel rolling out of itself." And in Eckhart's own words: "This divine ground is a unified stillness, immovable in itself. Yet from this immobility all things are moved and receive life."

The Hindu from whom I wish to quote is Aurobindo, who died only a few years ago. There is no doubt in my mind that he himself experienced the mystical vision in full measure. He says:

> Those who have thus possessed the calm within can perceive always welling out from its silence the perennial supply of the energies which work in the world.

I wish to comment on this sentence. "Those who have thus possessed the calm within" means those who have possessed mystical vision. "Can perceive always welling out from its silence"—"silence" is the motionlessness, the stillness, the inactivity of the divine. "The perennial supply of the energies which work in the world" refers to the creative activity of the divine. These creative energies are said to "well out from the silence." In other words, they issue out of the empty void. Finally, we see the paradox of the static and the dynamic directly stated as an *experience*. The word "perceive" is used. This is not an intellectual proposition, a theory, an intellectual construction, a philosophical opinion. It is a direct perception or vision of reality.

My last example is Suzuki, the well-known Zen Buddhist mystic, now teaching in New York. He writes:

It is not the nature of "prajna" to remain in the state of "sunyata," absolutely motionless.

("Prajna" is the word for mystical intuition, while "sunyata" means the void.) So he is saying it is not the nature of mystical consciousness to remain in a state of void, absolutely motionless.

It demands of itself that it differentiate itself unlimitedly and, at the same time, it deserves to remain in itself undifferentiated. This is why "sunyata" is said to be a reservoir of infinite possibility, and not just a state of mere emptiness. Differentiating itself and yet remaining in itself undifferentiated, it goes on eternally in the work of creation. We can say of it that it is creation out of nothing. "Sunyata" is not to be conceived statically but dynamically, or better, as at once static and dynamic.

David Hume asked ironically, "Have you ever seen a world created under your eyes—have you ever observed an act of creation of the world?" The answer is: Yes, there are men who have seen this.

I conclude that these contradictions and paradoxes are impossible of logical adjustment or resolution. What, then, should we think about the matter? Should we say that there is contradiction in the nature of God himself, in the ultimate being? Well, if we were to say that, I think that we shouldn't be saying anything very unusual or very shocking. Many people have said this or at any rate implied it. Does not the Christian doctrine of the Trinity itself imply this? What could be a greater paradox than that? And it is not to be believed that the three-in-one, the three which is one and the one which is three, could be understood or explained by a super-Einstein, or by a higher mathematics than has yet been invented. It is irremovable and an absolute paradox. Also one might quote the words of Jacob Boehme suggesting that there is contradiction in the heart of things, in the ultimate itself. Schwegler, a distinguished German historian of philosophy, writes this:

The main thought of Boehme's philosophizing is this: that self-distinction, inner diremption is the essential characteristic of spirit, and, consequently of God. God is the living spirit only if and insofar as he comprehends within himself difference from himself.

One might also perhaps quote Boehme's well-known statement that God is both "the Eternal Yea" and "the Eternal Nay," but this perhaps might also be taken simply as a brief expression of the negative-positive paradox.

Although I do not think it would be anything seriously erroneous if we would say that there is contradiction in the Ultimate, yet I would prefer myself to use other language. I should say that the contradiction is in us, in our intellect, and not in God. This means that God is utterly and forever beyond the reach of the logical intellect or of any intellectual comprehension, and that in consequence when we try to comprehend his nature intellectually, contradictions appear in our thinking. Let me use a metaphor to express this. We speak of God as the "Infinite" and of ourselves as "finite" minds. As a matter of fact what the word "infinite" means in this connection is itself a difficult problem in the philosophy of religion. It is certain that the word "infinite," when applied to God, is not used in the same sense as when we speak of infinite time or infinite space or the infinite number series. What it does mean is a problem. I believe that it can be solved, that is to say, it is possible to give a clear meaning to the word "infinite"—different from the infinity of space and time—as the word is applied to God. However, if I am allowed to use this language of finite and infinite, my metaphor is that if you try to pour the infinite into the finite vessels which are human minds, these finite vessels split and crack, and these cracks and splits are the contradictions and paradoxes of which I have been talking. Therefore this amounts to saying that God is utterly incomprehensible, incapable of being intellectually understood. In order to make my final point I will use the word "unknowable." It means that God is, in a sense, unknowable. But we must be very careful of this. If God were absolutely unknowable, and in no sense knowable, then there could be no such thing as religion, because in some sense or other religion is the knowledge of God.

The explanation of this is that he is unknowable to *the logical intellect,* but that he can be known in direct religious or mystical experience. Perhaps this is much the same as saying that he can be known by "faith" but not by "reason." Any attempt to reach God through logic, through the conceptual, logical intellect, is doomed, comes up against an absolute barrier; but this does not mean the death of religion— it does not mean that there is no possibility of that knowledge and communion with God which religion requires. It means that the knowledge of God which is the essence of religion is not of an intellectual kind. It is rather the direct experience of the mystic himself. Or if we are not mystics, then it is whatever it is that you would call religious experience. And this experience of God—in the heart, shall we say, not any intellectual understanding or explanation—this experience of God is the essence of religion.

NOTES

1. *Religion, Philosophy, and Psychical Research,* pp. 172–173.
2. Rudolph Otto in his *Mysticism East and West* claims it is a superiority of the Christian God over the Hindu, that the latter is merely static, the former dynamic. He has missed the paradox and been misled by the frequent statements that Brahman is inactive.

26 Is There Life after Death?

Plato & Ducasse

The question of immortality—whether or not one's personal consciousness and identity can survive death—is to some people the most important question of all. The prospect of death, the possible dissolution of the self into nothingness is, according to writers like Schopenhauer and Camus, what makes philosophers of us all. Most religions have adhered to a belief in personal immortality (Hinayana Buddhism is one of the few that does not) and a number of the great philosophers, including Socrates, Saint Augustine, Saint Thomas Aquinas, Descartes, Kant, and James, have presented arguments to support it.

In *The Apology,* Socrates raised the possibility of conscious personal immortality, but he also faced the possibility of death's being a dreamless sleep. Later in the *Phaedo,* which describes his conversation shortly before his death, he (or Plato) argued at length for the soul's indestructibility on the basis of its nature as immaterial, incorruptible, indivisible, and as the spiritual animator of the body separable from it. The last portion of Socrates' argument is given here, along with the description of how Socrates faced his own death with complete confidence.

Other philosophers, such as Epicurus, Hume, Schopenhauer, Dewey, and Russell, have denied that the belief in immortality has any rational or empirical basis. Schopenhauer, for example, considered the belief to spring from a combination of terror over the prospect of annihilation, exploitation of the fears and ignorance of the masses by crafty religious authorities, and plain wishful thinking. And Russell wrote that "to expect a personality to survive the dissolution of the brain is like expecting a cricket club to survive when all its members are dead."

Of the arguments that have been given for and against immortality some are much weaker than others. An American philosopher, Edgar Sheffield Brightman (1884–1953), who himself viewed the belief in immortality to be an extension of our experience of purpose, collated the arguments for personal survival after death in his *Philosophy of Religion*. He rejected as being weak arguments that the belief is true because it is universal, based on consensus, inspiring, or supported by revelation. Equally weak are the arguments that the belief is false because many scientists disbelieve it; that if it were true "the universe would eventually be overcrowded with souls"; and that "an individual's lasting social influence is an adequate substitute for immortality."[1] The crucial empirical argument against immortality for Brightman was the argument based on the so-called facts of physiological psychology; for as consciousness depends upon the functioning of the brain, when it is damaged or destroyed consciousness is also destroyed. This materialistic hypothesis, if true, would be fatal to a belief in immortality, but Brightman took issue with it. As a personalist, an idealist who stressed the primacy of humans, and who saw individual purpose as related inextricably with cosmic purpose, Brightman argued that "the facts of consciousness are clues to the nature of all reality."[2] If materialism cannot explain adequately the nature of our conscious experience, by what right can it claim that the death of the body affects or destroys this consciousness? As Brightman wrote:

> The more closely we inspect conscious experience, the more difficulties emerge for materialism. We experience personal identity, unity, memory; materialism offers no account of these facts that explains their characteristic features. We experience purpose; materialism has to try to explain purpose away. We experience values and ideals; materialists also experience them and often are loyal to them, but their philosophy renders the very experience of ideal value unintelligible and offers no theory of obligation. In short, materialism, based as it is on an exclusive preference for sensations, cannot in the nature of the case give a coherent description of experience as a whole, and cannot even include sensations themselves in the domain of matter.[3]

Brightman then went on to present what he considered to be the crucial rational argument for immortality—that "God as the conserver of values, must be God, the preserver of persons." If God did not exist, then there could be no personal immortality. But since, in Brightman's view, God does exist as an infinitely good but finite cosmic divine Person, He will preserve the highest purposive agent in the universe, man.

Curt Ducasse (1881–1969), the author of the following essay, would have agreed with Brightman's misgivings about materialism, but he did not make belief in immortality contingent on belief in God. The evidence which he found most relevant to immortality is the evidence of physical phenomena, a field which he explored and studied for years.

Can we answer with any finality the question, "Is there life after death?" One of the best-known recent writers on death and dying, Elisabeth Kubler-Ross, has spoken out for immortality on the basis of her studies of reported deathbed experiences. Another author, Raymond Moody, in *Life After*

Life, presents the view that there are veridical psychical experiences that "prove" immortality.

With hope, curiosity, and ultimate concern, in the Socratic spirit philosophers continue to wonder and sometimes to worry about death. A scholarly but gloomy Anglican Archbishop once said when questioned about immortality that he knew as much about the subject as any man living on earth, namely, nothing. When Confucius was similarly questioned, he replied, "We do not know anything about life; what can we know about death?" An existentialist might remind us that an escape from the confrontation with death, no matter how much we might long for immortality, is never justified; for an awareness of death is what makes us more authentic, more alive and vibrant, more determined to choose freely in order to make our lives count. "There is only one liberty, to come to terms with death. After that everything is possible," wrote Camus.

Socrates transcended death in that when it came, according to Phaedo's report, he faced it calmly, fully aware and in complete control of all his faculties. For he had either absolute confidence that he was going to survive the destruction of his body or the strong simple faith which he had expressed at his trial sustained him. "No harm can come to a good man," he had said to the jurors, "either in life or after death."

NOTES

1. See Edgar S. Brightman, *A Philosophy of Religion* (New York: Prentice-Hall, 1946), Chap. 13.
2. Ibid., p. 399.
3. Ibid., p. 400.

Death of Socrates

Plato

(*Speakers are Socrates and Cebes.*)

And now, he said, let us begin again; and do not you answer my question in the words in which I ask it: let me have not the old safe answer of which I spoke at first, but another equally safe, of which the truth will be inferred by you from what has been just said. I mean that if any one asks you 'what that is, of which the inherence makes the body hot,' you will reply not heat (this is what I call the safe and stupid answer), but fire, a far superior answer, which we are now in a condition to give. Or if any one asks you 'why a body is diseased,' you will not say from disease, but from fever; and instead of saying that oddness is the cause of odd numbers, you will say that the monad is the cause of them: and so of things in general, as I dare say that you will understand sufficiently without my adducing any further examples.

Yes, he said, I quite understand you.

Tell me, then, what is that of which the inherence will render the body alive?

The soul, he replied.

And is this always the case?

Yes, he said, of course.

Then whatever the soul possesses, to that she comes bearing life?

Yes, certainly.

And is there any opposite to life?

From Plato, the *Phaedo*, in *The Dialogues of Plato*, trans. Benjamin Jowett, 3d ed. (New York: Oxford University Press, 1898).

There is, he said.

And what is that?

Death.

Then the soul, as has been acknowledged, will never receive the opposite of what she brings.

Impossible, replied Cebes.

And now, he said, what did we just now call that principle which repels the even?

The odd.

And that principle which repels the musical or the just?

The unmusical, he said, and the unjust.

And what do we call that principle which does not admit of death?

The immortal, he said.

And does the soul admit of death?

No.

Then the soul is immortal?

Yes, he said.

And may we say that this has been proven?

Yes, abundantly proven, Socrates, he replied.

Supposing that the odd were imperishable, must not three be imperishable?

Of course.

And if that which is cold were imperishable, when the warm principle came attacking the snow, must not the snow have retired whole and unmelted—for it could never have perished, nor could it have remained and admitted the heat?

True, he said.

Again, if the uncooling or warm principle were imperishable, the fire when assailed by

(Socrates, Cebes, Simmias.)

cold would not have perished or have been extinguished, but would have gone away unaffected?

Certainly, he said.

And the same may be said of the immortal: if the immortal is also imperishable, the soul when attacked by death cannot perish; for the preceding argument shows that the soul will not admit of death, or ever be dead, any more than three or the odd number will admit of the even, or fire, or the heat in the fire, of the cold. Yet a person may say: 'But although the odd will not become even at the approach of the even, why may not the odd perish and the even take the place of the odd?' Now to him who makes this objection, we cannot answer that the odd principle is imperishable; for this has not been acknowledged, but if this had been acknowledged, there would have been no difficulty in contending that at the approach of the even the odd principle and the number three took their departure; and the same argument would have held good of fire and heat and any other thing.

Very true.

And the same may be said of the immortal: if the immortal is also imperishable, then the soul will be imperishable as well as immortal; but if not, some other proof of her imperishableness will have to be given.

No other proof is needed, he said; for if the immortal, being eternal, is liable to perish, then nothing is imperishable.

Yes, replied Socrates, and yet all men will agree that God, and the essential form of life, and the immortal in general, will never perish.

Yes, all men, he said—that is true; and what is more, gods, if I am not mistaken, as well as men.

Seeing then that the immortal is indestructible, must not the soul, if she is immortal, be also imperishable?

Most certainly.

Then when death attacks a man, the mortal portion of him may be supposed to die, but the immortal retires at the approach of death and is preserved safe and sound?

True.

Then, Cebes, beyond question, the soul is immortal and imperishable, and our souls will truly exist in another world!

I am convinced, Socrates, said Cebes, and have nothing more to object; but if my friend Simmias, or any one else, has any further objection to make, he had better speak out, and not keep silence, since I do not know to what other season he can defer the discussion, if there is anything which he wants to say or to have said.

But I have nothing more to say, replied Simmias; nor can I see any reason for doubt after what has been said. But I still feel and cannot help feeling uncertain in my own mind, when I think of the greatness of the subject and the feebleness of man.

Yes, Simmias, replied Socrates, that is well said: and I may add that first principles, even if they appear certain, should be carefully considered; and when they are satisfactorily ascertained, then, with a sort of hesitating confidence in human reason, you may, I think, follow the course of the argument; and if that be plain and clear, there will be no need for any further enquiry.

Very true.

But then, O my friends, he said, if the soul is really immortal, what care should be taken of her, not only in respect of the portion of time which is called life, but of eternity! And the danger of neglecting her from this point of view does indeed appear to be awful. If death had only been the end of all, the wicked would have had a good bargain in dying, for they would have been happily quit not only of their body, but of their own evil together with their souls. But now, inasmuch as the soul is manifestly immortal, there is no release or salvation from evil except the attainment of the highest

(Socrates, Crito.)

virtue and wisdom. For the soul when on her progress to the world below takes nothing with her but nurture and education; and these are said greatly to benefit or greatly to injure the departed, at the very beginning of his journey thither. . . .

A man of sense ought not to say, nor will I be very confident, that the description which I have given of the soul and her mansions is exactly true. But I do say that, inasmuch as the soul is shown to be immortal, he may venture to think, not improperly or unworthily, that something of the kind is true. The venture is a glorious one, and he ought to comfort himself with words like these, which is the reason why I lengthen out the tale. Wherefore, I say, let a man be of good cheer about his soul, who having cast away the pleasures and ornaments of the body as alien to him and working harm rather than good, has sought after the pleasures of knowledge; and has arrayed the soul, not in some foreign attire, but in her own proper jewels, temperance, and justice, and courage, and nobility, and truth—in these adorned she is ready to go on her journey to the world below, when her hour comes. You, Simmias and Cebes, and all other man, will depart at some time or other. Me already, as a tragic poet would say, the voice of fate calls. Soon I must drink the poison; and I think that I had better repair to the bath first, in order that the women may not have the trouble of washing my body after I am dead.

When he had done speaking. Crito said: And have you any commands for us, Socrates— anything to say about your children, or any other matter in which we can serve you?

Nothing particular, Crito, he replied: only, as I have always told you, take care of yourselves; that is a service which you may be ever rendering to me and mine and to all of us, whether you promise to do so or not. But if you have no thought for yourselves, and care not to walk according to the rule which I have prescribed for you, not now for the first time, however much you may profess or promise at the moment, it will be of no avail.

We will do our best, said Crito: And in what way shall we bury you?

In any way that you like; but you must get hold of me, and take care that I do not run away from you. Then he turned to us, and added with a smile:—I cannot make Crito believe that I am the same Socrates who have been talking and conducting the argument: he fancies that I am the other Socrates whom he will soon see, a dead body—and he asks, How shall he bury me? And though I have spoken many words in the endeavour to show that when I have drunk the poison I shall leave you and go to the joys of the blessed,—these words of mine, with which I was comforting you and myself, have had, as I perceive, no effect upon Crito. And therefore I want you to be surety for me to him now, as at the trial he was surety to the judges for me: but let the promise be of another sort; for he was surety for me to the judges that I would remain, and you must be my surety to him that I shall not remain, but go away and depart; and then he will suffer less at my death, and not be grieved when he sees my body being burned or buried. I would not have him sorrow at my hard lot, or say at the burial, Thus we lay out Socrates, or, Thus we follow him to the grave or bury him; for false words are not only evil in themselves, but they infect the soul with evil. Be of good cheer then, my dear Crito, and say that you are burying my body only, and do with that whatever is usual, and what you think best.

When he had spoken these words, he arose and went into a chamber to bathe; Crito followed him and told us to wait. So we remained behind, talking and thinking of the subject of discourse, and also of the greatness of our sorrow; he was like a father of whom we were being bereaved, and we were about to pass the rest of our lives as orphans. When he had taken

(*Socrates, Crito, The Jailer.*)

the bath his children were brought to him—(he had two young sons and an elder one); and the women of his family also came, and he talked to them and gave them a few directions in the presence of Crito; then he dismissed them and returned to us.

Now the hour of sunset was near, for a good deal of time had passed while he was within. When he came out, he sat down with us again after his bath, but not much was said. Soon the jailer, who was the servant of the Eleven, entered and stood by him, saying:—To you, Socrates, whom I know to be the noblest and gentlest and best of all who ever came to this place, I will not impute the angry feelings of other men, who rage and swear at me, when, in obedience to the authorities, I bid them drink the poison—indeed, I am sure that you will not be angry with me; for others, as you are aware, and not I, are to blame. And so fare you well, and try to bear lightly what must needs be—you know my errand. Then bursting into tears he turned away and went out.

Socrates looked at him and said: I return your good wishes, and will do as you bid. Then turning to us, he said, How charming the man is: since I have been in prison he has always been coming to see me, and at times he would talk to me, and was as good to me as could be, and now see how generously he sorrows on my account. We must do as he says, Crito; and therefore let the cup be brought, if the poison is prepared: if not, let the attendant prepare some.

Yet, said Crito, the sun is still upon the hilltops, and I know that many a one has taken the draught late, and after the announcement has been made to him, he has eaten and drunk, and enjoyed the society of his beloved; do not hurry—there is time enough.

Socrates said: Yes, Crito, and they of whom you speak are right in so acting, for they think that they will be gainers by the delay; but I am right in not following their example, for I do not think that I should gain anything by drinking the poison a little later; I should only be ridiculous in my own eyes for sparing and saving a life which is already forfeit. Please then to do as I say, and not to refuse me.

Crito made a sign to the servant, who was standing by; and he went out, and having been absent for some time, returned with the jailer carrying the cup of poison. Socrates said: You, my good friend, who are experienced in these matters, shall give me directions how I am to proceed. The man answered: You have only to walk about until your legs are heavy, and then to lie down, and the poison will act. At the same time he handed the cup to Socrates, who in the easiest and gentlest manner, without the least fear or change of colour or feature, looking at the man with all his eyes, Echecrates, as his manner was, took the cup and said: What do you say about making a libation out of this cup to any god? May I, or not? The man answered: We only prepare, Socrates, just so much as we deem enough. I understand, he said: but I may and must ask the gods to prosper my journey from this to the other world—even so—and so be it according to my prayer. Then raising the cup to his lips, quite readily and cheerfully he drank off the poison. And hitherto most of us had been able to control our sorrow; but now when we saw him drinking, and saw too that he had finished the draught, we could no longer forbear, and in spite of myself my own tears were flowing fast; so that I covered my face and wept, not for him, but at the thought of my own calamity in having to part from such a friend. Nor was I the first; for Crito, when he found himself unable to restrain his tears, had got up, and I followed; and at that moment, Apollodorus, who had been weeping all the time, broke out in a loud and passionate cry which made cowards of us all. Socrates alone retained his calmness: What is this strange outcry? he said. I sent away the women mainly in order that they might not misbehave in this

(Socrates, Crito, Phaedo.)

way, for I have been told that a man should die in peace. Be quiet then, and have patience. When we heard his words we were ashamed, and refrained our tears; and he walked about until, as he said, his legs began to fail, and then he lay on his back, according to the directions, and the man who gave him the poison now and then looked at his feet and legs; and after a while he pressed his foot hard, and asked him if he could feel; and he said, No; and then his leg, and so upwards and upwards, and showed us that he was cold and stiff. And he felt them himself, and said: When the poison reaches the heart, that will be the end. He was beginning to grow cold about the groin, when he uncovered his face, for he had covered himself up, and said —they were his last words—he said: Crito, I owe a cock to Asclepius; will you remember to pay the debt? The debt shall be paid, said Crito; is there anything else? There was no answer to this question; but in a minute or two a movement was heard, and the attendants uncovered him; his eyes were set, and Crito closed his eyes and mouth.

Such was the end, Echecrates, of our friend; concerning whom I may truly say, that of all the men of his time whom I have known, he was the wisest and justest and best.

Is a Life after Death Possible?

C. J. Ducasse

The question whether human personality survives death is sometimes asserted to be one upon which reflection is futile. Only empirical evidence, it is said, can be relevant, since the question is purely one of fact.

But no question is purely one of fact until it is clearly understood; and this one is, on the contrary, ambiguous and replete with tacit assumptions. Until the ambiguities have been removed and the assumptions critically examined, we do not really know just what it is we want to know when we ask whether a life after death is possible. Nor, therefore, can we tell until then what bearing on this question various facts empirically known to us may have.

To clarify its meaning is chiefly what I now propose to attempt. I shall ask first why a future life is so generally desired and believed in. Then I shall state, as convincingly as I can in the time available, the arguments commonly advanced to prove that such a life is impossible. After that, I shall consider the logic of these arguments, and show that they quite fail to establish the impossibility. Next, the tacit but arbitrary assumption, which makes them nevertheless appear convincing, will be pointed out. And finally, I shall consider briefly a number of specific forms which a life after death might take, if there is one.

From Curt J. Ducasse, "Is a Life after Death Possible?," *Newsletter of the Parapsychology Foundation*, Vol. 3, No. 1 (January–February, 1956), pp. 3–8. (Notes are omitted. *Ed.*)

Let us turn to the first of these tasks.

To begin with, let us note that each of us here has been alive and conscious at all times in the past which he can remember. It is true that sometimes our bodies are in deep sleep, or made inert by anesthetics or injuries. But even at such times we do not experience unconsciousness in ourselves, for to experience it would mean being conscious of being unconscious, and this is a contradiction. The only experience of unconsciousness in ourselves we ever have is, not experience of total unconsciousness, but of unconsciousness *of this or that*; as when we report: "I am not conscious of any pain," or "of any bell-sound," or "of any difference between those two colors," etc. Nor do we ever experience unconsciousness in another person, but only the fact that, sometimes, some or all of the ordinary activities of his body cease to occur. That consciousness itself is extinguished at such times is thus only a hypothesis which we construct to account for certain changes in the behavior of another person's body or to explain in him or in ourselves the eventual lack of memories relating to the given period.

Being alive and conscious is thus, with all men, a lifelong experience and habit; and conscious life is therefore something they naturally —even if tacitly—expect to continue. As J. B. Pratt has pointed out, the child takes the continuity of life for granted. It is the fact of death that has to be taught him. But when he has learned it, the idea of a future life is then put explicitly before his mind, it seems to him the most natural thing in the world.

The witnessing of death, however, is a rare experience for most of us, and, because it breaks so sharply into our habits, it forces on us the question whether the mind, which until then was manifested by the body now dead, continues somehow to live on, or, on the contrary, has become totally extinct. This question is commonly phrased as concerning "the immortality of the soul," and immortality, strictly speaking, means survival forever. But assurance of survival for some considerable period—say a thousand, or even a hundred, years—would probably have almost as much present psychological value as would assurance of survival strictly forever. Most men would be troubled very little by the idea of extinction at so distant a time—even less troubled than is now a healthy and happy youth by the idea that he will die in fifty or sixty years. Therefore, it is survival for some time, rather than survival specifically forever, that I shall alone consider.

The craving for continued existence is very widespread. Even persons who believe that death means complete extinction of the individual's consciousness often find comfort in various substitute conceptions of survival. They may, for instance, dwell on the continuity of the individual's germ plasm in his descendants. Or they find solace in the thought that, the past being indestructible, their individual life remains eternally an intrinsic part of the history of the world. Also—and more satisfying to one's craving for personal importance—there is the fact that since the acts of one's life have effects, and these in turn further effects, and so on, therefore what one has done goes on forever influencing remotely, and sometimes greatly, the course of future events.

Gratifying to one's vanity, too, is the prospect that, if the achievements of one's life have been great or even only conspicuous, or one's benefactions or evil deeds have been notable, one's name may not only be remembered by acquaintances and relatives for a little while, but may live on in recorded history. But evidently survival in any of these senses is but a consolation prize—but a thin substitute for the continuation of conscious individual life, which may not be a fact, but which most men crave nonetheless.

The roots of this craving are certain desires which death appears to frustrate. For some, the chief of these is for reunion with persons dearly loved. For others, whose lives have been wretched, it is the desire for another chance at the happiness they have missed. For others yet, it is desire for further opportunity to grow in ability, knowledge or character. Often, there is also the desire, already mentioned, to go on counting for something in the affairs of men. And again, a future life for oneself and others is often desired in order that the redressing of the many injustices of this life shall be possible. But it goes without saying that, although desires such as these are often sufficient to cause belief in a future life, they constitute no evidence at all that it is a fact.

In this connection, it may be well to point out that, although both the belief in survival and the belief in the existence of a god or gods are found in most religions, nevertheless there is no necessary connection between the two beliefs. No contradictions would be involved in supposing either that there is a God but no life after death or that there is a life after death but no God. The belief that there is a life after death may be tied to a religion, but it is no more intrinsically religious than would be a belief that there is life on the planet Mars. The after-death world, if it exists, is just another region or dimension of the universe.

But although belief in survival of death is natural and easy and has always been held in one form or another by a large majority of mankind, critical reflection quickly brings forth a number of apparently strong reasons to regard that belief as quite illusory. Let us now review them.

There are, first of all, a number of facts which definitely suggest that both the existence and the nature of consciousness wholly depend on the presence of a functioning nervous system. It is pointed out, for example, that wherever consciousness is observed, it is found associated with a living and functioning body. Further, when the body dies, or the head is struck a heavy blow, or some anesthetic is administered, the familiar outward evidences of consciousness terminate, permanently or temporarily. Again, we know well that drugs of various kinds— alcohol, caffein, opium, heroin, and many others—cause specific changes at the time in the nature of a person's mental state. Also, by stimulating in appropriate ways the body's sense organs, corresponding states of consciousness—namely, the various kinds of sensations— can be caused at will. On the other hand, cutting a sensory nerve immediately eliminates a whole range of sensations.

Again, the contents of consciousness, the mental powers, or even the personality, are modified in characteristic ways when certain regions of the brain are destroyed by disease or injury or are disconnected from the rest by such an operation as prefrontal lobotomy. And that the nervous system is the indispensable basis of mind is further suggested by the fact that, in the evolutionary scale, the degree of intelligence of various species of animals keeps pace closely with the degree of development of their brain.

That continued existence of mind after death is impossible has been argued also on the basis of theoretical considerations. It has been contended, for instance, that what we call states of consciousness—or more particularly, ideas, sensations, volitions, feelings, and the like—are really nothing but the minute physical or chemical events which take place in the tissues of the brain. For, it is urged, it would be absurd to suppose that an idea or a volition, if it is not itself a material thing or process, could cause material effects such as contractions of muscles.

Moreover, it is maintained that the possibility of causation of a material event by an immaterial, mental cause is ruled out *a priori* by the principle of the conservation of energy; for such causation would mean that an additional quantity of energy suddenly pops into the nervous system out of nowhere.

Another conception of consciousness, which is more often met with today than the one just mentioned, but which also implies that consciousness cannot survive death, is that "consciousness" is only the name we give to certain types of behavior, which differentiate the higher animals from all other things in nature. According to this view, to say, for example, that an animal is conscious of a difference between two stimuli means nothing more than that it responds to each by different behavior. That is, the difference of *behavior* is what consciousness of difference between the stimuli *consists in;* and is not, as is commonly assumed, only the behavioral *sign* of something mental and not public, called "consciousness that the stimuli are different."

Or again, consciousness, of the typically human sort called thought, is identified with the typically human sort of behavior called speech; and this, again not in the sense that speech *expresses* or *manifests* something different from itself, called "thought," but in the sense that speech—whether uttered or only whispered—*is* thought itself. And obviously, if thought, or any mental activity, is thus but some mode of behavior of the living body, the mind cannot possibly survive death.

Still another difficulty confronting the hypothesis of survival becomes evident when one imagines in some detail what survival would have to include in order to satisfy the desires which cause man to crave it. It would, of course, have to include persistence not alone of consciousness, but also of personality; that is, of the individual's character, acquired knowledge, cultural skills and interests, memories, and awareness of personal identity. But even this would not be enough, for what man desires is not bare survival, but to go on living in some objective way. And this means to go on meeting new situations and, by exerting himself to deal with them, to broaden and deepen his experience and develop his latent capacities.

But it is hard to imagine this possible without a body and an environment for it, upon which to act and from which to receive impressions. And, if a body and an environment were supposed, but not material and corruptible ones, then it is paradoxical to think that, under such radically different conditions, a given personality could persist.

To take a crude but telling analogy, it is past belief that, if the body of any one of us were suddenly changed into that of a shark or an octopus, and placed in the ocean, his personality could, for more than a very short time, if at all, survive intact so radical a change of environment and of bodily form.

Such, in brief, are the chief reasons commonly advanced for holding that survival is impossible. Scrutiny of them, however, will, I think, reveal that they are not as strong as they first seem and far from strong enough to show that there can be no life after death.

Let us consider first the assertion that "thought," or "consciousness," is but another name for subvocal speech, or for some other form of behavior, or for molecular processes in the tissues of the brain. As Paulsen and others have pointed out, no evidence ever is or can be offered to support that assertion, because it is in fact but a disguised proposal to make the words "thought," "feeling," "sensation," "desire," and so on, denote facts quite different from those which these words are commonly employed to denote. To say that those words are but other names for certain chemical or behavioral events is as grossly arbitrary as it would be to say that "wood" is but another name for glass, or "potato" but another name for cabbage. What thought, desire, sensation, and other mental states are like, each of us can observe directly by introspection; and what introspection reveals is that they do not in the least resemble muscular contraction, or glandular secretion, or any other known bodily events. No tampering with language can alter the observable fact that thinking is one thing and muttering quite another; that the feeling called anger has no resemblance to the bodily behavior which usually goes with it; or that an act of will is not in the least like anything we find when we open the skull and examine the brain. Certain mental events are doubtless connected in some way with certain bodily events, but they are not those bodily events themselves. The connection is not identity.

This being clear, let us next consider the arguments offered to show that mental processes, although not identical with bodily processes, nevertheless depend on them. We are told, for instance, that some head injuries, or anesthetics, totally extinguish consciousness for the time being. As already pointed out, however, the strict fact is only that the usual bodily signs of consciousness are then absent. But they are also absent when a person is asleep; and yet, at the same time, dreams, which are states of consciousness, may be occurring.

It is true that when the person concerned awakens, he often remembers his dreams, whereas the person that has been anesthetized or injured has usually no memories relating to the period of apparent blankness. But this could mean that his consciousness was, for the time, dissociated from its ordinary channels of manifestation, as was reported of the co-conscious personalities of some of the patients of Dr. Morton Prince. Moreover, it sometimes occurs that a person who has been in an accident reports lack of memories not only for the period during which his body was unresponsive but also for a period of several hours *before* the accident, during which he had given to his associates all the ordinary external signs of being conscious as usual.

But, more generally, if absence of memories relating to a given period proved unconsciousness for that period, this would force us to conclude that we were unconscious during the first few years of our lives, and indeed have been so most of the time since; for the fact is that we have no memories whatever of most of our days. That we are alive and conscious on any long past specific date is, with only a few exceptions, not something we actually remember, but only something which we infer must be true.

Another argument advanced against survival was, it will be remembered, that death must extinguish the mind, since all manifestations of it then cease. But to assert that they invariably then cease is to ignore altogether the considerable amount of evidence to the contrary, gathered over many years and carefully checked by the Society for Psychical Research. This evidence, which is of a variety of kinds, has been reviewed by Professor Gardner Murphy in an article published in the Journal of the Society. He mentions first the numerous well-authenticated cases of apparition of a dead person to others as yet unaware that he had died or even been ill or in danger. The more strongly evidential cases of apparition are those in which the apparition conveys to the person who sees it specific facts until then secret. An example would be that of the apparition of a girl to her brother nine years after her death, with a conspicuous scratch on her cheek. Their mother then revealed to him that she herself had made that scratch accidentally while preparing her daughter's body for burial, but that she had then at once covered it with powder and never mentioned it to anyone.

Another famous case is that of a father whose apparition some time after death revealed to one of his sons the existence and location of an unsuspected second will, benefiting him, which was then found as indicated. Still another case would be the report by General Barter, then a subaltern in the British Army in India, of the apparition to him of a lieutenant he had not seen for two or three years. The lieutenant's apparition was riding a brown pony with black mane and tail. He was much stouter than at their last meeting, and, whereas formerly clean-shaven, he now wore a peculiar beard in the form of a fringe encircling his face. On inquiry the next day from a person who had known the lieutenant at the time he died, it turned out that he had indeed become very bloated before his death; that he had grown just such a beard while on the sick list; and that he had some time before bought and eventually ridden to death a pony of that very description.

Other striking instances are those of an apparition seen simultaneously by several persons. It is on record that an apparition of a child was perceived first by a dog, that the animal's rushing at it, loudly barking, interrupted the conversation of the seven persons present in the room, thus drawing their attention to the apparition, and that the latter then moved through the room for some fifteen seconds, followed by the barking dog.

Another type of empirical evidence of survival consists of communications, purporting to come from the dead, made through the persons commonly called sensitives, mediums, or automatists. Some of the most remarkable of these communications were given by the celebrated American medium, Mrs. Piper, who for many years was studied by the Society for Psychical Research, London, with the most elaborate precautions against all possibility of fraud. Twice, particularly, the evidences of identity supplied by the dead persons who purportedly were thus communicating with the living were of the very kinds, and of the same precision and detail, which would ordinarily satisfy a living person of the identity of another living person with whom he was not able to communicate directly, but only through an intermediary, or by letter or telephone.

Again, sometimes the same mark of identity of a dead person, or the same message from him, or complementary parts of one message, are obtained independently from two mediums in different parts of the world.

Of course, when facts of these kinds are recounted, as I have just done, only in abstract summary, they make little if any impression upon us. And the very word "medium" at once brings to our minds the innumerable instances of demonstrated fraud perpetuated by charlatans to extract money from the credulous bereaved. But the modes of trickery and sources of error, which immediately suggest themselves to us as easy, natural explanations of the seemingly extraordinary facts, suggest themselves just as quickly to the members of the research committees of the Society for Psychical Research. Usually, these men have had a good deal more experience than the rest of us with the tricks of conjurers and fraudulent mediums, and take against them precautions far more strict and ingenious than would occur to the average skeptic.

But when, instead of stopping at summaries, one takes the trouble to study the detailed, original reports, it then becomes evident that they cannot all be just laughed off; for to accept the hypothesis of fraud or mal-observation would often require more credulity than to accept the facts reported.

To *explain* those facts, however, is quite another thing. Only two hypotheses at all adequate to do so have yet been advanced. One is that the communications really come, as they purport to do, from persons who have died and have survived death. The other is the hypothesis of telepathy—that is, the supposition, itself startling enough, that the medium is able to gather information directly from the minds of others, and that this is the true source of the information communicated. To account for all the facts,

however, this hypothesis has to be stretched very far, for some of them require us to suppose that the medium can tap the minds even of persons far away and quite unknown to him, and can tap even the subconscious part of their minds.

Diverse highly ingenious attempts have been made to devise conditions that would rule out telepathy as a possible explanation of the communications received; but some of the most critical and best-documented investigators still hold that it has not yet been absolutely excluded. Hence, although some of the facts recorded by psychical research constitute, prima facie, strong empirical evidence of survival, they cannot be said to establish it beyond question. But they do show that we need to revise rather radically in some respects our ordinary ideas of what is and is not possible in nature.

Let us now turn to another of the arguments against survival. That states of consciousness entirely depend on bodily processes, and therefore cannot continue when the latter have ceased, is proved, it is argued, by the fact that various states of consciousness—in particular, the several kinds of sensations—can be caused at will by appropriately stimulating the body.

Now, it is very true that sensations and some other mental states can be so caused; but we have just as good and abundant evidence that mental states can cause various bodily events. John Laird mentions, among others, the fact that merely willing to raise one's arm normally suffices to cause it to rise; that a hungry person's mouth is caused to water by the idea of food; that feelings of rage, fear or excitement cause digestion to stop; that anxiety causes changes in the quantity and quality of the milk of a nursing mother; that certain thoughts cause tears, pallor, blushing or fainting; and so on. The evidence we have that the relation is one of cause and effect is exactly the same here as where bodily processes cause mental states.

It is said, of course, that to suppose something nonphysical, such as thought, to be capable of causing motion of a physical object, such as the body, is absurd. But I submit that if the heterogeneity of mind and matter makes this absurd, then it makes equally absurd the causation of mental states by stimulation of the body. Yet no absurdity is commonly found in the assertion that cutting the skin causes a feeling of pain, or that alcohol, caffein, bromides, and other drugs, cause characteristic states of consciousness. As David Hume made clear long ago, no kind of causal connection is intrinsically absurd. Anything might cause anything; and only observation can tell us what in fact can cause what.

Somewhat similar remarks would apply to the allegation that the principle of the conservation of energy precludes the possibility of causation of a physical event by a mental event. For if it does, then it equally precludes causation in the converse direction, and this, of course, would leave us totally at a loss to explain the occurrence of sensations. But, as Keeton and others have pointed out, that energy is conserved is not something observation has revealed or could reveal, but only a postulate— a defining postulate for the notion of an "isolated physical system."

That is, conservation of energy is something one has to have if, but only if, one insists on conceiving the physical world as wholly self-contained, independent, isolated. And just because the metaphysics which the natural sciences tacitly assume does insist on so conceiving the physical world, this metaphysics compels them to save conservation by postulations *ad hoc* whenever dissipation of energy is what observation reveals. It postulates, for instance, that something else, which appears at such times but was not until then regarded as energy, is energy too, but it is then said, "in a different form."

Furthermore, as Broad has emphasized, all that the principle of conservation requires is that when a quantity Q of energy disappears at one place in the physical world an equal quantity of it should appear at some other place there. And the supposition that, in some cases, what causes it to disappear here and appear there is some mental event, such perhaps as a volition, does not violate at all the supposition that energy is conserved.

A word, next, on the parallelism between the degree of development of the nervous systems of various animals and the degree of their intelligence. This is alleged to prove that the latter is the product of the former. But the facts lend themselves equally well to the supposition that, on the contrary, an obscurely felt need for greater intelligence in the circumstances the animal faced was what brought about the variations which eventually resulted in a more adequate nervous organization.

In the development of the individual, at all events, it seems clear that the specific, highly complex nerve connections which become established in the brain and cerebellum of, for instance, a skilled pianist are the results of his will over many years to acquire the skill.

We must not forget in this context that there is a converse, equally consistent with the facts, for the theory, called epiphenomenalism, that mental states are related to the brain much as the halo is to the saint, that is, as effects but never themselves as causes. The converse theory, which might be called hypophenomenalism, and which is pretty well that of Schopenhauer, is that the instruments which the various mechanisms of the body constitute are the objective products of obscure cravings for the corresponding powers; and, in particular, that the organization of the nervous system is the effect and material isomorph of the variety of mental functions exercised at a given level of animal or human existence.

We have now scrutinized . . . the reasons mentioned earlier for rejecting the possibility of survival, and we have found them all logically weak. . . . It will be useful for us to pause a moment and inquire why so many of the persons who advance those reasons nevertheless think them convincing.

It is, I believe, because these persons approach the question of survival with a certain unconscious metaphysical bias. It derives from a particular initial assumption which·they tacitly make. It is that *to be real is to be material.* And to be material, of course, is to be some process or part of the perceptually public world, that is, of the world we all perceive by means of our so-called five senses.

Now the assumption that to be real is to be material is a useful and appropriate one for the purpose of investigating the material world and of operating upon it; and this purpose is a legitimate and frequent one. But those persons, and most of us, do not realize that the validity of that assumption is strictly relative to that specific purpose. Hence they, and most of us, continue making the assumption, and it continues to rule judgment, even when, as now, the purpose in view is a different one, for which the assumption is no longer useful or even congruous.

The point is all-important here and therefore worth stressing. Its essence is that the conception of the nature of reality that proposes to define the real as the material is not the expression of an observable fact to which everyone would have to bow, but is the expression only of a certain direction of interest on the part of the persons who so define reality—of interest, namely, which they have chosen to center wholly in the material, perceptually public world. This specialized interest is of course as legitimate as any other, but it automatically ignores all the facts, commonly called facts of mind, which only introspection reveals. And that specialized interest is what alone compels persons in its grip to employ the word "mind" to denote, instead of what it commonly does denote, something else altogether, namely, the public behavior of bodies that have minds.

Only so long as one's judgment is swayed unawares by that special interest do the logically weak arguments against the possibility of survival, which we have examined, seem strong.

It is possible, however, and just as legitimate, as well as more conducive to a fair view of our question, to center one's interest at the start on the facts of mind as introspectively observable, ranking them as most real in the sense that they are the facts the intrinsic nature of which we most directly experience, the facts which we most certainly know to exist; and moreover, that they are the facts without the experiencing of which we should not know any other facts whatever—such, for instance, as those of the material world. . . .

27 Beyond Scepticism

James

In developing a philosophy to live by and a faith by which to die, the American philosopher William James (1842–1910) confronted the most extreme scepticism and found his own way of meeting it. The traditional rationalist attempts to meet sceptical arguments with logical refutations. This approach has never succeeded in reducing the amount of general scepticism, James pointed out, because scepticism is not a purely logical affair but rather, in his words, "the live mental attitude of refusing to conclude."[1] The consistent sceptic is no fool or ignoramus. He is usually shrewd enough not to commit himself to a dogmatic position which asserts that "there is nothing certain" or "I know nothing." Instead, like Montaigne, he may refuse to commit himself to an affirmative position. He may merely sum up his sceptical attitude in a question such as, What do I know? or, Who knows anything? The true sceptic, James realized, simply chooses his scepticism as a habit. It thus becomes "a permanent torpor of the will, renewing itself in detail toward each successive thesis."[2] This torpor can never be dispelled by clear and distinct ideas, dissipated by rational argument, or destroyed by force. The nature of scepticism is such that rational argument cannot logically defeat it.

Is there no way then to deal with scepticism? James asserted that there is, but this way necessitates assuming a new concept of the task of philosophy, a new approach to thinking about the nature of the universe, and a new method of arriving at the truth.

First, James urged that we should not expect from philosophy final answers to life's problems, a universal truth to believe in, or an absolutely certain system by which we may explain everything. What we can expect is help in developing "the habit of always seeing an alternative, of not taking the usual for granted, of making conventionalities fluid again, of imagining foreign states of mind."[3] James held that philosophy "means the possession of mental perspective."[4] A study of philosophy can instill in us a flexible, open-minded frame of mind that will not be unduly disturbed by scepticism; in fact, it is vitally imbued with the best sceptical spirit. Rejecting both dogmatism and excessive scepticism, it is free to venture, even into transcendental concerns.

In his own philosophical and religious venturing, James developed a new way of thinking about the universe. He called it *radical empiricism.* As *empiricism,* this viewpoint considers beliefs about matters of fact to be simply "hypotheses liable to modification in the course of future experience."[5] It is *radical* because it rejects philosophical monism or the explanation of reality as a complete, self-contained system or absolute unity. Instead, radical empiricism emphasizes the multiplicity of things, the complexity, the manifoldness, even the crudity of the world of real, experienced things. Unlike other philosophic approaches, it can do justice to, not distort, dismiss, or rationalize life as it appears to the ordinary man. Rejecting monistic explanations, it is able to take into account "real possibilities, real indeterminations, real beginnings, real ends, real evil, real crises, catastrophes, and escapes, a real God, and a real moral life just as common sense conceives these things."[6] James's radical empiricism aimed at creating a "mosaic philosophy, a philosophy of plural facts,"[7] which starts with parts rather than with wholes and universals in building up a conception of reality. It is thus basically pluralistic rather than monistic in its orientation.

Finally, James proposed and developed a method of defining and testing the truth of a concept, idea, or proposition that had been formulated by one of his contemporaries, the mathematician and philosopher Charles S. Peirce. This is the method of *pragmatism* (from the Greek *pragma,* practice). "True ideas," according to James's pragmatic method, "are those that we can assimilate, validate, corroborate, and verify." "False ideas," on the other hand, "are those that we cannot."[8] Thus truth is not some static inherent property of an idea. "Truth *happens* to an idea."[9] An idea becomes true if and only if it is made true by the events or consequences by which it is verified. "The true," James wrote, summing up his view, "is only the expedient in the way of our thinking, just as the right is only the expedient in the way of our behaving."[10]

James's will to believe can best be understood against the background of his dynamic conception of philosophy, his radical empiricism, and, above all, his pragmatic approach to the definition and test of truth.

NOTES

1. William James, *The Meaning of Truth* (London: Longmans, Green & Co., 1912), p. 180.

2. Ibid.

3. Quoted in Horace M. Kallen, ed., *The Philosophy of William James* (New York: Random House, n.d.), p. 58.

4. Ibid.
5. Ibid., p. 60.
6. Ibid., p. 61.
7. William James, *Essays in Radical Empiricism* (London: Longmans, Green & Co., 1912), pp. 41–42.
8. James, *The Meaning of Truth*, v–viii.
9. Ibid.
10. Ibid., p. 166.

The Will to Believe

In the recently published Life by Leslie Stephen of his brother, Fitz-James, there is an account of a school to which the latter went when he was a boy. The teacher, a certain Mr. Guest, used to converse with his pupils in this wise: "Gurney, what is the difference between justification and sanctification?—Stephen, prove the omnipotence of God!" etc. In the midst of our Harvard free-thinking and indifference we are prone to imagine that here at your good old orthodox College conversation continues to be somewhat upon this order; and to show you that we at Harvard have not lost all interest in these vital subjects, I have brought with me tonight something like a sermon on justification by faith to read to you,—I mean an essay in justification *of* faith, a defense of our right to adopt a believing attitude in religious matters, in spite of the fact that our merely logical intellect may not have been coerced. "The Will to Believe," accordingly, is the title of my paper.

I have long defended to my own students the lawfulness of voluntary adopted faith; but as soon as they have got well imbued with the logical spirit, they have as a rule refused to admit my contention to be lawful philosophically, even though in point of fact they were personally at the time chock-full of some faith or other themselves. I am all the while, however, so profoundly convinced that my own

From William James, *The Will to Believe and Other Essays in Popular Philosophy* (London: Logmans, Green & Co., 1897), pp. 1–31 (with omissions).

position is correct, that your invitation has seemed to me a good occasion to make my statements more clear. Perhaps your minds will be more open than those with which I have hitherto had to deal. I will be as little technical as I can, though I must begin by setting up some technical distinctions that will help us in the end. . . .

Let us give the name of *hypothesis* to anything that may be proposed to our belief; and just as the electricians speak of live and dead wires, let us speak of any hypothesis as either *live* or *dead*. A live hypothesis is one which appeals as a real possibility to him to whom it is proposed. If I ask you to believe in the Mahdi, the notion makes no electric connection with your nature—it refuses to scintillate with any credibility at all. As an hypothesis it is completely dead. To an Arab, however (even if he be not one of the Mahdi's followers), the hypothesis is among the mind's possibilities: it is alive. This shows that deadness and liveness in an hypothesis are not intrinsic properties, but relations to the individual thinker. They are measured by his willingness to act. The maximum of liveness in an hypothesis means willingness to act irrevocably. Practically, that means belief; but there is some believing tendency wherever there is willingness to act at all.

Next, let us call the decision between two hypotheses an *option*. Options may be of several kinds. They may be—1. *living* or *dead;* 2. *forced* or *avoidable;* 3. *momentous* or *trivial;* and for our purposes we may call an option a *genuine* option when it is of the forced, living, and momentous kind.

1. A living option is one in which both hypotheses are live ones. If I say to you: "Be a theosophist or be a Mohammedan," it is probably a dead option, because for you neither hypothesis is likely to be alive. But if I say: "Be an agnostic or be a Christian," it is otherwise: trained as you are, each hypothesis makes some appeal, however small, to your belief.

2. Next, if I say to you: "Choose between going out with your umbrella or without it," I do not offer you a genuine option, for it is not forced. You can easily avoid it by not going out at all. Similarly, if I say, "Either love me or hate me," "Either call my theory true or call it false," your option is avoidable. You may remain indifferent to me, neither loving nor hating, and you many decline to offer any judgment as to my theory. But if I say, "Either accept this truth or go without it," I put on you a forced option, for there is no standing place outside of the alternative. Every dilemma based on a complete logical disjunction, with no possibility of not choosing, is an option of this forced kind.

3. Finally, if I were Dr. Nansen and proposed to you to join my North Pole expedition, your option would be momentous; for this would probably be your only similar opportunity, and your choice now would either exclude you from the North Pole sort of immortality altogether or put at least the chance of it into your hands. He who refuses to embrace a unique opportunity loses the prize as surely as if he tried and failed. *Per contra*, the option is trivial when the opportunity is not unique, when the stake is insignificant, or when the decision is reversible if it later prove unwise. Such trivial options abound in the scientific life. A chemist finds an hypothesis live enough to spend a year in its verification: he believes in it to that extent. But if his experiments prove

inconclusive either way, he is quit for his loss of time, no vital harm being done.

It will facilitate our discussion if we keep all these distinctions in mind. . . .

In Pascal's *Thoughts* there is a celebrated passage known in literature as Pascal's wager. In it he tries to force us into Christianity by reasoning as if our concern with truth resembled our concern with the stakes in a game of chance. Translated freely his words are these: You must either believe or not believe that God is—which will you do? Your human reason cannot say. A game is going on between you and the nature of things which at the day of judgment will bring out either heads or tails. Weigh what your gains and your losses would be if you should stake all you have on heads, or God's existence: if you win in such case, you gain eternal beatitude; if you lose, you lose nothing at all. If there were an infinity of chances, and only one for God in this wager, still you ought to stake your all on God; for though you surely risk a finite loss by this procedure, any finite loss is reasonable, even a certain one is reasonable, if there is but the possibility of infinite gain. Go, then, and take holy water, and have masses said; belief will come and stupefy your scruples,—*Cela vous fera croire et vous abêtira.* Why should you not? At bottom, what have you to lose? . . .

The thesis I defend is, briefly stated, this: *Our passional nature not only lawfully may, but must, decide an option between propositions, whenever it is a genuine option that cannot by its nature be decided on intellectual grounds; for to say, under such circumstances, "Do not decide, but leave the question open," is itself a passional decision,—just like deciding yes or no,—and is attended with the same risk of losing the truth.* The thesis thus abstractly expressed will, I trust, soon become quite clear. . . .

And now, after all this introduction, let us go straight at our question. I have said, and now repeat it, that not only as a matter of fact do we find our passional nature influencing us in our opinions, but that there are some options between opinions in which this influence must be regarded both as an inevitable and as a lawful determinant of our choice.

I fear here that some of you my hearers will begin to scent danger, and lend an inhospitable ear. Two first steps of passion you have indeed had to admit as necessary,—we must think so as to avoid dupery, and we must think so as to gain truth; but the surest path to those ideal consummations, you will probably consider, is from now onwards to take no further passional step.

Well, of course, I agree as far as the facts will allow. Wherever the option between losing truth and gaining it is not momentous, we can throw the chance of *gaining truth* away, and at any rate save ourselves from any chance of *believing falsehood,* by not making up our minds at all till objective evidence has come. In scientific questions, this is almost always the case; and even in human affairs in general, the need of acting is seldom so urgent that a false belief to act on is better than no belief at all. Law courts, indeed, have to decide on the best evidence attainable for the moment, because a judge's duty is to make law as well as to ascertain it, and (as a learned judge once said to me) few cases are worth spending much time over: the great thing is to have them decided on *any* acceptable principle, and got out of the way. But in our dealings with objective nature we obviously are recorders, not makers, of the truth; and decisions for the mere sake of deciding promptly and getting on to the next business would be wholly out of place. Throughout the breadth of physical nature facts are what they are quite independently of us, and seldom is there any such hurry about them that the risks of being duped by believing a premature theory need be faced. The questions here are always trivial options, the hypotheses are hardly living (or any rate not living for us spectators), the choice between believing truth or falsehood is seldom forced. The attitude of sceptical balance is therefore the absolutely wise one if we

would escape mistakes. What difference, indeed, does it make to most of us whether we have or have not a theory of the Röntgen rays, whether we believe or not in mind-stuff, or have a conviction about the causality of conscious states? It makes no difference. Such options are not forced on us. On every account it is better not to make them, but still keep weighing reasons *pro et contra* with an indifferent hand.

I speak, of course, here of the purely judging mind. For purposes of discovery such indifference is to be less highly recommended, and science would be far less advanced than she is if the passionate desires of individuals to get their own faiths confirmed had been kept out of the game. See for example the sagacity which Spencer and Weismann now display. On the other hand, if you want an absolute duffer in an investigation, you must, after all, take the man who has no interest whatever in its results: he is the warranted incapable, the positive fool. The most useful investigator, because the most sensitive observer, is always he whose eager interest in one side of the question is balanced by an equally keen nervousness lest he become deceived. Science has organized this nervousness into a regular *technique,* her so-called method of verification; and she has fallen so deeply in love with the method that one may even say she has ceased to care for truth by itself at all. It is only truth as technically verified that interests her. The truth of truths might come in merely affirmative form, and she would decline to touch it. Such truth as that, she might repeat with Clifford, would be stolen in defiance of her duty to mankind. Human passions, however, are stronger than technical rules. *Le coeur a ses raisons,* as Pascal says, *que la raison ne connait pas;* and however indifferent to all but the bare rules of the game the umpire, the abstract intellect, may be, the concrete players who furnish him the materials to judge of are usually, each one of them, in love with some pet 'live hypothesis' of his own. Let us agree, however, that wherever there is no forced option, the dispassionately judicial intellect with no pet hypothesis, saving us, as it does, from dupery at any rate, ought to be our ideal.

The question next arises: Are there not somewhere forced options in our speculative questions, and can we (as men who may be interested at least as much in positively gaining truth as in merely escaping dupery) always wait with impunity till the coercive evidence shall have arrived? It seems *a priori* improbable that the truth should be so nicely adjusted to our needs and powers as that. In the great boardinghouse of nature, the cakes and the butter and the syrup seldom come out so even and leave the plates so clean. Indeed, we should view them with scientific suspicion if they did. . . .

Moral questions immediately present themselves as questions whose solution cannot wait for sensible proof. A moral question is a question not of what sensibly exists, but of what is good, or would be good if it did exist. Science can tell us what exists; but to compare the *worths,* both of what exists and of what does not exist, we must consult not science, but what Pascal calls our heart. Science herself consults her heart when she lays it down that the infinite ascertainment of fact and correction of false beliefs are the supreme goods for man. Challenge the statement, and science can only repeat it oracularly, or else prove it by showing that such ascertainment and correction bring man all sorts of other goods which man's heart in turn declares. The question of having moral beliefs at all or not having them is decided by our will. Are our moral preferences true or false, or are they only odd biological phenomena, making things good or bad for *us*, but in themselves indifferent? How can your pure intellect decide? If your heart does not *want* a world of moral reality, your head will assuredly never make you believe in one. Mephistophelian scepticism, indeed, will satisfy the head's play-instincts much better than any rigorous idealism can. Some men (even at the student age) are so naturally cool-hearted that the moralistic hypothesis never has for them any pungent life,

and in their supercilious presence the hot young moralist always feels strangely ill at ease. The appearance of knowingness is on their side, of naïveté and gullibility on his. Yet, in the inarticulate heart of him, he clings to it that he is not a dupe, and that there is a realm in which (as Emerson says) all their wit and intellectual superiority is no better than the cunning of a fox. Moral scepticism can no more be refuted or proved by logic than intellectual scepticism can. When we stick to it that there *is* truth (be it of either kind), we do so with our whole nature, and resolve to stand or fall by the results. The sceptic with his whole nature adopts the doubting attitude; but which of us is the wiser, Omniscience only knows.

Turn now from these wide questions of good to a certain class of questions of fact, questions concerning personal relations, states of mind between one man and another. *Do you like me or not?*—for example. Whether you do or not depends, in countless instances, on whether I meet you half-way, am willing to assume that you must like me, and show you trust and expectation. The previous faith on my part in your liking's existence is in such cases what makes your liking come. But if I stand aloof, and refuse to budge an inch until I have objective evidence, until you shall have done something apt, as the absolutists say, *ad extorquendum assensum meum,* ten to one your liking never comes. How many women's hearts are vanquished by the mere sanguine insistence of some man that they *must* love him! He will not consent to the hypothesis that they cannot. The desire for a certain kind of truth here brings about that special truth's existence; and so it is in innumerable cases of other sorts. Who gains promotions, boons, appointments, but the man in whose life they are seen to play the part of live hypotheses, who discounts them, sacrifices other things for their sake before they have come, and takes risks for them in advance? His faith acts on the powers above him as a claim, and creates its own verification.

A social organism of any sort whatever, large

or small, is what it is because each member proceeds to his own duty with a trust that the
other members will simultaneously do theirs.
Wherever a desired result is achieved by the
co-operation of many independent persons, its
existence as a fact is a pure consequence of the
precursive faith in one another of those immediately concerned. A Government, an army, a
commercial system, a ship, a college, an athletic
team, all exist on this condition, without which
not only is nothing achieved, but nothing is
even attempted. A whole train of passengers
(individually brave enough) will be looted by
a few highwaymen, simply because the latter
can count on one another, while each passenger
fears that if he makes a movement of resistance,
he will be shot before any one else backs him
up. If we believed that the whole car-full would
rise at once with us, we should each severally
rise, and train-robbing would never even be
attempted. There are, then, cases where a fact
cannot come at all unless a preliminary faith
exists in its coming. *And where faith in a fact
can help create the fact,* that would be an insane logic which should say that faith running
ahead of scientific evidence is the 'lowest kind
of immorality' into which a thinking being can
fall. Yet such is the logic by which our scientific absolutists pretend to regulate our lives! . . .

In truths dependent on our personal action,
then, faith based on desire is certainly a lawful
and possibly an indispensable thing.

But now, it will be said, these are all childish
human cases, and have nothing to do with
great cosmical matters, like the question of religious faith. Let us then pass on to that. Religions differ so much in their accidents that in
discussing the religious question we must make
it very generic and broad. What then do we
now mean by the religious hypothesis? Science
says things are; morality says some things are
better than other things; and religion says essentially two things.

First, she says that the best things are the
more eternal things, the overlapping things, the
things in the universe that throw the last stone,
so to speak, and say the final word. "Perfection
is eternal,"—this phrase of Charles Secrétan
seems a good way of putting this first affirmation of religion, an affirmation which obviously
cannot yet be verified scientifically at all.

The second affirmation of religion is that we
are better off even now if we believe her first
affirmation to be true.

Now, let us consider what the logical elements of this situation are *in case the religious
hypothesis in both its branches be really true.*
(Of course, we must admit that possibility at
the outset. If we are to discuss the question
at all, it must involve a living option. If for any
of you religion be a hypothesis that cannot, by
any living possibility be true, then you need go
no farther. I speak to the 'saving remnant'
alone.) So proceeding, we see, first, that religion offers itself as a *momentous* option. We
are supposed to gain, even now, by our belief,
and to lose by our non-belief, a certain vital
good. Secondly, religion is a *forced* option, so
far as that good goes. We cannot escape the issue by remaining sceptical and waiting for
more light, because, although we do avoid error
in that way *if religion be untrue,* we lose the
good, *if it be true,* just as certainly as if we positively chose to disbelieve. It is as if a man
should hesitate indefinitely to ask a certain
woman to marry him because he was not perfectly sure that she would prove an angel after
he brought her home. Would he not cut himself
off from that particular angel-possibility as de-
cisively as if he went and married some one
else? Scepticism, then, is not avoidance of option; it is option of a certain particular kind of
risk. *Better risk loss of truth than chance of
error,*—that is your faith-vetoer's exact position.
He is actively playing his stake as much as the
believer is; he is backing the field against the
religious hypothesis, just as the believer is backing the religious hypothesis against the field. To
preach scepticism to us as a duty until 'sufficient
evidence' for religion be found, is tantamount
therefore to telling us, when in presence of the

religious hypothesis, that to yield to our fear of its being error is wiser and better than to yield to our hope that it may be true. It is not intellect against all passions, then; it is only intellect with one passion laying down its law. And by what, forsooth, is the supreme wisdom of this passion warranted? Dupery for dupery, what proof is there that dupery through hope is so much worse than dupery through fear? I, for one, can see no proof; and I simply refuse obedience to the scientist's command to imitate his kind of option, in a case where my own stake is important enough to give me the right to choose my own form of risk. If religion be true and the evidence for it be still insufficient, I do not wish, by putting your extinguisher upon my nature (which feels to me as if it had after all some business in this matter), to forfeit my sole chance in life of getting upon the winning side, —that chance depending, of course, on my willingness to run the risk of acting as if my passional need of taking the world religiously might be prophetic and right.

All this is on the supposition that it really may be prophetic and right, and that, even to us who are discussing the matter, religion is a live hypothesis which may be true. Now, to most of us religion comes in a still further way that makes a veto on our active faith even more illogical. The more perfect and more eternal aspect of the universe is represented in our religions as having personal form. The universe is no longer a mere *It* to us, but a *Thou*, if we are religious; and any relation that may be possible from person to person might be possible here. For instance, although in one sense we are passive portions of the universe, in another we show a curious autonomy, as if we were small active centers on our own account. We feel, too, as if the appeal of religion to us were made to our own active good-will, as if evidence might be forever withheld from us unless we met the hypothesis half-way. To take a trivial illustration: just as a man who in a company of gentlemen made no advances, asked a warrant for every concession, and believed no one's

word without proof, would cut himself off by such churlishness from all the social rewards that a more trusting spirit would earn,—so here, one who should shut himself up in snarling logicality and try to make the gods extort his recognition willy-nilly, or not get it at all, might cut himself off forever from his only opportunity of making the gods' acquaintance. This feeling, forced on us we know not whence, that by obstinately believing that there are gods (although not to do so would be easy both for our logic and our life) we are doing the universe the deepest service we can, seems part of the living essence of the religious hypothesis. If the hypothesis *were* true in all its parts, including this one, then pure intellectualism, with its veto on our making willing advance, would be an absurdity; and some participation of our sympathetic nature would be logically required. I, therefore, for one, cannot see my way to accepting the agnostic rules for truth-seeking, or willfully agree to keep my willing nature out of the game. I cannot do so for this plain reason, that *a rule of thinking which would absolutely prevent me from acknowledging certain kinds of truth if those kinds of truth were really there, would be an irrational rule.* That for me is the long and short of the formal logic of the situation, no matter what the kinds of truth might materially be.

I confess I do not see how this logic can be escaped. But sad experience makes me fear that some of you may still shrink from radically saying with me, *in abstracto,* that we have the right to believe at our own risk any hypothesis that is live enough to tempt our will. I suspect, however, that if this is so, it is because you have got away from the abstract logical point of view altogether, and are thinking (perhaps without realizing it) of some particular religious hypothesis which for you is dead. The freedom to 'believe what we will' you apply to the case of some patent superstition; and the faith you think of is the faith defined by the schoolboy when he said, "Faith is when you believe something that you know ain't true." I can only repeat that this is misapprehension. *In concreto,* the freedom to believe can only cover living options which the intellect of the individual cannot by itself resolve; and living options never seem absurdities to him who has them to consider. When I look at the religious question as it really puts itself to concrete men, and when I think of all the possibilities which both practically and theoretically it involves, then this command that we shall put a stopper on our heart, instincts, and courage, and *wait*—acting of course meanwhile more or less as if religion were *not* true—till* doomsday, or till such time as our intellect and senses working together may have raked in evidence enough,—this command, I say, seems to me the queerest idol ever manufactured in the philosophic cave. Were we scholastic absolutists, there might be more excuse. If we had an infallible intellect with its objective certitudes, we might feel ourselves disloyal to such a perfect organ of knowledge in not trusting to it exclusively, in not waiting for its releasing word. But if we are empiricists, if we believe that no bell in us tolls to let us know for certain when truth is in our grasp, then it seems a piece of idle fantasticality to preach so solemnly our duty of waiting for the bell. Indeed we *may* wait if we will,—I hope you do not think that I am denying that,—but if we do so, we do so at our peril as much as if

* Since belief is measured by action, he who forbids us to believe religion to be true, necessarily also forbids us to act as we should if we did believe it to be true. The whole defence of religious faith hinges upon action. If the action required or inspired by the religious hypothesis is in no way different from that dictated by the naturalistic hypothesis, then religious faith is a pure superfluity, better pruned away, and controversy about its legitimacy is a piece of idle trifling, unworthy of serious minds. I myself believe, of course, that the religious hypothesis gives to the world an expression which specifically determines our reactions, and makes them in a large part unlike what they might be on a purely naturalistic scheme of belief.

we believed. In either case we *act,* taking our life in our hands. No one of us ought to issue vetoes to the other, nor should we bandy words of abuse. We ought, on the contrary, delicately and profoundly to respect one another's mental freedom: then only shall we bring about the intellectual republic; then only shall we have that spirit of inner tolerance without which all our outer tolerance is soulless, and which is empiricism's glory; then only shall we live and let live, in speculative as well as in practical things.

I began by a reference to Fitz-James Stephen; let me end by a quotation from him. "What do you think of yourself? What do you think of the world? . . . These are questions with which all must deal as it seems good to them. They are riddles of the Sphinx, and in some way or other we must deal with them. . . . In all important transactions of life we have to take a leap in the dark. . . . If we decide to leave the riddles unanswered, that is a choice; if we waver in our answer, that, too, is a choice: but whatever choice we make, we make it at our peril. If a man chooses to turn his back altogether on God and the future, no one can prevent him; no one can show beyond reasonable doubt that he is mistaken. If a man thinks otherwise and acts as he thinks, I do not see that any one can prove that *he* is mistaken. Each must act as he thinks best; and if he is wrong, so much the worse for him. We stand on a mountain pass in the midst of whirling snow and blinding mist, through which we get glimpses now and then of paths which may be deceptive. If we stand still we shall be frozen to death. If we take the wrong road we shall be dashed to pieces. We do not certainly know whether there is any right one. What must we do? 'Be strong and of a good courage.' Act for the best, hope for the best, and take what comes. . . . If death ends all, we cannot meet death better."*

* Fitz-James Stephen, *Liberty, Equality, Fraternity,* 2d ed. (London, 1874), p. 353.

RELATED READING

Alvarez, A. *The Savage God*. New York: Bantam Books, 1971.

Berger, Peter L. *The Sacred Canopy: Elements of a Sociological Theory of Religion*. Garden City, N.Y.: Doubleday & Co., 1969.

Bertocci, Peter. *Introduction to Philosophy of Religion*. Englewood Cliffs, N.J.: Prentice-Hall, 1960.

Bierce, Ambrose, *The Devil's Dictionary*. New York: Dover Publications, 1957.

Brightman, Edgar S. *A Philosophy of Religion*. Englewood Cliffs, N.J.: Prentice-Hall, 1940.

Buber, Martin. *I and Thou*, trans. R. G. Smith. Edinburgh: Clark, 1937.

Cahn, Steven M., ed. *Philosophy of Religion*. New York: Harper & Row, 1970.

Choron, Jacques. *Modern Man and Death*. New York: Macmillan, 1964.

———. *Death and Western Thought*. New York: Collier, 1963.

———. *Suicide*. New York: Charles Scribner's Sons, 1972.

Clemens, Samuel L. (Mark Twain). *Letters from the Earth*, edited by Bernard De Voto. New York: Fawcett, 1962.

Cox, Harvey. *Feast of Fools*. New York: Harper & Row, 1969.

———. *The Secular City*. New York: Macmillan, 1965.

De Ropp, Robert. *The Master Game: Pathways to Higher Consciousness Beyond the Drug Experience*. New York: Dell Publishing Co., 1968.

Dewey, John. *A Common Faith*. New Haven, Conn.: Yale University Press, 1934.

Ducasse, Curt J. *A Critical Examination of the Belief in a Life after Death*. Springfield, Ill.: Charles C Thomas, 1961.

Feifel, Herman, ed. *The Meaning of Death*. New York: McGraw-Hill, 1959.

Harrington, Alan. *The Immortalist*. New York: Random House, 1969.

Hick, John. *Philosophy of Religion*. Englewood Cliffs, N.J.: Prentice-Hall, 1963.

Hook, Sidney, ed. *Religious Experience and Truth*. New York: New York University Press, 1961.

Hume, David. *Dialogues Concerning Natural Religion*. New York: Hafner Press, 1948.

Huxley, Aldous. *The Perennial Philosophy*. New York: Harper & Row, 1944.

———. *The Doors of Perception and Heaven and Hell*. New York: Harper & Row, 1963.

Huxley, Julian. *Religion without Revelation*. New York: Harper & Row, 1957.

Huxley, Laura. *This Timeless Moment*. New York: Farrar, Straus & Giroux, 1968.

James, William. *The Varieties of Religious Experience*. New York: Collier, 1961.

Kaufman, Walter A. *Critique of Religion and Philosophy*. New York: Harper & Row, 1958.

———. *The Faith of a Heretic*. New York: Doubleday & Co., 1961.

Keen, Sam. *To a Dancing God.* New York: Harper & Row, 1970.

Kierkegaard, Sören. *A Kierkegaard Anthology* edited by Robert Bretall. New York: Modern Library, 1946.

Koestenbaum, Peter. *Is There an Answer to Death?* Englewood Cliffs, N.J.: Prentice-Hall, 1976.

Kubler-Ross, Elisabeth. *On Death and Dying.* New York: Macmillan, 1969.

Lamont, Corliss. *The Illusion of Immortality.* New York: G. P. Putnam's Sons, 1935.

Maslow, Abraham. *Religions, Values and Peak Experiences.* Columbus, Ohio: Ohio University Press, 1964.

Masters, R. E. L., and Jean Huston. *The Varieties of Psychedelic Experience.* New York: Holt, Rinehart & Winston, 1966.

Mehta, Ved. *The New Theologian.* New York: Harper & Row, 1965.

Miller, David. *Gods and Games: Toward a Theology of Play.* New York: Harper & Row, 1970.

Moody, Raymond A., Jr. *Life After Life.* New York: Bantam Books, 1975.

Niebuhr, Reinhold. *Moral Man and Immoral Society.* New York: Charles Scribner's Sons, 1932.

O'Brien, John A. *Truths Men Live By.* New York: Macmillan, 1946.

Otto, Rudolph. *The Idea of the Holy,* 2nd ed. New York: Oxford University Press, 1950.

Plantinga, Alvin, ed. *The Ontological Argument.* New York: Doubleday & Co., 1965.

Russell, Bertrand. *Why I Am Not a Christian.* New York: Simon & Schuster, 1959.

———. *Mysticism and Logic.* New York: Doubleday & Co., 1957.

Sheen, Fulton J. *Philosophy of Religion.* New York: Appleton-Century-Crofts, 1948.

Smith, Huston. *The Religions of Man.* New York: Harper & Row, 1958.

Stace, Walter. *The Teachings of the Mystics.* New York: New American Library, 1960.

Suzuki, D. T. *Introduction to Zen Buddhism.* London: Rider, 1960.

Tillich, Paul. *The Courage to Be.* New Haven, Conn.: Yale University Press, 1952.

———. *The Dynamics of Faith.* New York: Harper & Row, 1957.

Ward, Hiley H. *Religion 2101 A.D.* Garden City, N.Y.: Doubleday & Co., 1975.

Weil, Andrew. *The Natural Mind.* Boston: Houghton Mifflin, 1972.

White, John, ed. *The Highest State of Consciousness.* New York: Doubleday & Co., 1972.

Wieman, Henry Nelson. *Man's Ultimate Commitment.* Carbondale, Ill.: Southern Illinois University Press, 1958.

Wilson, Nancy, ed. *The World of Zen: An East-West Anthology.* New York: Vintage, 1960.

Zaehner, R. C. *Mysticism, Sacred and Profane.* New York: Oxford University Press, 1961.

Part 6

CONFRONTATION WITH THE FUTURE

Commitment to Present Amelioration

Today as never before we need a multiplicity of visions, dreams, and prophecies — images of potential tomorrows.

Alvin Toffler

The future cannot be predicted, but futures can be invented.

Dennis Gabor

If you have built castles in the air, your work need not be lost; that is where they should be. Now put foundations under them.

Henry D. Thoreau

To predict the future we need logic; but we also need faith and imagination which can sometimes defy logic itself.

Arthur C. Clarke

I hold that man is in the right who is most closely in league with the future.

Henrik Ibsen

Every intelligent and active-minded person is to some degree a utopian.

Arthur E. Morgan

Change in the climate of the imagination is the precursor of the changes that affect more than the details of life.

John Dewey

All living things act to anticipate the future; this is what distinguishes them from lifeless things.

Jacob Bronowski

It has usually been lack of imagination, rather than excess of it, that caused unfortunate decisions and missed opportunities.

Herman Kahn and Anthony Wiener

Introduction: Alternative Futures

"Philosophy . . . is the most effective of all the intellectual pursuits. It builds cathedrals before the workmen have moved a stone, and it destroys them before the elements have worn down their arches. It is the architect of the buildings of the spirit, and it is also their solvent."[1] The following selections, which correspond to the preceding five parts of this book, are "buildings of the spirit," rational and imaginative assessments of the future.

Part One considered the characteristics of the human condition which lead thinkers into examining alternative beliefs, assessing arguments, and confronting doubts in various ways. For Socrates, the examined life was central. Many today believe it is also crucial to examine all aspects of the projected future conditions if we are to avoid worldwide catastrophes. Speculating on the human condition in the future, the political scientist Robert Heilbroner holds out little hope for finding overall solutions to such problems as the world's population growth, war, pollution of our environment, and our limited energy resources. The lag between our advanced technology and our lifestyles and political institutions presents a dim prospect for the human condition. Radical changes in human attitudes, and the reorganization of society and industry, will be necessary if we are to save ourselves and our world from a bleak future of deprivation and decline.

George Wald's indictment of the present is even more sweeping. Because the multinational corporations have taken the reins, human suffering and starvation as well as nuclear threat will increase. The people of the world should unite to take power away from the selfish vested interests of the corporations which are, because of their indifference to the human plight, destroying us and the earth in the pursuit of profit and power.

A more optimistic prospect is presented by Herbert Kahn. He thinks that an improved approach to planning for the future using all of the old and new techniques available is the only solution to human problems. Our images of the future do affect the future, and an imaginative anticipation of future trends can enable us to respond adequately to new challenges in the decades ahead. The proponents of limited economic growth may be hasty in their gloomy conclusions regarding the future.

In Part Two, various perspectives on human nature related to animal drives, social needs, spiritual aspirations, and material conditions were given. Human nature was examined and the prospect of radically altering man's behavior was raised. In the section on the Transformation of Human Nature, Norman Cousins senses the unparalleled significance of the now possible violent extinction of all of life on this planet. He raises questions about war and human aggression and points to the growing bifurcation of science and morality; gadgetry and wisdom; and intellect and conscience. Human nature can and must change in order to adjust itself to this new condition. An increase in our critical intelligence and a move toward world government are only some of the adjustments needed for our survival.

Sam Keen turns our attention to the inner dimensions of human nature and the need for an authentic life in an alienating and empty human environment. He calls for a new model of human nature in which our sense of wonder is balanced with our willingness for action; our imaginative abilities with our practical nature; and our capacity for dreams with the recognized need for hard decisions. The last selection considers genetic engineering as a means for reshaping human nature. The possible use of such biomedical technology and other techniques of behavioral and chemical control is raising difficult questions regarding free choice and human conditioning, which are not only ethical problems but also legal and political issues. Human nature may be on the verge of becoming something decreed and designed rather than something given.

The question raised in Part Three regarding our commitment to the Good Life is raised again within the context of a fast-changing society filled with what many feel is an impersonal emptiness and with difficulties in finding meaning and relatedness. Rollo May explores the psychological dimensions of living in the modern world and the decreasing capacity many have for loving. Love should be our common will, our common good, for it "elicits in us the capacity to reach out, to let ourselves be grasped, to perform and mold the future." Using the sexual relationship as his major paradigm, May believes that love begets tenderness, sense of identity, personal enrichment, receptivity, and the feeling of communion and unity that so many seek today. Herbert Otto would agree with May that "in every act of love and will—and in the long run they are both present in each genuine act—we mold ourselves and our world simultaneously. This is what it means to embrace the future." Otto calls for a regeneration of love as a force in today's society, and he has many practical suggestions as to how to accomplish this. At the top of his list is a reshaping of our social institutions.

In the section entitled "Democracy: The Open and Anticipatory Society," Charles Frankel and Alvin Toffler speak of two aspects of democracy. Although sceptical regarding the justification of political ideologies, Frankel believes that the importance of the democratic political methods is considerable. They foster personal liberties and the virtues of independent judgment and dissent; they socialize conflict; and they establish the situation in which the condition for holding power is a condition which educates the holders of power. Democracy is a substantial contributor to education. Moreover, within a democracy, politics is limited in its scope with respect to the rest of the civilization and populace, a populace which is free, diverse, aware of human fallibility, and open to freedom of inquiry.

Toffler would agree with the spirit of what Frankel has to say; however, in a technological society such as ours, democracy is severely curtailed in fact because of the lack of citizen participation and a proper awareness of the future. Our society and political system float from crisis to crisis. Anticipatory democracy conjoins the two necessary ingredients for us to deal with the change and complexity of today's society: greater citizen participation and increased future consciousness. Toffler suggests concrete methods to accomplish this, including better use of news media and more referenda, and public meetings. The super-industrial society, which is now emerging from the old industrial society, will require flexible, decentralized planning as well as the expertise necessary for rational decisions. All must help to "destandardize, decentralize, deconcentrate, descale, and democratize planning."[2]

Looking to the future of religion, it seems that the search for transcendence will continue but with some differences. All of the selections on religion suggest that there will be radical changes in religion and religious institutions. Leon Putnam believes that religion based upon ignorance, fear, and authoritarianism will decline; religious institutions and sects will become more diverse, and the focus of religious concern will become more interdisciplinary. Whatever the changes, the basic religious question of the nature of life's meaning and value will remain a part of the human condition. Change is the focus of the discussion "Religion in the Year 2000" in which the panelists admit that science as a mode of thinking is serving as an "acid solvent" for many of the traditional religious beliefs. In the future, religion will be increasingly disassociated from the church and will serve, according to Harvey Cox, as a source of hope, a critic of society, and a place for festivity, celebration, and vision.

Many people today have a sense of living in a world in which the old distinctions are no longer clear: mind and body; man and society; man and nature; earth and universe. Along with this is the strong presentiment that everything can be changed. The physical environment, the biological organism, consciousness, society, culture, religion, art, and philosophy—in short, everything that has been thought fixed enough to yield a stable definition of the human condition is subject to human intervention and manipulation. The issue now is not primarily whether we initiate techniques for change upon the inner man or his external environment. In many ways this distinction between inner and outer no longer makes sense. The question today is which direction change in the future will take. This is not a question of facts but of values. It is not "What kind of future must we have?" but "What kind of future do we want? What kind of future ought we to try to create?" As Rainer Maria Rilke wrote in one of his *Letters to a Young Poet,* "The future enters into us in order to transform itself in us long before it happens."[3]

Many people confuse futurology with prophecy, which was aptly defined in Ambrose Bierce's *Devil's Dictionary* as "the art and practice of selling one's credibility for future delivery." But futurology, as it is now being developed and practiced, is becoming more like scientific investigation than prophecy. Its most reputable practitioners attempt to base their hypotheses about alternative futures on extensive scientific data. They are systematic, critical, and interdisciplinary in their approach. And they usually stress the tentativeness and possible inadequacy of their conclusions. They try to emulate scientific probers rather than religious prophets and pundits. But many, such as Herman Kahn and Alvin Toffler, are willing to make informed guesses about the future, and are not afraid to use imagination as well as reason in passing back and forth between present and future.

In *Future Shock* Alvin Toffler stresses the importance of envisaging and examining alternative futures by utopian speculation, futuristic games-playing, and other means. An examination of alternatives is valuable in that it serves as preparation for what is expected to happen. Even if our expectation fails, we will be better able to cope than if we were caught unaware. Examination of alternatives can also call attention to paths of action that might be overlooked in hasty commitments to action. Finally, such examination supports attitudes of openmindedness and comprehensiveness without which one cannot be either rational or reasonable. The challenge of future shock, as Toffler describes it, can only be met if we confront it with "a dramatically new, a more deeply rational response toward change."[4] To do this is to confront its challenge philosophically.

If history, as H. G. Wells once said, is becoming more and more a race between education and catastrophe, it is urgent that we get on with our education, not just by accumulating new knowledge and techniques, but by examining our present commitments and relating them to our ultimate concerns. As an indispensable part of education, philosophy can help us to look to the future with clearer concepts, wider interests, and more realistic goals. Philosophy may begin in wonder and it may end in hope.

NOTES

1.   Alfred North Whitehead, *Science and the Modern World* (New York: Macmillan, 1925), pp. viii–ix.

2.   "Toffler Speaks on Futurism in Politics," *The Futurist,* IX (October, 1975), p. 229.

3.   Rainer Maria Rilke, *Letters to a Young Poet,* trans. M. D. Herter Norton (New York: W. W. Norton & Co., 1934), p. 65.

4.   Alvin Toffler, *Future Shock* (New York: Random House, 1971), p. 429.

28 Appraisals of the Future Human Condition: A Dismal Future Prospect?

Heilbroner & Wald

Is there hope for man? This is the question Robert Heilbroner attempts to answer in *An Inquiry into the Human Prospect*. An economist and social philosopher, Heilbroner begins his inquiry by attempting to trace the sources of the anxieties characteristic of many Americans (and others) living in this last quarter of the twentieth century. Certain shocking events such as the Vietnam War, the increase in street violence, airplane hijackings, and assassinations have undermined American confidence. The traditional belief in progress has been challenged by continuing poverty, prejudice, and inflation. At the same time, there is increasing awareness that despite stress on a higher and higher standard of living, the physical environment is deteriorating rapidly and our quality of life seems to be steadily declining. In addition, we are suffering from a "civilizational malaise," Heilbroner believes, which reflects the fact that our cherished "American Way of Life" is failing to satisfy what Erich Fromm calls our "uniquely human needs."

With further analysis of our external and internal predicaments, Heilbroner formulates and suggests solutions to the three major challenges of this "age of anxiety": the problems of population, war, and environmental deterioration. These problems have become acute because of an accelerating advance of science and technology unregulated and unguided by equal advancements in mechanisms of social control. Our civilization is lopsided: highly developed technologically, and inadequately developed humanistically. Neither capitalism nor socialism has succeeded in developing the humanistic dimensions of civilized life. Since both capitalism and social-

445

ism rely upon the increase of industrial production to achieve their social goals, Heilbroner thinks that both ultimately cannot meet the external socio-economic challenges of our times. Internationally, what is required is continued industrialization, but this effort is confronting the very real limited capacity of our resources.

What is needed in a post-industrial society is a reorganization of the modes of production, leading to the restriction, control, and reduction of production over a period of time. We must overcome the urge to consume and habits of wastefulness. We must learn to simplify and conserve if we are to survive. Heilbroner is not optimistic regarding changes in human nature. Man, in his view, manifests two strong inclinations—to obey and to identify—thus providing a basis in human nature for political authority and political identification (e.g., nationalism). However, we must make do with less rather than to constantly expect more. As he makes clear in the following selection, Heilbroner admires the stoical fortitude of Atlas rather than the restless and defiant spirit of Prometheus. "To accept the limitations of our abilities both as individuals and as a collectivity, seems to be the most difficult idea that Promethean man must learn."[1]

Some critics of Heilbroner's *Inquiry* considered him to be a Neo-Malthusian prophet of doom, but Heilbroner considers his conclusions to reflect neither a gloomy nor a pessimistic attitude toward man and his future. They reflect a realistic appraisal of rational self-interest and moral responsibility. The question, "Is there hope for man?" means more than, "Can man survive?" It also means, for Heilbroner, "Can man develop the awareness of his plight and use the means at his disposal to cope with it before it is too late?"

In a later essay, "What has posterity ever done for me?" Heilbroner sums up his position:

> Of course, there are moral dilemmas to be faced even if one takes one's stand on the "survivalist" principle. Mankind cannot expect to continue on earth indefinitely if we do not curb population growth, thereby consigning billions or tens of billions to the oblivion of nonbirth. Yet, in this case, we sacrifice some portion of life-to-come in order that life itself may be preserved. This essential commitment to life's continuance gives us the moral authority to take measures, perhaps very harsh measures, whose justification cannot be found in the precepts of rationality, but must be sought in the unbearable anguish we feel if we imagine ourselves as the executioners of mankind.[2]

Where Heilbroner's focus is on America and his call is for the abandonment of the dangerous mentality of industrial civilization, George Wald's messages is to the people of the world. He calls for a total revolution in which power is wrested from the multinational corporations which he believes are bringing us all to our doom. Wald, a Nobel Prize Laureate for physiology in 1967, calls our attention to the balance of terror which *is* the arms race and how the present situation is dominated by vested interests such as our defense establishment and big indusrty. President Eisenhower had already warned us against the acquisition of unwarranted influence by the military-industrial complex, but Wald believes that this call for vigilance has not been heeded. The big multinational corporations are already running things and have transcended party politics and even political ideologies. The time for our awareness of what is taking place is past. Our first priority is the survival of people everywhere.

The most immediate threat and one which has become a part of our consciousness is the military nuclear arsenal which is closely tied with other destructive devices. Ironically, the threat to us as citizens of the world has not created the basis for world unity; the politics of the real world carries on business as usual despite the fact that, through sales, additions to the nuclear bomb club increase the chances of disaster by accident or by miscalculation.

Wald's analysis of the world's food crisis is similar to his analysis of the nuclear proliferation crisis. The waste and misallocation of food resources exist because they are in the hands of agribusiness. Unemployment, ecological problems, and starvation are the results of the way in which we have allowed our political and social structure to be organized by vested interests. Professor Wald has raised the question, "Who's to be in charge of human destiny?" "All power to the people!" would be his reply.

NOTES

1. Robert L. Heilbroner, *An Inquiry into the Human Prospect* (New York: W. W. Norton & Co., 1974), p. 168.

2. Ibid., p. 174.

Final Reflections on the Human Prospect

Robert L. Heilbroner

What is needed now is a summing up of the human prospect, some last reflections on its implications for the present and future alike.

The external challenges can be succinctly reviewed. We are entering a period in which rapid population growth, the presence of obliterative weapons, and dwindling resources will bring international tensions to dangerous levels for an extended period. Indeed, there seems no reason for these levels of danger to subside unless population equilibrium is achieved and some rough measure of equity reached in the distribution of wealth among nations, either by great increases in the output of the underdeveloped world or by a massive redistribution of wealth from the richer to the poorer lands.

Whether such an equitable arrangement can be reached—at least within the next several generations—is open to serious doubt. Transfers of adequate magnitude imply a willingness to redistribute income internationally on a more generous scale than the advanced nations have evidenced within their own domains. The required increases in output in the backward regions would necessitate gargantuan applications of energy merely to extract the needed resources. It is uncertain whether the requisite energy-producing technology exists, and, more serious, possible that its application would bring

Reprinted from *An Inquiry into the Human Prospect* by Robert L. Heilbroner. By permission of W. W. Norton & Company, Inc. Copyright © 1975, 1974 by W. W. Norton & Company, Inc.

us to the threshold of an irreversible change in climate as a consequence of the enormous addition of man-made heat to the atmosphere.

It is this last problem that poses the most demanding and difficult of the challenges. The existing pace of industrial growth, with no allowance for increased industrialization to repair global poverty, holds out the risk of entering the danger zone of climatic change in as little as three of four generations. If that trajectory is in fact pursued, industrial growth will then have to come to an immediate halt, for another generation or two along that path would literally consume human, perhaps all, life. That terrifying outcome can be postponed only to the extent that the wastage of heat can be reduced, or that technologies that do not add to the atmospheric heat burden—for example, the use of solar energy—can be utilized. The outlook can also be mitigated by redirecting output away from heat-creating material outputs into the production of "services" that add only trivially to heat.

All these considerations make the designation of a timetable for industrial deceleration difficult to construct. Yet, under any and all assumptions, one irrefutable conclusion remains. The industrial growth process, so central to the economic and social life of capitalism and Western socialism alike, will be forced to slow down, in all likelihood within a generation or two, and will probably have to give way to decline thereafter. To repeat the words of the text, "whether we are unable to sustain growth or unable to tolerate it," the long era of industrial expansion is now entering its final stages, and we must anticipate the commencement of a new era of stationary total output and (if population growth continues or an equitable sharing among nations has not yet been attained) declining material output per head in the advanced nations.

These challenges also point to a certain time frame within which different aspects of the human prospect will assume different levels of importance. In the short run, by which we may speak of the decade immediately ahead, no doubt the most pressing questions will be those of the use and abuse of national power, the vicissitudes of the narrative of political history, perhaps the short-run vagaries of the economic process, about which we have virtually no predictive capability whatsoever. From our vantage point today, another crisis in the Middle East, further Vietnams or Czechoslovakias, inflation, severe economic malfunction—or their avoidance—are sure to exercise the primary influence over the quality of existence, or even over the possibilities for existence.

In a somewhat longer time frame—extending perhaps for a period of a half century—the main shaping force of the future takes on a different aspect. Assuming that the day-to-day, year-to-year crises are surmounted in relative safety, the issue of the relative resilience and adaptive capabilities of the two great socio-economic systems comes to the fore as the decisive question. Here the properties of industrial socialism and capitalism as ideal types seem likely to provide the parameters within which and by which the prospect for man will be formed. We have already indicated what general tendencies seem characteristic of each of these systems, and the advantages that may accrue to socialist—that is, planned and probably authoritarian social orders—during this era of adjustment.

In the long run, stretching a century or more ahead, still a different facet of the human prospect appears critical. This is the transformational problem, centered in the reconstruction of the material basis of civilization itself. In this period, as indefinite in its boundaries but as unmistakable in its mighty dimension as a vast storm visible on the horizon, the challenge devolves upon those deep-lying capabilities for political change whose roots in "human nature" have been the subject of our last chapter.

It is the challenges of the middle and the long run that command our attention when we speculate about the human prospect, if only because those of the short run defy our prognostic grasp entirely. It seems unnecessary to add more than a word to underline the magnitude of these still distant problems. No developing country has fully confronted the implications of becoming a "modern" nation-state whose industrial development must be severely limited, or considered the strategy for such a state in a world in which the Western nations, capitalist and socialist both, will continue for a long period to enjoy the material advantages of their early start. Within the advanced nations, in turn, the difficulties of adjustment are no less severe. No capitalist nation has as yet imagined the extent of the alterations it must undergo to attain a viable stationary socio-economic structure, and no socialist state has evidenced the needed willingness to subordinate its national interests to supra-national ones.

To these obstacles we must add certain elements of the political propensities in "human nature" that stand in the way of a rational, orderly adaptation of the industrial mode in the directions that will become increasingly urgent as the distant future comes closer. There seems no hope for rapid changes in the human character traits that would have to be modified to bring about a peaceful, organized reorientation of life styles. Men and women, much as they are today, will set the pace and determine the necessary means for the social changes that will eventually have to be made. The drift toward the strong exercise of political power—a movement given its initial momentum by the need to exercise a much wider and deeper administration of both production and consumption—is likely to attain added support from the psychological insecurity that will be sharpened in a period of unrest and uncertainty. The bonds of national identity are certain to exert their powerful force, mobilizing men for the collective efforts needed but inhibiting the international sharing of burdens and wealth. The myopia that confines the present vision of men to the short-term future is not likely to disappear overnight, rendering still more difficult a planned and orderly retrenchment and redivision of output.

Therefore the outlook is for what we may call "convulsive change"—change forced upon us by external events rather than by conscious choice, by catastrophe rather than by calculation. As with Malthus's much derided but all too prescient forecasts, nature will provide the checks, if foresight and "morality" do not. One such check could be the outbreak of wars arising from the explosive tensions of the coming period, which might reduce the growth rates of the surviving nation-states and thereby defer the danger of industrial asphyxiation for a period. Alternatively, nature may rescue us from ourselves by what John Platt has called a "storm of crisis problems."[1] As we breach now this, now that edge of environmental tolerance, local disasters—large-scale fatal urban temperature inversions, massive crop failures, resource shortages—may also slow down economic growth and give a necessary impetus to the piecemeal construction of an ecologically and socially viable social system.

Such negative feedbacks are likely to exercise an all-important dampening effect on a crisis that would otherwise in all probability overwhelm the slender human capabilities for planned adjustment to the future. However brutal these feedbacks, they are apt to prove effective in changing our attitudes as well as our

actions, unlike appeals to our collective foresight, such as the exhortations of the Club of Rome's *Limits to Growth,* or the manifesto of a group of British scientists calling for an immediate halt to growth.[2] The problem is that the challenge to survival still lies sufficiently far in the future, and the inertial momentum of the present industrial order is still so great, that no substantial voluntary diminution of growth, much less a planned reorganization of society, is today even remotely imaginable. What leader of an underdeveloped nation, particularly one caught up in the exhilaration of a revolutionary restructuring of society, would call a halt to industrial activity in his impoverished land? What capitalist or socialist nation would put a ceiling on material output, limiting its citizens to the well-being obtainable from its present volume of production?

Thus, however admirable in intent, impassioned polemics against growth are exercises in futility today. Worse, they may even point in the wrong direction. Paradoxically, perhaps, the priorities for the present lie in the temporary encouragement of the very process of industrial advance that is ultimately the mortal enemy. In the backward areas, the acute misery that is the potential source of so much international disruption can be remedied only to the extent that rapid improvements are introduced, including that minimal infrastructure needed to support a modern system of health services, education, transportation, fertilizer production, and the like. In the developed nations, what is required at the moment is the encouragement of technical advances that will permit the extraction of new resources to replace depleted reserves of scarce minerals, new sources of energy to stave off the collapse that would occur if present energy reservoirs were exhausted before substitutes were discovered, and, above all, new techniques for the generation of energy that will minimize the associated generation of heat.

Thus there is a short period left during which we can safely continue on the present trajectory. It is possible that during this period a new direction will be struck that will greatly ease the otherwise inescapable adjustments. The underdeveloped nations, making a virtue of necessity, may redefine "development" in ways that minimize the need for the accumulation of capital, stressing instead the education and vitality of their citizens. The possibilities of such an historic step would be much enhanced were the advanced nations to lead the way by a major effort to curtail the enormous wastefulness of industrial production as it is used today. If these changes took place, we might even look forward to a still more desirable redirection of history in a diminution of scale, a reduction in the size of the human community from the dangerous level of immense nation-states toward the "polis" that defined the appropriate reach of political power for the ancient Greeks.

All these are possibilities, but certainly not probabilities. The revitalization of the polis is hardly likely to take place during a period in which an orderly response to social and physical challenges will require an increase of centralized power and the encouragement of national rather than communal attitudes. The voluntary abandonment of the industrial mode of production would require a degree of self-abnegation on the part of its beneficiaries—managers and consumers alike—that would be without parallel in history. The redefinition of development on the part of the poorer nations would require a prodigious effort of will in the face of the envy and fear that Western industrial power and "affluence" will arouse.

Thus in all likelihood we must brace ourselves for the consequences of which we have spoken—the risk of "wars of redistribution" or of "preemptive seizure," the rise of social tensions in the industrialized nations over the division of an ever more slow-growing or even diminishing product, and the prospect of a far more coercive exercise of national power as the means by which we will attempt to bring these disruptive processes under control.

From that period of harsh adjustment, I can see no realistic escape. Rationalize as we will, stretch the figures as favorably as honesty will permit, we cannot reconcile the requirements for a lengthy continuation of the present rate of industrialization of the globe with the capacity of existing resources or the fragile biosphere to permit or to tolerate the effects of that industrialization. Nor is it easy to foresee a willing acquiescence of humankind, individually or through its existing social organizations, in the alterations of lifeways that foresight would dictate. If then, by the question "Is there hope for man?" we ask whether it is possible to meet the challenges of the future without the payment of a fearful price, the answer must be: No, there is no such hope.

At this final stage of our inquiry, with the full spectacle of the human prospect before us, the spirit quails and the will falters. We find ourselves pressed to the very limit of our personal capacities, not alone in summoning up the courage to look squarely at the dimensions of the impending predicament, but in finding words that can offer some plausible relief in a situation so bleak. There is now nowhere to turn other than to those private beliefs and disbeliefs that guide each of us through life, and whose disconcerting presence was the first problem with which we had to deal in appraising the prospect before us. I shall therefore speak my mind without any pretense that the words I am about to write have any basis other than those subjective promptings from which I was forced to begin and in which I must now discover whatever consolation I can offer after the analysis to which they have driven me.

At this late juncture I have no intention of sounding a call for moral awakening or for social action on some unrealistic scale. Yet, I do not intend to condone, much less to urge, an attitude of passive resignation, or a relegation of the human prospect to the realm of things we choose not to think about. Avoidable evil remains, as it always will, an enemy that can be defeated; and the fact that the collective destiny of man portends unavoidable travail is no reason, and cannot be tolerated as an excuse, for doing nothing. This general admonition applies in particular to the intellectual elements of Western nations whose privileged role as sentries for society takes on a special importance in the face of things as we now see them. It is their task not only to prepare their fellow citizens for the sacrifices that will be required of them but to take the lead in seeking to redefine the legitimate boundaries of power and the permissible sanctuaries of freedom, for a future in which the exercise of power must inevitably increase and many present areas of freedom, especially in economic life, be curtailed.

Let me therefore put these last words in a somewhat more "positive" frame, offsetting to some degree the bleakness of our prospect, without violating the facts or spirit of our inquiry. Here I must begin by stressing for one last time an essential fact. The human prospect is not an irrevocable death sentence. It is not an inevitable doomsday toward which we are headed, although the risk of enormous catastrophes exists. The prospect is better viewed as a formidable array of challenges that must be overcome before human survival is assured, before we can move *beyond doomsday*. These challenges can be overcome—by the saving intervention of nature if not by the wisdom and foresight of man. The death sentence is therefore better viewed as a contingent life sentence—one that will permit the continuance of human society, but only on a basis very different from that of the present, and probably only after much suffering during the period of transition.

What sort of society might eventually emerge? As I have said more than once, I believe the long-term solution requires nothing less than the gradual abandonment of the lethal techniques, the uncongenial life-ways,

and the dangerous mentality of industrial civilization itself. The dimensions of such a transformation into a "post-industrial" society have already been touched upon, and cannot be greatly elaborated here: in all probability the extent and ramifications of change are as unforeseeable from our contemporary vantage point as present-day society would have been unimaginable to a speculative observer a thousand years ago.

Yet I think a few elements of the society of the post-industrial era can be discerned. Although we cannot know on what technical foundation it will rest, we can be certain that many of the accompaniments of an industrial order must be absent. To repeat once again what we have already said, the societal view of production and consumption must stress parsimonious, not prodigal, attitudes. Resource-consuming and heat-generating processes must be regarded as necessary evils, not as social triumphs, to be relegated to as small a portion of economic life as possible. This implies a sweeping reorganization of the mode of production in ways that cannot be foretold, but that would seem to imply the end of the giant factory, the huge office, perhaps of the urban complex.

What values and ways of thought would be congenial to such a radical reordering of things we also cannot know, but it is likely that the ethos of "science," so intimately linked with industrial application, would play a much reduced role. In the same way, it seems probable that a true post-industrial society would witness the waning of the work ethic that is also intimately entwined with our industrial society. As one critic has pointed out, even Marx, despite his bitter denunciation of the alienating effects of labor in a capitalist milieu, placed his faith in the presumed "liberating" effects of labor in a socialist society, and did not consider a "terrible secret"—that even the most creative work may be only "a neurotic activity that diverts the mind from the diminution of time and the approach of death."[3]

It is therefore possible that a post-industrial society would also turn in the direction of many pre-industrial societies—toward the exploration of inner states of experience rather than the outer world of fact and material accomplishment. Tradition and ritual, the pillars of life in virtually all societies other than those of an industrial character, would probably once again assert their ancient claims as the guide to and solace for life. The struggle for individual achievement, especially for material ends, is likely to give way to the acceptance of communally organized and ordained roles.

This is by no means an effort to portray a future utopia. On the contrary, many of these possible attributes of a post-industrial society are deeply repugnant to my twentieth-century temper as well as incompatible with my most treasured privileges. The search for scientific knowledge, the delight in intellectual heresy, the freedom to order one's life as one pleases, are not likely to be easily contained within the tradition-oriented, static society I have depicted. To a very great degree, the public must take precedence over the private—an aim to which it is easy to give lip service in the abstract but difficult for someone used to the pleasures of political, social, and intellectual freedom to accept in fact.

These are all necessarily prophetic speculations, offered more in the spirit of providing some vision of the future, however misty, than as a set of predictions to be "rigorously" examined. In these half-blind gropings there is, however, one element in which we can place credence, although it offers uncertainty as well as hope. This is our knowledge that some human societies have existed for millennia, and that others can probably exist for future millennia, in a continuous rhythm of birth and coming of age and death, without pressing toward those dangerous ecological limits, or engendering those dangerous social tensions, that threaten present-day "advanced" societies.

In our discovery of "primitive" cultures, living out their timeless histories, we may have found the single most important object lesson for future man.

What we do not know, but can only hope, is that future man can rediscover the self-renewing vitality of primitive culture without reverting to its levels of ignorance and cruel anxiety. It may be the sad lesson of the future that no civilization is without its pervasive "malaise," each expressing in its own way the ineradicable fears of the only animal that contemplates its own death, but at least the human activities expressing that malaise need not, as is the case in our time, threaten the continuance of life itself.

All this goes, perhaps, beyond speculation to fantasy. But something more substantial than speculation or fantasy is needed to sustain men through the long trials ahead. For the driving energy of modern man has come from his Promethean spirit, his nervous will, his intellectual daring. It is this spirit that has enabled him to work miracles, above all to subjugate nature to his will, and to create societies designed to free man from his animal bondage.

Some of that Promethean spirit may still serve us in good stead in the years of transition. But it is not a spirit that conforms easily with the shape of future society as I have imagined it; worse, within that impatient spirit lurks one final danger for the years during which we must watch the approach of an unwanted future. This is the danger that can be glimpsed in our deep consciousness when we take stock of things as they now are: the wish that the drama run its full tragic course, bringing man, like a Greek hero, to the fearful end that he has, however unwittingly, arranged for himself. For it is not only with dismay that Promethean man regards the future. It is also with a kind of anger. If after so much effort, so little has been accomplished; if before such vast challenges, so little is apt to be done—

then let the drama proceed to its finale, let mankind suffer the end it deserves.

Such a view is by no means the expression of only a few perverse minds. On the contrary, it is the application to the future of the prevailing attitudes with which our age regards the present. When men can generally acquiesce in, even relish, the destruction of their living contemporaries, when they can regard with indifference or irritation the fate of those who live in slums, rot in prison, or starve in lands that have meaning only insofar as they are vacation resorts, why should they be expected to take the painful actions needed to prevent the destruction of future generations whose faces they will never live to see? Worse yet, will they not curse these future generations whose claims to life can be honored only by sacrificing present enjoyments; and will they not, if it comes to a choice, condemn them to nonexistence by choosing the present over the future?

The question, then, is how we are to summon up the will to survive—not perhaps in the distant future, where survival will call on those deep sources of imagined human unity, but in the present and near-term future, while we still enjoy and struggle with the heritage of our personal liberties, our atomistic existences.

At this last moment of reflection another figure from Greek mythology comes to mind. It is that of Atlas, bearing with endless perseverance the weight of the heavens in his hands. If mankind is to rescue life, it must first preserve the very will to live, and thereby rescue the future from the angry condemnation of the present. The spirit of conquest and aspiration will not provide the inspiration it needs for this task. It is the example of Atlas, resolutely bearing his burden, that provides the strength we seek. If, within us, the spirit of Atlas falters, there perishes the determination to preserve humanity at all cost and any cost, forever.

But Atlas is, of course, no other but ourselves. Myths have their magic power because they cast on the screen of our imaginations, like the figures of the heavenly constellations, immense projections of our own hopes and capabilities. We do not know with certainty that humanity will survive, but it is a comfort to know that there exist within us the elements of fortitude and will from which the image of Atlas springs.

NOTES

1. John Platt, "What We Must Do," *Science*, Nov. 28, 1969, p. 1115.

2. "Blueprint for Survival," *The Ecologist*, Jan. 1972.

3. John Diggins, "Thoreau, Marx, and the Riddle of Alienation," *Social Research*, Winter 1973, p. 573.

Arise, Ye Prisoners of Extinction

George Wald

Human life is now threatened as never before, not by one, but by many, perils—each in itself capable of destroying us, but all interrelated, and all coming upon us together. I am one of those scientists who does not see how to bring the human race much past the year 2000. If we perish—as seems more and more possible —in a nuclear holocaust, that will be the end, not only for us, but for much of the rest of life on Earth.

We live—while that is permitted us—in a balance of terror. The U.S. and the Soviet Union together have already stockpiled nuclear weapons with the explosive force of 10 tons of TNT for every man, woman, and child on Earth. One might think that enough, but both countries are now in the midst of further escalation, replacing every single nuclear warhead with multiple warheads, and devising new and more devastating weapons.

The U.S., at present, is making three new hydrogen warheads per day, while the Soviet Union keeps pace with us. We are told that our security (strange thought) lies in Mutual Assured Destruction—MAD. It is well-named.

The bomb that destroyed Hiroshima, killing about 100,000 persons, was a small one by present standards, with the explosive power of about 15,000 tons of TNT.

One of my friends about 10 years ago was able to look up what we then had targeted

upon a Russian city about the size of Hiroshima. It was in the megaton range, several hundred times as large. Why? One can only destroy a city. One can only kill a person. It is insane—but the insanity of the practical and calculating persons who run our lives. It is insane—unless ones holds an arms contract. Then it is business, and the bigger the better.

The U.S. now budgets about $22,000,000,000 a year on new arms. A rapid rate of turnover assures that this business will go on. Our arms sales abroad doubled in 1973–74 over the year before—to $8,500,000,000, about $7,000,000,000 going to the Middle East. Early in 1971, when the Joint Economic Committee of Congress asked a representative of the Department of Defense how much military hardware the department then held that had been declared surplus, mainly to be sold as scrap, he replied that it amounted to $17,000,000,000 worth.

The nuclear arms contracts alone are worth about $7,000,000,000 a year. That sum talks more loudly than any number of humanitarian declarations or terrified people or children facing extinction. That money is real, hard cash. Where it changes hands, those consequences are out of sight, hence out of mind—mere abstractions.

THE BIG HUNGER

However, arms, war, and nuclear weapons are only part of the crisis. The big hunger is

From George Wald, "Arise, Ye Prisoners of Extinction," *Intellect*, April 1976, pp. 501–502.

now upon us, the great famines that scientists have been predicting for years past—hunger among the poor in the developed countries and starvation in Africa, South Asia, and South America.

The Green Revolution, so recently begun, has already collapsed. It depended on huge supplies of cheap oil and coal to prepare the artificial fertilizers and pesticides that alone made it work, and oil and coal are no longer cheap. The profits of the major oil companies —which also own most of the coal and are now developing nuclear power—doubled and tripled during the past year as the peoples of the Third World began to starve. It seems possible that 20,000,000 persons will die of famine during the next 12 months in India, Pakistan, and Bangladesh alone.

All of these problems are made more terrible by the population explosion. We have not yet quite taken in what that means. Even if all the developed nations reached the replacement level—an average of two children per producing pair—by the year 2000, and if all the nations of the Third World came to the same state by 2050 (both conditions highly unlikely), then the world population, which is now at about 3,700,000,000, would rise by 2120 to about 13,000,000,000.

Development, so-called, has meant mechanization. The work that used to be done by human and animal muscle is increasingly done by machines. That is true even in agriculture. It is another aspect of the Green Revolution. Farming is rapidly being replaced by "agribusiness."

In the U.S., the same huge corporations that make aircraft, control our oil and gas, and run our transportation also grow our food. Such agribusiness now controls 51% of our vegetable production, 85% of our citrus crops, 97% of our chicken-raising, and 100% of our sugar cane. That is happening all over the world. It means more food, but many fewer jobs, and

only those who find work can eat and feed their families. Unemployment, that child of the Industrial Revolution, is rising throughout the world.

Moreover, a new phenomenon has developed that is much worse. With increasing mechanization, increasing numbers of persons have become not only unemployed, but superfluous. There is no use for them in the free-market economy. They are wanted neither as workers nor customers. They are not wanted at all. Their existence is a burden, an embarrassment. It would be a relief if they vanished—parents and children.

In his report to the International Bank for Reconstruction and Development (World Bank) in September, 1970, its president, Robert McNamara, former Ford executive and U.S. Secretary of Defense, spoke of such persons as "marginal men." He estimated that, in 1970, there were 500,000,000 of them—twice the population of the U.S.—and that by 1980 there would be 1,000,000,000; by 1990, 2,000,-000,000. That would be half the world's population.

THE LAST CHANCE—THE NEED FOR POLITICAL POWER

It is too late for declarations, for popular appeals, here or anywhere. All that matters now is political power.

We call here for the abolition of nuclear weapons. Even in the remote chance that that would happen, it would not protect us from nuclear war. Those nations that have already learned how to make nuclear weapons could produce them in quantity within a few months of the outbreak of a new war. Getting rid of the nuclear stockpiles would defuse the present threat of instant annihilation, and would gain us a little time. That would be an important gain, but only a step toward what must be the ultimate aim—to abolish war. War is obsolete in the modern world. It has become intolerably dangerous.

The only thing that can save us now is political power—for the peoples of this world to take that power away from their present masters, who are leading our world to destruction.

Who are our masters? In the so-called "free world," it is not the governments. They are only the servants, the agents. Nor is it the generals. They, too, are only servants.

The free world is run by such enterprises as General Motors, ITT, the Chase Manhattan Bank, Exxon, Dutch Shell and British Petroleum, Mitsubishi and Mitsui. Their wealth and power exceed any previously known throughout human history.

We think of General Motors as a private business, but only 18 nations in the world have gross national products as large as the annual sales of General Motors—$36,000,000,000 in 1973.

Those giant corporations can buy and sell, can make and break governments. They stop at nothing. In 1973, Chile was taken over by a military junta, its President Allende murdered, its great folk singer Victor Jara beaten to death. Yet, ITT, which offered the CIA $1,000,000 to keep Allende from becoming president, now can operate freely; and Anaconda Copper has settled its claims with the new Chilean dictatorship for $253,000,000.

What of the "socialist" world? It offers us an imperialism of the left to balance that of the right. We have had hard lessons to learn during the past years. One of them is that private wealth and personal political power are interchangeable, bureaucracies are interchangeable, generals and admirals, corporate executives and industrial commissars—all are interchangeable.

Hence, no nation so closely resembles the U.S. as does the Soviet Union. That is what Andrei Sakharov told us a few years ago, as he proposed that both nations now join forces to work for the good of humanity. For that, he is virtually a prisoner in his own country. Policy in the modern world—right or left—is not made by the Sakharovs.

We are often told that even the experts do not know how to deal with the problems that now threaten worldwide disaster, that "all the facts are not yet in," that more research must be done, and more reports written.

By all means, let us have more research, but that must not be allowed to become a trap, an excuse for endlessly putting off action. We already know enough to begin to deal with all our major problems: nuclear war, overpopulation, pollution, hunger, and despoliation of the planet Earth.

The present crisis is a crisis not of information, but of policy. We could begin to cope with all the problems that now threaten our lives, but we can not cope with any of them while maximizing profits. A society that insists before all on maximizing profits for the few thereby threatens disaster for all—but not for all at the same time.

As matters now stand, the peoples of the Third World are to perish first. They have already begun to starve. All that is asked of them is to starve quietly. If they make trouble, they will be exterminated by other means.

The developed nations are armed to the teeth, and they mean not only to hold on to what they have, but to grasp whatever more they can, while they can—for example, the last of the world's rapidly dwindling natural resources. Another example is that, as the great famines begin, the grain that might feed a hungry peasantry throughout the Third World is fed instead to cattle and hogs to supply the rapidly increasing demand for beef and pork in the affluent countries. However, the developed nations' turn will come too—first, of course, to their poor, already hard-hit by worldwide inflation and unemployment. Of course, if there should be another major war, as seems likely, a nuclear holocaust would swallow up everything.

Unless the people of this world can come together to take control of their lives, to wrest political power from those of its present masters who are pushing it toward destruction, then we are lost—we, our children, and their children.

Arise, ye prisoners of extinction. Peoples of the world, unite. You have nothing to lose but your terror, your exploitation, and ceaseless deception; your alienation and dehumanization; your helplessness and hopelessness.

And a world to win.

29 Appraisals of the Future Human Condition: An Optimistic Prospect

Kahn

Sometimes called a one-man think tank, the nuclear physicist, mathematician, and futurist Herman Kahn (1922–) has made a vocation of thinking about the unthinkable. Now director of a private policy research organization called the Hudson Institute, Kahn first became widely known for his work *On Thermonuclear War* in which he discussed unflinchingly the conceivable precipitating causes and possible consequences of an atomic war. Some of the questions he raised and answered in that book were so disturbing that some critics objected to his even asking them. Kahn, however has insisted that it is of utmost importance in a democratic society that questions of warfare and survival not be left to politicians and military experts. These questions should be discussed and debated rationally, extensively, and publicly. He would agree with the view that "the study of war is an absolute prerequisite to the avoidance of war."

As Socrates advised, in searching for rational alternatives we must follow the argument wherever it may lead. Thinking about the unthinkable must be coupled with the most vigorous logic of rational discourse and the use of a number of unconventional aids such as abstract models of possible situations, "scenarios" or descriptions of hypothetical sequences of events, war and peace games, as well as instructive examples taken from history and literature.

Before making their conjectures about the future, Kahn and associates at the Hudson Institute identify long term social trends, study clusters of significant events by time intervals, and abstract statistical data from which to project key variables and their growth rate. On this foundation, they extrapolate current trends to create "surprise-free projections," and describe a "standard world of the future" along with some possible "canonical variations." For example, they described in 1966 a basic long term trend toward an increasing "sensate" culture, that is, a culture that is empirical, secular, humanistic, and hedonistic; toward worldwide industrialization and modernization; and toward increasing urbanization, affluence, and leisure.[1] They also noted the continuing growth of population, the development of bureaucratic elites, and the acceleration and institutionalization of change. Along with the increase of education and literacy, they also called attention to the increase in the capacity for mass destruction. They were reasonably sure that these trends would continue for the rest of this century and would become universalized.

In their treatment of science and technology, Kahn and his associates made specific predictions of a hundred innovations likely to occur in the last third of the twentieth century. These ranged from new and improved structural materials, fabrics, and appliances to new techniques in child education, genetic control, and biological warfare. They recognized that some of these would be considered "unambiguous examples of progress" while others would be clearly controversial. All are important enough to bring about significant changes in the world in which we live, and Kahn is as interested in change as he is in continuity.

According to one commentator, Herman Kahn "labors under the burden of being an optimist in a period when pessimism is more fashionable in intellectual circles."[2] His view of the human prospect certainly seems strongly optimistic compared with that of Robert Heilbroner, for, unlike Heilbroner, Kahn believes that we can find the means in the years ahead to continue to meet mankind's needs for energy, resources, and technical ability. Such a prospect, to Kahn, is not optimistic but realistic.

Whether or not the best possible future for the world is realized will depend upon political and institutional factors. He carefully catalogs the various mechanisms which can bring about undesirable results in social processes—"pitfalls" to progress. Narrow decisions, inadequate thought, bad luck, inappropriate models and values—these are some of the reasons decisions are distorted and the best consequences are not achieved. The objective of Kahn's future-oriented policy research is to remove such obstacles. Realistic futurists, can, he believes, "stimulate and stretch the imagination," clarify major issues, design alternative policies, and improve communication and cooperation. The responsible futurist is willing to run the risk of wasting time by considering "unfashionable improbabilities" in the hope of gaining new insights to cope with new problems. "In any case, it has usually been the lack of imagination, rather than the excess of it, that caused unfortunate decisions and missed opportunities."[3]

From his imaginative and informed probes into the future, Kahn is convinced that many of the issues considered central today will be considered peripheral in the long run. Population, energy, pollution—these problems, to Kahn, can and probably will be solved in the near future.

They are "transitory issues of a transitory era, the problems of a time between world poverty and world prosperity."[4]

NOTES

1. See Herman Kahn and Anthony J. Wiener, *The Year 2000: A Framework for Speculation on the Next Thirty-Three Years* (New York: Macmillan, 1967).

2. *Futurist,* Vol. IX, No. 6 (Dec. 1975), p. 286.

3. Kahn and Wiener, *The Year 2000,* p. 400.

4. Ibid., p. 25.

An Interview with Herman Kahn

Paul Kurtz

HUMANISM

PAUL KURTZ: You have said that you are a "humanist."

HERMAN KAHN: I say that with many reservations.

KURTZ: Really? You have recently defended the heroic humanist virtues.

KAHN: I should explain. First of all, there are two uses of the term "humanist." There is the term employed roughly since the sixteenth century, which refers to values of the twelfth and thirteenth century Renaissance and its attempt to return to its conception of Greek and Roman values of heroism and reason. The recent American use of the term "humanist," on the other hand, has typically meant "joy," "love," "counterculture," and "spontaneity." It is "anti-hangup," and reason and heroism are considered to be hangups. This is a completely American concept that is expressed, for example, in the *New York Review of Books*. Now the use of the term by *The Humanist* magazine is the more traditional one.

KURTZ: There are those within the American humanist movement who represent the Greek or Renaissance meaning, as John Dewey did.

KAHN: You have there the more traditional

This article first appeared in *The Humanist*, November–December, 1973, pp. 42–50, and is reprinted by permission.

meaning which, by the way, is the way Europeans still use the word today. The typical American use reminds me a little of the word "liberalism," which also reversed its meaning from the nineteenth to the twentieth century, so that now the exponent of nineteenth-century liberalism has to say, "I'm a classical liberal," or something like that. Thus, I want to argue that I am a classical humanist.

KURTZ: What are the heroic virtues that you personally have as a classical humanist?

KAHN: There are a lot of heroic virtues that I feel I have—though my wife says the opposite. My basic self-image is that of a stoic. My wife's position is that you can't be a three-hundred-pound stoic. So, I think of myself as a neo-stoic.

KURTZ: A stoic in what sense?

KAHN: The stoics have a lot of positions. First of all, they believe that every man counts. Second, there is the notion that man ought to be able to endure any kind of pain or agony without complaint. I'm not sure that I'm in that class, but I might be. Their basic accomplishment, as far as I'm concerned, was that they kept the Roman system running. The tradition of stoicism ran in certain families in the Roman period, and these people maintained the system. The Stoics essentially ran the Roman Empire from after Augustus right through Marcus Aurelius (and this includes Nero) for about three hundred years. They ran it incredibly well. There is general agreement, quite apart from Gibbon, that this was one of the best-governed periods in the history of mankind. There may be some periods in Chinese history that are equivalent. The Romans felt that it was important that the system work, and they tried to make it work. They had all the stoic virtues, not just the well-known one of being able to bear enormous pain but also the idea that every man does his duty.

KURTZ: Are you a "neo-Stoic" in the sense that you think there exists in human affairs failure, defeat, and the tragic, as part of the total system of things?

KAHN: Let us say that often success is failure. This is a kind of central notion in many of our studies. The basic idea of the Stoics was not to do your duty as a soldier—the soldier wants to win—but to do it as an actor in a play. It's up to the author whether the actor wins or loses. The actors still have to perform as best they can with the lines they are given. Now I am more like a soldier than an actor. Nothing would depress me more than to go down dramatically with flags flying. An actor wouldn't mind doing this and neither would a stoic. So, I am a neo-Stoic in that sense, too. Yet I also recognize that, in the long run, few things fail like success.

KURTZ: Would you say the neo-Stoic is basically optimistic or pessimistic?

KAHN: Pessimistic. The Stoic was a democrat who ran an empire. He was a pacifist who ran an army. He believed in democracy, but he had a slave state. He believed in the triviality of sensuality; yet his was one of the most materialistic and sensual cultures of all time. Completely pessimistic.

KURTZ: In your own thinking about the present situation, are you still a neo-Stoic?

KAHN: Yes, except I expect to win in the short and medium run. I expect to make things come out right. Also I don't put great

emphasis on the ability of individuals to bear pain as opposed to hardship and inconvenience. Pain really isn't much of an issue in our culture anyway. One exception is obviously war.

KURTZ: The two heroic virtues that you talked about were courage and reason.

KAHN: The heroic virtues imply more than courage. First of all, heroic virtues imply a heroic conception of life: there are things worth doing that are more important than individual human beings. One of the oddities of the humanist picture today is that the modern American humanist says that the human being is all-important and that there is no cause, no task, that justifies the sacrifice of human lives or even comfort. That's the modern American usage of "humanism."

KURTZ: But you are referring again to only one wing of the humanist movement.

KAHN: Yes and no. You and I are clear about the misuse of the word "humanism." You know what the word "humanist" means, and at the same time you edit a magazine for the American Humanist Association and the American Ethical Union. That is why you feel that your use of the word roughly corresponds to the American usage. But, in fact, you're wrong to consider that this use is acceptable in most American literary circles today.

KURTZ: You are talking about the usage of the word "humanism" that has developed in the last five or seven years?

KAHN: The last five years.

KURTZ: You are identifying humanism with the humanist New Left?

KAHN: I'm saying that a general American usage of the word has been determined by, say, the more widely reviewed writers and professors at prestige universities. When I talk about the American usage of that term, I am talking about its usage by the influential literary and intellectual figures. In these groups, humanism would be opposed to heroism. Heroism would mean to them the sacrifice of human values for a hangup or an unworthy goal. The younger members of these groups are increasingly opposed to reason in much the same way that the Nazis were opposed to reason—as cold, unemotional, without real feeling, and unsatisfying. Reason dries up the human juices.

KURTZ: This is the existential aspect of humanism, which is supposed to liberate the individual.

KAHN: Right. Even Norman Mailer, one of the best minds of the twentieth century, used to go around saying something like, "I am only alive when I'm beating up somebody."

KURTZ: So, it's the passionate and the irrational aspect that you are objecting to?

KAHN: In part, the passionate, irrational state of mind. The mystic state of mind. The transcendental state of mind. Actually, I object mainly to their proselytizing and to their hostility to my state of mind—otherwise I would tend to say live and let live.

KURTZ: Do you disagree because you're emphasizing intelligence?

KAHN: I'm saying that we have here a complete misuse of the term "humanist." Yet I concede that temporarily the group we have been talking about has won the right to determine the word's meaning. But you can't, because you're a member of the American Humanists, and they don't use the word in the way that we agree is right.

KURTZ: We have many people who do. There's a split on that point, of course.

KAHN: Isn't it annoying when somebody takes a word that you like and distorts it?

KURTZ: Well, this is what's happening all the time—the corruption of words. . . . How would you deal with someone like Sidney Hook, for example?

KAHN: Sidney Hook is definitely a humanist in the original sense, but he is an older man. If you use the term "humanism" in the pre-World War II sense, there is no question what the word means. It's the same use of the word that the Europeans have had.

KURTZ: So your sense of humanism, then, would emphasize intelligence as a key method or end?

KAHN: Reason, not intelligence. One can be very bright and completely non-humanist, if you will. Common sense is an element of humanism. Humanism was originally opposed to the Catholic Church, to the idea that the only purpose of man is to serve God. The heroic emphasis meant human purposes as opposed to God's purposes. But today such human purposes would be held to be disreputable.

KURTZ: Held to be disreputable by whom?

KAHN: By the New Left. The only legitimate human purpose to them is self-actualization.

KURTZ: You mean individual self-actualization?

KAHN: Yes. There were two Maslows. The early Maslow uses the word "self-actualization" the way I would use it, as an additional motivation to those provided by guilt, fear, shame, punishment, and reward. But he realized that you never forget about the need for some combination of guilt, fear, shame, punishment, reward, and self-actualization. The later Maslow thinks of guilt, fear, shame, punishment, and reward as sick and says you shouldn't use them.

KURTZ: He wants to get rid of repression.

KAHN: Yes, any kind of repression. But in so doing he was probably misreading Freud. Freud made three very basic remarks. First, "Civilization is repression." That goes with all of Freud. Second, "You must socialize the child at any cost." Third, having made those two decisions, "You must reduce the cost of socialization." There are cheap and expensive ways to socialize the child. Now the only idea the Americans heard was the third—how can you reduce the cost? Many psychoanalysts, psychiatrists, and professional Freudians, in fact, haven't read Freud very accurately or deeply.

KURTZ: You said earlier that you would be willing to sacrifice persons to a cause.

KAHN: In my definition of the word "humanism," there are many causes that require the sacrifice of human lives and human values. I admire the American colonel, for example, who is willing to sacrifice his life and liberty and who is prepared, at the least, to spend many years away from home. His family often feels this sense of sacrifice very acutely. In the modern American milieu, the family feels abused. But this doesn't stop the colonel from performing very well.

KURTZ: These other humanists refuse to make sacrifices for a cause because it's the human being that they wish to actualize.

KAHN: Yes. Their basic definition of humanism is self-actualization. What do I, as a human being, want to do? In my view that is almost total selfishness, total self-indulgence. The current word "humanism" is a recipe for self-indulgence and selfishness. This is not always and not completely so bad, for self-indulgence and selfishness can be disciplined and can be very useful. For instance, I like the work I do, but I'm not completely self-indulgent. I get pleasure and benefits from my work, but I'm not completely selfish. So, I am not objecting to self-actualization as necessarily degenerate; however, if self-actualization is set above everything else, I think it's degenerate.

KURTZ: As a neo-Stoic, then, you believe that we have to commit ourselves to certain values in running the system?

KAHN: Yes, and these values don't necessarily overlap a great deal with self-indulgence or with the kind of self-actualization that permits everyone to do his own thing, as the saying goes.

KURTZ: You seem to express a strong "conservative" value here, a "sense of duty."

KAHN: A sense of duty and obligation.

KURTZ: Why do you have a sense of duty and obligation?

KAHN: I believe they have a high survival value. Perhaps I overvalue the necessity of putting emphasis on this quality, but I don't believe so. The nastiest remark I think anyone ever made about anybody was made by Bertrand Russell about Nietzsche. Russell said, "Never have the ideas of a Bavarian nursemaid been put so well." He was clearly being nasty. Russell might have said about my work that never have the ideas of a Bronx middle-class Jew with bourgeois values been put so well. There are certain values that I hold very strongly, but I don't think of them as relevant or necessary to the culture or the future. That's the Bavarian nursemaid part. But I do not believe my emphasis on the national interest, on survival, or on social contrast is irrelevant or idiosyncratic.

KURTZ: Aren't these the values that you have been brought up on?

KAHN: Yes, and there are other values I've been brought up on, which are actually central for both me and my culture.

KURTZ: Which are these?

KAHN: A sense of duty and obligation. A sense that it is important, if possible, for people to have a high material level of life without over-emphasizing the material level of life. That is, I am perfectly prepared to believe that people could be happy and poor. But most cultures today require a high material level of life. The number one thing that makes a Western standard of living possible is a basic sense of what people call the "work ethic," including both achievement orientation and work orientation. I don't believe that these two last virtues, or values, are essential for mankind. I think they're useful and almost essential for the current state of man. I don't mean that this is uniformly correct, but I do think that the basic theme of the culture is still the work ethic. Thus, I look on the current attempts to limit work orientation as kind of sick. These efforts are not necessarily sick on an individual basis, but from the standpoint of the culture as a whole they're unhealthy. Yet eventually—probably in the next one hundred years—I believe that there will be a reaction against the work ethic and that then it may well be healthy.

KURTZ: Do you think that this reaction against work is worldwide or is it strong primarily in this country?

KAHN: To a greater or lesser extent, this reaction is worldwide. The prestigious schools are anti-work ethic today, anti-growth. This is a worldwide issue. The anti-work ethic, anti-growth position is felt to be one of the images of the future. The Club of Rome is one of the agents acting to create such an image of the future.

THE RESTRICTION OF ECONOMIC GROWTH

KURTZ: What do you think about the image of the future advocated by The Club of Rome, that is, the necessity to restrict economic growth?

KAHN: I think that it is almost unbelievably childish. More specifically, I think it reflects narrow technicism and an even narrower class interest. We've spent a fair amount of time examining the report but, while I happened to like the people who did the study as individuals, it's just not professionally done. It is not a well-done study in any way that I would care to name, except that it states one of the important problems. They say, in effect, that it's hard to look at the interests of our grandchildren and great-grandchildren, and they are trying to do this. That's legitimate enough, and that's

its great virtue. It has also attracted much attention to the current pollution problems, but in a way that is often counterproductive rather than productive.

KURTZ: It's futurist oriented, but in that sense . . .

KAHN: In any other sense it has no virtues. It does not understand the whole system; it's not a good computer study; its assumptions are awful; its technique is bad.

KURTZ: Now what about their notion concerning the use of energy, resources, and production; that is, if it continues at the same rate, by the year 2000 we'll be in a terrible energy and ecological crisis.

KAHN: Absolutely not, given only one caveat: you don't do things that are incredibly dumb. There are two kinds of problems you can get into. One kind of problem is similar to the thalidomide problem. You introduce a drug and a lot of people got crippled. Now that drug also did a lot of useful things, by the way. It may have done more useful things than harm. But the harm is very visible and we don't care to have it. Some aspects of industry are like that. They do both good and harm. There are mistakes like the methyl mercury problem in the United States. With this kind of problem it takes a long time for the effects to show up.

KURTZ: On the fish you mean?

KAHN: On human beings also. And if you don't watch and move fast you can poison a lot of rivers, and it can be very hard to unpoison them, though this can be done. Now, assuming that we will at least learn from the more obvious mistakes, it doesn't take very high-quality decision-making to make sure that we don't run into pollution deaths of any great magnitude or that we don't have mass starvation on the order of hundreds of millions of people. Let's go to the next one hundred years. If the population grows 2.1 per cent per year, and if it continues unchecked, we'll have 54 billion people by 2100. We don't expect to hit that. We expect to taper off way before that, probably at around 10 or 15 billion.

KURTZ: When?

KAHN: I'll say probably 10 or 20 billion in the early or mid-twenty-first century and very slow growth or a decline after that.

KURTZ: Well how come the predictions that we may be overwhelmed by 2020? We hear a great deal about that.

KAHN: It could happen, but I don't think it will. I think there is a systematic overestimate of the likely future rate of population growth.

KURTZ: Well how do you explain this great concern? Is this country in the throes of a great hysteria worrying about the future?

KAHN: The hysteria has to do with a number of issues put together and it originates with an attitude held by a certain class of people. These people want to believe certain kinds of things for various reasons. The most obvious reason is self-interest. Say you are living on 10, 15, or 20 thousand dollars a year in a country like Portugal, Spain, Mexico, or Brazil. You live very well. First of all, you have two to five live-in servants. (Incidentally, one good servant is better than a household full of appliances.) Second, you have easy access to the more sensual pleasures of life, including girlfriends or mistresses. Third, you have immunity from the petty cares of life. You have cars without traffic jams, you have status, you have importance, you have a kind of safety, when other people have none of these things. Now, compare this life to that of someone making 50 thousand dollars in the United States. Who do you think lives better?

KURTZ: Who does?

KAHN: The guy who is making 10 to 20 thousand dollars a year in Portugal and has the servant is living better than the American who makes 50 thousand dollars a year. If you are one of the 5 per cent who have cars, you're living great. If you have a Cadillac, maybe you also have a Chevy.

KURTZ: But there is only a small class in Portugal which lives like this.

KAHN: That's right. All I'm saying is that the standard of living in upper-class elites all around the world goes down both absolutely and relatively as the world gets richer. And they recognize it. Now why are our middle class young in the United States playing poor? They play at being poor in order to differentiate themselves from the lower-middle-class kids who are proud of no longer being poor and who like to dress and act in a way that shows off their affluence. Playing poor is a form of snobbishness directed against the lower middle class. Nobody plays poor in a country where there are really poor people. All the hippies come from very well-off countries in which the poor basically don't exist.

KURTZ: The affluent societies?

KAHN: Not only affluent, but affluent with almost an absence of the absolutely poor. Now they think of themselves as having poor, because they define poor as three to four thousand dollars a year. But I mean poor as the world uses the term.

KURTZ: Then don't you think that there is a class of poor people in this country?

KAHN: No, there's practically no poverty in the United States.

KURTZ: You think poverty is just relative?

KAHN: There is relative poverty in the United States, which will presumably continue throughout history, but very little absolute poverty.

KURTZ: Is poverty another notion that in your view needs to be discarded?

KAHN: No. You do have some very poor people in Appalachia and the South, but throughout the country the improverished tend to be people who can't, who don't know how to, or who don't want to cope with the system. That is, there are people who really know how to fill out the forms, but just don't want to fill out the forms, or people whose state is conspiring against them, as may be the case in some parts of Mississippi and Louisiana.

KURTZ: Then how do you explain the well-nigh mass hysteria which has invaded the advanced industrial nations? You've got people like John D. Rockefeller III arguing that growth is the overwhelming problem and that the industrial nations have to restrict their growth.

KAHN: You've put it quite clearly. This is mass hysteria.

KURTZ: Where does it come from?

KAHN: The issue is very complicated. The first thing to recognize is that for the upper-middle-class guy, not for John D. Rockefeller III, growth is a disaster. Now take myself; we were poor, not middle class, when I was a kid, but I lived better than most kids ever lived. We went to California, and I've worked since I was about 13 earning a man's salary. When I was 14 I bought my own car—a Model A, for 75 bucks. I used to drive down to Mexico for Mexican meals and up to San Francisco for Chinese meals. When we went up to the beach, we went to Malibu where the movie stars live now and had the whole beach to ourselves. If anyone else came, we went north to another beach. We used to hike in the High Sierras. If we met someone there on the trail, the day was ruined. Now that's the way you could live if you wanted to 30 or 40 years ago.

KURTZ: As you describe it, it sounds like a beautiful life.

KAHN: In any level of income, these modern kids could not live this way. I make roughly 20 times as much now, and I can't live as well.

KURTZ: Isn't this due to over-population and the underdevelopment of the country?

KAHN: It isn't the population; it's wealth. Really poor people don't disturb anybody. They are quiet; they don't move around; they don't take up much space. It's people with money who cause problems. People with money to buy cars and boats and who have time for vacations and travel. These are the ones who fill the country.

KURTZ: This level of affluence is growing; it is worldwide; and it may continue to grow.

KAHN: Yes, and that means a loss to many with upper-middle-class values. But the middle class will enjoy it. The middle class doesn't mind applying ahead of time to get into a national park. I do, I will not go to a national park if I have to apply ahead of time. It's got to be there when the mood moves me.

KURTZ: Do you think it's the impatience of the upper class?

KAHN: The upper classes want privileges; they want spontaneity, large amounts of privacy; they want to be able to do what they please when they feel like it. They don't like traffic jams.

KURTZ: And that's why they are worried about growth, you mean.

KAHN: Partly, yes. They lose by growth. Some of them don't like suburban sprawl. Eighty-five per cent of Americans have a huge commitment to suburban sprawl. You know how in most European countries people used to live in villages and go out to the farm? In our country farmers always lived in widely separated houses—even during pioneer days—and this meant accepting high risks of Indians, and so on. And that commitment to suburban sprawl has continued right up to today. Now I doubt if you could find many city planners who think suburban sprawl is a good thing. Most city planners hate suburban sprawl. They want Le Corbusier-type ribbon cities; they want green belts. They do not want Levittown; unfortunately, the middle class does.

KURTZ: In your book *The Year 2000* or *Things to Come,* you talk about the eventual overflowing of the technological bathtub.

KAHN: We talk there about the dangers of growth. They are very real. I talk about the 1985 technological crisis. In one part I list seventy problems which could really cause terrible troubles in the next ten to twenty years.

KURTZ: But are these not caused by growth?

KAHN: They are caused by growth. In this world nothing comes for free.

KURTZ: Is the problem then, not to limit growth, but to redirect it?

KAHN: Not so much redirect it as control it. As a matter of fact, I would be willing to limit growth if we could do so safely and equitably. But I'm relatively well off; I'm not poor. I'm not sure how I would vote if I were making five thousand dollars a year. I am perfectly prepared to say that a number of problems are made easier if you limit growth. And few problems get more difficult for me personally if you limit growth.

KURTZ: The growth of others you mean.

KAHN: The growth of everybody. I want to include others. Absolutely. The argument for limiting growth is, I think, fairly good. But there are also very good arguments against limiting growth. It's very hard to get a reasonable balance. All I'm saying is (a) that you can't totally limit growth, and (b) that the plusses for increased growth are probably overwhelming. On the other hand, many problems are alleviated by slowing down growth. But that's mainly true in the rich world. In the poor world you have the population problem. I believe the only way to solve this problem is to make people rich. In other words, the American girl that normally has about two children limits the number of her children not because of pollution or starvation but because of wealth. Middle-class people simply don't want too many children. Benjamin Franklin once made the comment that the easiest way for a young man to get rich was to marry a widow with seven children. That is a formula for bankruptcy today. If you want to stop the population growth, I believe you have to make the poor countries richer. And the easiest and fastest way to make them richer is to make the rich countries richer. One major argument for making the rich countries very rich is to increase the gap, which pulls up the poor countries.

KURTZ: Yes, but isn't the gap supposed to be increasing?

KAHN: It is increasing. The dumbest argument that was ever made by middle-class Americans and AID people is the following calculation which they make every year: the rich people make two thousand dollars per capita, poor people make two hundred dollars per capita, the gap is eighteen-hundred dollars. In one or two decades both incomes will be double. The rich will make four thousand dollars, the poor four hundred. The gap will then be thirty-six hundred and they will be twice as badly off. You can't make a dumber remark than that. The poor people of the world are delighted to double their income from two hundred to four hundred dollars. You know something? They don't care what the rich countries make.

KURTZ: As long as they can increase their own?

KAHN: Yes. They couldn't care less whether you doubled, tripled, quadrupled, or halved your income. Their interest is solely in increasing their income. Now let me discuss gaps, because the concept is important to understand. The greatest gap in the world is basically between the first and second son of the king. One heartbeat away from everything. He feels the gap. The two vice-presidents, only one of whom makes president; the two authors, only one of whom gets the prize. Intellectuals really feel gaps, careerists do, and so on. And they think that everybody feels the same way. The next big gap is where somebody who has been up has gone down. England felt a big gap when the Germans and French passed them. They are going to feel even worse. In 1985 very likely Italy, Portugal, and Spain will have a higher per capita income than England. That's a gap.

KURTZ: Spain and Portugal will have a higher income than England?

KAHN: It's a reasonable statement—per capita income.

KURTZ: And the English will feel very bad about this.

KAHN: Older Englishmen, yes. The young Englishmen much less so. They have no idea why the older Englishman turns white, blue, green, and orange when you say this. They're used to thinking of themselves as a second-class nation—or, better, not thinking in terms of hierarchy. Older Englishmen just can't stand the idea. The possibility of being patronized by visiting Italians or Portuguese horrifies them. But, let me say this, the gap thing is kind of important. A lot of things revolve around the idea of social gaps.

Now take a chauffeur from the Rockefeller estate. He is not depressed because Rockefeller lives many times better than he does. You know, he expects it; he couldn't care less. He's not even depressed if the upstairs maid makes 50 per cent more than he does. He knows that upstairs maids are scarce. You tell him though that another chauffeur makes 10 cents an hour more, and he gets ulcers. That's the gap. It's the gaps within your own socio-economic status group that are really felt. Now if you're rich, you may not understand that. Rich men's children often have trouble talking to chauffeurs; they feel guilty about their money. But that's the kid's problem, not the chauffeur's.

KURTZ: But you don't think that the advanced countries ought to limit growth at this point?

KAHN: Just the opposite. They have a duty to make the rest of the world rich.

KURTZ: And you think if they grow they will export?

KAHN: It is the so-called trickle-down theory. And the trickle-down theory has worked in all cases. I don't know of any case where it doesn't work. The fact that the people don't want to believe that it works is again a problem that the people have, not an objective problem.

KURTZ: You mean if advanced countries limit growth, then this will tend to limit growth in the underdeveloped countries?

KAHN: Absolutely.

THE ENERGY CRISIS

KURTZ: But take the energy crisis of today. Suddenly great shortages have occurred in this country. You've been predicting it; other people have been predicting it.

KAHN: Actually, we've been very lucky. If we had had one very cold winter or one very hot summer, we would have had a shutdown altogether. In fact, several months ago the Middle West had a shutdown. They were saved only by unseasonably warm weather on the East Coast.

KURTZ: But doesn't this suggest that the problems of growth are getting out of hand?

KAHN: The problems of mismanagement. Here's an important example of mismanagement: We took something like natural gas, which is the most convenient fuel you can have, and we priced it at twenty cents a thousand cubic feet. It was severely underpriced. The average price of gas today is twenty-five cents a thousand cubic feet. This is fuel which clearly should be sold at one dollar per thousand cubic feet. So naturally everybody uses gas instead of oil or coal, and you get a complete distortion of the market. This is not the same as a real shortage.

KURTZ: Do you think there are new sources of energy that can be used?

KAHN: There's plenty of energy in the world, but there will be a more or less permanent shortage of very cheap energy. In fact it's a reasonably good bet that energy at twenty cents a million BTUs will no longer be available, except in the Far East and Middle East. If you are willing to pay a dollar for the same amount, there's all you want for at least a century or two. If you want to pay two or three dollars a million BTUs, there is all that you want for the rest of history. If you are rich you can afford to pay the higher price. Now one of the big advantages that the United States has is that if we want to produce our own oil we can mine about two or three trillion tons of coal, which would produce about ten trillion barrels of oil. The most oil you have in the world from undiscovered oil is two or three trillion. From coal alone we could get three times as much in U.S. oil.

KURTZ: Wouldn't this process be costly?

KAHN: It would cost five or six dollars a barrel. This is what we expect we are going to have to pay for oil anyway. So we don't have to buy it from abroad if we don't want to. Now in oil shale we have about two trillion barrels available. We do have serious problems of strip mining but I think they can be worked out. They are serious problems, but they are hopeful problems— that is, they can be solved, and their solutions do not lead to worldwide death and destruction. The difficulty is that you may have to sacrifice major portions of at least four or five states, including Colorado and Wyoming. Wyoming has unbelievably big coal deposits, and Colorado has both coal shale and gas reserves.

KURTZ: Do you think that the energy problem has been manufactured by the media for the public?

KAHN: No, it is a serious problem. You have a serious shortage of refinery capacity in the United States. We haven't built a single refinery in this country for four years, and we currently have no plans for building any.

KURTZ: Is this in part because of efforts to repeal the oil depletion tax allowance?

KAHN: It has nothing to do with taxes. It's because of the environmental objections. For example, you can build a road. No matter where you build it, anybody who lives right near that road is unhappy. Anybody a little distance away is very happy. The road is clearly good for almost everybody, but it's definitely bad for the guy whose house is torn down. The state doesn't want the refinery, for it louses up the larger area. Now I agree with the right of every state to protest refineries. But I don't think their protests should always be successful. In other words, this is the eminent domain issue. Often, somebody has to be hurt.

KURTZ: Do you think the objections of environmentalists, and the over-emphasis of dangers by groups such as the Sierra Club will have negative consequences?

KAHN: Well, both negative and positive. You do have to worry about the environment, and it's very good to have movements that are worried about it. But the way these groups act is counterproductive. Ninety-five per cent of the American people used to support environmental protection. Now it's eighty-five per cent. They've been driven out of the movement by the excesses of environmentalists. They are really acting irrationally. But it may be good to have some conflict in such situations. If you want a lot of pressure groups on both sides, even extremist movements can be useful. On the other hand, the leading environmentalists appear to some people as if they had gone crazy.

KURTZ: So you need some balance on this?

KAHN: Yes.

IMAGES OF THE FUTURE

KURTZ: Well, I wonder if we can get back to images of the future. Do you think that in some sense the images that we have of the future determine the kind of future we have?

KAHN: They affect the future. Obviously, there are both self-fulfilling and self-defeating prophecies, and it is possible for the two to cancel each other out. On balance, however, I believe that self-fulfilling prophecies are more important.

KURTZ: I'm interested in the images of the future that you think will emerge.

KAHN: Let me give you one commonly held image—the neo-Malthusian theory. Resources are running out. Pollution is going to kill a lot of people soon. Disastrous gaps are opening between the rich and the poor. The humanist left would add that, not only are the rich countries in trouble, but they were bastards who got rich by criminally exploiting men and the environment. This is an inflexible position. The progressive center sometimes says that there are different kinds of growth and it tries to weasel about the situation. This more moderate position, I think, is closer to being correct.

KURTZ: And you hold the position that almost everyone is getting richer, some faster than others, and if growth is properly managed, there will be plenty of resources. Is that your image of the future?

KAHN: That is the image I hold. It is completely accurate. It's carefully stated and not an extreme view. I can give you all the supporting data you want on it. Now there are some converts to my position. The future we foresee looks all right by middle-class stan-dards and middle-class interests—not upper-middle-class standards or interests. You do have to worry about some far-fetched and unlikely but terribly important problems. It takes a moderate level of decision-making to overcome the problems we can imagine, but no extraordinarily good behavior. And I do not promise that if you're rich you'll be well off. In fact, my basic point is that miseries of the future are likely to be due to the ambiguities of wealth, rather than to the pressures of poverty.

KURTZ: By the ambiguity you mean the psychological problems?

KAHN: There are all kinds of problems in the world. Wealth is not necessarily good for people.

KURTZ: Then your image is fairly optimistic.

KAHN: Optimistic at the material level with important subjective problems. For example, we talk about a technological crisis in 1985. This crisis brings with it a lot of subjective problems, such as the loss of privacy. That's ten to twenty years away, not fifty or one hundred. It's with us right now.

KURTZ: Is your view concerned with the need for population restriction?

KAHN: I think population restriction is something like the fourth most important problem. For many poor countries, population restriction is crucial. For India, for example, it's very important. For China, it's useful. For countries like the United States and Japan, it's merely nice. It may or may not be good for a country. It's just not equally important for all countries.

KURTZ: So in your view, ten billion people by the year 2020 is not a disaster?

KAHN: Not a disaster by middle-class standards.

KURTZ: And you think ten billion is likely by 2020?

KAHN: Ten to fifteen billion is a fairly reasonable number for 2020 or 2025, given the expected tapering off of growth rates.

KURTZ: Although population is a major world problem, you don't consider it as the first problem. What is then?

NUCLEAR WAR

KAHN: The first problem facing the world has been with us for some time now. It is the issue of war or peace. This problem seemed to recede in the sixties. We generally felt that the world was relatively safe then regardless of what governments did. The risk of serious war is now starting to go up again, precisely because people are not worrying about the problem.

KURTZ: Now, what about the efforts toward disarmament? Do you think that this is an illusion? What about the SALT talks?

KAHN: The SALT talks were both good and bad. They were what we call a fair-weather policy. The policy will work very well if it is not challenged and things go well. It's not a hedge against problems, and it helps to create the problems it's supposed to be a hedge against. But it also helps to create the fair-weather atmosphere. So it's hard to say. Some of the things agreed to were crazy from both the Soviet and the American point of view.

KURTZ: Senator Jackson, who is extremely critical of Nixon's policies concerning the Soviet Union, seems to be the only one in this country aware of that.

KAHN: Everyone would be aware of it if they understood it. Take the number one point of the SALT talks, the number of missiles each side has. We don't even know if the negotiators knew what the Russians had. At no point did the Russians agree to any statement of ours as to what they had. We say it had been limited to so many missiles. We would start by saying, "You now have three hundred missiles." They would say, "That's a very interesting number." They

didn't agree to it. Even in the final agreement the Soviet Union made no statement of how many missiles they had.

KURTZ: Then, in your judgment, we don't know what they have for sure.

KAHN: We probably do know; but it's crazy to sign any agreement that in principle doesn't require open . . .

KURTZ: Inspection?

KAHN: Not even inspection. Just verification of what the number is. I'm willing to trust their word for it, but they haven't given their word. Throughout the entire agreement there is no admission by the Russians of what they have. Thus, if we accused them of building new silos, they could claim that they were old silos that the United States just never noticed before. You're practically asking them to cheat. This is the worst kind of agreement we can have—one that breeds suspicion.

KURTZ: Do you think then that the ideological crisis that we lived through in the fifties and sixties will emerge again in the future?

KAHN: No, I think it's winding down. The so-called domino theory is basically correct even in reverse. The defeat of Communism in Vietnam and the detente between the United States and the Soviet Union has made Communism everywhere in the world a defeated ideology. There's no place in the world where the Communists have high morale, even though a good deal of the world is hostile to the United States. Look at Latin America; Communist ideology is the prevailing ideology if you except Brazil, Mexico, and Colombia. Nevertheless there's no active movement to rally round. There's no radical ideology with any kind of dynamism. Castroism is dead; Maoism is dead; Russian Stalinism is dead. (However, it's possible to write scenarios for the revival of Communist morale.)

KURTZ: Well, does this suggest a decline of

Communist ideology over the next ten to twenty years?

KAHN: We don't know. But we do know that at the moment there are no left-wing Communist movements with high morale anywhere.

KURTZ: But then why do you think the problem of war and peace is still crucial?

KAHN: One, the nuclear weapons are becoming easier to buy. Technology is producing some very dangerous products here. Two, the kind of balance achieved by World War II is gradually weakening.

KURTZ: Your reputation suffered during the days of the Rand Corporation when you were "thinking the unthinkable," and you came under heavy personal attack.

KAHN: Our study on this is now a standard textbook at dozens of universities. As far as I know, there are no serious errors that wreck any part of its argument.

KURTZ: So you think that it was a kind of "moralism" in your critics when they reacted so bitterly to what you were doing?

KAHN: Nuclear weapons are extraordinarily unpleasant things and most people didn't want to talk about them. Unless you believe in unilateral disarmament, however, and are willing to accept the consequences of this policy, you have to consider the problem. If you believe in unilateral disarmament, you can say "to hell with the Bomb, I don't want to talk about it." As far as I'm concerned, I think we're just lucky that we didn't have a war during the 1950's. We maintained our strength, and we prevented accidental wars without really knowing what we were doing.

KURTZ: But what about the 1970's and 1980's?

KAHN: As I said, I think that the probability of war will rise, in part because people don't take it seriously.

KURTZ: Does the China-Russia situation bother you?

KAHN: If I had to guess where the Bomb would first be used, I guess it would be Japan versus China. That's the most serious danger. The next would be China versus Russia. Of course, the Japanese and Chinese may succeed in avoiding war, but the problem is basically that Japan and China are going to compete for Asia. And Japan has the edge. Yet it's hard to imagine the Chinese taking a second place to Japan.

MEANING AND PURPOSE

KURTZ: Now what do you think is the next major problem facing the world?

KAHN: If the first problem is nuclear war and the second is the problem of accelerated growth, the next problem is the lack of a sense of meaning and purpose. Low morale is and will be a problem for the United States and the developed world. There is the whole question of what kind of character structure you want, the issue of what you mean by humanism, the problem of values for the United States. There's a terrible split between what I call the "high culture" and "middle cultures." People in the "high culture" simply do not understand the value structure of the middle class. The next split is associated with the meaning and purpose of life.

KURTZ: In your view is the emergence of the humanist left also part of the problem?

KAHN: The humanist left is the most characteristic symptom of the problem.

KURTZ: Is not the humanist left a response to this loss of meaning and purpose?

KAHN: It is a response which only exacerbates the problem. It is many things—a symptom of the problem, a part of the problem and a response to the problem.

KURTZ: You think the basic question is that of intellectual ideals, goals, and purposes?

KAHN: Yes, but I think the President is in a position to do something to alter the basic attitudes and self-images of Americans, even if such action does not normally fall within the President's domain.

KURTZ: This is a larger issue than the political one?

KAHN: Yes. Once in a while you have a situation in history where a gimmick makes a night-and-day difference. The bicameral legislature in the early days of the Republic was basically a gimmick, but without it you never would have gotten the Constitution accepted. No gimmick—no Constitution. I think there's a gimmick that can be used to fix up the country, which is the bicentennial celebration in 1976.

KURTZ: Do we need a reassessment of purpose?

KAHN: A reassessment. Let me describe it in terms of the Hudson Institute program, which is broader than this. We did a study we called "The Prospects of Mankind." We make much stronger statements than anyone else has made. We claim that with current technology we can support a worldwide population of 20 billion people with 20 thousand dollars per capita. That's a surprise. The most surprising part is that we require no faith in the continued improvement of technology on a worldwide basis. We can do it with what we have now. That's the point we want to make. We had thought it would take improvements in technology.

KURTZ: We can do this with current technology and with the use of resources?

KAHN: That's right. Now, it's clear that improved technology is going to make things even better. It should be easy, not hard. The Hudson Institute believes that we can support 20 billion people at 20 thousand dollars per capita.

KURTZ: This will be a startling study when it's done.

KAHN: The general public should be made aware of this, and the 1976 Bicentennial should be the means by which these pros-

pects are made known. Now in the Bicentennial, the President has the right to look back two hundred years, and he has the right to look ahead to the year 2000—which is only twenty-five years ahead. When you look at the United States on that time scale, things look very good. In twenty-five years you can fix every problem in America—pollution, growth, traffic, housing, you name it.

KURTZ: You said you're a neo-Stoic. You're really a buoyant optimist.

KAHN: No. This is sober realism. There's no problem you can't fix in twenty-five years. What upsets people is the fact that you can't solve problems in five to ten years.

KURTZ: Your trademark is that you've got great confidence. Every problem can be solved.

KAHN: No, I don't say that about the fundamental human problems. But remember the problems people are talking about—they're screaming about the slums, the roads, pollution, you name it. They are material problems. They can all be solved. It just takes money and appropriate planning. All of the country's material problems, as we currently worry about them, can be solved by middle-class standards. And the President has a right to make this observation at the Bicentennial. But he can't make it now, because many will think him dumb, credulous, or deceptive. "Twenty-five years from now! Whom are you kidding?" But during a Bicentennial such "visionary" thinking is acceptable, if not required. He can make the second observation that the worldwide poverty problems, except for that of the hardcore poor, will be mostly solved, and quickly, mainly because of the rapid growth of the U.S. and Japan.

KURTZ: On a worldwide basis?

KAHN: Yes, on a worldwide basis. The employment data is that everybody should have at least about five thousand dollars per capita, by current U.S. and European standards, and everybody should have it by the end of the twenty-first century. It might be even much higher. Now, there will be a few exceptions—mainly those people who don't want it or are feckless. Okay, I can't help that. So that's the basic picture. There are ecologists who picture those people who "drop out" as doing God's work: they are not polluting or using up resources. They then portray those people who work in industry as doing the devil's work by making the world uninhabitable. These ecologists are not helping things. They hold up a project, they prevent refineries from being built, and they see this as God's work.

KURTZ: These are the "moralist" ecologists?

KAHN: Yes, and the point is, they are morally wrong and their opponents should *say* that they are morally wrong.

KURTZ: And the morally right position should be to try to get rid of poverty and to continue growth?

KAHN: Continue growth. That's absolutely right. Now, I'm not saying that growth is without problems. Remember the technological crisis of 1985—if there is terrible growth, it causes all kinds of terrible problems.

KURTZ: Not to grow would be a greater disaster?

KAHN: Yes. The main point is that you don't have to stop growing; you have a choice. The mechanism is there; you've got to steer it.

30 The Transformation of Human Nature

Cousins, Keen, Tunney & Levine

"Man is something to be overcome," wrote Friedrich Nietzsche in *Thus Spake Zarathustra*. Although God is dead, according to Nietzsche, and man can only pin his faith on man, this faith is on man not as he is but as he can become, or as he can overcome his present nature, transform himself into a superior, more admirable form of humanity—the *Übermensch* or Superman. In his present state, man is as inferior to the man-yet-to-be as the monkey is inferior to the present *homo sapiens*. "Man is a rope fastened between animal and Superman—a rope over the abyss . . . What is great in man is that he is a bridge and not a goal."[1]

Nietzsche makes it clear, however, that the coming transformation of man into superman is to be accomplished not by eugenics (or bionics) but by a profound spiritual revolution in humanity, a "transvaluation of all values." The Christian values of the past which consisted of such virtues as love, kindness, humility, and resignation constituted, in Nietzsche's view, a "slave morality." What is needed to meet the challenge of the future is a superior master morality glorifying such virtues as self-overcoming which springs not from the will to suffer or to be resigned, but from the will to power, to overcoming. The new man of the future will be in his nature both rational (Apollonian) and spontaneous (Dionysian). He will no longer be at war with himself and with others as he will have achieved the highest level of discipline over his impulses. His impulses will be channeled toward powerful creative outlets which will enable him to continue to transform himself and the world.

This view that man is something to be overcome did not originate with Nietzsche, although few have expressed it so powerfully and influentially. The Old Testament prophets condemned the excesses of human behavior

477

because they lead to defiance and disobedience of God. The prophets envisaged a radically reformed man who would be fearful of God and obedient to His will. In the *Republic,* Plato outlined his proposals for transforming human nature by instituting both fundamental educational reforms and a state-controlled eugenics program. The ideal man of the future would be sturdy in body, sensitive in feeling, and enlightened in mind. He would be a lover of wisdom rather than a lover of pleasure, an individual directed by reason to achieve harmonious self-actualization within a utopian social setting. This could not come about, however, until philosophers rather than politicians became the rulers of states (see Part Three).

The question today is no longer, "Can human nature be modified?" but, rather, "Should it be modified?" and "According to what model of human nature should this modification be undertaken?" Norman Cousins' essay, "Modern Man Is Obsolete," written after the first atomic bomb was dropped on Japan, concludes that man as we have known him is obsolete and needs radical transformation. A creature that, despite his astonishing scientific advances, has reached the point of being quite capable and even willing to risk the possible extinction of his kind in atomic warfare is a threat both to himself and to life on earth. At the end of his essay, Cousins suggests the changes that must be brought about if man is to survive and prosper in the future. But he recognizes that the alternative—total extinction of civilization or the human race—has become for the first time in history a real possibility. Before we can develop a positive idea of what human nature ought to be, we must remove the social, political, and economic obstacles that prevent us from pursuing truly humanistic goals.

Another model of human nature, representative of a rich and growing body of investigations sometimes called the New Consciousness, is suggested by the selection from Sam Keen. In his *Apology for Wonder,* Keen explains two previous conceptions or models of traditional and modern man. These are *homo admirans* (man the wonderer) and *homo faber* (man the producer). Neither of these conceptions of man or modes of being in the world, in Keen's view, is adequate to define the nature of authentic existence, of a healthy personality. Keen's model of human nature is one in which a balance is achieved between receptivity and manipulation and between wonder and action. As an alternative normative model of human nature, Keen proposes *homo tempestivus,* "the timely, seasonable, or opportune man" in whom the Apollonian virtue of wonder and the Dionysian virtue of action are synthesized in a meaningful lifestyle.

But *homo faber* has had the upper hand in this century, as evidenced by the impact of science and technology. Twentieth-century utopian visions of transformed man and the social order have tended to rely upon scientists instead of philosophers or sages as creators and managers of utopias. Huxley's vision of a Brave New World in which people would no longer be born but decanted in state hatcheries and their bodies and minds biologically programmed by genetic manipulation was intended as a dystopian proposal. However, many today would see genetic engineering as one of the major hopes for, if not a totally transformed human nature, at least an improved organism, one less prone to disease and defect. Superman may no longer be an eccentric ideal or a character in a television series but an actual possibility.

The article on eugenics which completes this section was co-authored by a Senator from California, and it focuses on some of the ethical, legal, and political issues involved in proposals for experiments in genetic modification. As the *New York Times* recently pointed out in an editorial entitled "Letting the Gene Out of the Bottle," ". . . within the scientific community genetic engineering has produced the widest philosophical debate since the splitting of the atom."[2] If this is an accurate statement it is so because the manipulation of human nature, man in control of his own evolution, would have repercussions on all aspects of the future of life in the universe.

NOTES

1.   Friedrich Nietzsche, *Thus Spoke Zarathustra,* trans. R. J. Hollingdale (Baltimore, Md.: Penguin Books, 1961), pp. 43–44.

2.   *New York Times,* March 11, 1977.

Modern Man Is Obsolete

Norman Cousins

Whatever elation there is in the world today because of final victory in the war is severely tempered by fear. It is a primitive fear, the fear of the unknown, the fear of forces man can neither channel nor comprehend. This fear is not new; in its classical form it is the fear of irrational death. But overnight it has become intensified, magnified. It has burst out of the subconscious and into the conscious, filling the mind with primordial apprehensions. It is thus that man stumbles fitfully into a new age of atomic energy for which he is as ill-equipped to accept its potential blessings as he is to counteract or control its present dangers.

Where man can find no answer, he will find fear. While the dust was still settling over Hiroshima, he was asking himself questions and finding no answers. The biggest question of these concerns the nature of man. Is war in the nature of man? If so, how much time has he left before he employs the means he has already devised for the ultimate in self-destruction—extinction? And now that the science of warfare has reached the point where it threatens the planet itself, is it possible that man is destined to return the earth to its aboriginal incandescent mass blazing at fifty million degrees? If not—that is, if war is not in the nature of man—then how is he to interpret his own experience, which tells him that in all of

From *The Saturday Review*, August 1, 1970. The original editorial appeared in 1945, after the atomic destruction of Hiroshima.

recorded history there have been only 300 years in the aggregate during which he has been free of war?

Closely following upon these are other questions, flowing out endlessly from his fears and without prospect of definitive answer. Even assuming that he could hold destructive science in check, what changes would the new age bring or demand in his everyday life? What changes would it bring or demand in his culture, his education, his philosophy, his religion, his relationships with other human beings?

In speculating upon these questions, it should not be necessary to prove that on August 6, 1945, a new age was born. That day marks the violent death of one stage in man's history and the beginning of another. Nor should it be necessary to prove the saturating effect of the new age, permeating every aspect of man's activities, from machines to morals, from physics to philosophy, from politics to poetry; in sum, it is an effect creating a blanket of obsolescence not only over the methods and the products of man but over man himself.

It is a curious phenomenon of nature that only two species practice the art of war—men and ants, both of which, ironically, maintain complex social organizations. This does not mean that only men and ants engage in the murder of their own kind. Many animals of the same species kill each other, but only men and ants have practiced the science of organized destruction, employing their massed numbers in violent combat and relying on strategy and tactics to meet developing situations or to capitalize on the weaknesses in the strategy and tactics of the other side. The longest continuous war ever fought between men lasted thirty years. The longest ant war ever recorded lasted six-and-a-half weeks, or whatever the corresponding units would be in ant reckoning.

It is encouraging to note that while all entomologists are agreed that war is instinctive with ants, not all anthropologists and biologists are agreed that war is instinctive with men. The strict empiricists, of course, find everything in man's history to indicate that war is locked up with his nature. But a broader and more generous, certainly more philosophical, view is held by those scientists who claim that the evidence to date is incomplete and misleading, and that man *does* have within him the power of abolishing war. Prominent among these is Julian Huxley, who draws a sharp distinction between human nature and the *expression* of human nature. Thus, war is not a reflection but an expression of his nature. Moreover, the expression may change, as the factors that lead to war may change. "In man, as in ants, war in any serious sense is bound up with the existence of accumulations of property to fight about. . . . As for human nature, it contains no specific war instinct, as does the nature of harvester ants. There is in man's makeup a general aggressive tendency, but this, like all other human urges, is not a specific and unvarying instinct; it can be molded into the most varied forms."

But even if this gives us a reassuring answer to the question—is war inevitable because of man's nature?—it still leaves unanswered the question concerning the causes leading up to war. The expression of man's nature will continue to be warlike if the same conditions are continued that have provoked warlike expressions in him in the past. And since man's survival on earth is now absolutely dependent on

his ability to avoid a new war, he is faced with the so-far insoluble problem of eliminating those causes.

In the most primitive sense, war in man is an expression of his competitive impulses. Like everything else in nature, he has had to fight for existence; but the battle against other animals, once won, gave way in his evolution to battle against his own kind. Darwin called it the survival of the fittest, and its most overstretched interpretation is to be found in *Mein Kampf*, with its naked glorification of brute force and the complete worship of might makes right. In the political and national sense, it has been the attempt of the "have-nots" to take from the "haves," or the attempt of the "haves" to add further to their lot at the expense of the "have-nots." Not always was property at stake; comparative advantages were measured in terms of power, and in terms of tribal or national superiority. The good luck of one nation became the hard luck of another. The good fortune of the Western powers in obtaining "concessions" in China at the turn of the century was the ill fortune of the Chinese. The power that Germany stripped from Austria, Czechoslovakia, Poland, and France at the beginning of World War II, she added to her own.

What does it matter, then, if war is not in the nature of man so long as man continues through the expression of his nature to be a viciously competitive animal? The effect is the same, and therefore the result must be as conclusive—war being the effect, and complete obliteration of the human species being the result.

If this reasoning is correct, then modern man is obsolete, a self-made anachronism becoming more incongruous by the minute. He has exalted change in everything but himself. He has leaped centuries ahead in inventing a new world to live in, but he knows little or nothing about his own part in that world. He has surrounded and confounded himself with gaps—gaps between revolutionary science and evolutionary anthropology, between cosmic gadgets and human wisdom, between intellect and conscience. The struggle between science and morals that Henry Thomas Buckle foresaw a century ago has been all but won by science. Given time, man might be expected to bridge those gaps normally; but by his own hand, he is destroying even time. Communication, transportation, war no longer wait on time. Decision and execution in the modern world are becoming virtually synchronous. Thus, whatever bridges man has to build and cross he will have to build and cross immediately.

This involves both biology and will. If he lacks the actual and potential biological equipment to build those bridges, then the birth certificate of the Atomic Age is in reality a *memento mori*. But even if he possesses the necessary biological equipment, he must still make the decision which says that he is to apply himself to the challenge. Capability without decision is inaction and inconsequence.

Man is left, then, with a crisis in decision. The main test before him involves his will to change rather than his ability to change. That he is capable of change is certain. For there is no more mutable or adaptable animal in the world. We have seen him migrate from one extreme clime to another. We have seen him step out of backward societies and join advanced groups. We have seen, within the space of a single generation, tribes of head-hunters spurn their acephalous pastimes and rituals and become purveyors of the Western arts. This is not to imply that the change was necessarily for the better; only that change was possible. Changeability with the head-hunters proceeded from external pressure and fear of punishment, true, and was only secondarily a matter of voluntary decision. But the stimulus was there; and mankind today need look no further for stimulus than its own desire to stay alive. The critical power of change, says

Spengler, is directly linked to the survival drive. Once the instinct for survival is stimulated, the basic condition for change can be met.

That is why the quintessence of destruction as potentially represented by modern science must be dramatized and kept in the forefront of public opinion. The full dimensions of the peril must be seen and recognized. Then and only then will man realize that the first order of business is the question of continued existence. Then and only then will he be prepared to make the decisions necessary to assure that survival.

In making these decisions, there are two principal courses that are open to him. Both will keep him alive for an indefinite or at least a reasonably long period. These courses, however, are directly contradictory and represent polar extremes of approach.

The first course is the positive approach. It begins with a careful survey and appraisal of the obsolescences that constitute the afterbirth of the new age. The survey must begin with man himself. "The proper study of Mankind is Man," said Pope. No amount of tinkering with his institutions will be sufficient to insure his survival unless he can make the necessary adjustments in his own relationship to the world and to society.

The first adjustment or mutation needed in the expression of his nature, to use Huxley's words, is his savagely competitive impulses. In the pre-Atomic Age, those impulses were natural and occasionally justifiable, though they often led to war. But the rise of materialistic man had reasons behind it and must be viewed against its natural setting. Lyell, Spencer, Darwin, Lamarck, Malthus, and others have concerned themselves with various aspects of this natural setting, but its dominant feature was an insufficiency of the goods and the needs of life. From biblical history right up through the present, there was never time when starvation and economic suffering were not acute somewhere in the world.

This is only part of the story, of course, for it is dangerous to apply an economic interpretation indiscriminately to all history. Politics, religion, force for force's sake, jealousy, ambition, love of conquest, love of reform—all these and others have figured in the equations of history and war. But the economic factor was seldom if ever absent, even when it was not the prime mover. Populations frequently increased more rapidly than available land, goods, or weath. Malthus believed that they increased so rapidly at times that war or plague became nature's safety valve. This interpretation has undergone some revision, but it is not the interpretation but the circumstances that raise the problem.

Yet, all this has been—or can be—changed by the new age. Man now has it within his grasp to emancipate himself economically. If he wills it, he is in a position to refine his competitive impulse; he can take the step from competitve man to cooperative man. He has at last unlocked enough of the earth's secrets to provide for his needs on a world scale. The same atomic and electrical energy that can destroy a city can also usher in an age of economic sufficiency. It need no longer be a question as to which peoples shall prosper and which shall be deprived. There is power enough and resources enough for all.

It is here that man's survey of himself needs the severest scrutiny, for he is his own greatest obstacle to the achievement of those attainable and necessary goals. While he is willing to mobilize all his scientific and intellectual energies for purposes of death, he is unwilling to undertake any comparable mobilization for purposes of life. He has shattered the atom and harnessed its fabulous power to a bomb, but he balks—or allows himself to be balked—when it comes to harnessing that power for human progress. Even as man stands on the threshold of a new age, he is being pulled back

by his coattails and told to look the other way, told that he must not allow his imagination to get out of hand—all this at a time when he should know almost instinctively that if he can put the same courage, daring, imagination, ingenuity, and skill that he demonstrated in winning the war into meeting the problems of the new age, he can win the peace as well.

He must believe, too, that mobilization of science and knowledge in peace should not be confined to cosmic forces, but must be extended to his other needs, principally health. What a fantastic irony that organized science knows the secret of the atom but as yet knows not a fig about the common cold! Who can tell what advances in medical knowledge might accrue to the welfare of mankind if as much mobilized effort were put into the study of man as there has been of matter! Cancer, heart disease, nephritis, leukemia, encephalitis, poliomyelitis, arteriosclerosis, aplastic anemia—all these are anomalies in the modern world; there is no reason why mobilized research should not be directed at their causes and cure. Nor is there any reason why even old age should not be regarded as a disease to be attacked by science in the same intensive fashion.

Surveying other adjustments he will have to make if he chooses the positive course, man must consider himself in relation to his individual development. He can have the limitless opportunities that can come with time to think. The trend during the last fifty years toward shorter work weeks and shorter hours will be not only continued but sharply accelerated. Not more than half of each week will be spent earning a living. But a revolution is needed in his leisure-time activities—which so far have come to be associated almost entirely with the commodities of vended amusement. Once before, the world knew a Golden Age where the development of the individual —his mind and his body—was considered the first law of life. In Greece, it took the form of the revolution of awareness, the emancipation of the intellect from the limitations of corroding ignorance and prejudice.

Once again, if man wills it, he can be in a position to restore that first law of life. But he will have to effect a radical transformation in his approach to and philosophy of education, which must prepare him for the opportunities and responsibilities of not only his chosen work but the business of living itself. The primary aim should be the development of a critical intelligence. The futile war now going on between specialization and general study must be stopped. There need no longer be any conflict between the two. The individual will need both—specialization for the requirements of research, general knowledge for the requirements of living.

We have saved for last the most crucial aspect of this general survey relating to the first course: the transformation or adjustment from national man to world man. Already he has become a world warrior; it is but one additional step—though a long one—for him to develop a world conscience. This is not vaporous idealism, but sheer driving necessity. It bears directly on the prospects of his own survival. He will have to recognize the flat truth that the greatest obsolescence of all in the Atomic Age is national sovereignty. Even back in the old-fashioned rocket age before August 6, 1945, strict national sovereignty was an anomalous and preposterous holdover from the tribal instinct in nations. If it was anomalous then, it is the quintessence of anomaly now. The world is a geographic entity. This is not only the basic requisite for world government but the basic reason behind the need. A common ground of destiny is not too large a site for the founding of any community.

Reject all other arguments for *real* world government—reject the economic, the ideological, the sociological, the humanitarian arguments, valid though they may be. Consider only the towering problem of policing the atom—the problem of keeping the smallest particle of matter from destroying all matter. We are building on soap bubbles if we expect this problem to be automatically solved by having America, Britain, and Canada keep the secret to themselves. That is not only highly improbable, but would in itself stimulate the other nations to undertake whatever additional research might be necessary over their present experimentation to yield the desired results. In all history, there is not a single instance of a new weapon being kept exclusively by any power or powers; sooner or later either the basic principles become generally known or parallel devices are invented. Before long, the atomic bomb will follow the jet plane, the rocket bomb, radar, and the flame thrower into general circulation. We must not forget that we were not the only horse in the atomic derby; we just happened to finish first. The others will be along in due time.

Nor can we rely on destructive atomic energy to take care of itself. Already there is the tempting but dangerous notion to the effect that the atomic bomb is so horrible and the terror of retaliation so great that we may have seen the last of war. Far from banishing war, the atomic bomb will in itself constitute a cause of war. In the absence of world control as part of world government, it will create universal fear and suspicion. Each nation will live nervously from one moment to the next, not knowing whether the designs or ambitions of other nations might prompt them to attempt a lightening blow of obliteration. The ordinary, the inevitable differences among nations that might in themselves be susceptible of solution might now become the signals for direct action, lest the other nation get in the first and decisive blow. Since the science of warfare will no longer be dependent upon armies but will be waged by push-buttons, releasing radio-controlled rockets carrying cargoes of atomic explosives, the slightest suspicion may start all the push-buttons going.

No; there is no comfort to be derived from

the war-is-now-too-horrible theory. There is one way and only one to achieve effective control of destructive atomic energy and that is through centralized world government. Not loose, informal organization. Not even through an international pool, or through an international policing agreement. A police force is no better than its laws, and there can be no laws without government. Finally, the potency of the weapon must dictate the potency of its control.

There is no need to discuss the historical reasons pointing to and arguing for world government. There is no need to talk of the difficulties in the way of world government. There is need only to ask whether we can afford to do without it. All other considerations become either secondary or inconsequential.

It would be comforting to know that the world had several generations in which it might be able to evolve naturally and progressively into a single governmental unit. In fact, even as late as August 5, 1945, it seemed that the Charter of the United Nations had made an adequate beginning in that direction, providing the machinery for revision that might lead within fifteen or twenty years to a real world structure. But the time factor has been shattered. We no longer have a leeway of fifteen or twenty years; whatever must be done must be done with an immediacy that is in keeping with the urgency. Once the basic peace settlements are arranged, the United Nations must convene again for an Atomic Age inventory, undertaking an overall examination of the revolutionary changes in the world since its conference in San Francisco in the long-ago spring of 1945.

If all this sounds like headlong argument, posing methods or solutions that seem above the reach of mortal man, the answer must be that mortal man's reach was long enough apparently to push science and invention ahead by at least five hundred years during five years of experimentation on atomic energy. His abil-

ity to do this not only indicates that he can extend or overextend himself when pressed but emphasizes the need to do the same with government.

Man must decide what is more important —his differences or his similarities. If he chooses the former, he embarks on a path that will, paradoxically, destroy the differences and himself as well. If he chooses the latter, he shows a willingness to meet the responsibilities that go with maturity and conscience. Though heterogeneity is the basic manifestation of nature, as Spencer observed, a still greater manifestation is the ability of nature to create larger areas of homogeneity that act as a sort of rim to the spokes of the human wheel.

True, in making the jump to world government, man is taking a big chance. Not only does he have to create the first world authority, but he shall have to make sure that this authority is wisely used. All through history there has been too great a contradiction between ideals and institutions and the forces that have taken over those ideals and institutions. We have too often allowed the best ideas to fall into the hands of the worst men. There has not been a great ideal or idea that has not been perverted or exploited at one time or another by those who were looking for means to an end— the end being seldom compatible with the idea itself.

This is the double nature of the challenge: to bring about world government and to keep it pure. It is a large order, perhaps the largest order man has had to meet in his 50,000-odd years on earth, but he himself has set up the conditions that have made the order necessary.

All these are the various mutations and adjustments needed in the expression of man's nature, in his way of life, his thinking, his economics, his education, his conditioning and orientation, and his concept of government in an Atomic Age. But if he rejects this, the first course, there is yet another way, an alternative to world government. This is the second course. Preposterous as this second course may seem, we describe it in all seriousness, for it is possible that through it man may find a way to stay alive—which is the central problem under consideration in this editorial.

The second course is relatively simple. It requires that man destroy, carefully and completely, everything relating to science and civilization. Let him destroy all machines and the knowledge that can build or operate those machines. Let him raze his cities, smash his laboratories, dismantle his factories, tear down his universities and schools, burn his libraries, rip apart his art. Let him murder his scientists, his doctors, his teachers, his lawmakers, his mechanics, his merchants, and anyone who has anything to do with the machinery of knowledge or progress. Let him punish literacy by death. Let him abolish nations and set up the tribe as sovereign. In short, let him revert to his condition in society in 10,000 B.C. Thus emancipated from science, from progress, from government, from knowledge, from thought, he can be reasonably certain of safeguarding his existence on this planet.

This is the alternative to world government —if modern man wishes an alternative.

Wonder and the Authentic Life: Homo Tempestivus

Sam Keen

We are now in a position to gather up many suggestions and clues and answer the question with which this chapter began: What is the place of wonder within the economy of the authentic life? By constructing a broad typology of pathology we have been led to the conclusion that the delicate balance of human existence may be upset by either too little or too much wonder. If the Apollonian personality minimizes wonder in the tightly controlled world it has domesticated by the imposition of philosophical, psychological, or social necessity, the Dionysian personality is inundated by the mysterious givenness of things and is awash in the endless possibilities of the oceanic consciousness.

While we are able to agree with the advocates of the Dionysian consciousness that the dominant personality type in contemporary Western society is repressively Apollonian, and our culture stands in danger of losing the virtues of enthusiasm, hope, spontaneity, celebration, and wonder, we cannot believe that the death of Apollo will lead to their recovery. The apocalyptic demands of the advocates of Dionysus neglect the reality of the psychological and political present by refusing to take responsibility for articulating any appropriate means for moving step by step to freer per-

From Sam Keen, *Apology for Wonder*. Copyright © 1969 by Sam Keen. By permission of Harper & Row, Publishers, Inc.

sonality and social structures. They do not speak to the problem of creating a personality structure and social order within which it might become possible to carry on the day-to-day responsibilities of making a living, raising children, and creating a community in a more spontaneous and graceful manner. Away with all permanent structures! Down with the ego and repression! Freedom now! Tune in, turn on, and drop out! While such slogans intoxicate the young and set them to dancing for a time, they tell nothing of the triumph and quiet ecstasy that result from seeing the pursuit of justice prepare the ground for the advent of love, the discipline of five-finger exercises yielding to the creative moment, or patient and courageous decisions resulting in sustained *growth* toward mature freedom. It was wisdom that led the Greek spirit to require the temple at Delphi to be shared by Apollo and Dionysus. Either god worshiped alone leads to madness.

HEALTH AS BALANCE: WONDER AND ACTION

As a guiding star to that balance which is the essence of both sanity and authentic life, we may adopt as a maxim Chesterton's statement, with which this chapter was prefaced. These twin demands of the human spirit for wilderness and home, wonder and welcome, adventure and security, or Dionysus and Apollo may be considered structural principles of the authentic life, as they are also the essential components of all rationality. In defining what he calls "the sentiment of rationality," William James maintains that the philosophic attitude consists of a balance between two cravings. There is, first, the passion for distinguishing—for being acquainted with the particulars, in all their chaotic multiplicity. And second, there is the passion for simplification—for unification of diverse particulars under one universal law. A philosophy which listens only to heterogeneous particulars—which remains in wonder before the givenness of things—fails to get us out of the "empirical sand-heap world"; it leaves us with utter pluralism, which is the psychological equivalent of schizophrenia and the philosophical equivalent of nihilism. Likewise, a philosophy which forces all particulars into an abstract explanatory synthesis, and thus eliminates multiplicity, makes of the world a monotonous plenum in which there is no room for novelty or surprise. An adequate philosophy must preserve the adventure of standing in wonder before the mystery of the given as well as the security of explanations, boundaries, and limits which domesticate chaos.

If authentic life is defined as requiring a balance of Dionysian and Apollonian elements, we may conclude that neither *homo admirans* nor *homo faber* is an adequate model of man. *Homo admirans* accepted the world as a gift and affirmed that the highest and most appropriate human act was contemplation and celebration; however, he refused to assume full responsibility for remaking the world closer to the heart's desire. Poverty, suffering, and the wanton ravages of flood, erosion, and disease have too often been accepted by traditional cultures of East and West as unalterable aspects of the giveness of life with which it is impious to tamper. *Homo faber* has abandoned the notion of the impious and has assumed total responsibility for molding the chaos of nature into the secular city, but in so doing has lost the ability to celebrate anything other than the products of his own hands. The wilderness is not the source of gifts for *homo faber;* it is only chaos waiting to be fabricated into something of meaning. Thus he fears all areas in which wilderness and spontaneity reign—the dream, the dance, the moment of wonder. If traditional man evaded his responsibility by devoting himself too largely to the Dionysian enthusiasm, modern man has exalted his power to discipline the world to such an extent that he fears and suspects anything grace-ful or gratuitous.

We are in need of a new model of man which will allow us to preserve the valid insights of both traditional and modern, Dionysian and Apollonian, models of man. An adequate model must make clear that what have often been taken as mutually exclusive models of man are more properly seen as different moments in perception and action which must achieve a balance for vivid, full human life to be sustained. In summary, the elements that must be components of an adequate model of man may be represented schematically as those belonging to what we may call the principles of wonder and action.

Wonder

The Dionysian mode of being in the world.

Man-the-dancer responds to experience as it is given in its multiplicity. *Homo ludens* is oriented toward play, levity, fantasy, spontaneity; he is libidinal, erotic, living primarily in feeling and sensation, destroying boundaries and exploring diversity.

Action

The Apollonian mode of being in the world.

Man-the-maker fabricates an environment from the raw material of nature. *Homo faber* is oriented toward work, seriousness, realism, regularity; he is governed by a strong ego, living primarily by thinking and willing, by erecting boundaries, giving form, intellectual and material possession.

Without wonder there is no knowledge of the *world*. Thus, one axis of knowledge is: intuition, silence, welcoming receptivity, relaxation in the presence of the other. In wonder man attends to the kaleidoscopic plurality of the world; he juxtaposes and savors particulars. Wondering knowledge is immediate, sensuous, enthusiastic, a matter of participation and union, an overcoming of the estrangement between subject and object.

In wonder, value and meaning are discovered as given in the encounter. Authentic life involves the "feminine" moment of opening to, welcoming, nurturing the meanings which are given in the immediacy of sensation, relationship, environment, personality; it involves letting things happen, listening in silence for the meaning that is prior to the word.

Personality begins with the gift of relationship. In the beginning is the breast, the world of total succor. The world of primal experience is a matrix of gift and limitation.

Appropriate responses to the world as given in wonder are: admiration, gratitude, appreciation, celebration, contemplation.

This mode of perception and being in the world has traditionally been championed by religion and the arts.

Without action there is no *knowledge* of the world. Thus, one axis of knowledge is: judgment, abstraction, categorization, synthesis. Laboring reason goes beyond immediacy in a search for understanding. Intelligence acting upon the world to reduce the chaos of plurality to terms that are manageable. Laboring reason searches for coherence, simplicity, unity, and usefulness. The knowledge which results from laboring reason is pragmatic, objective, universal, and verifiable.

In acting, man creates values and meanings by his vows, covenants, contracts, projects. Authentic life involves the "masculine" moment of aggressive control, of projecting and realizing a world; it involves making things happen, speaking the words that shape the world.

Identity begins with decision and action. To separate the self from the matrix one must pass from what is imposed to what is chosen. In the world of mature experience chosen and given limits are in harmony.

Appropriate responses to the world which must be created by human action are: problematic questioning, searching for explanations, solutions, causes.

This mode of perception and being in the world has become dominant in the West with the development of secular science and technology.

A philosophical definition of health, creative life, or authentic selfhood must incorporate the dominant emphases of these two modes of being in the world and their respective models of man. The philosopher must resist the ideological demands of religious and secular orthodoxies which create pressure toward the adoption of a model of man which requires the rejection of the insights of all competing models. Health is to be found in balance, in wholeness—in polychrome existence. Orthodoxy always demands purity of heart and foolish consistency. Thus, medieval Christendom created an atmosphere in which it was difficult for the individual to credit his longings for and experience of potency to recreate the world through investigation and action. And in a parallel manner,

secular technocracy creates a spiritual climate within which investigation and action are approved, but wonder, hope, and basic trust are suspect. The repressive demand that forces us to choose between wonder or action, grace or responsibility, and gratitude for the gift of life or radical freedom in a contingent world leads to the destruction of the synthesis which is the essence of creative personality. The task of philosophy is to see life steadily and whole; therefore is has the prophetic responsibility of protesting against any ideological castration of man.

THE PRINCIPLE OF OSCILLATION

There is increasing evidence that healthy personality is structured upon a principle of oscillation. Studies reveal that creativity arises out of the interplay between primary and secondary process-thinking (id and ego). The creative process is an oscillation between play and work, fantasy and realism, and imagination and conceptualization. Also, as we saw in dealing with wonder and the growth of reason in children, there is a rhythm in the development of a healthy child between juxtaposing and syncretism, or between incorporating the concrete new items that are given in raw experience and the creation of an overall schema of understanding and explanation. This same process characterizes the ideal harmony of creative adult life. Creative perception and creative action go hand in hand; sensitive perception of concrete particulars is bound up with the creation of wider and more meaningful patterns of explanation and relationship. It is an illusion to believe that we can have one of these modes of relating to the world without the other. Pathology involves just such an effort to deny wonder-openness-novelty-possibility or action-decision-regularity-necessity. Health lies in the both/and (not the either/or): in granting proper reverence to both Dionysus and Apollo. In the mature personality the pendulum is constantly swinging between wonder and action, and the further it swings in one direction, the further it may go in the opposite direction. The more the self is at home in the world it has created by accepting and defining its gifts and limits, the freer it is to wander and appreciate strangeness. Ontological security and ontological wonder increase proportionately. It is the insecure self that lives in anxiety and defensiveness, protecting itself from the intrusion of any novelty which threatens its tenuous integration. Having the security of a home is the source of the psychological strength necessary to undertake an adventure. In the creative personality the lion and the lamb lie down together without ceasing to be lion and lamb; the gypsy and the homesteader live side by side in peace.

WISDOM AS TIMELINESS

The question naturally arises: How is it possible to combine the virtues of Dionysus and Apollo within a single model of man? By way of answering this we must point out that *both Dionysian and Apollonian models of man are governed by spatial metaphors.* The Dionysian way advises that we break down the *boundaries.* The Apollonian way insists that we observe the *limits* of the possible as they have been set forth by metaphysical vision, social convention, or religious tradition. There is, in the history of philosophy, another organizing principle which cannot be neglected. The wisdom tradition maintains that *time* rather than *space* is the organizing principle for the authentic life. The unity of the authentic life is plural; its wisdom lies in understanding the necessity for the changing moments and seasons of life.

> For everything there is a season, and a time
>   for every matter under heaven:
> a time to be born, and a time to die;
> a time to plant, and a time to pluck up what
>   is planted;
> a time to kill, and a time to heal;
> a time to break down, and a time to build
>   up;
> a time to weep, and a time to laugh;
> a time to mourn, and a time to dance;
> a time to cast away stones, and a time to
>   gather stones together;
> a time to embrace, and a time to refrain
>   from embracing;
> a time to seek, and a time to lose;
> a time to keep, and a time to cast away;
> a time to rend, and a time to sew;
> a time to keep silence, and a time to speak;
> a time to love, and a time to hate;
> a time for war, and a time for peace.

Wisdom comes, usually with age, when a man can look back over his years and realize that there is an economy to the seasons of life. He sees that the times of strife, suffering, and waiting which seemed so difficult to endure were as necessary to the formation of personality as the times of love, joy, and ecstasy. To love and accept the self as it is, is to accept all the moments that formed it.

The difference between the wise man and the fool lies in the sense of timing. *The wise man knows what time it is in his own life and in the life of the community.* He knows that sensing the *kairos* (the prepared or ripe moment) is more important than conforming to the compulsive rhythm of chronological time. Thus, the wise man is able to give himself gracefully to seemingly contradictory experiences, because he knows that they belong to different seasons of life, all of which are necessary to the whole. Spring and winter, growth and decay, creativity and fallowness, health and sickness, power and impotence, and life and death all belong within the economy of being. The fool distrusts the polychrome character of life and hence is always trying to hold on to what is past or to grasp prematurely what is coming. Because of his basic distrust and resentment of the economy of the seasons, the fool loses even the ability to move gracefully within the present. Folly is founded on the conviction that time bears us only toward death and gradually destroys all that is of value to the individual, and therefore it must be resisted. The life of the fool, then, becomes the vain effort to run from death by using the energies of life to create a monument or a memory. Being unable to accept the gracefulness of time, the fool seeks to stem its flow.

THE TIMELY MAN— HOMO TEMPESTIVUS

For the sake of convenience we may christen the model of man recommended by the wisdom tradition in philosophy with the title, *homo tempestivus*—the timely or opportune man, the man for all seasons. In using this designation, we must be careful to guard against the negative connotations which have become associated with opportunism. The opportunist is reckoned to have no integrity or moral purposiveness, hence in any moment—like a chameleon—he changes his moral coloration to blend in with the background in order to serve his own selfish interests. The word "opportune," however, may easily bear the connotation of a strong, but flexible, moral stance. Webster defines opportune as "1. right for the purpose; fitting in regard to circumstances; said of time. 2. happening or done at the right time; seasonable; well timed; timely." Thus, *homo tempestivus* is a proper designation for the man whose wisdom consists of knowing what time (*kairos*) it is. The opportunist belongs to what Kierkegaard called the "aesthetic" mode of existence in which the self, being empty of moral decisiveness and purpose, must be filled from without by the happenings of the moment. The opportune man, on the other hand, has a strong ethical commitment and an equally strong sense of the ambiguities of the situation within which his ethical commitment must be lived out. Given both the wondering sensitivity to the situation and the impulse toward ethical activity and responsibility, *homo tempestivus* seeks to act *appropriately*. Indeed, we may say that the prime ethical ideal of the wise man is appropriate response.

It is, in principle, impossible to create a casuistry of appropriate responses. Perhaps the best metaphor to illuminate the ethical style of *homo tempestivus* is that of the dance. The wise man is a dancer; he hears the music issuing from his situation, he is sensitive to his partners, and he moves boldly to commit himself to the rhythmic patterns that emerge in the dance. The fool always wants the certainty of knowing all the steps before he will commit himself to the dance; thus he is too timid to learn to trust himself to be appropriately moved by the music and the motion.

The sense of timing which is the essence of wisdom comes only when one trusts oneself to the dance. One of the great moments in modern literature is when the repressed Apollonian character of "the boss" in Kazantzakis's novel turns to the Dionysian Zorba and says, "Zorba—teach me to dance," for he has then realized that the touch of madness necessary to authentic life is identical with the decision to trust the self to move gracefully when there is no rule of casuistry.

Homo tempestivus avoids the extremes that lead to the Apollonian and Dionysian pathologies without sacrificing the virtues of either god. He is sufficiently endowed with a sense of wonder to refuse to make any premature closure of the limits of the possible. In wondering he finds hope, because he recognizes that to be exiled within the limiting structures of temporal existence is to be ignorant about the range of ultimate possibilities. Because the future is open, he can throw the full weight of his freedom behind the project to which he commits himself, knowing it is impossible to determine in advance the range of novelty that is possible. On the other hand, *homo tempestivus* is sufficiently Apollonian to be aware of the provisional limits which are currently the defining structures of human personality, culture, and historical existence. There is a time to die, and this means that all human existence is under the necessity of defining its limits within the known horizons of the penultimate. There may be grounds for the wise man to hope, since the ultimate context of human existence is unknown and unknowable, but the penultimate necessity of death demands a radical decisiveness and resignation to limited possibilities. Both the timeless imagination of the id and the tragic realism of the ego are necessary—both dreams and decisions, wonder and action.

When I was a boy I used to swim in the Indian River Inlet in southern Delaware. Where the outgoing water from the bay met the incoming surge from the ocean, the currents were swift and the waves wild and irregular. Many people lost their lives in these waters, and the inlet was rightly considered extremely treacherous. With a confidence born of folly, I played with the irresistible danger. However, having survived the folly of repeated swimming in dangerous tides, I can now see that I learned something of the principles (if not the practice) of wisdom in those waters. The outgoing currents were too swift to swim against, but if you would only yield yourself to them they would carry you to a point beyond the inlet, where it was possible to swim cross-current and come back to shore in the calm waters in the lee of the jetty that formed the south boundary of the inlet. When swimming in turbulent waters, wisdom lies in knowing when to relax and when to struggle.

Genetic Engineering

John V. Tunney & Meldon E. Levine

The cry has been raised by many that the impact of science has been too fruitful. It has been raised by some with regard to the nuclear sciences. It might well be reiterated in the near future with regard to the biomedical sciences.

The biomedical sciences have provided man with the increasing ability to modify and to alter human genes. These developments touch upon the most fundamental issues of human life. They portend the ability to reshape man.

Accepted attitudes about the inviolable nature of man's genetic endowment now stand challenged by science. The political impact of this challenge might be just as powerful as the scientific impact. Unless the potential provided by the biomedical sciences is properly understood, the inevitable social response might be fashioned out of fear. When complex problems appear too terrifying or mysterious, some people might seek simple solutions that prove inadequate or improper.

If people become sufficiently frightened—if they feel the need to be rescued from a menace they do not understand—they are more likely to delegate freedoms and less likely to respond with reason. If the polity responds to the scientific community through fear and mistrust, we could witness the erosion of our most precious freedoms. Political

From *Saturday Review*, August 5, 1972, pp. 23–28.

alteration—like genetic alteration—might be irreversible. If our personal liberty is ever lost, it might never be recovered.

Consequently, the most important and enduring of our freedoms are linked with the manner in which the biomedical sciences are understood and applied. The issues raised by the biomedical sciences must be exposed to public scrutiny. They must be discussed candidly, openly, and at once.

In approaching these issues, we the authors must of necessity wear several "hats." The first "hat," if you will, is a multifaceted one, fashioned around our own personal backgrounds—our social, philosophical, and ethical beliefs. The second "hat" is a legal one, obtained after studying the law and participating in it over a period of years. The third is a legislative one, obtained from the unique perspective to which we are exposed in helping to propose, evaluate, and create the laws of this land.

It is important to recognize that all political figures wear "hats" of this nature. They are all different, depending upon the individual background and experience of the person, but they influence him as he evaluates and determines policy, especially in an area as sensitive and as potentially explosive as genetic engineering.

Before we discuss the ethical, legal, or legislative view, however, it is important to set forth the most salient aspects of genetic engineering and to indicate our assessment of the state of the art in each of these aspects.

ABORTION AND AMNIOCENTESIS. The technique of amniocentesis—prenatal sampling of the amniotic fluid surrounding the fetus—is frequently used to provide advice on therapeutic abortions. The procedure is relatively safe, but we do not yet have the ability, with amniocentesis, to detect all genetic defects. Within five years most monogenic defects that we understand will be detectable thereby, but even then questions will remain unanswered as to whether amniocentesis affects the eventual intelligence of the child.

MASS GENETIC SCREENING. In this, too, we appear to be on the threshold. The technique is available for many diseases, although not for some others. However, it has already become evident that many people will oppose mass genetic screening—whether of children or adults—for a variety of personal reasons. Some feel it is an invasion of personal rights; others do not want children genetically defective to find out that they are so afflicted. Again, however, the technology is increasingly available.

MONOGENIC GENE THERAPY. Modification of certain cells in terms of their genes, or monogenic gene therapy, we have been advised, has not yet been performed successfully. It should, however, be a possibility for certain diseases within five years. As we gain more knowledge about monogenic defects, the possibility of monogenic gene therapy will become more of a reality in broader areas.

IN VITRO FERTILIZATION. Both in vitro fertilization and reimplantation in the uterus have been performed successfully in experimental animals. If the research in this area is not seriously inhibited by external controls, the technology for in vitro fertilization and for reimplantation in human beings should be available within five to ten years, or perhaps even earlier. Recently a Yugoslav scientist advised a conference in Tokyo that he had developed an instrument for oöcyte (egg) transplant into the uterus.

CLONING. Cloning of frogs, where a replica of an individual is developed from one of its somatic cells, has already been successful. The technology for the cloning of mammals will be available within five years, and, unless research is stopped, the technology for the cloning of human beings might be available within anything from ten to twenty-five years.

POLYGENIC GENE THERAPY. We are very far away from achieving polygenic gene therapy —perhaps 50 to 100 years. Our understanding of polygenic gene defects still is extremely primitive. For a variety of reasons it is considerably more complicated to isolate and trace a polygenic trait than to isolate and trace a monogenic trait.

One of the most powerful arguments presented in favor of employing one or more of the technologies of genetic engineering in the direction of genetic intervention is that man's genetic load is increasing. In other words, the total number of genetic defects carried by man has been increasing. This has been occurring as a result of the increased mutation rate that accompanies population growth and the decreased natural selection rate occasioned by modern medicine and technology. About one child in twenty, for example, is now said to be born with a discernible genetic defect.

The question then arises: Should the human species attempt to employ these new technologies to deal with this increased genetic load? Paul Ramsey of Yale has stated that "it is no answer to say that changes are already taking place in humankind or that men are constantly modifying themselves by changes now consciously or unconsciously introduced. . . ." He argues, as a Protestant theologian, that scientific intervention in this area is a questionable human aspiration, as he puts it, "to Godhood." Regardless of the merits of Ramsey's position, the very vigor with which he defends it suggests the extent to which ethical issues are at stake.

The ethical questions raised by the possibilities implicit in genetic engineering are no less fundamental than the issues of free choice, the quality of life, the community of man, and the future of man himself. Thus, it becomes evident that one's own sense of ethics, one's personal view of right and wrong, one's own standard of conduct or moral code, are essential components of decision making in this extremely sensitive area.

Many political scientists like to believe that political decision making can be objectified, that a process can be delineated by which political decisions are made. Through such a process, it is assumed, decisions and actions can be predicted. The wisdom of these political scientists is questionable for a variety of reasons. One of the most important is the significant subjective component of political decision making—the large realm left to one's own values and ethics.

This realm affects all aspects of lawmaking. It is especially important in any political or even legal approach to genetic engineering. One's own values or ethics must inevitably be brought to bear upon a variety of important questions in this area, questions that can be evaluated only by subjective criteria. In an effort to rationalize some of the issues involved, we will attempt to draw some distinctions and to articulate some criteria for analysis. Some of these criteria have been suggested by others; some are our own. We suggest them not as a definitive list but as a reminder that it will be very important to apply criteria such as these to any legislative or legal analysis of the implications of genetic engineering.

Let us posit a list of ten general considerations suggesting possible ethical distinctions:

First, if we are to engage in any eugenics, negative or positive, we must confront three vital questions that pervade this entire subject: What traits are to be considered desirable? Who is to make that determination? When in the course of human development will the choice be made? These questions cannot be underestimated in their importance to the future of man, particularly when we are considering biological alternatives that might not be reversible.

Second, we must ask whether the genetic engineering or "improvement" of man would affect the degree of diversity among men. Does it presume a concept of "optimum" man? Is diversity important as a goal in itself? Does—or should—man seek an "optimum," or does he seek a "unique"? What would the quest for an "optimum" do for our sense of tolerance of the imperfect? Is "tolerance" a value to be cherished?

Third, we should consider whether it might be appropriate to delineate different biological times or moments—at least in humans—during which experimentation might occur. Do different ethical considerations apply if we attempt to distinguish between experimentation on an unfertilized sperm or egg, a fertilized sperm or egg, a fetus, an infant, a child, or an adult? Might the factors to be balanced in making a decision as to whether experimentation is proper vary at different stages of human development?

Fourth, is there a workable difference between, on the one hand, genetic "therapy" to correct genetic factors known to cause somatic disease and, on the other hand, genetic "engineering," defined as techniques to alter man in terms of some parameters other than somatic disease? Might it be appropriate to attempt such a distinction in definitions in this emotionally charged area? Might the term "genetic therapy" evoke less emotionally charged reactions than the term "genetic engineering"? Might it, in fact, be preferable to respond more receptively to those areas of genetic work that are primarily "therapeutic"? Or is such a distinction unworkable?

Fifth, it would seem to be advisable to ask whether a particular technique or technology is devised for the therapeutic treatment of an individual or whether it is designed to have a broader societal impact. This potential distinction has a variety of ramifications. For example, it should be asked whether techniques developed for the therapy of an individual patient automatically diffuse into the general public for purposes other than this therapy. Are physicians operationally capable of restricting the use to one group, or does societal pressure make them semiautomatic dispensers of seemingly desirable technologies?

Sixth, we might ask whether any eugenics program—whether positive or negative, voluntary or compulsory—does not imply a certain attitude toward "normalcy," toward a proper norm for human activity and behavior, and toward expectations with regard to the behavior of future generations of human beings. Implicit in this question are distinctions with regard to positive versus negative eugenics programs and also with regard to compulsory versus voluntary eugenics programs.

Seventh, how are words such as "normal," "abnormal," "health," "disease," and "improvement" defined? Are they words that can be operationally used to determine what should be done in the area of genetic engineering?

Eighth, we must ask if the quest for genetic improvement would be continuous. Would it invariably make all children "superior" to their parents? What would be the social consequences of this? Would it institutionalize generation gaps and isolate communities by generations?

Ninth, we should consider whether the institutionalization of a quest for genetic improvement of man is likely to lead to his perception of himself as lacking any worth in the state in which he is. What does this do to the concept of the dignity of the human being in his or her own right, regardless of some "index of performance"?

Tenth, if we have a well-developed ability to perform genetic therapy as an assault upon certain diseases but such therapy is not available for all who have the affliction or who desire the "cure," the question will immediately arise as to how to determine which patients will receive it. Are some classes or groups of people more desirable patients or more worthy of treatment? How will selection be made? By what criteria will those decisions be reached?

Questions such as these ten can be answered only by appealing to ethical, or so-called moral, arguments. When we enter this realm, it is important to remember that no one has a greater claim to wisdom than anyone else. All men have a stake in this area, and all men have a right to be heard.

We would like to offer three additional thoughts that might affect all of the ethical judgments involved. Two are caveats, and one might be a preliminary guide for analysis.

The two caveats are reminders of the imprecision of measurement and the difficulty of meaningful analysis in this area. As for the imprecision of measurement (caveat number one), Ramsey states that "many or most of the proposals we are examining are exercises in 'what to do when you don't know the names of the variables.'" While that might be somewhat harsh, he is accurate in his suggestion that prediction of behavior or even of most genetic disease will be very difficult, owing not only to polygenic factors but also to such other imponderables as pinpointing a recessive trait in its heterozygous state and predicting the influence of environmental factors.

The second caveat is the difficulty of meaningful analysis. Some values we will be asked to compare will be like comparing apples and oranges. How can one, for example, compare the possible deep satisfaction experienced by an infertile woman carrying and bearing a child that was fertilized in vitro and reimplanted in her uterus with the 1 or 2 or 5 per cent chance that the child will be deformed? In measuring eugenic traits to be cherished, how can one compare intelligence (even assuming it can be defined) with love?

In making genetic choices—and in selecting those who will make them—one should not forget such caveats.

The last of these attempts at ethical classification is an effort to ask the question of just where in the broad field of genetic engineering the ethical issues will arise. At what level in the process? Professor Abram Chayes of Harvard Law School has suggested that at least three levels can be discerned at which the questions posed above might arise:

First, the general level of research. Should research be pursued that might lead to technologies that will give science the genetic capability to engineer human beings?

Second, the level of treating human disease. Questions will, of course, be raised as to what exactly is a disease—and how it is defined. (Should socially undesirable or disruptive behavior be treated as an illness? Are some forms of mental illness proper candidates for genetic therapy?) Even assuming that those questions can be answered, ethical considerations will arise with regard to whether the disease should be treated with a newly available genetic technique.

Third, the broad level of attempting to affect society—the level of what some will consider an improvement of the human species.

These levels overlap to some degree with the questions we have already raised, and it appears clear that the ethical pressures that will be directed against the continuation of the activity will become increasingly strong

as we move from the first to the second and then to the third level. While these considerations by no means exhaust the ethical realm, they do suggest the enormity of the problems with which we are attempting to deal. Perhaps the attempt—however primitive—at ethical classification might also offer the lawyer some general guidance.

It might be asked, for example, whether there are legal as well as ethical distinctions between negative and positive eugenics. Are there legal differences between an attempt, on the one hand, to treat an individual for disease by either monogenic or polygenic gene therapy and an attempt, on the other hand, to control behavior or otherwise alter society's norms? Does it matter—legally—at what point in the state of human development the therapy or the engineering is conducted: whether in the stage of birth control, in the realm of abortion, in treating a minor or an adult? Does it matter—legally—how the therapy or the engineering is conducted, whether it is voluntary or compulsory, whether for punitive or eugenic reasons, or whether the physician has freely and openly obtained the consent of the patient?

Clearly, these distinctions ought to be important—legally as well as ethically. They touch upon fundamental and traditional legal principles, principles that have been applied in Anglo-American jurisprudence for a number of years. They offer the lawyer a variety of factors that will help in his analysis.

Law, at least in the United States, can be said to operate on three broad tiers or levels. First, we have constitutional law, or the legal framework set forth by the Constitution of the United States and by the courts in interpreting the Constitution. Second, we have statutory law, or law that is enacted by statute —either of a state or of the federal government. No statute can contravene a constitutional requirement. But, in the absence of a constitutional prohibition or pre-emption, federal and state legislatures can enact statutory standards to respond to a variety of needs, such as those that arise in the areas of health and welfare. Third, in the absence of a controlling constitutional or statutory provision, the courts rely upon the body of law known as the common law—those legal principles that have emerged from judicial decisions. The issues raised by the technology of genetic engineering affect constitutional, statutory, and common-law principles. We shall briefly consider each of these legal tiers.

At least three constitutional factors clearly emerge when one considers the general subject of genetic engineering. The first is the right to privacy. The Fourth Amendment to the Constitution declares that "the right of the people to be secure in their persons, houses, papers, and effects, against unreasonable searches and seizures, shall not be violated. . . ." This language has been interpreted to guarantee to the individual a constitutional right of privacy. Genetic engineering raises questions with regard to the extent and inviolability of that right. The second factor involves the rights protected in the Fifth and Fourteenth amendments, which guarantee that no person shall be deprived of life, liberty, or property without due process of law. Third, and perhaps the most important factor that the Constitution brings to bear upon genetic engineering, is the *approach* of constitutional law—the method of analysis that courts have developed for dealing with constitutional issues. Apart from the technicalities inherent in whether state action is or is not involved—a threshold question in any constitutional analysis—constitutional law requires the government to show a more compelling governmental need when the abridgment of fundamental freedoms is involved.

Let us take two examples. Contrast, for instance, a government-sponsored compulsory program of negative eugenics, designed to eliminate a certain genetic disease, with a government-sponsored compulsory program of positive eugenics, designed to control behavior. As both programs are compulsory, both could infringe the fundamental freedom of procreation and possibly of marriage. However, compelling state interest could be advanced as a more legitimate argument in eliminating a disease rather than in controlling or altering behavior. The eradication of disease has long been accepted as a vital social objective. We do not offer this dichotomy in an effort to support the negative eugenics program. In fact, we would probably oppose it. But we do think that a constitutional analysis of the two approaches would bring different factors into being and might yield different results in the two cases.

To move from constitutional law to statutory law, it should be noted at the outset that a variety of statutes in numerous American jurisdictions have attempted to impose eugenics controls. Professor William Vukowich of Georgetown has written: "In the early 1900s, many states enacted laws that prohibited marriage by criminals, alcoholics, imbeciles, feebleminded persons, and the insane. Today most states prohibit marriage by persons with venereal disease but only a few states have laws which are similar to those of the early 1900s. Washington and North Dakota, however, still prohibit marriage by women under forty-five and men of any age, unless they marry women over forty-five, if they are an imbecile, insane, a habitual criminal, a common drunkard, feebleminded or [a] person who has . . . been afflicted with hereditary insanity."

A number of the more recent developments in the field of genetic engineering, however, go entirely unregulated. Sperm banks—which may be used as a reserve of sperm for artificial insemination by third-party donors, for example—are an excellent example of institutions for which pertinent statutes do not exist.

Their administration is entirely up to the persons operating them.

That is an instance in which our third legal tier, the tier of the common law, must be our guide. In the absence of constitutional or statutory guidance, we must turn to the common law for our standards. Here again the law is neither silent nor comprehensive. It falls somewhere in between. Assume this set of possibilities: Amniocentesis is an everyday practice, held by most doctors to be free of harmful effects such as infection. A woman who has not been offered amniocentesis gives birth to a Mongoloid child. Is her obstetrician liable for malpractice?

Common-law tort principles of malpractice would probably hold that the doctor would, in fact, be liable. This is so because the common law in determining negligence tends to follow whatever is the accepted medical practice for a particular community. But is this a viable solution? Would it be appropriate to require amniocentesis even if the mother— or the doctor—has strong religious convictions that preclude consideration of an abortion under any circumstances? What about offering amniocentesis under those circumstances? And what about the legal rights of an egg that has been fertilized and grown in a test tube? Does the *father* have any rights? What rights does the *mother* have? Or the doctor? Do common-law tort or property rights apply to this question?

However one evaluates these issues, they must be faced. If one does not wish to face them with the exclusive guidance of the common law, the result will be the consideration of new legislation. To the extent that current law is inadequate, legislation must be developed.

In considering the possibility that legislation must be developed, we both are painfully aware of the potential inadequacy of the legal and the legislative processes in responding to issues presented by science. In the area of genetic engineering, science may be outpacing the legal and legislative processes. It may be presenting challenges to which our lawyers and legislators are ill-equipped to respond. Our legislative system may be poorly equipped to respond to these problems because of at least two inherent difficulties: its speed and its scope.

Our legislative process generally works slowly. Sen. Walter Mondale, for example, first introduced legislation that called for a commission to study the effects of genetic engineering almost five years ago. That bill passed the Senate unanimously last year, but it has not yet been acted upon by the House of Representatives. Just initiating a study commission on so momentous a subject has already, then, taken longer than five years.

Not only is our political system slow. It is, obviously, only national in scope. Generally, that is not a significant problem to the people in Washington who are considering various legislative proposals. Most proposals are only national in scope—or less. Genetic engineering, however, is clearly a matter of international concern. It will require, if any controls or guidelines are to be effectively suggested, international agreements. This also will serve as a political or legislative constraint.

Recognizing these constraints, we still believe that certain constructive steps can be taken—steps that will begin to offer legislative rationalization to the field. If the legislative system begins to consider these problems now, it might be possible to respond politically and legislatively before it is too late.

Conversely, we fear the consequences that could be wrought if informed legislative consideration of the issues inherent in genetic engineering does not soon begin. If the legislation comes as a result of dramatic scientific breakthroughs that scare the public, the outcome might be hasty and unwise political decisions predicated upon inadequate information and upon fear. If debates and discussions begin now, however, the ultimate legislation might emanate from deliberate and reasoned political, social, and scientific analysis. We do not believe that, at this point, it would be appropriate to suggest answers to the momentous issues raised by genetic engineering. But we do believe that we know enough to undertake certain legislative initiatives. Let us suggest three.

First, Congress should enact the Mondale bill [S. J. Res. 75], which provides for a study and evaluation of the ethical, social, and legal implications of advances in biomedical research and technology. The proposed study commission might serve as a preliminary vehicle for educating the public about the foreseeable social consequences of biological advances. Such a commission might best be an international one, but that is logically a second step.

Second, and perhaps equally important, is the initiation of technology assessment in all institutions that disburse funds, direct research, or provide grants that are related to biomedical concerns. It has long been obvious that technological developments have implications that affect society in a variety of ways and that their impact cannot be limited to an analysis of the technical aspects of the product or of the innovation. Similarly, the myriad implications of the developments of biomedical research reach out to all segments of society. Technological assessment should be a part of any analysis of any project that involves a potentially new biomedical development.

Third, it might be appropriate for Congress to earmark a small proportion of health research funds (say one-quarter or one-half of 1 per cent) for research into possible social consequences of biological technologies either presently available of foreseeable.

It is not only the legislature, however, that can initiate improvement in communication between the scientific community and the general public as well as expansion of public awareness of and concern with these issues. Four other suggestions might be worthy of consideration:

First, private foundations should be urged to initiate programs to bridge presently existing gaps between the sciences and the humanities, exposing people in each area to people in the other, and making the ideas of each readily available and understandable to the other.

Second, universities should consider establishing additional programs whereby students in the humanities would be exposed to the methodologies familiar to those in the scientific disciplines, and vice versa. The two general groups should feel a closer relation to and understanding of each other in universities as well as elsewhere. The effective separation of these two groups in universities—particularly at the graduate level, but even at the undergraduate level—establishes a line of demarcation between those in the sciences and those in the humanities, with very inadequate and narrow bridges to unite the two general areas.

Third, research proposals in the biological area should perhaps be assessed by institutional research review committees that include nonscientists. Some form of technological assessment, in other words, or consideration of the ethical moral, and social implications of biological projects—by nonscientists —should be considered at the level of all research proposals in this general area.

Fourth, it might be appropriate for the medical profession itself to study the ways in which the technologies it uses for the benefit of individual patients may affect society as a whole if used for purposes other than the cure of individual patients. The "individual treatment versus social engineering" dichotomy should be considered clearly and carefully by the medical profession and should probably be emphasized more strongly than it currently is.

These efforts to bring society and the biomedical sciences closer together are, in our opinion, essential. Dr. Andre Hellegers, director of the Joseph and Rose Kennedy Institute for the Study of Human Reproduction and Bioethics of Georgetown University, has testified before the Senate that "nothing could be worse than that society should come to fear scientific progress. . . . I can foresee that the occasional, seemingly sensational scientific episode will so frighten society as to undermine the very support [that] science needs in order to continue to make contributions to improve the lot of mankind. . . . It is high time that there be started an educative process that explains to the country the precise nature and limitations of the scientific process and the place it occupies in man's control of his environment. . . . No segment can stand apart in this interdependent society. If it attempts to do so, it is bound to cease being supported. The sooner the relationship of science to society is examined and explained for all to see the better it will be both for science and for society."

This testimony touches upon two very important facts of American political life, neither of which should be forgotten. First is the theory of political accountability; if the public supports something financially, the public is entitled to know what it is that it is supporting. Second is the foundation of political democracy; thoughts, suggestions, proposals, and policies should be scrutinized in the market place of ideas. Political debate and public discussion are healthy and are conducive to the best analysis of any position. Particularly in an area as fraught with subjectivity as this one, it is vital that the issues raised be aired, discussed, and debated. We are dealing in an area in which there is no monopoly of expertise. Rather, it is a field in which men trained in a variety of different areas, or even in no special area, bring to bear their own unique perspective, or, if you will, "expertise." We are dealing with a subject in which morality, or one's own subjective sense of ethics, is pervasive. We are, therefore, dealing with an area in which all persons have a right and a special claim to be heard.

There are certain suggestions that we would offer in any debate on this subject. We would suggest that among the values that man ought to protect most fully are the values of humility, of compassion, of diversity, and of skepticism. We would suggest that any scientific or technical initiatives of one generation that would foreclose or eliminate the options of future generations—any decision today that implies an ability to predict the human traits that will be most cherished tomorrow —smacks of arrogance and should be avoided. We would suggest that man should exercise the utmost caution in this sensitive field and that decisions that will be genetically irreversible might require a wisdom we do not possess. We would also suggest that there is no reason why the ethics or morality of any one of us is better than that of any other. In the realm of morality each of us has an equal claim to wisdom.

Therefore, the issues raised by the biomedical scientists must be debated, and the debate must begin now. If we postpone debate in this area, we might face irreversible trends not only in genetics but also in political freedoms.

All segments of society should be involved in the debate these new technologies demand. The techniques must be discussed and debated among lawyers, doctors, theologians, legislators, scientists, journalists, and all other segments of society. The issues raised require interdisciplinary attention. We cannot begin too soon to consider them.

31   Love in the Future Good Life

May & Otto

The contemporary existential psychotherapist Rollo May seeks to probe human feelings in order to understand the present human condition and our future prospects. Today people are increasingly experiencing feelings of emptiness, loneliness, powerlessness, and anxiety. These feelings, May believes, are symptoms of deep and often traumatic changes in western civilization, changes that have occurred so rapidly that people have either not been aware of them or so far been unable to find ways of coping with them.

In *Man's Search for Himself*, May traces "the roots of our malady" to a number of losses that we have experienced in our time: the loss of a center of value in our society; the loss of a sense of self; the loss of language for personal communication; the loss of a sense of relatedness to nature; and the loss of the sense of tragedy.[1] As a result of his analysis of the contemporary human predicament, May gives our condition a bleak diagnosis, but this does not necessarily mean, he points out, that we have a bleak prognosis.

In order to move toward recovery, human beings must rediscover within themselves the sources of strength, integrity, and meaning. They must rediscover their selfhood by learning again what it means to be an authentic human being. This, May recognizes, is not easy. First of all, people must face their feelings honestly and unflinchingly, learning to distinguish between, for example, normal and neurotic anxiety and between feelings of narcissism and feelings of self-worth. They must learn that consciousness of self is not the same as introversion, and that before they can achieve inner wholeness they must recover their relation with the unconscious aspects of the self. One must not reject all suffering as evil and undesirable, but recognize that some suffering is inevitable in the struggle to be, to become a free and self-directing person. It is painful to cut one's emotional umbilical cord and to take complete responsibility for one's self. But, like Erich Fromm, May sees no other way to achieve selfhood except to become one's own father, mother, a child. As May puts it, "the continuum of differentiation which is the life pilgrimmage of the human being requires developing away from incest and toward the capacity to 'love outwardly'."[2]

Along with other existentialists, May is mainly concerned with the struggle to be, the effort to find a meaning that is created through effort and choice. Human existence precedes human essence, and what a person becomes will depend for the most part on what he does—the extent to which he can use the freedom he possesses. While May is not an extreme indeterminist, he does believe that human beings have some important degree of freedom, which is "man's capacity to take a hand in his own development."[3] Further, one's sense of freedom increases with one's consciousness of self. May agrees with Nietzsche, who said that freedom is the capacity "to become what we truly are." Of course, May recognizes the factors which can sometimes limit the degree of freedom we possess: for example, our heredity, our environment, our aptitudes, and the time and culture in which we live. Freedom always occurs within a structure. It is incompatible with either anarchy or despotism.

In his discussion of human problems, May stresses not only the psychological but also the ethical dimensions of the quest for self-knowledge and self-fulfillment. "Man is the ethical animal," he points out, and thus he devotes considerable attention to the development in man of a "creative conscience," a conscience that accepts responsibility without being overburdened by excessive guilt, a conscience that can judge without being dogmatic and can guide without being autocratic, a conscience that is aware, mature, liberated. To develop this kind of conscience, May recognizes, takes courage, the courage "not to assert one's self but to give one's self."[4] In a word, it takes commitment. Socrates, in May's view, admirably manifested that kind of courage, and we too may learn to develop it with increased self-awareness, self-discipline, and self-transcendence.

When one learns to become a person in his own right, then and only then is he capable of giving and receiving mature love. May views his book *Man's Search for Himself* to be a "preface to love," in that "the real problem for people in our day is preparatory to love itself, namely to become *able* to love."[5] Love, as May defines it initially, is a "delight in the presence of the other person and an affirming of his value and development as much as one's own."[6] Love is not narcissism; it is not dependency; it is not self-abnegation. May devoted another book, *Love and Will*, to exploring more fully the nature of love and to differentiating its various forms. In that book, as in *Man's Search for Himself*, he expresses his conviction that even in the turmoil of the contemporary world one does not have to feel lost, lonely, or alienated as one cultivates awareness and commits himself to the painful but rewarding task of self-creation. As he puts it,

> Does not the uncertainty of our time teach us the most important lesson of all—that the ultimate criteria are the honesty, integrity, courage, and love of a given moment of relatedness? If we do not have that, we are not building for the future anyway; if we do have it, we can trust the future to itself.[7]

In agreement with Rollo May, Herbert A. Otto believes that the growth of personality and the development of our potential require love from conception (alpha) to death (omega). But we need to nourish love by means of concrete programs of action. We need to develop an intensive, interdisciplinary study of love and its function in human life starting with the important love of the infant for the mother, an all-encompassing love which Otto calls primary narcissism. There must also be studies of the relation of love to religious mysticism, the nonverbal communication of love, love and the communal movement, and the relation of love to current mental health care. With proper funding, new approaches and new questions could be explored. The growth of T-Groups and encounter experiences have not, generally, been successful in transmitting how love, sensitive caring, may be more important to people and their relationships. But these techniques need to be sharpened, increased, and enhanced. Love Team centers or projects where misconceptions of love are dispelled could be encouraged. A renaissance of love and the regeneration of our society are interdependent, and both are necessary to the growth of the individual in our society. These practical steps could go a long way, Otto thinks, toward the amelioration of a society in which people are alienated not only from others but also from themselves.

NOTES

1. See Rollo May, *Man's Search for Himself* (New York: Signet, 1953), Chap. 2.
2. Ibid., p. 136.
3. Ibid., p. 160.
4. Ibid., p. 227.
5. Ibid., p. 238.
6. Ibid., p. 241.
7. Ibid., p. 276.

Communion of Consciousness

Rollo May

Let them render grace for grace,
Let love be their common will.
　　—Athena, summing up the duty of
　　　the Athenians, in the *Orestia* of
　　　Aeschylus.

When we look for answers to the questions we have been discussing, we find, curiously enough, that every answer seems to somehow impoverish the problem. Every answer sells us short; it does not do justice to the depth of the question but transforms it from a dynamic human concern into a simplistic, lifeless, inert line of words. Hence, Denis de Rougement says, at the end of his *Love in the Western World,* that there "probably aren't any answers."

The only way of resolving—in contrast to solving—the questions is to transform them by means of deeper and wider dimensions of consciousness. The problems must be embraced in their full meaning, the antinomies resolved even with their contradictions. They must be built upon; and out of this will arise a new level of consciousness. This is as close as we shall ever get to a resolution: and it is all we need to get. In psychotherapy, for example, we do not seek answers as such, or cut-and-dry solutions to the question—which would leave the patient worse off than he

originally was in his struggling. But we seek to help him take in, encompass, embrace, and integrate the problem. With insight, Carl Jung once remarked that the serious problems of life are never solved, and if it seems that they have been solved, something important has been lost.

This is the "message" of all three of the central emphases in this book: eros, the daimonic, and intentionality. As the function of eros, both within us and in the universe itself, is to draw us toward the ideal forms, it elicits in us the capacity to reach out, to let ourselves be grasped, to perform and mold the future. It is the self-conscious capacity to be responsive to what *might* be. The daimonic, that shadowy side which, in modern society, inhabits the underground realms as well as the transcendent realms of eros, demands integration from us on the personal dimension of consciousness. Intentionality is an imaginative attention which underlies our intentions and informs our actions. It is the capacity to participate in knowing or performing the art proleptically—that is, trying it on for size, performing it in imagination. Each of these emphases points toward a deeper dimension in human beings. Each requires a participation from us, an openness, a capacity to give of ourselves and receive into ourselves. And each is an inseparable part of the basis of love and will.

The new age which knocks upon the door is as yet unknown, seen only through beclouded windows. We get only hints of the

Reprinted from *Love and Will* by Rollo May. By permission of W. W. Norton & Company, Inc. Copyright © 1969 by W. W. Norton & Company, Inc.

new continent into which we are galloping: foolhardy are those who attempt to blueprint it, silly those who attempt to forecast it, and absurd those who irresponsibly try to toss it off by saying that the "new man will like his new world just as we like ours." There is plenty of evidence that many people do not like ours and that riots and violence and wars are necessary to force those in power to change it. But whatever the new world will be, we do not choose to back into it. Our human responsibility is to find a plane of consciousness which will be adequate to it and will fill the vast impersonal emptiness of our technology with human meaning.

The urgent need for this consciousness is seen by sensitive persons in all fields and is especially made real by the new consciousness in race relations, where we live if we transcend racial differences and die if we do not. I quote James Baldwin: "If we—and now I mean the relatively conscious whites and the relatively conscious blacks, *who must, like lovers insist on, or create, the consciousness of the others*—do not falter in our duty now, we may be able, handful that we are, to end the racial nightmare, and achieve our country, and change the history of the world. If we do not now dare everything, the fulfillment of that prophecy, re-created from the Bible in song by a slave, is upon us: 'God gave Noah the rainbow sign, No more water, the fire next time.' "[1]

Love and will are both forms of communion of consciousness. Both are also *affects* —ways of *affecting* others and our world. This play on words is not accidental: for affect, meaning affection or emotion, is the same word as that for *affecting* change. An affect or affection is also the way of making, doing, forming something. Both love and will are ways of creating consciousness in others. To be sure, each may be abused: love may be used as a way of clinging, and will as a way of manipulating others in order to en-

force a compliance. Possibly always some traces of clinging love and manipulating will crop up in the behavior of all of us. But the abuse of an affect should not be the basis for its definition. The lack of both love and will ends up in separation, putting a distance between us and the other person; and in the long run, this leads to apathy.

LOVE AS PERSONAL

In the embracing and transformation of the antinomies of love and will, we have discovered that sexual love moves through *drive* to *need* to *desire*. Freud began with sex conceived as a drive, a push from the past, a stored-up set of energies. This concept came largely from the fact that his patients were victims of Victorian repression. But we now know that sexual love can evolve from drive, through primary need, to desire. As a *drive*, sexuality is essentially biological, has the character of force, and is physiologically insistent. *Need* is a less imperative form of drive. So long as a need is repressed, it tends to become a drive. We shall lump the two together here, as *need*, contrasting them both with *desire*.

The need is physiological in origin, but becomes imperious because of the constant stimulation of sexuality all about us. In contrast, the desire is psychological, and arises from human (in a total organismic sense) rather than physiological experience. The first is an economy of scarcity; the second is an economy of abundance. The need pushes us from the rear—we try to get back to something, to protect something, and we are then *driven* by this need. The desire, on the other hand, pulls us ahead to new possibilities. The need is negative, the desire positive. To be sure, if sexual love, or specifically sex, is unrelieved when the person is in a constant state of stimulation over a period of time, it reverts to its earlier status as a compelling need and may then become a drive.

We find, from sources where we would least expect, impressive evidence that even on infrahuman levels, sex is not the primary need we have thought it to be. In Harry Harlow's extensive work with rhesus monkeys, it becomes clear that the monkeys' need for contact, touch, and relationship takes precedence over the "drive" toward sex. The same is true of Masserman's experiments with monkeys, where sex turns out not to be the primary, all-encompassing drive. To be sure, sex *is* a primary need for the race, and its biological survival depends on sex. But as our world becomes less and less bound by the exigencies of that kind of biological survival—indeed *overpopulation* is our threat—and more and more open to the development of human values and choices, we find that this emphasis is not constructive, and that the individual does not depend upon sexuality as a primary need.

Now it is in the shift from drive to desire that we see *human* evolution. We find love as personal. If love were merely a *need,* it would not become personal, and will would not be involved: choices and other aspects of self-conscious freedom would not enter the picture. One would just fulfill the needs. But when sexual love becomes *desire,* will is involved; one chooses the woman, is aware of the act of love, and how it gets its fulfillment is a matter of increasing importance. Love and will are united as a task and an achievement. For human beings, the more powerful need is not for sex per se but for relationship, intimacy, acceptance, and affirmation.

This is where the fact that there are men and women—the polarity of loving—becomes ontologically necessary. The increased personal experience goes along with the increased consciousness; and consciousness is a polarity, an either/or, a saying "yes" to this and "no" to that. This is why, in an earlier chapter, we

referred to the negative-positive polarity held in the theories of both Whitehead and Tillich. The paradox of love is that it is the highest degree of awareness of the self as a person and the highest degree of absorption in the other. Pierre Teilhard de Chardin asks, in *The Phenomenon of Man,* "At what moment do lovers come into the most complete possession of *themselves,* if not when they are *lost* in each other?"[2]

The polarity which is shown ontologically in the processes of nature is also shown in the human being. Day fades into night and out of darkness day is born again; yin and yang are inseparable and always present in oscillation; my breath expires and I then inspire again. The systole and diastole of my heartbeat echo this polarity in the universe; it is not mere poetry to say that the beat of the universe, which constitutes its life, is reflected in the beating of the human heart. The continuous rhythm of each moment of existence in the natural universe is reflected in the pulsating blood stream of each human being.

The fact that love is personal is shown in the love act itself. Man is the only creature who makes love *face to face,* who copulates *looking* at his partner. Yes, we can turn our heads or assume other positions for variety's sake, but these are variations on a theme—the theme of making love vis-à-vis each other. This opens the whole front of the person— the breasts, the chest, the stomach, all the parts which are most tender and most vulnerable— to the kindness or the cruelty of the partner. The man can thus see in the eyes of the woman the nuances of delight or awe, the tremulousness or the angst; it is the posture of the ultimate baring of one's self.

This marks the emergence of man as a psychological creature: it is the shift from animal to man. Even monkeys mount from the rear. The consequences of this change are great indeed. It not only stamps the love act as irrevocably *personal,* with all the implications of that fact, one of which being that the lovers can speak if they wish. Another consequence is the accentuation of the experience of intimacy in giving the side of the person closest to "ourselves" in the sexual experience. The two chords of love-making—one's experience of himself and his experience of the partner—are temporarily merged here. We feel our delight and passion and we look into the eyes of the partner also reading there the meaning of the act—and I cannot distinguish between her passion and mine. But the looking is fraught with intensity; it brings a heightened consciousness of relationship. We experience what we are doing—which may be play, or exploitation, or sharing of sensuality, or fucking, or love-making, or any form thereof. But at least the norm given by this position is personal. We have to block something off, exert some effort, to make it *not* personal. This is ontology in the psychological area: the capacity for self-relationship constitutes the genus *Homo sapiens.*

The banal word "relating" is lifted to an ontological level in this act which is anything but banal, in which male and female re-enact their counterpart of the age-old cosmic process, each time virginally and with surprise as though it were the first time. When Pythagoras talks of the music of the stars, he refers to a music which has as its obligato the basic act of sexual love.

One result of this personal aspect of sexual love is the variety it gives us. Consider, as an analogy, Mozart's music. In some portions of his music Mozart is engaged in elegant play. In other portions his music comes to us as pure sensuous pleasure, giving us a sheer delight. But in other portions, like the death music at the end of *Don Giovanni* or in his quintets, Mozart is profoundly shaking: we are gripped by fate and the daimonic as the inescapable tragedy rises before us. If Mozart had only the first element, play, he would sooner or later be banal and boring. If he presented only pure sensuality, he would become cloying; or if only the fire and death music, his creations would be too heavy. He is great because he writes on all three dimensions; and he must be listened to on all these levels at once.

Sexual love similarly can not only be play, but probably an element of sheer play should be regularly present. By this token, casual relationships in sex may have their gratification or meaning in the sharing of pleasure and tenderness. But if one's whole pattern and attitude toward sex is only casual, then sooner or later the playing itself becomes boring. The same is true of sensuality, obviously an element in any gratifying sexual love: if it has to carry the whole weight of the relationship, it becomes cloying. If sex is only sensuality, you sooner or later turn against sex itself. The element of the daimonic and tragic gives the depth and the memorable quality to love, as it does to Mozart's music.

ASPECTS OF THE LOVE ACT

Let us summarize how the love act contributes to the deepening of consciousness. First, there is the tenderness which comes out of an awareness of the other's needs and desires and the nuances of his feelings. The experience of tenderness emerges from the fact that the two persons, longing, as all individuals do, to overcome the separateness and isolation to which we are all heir because we are individuals, can participate in a relationship that, for the moment, is not of two isolated selves but a union. In this love act, the lover often cannot tell whether a particular sensation of delight is felt by him or his loved one—and it doesn't make any difference. A sharing takes place which is a new *Gestalt,* a new field of magnetic force, a new being.

The second aspect of the deepened consciousness comes from the affirmation of the self in the love act. Despite the fact that many people in our culture use sex to get a short-circuited, ersatz identity, the love act can and ought to provide a sound and meaningful avenue to the sense of personal identity. We normally emerge from love-making with renewed vigor, a vitality which comes not from triumph or proof of one's strength but from the expansion of awareness. Probably in love-making there is always some element of sadness—to continue an analogy suggested in an earlier chapter—as there is in practically all music no matter how joyful (precisely because it does not last; one hears it at that moment or it is lost forever). This sadness comes from the reminder that we have not succeeded absolutely in losing our separateness; and the infantile hope that we can recover the womb never becomes a reality. Even our increased self-awareness can also be a poignant reminder that none of us ever overcomes his loneliness completely. But by the replenished sense of our own personal significance in the love act itself, we can accept these limitations laid upon us by our human finiteness.

This leads immediately to the third aspect, the enrichment and fulfillment—so far as this is possible—of personality. Beginning with the expansion of awareness of our own selves and our feelings, this consists of experiencing our capacity to give pleasure to the other person, and thereby achieving an expansion of meaning in the relationship. We are carried beyond what we were at any given moment; I become literally more than I was. The most powerful symbol imaginable for this is *pro-creation*—the fact that a new being may be conceived and born. By new being I mean not simply a literal "birth," but the birth of some new aspect of one's self. Whether literal or partially metaphorical, the fact remains that the love act is distinguished by being procreative; and whether casual and ephemeral or faithful and lasting, this is the basic symbol of love's creativity.

A fourth aspect of new consciousness lies in the curious phenomenon that being able to give to the other person in love-making is essential to one's own full pleasure in the act. This sounds like a banal moralism in our age of mechanization of sex and emphasis on "release of tension" in sexual objects. But it is not sentimentality; it is rather a point which anyone can confirm in his own experience in the love act—that to give is essential to one's own pleasure. Many patients in psychotherapy find themselves discovering, generally with some surprise, that something is missing if they cannot "do something for," give something to, the partner—the normal expression of which is the giving in the act of intercourse itself. Just as giving is essential to one's own full pleasure, the ability to receive is necessary in the love relationship also. If you cannot receive, your giving will be a domination of the partner. Conversely, if you cannot give, your receiving will leave you empty. The paradox is demonstrably true that the person who can only receive becomes empty, for he is unable actively to appropriate and make his own what he receives. We speak, thus, not of receiving as a passive phenomenon, but of *active receiving:* one knows he is receiving, feels it, absorbs it into his own experience whether he verbally acknowledges it or not, and is grateful for it.

A corollary of this is the strange phenomenon in psychotherapy that when the patient feels some emotion—eroticism, anger, alienation, or hostility—the therapist normally finds himself feeling that same emotion. This inheres in the fact that when a relationship is genuine, they empathetically share a common field of emotion. This leads to the fact that, in everyday life, we normally tend to fall in love with those who love us. The meaning of "wooing" and "winning" a person is to be found here. The great "pull" to love someone comes precisely from his or her loving you. Passion arouses an answering passion.

Now I am aware of all the objections which will immediately be raised to this statement. One is that people are often repulsed by someone's loving them. Another is that my statement does not take into account all the added things one is motivated to *do* for the beloved and that it places too great an emphasis on passivity. The first objection, I answer, is the reverse proof of my point: we inhabit a *Gestalt* with the one who loves us, and to protect ourselves against his emotion, possibly with good reason, we react with revulsion. The second objection is merely a footnote to what I am already saying—that if someone loves us, he *will* do the many things necessary to show us that this is so; the actions are not the cause, however, but part of the total field. And the third objection will be made only by people who still separate passive and active and who have not accepted or understood active receiving. As we all know, the love experience is filled with pitfalls and disappointments and traumatic events for most of us. But all the pitfalls in the world do not gainsay the point that the given affect going out to the other does incite a response, positive or negative, in him. To quote Baldwin again, we are "like lovers [who] insist on, or create, the consciousness of the others." Hence, *making* love (with the verb being neither a manipulative nor accidental one) is the most powerful incentive for an answering emotion.

There is, finally, the form of consciousness which occurs ideally at the moment of climax in sexual intercourse. This is the point when the lovers are carried beyond their personal isolation, and when a shift in consciousness occurs which they experience as uniting them with nature itself. There is an accelerating experience of touch, contact, union to the point where, for a moment, the awareness of separateness is lost, blotted out in a cosmic feeling of oneness with nature. In Hemingway's novel, *For Whom the Bell Tolls,* the older woman, Pilar, waits for the hero and the girl he loves when they have gone ahead into the mountain to make love; and when they return, she asks, "Did the earth shake?" This seems to be a normal part of the momentary loss of awareness of the self and the surging up of a sudden consciousness that includes the earth as well. I do not wish my account to sound too "ideal," for I think it is a quality, however subtle, in all love-making except the most depersonalized sort. Nor do I wish it to sound simply "mystic," for despite limitations in our awareness, I think it is an inseparable part of actual experience in the love act.

CREATING OF CONSCIOUSNESS

Love pushes us toward this new dimension of consciousness because it is based on the original "we" experience. Contrary to the usual assumption, we all begin life not as individuals, but as "we"; we are created by the union of male and female, literally of one flesh, produced by the semen of the father fertilizing the egg of the mother. Individuality emerges *within* this original "we," and by virtue of this "we." True, no one of us would actualize himself at all if he did not, sooner or later, become an individual, did not assert his own identity against his mother and father. Individual consciousness is essential for that. Though we do not begin as lonely selves, it is necessary—as we have lost the first freedom, the Garden of Eden at our mother's breast—that we be able to affirm our individuality as the Garden crumbles and the beginning of a man emerges. As the "we" is original *organically,* the "I" is original in human *conscious-*

ness. This individual is a man because he can accept the crumbling of the first freedom, painful as it is, can affirm it, and can begin his pilgrimage toward full consciousness. The original "we" is always a backdrop against which we conduct the pilgrimage. As W. H. Auden puts it:

Whatever view we hold, it must be shown
Why every lover has a wish to make
Some other kind of otherness his own:
Perhaps, in fact, we never are alone.[3]

We have said that sex is saved from self-destruction by eros, and that this is the normal condition. But eros cannot live without philia, brotherly love and friendship. The tension of continuous attraction and continuous passion would be unbearable if it lasted forever. Philia is the relaxation in the presence of the beloved which accepts the other's being as being; it is simply liking to be with the other, liking to rest with the other, liking the rhythm of the walk, the voice, the whole being of the other. This gives a width to eros; it gives it time to grow; time to sink its roots down deeper. Philia does not require that we do anything for the beloved except accept him, be with him, and enjoy him. It is friendship in the simplest, most direct terms. This is why Paul Tillich makes so much of acceptance, and the ability—curious loss for modern man that this will sound strange—to *accept acceptance.*[4] We are the independent men who, often taking our powers too seriously, continuously act and react, unaware that much of value in life comes only if we don't press, comes in quietly when it is not pushed or required, comes not from a drive from behind or an attraction from in front, but emerges silently from simply being together. This is what Matthew Arnold refers to in his lines,

Only—but this is rare—
When a belovéd hand is laid in ours,

When, jaded with the rush and glare
Of the interminable hours,
Our eyes can in another's eyes read clear,
When our world-deafened ear
Is by the tones of a loved voice caressed—
A bolt is shot back somewhere in our
    breast,
And a lost pulse of feeling stirs again;
The eye sinks inward, and the heart lies
    plain,
And what we mean, we say, and what we
    would, we know.
A man becomes aware of his life's flow.[5]

Hence Harry Stack Sullivan emphasized the "chum" period in human development. This period includes the several years, from about eight to twelve, before the heterosexual functioning of the boy or girl begins to mature. It is the time of genuine liking of the same sex, the time when boys walk to school with arms around each other's shoulders and when girls are inseparable. It is the beginning of the capacity to care for someone else as much as for yourself. If this "chum" experience is missing, holds Sullivan, the person cannot love heterosexually afterwards. Furthermore, Sullivan believed that the child cannot love *before* the "chum" period, and held that if one forces it, one can get him to *act* as though he loves someone, but it will be a pretense. Whether or not one accepts these beliefs in their extreme form, the import is still clear.

An added confirmation of the importance of philia is also given in the experiments of Harry Harlow with rhesus monkeys.[6] Harlow's monkeys, who were not permitted to make friends in their childhood, who never learned to play with siblings or "friends" in all sorts of free and nonsexual ways, were those who later could not adequately function sexually. The period of play with peers is, in other words, an essential prerequisite to the learning of adequate sexual attraction and response to the opposite sex later. In his article, Harlow says, "We believe that the role of affection in the socialization of primates can only be understood by conceiving love as a number of love or affectional systems and not as a single emotion."

In our hurried day, philia is honored as a kind of vestige of bygone periods when people had time for friendship. We find ourselves so rushed, going from work to meetings to a late dinner to bed and up again the next morning, that the contribution of philia to our lives is lost. Or we get it mistakenly connected with homosexuality; American men are especially afraid of male friendship lest it have in it some trace of the homosexual. But, at least, we must recall that the importance of philia is very great in helping us to find ourselves in the chum period and begin the development of identity.

Philia, in turn, needs agapé. We have defined agapé as esteem for the other, the concern for the other's welfare beyond any gain that one can get out of it; disinterested love, typically, the love of God for man. Charity, as the word is translated in the New Testament, is a poor translation, but it does contain within it the element of selfless giving. It is an analogy—though not an identity—with the biological aspect of nature which makes the mother cat defend to her death her kittens, and the human being love his own baby with a built-in mechanism without regard for what that baby can do for him.

Agapé always carries with it the risk of playing god. But this is a risk that we need to take and can take. We are aware that no human being's motivations are purely disinterested, that everyone's motivations are, at best, a blending of these different kinds of love. Just as I would not like someone to "love" me purely ethereally, without regard for my body and without any awareness of whether I am male or female, I also don't want to be loved *only* for my body. A child

senses the lie when he is told that adults do something "only for your good," and everyone dislikes being told he is loved only "spiritually."

Each kind of love, however, presupposes care, for it asserts that something does matter. In normal human relations, each kind of love has an element of the other three, no matter how obscured it may be.

LOVE, WILL, AND THE FORMS OF SOCIETY

Love and will take place within the forms of the society. These forms are the myths and symbols viable at that period. The forms are the channels through which the vitality of the society flows. Creativity is the result of a struggle between vitality and form. As anyone who has tried to write a sonnet or scan poetry is aware, the forms ideally do not take away from the creativity but may add to it. And the present revolt against forms only proves the point in reverse: in our transitional age, we are hunting, exploring, reaching about, struggling to assert whatever we can find in the experiment for some new forms. In a homely illustration, Duke Ellington recounts that when he writes music, he must keep in mind that his trumpeter cannot hit the very high notes securely, whereas the trombonist is very good at them; and writing under these impediments, he remarks, "It's good to have limits." Not only with libido and eros, but other forms of love as well: full satisfaction means the death of the human being; love runs itself out with the death of the lovers. It is the nature of creativity to need form for its creative power; the impediment thus has a positive function.

These forms of the society are molded and presented first of all by the artists. It is the artists who teach us to see, who break the ground in the enlargement of our consciousness; they point the way toward the new dimensions of experience which we have, in any given period, been missing. This is why looking at a work of art gives us a sudden experience of self-recognition. Giotto, precursor to that remarkable birth of awareness known as the Renaissance, saw nature in a new perspective and for the first time painted rocks and trees in three-dimensional space. This space had been there all the time but was not seen because of medieval man's preoccupation with his vertical relationship to eternity reflected in the two-dimensional mosaics. Giotto enlarged human consciousness because his perspective required an individual man standing at a certain point to see this perspective. The individual was now important; eternity was no longer the criterion, but the individual's own experience and his own capacity to look. The art of Giotto was a prediction of the Renaissance individualism which was to flower a hundred years later.

The new view of space pictured by Giotto was basic for the new geographical explorations of oceans and continents by Magellan and Columbus, which changed man's relation to his world, and for the explorations in astronomy by Galileo and Copernicus, which changed man's relation to the heavens. These new discoveries in space resulted in a radical upheaval of man's image of himself. Ours is not the first age to be confronted with loneliness arising from man's discovery of new dimensions of external space and similarly requiring new extensions of his own mind. The psychological upheaval and spiritual loneliness in this period was expressed by the poet John Donne,

> And freely men confesse that this world's
>   spent,
> When in the Planets, and the Firmament
> They seeke so many new; . . .
> 'Tis all in pieces, all cohærence gone;
> All just supply, and all Relation:

> Prince, Subject, Father, Sonne, are things
>   forgot,
> For every man alone thinkes he hath got
> To be a Phoenix. . . .[7]

The loneliness was also expressed in the philosopher Leibnitz's doctrine of isolated monads with no doors or windows by which one could communicate with the other. And by the scientist Pascal:

> On beholding the blindness and misery of man, on seeing all the universe dumb, and man without light, left to himself, as it were astray in this corner of the universe, knowing not who has set him here, what he is here for, or will become of him when he dies, incapable of all knowledge, I begin to be afraid, as a man who has been carried while asleep to a fearful desert island, and who will awake not knowing where he is and without any means of quitting the island.[8]

But just as these men were able to find the new planes of consciousness which did, to some extent, fill the new reservoirs of space, so in our day a similar shift is necessary.

Cézanne, at the beginning of our century, saw and painted space in a new way, not in perspective now but as a spontaneous totality, an immediate apprehension of form in space. He painted the *being* of space rather than its *measurements*. As we look at the rocks and trees and mountains on his canvases, we do not find ourselves thinking, "This mountain is behind this tree," but we are grasped by an immediate whole which is mythic in that it encompasses near and far, past and present, conscious and unconscious in one immediate totality of our relationship to the world. Indeed, I was recently intrigued to notice, when looking at one of Cézanne's oils in London, *Le Lac d'Annecy* (which I had never seen before), that he actually paints brushstrokes of the mountain *over* the tree, in complete contradiction to the literal fact that the mountain, as he looked at it, was twenty miles away. In Cézanne, the forms are not before us as compartmentalized items to be added up, but as a presence that grips us. The same is true in Cézanne's portraits—the subject is presented to us not as a face with a forehead and two ears and a nose, but as a presence. The eloquence of this presence beggars our naïve slavery to literalism, and reveals to us *more* truth about the human being than does realism. The significant point is that it *requires our participation in the picture itself if the painting is to speak to us.*

In Cézanne, we see this new world of spaces and stones and trees and faces. He tells us the *old* world of mechanics is gone and we must see and live in the *new* world of spaces. This is evident even with his seemingly banal apples and peaches on a table. But it is particularly clear and eloquent in his paintings of trees. In my college days, I used to walk to classes across the campus of my college under tall elms, whose size and strength I admired. Nowadays, I walk to my office under elm trees on Riverside Drive. Between these two, I saw and learned to love Cézanne's paintings of elms in their architectural grandeur, and what I now each morning see—or rather experience—is altogether different from the college campus. Now the trees are part of a musical movement of forms which has nothing to do with literal measurements of trees. The triangular white forms of the sky are as important as the tree limbs which give them their form; the sheer power hanging in the air has nothing to do with the size of the trees but consists of the lines the branches block in on the gray-blue of the Hudson River.

The new world which Cézanne reveals is characterized by a transcendence of cause and effect. There is no linear relationship in the sense of "A" produces "B" produces "C"; all aspects of the forms are born in our vision simultaneously—or not at all. This demonstrates the new form which will takes in our

day. The painting is mythic, not literalistic or realistic: all categories of time, past, present, and future, conscious and unconscious, are included. And most important of all, I cannot even *see* the painting if I stand totally outside it; it communicates only if I *participate* in it. I cannot see Cézanne by observing his rocks as an accurate rendering of rocks, but only by looking at the rocks as patterns of forms which speak to me through my own body and my feelings and my perceptions of my world. This is the world that I must empathize with. I must give myself to it in a universe of basic forms in which my own life is grounded. This is the challenge to my consciousness which these paintings give.

But how do I know I will find myself again if I let myself go into the orbit of Cézanne's new forms and spaces? This question explains much of the rabid, irrational, and violent opposition many people feel toward modern art; it *does* destroy their old world, and must, therefore, be hated. They can never see the world in the old way again, never experience life in the old way; once the old consciousness is shattered, there is no chance of building it up again. Though Cézanne, bourgeois that he was, seems to present strong, solid forms on which life could look secure, we should not be lulled into failing to realize that in his paintings a radically different language obtains. It was a degree of consciousness which drove Van Gogh into psychosis a few years previously and with which Nietzsche struggled at great cost.

Cézanne's works are the opposite of the "divide-and-conquer" fragmentation which has characterized modern man's relation to nature since Bacon and has led us to the brink of catastrophe. There is in Cézanne a statement that we can, and must, *will* and *love* the world as an immediate, spontaneous totality. In Cézanne and his fellow artists, there is a new language of myth and symbol which will be more adequate to love and will in the new conditions we must confront.

It is the passion of the artist, of whatever type or craft, to communicate what he experiences as the subconscious and unconscious significance of his relation to his world. "Communicate" is related to "commune," and, in turn, both are avenues to the experience of communion and community with our fellowmen.

We love and will the world as an immediate, spontaneous totality. We *will* the world, create it by our decision, our fiat, our choice; and we *love* it, give it affect, energy, power to love and change us as we mold and change it. This is what it means to be fully related to one's world. I do not imply that the world does not exist *before* we love or will it; one can answer that question only on the basis of his assumptions, and, being a mid-westerner with inbred realism, I would assume that it does exist. But it has no reality, no relation to me, as I have no effect upon it; I move as in a dream, vaguely and without viable contact. One can choose to shut it out—as New Yorkers do when riding the subway—or one can choose to see it, create it. In this sense, we give to Cézanne's art or the Cathedral at Chartres the power to move us.

What does this mean concerning our personal lives, to which, at last, we now return? The microcosm of our consciousness is where the macrocosm of the universe is *known*. It is the fearful joy, the blessing, and the curse of man that he can be conscious of himself and his world.

For consciousness surprises the meaning in our otherwise absurd acts. Eros, infusing the whole, beckons us with its power with the promise that it may become our power. And the daimonic—that often nettlelike voice which is at the same time our creative power —leads us into life if we do not kill these daimonic experiences but accept them with a sense of the preciousness of what we are and what life is. Intentionality, itself consisting of the deepened awareness of one's self, is our means of putting the meaning surprised by consciousness into action.

We stand on the peak of the consciousness of previous ages, and their wisdom is available to us. History—that selective treasure house of the past which each age bequeaths to those that follow—has formed us in the present so that we may embrace the future. What does it matter if our insights, the new forms which play around the fringes of our minds, always lead us into virginal land where, like it or not, we stand on strange and bewildering ground? The only way out is ahead, and our choice is whether we shall cringe from it or affirm it.

For in every act of love and will—and in the long run they are both present in each genuine act—we mold ourselves and our world simultaneously. This is what it means to embrace the future.

Love—the Alpha and Omega

Herbert A. Otto

We are at a point in our development where a massive nourishing and flourishing of love has become a necessity if we are to survive as a species. How then are we to foster this massive nourishment and increased emergence of love in today's society? It is in this context that the contributions to *Love Today* become especially meaningful.

On reading the various essays it is once more clear that love and love relationships play a central and dynamic role from inception and birth until our death, and perhaps beyond. Since most people are surrounded by a loving and caring climate at their birth as well as at the time of their death, and since for most people the moment of conception is also a moment of love, love then can be said to be the beginning and the end, the alpha and omega of our being.

Within that context, personality growth and the actualizing of personal potential is our most engrossing lifelong adventure. Many of the contributors to this volume share insights, findings and conclusions *which are directly relevant to this task of expanding our own awareness and self-understanding.*

In turn, this increased self-awareness and understanding can be a means toward our becoming more loving beings. David Orlinsky's conclusion that "love relationships are

From Herbert A. Otto, "Epilogue: Love—The Alpha and Omega," pp. 268–274 in *Love Today: A New Exploration*, Herbert A. Otto, Editor. New York: Association Press, 1972.

. . . necessary links in the process of personal growth" is especially relevant. Alexander Lowen adds to this, "Love has the stabilizing element of the eternal. It is this quality in love that makes growth possible." To complete the picture David Jones finds that love and life goals are "inextricably woven together." The reaffirmation of the centrality of love by the contemporary behavioral scientists and thinkers who have contributed to this volume establishes a sound basis for a number of *action alternatives* which will be of special interest to those who believe the regeneration of love as a force in today's society should receive priority. One action alternative is the intensive study of love.

Specific chapters in this volume pose a variety of fascinating questions and furnish leads to inquiries which can more fully illuminate our understanding of love and its function. The work of the late Pitirim Sorokin, one of our profoundest contemporary students of the subject, invites us to explore the practical applications of his five-dimensional system of love to contemporary living. Alexander Lowen's contribution raises the whole question of the relationship between body motility and the capacity for love. How can we help people toward greater proficiency in the "practice of the love arts" as defined by David Jones—and are there other components of these arts yet to be discovered? Henry Winthrop invites us to focus attention on the relationship between the forms of love and companionship. In his essay on creativity and love Lowell Colston opens the door to a whole series of inquiries. Most intriguing to me are the questions "By what means can our love relationship become more of a bridge for the unfolding of our creative potential?" and "In what ways can we help our creative flow to nourish love and loving behavior in us?"

Other lines of inquiry which are suggested by the contributors are studies of the nonverbal communication of love, inquiries into the relationship between a healthy sensuality and sexuality and the capacity to give and receive love, etc.

I personally believe the phenomenon of "primary narcissism" offers one of the most promising lines of inquiry. Primary narcissism is the love of the infant for the mother, a very powerful undifferentiated emotion; undifferentiated because the infant loves himself, the mother *and* the world without separating one from the other. To the infant this love "encompasseth all things." This is a universal reservoir of goodwill, caring, affection, and perhaps the bedrock on which man's capacity to love is built. There is reason to believe that this reservoir of loving feelings can in some manner be reawakened so that this force will play a more active role in the total personality functioning. The Primal Sensory Experience[1] which I have developed for use in small groups and field-tested over the past three years seems to be a step in the right direction. I am convinced that a whole range of techniques and methods can be devised and researched which will reawaken this primal love. This is a dynamic source, slumbering in every person, which can be tapped and utilized so that we will love ourselves more and be able to love our neighbor more.

The presence within our society of a considerable potential for violence and destruction is paralleled by the presence of an equal if not greater potential for caring and loving. There are many signs that young people especially are aware of this fact and are searching for life-affirmative directions. Significant segments of the younger generation in the United States especially and to a heretofore unsurpassed degree have chosen love and cultivation of loving behavior as a way of life. This appears to be an outgrowth of a strong spiritual thrust into the Eastern and Western religions, philosophy and mysticism which continues to gather momentum. Unfortunately, the media focus most attention on the bizarre and violent aspects of what has come to be called "the youth culture." The end result is the creation of an image which does not correspond to reality—young people emerge as bizarre types, prone to violence or committed to violent change. My association with young people, particularly during my study of the commune movement in this country in 1970, has convinced me *that the media's image effectively denies the most dynamic component of the youth culture—love.* Is it possible that our fear of love surpasses our fear of violence?

A concerted interdisciplinary approach to the study of love is urgently needed and at this point in man's development should be very much higher on the list of priorities than the innumerable inquiries into personality pathology and dysfunction which seem to preoccupy behavioral scientists and members of the helping professions and the mental health movement. The regeneration of love has broad preventive applications and can form the base for the development of a number of far-ranging preventive programs. Hopefully the mental health movement is now at a point in its evolution where there will be increasing recognition that more resources and effort need to be invested in the preventive area.

One action alternative is directly and indirectly suggested both by the nature of the contributions to this volume and some of the writers themselves. This is a multifaceted extensive research approach to the phenomenon of love utilizing the best tools, techniques and resources at our disposal. Adequate funding for such research is a prime requisite. And hopefully this is a field in which private foundations will become interested, and to which the National Institute of Health will be more generous in giving support.

Underlying a concerted research approach would be the following basic questions: (1) What is the role of love in personality functioning and the actualizing of human potential? (2) What is the role of our social institutions vis-à-vis the emergence of caring and loving relationships between members of our society? (3) What generates fear of love and what prevents love from developing in man? (4) What means and approaches can we utilize and develop (including regeneration of our institutions) to help man today to become more of a loving and caring being?

The interdisciplinary team approach to the study of love needs to be particularly concerned with the key question, "How can two of our most powerful institutions—the schools and our religious organizations and churches—be helped to make love more functional in the lives of their members?" Certainly the school curriculum from grade school through college needs to be reexamined in the light of the above question. Where in the maze of classes, information giving and lectures do we explicitly foster the emergence and nurture of love as an ongoing part of the total educational experience? Similarly, sermonizing and the proscriptions and prescriptions from the pulpit utilized by so many religious organizations and institutions have not been very successful in fostering loving behavior in their members. Nor have these religious institutions been notably successful in helping their members to bring religious beliefs and value structures into close consonance with their daily lives and functioning. ("Living what we believe.")

Over the past decade, an increasing number of schools and religious institutions have used small group experiences as a means of coming to grips with man's estrangement from himself and his fellow man. T-group, sensitivity and encounter experiences have proliferated in many institutions. Unfortunately, over the past five years especially, an increasing number of institutions have been disillusioned with the sensitivity and encounter group approach. In most such instances, the many angry confrontations between group members and the consistent emphasis on problems and "hang-ups" has accounted for the strong backlash directed toward this type of group experience.

This ongoing angry, if not hostile, interaction is by no means characteristic of all encounter groups. A major variable here seems to be the facilitator's personality and leadership style which calls forth this consistent response. Institutions which are discontinuing the use of all small group approaches due to their negative experience with "sensitivity" or "encounter" are throwing out the baby with the bath water. A number of small group approaches exist which emphasize the development of a loving and caring climate. These approaches focus on the strengths and potentials of the participants. Problems are dealt with in this context and there is an emphasis on open communication, emotional honesty, and the development of empathy. Dr. Stewart B. Shapiro's program of positive experiencing[2] and the Developing Personal Potential program[3] begun at the University of Utah in 1960 and currently offered by a number of universities and educational institutions are samples. The continued development of group experiences and programs which foster the emergence of love and caring in the participants and *making these or similar programs widely available to as many people as possible offers another major action alternative.*

A final action alternative is the organization of Love Team Centers and the initiation of Love Team Projects, a concept sparked by teacher Arleen Lorrance's program at

Thomas Jefferson High School, Brooklyn, New York. Love Team Centers and Projects can be a means of personal and social regeneration involving many segments and aspects of society including adolescents, college students, school children, minority groups, professionals, senior citizens, etc. Love Team Centers could be organized within schools, churches, clubs, and mental health clinics. These organizations would provide leadership and a physical meeting place for the Love Teams. The teams (with anywhere from five to twelve members) would have two major objectives—to create a loving and caring group climate which will enable participants to give to themselves and to each other and to formulate and carry out specific projects within the larger community expressing the spirit of giving, caring, and loving which has been created within the team.

The Love Team Center concept is based on the recognition that (a) to give love to others, it is best to begin by giving ourselves more love, (b) love is manifest through action, (c) to give and receive love is a means of developing respect for oneself and others, and (d) to give and receive love is a means of joyous and vital living and a way of communing with the essence of being and becoming.

Deep within some core of our being, most of us recognize that although we are led to believe we have only so much love to offer, *the more love we give, the more we have to give.* As Ashley Montagu so well expressed it during a Los Angeles address: "As a result of our misunderstanding of what we are on this earth for, we have brought ourselves very near to the edge of doom. I regard most people as dead, simply as creatures wandering around, having no realization of why they are on this earth. They have no idea that *the only reason for being on this earth is to live to love.*" (Italics added.)

It is within our power to create a renaissance of love—a climate of sensitive caring which cradles each man in the recognition that his relatedness to the other is the means of growth, of becoming, of unfoldment. The shaping of this renaissance offers us an opportunity to join in an act of creation unparalleled in history: fostering the flowering of love in man and utilizing everything we have learned to date in the process, including the resources of our science and technology. In this particular period of explosive social change, our massive investment in the regeneration of love will create optimum conditions for the evolutionary process in which we are engaged. *It is by a massive investment in the regeneration of love that rapid social evolution will fail to turn into the violence of disintegrative revolution.*

If we examine our situation clearly, it becomes very evident that the renaissance of love and the regeneration of our social institutions are different faces of the same coin and are in fact inseparable. It is only when we share our social institutions so that they will allow for the unfoldment and foster the development of love and deep caring of one human being for another that man's best qualities and deeper powers will make their appearance. It is only then that man begins to be in a position to realize his full potential. Paradoxically, the process of institutional regeneration begins with our own regeneration.

The renaissance of love is not a utopian dream. There exists a large array of facts, approaches and techniques which can bring about a rebirth of love, and the research suggested previously will add immeasurably to what we already have. The means are at hand for each man to transform himself into a more caring, loving human being.

Love is the most powerful agent for the transformation of man and his institutions. By learning to let love flow freely we gain both new dimensions of freedom and new responsibility (response-ability) in relation to ourselves and the world we live in. At this turning point in our history the·renaissance of love can bring to this living entity we call earth a new health, beauty and oneness—the preconditions for the next step in man's growth.

NOTES

1.   Herbert A. Otto, *Group Methods to Actualize Human Potential* (Holistic Press, 160 S. Robertson Blvd., Beverly Hills, Calif.), second edition, pp. 360–363.

2.   Stewart B. Shapiro, "Tradition Innovation," in *Encounter,* Arthur Burton, ed. (San Francisco, Jossey-Bass, Inc., 1969), p. 177.

3.   Herbert A. Otto, *op. cit.,* pp. 1–23.

32 The Open and Anticipatory Society

Frankel & Toffler

To develop a new philosophical perspective on democracy, Charles Frankel thinks we must look critically and analytically at the contemporary social environment within which democratic ideals supposedly lack efficacy or relevance. At the basis of what he calls "the politics of malaise" is a feeling on the part of many people that we cannot control the powerful tendencies of our time, the radical changes, and new challenges which can lead to what Toffler later called "future shock." The older liberalism seems to be incapable of coping with current economic and social problems. A sense of purposelessness, a feeling of alienation from the machinery of government and from those who control and manipulate it, and an underlying conviction of helplessness seem to have eroded the faith in liberalism. What is missing, Frankel believes, is a new conception of democracy that will bring new inspiration to liberal efforts and provide a basis for organizing new programs of social action. Only this can help us to begin to overcome the politics of malaise, "the politics of unfocused worries and moral ennui."[1]

Before we can get a clear idea of what democracy means or should mean, we must not only review its natural history but also we must examine carefully the meaning of its most cherished terms such as "majority rule," "consent of the governed," and "democratic consensus." We must try to understand the "democratic bias" that underlies the use of these terms. It is a feeling or sentiment that may be difficult to characterize because it constitutes an attitude or emotional posture rather than a conceptual or rational judgment. A person having a genuinely democratic attitude judges his fellow humans not in terms of their status or rank but in terms of their membership in a community within which

521

everyone has common rights and responsibilities. He does not try to define the good life for everyone or demand that everyone live the way he does. "He is ready to assign all men the same rights without insisting they all live by the same rights."[2] Generally, the continental tradition of democracy, Frankel points out, has stressed equality and fraternity whereas the Anglo-Saxon tradition (see Mill in Part Four) has stressed liberty.[3] Both are essential to an adequate conception of democracy. They are, in fact, the twin attitudes from which spring democracy's characteristic ideals.

One of the greatest challenges to the democratic prospect today is the problem of preserving individual freedom and self-direction despite the rapid growth of industrialization, mass production, and large impersonal bureaucracies. In light of these challenges Frankel gives considerable attention to what he calls "the civilizing of technology." He thinks that we should try to find ways within the system of industrial production to give increased autonomy and choice to the citizen and worker. Hugeness of organization can be controlled by new approaches to decentralization. The work process can be better analyzed and reformed. A new ideal of work and play can be developed that takes into account the importance of self-discipline and self-realization. People can be educated not just to work but to play more productively so that work will not become drudgery and play will not be frivolous.

Frankel intentionally uses the term "democratic prospect" not in a prophetic sense but to refer to three different meanings: the extent to which democratic ideals have been realized in contemporary America, the democratic prospect on life and man, and the appropriate business of democracy in the immediate future.[4] Taking issue with Plato's low estimate of democratic forms of government (see Part Three), Frankel undertakes his defense of democracy by carefully delineating the conditions that have produced and sustained it, the challenges it has attempted to meet, and the framework within which it operates. The essential ideals of what he calls "the democratic revolution—government by consent, an open society, the autonomous individual, and the responsible control by human beings of their own history"[5]—are by no means anachronisms or irrelevant to our time. What is needed is a fresh and extensive re-examination of the basic features of democracy and proposals for a reorganization of society so that democracy can meet the new demands and continue to renew itself. To accomplish this Frankel thinks that the values of individual freedom and human worth must be placed above all else. This does not mean that scientific and technological advancement must be denigrated or isolated from the total human domain. It means that somehow we must find a way of combining the spirit of the humanities with the spirit of the sciences. As John Dewey stressed, we must recognize that experience is continuous. We must not compartmentalize.

the human and the mundane, the cultural and the natural, the world of value and the world of fact.

Throughout his discussion of the democratic prospect, Frankel says much that Alvin Toffler would agree with: democratic government must above all be responsible government. Responsible government is accountable government, open in its activities, its decision-makers identifiable and competent, encouraging effective communication between the governing groups and their constituencies and critics.[6] At the conclusion of *Future Shock*, Toffler calls for "a revolution in the very way we formulate our social goals."[7] This is needed, he argues, to counteract the limitations of the technocratic planners who suffer increasingly from what Toffler calls "econo-think," "my-opia," and "the virus of elitism."[8] What is lacking, and this is especially evident in city planning, are plans for different aspects of the city—its economic, social, educational, and cultural life—to support rather than contradict one another. Such plans can only be developed on the basis of rationally integrated goals that can help city planners to bring order out of chaos.[9] Otherwise, we all will be unable to cope with the accelerated change characteristic of our time.

In the following selection, "anticipatory democracy" is one of the strategies for survival Toffler recommends as a possible antidote to future shock. As change accelerates, an improved social information system can be designed that is more like a loop than a ladder.[10] The question, "Where do we want to go from here?" will be asked and discussed openly, and its answer ultimately will require the approval of the people.

NOTES

1. Charles Frankel, *The Democratic Prospect* (New York: Harper & Row, 1962), p. 3.
2. Ibid., p. 32.
3. Ibid.
4. Ibid., p. ix.
5. Ibid., p. xi.
6. Ibid., p. 158.
7. Alvin Toffler, *Future Shock* (New York: Bantam Books, 1970), p. 416.
8. Ibid.
9. Ibid., p. 417.
10. Ibid., p. 421.

Why Choose Democracy?

Charles Frankel

We have been overexposed to ideologies and political abstractions in this century, and have seen how much men are willing to sacrifice for the sake of ideological certainty. It is not surprising that sensitive men have developed something close to an ideology of uncertainty, and should look with a jaundiced eye on all questions about the justification of political systems. Why choose democracy? Trained in a hard school that has taught us the perils of belief, can we say anything more than that fanaticism is odious and that democracy should be chosen because it asks us to believe in very little?

On the contrary, it asks us to believe in a great deal. I do not believe we can show that the inside truth about the universe, human history, or the human psyche commands us to adopt democratic ideals. Choosing a political ideal is not like demonstrating the truth of a theorem in some geometry, and those who think that democracy needs that kind of justification are indirectly responsible for the uncertainty about it. Despite the semantic inflation from which the current discussion of political ideals suffers, the reasons for choosing democracy are neither mysterious nor difficult. But they are unsettling reasons, and they ask those who accept them to bet a great deal on their capacity to live with what they have chosen.

From Charles Frankel, *The Democratic Prospect.* Copyright © 1962 by Charles Frankel. By permission of Harper & Row, Publishers, Inc.

THE SIGNIFICANCE OF THE DEMOCRATIC POLITICAL METHOD

In an area so full of grandiose claims, it is safest to begin by using the word "democracy" in its narrowest sense. So conceived, democracy is the method of choosing a government through competitive elections in which people who are not members of the governing groups participate. Whatever may be said for or against democracy so conceived, it is surely not a supreme ideal of life. It is doubtful that anyone has ever treated the right to cast a ballot once every year or so as an end in itself. A society in which the democratic political method has been consolidated, to be sure, has a tremendous source of reassurance. It possesses a peaceful method for determining who shall hold power and for effecting changes in the structure of power. Yet even peace is only one value among others. It is worth something to have security and order, but how much it is worth depends on the kind of security and order it is. The importance of the democratic political method lies mainly in its nonpolitical by-products. It is important because a society in which it is well established will probably be different in at least four respects—in the conditions that protect its liberties, in the kind of consensus that prevails, in the character of the conflicts that go on within it, and in the manner in which it educates its rulers and citizens.

First, liberties. Construed strictly as a

method for choosing governments, democracy does not guarantee the citizen's personal liberties. Democratic governments have attacked personal liberties, as in colonial New England, and undemocratic governments have often protected them, as in Vienna before World War I. Yet competitive elections have their points, and it is only one of their points that they allow a society to choose its government. For in order to maintain competitive elections, it is necessary to have an opposition, the opposition must have some independent rights and powers of its own, the good opinion of some people outside government must be sought, and at least some members of the society must have protections against the vengefulness of the powers that be. And this carries a whole train of institutions behind it —courts, a press not wholly devoted to promoting the interests of those in power, and independent agencies for social inquiry and criticism.

It is these necessitating conditions for elections that give elections their long-range significance. So far as political democracy is concerned, these conditions are only means to ends: they make competitive elections possible. But it is because a system of competitive elections requires and fosters such conditions that it justifies itself. The conditions required for maintaining an honest electoral system are the best reasons for wishing to maintain it. Indeed, a man might value such a system even though he thought all elections frivolous and foolish. He would have as good a reason to do so, and perhaps a better reason, than the man who always finds himself voting happily for the winning side. The outsider and the loser are the peculiar beneficiaries of a political system that creates institutions with a vested interest in liberty.

The democratic political method, furthermore, helps to foster a different kind of social consensus. There have been many kinds of political arrangement that have allowed men to feel that the government under which they live is *their* government. There is no clear evidence that democracy is necessarily superior to other systems in promoting a sense of oneness between rulers and ruled. But the special virtue of a democratic political system is that it permits men to feel at home within it who do not regard their political leaders as their own kind, and who would lose their self-respect, indeed, if they gave their unprovisional loyalty to any human institution. Despite all that is said about democratic pressures towards conformity—and a little of what is said is true—the democratic political system ceremonializes the fact of disagreement and the virtue of independent judgment. If it is to work, it requires an extraordinary sophisticated human attitude—loyal opposition. The mark of a civilized man, in Justice Holmes' famous maxim, is that he can act with conviction while questioning his first principles. The ultimate claim of a democratic government to authority is that it permits dissent and survives it. In this respect, it dwells on the same moral landscape as the civilized man.

The democratic political method also changes the character of the conflicts that take place in a society. The perennial problem of politics is to manage conflict. And what happens in a conflict depends in part on who the onlookers are, how they react, and what powers they have. A significant fact about political democracy is that it immensely expands the audience that looks on and that feels itself affected and involved. This is why democratic citizens so often find democracy tiring and feel that their societies are peculiarly fragile. Hobbes, who said that he and fear were born as twins, recommended despotism in the interests of psychological security as well as physical safety.

But to say that democracy expands the scope of a conflict is also to say that democracy is a technique for the socialization of conflict. It brings a wider variety of pressures to bear on those who are quarreling and extends public control over private fights and private arrangements. And it does so whether these private fights are inside the government or outside. The association of democracy with the conception of private enterprise has something paradoxical about it. In one sense, there is more important enterprise that is private—free from outside discussion and surveillance—in totalitarian systems than in democratic systems. The persistent problem in a democratic system, indeed, is to know where to draw the line, where to say that outside surveillance is out of place. That line is drawn very firmly by those who make the important decisions in totalitarian societies.

But the final contribution that the democratic political method makes to the character of the society in which it is practiced is its contribution to education. Begin with the impact of political democracy on its leaders. The democratic method, like any other political method, is a system of rules for governing political competition. And such rules have both a selective and an educational force. They favor certain kinds of men, and make certain kinds of virtue more profitable and certain kinds of vice more possible. From this point of view, the significant characteristic of democratic rules of competition is that the loser is allowed to lose with honor, and permitted to live and try again if he wants. The stakes are heavy but limited. Such a system of competition gives men with sporting moral instincts a somewhat better chance to succeed. Even its typical kind of corruption has something to be said in its favor. The greased palm is bad but it is preferable to the mailed fist.

The democratic political method, furthermore, rests on methods of mutual consultation between leaders and followers. There are various ways in which support for the policies of political leaders is obtained in a democracy, but one of the most important is that of giving men the sense that they have been asked for their opinions and that their views have been taken into account. This makes leadership in a democracy a nerve-wracking affair. One of the great dangers in a democratic political system, in fact, is simply that leaders will not have the privacy and quiet necessary for serene long-range decisions. But this is the defect of a virtue. In general, power insulates. The democratic system is a calculated effort to break in on such insulation. The conditions under which democratic leaders hold power are conditions for educating them in the complexity and subtlety of the problems for which they are responsible.

And the coin has its other side. "We Athenians," said Pericles, "are able to judge policy even if we cannot originate it, and instead of looking on discussion as a stumbling-block in the way of action, we think it an indispensable preliminary to any wise action at all." But the fruits of free discussion do not show themselves only in public policy. They show themselves in the attitudes and capacities of the discussants. Democratic political arrangements are among the factors that have produced one of the painful and more promising characteristics of modern existence—men's sense that their education is inadequate, men's assertion that they have a right to be educated. And democratic politics help to promote a classic conception of education—it must be social as well as technical, general as well as special, free and not doctrinaire. We can can reverse the classic conception of the relation of education to democracy and not be any further from the truth: education is not simply a prerequisite for democracy; democracy is a contribution to education.

USES OF DEMOCRACY

But enough of political systems. In any liberal view of men's business, politics is a subordinate enterprise. It has its soul-testing challenges and pleasures, and its great work to do. But like the work of commerce and industry, the work of politics is essentially servile labor. The State is not the place to turn if you want a free commentary on human experience, and governments do not produce science, philosophy, music, literature, or children —or at any rate they do not produce very convincing specimens of any of these things. Politics may achieve its own forms of excellence, but the more important human excellences are achieved elsewhere. And it is from this point of view, I think, that democracy should in the end be considered.

For the democratic idea is based on the assumption that the important ends of life are defined by private individuals in their own voluntary pursuits. Politics, for liberal democracy, is only one aspect of a civilization, a condition for civilization but not its total environment. That is probably why the air seems lighter as one travels from controlled societies to free ones. One receives an impression of vitality, the vitality of people who are going about their own business and generating their own momentum. They may be going off in more different directions than the members of a centrally organized society, but the directions are their own. The best reasons for choosing democracy lie in the qualities it is capable of bringing to our daily lives, in the ways in which it can furnish our minds, imaginations, and consciences. These qualities, I would say, are freedom, variety, self-consciousness, and the democratic attitude itself.

That democracy is hostile to distinction and prefers mediocrity is not a recent view. And there is an obvious sense in which it is true that democracy makes for homogeneity. Democracy erodes the clear distinctions between classes. It destroys ready-made status-symbols so rapidly that the manufacture of new ones becomes the occupation of a major industry. Most obvious of all, democracy in-

creases the demand for a great many good things, from shoes to education. By increasing the demand, it also puts itself under pressure to cheapen the supply.

Yet certain pertinent facts must be set against these tendencies. First, more good things *are* more generally available in democracies. Second, egalitarianism's twin is the morality of achievement. There is a tension between the democratic suspicion of the man who sets himself apart and the democratic admiration for the man who stands out, but the egalitarian hostility towards ostentatious social distinctions is normally rooted in the belief that each man should be given a chance on his own to show what he can do. And finally, pressures towards uniformity are great in all societies. Is suspicion of the eccentric in egalitarian metropolitan America greater than in an eighteenth-century village? It is difficult to think so. "The fallacy of the aristocrat," Bertrand Russell has remarked, "consists in judging a society by the kind of life it affords a privileged few." Standing alone takes courage anywhere. Usually it also takes money; almost invariably it requires the guarantee that the individual will still retain his basic rights. In these respects modern liberal democracy, despite all the complaints about conformity, has made it easier for the ordinary unprivileged man to stand alone, if he has the will to do so, than any other kind of society known in history.

For however ambiguous some of the facts may be, the official commitment of liberal democracy is to the view that each man has his idiosyncrasies, that these idiosyncrasies deserve respect, and that if the individual does not know what is good for him, it is highly unlikely that a self-perpetuating elite will know better. And this is not just an official commitment. The institutions of liberal democracy go very far in giving it concrete embodiment. Assuming that the members of a democratic society have minimal economic

securities, there is a flexibility in their situation which not many ordinary men have enjoyed in the past. If they fall out of favor
with one set of authorities, they have a
chance to turn around and look elsewhere.

It is unquestionable that there are great
constellations of concentrated power in contemporary democratic societies; it is equally
unquestionable that there is some freedom in
any society. For in dealing with power, bright
men learn how to work the angles. But in a
democratic society there are more angles to
work. Individual freedom of choice is not an
absolute value. Any society must limit it;
indeed, one man's freedom often rests on restricting the next man's. But while freedom
of choice is not an absolute value, the democratic doctrine that each man has certain
fundamental rights assigns an intrinsic value
to his freedom of choice. If it has to be limited, it is recognized that something of value
has been sacrificed. Social planning in a
democracy is for this reason fundamentally
different from social planning in undemocratic
environments. The vague phrase "social utility," in a democratic setting, implicitly includes as one of its elements the value of
freedom of choice.

What difference does this make? One difference is that variety is promoted; a second
is that individuals are educated in self-consciousness. Needless to say, variety, too, has
its limits. We do not have to protect dope
peddlers in its name. But the full import of
variety, of the mere existence of differences
and alternatives, is frequently overlooked. It
does not merely give us more choices, or offer
us a break in the routine. It affects the immediate quality of our experience; it changes
our relation to whatever it is that we choose
to have or do or be. This is what is forgotten
when freedom is defined simply as the absence of felt frustrations, or when it is said
that if a man has just what he wants, it makes
little difference whether he has any choice or

not. A good that is voluntarily chosen, a
good which a man is always free to recon-
sider, belongs to him in a way that a passively accepted good does not. It is his
responsibility.

And this means that democratic variety has
another use as well. No one can say with
assurance that democracy makes people wiser
or more virtuous. But political democracy invites men to think that there may be alternatives to the way they are governed. And social
democracy, in reducing the barriers of class,
caste, and inherited privilege that stand between men, adds to the variety of people and
occasions the individual meets and puts greater
pressure on his capacity to adapt to the new
and different. Political democracy and a socially mobile society thus invite the individual to a greater degree of consciousness about
the relativity of his own ways and a greater
degree of self-consciousness in the choice of
the standards by which he lives. These are
conditions for intensified personal experience.
The role of democracy in the extension of
these attitudes represents one of its principal
contributions to the progress of liberal civilization.

The extension of such attitudes, to be sure,
has its risks, which explains much of our uneasiness about what the democratic revolution means. Fads and fashions engage and
distract larger groups in modern democratic
societies. And social mobility, though it gives
breadth and variety to men's experience, may
well foreshorten their sense of time. Cut loose
from fixed ranks and stations, each with its
legends, rationale, and sense of historic vocation, the citizens of a modern democracy face
a peculiar temptation to live experimentally,
with the help of the latest book, as though
no one had ever lived before. But these are
the risks not simply of democracy but of
modernity, and they can be controlled. The
courts, the organized professions, the churches,
and the universities are storehouses of funded

experience. In a society in which they are given independence from the political urgencies of the moment, they can serve as protections against the dictatorship of the specious present. Modernity implies a revolution in human consciousness. Democratic social arrangements reflect that revolution and accept it; but they also provide instruments for guiding and controlling it. None of democracy's contemporary rivals possess these two qualities to the same extent.

In the end, indeed, the risks of democracy are simply the risks implicit in suggesting to men that the answers are not all in. Democracy gives political form to the principle that also regulates the scientific community—the principle that inquiry must be kept open, that there are no sacred books, that no conclusion that men have ever reached can be taken to be the necessary final word. Cant, obscurantism, and lies are of course a good part of the diet of most democracies. Man is a truth-fearing animal, and it would be a miracle if any social system could quickly change this fact. But the institutions of liberal democracy are unique in that they require men to hold no irreversible beliefs in anything except in the method of free criticism and peaceful change itself, and in the ethic on which this method rests. Such a social system permits men to give their highest loyalty, not to temporary human beliefs or institutions, but to the continuing pursuit after truth, whatever it may be. The intellectual rationale of democracy is precisely that it does not need to make the foolish and arrogant claim that it rests on infallible truths. Men can believe in it and still believe that the truth is larger than anything they may think they know.

Yet the question that probably gnaws at us most deeply still remains. Freedom, variety, self-consciousness, a sane awareness of human fallibility, and loyalty to the principle that inquiry must be kept open—obviously, these have much in their favor. But they are re-fined values. Has liberal democracy priced itself out of the competition? Does it have anything to say, not to those who already know and enjoy it, but to the many more who must come to want it if human liberties are to be a little more secure in the world than they now are?

One of the debilitating illusions of many Western liberals is that the values of liberal culture are only our own values, that they have little point for those who look at the world differently, and no point at all for those whose lives are poor, mean, brutish, and short. Although colonialists used this view for different purposes, they shared it, and it betrays an inexact understanding of the nature of liberal values. Freedom, variety, self-consciousness, and the chance to seek the truth are all taxing experiences. Their virtues may be hard to conceive by those who have never enjoyed them. Yet in spite of the discomforts these values bring, the evidence indicates, I think, that most men would be happy to have them, and would think their lives enhanced. The difficulty with the most characteristic liberal values is not that they are parochial values. The difficulty is that men have other more imperious wants, like the need for medicines, schooling, bread, release from usurers, or a chance to get out from under corrupt and exploitative regimes. Illiberal programs promise these substantial material improvements and frequently deliver. And liberal programs, if they speak of freedom and leave out the usury and corruption, do not generally bring freedom either.

But let us assume, as there is every reason to assume, that liberal programs, if they are willing to recognize that they, too, must make a revolution, can also improve men's material condition. What can be said to the young man or the young—or old—nation in a hurry? What good reasons can we give, reasons that take account of their present condition and justified impatience, when we try to explain to them —and to ourselves—why the liberal path, despite its meanderings, is preferable to the authoritarian path?

One thing that can be said, quite simply, is that the authoritarian path closes up behind the traveler as he moves. The virtue of liberal democracy is that it permits second thoughts. To choose an authoritarian regime is to bet everything on a single throw of the dice; if the bet is bad, there is no way out save through violence, and not much hope in that direction. To choose a liberal approach, while it does not guarantee against errors, guarantees against the error so fatal that there is no peaceful way out or back. But there is another reason as well. The reason for choosing democracy is that it makes democrats.

Imagine a regime wholly committed to the welfare of those it rules. Imagine, against all the practical difficulties, that it is intelligent, honest, courageous, and that it does not have to enter into any deals with any of the international blocs that dominate the modern scene. And imagine, too, that this regime aims, in the end, to bring democracy and liberal values to the country it rules. But assume only that it claims, for the present, to be the one true spokesman for the public interest, the only group in the society that knows what truth and justice mean. What is the consequence? The consequence is that a democratic attitude is impossible. That attitude has been described in various ways—as a love for liberty, equality, and fraternity, as respect for the dignity of the individual, as a consistent regard for individual rights. The descriptions are not wrong, but they overintellectualize the attitude. At bottom, the democratic attitude is simply an attitude of good faith plus a working belief in the probable rationality of others. And that is what political authoritarianism destroys. Once a society is governed by the doctrine that some one group monopolizes all wisdom, it is divided into the Enlightened and the Unenlightened, and the

Enlightened determine who shall be accorded membership in the club. In a modern State this makes almost impossible the growth of that mutual trust between opposing groups which is a fundamental condition for the growth of a strong political community that is also free.

The competition that takes place in a democracy is an instance of cooperative competition. It is a struggle in which both sides work to maintain the conditions necessary for a decent struggle. Accordingly, it rests on the assumption that there are no irreconcilable conflicts, that differences can be negotiated or compromised, if men have good will. Such a system requires men to deal with one another honestly, to make a serious effort to reach agreements, and to keep them after they have been made. It requires them to recognize, therefore, that the other side has its interests and to be prepared to make concessions to these interests when such concessions are not inconsistent with fundamental principles. A democratic ethic does not ask men to be fools. They do not have to assume that their opponents have put all their cards on the table. But democratic competition is impossible if the parties to the competition cannot assume that their opponents will recognize their victory if they win and will cooperate with them afterwards. The intention to annihilate the opposition or to win at all costs destroys the possibility of a regulated struggle. In this sense democracy is an exercise in the ethic of good faith. It is a system that makes it possible for men, not to love their enemies, but at least to live without fearing them. That kind of mutual trust between enemies is what authoritarianism destroys.

No doubt, such an argument may seem pathetically beside the point to men who live in societies that have been torn by distrust for centuries and that have known government only as a name for cruelty and dishonesty. If such men succeed in installing democratic regimes in their countries, they will do so by recognizing their enemies and distrusting them. But the harshness that goes with any deep social revolution is one thing if it is recognized as a bitter and dangerous necessity and is kept within limits. It is another if the violence is doctrinal, and the assumption is made that men can never cooperate unless they have the same interests and ideas. Such an assumption, as all the evidence suggests, encourages the adoption of terror as an official policy and condemns a society to an indefinite period in which power will be monopolistically controlled. In a diversified modern society, indeed in any society that has even begun the movement towards modernity, the doctrine of governmental infallibility trains men in suspiciousness and conspiracy. Perhaps other objectives will be achieved, but under such circumstances their taste will be sour.

Nor does the doctrine of infallibility destroy only good faith. It is also incompatible with a belief in the probable rationality of others. To hold a democratic attitude is to proceed on the assumption that other men may have their own persuasive reasons for thinking as they do. If they disagree with you, this does not necessarily make them candidates for correction and cure. This is the homely meaning of the oft-repeated assertion that democracy has faith in the reasonableness and equality of human beings. The faith does not assert that all men are in fact reasonable, or that they are equal in the capacity to think well or live sensibly. The faith is pragmatic:

it expresses a policy. And the policy is simply to credit others with minds of their own, and to hold them responsible for their actions, until there are strong and quite specific reasons for thinking otherwise. Such a policy allows room for the idiosyncrasies of men and permits the varieties of human intelligence to be recognized and used.

In the end, the man who asks himself why he should choose democracy is asking himself to decide with which of two policies he would rather live. One is the policy of normally thinking that his fellows are dangerous to him and to themselves. The other is the policy of thinking that they are reasonable until they show themselves dangerous. To act on either policy has its risks. Why should a man choose one rather than the other? One reason can be found if he asks himself about the consequences the policy he adopts will have for the elementary feelings he will entertain towards his fellows, not in some transfigured world to come, but here and now. The point of the democratic policy is that it makes for democratic feelings. Those who do not wish to see human society divided into exploiters and exploited, those who wish to see each man come into his own free estate, believe that in that ultimate condition men will treat each other with the respect and fellow-feeling that equals show to equals. It is in the name of such moral attitudes that they seek democracy. The final reason for choosing the democratic method is that it provides a training ground, here and now, in just these attitudes.

What Is Anticipatory Democracy?

Alvin Toffler

Anticipatory democracy is a process—a way of reaching decisions that determine our future. It can be used to help us regain control over tomorrow.

Two crucial problems endanger the stability and survival of our political system today.

First: *Lack of future-consciousness.* Instead of anticipating the problems and opportunities of the future, we lurch from crisis to crisis. The energy shortage, runaway inflation, ecological troubles—all reflect the failure of our political leaders at federal, state, and local levels to look beyond the next election. Our political system is "future-blind." With but few exceptions, the same failure of foresight marks our corporations, trade unions, schools, hospitals, voluntary organizations, and communities as well. The result is political and social future shock.

Second: *Lack of participation.* Our government and other institutions have grown so large and complicated that most people feel powerless. They complain of being "planned upon." They are seldom consulted or asked for ideas about their own future. On the rare occasions when they are, it is ritualistic rather than real consultation. Blue-collar workers, poor people, the elderly, the youth, even the affluent among us, feel frozen out of the decision process. And as more and more millions

From *The Futurist*, October, 1975, pp. 224–227. By permission of the author.

feel powerless, the danger of violence and authoritarianism increases.

Moreover, if this is true within the country, it is even more true of the world situation in which the previously powerless are demanding the right to participate in shaping the global future.

Anticipatory democracy (A/D) is a way to tackle both these critical problems simultaneously. It connects up future-consciousness with real participation.

Thus the term "anticipatory" stresses the need for greater attention to the long-range future. The term "democracy" stresses the need for vastly increased popular participation and feedback.

There is no single or magical way to build a truly anticipatory democracy. In general, we need to support any program or action that increases future-awareness in the society, while simultaneously creating new channels for genuine, broad-based citizen participation. This means, among other things, an emphasis not on "elite" or "technocratic" futures work, but on mass involvement. We certainly need experts and specialists; they are indispensable, in fact. But in an anticipatory democracy, goals are not set by elites or experts alone. Thus, where futures activity exists, we need to open it to all sectors of society, making a special effort to involve women, the poor, working people, minority groups, young and old—and to involve them at all levels of leadership as well. Conversely, where participatory activities exist at community, state, or federal levels, or within various corporate or voluntary organizations, we need to press for attention to longer-range' futures.

A/D ACTIVITIES TAKE MANY FORMS

Anticipatory democracy may take many different forms, including the following:

1. Creation of city or statewide "2000" organizations. These bring thousands of citizens together to help define long-range goals. These goals are sometimes then embodied in legislation. Examples include Hawaii 2000, Iowa 2000, and Alternatives for Washington —all three at the state level; Seattle 2000 at the city level. Some sort of "2000" activity has been identified in over 20 states.

2. Certain important movements in American society are inherently pro-participative: they work to open the society to the full participation of women, ethnic minorities, the elderly, the poor, or others who are frequently excluded from decision processes in the system. Working with these movements to introduce greater future-consciousness, more attention to long-term goals, awareness of new technologies or social trends that may impact on them, contributes to the spread of A/D.

3. Media feedback programs. Radio and TV audiences are seldom given a chance to voice *their* views—particularly about the future. The use of TV, radio, cable TV, cassette, the print media and other communications systems to present alternative futures and provide channels for audience feedback simultaneously increases both participation and future consciousness.

4. Congressional reform. Passage of a "foresight provision" (HR 988) in the U.S. House of Representatives now for the first time requires that most standing committees engage in futures research and long-range analysis. By strengthening the Congress vis-à-vis the Executive Branch, it increases the potential for democratic participation as well. For example, anticipatory democracy organizations like Alternatives for Washington or Iowa 2000 could systematically feed citizens' views on the future into foresight discussions in Congress. We need "foresight provisions" in the Senate, and in state legislatures and city councils as well.

5. Community Action Programs. Nearly 900 CAPs exist in all parts of the nation. Aimed at combatting poverty, they all involve some form of participatory planning, often neighborhood based. Attempts to strengthen participation and to extend planning beyond the short term also help the move toward anticipatory democracy.

6. Referenda. There are many ways to link referenda to long-term future issues. (The British just made a long-range decision to stay in the Common Market—and relied on the referenda to tell Parliament how the country felt on the issue.)

7. Steps aimed at involving workers, consumers, minorities, women, and community groups in decision-making in industry and government—when linked to long-term planning—further the process of A/D. The Congressional Office of Technology Assessment, for example, has an active Citizens Advisory panel that becomes deeply involved in decisions about the very long-range effects of new technologies. Movements for worker participation or self-management in industry, for consumer watchdog agencies, for participatory management can all be encouraged to become more future-conscious. Unless participation affects the planning process, it has little impact.

8. Futurizing the programs of organiza

tions like the Young Women's Christian Association, the Red Cross, or the National Education Association—to choose three at random—helps spread the necessary awareness through the network of existing voluntary organizations.

9. Opening up global or transnational organizations to greater participation and future-consciousness. The United Nations conferences, especially the informal meetings that occur simultaneously with them, are opportunities for introducing A/D on the global scale. Such conferences as those devoted to the law of the sea in Caracas, population in Bucharest, environment in Stockholm, food in Rome, women in Mexico City, and the forthcoming one on human settlements in Vancouver are events at which globally-oriented people and non-governmental organizations with local constituencies can get together to exchange information and strategies, and to influence formal policy.

10. Creation of participatory planning mechanisms within community organizations. For example, bringing the entire membership of a church, or a broadly representative group of parents, teachers and students in a school, or patients, medical staff and service employees in a hospital into the planning process advances anticipatory democracy. Provided the process is truly participatory and the time horizon reaches beyond, say, 10 years, it strengthens A/D and helps educate people to play a more active role in the national political system as well.

11. Democratizing the World Future Society through expanding its membership to include groups now underrepresented, and to assure fully democratic internal procedures is yet another step in the direction of A/D. Preventing futurism from becoming prematurely academicized or super-professionalized helps avoid its use as a tool for mystification of the public.

These are all examples of A/D activity. They are not given in any order of precedence, but they reflect the diversity of possibilities. Dozens more could no doubt be cited. We need to *invent* many additional kinds of A/D activity. This will require the help of millions of people from every discipline, from every walk of life, every profession, ethnic and class background. A democracy that doesn't anticipate the future cannot survive. A society that is good at anticipating but allows the future to be captured by elites is no longer a democracy. As we move into the future, anticipatory democracies will be the only surviving kind.

POSSIBLE A/D PROGRAMS

Members of Alvin Toffler's A/D (Anticipatory Democracy) Network compiled the following list of possible A/D activities. They emphasize that these are some possibilities—not necessarily recommendations. It is up to *you* to decide whether any of them are appropriate. You may want to adapt them or, better yet, invent your own!
• Visit your city council or state legislature and urge passage of a "foresight provision" modelled after H.R. 988 in the House of Representatives.
• Set up "futurist consciousness teams" to attend political rallies and meetings. These teams would ask speakers to explain what effect their proposed programs might have on, say, the year 1985 or 2000. By pressing for a discussion of long-range consequences, the entire political discussion is raised to a higher level. Another question

that can be asked: "If we don't really know what effect your proposal will have by 1985, what procedures ought we to be following to find out?"

• Phone a radio talk show and suggest a program on the future, inviting listeners to suggest goals for the community over the next 15 or 25-year period. Such shows have already been tried out in San Diego, Dallas, Atlanta, New Orleans, and other cities. A good response can be used to get interested listeners together to form an A/D group.

• Contact the city or state planning agency and suggest citizen participation activities like Alternatives for Washington. Provide the agency with the names of individuals who will take the initiative in organizing these activities, and sources of information on previous activities of this kind.

• Get a group of futurists to visit the nearest Community Action Agency or Community Action Program and ask: 1. What the futurists can offer in the way of methods, insights, perspectives. 2. What the futurists can learn from community experiences with public participation in planning.

• Organize speaking teams for community groups that express an interest in A/D or futurism.

• Working with your local Bicentennial planning group, arrange for an anticipatory democracy booth at local events. Use booth to distribute A/D literature, but also to get ideas and criticism about the future of your community from the public.

• Approach major companies in your area and ask them to make public in at least a general sense their plans for new investment, jobs, technologies, etc. Publicize their reactions as well as their plans. Ask to what degree consumers, employees or public officials were consulted in drawing up the plans.

• Place ballot boxes in local supermarkets, shopping centers or movies, with ballots asking passersby to check off the three things they most like and the three things they most dislike about the community. Pass findings to local press and relevant officials. What are they doing now to preserve the good and eradicate the bad by 1985?

• Organize an open discussion of long-term goals in a church or synagogue to define its purposes in relation to the community over a 10 to 25-year period.

• Working with doctors, the nursing association, and other community health groups, try to organize a community-wide "health plebescite," asking, through the mass media and other channels, for ordinary people to tell what they think is wrong, and what they think will be needed to improve health services by 1985. Compare their priorities with the local health budget.

• Approach parent-teacher associations, teachers' organizations, and students to run an Education 1985 or Education 2000 Conference through which parents and teachers, as well as professionals, have a chance to voice problems, hopes and fears about the future and to suggest ways of futurizing education.

Anticipatory democracy is not a single "thing"—it is a process. It can be created in a wide variety of ways. It's up to you to create your own.

33 The Future of Religion

Putnam, Cox et al.

Sigmund Freud, in *The Future of an Illusion,* envisaged a time in the distant future when man would no longer rely upon religious faith to sustain him in suffering and to fulfill his hopes for happiness either in this life or in the future. Scientific rationalism would replace what Freud considered to be religious illusion, for "in the long run, nothing can withstand reason and experience, and the contradiction which religion offers to both is all too palpable."[1]

Karl Marx, another of the thinkers most influential on the twentieth century, dismissed religion as "the opiate of the masses," and looked forward to the day when religious institutions—churches, congregations, priests, and ecclesiastical hierarchies—all of which he considered obstructions to progress and supporters of an unjust *status quo,* would be swept away. After the socialist revolution the proletariat would rely upon scientific dialectical materialism instead of utopian and religious idealisms as the means of establishing the future communist heaven on earth.

In the post-revolutionary Soviet Union freedom of nonreligion and religion were supposedly guaranteed to the people. In fact, however, antireligious propaganda was widely distributed by state authority, religious freedom was often suppressed, and some churches were even turned into museums dedicated to the promulgation of atheism. The effort to associate religion in the minds of the masses with superstition, ignorance, fanaticism, and even insanity has continued. The utopian vision of communism is that under its aegis religion along with the state will eventually wither away. The orthodox Marxist, like the orthodox Freudian, believes religion has no future.

Despite such outright rejections of the value of religion and such confident predictions of its ultimate demise, there are those who would take strong issue with such attitudes and predictions. Far from foreseeing the decline and demise of religion in the future, they see it reviving and changing in order to meet the demands of the present and the challenges of the future. Some would agree with Theodore M. Hesburgh, president of the University of Notre Dame, that no matter what changes occur in the future, "we will still need faith in God, and indeed in His Providence, if this world is not to become a vast insane asylum."[2] Without religious faith, he argues, we cannot give our lives the kind of ultimate direction and transcendent definition needed to cope with instability, uncertainty, and future shock. Such religious faith can be established on the basis not only of Thomistic metaphysical arguments, Hesburgh believes, but upon unique yet universal religious experiences. Also from a naturalistic point of view, John Dewey sees a future for the religious consciousness, in the sense of a continuing dedication to and pursuit of ever increasing, ideal-directed growth, but not for religions or religious dogmas.

Other philosophers of religion emphasize other aspects of religion that will ensure its survival in the future. As long as man is human, Paul Tillich argues, he will experience the essence of religious faith which is his ultimate concern. Karl Jaspers sees the experience of boundary situations such as guilt, suffering, and death as definitive and universal parameters of the existential and religious situation. If someday man should succeed in conquering death, rendering suffering impossible, and purging all feeling of guilt from his psyche, he may be happier and no longer religious, but in Jaspers' view he will no longer be capable of achieving authentic existence which depends upon a continuing unflinching confrontation with boundary situations.

Albert Schweitzer saw religious consciousness surviving and increasing in the future only to the extent that there is a concommitant increase of ethical consciousness, the reverence for life. Erich Fromm would have found the permanent and universal basis for a humanistic religion in man's uniquely human need for a frame of orientation and devotion. These are only a few of the thinkers who, rejecting both the Freudian view that religion is a mere illusion and the Marxist view that it is a dangerous opiate, believe that religion will play an indispensable role in the world of tomorrow.

In attempting to answer the question as to the future of religion, thinkers have not just directed attention back to the fundamental nature of man's religious quest, they have also examined current practices and trends as a basis for their prognostication. Hiley Ward, author of *Religion 2101 A.D.*, gives a fascinating account of newly developed conceptions of man, God, the Church, Jesus, and religious worship. He gives a list of "today's supermarket of varieties of theology," including theologies that emphasize process, politics, liberation, criticism, bases of faith, particular situations, hope, personal experience, body awareness, celebration, play, and games.[3] The message for the future Ward sees in these theologies, aside from the suggestion of evolving pluralism, is that "they point to the preoccupation with the nonstructural elements of religion, away from a former building complex, and a turning in on a search for personal relationships, meaning, and societal improvement."[4] This empirical approach which attempts to forecast on the basis of current trends is the approach used in the following selection. It is important to some of the conclusions tentatively put forward by the panel of theologians in the second selection that "informed hunches" and a good deal of speculation also play a noteworthy and unpredictable role in the discussion.

NOTES

1. Sigmund Freud, *The Future of an Illusion* (Garden City, N.Y.: Doubleday & Co., 1964), p. 89.

2. Theodore Hesburgh, "Will There Still Be a God?" *Saturday Review World,* August 24, 1974, p. 89.

3. See Hiley Ward, *Religion 2101* A.D. (Garden City, N.Y.: Doubleday & Co., 1975), pp. 153–159.

4. Ibid., pp. 159–160.

Religion and the Future: An Overview

Leon J. Putnam

In a cartoon showing bits and pieces spread over a toy counter, the saleslady comments: "Madam, I can recommend this toy for your child. It will enable him to live in the world of the future. You see, no matter how you put it together it doesn't work!" Another cartoon depicts a woman talking to a friend in a movie theatre as they watch a wedding scene on the screen. She says: "She must not have read the book or she wouldn't go through with it." A final cartoonist's picture shows a man taking off his glasses in the optician's office and saying: "I want to see things less clearly."

These comments reflect some of our attitudes as we contemplate the question of what lies in the future. We find no clear pattern for putting it all together, we are mindful that hindsight is always easier than foresight, and, confronted by "future shock," we would like to shut out some of what we see now, and at least avoid present shock.

Yet, while we recognize that the future is beyond our total comprehension, we can discern some of the trends that may considerably mold the world of tomorrow. If the present is an effect of the past, it is also, in a sense, an effect of the future, for present attitudes and beliefs are shaped not only by what has been, but also by what we hope will be.

Since the turn of the mid-20th-century, there has been much speculation regarding

From *Intellect*, April 1976, pp. 335–338.

events leading up to the year 2000. In recent years, marked by rather abrupt changes, there has been increased anxiety and concern regarding the future of religion in particular.

If religion is regarded as the process of ultimate valuing in which we place reliance and trust on that which gives meaning and wholeness to our individual and social lives, then we might anticipate that religion, itself, would be affected in a period characterized by a confusion over values and a lack of balance and coherence among those still held. The disparity in our believing and behaving appears to some as a generation gap, a sign of hypocrisy, or, indeed, as a signal of the end of religion.

Tillich viewed the present age as one in which man lived more on the surface of life than in its depth, more concerned with the horizontal dimension of sensate objects and things than with the vertical dimension of meaning, value, and purpose.[1] However, such a dimension is never completely lost, and mankind abhors a meaning vacuum. So, in the past decade, we have witnessed many fads in religion, including the "death of God" movement, the theology of hope, the Jesus "freaks," interest in Eastern religions, astrology cults, witchcraft and demonism, the new morality, the theology of wonder, the upsurge of Pentecostalism, speaking in tongues, mysticism, and group-encounter movements. It is difficult to know whether we should be rejoicing in "a world come of age," or whether we should be in despair over man's dehumanization.

In the midst of these currents of change, it is not surprising that observers and forecasters differ in their particular outlooks toward the future. Let us suggest, however, four trends that are discernible in much of what the late Crane Brinton called "the literature of Whither Mankind."[2]

THE DECLINE OF AUTHORITARIANISM

Religion based on ignorance, fear, and authoritarianism will decline, with less emphasis placed on reward, punishment, and the afterlife. Contributing to this projection is the increase in educational levels achieved and the rapid growth of religion as a recognized field of humanistic study. Religious knowledge is no longer defined, by and large, as something beyond the scrutiny of other disciplines. Understanding and appreciation for a diversity of viewpoints has made indoctrination suspect, not only on educational grounds, but also on psychological grounds.

In *Can People Learn to Learn?*, Chisholm has urged that children's minds be protected from the certainty of rightness of any one religious viewpoint lest they react irrationally to the problems of future generations.[3] Chesen, in his book *Religion May Be Hazardous to Your Health*, likewise questions, on the basis of his psychiatric practice, the kind of early religious training that would provide absolute ("fail-safe") answers which "impede the development of flexible thinking processes."[4] Too often, this leads to the rigid religious thought patterns that contribute to emotional instability. Chesen comments that the person brought up on an authoritarian approach to religious beliefs has "accumulated a system of intrinsic attitudes that are quite unlike extrinsic reality. . . . Furthermore, because his

distorted perceptions force him to live and react within the extrinsic real world, a polarization of his personality footing results. . . . The stage is thus set for an infinite mass of double messages, and these can be too much for the mind to reconcile comfortably."[5]

In the past, religion has often perpetuated conformity to its doctrines on the basis of fear, especially that of doing wrong. If beliefs were not accepted and practiced, the threat of punishment (hell) was made, or, if they were accepted, a lasting reward would be achieved (heaven).[6] It is now recognized that, on the basis of such threats and rewards, one can be coerced into believing just about anything. Moreover, a religious orientation built on such an emotional basis tends to separate the desire to believe from the mental activity that informs an adult's critical and integrated response to life.

In terms of transactional analysis popularized by Eric Berne and Thomas Harris, religious truth will likely be translated from the parental mode into that of the adult who can help liberate the childlike faith that is open, responsive, and free.[7] Truths are not necessarily embodied in the authoritarian stances of the past. In the future, we will see religious belief structures developing out of an interplay of the parent-adult-child dimensions of the self, with the beliefs existentially verified through authentic experiences here and now.

This does not mean that faith in its future expressions will be defined exclusively by rational reflection of the mind or activity of the body, but, rather, that the religious orientation will involve all aspects of the self—body, mind, and spirit—in growing harmony. One's religion will refer not only to what he professes in words, but also to what he does and to what he feels. This blending of the dimensions will enable us to recognize that, if religion concerns the vision of ultimate values, then no one has God neatly and completely circumscribed. Questions will be as relevant as answers in confronting a changing world. Religion will be viewed as a process, and not a product.[8]

We may anticipate increased non-sectarian teaching *about* religion in the public schools (the fourth R), which will not replace the religious influence of one's family and friends, but will provide additional input into one's own frame of reference as he becomes aware of the emerging world community and its various traditions. The Western mind will be enriched through both giving and receiving.

The insights of Mead, in her *Twentieth Century Faith,* and Toynbee, in *Change and Habit* and *Surviving the Future,* are helpful in providing cultural and historical contexts for this widening religious perspective.[9]

Toynbee provides a fitting summary of our first trend:

> The intellect will always refuse, sooner or later, to take traditional doctrines on trust ... it has refused in the Western World since the 17th century. Since that century, the modern Western outlook has become the outlook of a world-wide Westernizing intelligentsia; and what the intelligentsia thinks today, the masses will think tomorrow. The modern Western mind's insistence on thinking for itself and on putting traditional doctrines to the test thus seems to be "the wave of the future" for the world.[10]

PLURALISM

Religious pluralism will continue to grow. While some have anticipated the arrival of a common religion uniting all peoples, this appears to be unrealistic as we contemplate the foreseeable future. However, with increased knowledge and, frequently, the gaining of first-hand experiences of other cultures, recognition and respect for other religious viewpoints could be expected to expand.

Communication of all types—*e.g.,* televi-sion, books, movies, and travel—will undoubtedly make a person pause before proclaiming that he has the final word for all. Dogma will become more flexible, and belief structures will be influenced by exposure to the traditions and practices of others. Signs of this are already evident, as interest in yoga, Zen, African religions, and the like has shown. Occult and esoteric faith cults, while they have remained out of the mainstream of American religious practice, nevertheless have been of interest to many—*e.g.,* magic, witchcraft, astrology, and theosophy.

Again, religion will be seen as primarily a verb, and not a noun. Becoming will be stressed over being. The interaction of culturally diverse forms of expression that is already observable in art, literature, music, and the cinema will spread to the more abstract and rigid areas of religious and philosophical beliefs and practices. One will have a heightened awareness of different forms of expression, but will also see his own peculiar traditions in new ways.

This will pose a threat to those who see religion primarily as a security against change, but the fear of the unknown will be reduced, in part, by communication itself. Dialogue between theologians and laymen of all faiths will increase, producing, if not agreement, a bond of understanding. Those who retreat to the older thought patterns will simply find themselves engaged in monologues, with few listening.

Ironically, a pluralistic environment will be able to support genuine religious commitment which springs from the inner convictions of the self that is able to recognize and respect differences of others, not only geographically, but also emotionally and ideologically.

We might speculate that pluralism will not simply increase in an objective, descriptive sense, but also will be intensified within a person. Ordinarily, ultimate values, by their very nature, are not subject to rapid and radical change. Accordingly, the word "God" has frequently been used to refer to what is unchanging and eternal. On the other hand, our awareness of the nature of God *does* change. For example, the feminine aspects of God have received more attention recently, due in part to the Women's Liberation Movement. Likewise, changes in life style on the part of a person have become evident, and Lifton has suggested the arrival of "Protean man," who changes his basic orientation more frequently in terms of beliefs, jobs, and values.[11]

Writing in regard to education and the future, Buchen has pointed out that there are limits to individuality, especially in a changing environment: "The whole person is not and cannot be totally individual; part of the whole —today more than ever—must be nonindividualized, communal, or 'collectivized.' "[12] The "collectivized individual," he explains, is multiple, really many selves, rather than one:

> If the traditional notion in the West has been one God, one love, one job, one identity, one country and one planet, the futuristic notion is many gods, many loves, many jobs, many identities, many countries and many planets. The collectivized individual . . . will be capable of sustaining many allegiances, without contradiction, on both a national and international scale, and be closer to being, especially through the concept of global perspective, a world citizen.[13]

THE INTERDISCIPLINARY NATURE OF RELIGION

Religion will be regarded as an interdisciplinary field as it engages with other disciplines in common concerns, especially those relating to ethical decisions prompted by scientific achievements.

The common ground uniting those of different persuasions in a pluralistic world is found precisely in their shared humanity. Issues emerging from the frontiers of the nat-

ural and social sciences already touch some of us personally, and all of us socially and politically, regardless of our ethnic or national or religious labels. We find decisions necessary, for example, regarding the achievement of peace, world population control, ecology, the creation of life, sperm banks, organ transplants, the prolongation of life, mind manipulation, chemical control of man's behavior, women's rights, and world government.

All of these areas now prompt a rethinking and re-evaluating of traditional ethical stances based frequently on religious beliefs concerning the nature of man. While courses of action in regard to particular concerns may vary, we share—simply because we are humans living on one planet—in the problems themselves. As someone remarked at a conference considering religion in the future: "The basic problem we have to solve is the problem-solving problem."[14]

As facts and values intersect in ethical decision-making, the lines will continue to narrow between disciplines, and concepts whose meaning was taken for granted will be seen in a new and sometimes challenging light. Traditional religious ideas—such as love, creation, resurrection, soul, guilt, miracles, prayer, and immortality—have been subject to this process in recent years, raising fundamental questions about the nature of man and religion itself.

Perhaps the first effect of this interdisciplinary approach will not be found in simple and uniform answers to ethical concerns, but, rather, in a reformulating of the very nature of religion as mature and immature forms of it are recognized. Religion that has often spoken unilaterally to other disciplines will inevitably find its own foundations challenged by the responding voices of others.

In the area of psychology, for example, assumptions of traditional beliefs have been met with serious, and oftentimes skeptical, reactions. What, for instance, distinguishes sin from sickness, neurosis from health, and even religion from psychology? Studies such as Strunk's *Mature Religion* and Anderson's *Your Religion: Neurotic or Healthy?* are examples of the critical reflections emerging from interdisciplinary dialogue which recognizes that all aspects of our social life—including ultimate valuing—are interrelated, and necessarily interact.[15]

Humanistic, agnostic, and traditional religious approaches to life intersect in at least one point—man himself. Any meaningful basis for valuing now or in the future will have to encompass this diversity of orientation and outlook. The days of the lone and immune thinker—religious or irreligious—are coming to a close. From his perspective as a professional theologian, Kenneth Cauthen has commented:

> . . . The individual theologian, the great thinker who produces the great system, will probably be less and less important. I think theology will have to be a more corporate enterprise, a team enterprise, in the future. . . . The theology that is most useful and vital will be that which is worked out in direct conversation, encounter, dialogue, not only with the thinkers but also with the shapers of the future. The interdisciplinary nature of theology will be increasingly important.[16]

THE CONTINUANCE OF RELIGION

As the last of our trends, we would suggest that religion itself will not come to an end. Regardless of the extent of our knowledge, the nature of life's meaning and ultimate value remains, for there is mystery in what we know, as well as in what we do not know.[17] Indeed, the mystery of the known grows as we learn more about ourselves and the world process. Man, in his self-awareness and his contemplation, is a self-transcending creature and creator. He sees himself and his

future partly in an objective way, but is never quite able to remove the dimension of subjectivity. He will continue to ask the basic questions which science can not resolve within its methodology: Who am I? What do I live for? What does the process of living, learning, and loving mean?

After discussing scientific approaches to religion, Glock and Stark conclude their book, *Religion and Society in Tension,* with the observation:

> In the end, the existence of the universe, of nature, and of mankind will remain unexplained. . . . The dilemma will thus be created as to how the need for a system of ultimate meaning is to be satisfied. Science itself cannot fill the gap. It cannot supply the glue—the values and norms—which holds societies together and which makes existence meaningful. . . . Knowledge of how man is determined can have the consequence of enhancing rather than reducing man's freedom. Knowing how determinism operates may enable man to transcend it and indeed exercise greater control over his destiny.[18]

Man will continue to seek a significance to his unique life—a story line—but one not found in any book or textbook. If such a book should be written, it would mark the end, not simply of religion, but of man.

NOTES

1. Paul Tillich, "The Lost Dimension in Religion," in Richard Thruelsen and John Kobler, eds., *Adventures of the Mind* (New York: Vintage Books, 1960), pp. 52–69.

2. Crane Brinton, "Reflections on the Literature of Whither Mankind," in Leroy Rouner, ed., *Philosophy, Religion, and the Coming World Civilization* (The Hague: Martinus Nijhoff, 1966), pp. 310–319.

3. Brock Chisholm, *Can People Learn to Learn?* (New York: Harper, 1958), p. 75.

4. Eli Chesen, *Religion May Be Hazardous to Your Health* (New York: Peter Wyden, 1972), p. 8.

5. Ibid., pp. 16–17.

6. For a recent defense of this view, see Leslie Woodson, *Hell and Salvation* (Old Tappan, N.J.: Revell, 1973). *Cf.* Chesen, *op. cit.*, pp. 125–126.

7. See, for example, John K. Bontrager, *Free the Child in You* (Philadelphia: Pilgrim Press, 1974).

8. This is a recurring theme in Thomas O'Meara and Donald Weiser, eds., *Projections: Shaping an American Theology for the Future* (New York: Doubleday, 1971).

9. Margaret Mead, *Twentieth Century Faith* (New York: Harper & Row, 1972); Arnold Toynbee, *Change and Habit* (New York: Oxford University Press, 1966); and Arnold Toynbee, *Surviving the Future* (New York: Oxford University Press, 1971).

10. Toynbee, *Change and Habit, op. cit.*, pp. 180–181.

11. Robert Jay Lifton, *History and Human Survival* (New York: Vintage Books, 1971), pp. 311–331.

12. Irving H. Buchen, "Humanism and Futurism: Enemies or Allies?," in Alvin Toffler, ed., *Learning For Tomorrow* (New York: Vintage Books, 1974), p. 136.

13. Ibid., pp. 136–137. *Cf.* S. Demezynski, *Automation and the Future of Man* (London: George Allen and Unwin, 1964), pp. 233–234.

14. "A Faculty Conversation," in *Bulletin of Crozer Theological Seminary*, 62:6, January, 1970.

15. Orlo Strunk, Jr., *Mature Religion* (New York: Abingdon Press, 1965); and George Christian Anderson, *Your Religion: Neurotic or Healthy?* (Garden City, N.Y.: Doubleday, 1970).

16. "A Faculty Conversation," *op. cit.*, p. 16.

17. Leon J. Putnam, "The Mystery of the Known," *International Journal of Religious Education*, 39:3, March, 1963.

18. Charles Y. Glock and Rodney Stark, *Religion and Society in Tension* (Chicago: Rand McNally, 1963), pp. 305–306.

Religion in the Year 2000

Panel Discussion

Participants: Professors Harvey Cox, Emil L. Fackenheim, Johannes B. Metz, and Thomas F. O'Dea

O'DEA: All of you are aware that predicting the year 2000 has become a highbrow and middlebrow occupation—and, for some, preoccupation—here in the United States. It was focused on in the 1966 issue of *The American Scholar*, the 1967 issue of *Daedalus*, as well as the book by Herman Kahn and Anthony J. Wiener, *The Year 2000*. And those of you who sit in front of the television set know that Walter Cronkite goes in for a bit of this on Sunday evenings too. We thought we might also try a hand at it.

Since 1776—the year that Adam Smith wrote *The Wealth of Nations* as well as the year the United States came into existence as a political entity—man has advanced his ability to control and manipulate his environment more than in all previous history. As a result, the growth curve of science and technology goes straight up today. And, in the next thirty or forty years, we can expect a continued enormous increase. Where once we adapted ourselves to the environment, we now adapt the environment to ourselves.

Reprinted with the permission of the publisher from Walter H. Capps, *The Future of Hope* (Philadelphia: Fortress Press, 1970), pp. 127–135. © 1970 by Fortress Press.

Since 1660—the date which represents the point at which the intense and often highly intolerant religiosity of the earlier seventeenth century gave way to skepticism as well as the time which marks the beginning of "the scientific revolution"—men have witnessed a continual diminution of religious belief in the West. The scientific revolution is instructive for us today not only because it made that technology possible but because the approach which it fostered has acted as a kind of acid solvent for traditional beliefs. Furthermore, it has tended to geometrize and mathematize thought, and has consigned conceptions which cannot be thus refracted to a limbo of subjectivity and second-class importance. One can say that religion has been on the defensive vis-à-vis science since the last quarter of the seventeenth century. I am not speaking now of that more obvious kind of defensiveness—such as a biological theory of evolution with respect to the religion of the nineteenth century, or the adjustments required by the heliocentric theory in the sixteenth and seventeenth centuries—but rather of the way in which the scientific mode of thinking has acted as a kind of demythologizing solvent.

I begin the discussion, then, with two questions. First, how will religion fare in the technological society thus projected? And, second, can man really believe in God in the twenty-first century? What would it mean? What will it mean? How will such a belief be approached?

Cox: First, let me say that it is very good to be back in the business of defining the future. This used to be the monopoly of theologians many years ago. They would cut open a pigeon, take out the entrails, and decide what the future was going to be. Or they would consult the oracle, or simply make a prophetic utterance. In recent years this field has been intruded into by sociologists and technicians, and I feel a little resentful.

O'Dea: It still takes guts though.

Cox: Yes, it still takes guts. . . . At the outset I'd like to say that I am very suspicious of any prediction of the future which is merely an extrapolation of the trends we see around us today. That procedure is not only inaccurate but also downright dangerous since it tends to become self-fulfilling prediction. Whatever the book tells us the year 2000 is going to be like is entirely open to question. What it is going to be like is what we will make it like. We can reverse trends. We can set aside particular tendencies in our society. We do not simply have to knuckle under to them.

I'm particularly concerned about certain aspects of technological development in this regard. Operating among us is a kind of technological fatalism which conditions us to move along according to inherent dynamic forces. It is perfectly clear, for example, that we can put a man on the moon. We can. My question is: Can we *not* put a man on the moon? Can we really decide now that we do not want to? That is a serious question.

And it brings us back to Professor O'Dea's question: What do we really want the twenty-first century to be like? What steps do we take now to form the kind of century we want it to be? What are we hoping for? Professor Metz has rightly emphasized, I think, that the proper posture for religious belief today is *hope*. The content and stance of religious belief is an expectant posture toward the future which has some hope of what it hopes to see there —a hope which activates movement and energy in the present. Let me turn to the two questions Professor O'Dea raised.

Will it really be a technological society in the twenty-first century? Is that the most accurate depiction? Certainly, some technological developments will begin to level off—the speed of airplanes, for example. After we develop the supersonic jet there will not be much point in going beyond it. Automobiles haven't gotten much faster in the last few years: we have come to a kind of optimum on that. The major breakthroughs will probably come in the pharmaceutical, microbiological, and medical fields. Mind-controlling substances, especially, will pose all sorts of interesting problems for ethics and religion.

I also want to question whether religion has in fact declined in significance over the last two hundred fifty or three hundred years—or, for that matter, over the last few years. It is incontestable, I think, that the power and position of the churches have diminished. But unless one accepts the notion that outside the church there is no salvation—unless one accepts that and identifies religion with what the churches are doing—it is impossible to say that religion has declined. If one is sensitive to non-ecclesiastical, nonchurchly religion, it becomes clear and significant that religion is no longer the monopoly of the churches and never will be again—if it ever was. From now on we will have a lot more "do-it-yourself religion"—collage-building religion. It might be a bit messy from an orthodox theological point of view, but I am sure we are in for it.

Finally, I wonder if the question "Is it possible to believe in God in the twenty-first century?" isn't to some extent a rather provincial, Western kind of question. We ask it as Westerners because religion is primarily associated for us with belief in God. This is the fundamental aspect. However, this characterization doesn't apply very well to some very important non-Western religious options. When you talk to a Hindu or a Buddhist and press them on this issue, you are told that the future of religion really belongs to Buddhism or Hinduism: these options teach one how he can be religious even if he cannot believe in God—or at least not in the traditional sense. It may be that we will be able to retain a belief in God, but it will not be the kind of belief in God we have inherited. It will be a different kind of belief. Possibly it will have many of the qualities of hopefulness rather than elements of intellectual credulity.

O'DEA: I'm really just supposed to be chairman here, but I feel a certain urge to get into this. I'd like to defend Wiener and Kahn, the sociologists, so-called. They are aware of what you say, I think, that it's not simply a matter of extrapolation. One cannot predict a future for the year 2000. One can predict several futures, but human decision will play a large role in determining which one comes about. It won't play the entire role, of course, since there are all kinds of unintended consequences, and man is not all-powerful.

Then second, I would like to raise a question in relation to Professor Cox's comments about the religion of the future. I think I can see Baal coming out of the woods when you talk about this religion of experience. I'd like to have you comment on that. I am sure it is possible for us to have a society in which we have a religion of experience; we could do all sorts of things to ourselves to induce as many-sided experiences as possible. This may be very attractive to a lot of people in America. But it may also be a lot of hokum. I tend to sympathize with Elijah in that confrontation. And I think that in three ways—religiously, ethically, and I might say, just from the point of common sense—such a religion could be a religion of nonsense in more than the positive sense of the word.

FACKENHEIM: Could I react to a couple of things? Professor Cox, as much as the people he attacks, seems to think that we are makers of the future. Let me just throw in an observation. If you think back fifty years or so, people then too understood themselves to be making the world. But wasn't it just about then, in 1914, that the whole mess started? And the unintended consequences of those actions—of our actions also—are vast. We can pretty well predict technological progress by itself. But how moral values come to be negotiated—for better or worse—is infinitely complex. We must always bear in mind the uncertainty of the world in which we live.

When I think about the year 2000 I am most interested in knowing how I would behave. I know that I would not fall in with every majority trend that might happen to come along. My people have often been forced to be a minority; perhaps Christians in the future will be in a similar position. There was a time not so long ago when the devil governed practically all of Europe. The great failure of the church then was in not standing up to be counted.

COX: I agree. It is very probable that Christians will be a much smaller minority than they are now because of the disappearance of Christendom, and so on. We ought to get used to that. One of the ways we become used to it is by reminding ourselves that Christianity is not American civic religion.

METZ: I react critically to an earlier remark of yours, Professor Cox, insofar as I think institutionalized religion belongs in the society of tomorrow. If religion is to become an effective critic in our society, the question arises as to who or what is the bearer and the subject of such criticism. Nothing is more irrelevant and without efficiency today in our anonymous society than the purely individual subject. And, therefore, I think we will be confronted anew with the problem of institutionalization. For this reason there is a future not only for religion but also for the church in the coming society.

O'DEA: Toynbee wrote a few years ago that Hellenistic Judaism offered the model not just for religious groups but for cultural groups in the future: the diaspora model. He observed that there was a kind of urban society, in a sense, in the Hellenistic world. The Jews were able to exist as a community within this kind of megapolis—not really a community but a collection of communities and isolated individuals. Toynbee suggested that this is the kind of model for culture in the urban and mobile society into which we are moving.

Perhaps it is true. In the urbanized and mobile society toward which we are moving what we will have, perhaps, are smaller, informal groups with their own traditions existing alongside each other. Because of mass media, because a multiplicity of functions will be operating simultaneously in the coming society, the problems of building brotherhood—real community and real brotherhood—will probably be done in bits and pieces. This seems to be what the diaspora model is saying. Whether you agree with this or not, it is something to reckon with when you try to look ahead, let us say,

to the cities which may exist in the year 2069.

COX: It is interesting to ask ourselves what kind of community and what kind of church we want in the year 2000, and what we do now to get that church. One of the executive leaders of the World Council of Churches said that he wants a church which is a mixture of Quaker and Greek Orthodox. This will combine the small face-to-face task-oriented groups—within which people get to know each other in an intimate way, and a wide variety of theological perspectives are both permitted and encouraged—with the celebrative, liturgical festive church which the Greeks have maintained so well. If I were designing a church for the twenty-first century, this is what I would want to have: task groups, study groups, encounter groups, all coming together occasionally in a festive atmosphere for which we would pull out all of the stops. But we won't get that kind of church simply by merging all existing denominations into one.

O'DEA: I feel like Karl Barth a little bit now.

COX: That's an unusual role for you.

O'DEA: It is an unusual role for me; it's a very peculiar feeling too. But I feel like crying out that we are talking about religion and churches. But what about God?

FACKENHEIM: It seems to me that the central question of this age is, What is required of us? The Psalmist celebrated when he said, "Unless it had been for the Lord God, I would have perished in my affliction." I agree with this. And I don't feel all that worried about not believing in God. For one thing, lots of people know what the Lord requires of us even if they don't believe in him. So, I think the central question is a commitment to a better world from the pretty grim world in which we now live. The people who share such a commitment will form a community which will not disappear in the diaspora. That, I think, is the central issue.

O'DEA: Perhaps the "general religion" of the twenty-first century, not the small, diaspora group kind, but popular religion, the kind popular among decision-makers, might be a kind of Prometheanism. The advocates begin to feel that with such terrific technology in their hands they have indeed stolen fire from the gods and are taking over the earth. Maybe this is an enormous *hybris* or pride.

COX: I am not as worried about that as some people are. There is a lot of talk about the Vietnam War as an instance of the arrogance of American power and American Prometheanism. That element is there, certainly. But there is also an element of being captive to forces beyond your control. That is the opposite of the Promethean notion: being unable to extricate yourself from things which you have started or in which you have been caught up, a helpless marionette in the hands of history.

But let me conclude with a statement of another kind. I hope for a church in the twenty-first century in which real festivity and celebration will take place—a church in which people can learn to celebrate.

American Protestant society today has lost the capacity to celebrate.

The other thing I hope the church will provide is the occasion and the place for vision, imagination, fantasy, and utopian thought. It should be a place in which one can really imagine the kind of city, society, university, family, or a world quite different from the way it is now. I think we have previously identified Christianity much too closely with rules for making decisions for the situation in which we find ourselves rather than as the energizer to visions, speculation, and thought about the kingdom of God: the coming new-world city, the New Jerusalem. In one sense our capacity for imagination and fantasy in our society has been atrophied, and we need to have the place and the occasion in which that gift, that side of man, can be nurtured. I repeat: the religion of the twenty-first century is not already in the books! We can't simply watch to see what it will become as we study the trends. In large measure the kind of church we will have in the twenty-first century will be the kind of church we want it to be. And this is really the sort of question we ought now to be asking.

RELATED READING

Baier, Kurt, and Nicholas Rescher. *Values and the Future*. New York: Free Press 1969.

Bell, Daniel, ed. *Toward the Year 2000*. Boston: Houghton Mifflin, 1968.

Bell, Wendell, and James A. Mau. *The Sociology of the Future*. New York: Russell Sage Foundation, 1971.

Berry, Adrian, ed. *The Next Ten Thousand Years: A Vision of Man's Future in the Universe*. New York: New American Library, 1974.

Best, Fred. *The Future of Work*. Englewood Cliffs, N.J.: Prentice-Hall, 1973.

Bundy, Robert. *Images of the Future: The Twenty-first Century and Beyond*. Buffalo, N.Y.: Prometheus Books, 1976.

Burhoe, Ralph W., ed. *Science and Human Values in the 21st Century*. Philadelphia: Westminster Press, 1971.

Brzezinski, Zbigniew. *Between Two Ages: America's Role in the Technetronic Era*. New York: Penguin Books, 1969.

Chase, Stuart. *The Most Probable World*. New York: Harper & Row, 1968.

Clarke, Arthur C. *Profiles of the Future*. New York: Harper & Row, 1963.

Cox, Harvey. *Turning East: The Promise and Peril of the New Orientalism*. New York: Simon & Schuster, 1977.

Darwin, Charles G. *The Next Million Years*. London: R. Hart-Davis, 1952.

Dunstan, Maryjane, and Patricia W. Garlan, eds. *Worlds in the Making: Probes for Students of the Future*. Englewood Cliffs, N.J.: Prentice-Hall, 1970.

Farmer, Richard N. *The Real World of 1984: A Look at the Foreseeable Future*. New York: David McKay Co., 1973.

Freud, Sigmund. *The Future of an Illusion*. Garden City, N.Y.: Doubleday & Co., 1964.

Gabor, Dennis. *Inventing the Future*. New York: Alfred A. Knopf, 1964.

Heilbroner, Robert L. *The Future as History*. New York: Grove Press, 1961.

Hellman, Hal. *The City in the World of the Future*. New York: M. Evans & Co., 1970.

Jaspers, Karl. *The Future of Mankind*. Chicago: University of Chicago Press, 1961.

Kahn, Herman. *Thinking about the Unthinkable*. New York: Avon Books, 1962.

———, and Anthony J. Weiner. *The Year 2000: A Framework for Speculation on the Next Thirty-Three Years*. New York: Macmillan, 1967.

———, et al. *The Next 200 Years*. New York: William Morrow & Co., 1976.

King-Hele, Desmond. *The End of the Twentieth Century*. New York: St. Martin's Press, 1970.

Kostelanetz, Richard, ed. *Social Speculations: Visions for Our Time*. New York: William Morrow & Co., 1971.

Kuhns, William. *The Post Industrial Prophets: Interpretations of Technology*. New York: Harper & Row, 1971.

Leinwald, Gerald. *The Future*. New York: Pocket Books, 1976.

Maddox, John. *The Doomsday Syndrome*. New York: McGraw-Hill, 1972.

May, Rollo. *The Courage to Create*. New York: W. W. Norton & Co., 1975.

McHale, John. *The Future of the Future*. New York: George Braziller, 1969.

Medawar, P. B. *The Future of Man*. New York: New American Library, 1959.

Morgan, Douglas N. *Love: Plato, the Bible and Freud*. Englewood Cliffs, N.J.: Prentice-Hall, 1964.

Muller, Herbert J. *Uses of the Future*. Bloomington, Ind.: University of Indiana Press, 1974.

Northrop, F. C. S. *The Meeting of East and West*. New York: Macmillan, 1946.

Pauwels, Louis, and Jacques Bergier. *Impossible Possibilities*. New York: Avon Books, 1968.

Rosen, Stephen. *Future Facts*. New York: Simon & Schuster, 1976.

Rostand, Jean. *Can Man Be Modified?* New York: Basic Books, 1959.

Russell, Bertrand. *Has Man a Future?* Baltimore, Md.: Penguin Books, 1961.

Schweitzer, Albert. *Philosophy of Civilization.* New York: Macmillan, 1956.

Sorokin, Petrim. *Social Philosophies in an Age of Crisis.* Boston: Beacon Press, 1950.

Spekke, Andrew A. *The Next 25 Years.* Washington, D.C.: World Future Society, 1975.

Spengler, Oswald. *The Decline of the West,* abridged edition by Helmut Werner. New York: Modern Library, 1962.

Stapledon, Olaf. *Last and First Men and Star Maker.* New York: Dover Publications, 1968.

Theobald, Robert. *Futures Conditional.* Indianapolis, Ind.: Bobbs-Merrill, 1972.

Toffler, Alvin. *Future Shock.* New York: Bantam Books, 1970.

————, ed. *The Futurists.* New York: Random House, 1972.

————, ed. *Learning for Tomorrow: The Role of the Future in Education.* New York: Random House, 1974.

Toynbee, Arnold. *Civilization on Trial.* New York: Oxford Book Co., 1948.

World Future Society. *The Future: A Guide to Information Sources.* Washington, D.C.: World Future Society, 1977.

PERIODICALS

Futures: The Journal of Forecasting and Planning (London: Unwin).

The Futurist: A Journal of Forecasts, Trends, and Ideas About the Future (Washington, D.C.: The World Future Society).

Epilogue

THE QUEST FOR UTOPIA

The choice is no longer between Utopia and the pleasant ordered world that our fathers knew. The choice is between Utopia and Hell.

Lord Beveridge

The human mind has always accomplished progress by its construction of utopias.

H. G. Wells

My utopia is actual life, here and anywhere, pushed to the limits of its ideal possibilities.

Lewis Mumford

There is nothing like dreams to create the future. Utopia today, flesh and blood tomorrow.

Victor Hugo

Utopianism is man's ability to give names to things absent to break the power of things present.

Ruben Alves

An acre in Middlesex is better than a principality in Utopia.

Thomas Babington Macaulay

The Utopians wonder how man should be so much taken up with the glaring doubtful lustre of a jewel or stone, that can look up to a star, or to the sun himself.

Sir Thomas More

Ah, love, could you and I with Him conspire
To grasp this sorry Scheme of Things entire,
Would not we shatter it to bits — and then
Re-mould it nearer to the Heart's desire!

The Rubaiyat of Omar Khayyam

Philosophers make imaginary laws for imaginary commonwealths, and their discourses are as the stars which give little light because they are so high.

Francis Bacon

Man is defined by his dreams, which far more than action, shape his reality.

Denis de Rougemont

34 Philosophy and Utopian Thinking

Toffler

As the end of this century approaches, people are giving more and more attention to the future. Conferences are being held on prospects to be looked forward to (or dreaded) in the new century; masses of data are being gathered; philosophers and scientists are making predictions; and academic courses are paying more attention to futurology. Prognostication has become a popular pastime, not just for the practitioners of occult sciences, but for business, industry, and government.

As one might expect in an age that has produced manned flights to the moon, a great deal of attention is being directed toward future scientific and technological advancements. In *Profiles of the Future*, Arthur C. Clarke, the author of the movie script and novel *2001: A Space Odyssey*, paints a glowing picture of this future world. Planetary landings and colonizations, interstellar probes and flights, contact and meetings with extra-terrestrials are conceivable within the next one hundred and fifty years. Artificial life and intelligence; telesensory devices; robots and cyborgs; control of weather, climate, gravity, and heredity; and space mining are some of the achievements that Clarke envisages as possible by 2100. For an encyclopedic treatment of possible and probable scientific and technological advances, as well as for myriad scenarios of possible future developments, one can go to Herman Kahn and Anthony Wiener's *The Year 2000: A Framework for Speculation about the Future*.

Meanwhile, in today's world many people, especially those in the so-called counterculture, have shown increasing disillusionment with the widespread idea that "science and technology can save us." Actual wars and threats of war, environmental pollution and senseless waste, violence and crime, and racism and social inequality have driven many to seek alternatives to the present organization of the technological society. Communes of almost every conceivable variety have sprung up throughout this country (about three thousand, according to one recent estimate) and in many parts of the world as attempts to perform "experiments in living." *Utopia or Oblivion,* the title of a recent book by the utopian thinker F. Buckminster Fuller, is a recurring theme in discussions of the perennial question, What is to be done?

Contrary to popular misconceptions, utopian proposals are not necessarily impractical and useless or a waste of time. Presented either in fictional form or in a program for action, utopias have often served as designs for actual reform, as blueprints for new societies, and as beacons to guide human affairs. To say that utopian thinkers are mere visionaries and that utopias are irrelevant to the actual world is to ignore the tremendous impact that thinkers, such as Jesus, Confucius, and Marx, have had on human thought and action and to discount the continuing influence of utopian works, such as Plato's *Republic,* More's *Utopia,* Bellamy's *Looking Backward,* and, more recently, Skinner's *Walden Two.* As Oscar Wilde wrote, "A map of the world that does not include Utopia is not worth even glancing at, for it leaves out the one country at which Humanity is always landing. And when Humanity lands there, it looks out, and seeing a better country, sets sail. Progress is the realisation of Utopias."[1]

In the following and final selection, from *Future Shock,* Alvin Toffler proposes utopian thinking as an essential stage in the strategy of social futurism. As a means for extending our time horizon, utopian speculation is a practical necessity in grappling with the problems of today and preparing to cope with the shape of things to come.

In the Appendix is a guide that you may wish to use, either alone or with a group, for engaging in utopian thinking. It includes questions on human nature, the good life, freedom, and other major topics of concern to futurists.

Make no little plans; they have no magic to stir men's blood and probably themselves will not be realized. Make big plans: aim high in hope and work, remembering that a noble, logical diagram, once recorded, will never die, but long after we are gone will be a living thing, asserting itself with ever growing insistency.[2]

NOTES

1. Oscar Wilde, *Intentions and The Soul of Man* (London: Methuen, 1908), p. 299.

2. Attributed to Daniel Burnham, 1846–1912.

Utopian Thinking

Today as never before we need a multiplicity of visions, dreams and prophecies—images of potential tomorrows. Before we can rationally decide which alternative pathways to choose, which cultural styles to pursue, we must first ascertain which are possible. Conjecture, speculation and the visionary view thus become as coldly practical a necessity as feet-on-the-floor "realism" was in an earlier time.

This is why some of the world's biggest and most tough-minded corporations, once the living embodiment of presentism, today hire intuitive futurists, science fiction writers and visionaries as consultants. A gigantic European chemical company employs a futurist who combines a scientific background with training as a theologian. An American communications empire engages a future-minded social critic. A glass manufacturer searches for a science fiction writer to imagine the possible corporate forms of the future. Companies turn to these "blue-skyers" and "wild birds" not for scientific forecasts of probabilities, but for mind-stretching speculation about possibilities.

Corporations must not remain the only agencies with access to such services. Local government, schools, voluntary associations and others also need to examine their potential futures imaginatively. One way to help them do so would be to establish in each com-

munity "imaginetic centers" devoted to technically assisted brainstorming. These would be places where people noted for creative imagination, rather than technical expertise, are brought together to examine present crises, to anticipate future crises, and to speculate freely, even playfully, about possible futures.

What, for example, are the possible futures of urban transportation? Traffic is a problem involving space. How might the city of tomorrow cope with the movement of men and objects through space? To speculate about this question, an imaginetic center might enlist artists, sculptors, dancers, furniture designers, parking lot attendants, and a variety of other people who, in one way or another, manipulate space imaginatively. Such people, assembled under the right circumstances, would inevitably come up with ideas of which the technocratic city planners, the highway engineers and transit authorities have never dreamed.

Musicians, people who live near airports, jack-hammer men and subway conductors might well imagine new ways to organize, mask or suppress noise. Groups of young people might be invited to ransack their minds for previously unexamined approaches to urban sanitation, crowding, ethnic conflict, care of the aged, or a thousand other present and future problems.

In any such effort, the overwhelming majority of ideas put forward will, of course, be absurd, funny or technically impossible. Yet

From *Future Shock*, by Alvin Toffler. Copyright © 1970 by Alvin Toffler. Reprinted by permission of Random House, Inc.

the essence of creativity is a willingness to play the fool, to toy with the absurd, only later submitting the stream of ideas to harsh critical judgment. The application of the imagination to the future thus requires an environment in which it is safe to err, in which novel juxtapositions of ideas can be freely expressed before being critically sifted. We need sanctuaries for social imagination.

While all sorts of creative people ought to participate in conjecture about possible futures, they should have immediate access—in person or via telecommunications—to technical specialists, from acoustical engineers to zoologists, who could indicate when a suggestion is technically impossible (bearing in mind that even impossibility is often temporary.)

Scientific expertise, however, might also play a generative, rather than merely a damping role in the imaginetic process. Skilled specialists can construct models to help imagineers examine all possible permutations of a given set of relationships. Such models are representations of real life conditions. In the words of Christoph Bertram of the Institute for Strategic Studies in London, their purpose is "not so much to predict the future, but, by examining alternative futures, to show the choices open."

An appropriate model, for example, could help a group of imagineers visualize the impact on a city if its educational expenditures were to fluctuate—how this would affect, let us say, the transport system, the theaters, the occupational structure and health of the community. Conversely, it could show how changes in these other factors might affect education.

The rushing stream of wild, unorthodox, eccentric or merely colorful ideas generated in these sanctuaries of social imagination must, after they have been expressed, be subjected to merciless screening. Only a tiny fraction of them will survive this filtering process. These few, however, could be of the utmost importance in calling attention to new possibilities that might otherwise escape notice. As we move from poverty toward affluence, politics changes from what mathematicians call a zero sum game into a non-zero sum game. In the first, if one player wins another must lose. In the second, all players can win. Finding non-zero sum solutions to our social problems requires all the imagination we can muster. A system for generating imaginative policy ideas could help us take maximum advantage of the non-zero opportunities ahead.

While imaginetic centers concentrate on partial images of tomorrow, defining possible futures for a single industry, an organization, a city or its sub-systems, however, we also need sweeping, visionary ideas about the society as a whole. Multiplying our images of possible futures is important; but these images need to be organized, crystallized into structured form. In the past, utopian literature did this for us. It played a practical, crucial role in ordering men's dreams about alternative futures. Today we suffer for lack of utopian ideas around which to organize competing images of possible futures.

Most traditional utopias picture simple and static societies—i.e., societies that have nothing in common with super-industrialism. B. F. Skinner's *Walden Two*, the model for several existing experimental communes, depicts a pre-industrial way of life—small, close to the earth, built on farming and handcraft. Even those two brilliant anti-utopias, *Brave New World* and *1984*, now seem oversimple. Both describe societies based on high technology and low complexity: the machines are sophisticated but the social and cultural relationships are fixed and deliberately simplified.

Today we need powerful new utopian and anti-utopian concepts that look forward to super-industrialism, rather than backward to simpler societies. These concepts, however, can no longer be produced in the old way. First, no book, by itself, is adequate to describe a super-industrial future in emotionally compelling terms. Each conception of a super-industrial utopia or anti-utopia needs to be embodied in many forms—films, plays, novels and works of art—rather than a single work of fiction. Second, it may now be too difficult for any individual writer, no matter how gifted, to describe a convincingly complex future. We need, therefore a revolution in the production of utopias: collaborative utopianism. We need to construct "utopia factories."

One way might be to assemble a small group of top social scientists—an economist, a sociologist, an anthropologist, and so on—asking them to work together, even live together, long enough to hammer out among themselves a set of well-defined values on which they believe a truly super-industrial utopian society might be based.

Each member of the team might then attempt to describe in nonfiction form a sector of an imagined society built on these values. What would its family structure be like? Its economy, laws, religion, sexual practices, youth culture, music, art, its sense of time, its degree of differentiation, its psychological problems? By working together and ironing out inconsistencies, where possible, a comprehensive and adequately complex picture might be drawn of a seamless, temporary form of super-industrialism.

At this point, with the completion of detailed analysis, the project would move to the fiction stage. Novelists, film-makers, science fiction writers and others, working closely with psychologists, could prepare creative works about the lives of individual characters in the imagined society.

Meanwhile, other groups could be at work on counter-utopias. While Utopia A might stress materialist, success-oriented values, Utopia B might base itself on sensual, hedonistic values, C on the primacy of aesthetic values, D on individualism, E on collectivism, and so forth. Ultimately, a stream of books, plays, films and television programs would flow from this collaboration between art, social science and futurism, thereby educating large

numbers of people about the costs and benefits of the various proposed utopias.

Finally, if social imagination is in short supply, we are even more lacking in people willing to subject utopian ideas to systematic test. More and more young people, in their dissatisfaction with industrialism, are experimenting with their own lives, forming utopian communities, trying new social arrangements, from group marriage to living-learning communes. Today, as in the past, the weight of established society comes down hard on the visionary who attempts to practice, as well as merely preach. Rather than ostracizing utopians, we should take advantage of their willingness to experiment, encouraging them with money and tolerance, if not respect.

Most of today's "intentional communities" or utopian colonies, however, reveal a powerful preference for the past. These may be of value to the individuals in them, but the society as a whole would be better served by utopian experiments based on super- rather than pre-industrial forms. Instead of a communal farm, why not a computer software company whose program writers live and work communally? Why not an education technology company whose members pool their money and merge their families? Instead of raising radishes or crafting sandals, why not an oceanographic research installation organized along utopian lines? Why not a group medical practice that takes advantage of the latest medical technology but whose members accept modest pay and pool their profits to run a completely new-style medical school? Why not recruit living groups to try out the proposals of the utopia factories?

In short, we can use utopianism as a tool rather than an escape, if we base our experiments on the technology and society of tomorrow rather than that of the past. And once done, why not the most rigorous, scientific analysis of the results? The findings could be priceless, were they to save us from mistakes or lead us toward more workable organiza-tional forms for industry, education, family life or politics.

Such imaginative explorations of possible futures would deepen and enrich our scientific study of probable futures. They would lay a basis for the radical forward extension of the society's time horizon. They would help us apply social imagination to the future of futurism itself.

Indeed, with these as a background, we must consciously begin to multiply the scientific future-sensing organs of society. Scientific futurist institutes must be spotted like nodes in a loose network throughout the entire governmental structure in the techno-societies, so that in every department, local or national, some staff devotes itself systematically to scanning the probable long-term future in its assigned field. Futurists should be attached to every political party, university, corporation, professional association, trade union and student organization.

We need to train thousands of young people in the perspectives and techniques of scientific futurism, inviting them to share in the exciting venture of mapping probable futures. We also need national agencies to provide technical assistance to local communities in creating their own futurist groups. And we need a similar center, perhaps jointly funded by American and European foundations, to help incipient futurist centers in Asia, Africa, and Latin America.

We are in a race between rising levels of uncertainty produced by the acceleration of change, and the need for reasonably accurate images of what at any instant is the most probable future. The generation of reliable images of the most probable future thus becomes a matter of the highest national, indeed, international urgency.

As the globe is itself dotted with future-sensors, we might consider creating a great international institute, a world futures data bank. Such an institute, staffed with top caliber men and women from all the sciences and social sciences, would take as its purpose the collection and systematic integration of predictive reports generated by scholars and imaginative thinkers in all the intellectual disciplines all over the world.

Of course, those working in such an institute would know that they could never create a single, static diagram of the future. Instead, the product of their effort would be a constantly changing geography of the future, a continually re-created overarching image based on the best predictive work available. The men and women engaged in this work would know that nothing is certain; they would know that they must work with inadequate data; they would appreciate the difficulties inherent in exploring the uncharted territories of tomorrow. But man already knows more about the future than he has ever tried to formulate and integrate in any systematic and scientific way. Attempts to bring this knowledge together would constitute one of the crowning intellectual efforts in history— and one of the most worthwhile.

Only when decision-makers are armed with better forecasts of future events, when by successive approximation we increase the accuracy of forecast, will our attempts to manage change improve perceptibly. For reasonably accurate assumptions about the future are a precondition for understanding the potential consequences of our own actions. And without such understanding, the management of change is impossible.

If the humanization of the planner is the first stage in the strategy of social futurism, therefore, the forward extension of our time horizon is the second. To transcend technocracy, we need not only to reach beyond our economic philistinism, but to open our minds to more distant futures, both probable and possible.

RELATED READING

Bellamy, Edward. *Looking Backward: 2000–1887*. New York: New American Library, 1960.

————. *Equality*. New York: D. Appleton Century Co., 1934.

Berneri, Mary Louise. *Journey Through Utopia*. London: Routledge & Kegan Paul, 1950.

Boguslaw, Robert. *The New Utopians: A Study of Systems Design and Social Change*. Englewood Cliffs, N.J.: Prentice-Hall, 1965.

Buber, Martin. *Paths in Utopia*. Boston: Beacon Press, 1949.

Butler, Samuel. *Erewhon* and *Erewhon Revisited*. New York: Modern Library, n.d.

Clarke, Arthur C. *Childhood's End*. New York: Harcourt Brace & World, 1953.

Disch, Thomas A., ed. *The Ruins of Earth*. New York: Berkley Publishing Corp., 1961.

Goodman, Paul. *Utopian Essays and Practical Proposals*. New York: Random House, 1964.

Goodman, Percival, and Paul Goodman. *Communitas: Means of Livelihood and Ways of Life*. New York: Vintage, 1960.

Harrison, Henry, ed. *The Year 2000*. New York: Berkley Publishing Corp., 1970.

Hillegas, Mark R. *The Future as Nightmare: H. G. Wells and the Anti-Utopians*. New York: Oxford Book Co., 1967.

Holloway, Mark. *Heavens on Earth: Utopian Communities in America*. New York: Dover Publications, 1966.

Huxley, Aldous. *Brave New World*. New York: Bantam Books, 1931.

————. *Brave New World Revisited*. New York: Bantam Books, 1958.

————. *Island*. New York: Harper & Row, 1962.

Kateb, George. *Utopia and Its Enemies*. New York: Free Press of Glencoe, 1963.

Manuel, Frank E., ed. *Utopias and Utopian Thought*. Boston: Houghton Mifflin, 1966.

More, Thomas. *Utopia*, trans. H. V. S. Ogden. New York: Appleton-Century-Crofts, 1949.

Morgan, Arthur. *Nowhere Was Somewhere*. Chapel Hill, N.C.: University of North Carolina Press, 1946.

Mumford, Lewis. *The Story of Utopias*. New York: Viking Press, 1962.

Negley, Glenn R., and J. Max Patrick. *The Quest for Utopia: An Anthology of Imaginary Societies*. Garden City, N.Y.: Doubleday & Co., 1962.

Orwell, George. *1984*. New York: Harcourt Brace & World, 1948.

Ozmon, Howard. *Utopias and Education*. Minneapolis, Minn.: Burgess Publishing Co., 1968.

Rand, Ayn. *Anthem*. New York: New American Library, 1946.

———. *Atlas Shrugged*. New York: Random House, 1957.

Richter, Peyton E., ed. *Utopia/Dystopia*. Morristown, N.J.: General Learning Press, 1975.

———, ed. *Utopias: Social Ideals and Communal Experiments*. Boston: Holbrook Press, 1971.

Skinner, B. F. *Walden Two*. New York: Macmillan, 1948.

Van Vogt, A. E. *The World of Null-A*. New York: Berkley Publishing Corp., 1945.

———. *The Players of Null-A*. New York: Berkley Publishing Corp., 1948.

Walsh, Chad. *From Utopia to Nightmare*. New York: Harper & Row, 1962.

Wells, H. G. *A Modern Utopia*. London: Chapman and Hall, 1905.

Young, Michael. *The Rise of the Meritocracy, 1879–2033*. New York: Random House, 1959.

Zamiatin, Eugene. *We*. New York: E. P. Dutton & Co., 1924.

Appendix

A Utopia Project:
Confronting the Future Today

Utopian speculation is often used in stimulating people to confront social and philosophical problems and to commit themselves to imaginative solutions to them. It can also help to bring various fields of knowledge into meaningful relationships, affording new perspectives from which to view past, present, and future experience. When the speculation takes place in small groups of people working together to design an imaginary commune or intentional community, it can contribute to the understanding and tolerance of divergent points of view and foster fellowship, cooperation, and compromise in reaching group decisions. In any case, utopian speculation, individual or collective, is usually engrossing, provocative, and fun.

The following directions may be useful as guidelines:

1. Your utopia may be written alone or with a group of fellow students. If with a group, discuss all questions together, keep notes, then assign different parts to be written by different persons. Finally, edit and integrate the various parts into a unified paper.
2. It may be written in the form of a dialogue, a report, an essay, a diary, letters, a short story, a novelette, a scrapbook, or in some other form you may think appropriate. For different successful approaches, see Plato's *Republic*, Thomas More's *Utopia*, Edward Bellamy's *Looking Backward*, H. G. Wells's *A Modern Utopia*, Aldous Huxley's *Island*, and B. F. Skinner's *Walden Two*.
3. Try to be feasible rather than fantastic. Attempt to explain how your utopia could come about and why it might succeed. Construct arguments for your solutions to problems rather than state the solutions dogmatically. Throughout your presentation, aim at coherence, clarity, consistency, and plausibility.
4. You may decide to write a dystopia or anti-utopia, in which case your task will be harder but even more challenging. You'll soon discover that you have to keep both your social criticism and your implied utopian solution or alternative simultaneously in mind if you expect

565

your dystopia to be effective. For examples of successful dystopias, see Ignatius Donnelly's *Caesar's Column*, Eugene Zamiatin's *We*, Aldous Huxley's *Brave New World*, George Orwell's *1984*, and Ayn Rand's *Anthem* and *Atlas Shrugged*.

5. The papers should be typed, double-spaced and with ample margins. Illustrations, clippings, diagrams, charts, and photographs will help bring it to life. As for length, individually written papers should be from ten to twenty pages long and group papers, a minimum of thirty pages long in light of the extensive list of questions.

6. For a source book containing extensive bibliographies on utopian speculation, see Peyton E. Richter, ed. *Utopias: Social Ideals and Communal Experiments* (Boston: Holbrook Press, 1971). Other relevant books are listed in the Related Readings within this book, especially the last one.

Guide to Constructing a Utopia

I. EDUCATION, METHODS AND BELIEFS

1. What are the purposes of education in your utopia?
2. Who will be educated? Why? How?
3. Describe your ideal school system—its goals, methodology, and curriculum.
4. What will be the ideal characteristics of your teachers, students, and administrators?
5. Would only one view of the nature of ultimate reality be taught in your educational system? If so, what will it be and how will its truth be justified?
6. What is the definition and test of truth in your utopia?
7. What would be the relationship between your educational system and the state? How free would your educational approaches be?
8. How might your utopian education deal with:
    a. racial prejudices and conflicts; b. drug taking; c. sex education; d. political activists among students and faculty; e. exceptional students; f. boundary situations (guilt, suffering, struggle, death)?

II. POLITICS, AUTHORITY, AND FREEDOM

1. What will be the form of government of your utopia? Justify your choice.
2. Will you have a written constitution? Why, or why not?
3. If your society has governing officials, how will they be selected, changed, or removed?
4. How will abuses of political power be avoided or dealt with?
5. What will be the rights and responsibilities of citizenship in your utopia?

6. What is the relative importance of freedom and authority in your utopia? Of innovation and tradition?
7. How will your political system deal with:
   a. racial discrimination; b. internal and external defense; c. differences between the sexes; d. civil disobedience; e. religious differences?

III.   THE GOOD LIFE

A.   PHYSICAL PLAN

1. Where will your utopia be located? Why?
2. Describe its distinctive geographical features and natural resources.
3. Describe or sketch examples of its physical appearance—kinds and styles of buildings, community or city plans, transportation systems, disposal systems, etc. (Be as concrete and detailed as you wish.)

B.   ECONOMICS

1. How are problems of production and distribution to be solved in your utopia?
2. Explain the relative importance of agriculture, handicrafts, and industrial production in your utopia.
3. How much economic planning and control will there be in your utopia?
4. Who will do the "dirty work" in your utopia? Why?
5. How will your economic system deal with:
   a. possible depressions; b. waste and pollution; c. trade; d. class conflicts; e. vested interests or power cliques; f. incentives; g. loafers?

C.   HUMAN RELATIONS AND MORALITY

1. What are the size and characteristics (racial, ethnic, age, etc.) of your utopia's population?
2. Are members of your utopia to be selected, or is there open-admission to all? Why?
3. What moral virtues are you trying to promote? How do your utopian institutions promote these virtues?
4. What is your utopian criterion for judging action to be morally right or wrong? Give several examples of how the criterion would be applied.
5. How are deviants from your social norms to be dealt with? Justify.

6. What mechanisms will operate in your society to keep it unified and cohesive yet diversified and flexible?
7. Will the nuclear family be retained? Why, or why not?
8. How will your utopians spend their leisure time?
9. How will conflicts among members or groups be avoided or resolved?
10. What will be your society's attitude toward and treatment of:
   a. marriage; b. premarital and extra-marital sex; c. divorce; d. mental illness and emotional problems; e. old age; f. funeral rites?

IV. HUMAN NATURE, SCIENCE, AND TECHNOLOGY

1. What assumptions about human nature are you making in constructing your utopia? Justify.
2. How important are science and technology in bringing about and maintaining your utopia?
3. What is the attitude of your utopians toward machines and machine production?
4. How much applied and pure scientific research would there be in your utopia? How would it be subsidized?
5. Would scientific education be stressed in schools? Why or why not? What would be the relationship between the sciences and the humanities in your education?
6. How would scientists be selected, trained, and rewarded in your utopia?
7. What would be the relationship or relevance of science and technology to these problems in your utopia:
   a. warfare or peace-keeping; b. over-population; c. weather-control; d. feeding, sheltering, and clothing people; e. ecological problems; f. eugenics; g. behavioral engineering?

V. RELIGION

1. How would religion be defined in your ideal society?
2. What would be its functions?
3. In your utopia, would there be religious institutions with officials, creeds, rites, rituals, and other collective activities? If so, what would they be, why would they exist, and how would they function?
4. What would be the relationship between religion and other aspects of your society—e.g., the state, science, education, morality, and art? What conflicts might arise between these and how would they be avoided or resolved?

5. Do your utopians believe in God? Why or why not? Do they believe in personal survival after death or some other form of immortality? Why, or why not?
6. What would be your utopian religion's stand (if any) on these: a. euthanasia; b. abortion; c. suicide; d. drug-induced mystical experiences; e. messianic individuals; f. religious schisms; g. premarital and extra-marital sex; h. divorce; i. atheism; j. miracles?

VI. ART, BEAUTY, AND CREATIVITY

1. How would art and beauty be defined in your utopia?
2. What roles would art play in the everyday life of inhabitants of your utopia?
3. Would any organized or official attempt be made to nurture and reward creative artists in your society? Why, or why not?
4. Would your utopians allow censorship of art? If so, for what reason and by whom?
5. Would your schools be engaged in "aesthetic education" for everyone? If so, describe it.
6. Would tragedy, comedy, and satire continue to exist in your utopia? Why, or why not?
7. Do you think great art, artistic geniuses, and creative rebels would exist in your utopia? Why, or why not?

NOTES

This brief syllabus is similar to, but not identical with, a larger syllabus for a utopia project developed by Peyton E. Richter and other members of the Division of Humanities at Boston University College of Basic Studies in the early 1950s (see James A. Fisher and Peyton E. Richter, "Education for Citizenship: A Utopian Approach to General Education," *Journal of Higher Education* XXVIII, April 1957, pp. 220–24). Professor Glenn R. Negley at Duke University had already instituted a similar project in his course in Social Philosophy and Utopian Ideals. For an example of a student-written utopia, see Glenn R. Negley and J. Max Patrick, eds. *The Quest for Utopia: An Anthology of Imaginary Societies* (Garden City, N.Y.: Doubleday and Co., 1962), Appendix.

INDEX

2306

2306

B
29
.P5254
1978

B
29
.P525

1978

99
30.57